PR is...

A goal of *The ABCs of Strategic Com*  communication practitioners – no n achieving *their* goals. To do that, diss mal" definition of *public relations*:

Public relations is as simple as a thank-you note and as complicated as a four-color brochure.

It's as specific as writing a news release and as general as sensing community attitudes.

It's as inexpensive as a phone call to an editor or as costly as a full-page advertisement.

It's as direct as a conversation between two people and as broad as a radio or television program reaching thousands of listeners or millions of viewers.

It's as visual as a poster and as literal as a speech.

HERE, MY FRIENDS, IS THE BIG QUESTION:
What **IS** *public relations*?

It is a term often used . . . seldom defined!

In its broadest sense, **public relations** is "good work, publicly recognized."

Believe me, there are no secret formulas. *Public relations* is simply: the group itself saying –

*   "This is who we are;

*   What we think about ourselves;

*   What we want to do; and

*   Why we deserve your support."

Larry Litwin and Ralph Burgio © 1971; © 1999

For information and *ABCs'* updates and additions:
www.larrylitwin.com

The ABCs of Strategic Communication

Communication

Thousands of terms, tips and techniques
that define the professions

Second Edition

by M. Larry Litwin, APR, Fellow PRSA
Rowan University

AuthorHouse™
1663 Liberty Drive, Suite 200
Bloomington, IN 47403
www.authorhouse.com
Phone: 1-800-839-8640

First published by AuthorHouse 12/20/07

ISBN: 978-1-4343-5983-4 (sc)

Printed in the United States of America
Bloomington, Indiana

This book is printed on acid-free paper.

Dedication

The ABCs is dedicated to my parents, Jean and Eddie Litwin and Nancy's parents, Janet and Lionel Perris. Their support has always been unconditional. I would be remiss if I didn't mention my mother, in particular. Jeannie was always known for her "isms" – thoughts and expressions, which she passed onto her children, grandchildren and great grandchildren. Two of our favorites: "Never say I *can't* as in 'I *can't* do it.' *Can't* should never be part of your vocabulary" and "If you dream it, you can achieve it."

Because any book I write also has to be dedicated to the thousands of students who have passed through my classes, here are a couple of Eddie Litwin's "isms" for *them* – "Always strive to be the best that you can be. And never be afraid to ask questions. Questions are a sign of strength, not weakness." For those who didn't know him, Eddie Litwin was truly bigger than life. And, he seemed to always have the right answer.

M. Larry Litwin, APR

M. Larry Litwin, APR, Fellow PRSA, was born in South Philadelphia, raised in Camden and Pennsauken, New Jersey, lived in rural Iowa for three years, suburban North Jersey for two years and now resides in Berlin, N.J. after living in Cherry Hill, N.J. for 35 years.

Litwin is an established strategic advisor, teacher, mentor, role model and ethicist, and an award-winning public relations counselor and broadcast journalist, who has left a lasting impression on thousands of students and professionals.

He is an associate professor of communication at Rowan (N.J.) University where his classroom is considered a "laboratory for practical knowledge." Litwin teaches public relations, advertising, radio, television and journalism.

For the past 10 years, he has been full time. For 25 years prior to that, he served as an adjunct.

He is a graduate of Parsons (Iowa) College with a bachelor's degree in business. He received his master's in communication – educational public relations – from Glassboro (N.J.) State College. In 2002, he earned his APR (Accredited in Public Relations) from the Public Relations Society of America (PRSA). In 2007, Litwin was inducted into PRSA's College of Fellows – one of only 445 members.

During his 41-years in the communication profession, Litwin has worked as a public relations director for two school districts and as a radio and TV reporter, editor and anchor for ABC News in New York and KYW in Philadelphia. He was education reporter at KYW Newsradio for 10 years. He spent nearly two years in the U.S. Department of Labor as a deputy regional director of information and public affairs during Elizabeth Dole's tenure as labor secretary. He has also served as a public relations and advertising consultant.

Litwin was a governor's appointee to serve as chair of the New Jersey Open Public Records Act Privacy Study Commission, which recommended cutting edge legislation to assure that government records would be available to the public without exposing personal information – such as home addresses and telephone numbers – that should remain private and out of the public domain.

He was secretary of the Philadelphia Sports Writers Association for 35 years before stepping down in 2006, chair of the board of trustees of the

South Jersey Baseball Hall of Fame and a member of the Cherry Hill Public Library Board of Trustees. He served on the Cherry Hill Economic Development Council and as president of the Township's Alliance on Drug and Alcohol Abuse. He was a member of the South Jersey Scholar-Athlete Committee sponsored by the *Courier-Post* and *Coca-Cola*.

Litwin has authored two books: *The Public Relations Practitioner's Playbook – A Synergized Approach to Effective Two-Way Communication* (Kendall/Hunt – 2008) and *The ABCs of Strategic Communication – Thousands of terms, tips and techniques that define the professions* (AuthorHouse – 2008). He is a contributor to several college textbooks and has written many articles for national magazines.

He is the 2006 recipient of the National School Public Relations Association's *Lifetime Professional Achievement Award* for "his excellence in the field of educational public relations, leadership and contributions to NJSPRA (New Jersey chapter) and PenSPRA (Pennsylvania chapter), dedication to NSPRA and the (public relations) profession, and advocacy for students and our nation's public schools." He has also been awarded the Sigma Delta Chi (Society of Professional Journalists) *Bronze Medallion for Distinguished Service in Journalism* and the first ever *Grand Award* presented by the International Radio Festival of New York.

In 2002, the Philadelphia chapter of PRSA honored Litwin with its *Anthony J. Fulginiti Award* for "Outstanding Contributions to Public Relations Education" – which honors a person who excels in education, either through their mentoring/teaching, their efforts to help shape the careers of future PR professionals or their contributions to PRSSA (student chapter). Philadelphia PRSA awarded Rowan University's PRSSA chapter its *Pepperpot* for "Excellence in Public Relations" in 2004 and 2006, the only non-professional organization or agency to ever be so honored. Litwin serves as the chapter advisor.

Larry and his wife Nancy have two children, Julie and Adam Seth. Julie is a second grade teacher in Atlanta. She and husband Billy Kramer, publisher of *Georgia Sports Monthly* and *Dawg Nation*, have a daughter Alana and son Aidan. Adam, a Massachusetts Institute of Technology (MIT) fellow, is working toward a doctorate in economics and business.

Foreword

Communications is a large and diverse industry with many facets. Advertisers, public relations practitioners, marketers, researchers, journalists and professionals in myriad other related or ancillary disciplines all have their own languages or jargon. *The ABCs of Strategic Communication* is a veritable Rosetta Stone for the entire field.

The ABCs of Strategic Communication is a treasure trove of easy-to-understand definitions for more than 6,000 communications terms, phrases, acronyms and abbreviations. It will prove invaluable to anyone who works in the communications business or has to work with someone who does.

Reading this book can help even the complete communications neophyte become conversant in the field. No one will ever have to be in the dark again, wondering what a particular term means. Aspiring young communicators who study the book will be rewarded as well. They will learn practical tips – the little things – that count toward success and will help them thrive in the business world.

For students, the *ABCs of Strategic Communication* is the *Cliffs Notes* of the language of communication. But even seasoned pros will want to keep this book close at hand for easy reference – right next to their *Associated Press Stylebook*.

Larry Litwin and his present and former Rowan University students who helped put this book together deserve our thanks and our applause. They have given us recipes for success. As we learn to use the common language of communication, we are learning life's lessons of business.

Anne Sceia Klein, APR, Fellow PRSA
President, Anne Klein Communications Group
Public Relations Counselors
Marlton, New Jersey

Preface and Acknowledgements

The ABCs of Strategic Communication is a prime example of quintessential teamwork. In just its second edition, it has quickly become the go to source for marketing communication terms.

The ABCs represents the accomplishments of an incredibly talented team of outstanding public relations practitioners and counselors led by the commitment and dedication of senior editor Amy Ovsiew. Amy headed a team of nose-to-the-grindstone researchers and persuasive strategic writers. They were joined by an award-winning graphics specialist. Together, we took a concept, honed it and then produced a major desk-top reference that reviewers believe is quickly becoming a standard for the industry – the many disciplines that comprise the communication professions.

It all began with the question: "Wouldn't it be great if there were a book of terms that all communicators would find valuable?" It was raised by Katie Hardesty, original senior editor of what has affectionately become known as Book No. 1 titled *The Public Relations Practitioner's Playbook* (Kendall/Hunt – 2008). That "outside-the-box" thinking, which included the unique approach of interspersing relationship marketing terms and techniques throughout, has evolved into *The ABCs of Strategic Communication* (Book No. 2).

Like *The Playbook*, *The ABCs* is jargon free and jam packed with communication ideas that work. What started as a 48 page booklet has grown to more than 700 pages because the communication professions are so integrated and dependent on one another.

The finished product could never have been accomplished without six other colleagues who took a concept, ran with it and motivated me every step of the way: Michael Gross served as senior editor and operations manager of the inaugural edition; Mark Marmur, researcher and first reader; Linda Alexander, Tara Lhulier and Arianna Stefanoni, editors; and Stephanie Biddle, graphic designer. Mark and Michael are agency account executives; Linda, a corporate PR executive; Tara, a school PR director; Arianna, a recipient of the "Outstanding Collegiate Public Relations Student in the Nation"; and Stephanie, owner and designer of *Corporate Imagination*.

All of us appreciate one of their mentors and my colleague, Professor Claudia Cuddy, ELS, for providing publications terms from her book *Communicating With QuarkXPress* (Word Nerds Publishing). Thank you to Professor Frank Hogan, general manager of Rowan Radio - WGLS-FM, for many of the electronic media terms used in *The ABCs*.

A personal thanks to Anne Sceia Klein, APR, Fellow PRSA, and her husband Jerry Klein, Esq. – Anne for crafting and writing the foreword and Jerry for his wisdom and advice. The Philadelphia-area firm, *Anne Klein Communications Group (Public Relations Counselors)* is among the most respected both in the United States and internationally where *AKA* is an active member and participant in *Pinnacle Worldwide*.

Special kudos and a tip of the editor's "green eye shade visor" go to my wife Nancy. She stuck with me and helped turn stumbling blocks into stepping stones and challenges into accomplishments. As deadlines approached, Nancy rolled up her sleeves, grabbed a red pen and joined the others at the editors' desk to help complete this massive project.

No acknowledgement could be complete without a mention of my late long-time friend, colleague and business partner Ralph Edward Burgio. His influence is woven into so many of my strategic decisions. For all intents and purposes, Ralph invented the rounded corner boxes used in this book and the term "blurb" – at least in my mind.

And, what kind of father would I be if I didn't recognize the patience of my "grown" children (Julie Beth and husband Billy, and son Adam Seth) and grandchildren, Alana and Aidan, for putting up with my "neglect" and wondering: "Does it have to be 'all book, all the time'?"

As a small boy, I was taught: "If you dream it, you can achieve it."

The ABCs was a dream that did, indeed, come true – thanks to the efforts and perseverance of so many. There is no way to fully express my gratitude.

M. Larry Litwin, APR, Fellow PRSA
January 2008
www.larrylitwin.com

Contents

Tips and Techniques to Succeed

All Tips and Techniques are on the *Companion CD* available at www.larrylitwin.com.

a la carte services – Rather than provide all advertising services for one price, an agency may provide only the services that a client wishes to purchase. Boutique or niche agencies are in and of themselves, a la carte service providers.

ABC – Abbreviation for Audit Bureau of Circulations, an organization that compiles statistics on circulation.

above the fold – Newspaper term meaning stories printed on the upper half of a section front page. Term derived from passersby who see stories carried above the fold on front pages on a newsstand rack or inside newspaper vending machines.

above the (Web) fold – The fold is jargon for how much of a Web page a person sees without having to scroll down. Fewer than 35 percent of computer users scroll *below the fold.*

above-the-line public relations – Employs one or all of the five main media – print, broadcast, Internet (Web sites), face-to-face and special events. See *below the-line public relations.*

absolute costs – The minimum costs that an organization must bear to remain in business.

absolute project costs – Costs associated with any project that cannot be avoided. They are much like fixed costs that firms and individuals face.

academic detailer – A sales representative hired to "tell the truth" about certain products. Term was coined at Harvard University during the controversy over pharmaceutical reps and the "gifts" they offer physicians in return for prescribing their products. An *academic detailer's* job is to give doctors objective information about the cost and benefits of all kinds of treatments. See *detailer; foot soldier; missionary selling; sales calls.*

A.C. Nielsen ratings – Nielsen Media Research is a world-famous television ratings company. It is active in more than 40 countries and offers television and radio audience measurement, print readership, Internet measurement and custom media research services. In the United States, Nielsen Media Research provides television audience estimates for broadcast and cable networks, television stations, national syndicators, regional cable television systems, satellite providers, advertisers and advertising agencies. Nielsen Media Research also provides competitive advertising intelligence information through Nielsen Monitor-Plus in the U.S. and 30 other markets worldwide. Through a network of affiliates, Nielsen's coverage is extended to more than 70 countries, representing 85 percent of the world's advertising spending. Nielsen also collects Internet usage and advertising information through a number of subsidiaries. Read more at *www.nielsenmedia.com.*

1 Tips to Succeed: Leaders make the best teachers

We've all heard this one: If you give a man a fish, he has no reason to learn how to fish, but if you teach him how to fish, he won't have to go hungry.

The point? Leaders ought to be the best teachers. For example, if an employee comes to you and gives you a problem, should you:

A. Simply offer the answer, or

B. Ask questions to determine if the employee can arrive at the solution him or herself?

The answer is a resounding "B." Helping an employee to solve a problem on their own, when time and circumstances allow, is, by far, the best choice.

Forget the Golden Rule. Instead, follow The Platinum Rule: "Do unto others as they would have done unto themselves." In other words, if you really want to motivate people, ask them what will help them do a better job.

Robert Rosner, California Job Journal
Newstrack Executive Information Service
www.news-track.com • 800-334-5771

accelerated test marketing – Market testing of consumer goods using a simulated store technique rather than an actual test market. It is also referred to as laboratory test markets and purchase laboratories.

acceptable price range – An expectation in the minds of consumers regarding price levels of a product category. Research has proven that consumers are reluctant to buy below the acceptable price range for fear that the product will be inferior, or above it because the expected benefit of the product is not worth the price. See *prestige pricing*.

access journalism – When a person or organization allows a reporter (or selective reporters) to attend what would otherwise be a private meeting or board session. Public relations practitioners do not condone such a practice, but do recognize its importance to some "agendas."

access journalist – A reporter who is given access to "private" meetings. A reporter who gets "special" treatment from sources that others do not.

accessibility – One of the four major requirements of useful *market segmentation* with actionability, measurability and substantiality. *Accessibility* expresses the notion that the segment targeted must be able to be reached and served adequately by the firm's promotion and distribution system. See *actionability; measurability; substantiality*.

accomplishment – Something completed successfully. An achievement. Also, an acquired skill or expertise, social poise and grace.

accordion insert – An ad insert that has been folded like an accordion (i.e. - /\/\/\/).

account director – Depending on an agency's flow chart, an *account director* could have the same responsibilities as an *account manager* – could oversee one or a number of accounts.

account executive – The agency employee responsible for maintaining the relationship between the agency and the client. A position usually below the account manager.

account management – The process an agency or supplier uses to manage the needs of a client.

account manager – A representative responsible for a major client account or group of major accounts. See *account director*.

2 Techniques to Succeed: Phone etiquette

Part of doing business means doing business over the phone. Because the phone is such an important instrument in our daily business, below are some helpful hints, and proven phone techniques, that will help to make your phone conversations more effective.

Create a Good First Impression

• Try to answer the phone on the second ring. Answering a phone too fast can catch the caller off guard and waiting too long can make the caller angry.

• Answer with a friendly greeting. (Example – "Good Afternoon, IMT Customer Service, Sherrie speaking, how may I help you").

• Smile – it shows, even through the phone lines.

• Ask the caller for their name, even if their name is not necessary for the call. This shows you have taken an interest in them. Make sure that if you ask for their name, that you use it.

• Speak clearly and slowly. Never talk with anything in your mouth. This includes gum.

• Lower your voice if you normally speak loud

• Keep the phone two-finger widths away from your mouth

Putting Callers on Hold

When putting a caller on hold, always ask permission. If they ask why, provide them with the answer.

Examples:

"Would you mind holding while I get your file?"

"Can you hold briefly while I see if Mr. Jones is available?"

When taking a caller off of hold, always thank them for holding.

Transferring a Caller

1. If the caller needs to speak to another person or department, please transfer the caller directly to the desired person's extension, not to the operator. This will save the caller having to explain his/her requests another time, and it will cut the number of times the caller needs to be transferred.

2. When transferring a caller, tell them who you are transferring them to, and announce the caller to the person you are transferring them to.

Taking Phone Messages

When taking a phone message for someone, always be sure to include the following information:

• Caller's name and company name if applicable.

• Time and date of call.

• What the call is regarding.

• If the caller wants a return phone call, and if so,

• Obtain a phone number that is best for the return.

Last Impressions

• Before hanging up, be sure that you have answered all the caller's questions.

• Always end with a pleasantry: "Have a nice day" or "It was nice speaking with you."

• Let the caller hang up first. This shows the caller that you weren't in a hurry to get off the phone with them.

Azusa Pacific University – Azusa, Calif.
Read more at www.apu.edu/imt/telecom/etiquette.php

account planner – The person responsible for the creation, implementation and modification of the strategy on which creative (advertising) work is based.

account team – The public relations or advertising agency staff assigned to a specific client, generally consisting of various members – often including an *account director*, *account manager*, senior account executive/account executive and account assistants or account representatives.

accountability – Answerable and/or responsible. A key component to practicing effective and reliable public relations.

Accredited in Public Relations (APR) – A certification earned by PR professionals after serving as a successful practitioner for at least five years and passing a comprehensive examination. Only 6,000 in the world have earned the distinction. Read more at *www.prsa.org*.

accumulation – An audience-counting method, where each person exposed to a specific vehicle is counted once within a certain time period. Often referred to as cume.

accuracy – Conformity to fact. Also, precision, exactness or the ability of a measurement to match the actual value of the quantity being measured.

acetate – Transparent plastic sheet frequently used for overlays in advertisement layouts.

acquisition – One company acquiring control of another by purchase of a majority shareholding.

action plan – A detailed plan, containing a goal, objectives, strategies and tactics, illustrating how major tasks will be accomplished, managed and implemented, and an evaluation. Plan includes who will do them, when they will be carried out and costs (time and materials). Can be called a program plan.

actionability – Elements of a public relations plan, or an individual's agenda, which encourage the practitioner to "do something" – take action. These elements are usually based on data gathered through primary and secondary research. See *accessibility; measurability; substantiality.*

active audience – Members of the public who are readily available to be persuaded or convinced. However, they are seeking more information to solidify their attitude.

active buyer – A buyer or customer who has made a purchase within the last 12 months. Active buyers are highly likely to buy again and are considered "hot" leads in direct marketing.

active listening – Listening that is more than passively hearing what the customer is saying. It implies the need for the listener, or message receiver, to think while listening and to evaluate what is being said.

activity audit – Independent verification of measured activity for a specified time period. Some of the key components validated are advertisement impressions, page impressions, Web site clicks, total Web site visits and unique users. An activity audit results in a report verifying data and serves as a success measure of public relations or other type of communication or business plan. Formerly known as a *count audit.*

activity reports – Reports requiring agency personnel to provide details (such as number of calls made, new accounts opened, meetings attended and so on) as a measure of their activity in a given period.

actuality – The recorded words of someone who is part of a radio news story (newsmaker). Also referred to as a *soundbite* or *voice cut.*

ad audience – The number of unique users exposed to an advertisement within a specified time period.

ad blocker – Software on a user's Internet browser which prevents pop-up advertisements from being displayed.

ad campaign audit – An activity audit for a specific advertising or public relations campaign – a complete analysis of vehicle and channel use and costs compared to the increase (or decrease) in sales.

ad click – A rating measurement of an Internet user's action responding to (such as clicking on) an ad element causing a re-direct to another Web site or another frame or page within the advertisement.

ad copy – See *advertising copy*.

ad creep – Advertising that finds its way into news and feature articles. Similar to product placement or embedded ads. Advertisers pay to have their names mentioned in news or feature articles. While placing advertising in features and on radio and television programs is acceptable, many professionals consider payment for news article placements unethical.

3 Techniques to Succeed: Be interview ready

Looking for a new job can be stressful, but once you get an interview, landing the job could come down to a few minor details.

• Lack of preparation – this runs the gamut from not knowing anything about the organization or the job you're interviewing for, to arriving late and not dressing appropriately for the interview. Research the firm on the Web, learn all you can about what it does. Also, get directions ahead of time and arrive at least 15 minutes early.

• Being unprepared for difficult questions – you need to prepare for any type of question, from "Tell me what you know about our firm" to "Describe your most difficult work scenario and how you handled it."

Think about potential questions and prepare yourself to have a response.

• Not having questions prepared for the interviewer – a good interview should be a conversation between the interviewer and the applicant.

A few questions you can ask include: Why is this position open? Where are you in your hiring process? Tell me about your experience here at XYZ company?

Dawn Anthony - Director with OfficeTeam
Division of Robert Half International
800-804-8367

ad driven publications – Catalogues designed to look like magazines where the articles are actually advertorials. An example would be *LUCKY – The Magazine About Shopping*.

ad hoc – For the specific purpose, case or situation at hand and for no other – a committee formed ad hoc to address the issue of salaries.

ad materials – Creative artwork and copy.

ad recall – A measure of advertising effectiveness that samples a respondent's exposure to an ad and at a later point tests his/her recall of the ad. See *targeted ad recall*.

ad slick – Print ad that is ready to be sent to the print media leaving a designated location for a local retailer to insert its name and location. See *camera-ready, laser print, matte, repro, slick* and *velox*.

 Techniques to Succeed: Resolving client reluctance

Here is a five-step process to help resolve client conflict:

- Anticipate objections. When preparing presentations or proposals, keep in mind any issues the client might raise – anything they may have said or might say now. Have a planned response.

- Listen carefully. Show your value as a problem-solver to the client by listening closely to their concerns. Never interrupt or get defensive – work with them.

- Understand the objection. If you are not 100 percent clear about the client's objection, ask questions. Always check your understanding by restating the problem in your own words.

- Answer questions fully and honestly. Issues aren't resolved by being evasive, by manipulating the client or by misrepresenting your intensions. Always preface answers by showing you understand that the concern is legitimate from the client's viewpoint. After responding, confirm that you've dealt with the objection and that the client has no other questions.

- Be flexible. Try to resolve an objection by staying flexible in your proposals. Partner with your client to reach agreement.

The more skilled you are in resolving objections, the more satisfied your clients will be.

www.dalecarnegie.com

ad space – The location on a newspaper, magazine or Web site where an advertisement (usually display ad) can be placed.

ad value – The worth placed on a news release which appears in print and/or broadcast in terms of advertising dollars – if it had been paid for.

ad view – When an advertisement is seen, makes an impression and is tested by ad recall.

adaptive advertising – A technique in advertising which calls for the advertising message to adapt to that of a target audience to maximize effectiveness.

adaptive selling – A deliberate attempt on the part of a salesperson to adjust his or her communication style to suit the personality of the buyer. See *style flexing*.

added value – A firm's increased worth as a result of positive public relations. Factors that help generate the additional value are features, benefits, quality, reputation, image and exclusiveness.

addressable advertising – Individualized (personalized) ads and commercials (using massive databases) sent to individual magazine, newspaper or cable subscribers. In print, it is sometimes referred to as *ink jet printing* because early personalized ads inserted an individual's (person's) name using an ink jet printer.

adese – Advertising copy that is full of clichés, superlatives, stock phrases and vague generalities. It is considered a violation of all the guidelines for writing effective copy.

adjacencies – The commercial spot immediately before and after a particular television or radio program.

adopted orphan (film) – A documentary produced and shot by an independent filmmaker and sold to a studio or distributor because of a lack of interest.

adopted orphans – Documentary films picked up by a distributor. Orphan films, on the other hand, are documentaries that no one is willing to purchase or underwrite for distribution.

adopter category – A ranking of users of a new product, rated according to their willingness and speed to embrace a new product. Adopter categories are normally listed as innovators, early adopters, early majority, late majority and laggards. Different strategic messages (campaigns) are used for each adopter category.

adoption – The choice of one product or service over another.

adoption process – The series of stages, including awareness, interest, evaluation, trial and adoption or rejection, which consumers go through in their decision-making process. It is also called the diffusion process or adoption sequence.

adversarial shopper – A consumer whose shopping behavior is characterized by a determination to get good value at a low price. This would include a bargain hunter – one who regards all prices as negotiable.

advertainment – Commercials that integrate *product placement* (*embedded advertisements*) directly into television programs and motion pictures. Two examples are Rolaids® on "The Bernie Mac Show" and Sears® on "Extreme Makeover: Home edition."

advertising – Paid, non-personal communication from an identified source (sponsor) using mass media to persuade or influence an audience.

advertising agency – A firm specializing in the creation, design and media placement of advertisements, as well as the planning and execution of promotional campaigns. See *full-service advertising agency; limited-service advertising agency.*

advertising allowance – Discounts a manufacturer or supplier gives a retailer for featuring their products or brands in ads or in in-store promotions. An example would be a major beverage company offering supermarkets or "big box" drug stores free products in addition to the purchased product when the stores give up floor space for an in-store promotion.

advertising budget – Money set aside by the advertiser to pay for advertising, usually on an annual basis.

advertising campaign – A comprehensive advertising plan for a series of different but related ads that appear in different media across a specified time period.

6 Tips to Succeed: Be a team player

When interviewing for a position, it is always important to talk about the success you've achieved with the help of others. This discussion will inevitably lead to how you've also helped others achieve their goals. Companies like to hire people they can count on to work well with others. You are trying to fit into an already existing puzzle. You need to prove that you are willing to help others succeed and are willing to take advice and assistance from your new co-workers.

Steven Malloy - Career Counselor - University of Colorado

advertising copy – The content and context of a message contained in an advertisement. The printed text or spoken words in an advertisement. Radio or television advertising is sometimes referred to as continuity. Same as *ad copy.*

advertising effectiveness – The influence that an advertisement or some other form of promotional activity might have, is having, or has had on consumers or on the usage of a product advertised.

advertising elasticity – The relationship between a change in advertising budget and the resulting change in product sales.

advertising exposure – One presentation (or facing) of an advertisement to an audience. Advertising managers must decide how many "exposures" will be required to achieve their goal or objective.

advertising message – The central, underlying idea or theme within an advertisement. Also known as a strategic message.

advertising objectives – Statements of the effect of the advertising message on the audience.

advertising plan – An explicit outline of what goals an advertising campaign should achieve, how to accomplish those goals and how to determine whether or not the campaign was successful in obtaining those goals. Proper plans, whether advertising, public relations or other communication plans, should contain a *goal, objectives* (measurable with a time frame), *strategies* (messages), *tactics* (vehicles) and an evaluation component.

Advertising Research Foundation (ARF) – A nonprofit trade association whose mission is profitable business through effective research and insights. Read more at *www.arfsite.org*.

Advertising Standards Council – A body comprising representatives from the retail trade, trade unions, academia, advertising agencies and the media established to administer voluntary advertising codes and to provide a vehicle for consumer complaints about advertising. (Not a U.S. Regulatory Council – forms of this regulatory body are located in Australia, Canada and England.)

advertising substantiation – A Federal Trade Commission regulatory program requiring advertisers to have documentation of the claims made in their ads. The Federal Trade Commission has ruled that claims must be based on fact.

advertising testing – Advertisements and messages shown to a selected audience, prior to the ad launch, to determine effectiveness.

advertising vehicle – Outlet or vehicle (newspapers, magazines, television, radio, billboards, etc.) used in communication between advertisers and consumers. Advertisers are constantly challenged to create new vehicles – some innovative vehicles include supermarket floors, public bathrooms, ATM receipts, beach sand, sidewalks and monitors at self-service gasoline pumps.

advertorial – An advertisement that has the appearance of a news article or editorial, in a print publication. See *infomercial.*

advocacy advertising – A communication or message which presents information or a point of view on a controversial public issue, idea or cause. Many times referred to as issue advertising. A message aimed at bringing about legislative change. Many of the guidelines for *political advertising* may be applied.

aerial advertising – Advertising using airplanes as skywriters or flying billboards (some planes carry banners behind them).

affectation – A deliberate pretense or exaggerated display – usually in speech patterns or speaking cadence – verbal editorializing through delivery rather than content.

affiliate – A television or radio station that contracts with a national network to carry network-originated programming during part of its schedule.

affinity marketing – Marketing targeted at individuals sharing common interests that predispose them toward a product (e.g. an auto accessories manufacturer targeting automobile magazine readers). Also, a campaign jointly sponsored by a number of different, possibly dissimilar organizations that are non-competitive but have a particular interest in common. See *partnering*.

affirmative disclosure – A disclosure of information in an advertisement, required by the Federal Trade Commission or other authority that may not be desired by the advertiser. This information frequently admits to some limitation in the product or the offer made in the advertisement. Also called a disclaimer. Many pharmaceutical products carry disclaimers in both print and broadcast advertising.

affordable luxuries – Trying to purchase prestigious brands without paying full price – through discounters or thrift shops. See *Trading Up*.

after-action memo – A brief document written following an event and prior to a debriefing meeting listing what worked and what didn't work successfully or to the organization's satisfaction.

agate line – A measure of newspaper advertising size – equal to one column wide and one fourteenth of an inch deep (and approximately six-point type).

7 Tips to Succeed: Know where you are headed!

"It's okay to hit the ground running, just make sure you are going in the right direction."

age compression – Young people leaving childhood sooner or "growing up" quicker – forsaking toys for such other pleasures as shopping.

agency – A business that serves another. Public relations agencies provide counseling, research, strategic planning, media relations, promotion, publicity, special event planning and crisis communication expertise. Advertising agencies create, design, produce and place advertisements that call public attention to its clients. The most effective method for choosing the right agency for a firm, organization or product is to talk to others in a similar profession or business and to visit Web sites. Public relations and advertising agencies are more than willing to conduct formal pitches to attract clients.

agency commission – An agency's fee for designing and placing advertisements. Historically, this was calculated as 15 percent of the amount spent to purchase space or time in the various media used for the advertising. In recent years, the commission has, in many cases, become negotiable and may even be based on some measure of the campaign's success.

agency of record – An advertising or public relations agency that has been officially designated as having responsibility for coordinating the promotion of one or more of an advertiser's products and/or services.

agenda – An attempt to influence a preconceived notion of how an event should end. Some reporters have been accused of weaving a preconceived idea or slant into a story to help influence an event's outcome. See *agenda setting.*

agenda setting – Sometimes used by journalists and other members of the media – a preconceived slant to the story. It is the creation of what the public thinks is important and/or the creation of public awareness and concern for an issue or issues. As far back as 1922, newspaper columnist Walter Lippmann (first to formally use the **MAC Triad** [Message-Audience-Channel]), was concerned that the media had the power to present images to the public. Research (McCombs and Shaw) first conducted in 1968 concluded that the mass media exerted a significant influence on what voters considered to be the major issues of the campaign. It was determined that "when quotes don't fit the story (slant), they probably won't get used."

agent – Someone who acts on behalf of someone else, usually for a fee.

AIDA (Attention, Interest, Desire, Action) – A four-step model describing the process that advertising or promotion is intended to initiate in the mind of a prospective consumer – create attention, generate interest, develop desire and initiate action.

aided recall – The need for additional information or a word or phrase to trigger the recall of information about an advertisement, product, service or brand without any prompting. A method of evaluating the effectiveness of a company's recent advertising. See *recall test, unaided recall test.*

AIO statements – Expressions of a person's attitudes toward, interests in and opinions of, a product. See *psychographics.*

air stairs – Steps used to enter an airline from the tarmac.

8 Tips to Succeed:
Online resources can improve writing

Writing well is more than just knowing the basics. A well-written letter, proposal or brochure could make or break a sale.

If you are not the best writer, the Internet offers many resources for helping create well-crafted materials.

These Web sites can help you with business or personal writing.

- www.onelook.com – An online resource where you can search almost 1,000 dictionaries.

- www.bartleby.com/100 – A listing of familiar quotations so you can find just the right phrase for the "write" occasion.

- www.c2.com/cgi/wiki?ChicagoManualOfStyle – The online home of the "Chicago Manual of Style" answers frequently asked questions about style.

- thesaurus.com – The online version of Roget's New Millennium Thesaurus helps you locate the right word for the idea you're trying to express.

Andrea C. Carrero - Word Technologies Inc., Cherry Hill, N.J. - 856-428-0925

airbrush – An artist's technique for creating a smooth gradation of color. It is often used to cover imperfections in a photograph (e.g., in a model's skin).

all-we-can-afford method – A simple method of determining a budget (for public relations, advertising, etc.) where the amount allocated is the amount that can be afforded. Also, called the What-We-Can Afford Method, the Affordable Method and the Arbitrary Method.

alliances – In politics, lists of candidates who run on the same platform. For example, there could be two columns of Democrats, each representing its own philosophy or platform. In non-partisan elections, alliances or lists don't necessarily carry a party banner. Also called *lists*.

alliteration – The repetition of the same sounds or of the same kinds of sounds at the beginning of words or in stressed syllables, as in "on scrolls of silver snowy sentences" (Hart Crane). Artful use of alliteration helps make speeches effective.

allocations – Divisions or proportions of advertising dollars among the various media.

allowance – A reduction off the (list) price offered by a producer to a buyer. There are five common types of discounts *allowances*; *cash discount*; *quantity discount*; *seasonal discount*; *trade discount.*

altruism – In communication – more specifically, public relations – terms, helping your boss solve a problem he/she doesn't have.

ambush marketing – A deliberate attempt by an organization to associate itself with an event, for profit or charity, to gain some of the benefits associated with being an official sponsor without incurring the costs of sponsorship.

American Academy of Advertising (AAA) – An association of educators, students, and former educators in advertising. Read more at *www.advertising.utexas.edu/AAA.*

Tips to Succeed: A user-friendly Web site

So many people flock to the Web that if your Web site is not user-friendly you may be sending potential clients elsewhere.

Here are some hints to assure your Web site is right for business:

• Can visitors find information easily?

• Is the navigation clear and consistent throughout the site?

• Can visitors easily find your contact information?

• Do the pages load quickly on a standard modem connection? Many users still have dial-up service.

• Are the most important elements of your site visible without scrolling up and down or side to side on computer monitors set to the 600 X 800 resolution size?

• Does the site look good and work with Netscape® and Internet Explorer® browsers?

• Can the visitor identify what your business does or what products you sell?

Research is clear, frustrated visitors leave difficult to navigate sites and may not return.

American Association of Advertising Agencies (AAAA) – A non–profit trade association dedicated to improving and strengthening the advertising agency business. Read more at *www.aaaa.org*.

American Marketing Association (AMA) – One of the largest professional associations for marketers, has 38,000 members worldwide in every area of marketing. For more than six decades the AMA has been a resource providing relevant marketing information. Read more at *www.marketingpower.com*.

amiable (social style) – One of the four social styles (with *analytical*, *driver* and *expressive*) used to classify salespeople and their customers. *Amiables* are relationship oriented and look for personal motives in the actions of others. See *analytical*, *driver* and *expressive*.

analysis paralysis – So much data being available and considered that it interferes with the purpose of the survey or project.

analytical – One of the four social styles (with *amiable*, *driver* and *expressive*) used to classify salespeople and their customers. *Analyticals* tends to ask questions, gather facts and consider data seriously. See *amiable*, *driver* and *expressive*.

anchor interview – An interview conducted live by a television news anchor with a newsmaker either inside or outside of the studio.

anchor store – A popular, major retailer located within a shopping mall to attract mall patronage.

angel – Someone who invests money in a new business. Unlike a *venture capitalist*, this is an individual who decides to "back a business" – in its early stages. Also called *business angel*. See *venture capitalist*. Read more at *www.angelcapitalassociation.org*.

angle – The particular approach a reporter takes in writing a story. In public relations, different angles can be used to pitch a story a reporter.

anecdotal research – Informal research rather than scientific – many times gathered through observation.

animatic – A preliminary version of a commercial with the storyboard frames recorded on videotape along with a rough sound track.

animation – A type of recording medium where objects are sketched and then filmed one frame at a time.

anniversary journalism – A genre that stems from a culture obsessed with dates. Examples might include the commemoration of the date President Richard M. Nixon resigned, the date of the Hindenburg disaster or the date the first enclosed shopping mall opened on the East coast.

answer print – The final edited version (print) of a television commercial – for approval by the client. It may still need color correction, etc.

anticipate – Foreseeing. A key component of public relations counseling. It is the *A* in the *ABCs* of effective public relations. For every public relation action there will be reaction. PR counselors must anticipate reactions – positive or negative – through research before making recommendations to superiors or clients. See *research*.

anticipatory pricing – The practice of setting a somewhat higher price than would otherwise have been chosen in expectation of increased cost (inflation), government price control or an environmental circumstance.

AP style – Standardized rules of grammar and writing style, issued by the Associated Press (news "wire" service/international news agency). Most media outlets follow this style, or have their own version of style.

aperture – The ideal moment (an opening) for exposing consumers to an advertising message.

aping – Women who look and act like other women or men emulating women.

appeal – Something that moves people or arouses interest. An advertisement's selling message that arouses interest, makes a request or moves consumers to act.

appearance – How an individual looks – but more importantly, how the individual is perceived by another.

applause line – Line in a speech expected to elicit applause or other audience reaction.

appointment television – Programs that air at a particular time that has viewers scheduling their day or evening to make certain they watch it.

Arbitron – Radio rating service that publishes listenership reports for selected markets. Read more at *www.arbitron.com/home/content.stm.*

Area of Dominant Influence (ADI) – A geographic area reached by radio or television stations.

10 Tips to Succeed:
Economical business trips

Business travel can cost a whole lot – or – a lot less. With a little planning, you can keep costs down.

Given today's technology – e-mail, phones, Web sites – you may think the best way to save money on business travel is to just stay home. Wrong! Nothing beats the power of a face-to-face meeting for closing a deal or maintaining an ongoing client relationship.

It pays to be aware of costs and alternatives before booking a hotel, rental car or airline ticket.

In my years as a frequent traveler, here are a few money-saving business travel tips I've picked up:

• Use alternate airports

• Check low-cost airlines

• Shop prices on the Internet, but also call hotels directly

• Check the airlines' own Web sites in addition to the major Internet travel sites

• Try moderately-priced, business-oriented motels

• NEVER pick up the hotel phone before you know the charges

• When staying in a sprawling urban area, rent a car

• Use your frequent flier miles for expensive business trips rather than inexpensive leisure travel

Travel is an important and necessary part of business life. Don't avoid it, but don't spend more than you have to either.

Rhonda Abrams - www.rhondaworks.com/

arm piece – A date, or two people who usually show up together at an event.

aroma (scent) marketing – The subliminal use of scent or smell to suggest the purchase of a product. "Got Milk" ads in bus shelters in San Francisco infused the scent of freshly baked chocolate chip cookies (using adhesive scent strips) within walking distance of a bakery. Years ago, movie theatres learned that popping popcorn near the auditorium's doors would increase sales of popcorn along with Coca-Cola®.) An example – one million *People* subscribers got a special Kraft-sponsored holiday issue featuring "rub-and-smell" ads for products such as cherry Jell-O® and white fudge Chips Ahoy! ® cookies.

art – The visual elements in an advertisement, including illustrations, photos, type, logos and signatures, and the layout. Photograph(s) and/or other graphics accompanying a newspaper story or other publication.

art director – The advertising agency employee responsible for creating artwork and layouts for advertisements.

art proof – The artwork for an advertisement, to be submitted for client approval.

article guidelines – Requirements, specifications and procedures used to standardize bylined articles for submission to a specific publication.

artwork – The visual components of an ad, not including the typeset text.

11 Tips To Succeed: Five Cs of Credit – Essential to obtaining a business loan

Looking for a loan? Be ready to show the bank you have the five Cs of credit.

Character – This includes personal finances, how you're viewed in the industry, what's on your credit report. If there are discrepancies in your credit report, be up front and explain. Do not try to hide them.

Capacity – How much debt can your business handle? What will be the debt to income ratio? Make sure the loan will help your business, not break your business.

Capital – This is your businesses' cash flow.

Conditions – This would explain what the loan is going to be used for. This includes start-up costs, equipment and inventory. This also includes external effects on your business, such as market trends, government regulations or the weather.

Collateral – This is a second form of guarantee to the bank which includes the business property, inventory and personal assets such as your home.

Heather Mihal - Assistant Vice President - Hudson United Bank

assembly – Putting the scenes of a motion picture in proper order after they are shot – usually in the order they will appear in the final version.

asset led marketing – Product strengths such as the name and brand image to sell and/or market both new and existing products. Marketing decisions are based on the needs of the consumer.

assignment editor – The person in broadcast media who reviews news from outside sources, determines "newsworthy ideas," then determines the priority of the various news stories and assigns reporters.

Associated Press style – Standardized rules of grammar and writing style, issued by the Associated Press (news "wire" service/international news agency). Most media outlets follow this style, or have their own version of style.

Association of National Advertisers (ANA) – The trade association serving the needs of advertisers and marketers by providing leadership in advertising and marketing trends and best practices. Read more at *www.ana.net*.

at-home TV shopping – A type of non-store retailing in which consumers order merchandise by mail, telephone or the Internet. Goods are shipped directly to their homes. It is also referred to as *direct-response marketing; direct-response selling.*

atmospherics – The combination of decor, physical characteristics and amenities provided by a retailer to develop a particular image and attract customers.

atomic clock – A very precise clock that operates using the elements cesium or rubidium. A cesium clock has an error of one second per million years. GPS satellites contain multiple cesium and rubidium clocks.

attack dog – Spokesperson chosen to communicate a candidate or organization's message and snuff out opponents' assaults.

attention – The concentration of the mental powers on an advertisement or commercial. Truly effective ads/commercials engage the mind (draw attention) and then deliver the strategic message. Also, the ability or power to concentrate mentally.

attentioner – A tactic used to gain the target audience's attention. Examples would include a newspaper front page promo, television bumpers and Internet pop-up ads. See *bumper.*

12 Tips To Succeed: Mind your Manners for a good first impression

It takes only three to five seconds to make a first impression, but it can take a whole career to undo it. Here's what you should keep in mind during those first fateful moments to make a positive impression at an interview, conference, party or any other time you meet new faces.

The tardiness taboo

The most important guideline is the most fundamental: Don't be late. Ever.

Figure out how long it takes to get to your meeting point and allow extra time. It's better to arrive early than risk tardiness. For interviews and other important events, do a practice run in advance to clock the drive and make sure you know the route.

If you arrive more than 10 minutes ahead of schedule, take a short walk before going inside. Arriving too early can rattle the person you're meeting.

Appearances

It's an unfortunate fact of human nature that before you even say hello, people form an opinion of you based on how you look.

In business settings, look sharp by dressing slightly more formally than the people you're meeting with. Avoid distracting accents, like excessive jewelry or a goofy tie.

Your clothes should not draw attention to you. And don't leave a bad impression by forgetting the rear view.

Check the back of your clothes in the mirror for rips and stains. Make sure you're tucked in where you should be. Also examine the back of your shoes for mud splashes or worn-down heels.

Presenting yourself

At events where you have a chance to make new contacts, take a proactive approach. Peter Post (Emily's grandson) says, "Go in with an attitude that says you're going to participate, you're going to be willing to go up and introduce yourself to people and start conversations."

It takes guts to approach strangers, but if you do it with charm, those you meet will be impressed by your sociability.

Post recommends four actions to ensure a positive first impression:

- Stand up to get on eye level with the person.
- Look them in the eye.
- Give a firm handshake, but don't "bone crush" them. Keep your shoulders and feet oriented toward the person.
- Repeat the person's name and say you're pleased to meet them.

Fine-tune and rehearse your self-introduction, a 10-second or less sound-bite (elevator speech) that includes your first and last name and a snippet of background information to kindle conversation. Example: Hello, I'm Denise Kersten, a careers columnist for *USATO-DAY*.com.

Making connections

Introducing others will make you seem gracious and well connected, but be sure to follow the proper protocol.

In social situations the order in which you introduce two people is based on gender and age (women and older people first).

In business settings the order is determined by rank.

Introduce the lower-ranking person to the higher-ranking person, then reverse the order, so you say each person's name two times. Try to add an interesting tidbit to start the conversation. If you were introducing Mrs. Smith, a vice president of the company, to Mr. Jones, a junior associate, for example, you might say:

If you are unsure who the more important person is, default to the gender and age guideline.

Don't panic if you forget a name. Most people will be happy to remind you and appreciate the introduction.

Chit chat

Conversation is more like a tennis match than a golf game. Hitting the ball too many times in a row is a serious faux pas. Instead, try to establish a back-and-forth volley.

Asking questions about the other person's background and mentioning that interesting item you read in the newspaper are tried-and-true chat starters or icebreakers. Stay away from politically charged or sensitive topics with people you've just met.

Also avoid alienating individuals with different professional backgrounds.

Stay away from industry language and acronyms. It may make you feel plugged in, but it can turn-off uninitiated listeners.

If you succeed at establishing rapport with a new contact, you may ask for their business card and offer yours. But only do so in the context of building a mutually-beneficial relationship, or you may come across as pushy.

The recovery

We all make etiquette slip-ups from time to time. Even Peter Post admits to the occasional oversight. But you can minimize the damage with a sincere apology.

"Acknowledge your mistake. Don't try to put it off on somebody else. Accept it as your mistake. Then correct it," Post says.

For the less serious offenses a simple "excuse me" goes a long way.

Denise Kersten - *USATODAY*.com
Dana May Casperson - Author of Power Etiquette:
What You Don't Know Can Kill Your Career

attitude – A learned predisposition to act. Inner feelings. Enduring favorable or unfavorable feelings, emotions and action tendencies toward an issue, person, subject or ideal. Expression of the attitude is the opinion.

attitude tracking – Measuring the degree of satisfaction with a product through an ongoing study of consumer attitudes toward it.

attribution – A line identifying the source of a quote.

audience – The intended receivers of a message. Audiences are segmented into active audiences, which seek information even though they might already be persuaded or even convinced, and passive audiences, which are uninterested and usually send surrogates (stand-ins) to get more information.

audience attention probability – The degree to which a target consumer is likely to pay attention to an advertisement in a particular media outlet. For example, the audience attention probability of an advertisement for a new male enhancement drug is likely to be greater in a men's or women's magazine than in a daily newspaper.

audience composition – An analysis of an audience based on characteristics relevant to an advertiser.

audience duplication – The number of people that read, view or hear an advertisement more than once.

13

Tips to Succeed:
Ad placement matters on the Web

According to Google, ads placed in particular areas of a (home) page will get noticed. The hottest spot for advertisers is in the middle of a page. Ads above the fold are also good. The fold is jargon for how much of a Web page a person sees without having to scroll down. But if a person must scroll to read an entire article, all hope is not lost. Advertisements at the end of articles perform well. That's because people want to do something else after reading an article.

Gannett News Service

audience power structure – Audiences within a community or organization can be segmented into elite, diffused and amorphous and illustrated by using a pyramid – elite is where the power is concentrated at the top (a few opinion leaders or key communicators); diffused is where the power is spread throughout and amorphous is where the power has yet to surface (e.g. a new condominium community).

audience profile – Based on *demographics*, *psychographics* and *geodemographics*.

audience tune-out – An occurrence when relatively large groups of a radio or TV audience drop concentration, or stop listening altogether. Audience tune-out may result from commercial clutter.

audilog – A diary kept by selected audience members to record which television programs they watched. It's one of the components used by A.C. Nielsen in rating television shows. Read more at *www.nielsen-media.com*.

audimeter – An electronic recording device used by A.C. Nielsen to track when a television set is in use, and to what station it is set – sometimes referred to as a people meter or black box. Read more at *www.nielsenmedia.com*.

audiovisuals (AV) – Presentation methods that use sight and sound to enhance the understanding of a topic. AV includes the use of electronic

14 Techniques to Succeed: Make the most of your ads

Give your proposed ad to several different people and ask them what product you are selling. Would it entice them to find out more, or even purchase your product?

Hand someone your flier and ask them to find your contact information. See how long it takes. If it takes them longer than five seconds, you need to make it bigger, or make the flier less busy. Hand someone your flier and have them look at it for five seconds. Then hide the flier and ask them what the flier said. If they had no idea, then your ad or flier is poorly written or too cluttered. Does the ad or flier excite the reader to call or buy? This can be done with a special offer, a discount, or something for FREE.

Fred Hueston and Lyna Farkas –
Hosts of the radio show "Growing Your Business" –
www.growingyourbusiness.net

devices, usually involving screen and visual images, as contrasted with printed material. One common AV method is PowerPoint®.

audit – Third party validation of log activity and/or measurement process associated with public relations activities, which measures results against the plan. Some audits evaluate Internet activity/advertising. Activity audits validate measurement counts. Process audits validate internal controls associated with measurement.

Audit Bureau of Circulations (ABC) – A company that audits the circulation of print publications, to insure that reported circulation figures are accurate. Read more at *www.accessabc.com.*

author's alterations (AAs) – Changes a customer requests after a print job has been submitted. Customers are usually charged extra for any AAs. Public relations practitioners and others who use printers should check their printer's policy about AAs. Ethical printers usually have the customer sign a new estimate with the new charges included.

auto (car) wraps – An advertising technique using silk-screened vinyl tightly wrapped around a car, truck, bus or just about any other vehicle

15

Tips to Succeed: Six tips for keeping PR pitches out of newsroom recycle bins

The whole attachment business when emailing reporters is a huge deal — don't send unsolicited attachments. Attachments could shut email down because the system gets clogged.

These tips might help ensure that your e-mail pitches don't get tossed — and help you boost your pickup rate among the media you target:

1. Hook journalists with brevity and timeliness. The best e-mails are the ones that are brief and that have great subject lines. That means the subject line conveys "just the facts." Like a newspaper headline, it needs to deliver details like "when and where" without going on. The point is to keep it straightforward — e.g., "Teens to Rally at 3:00 p.m. at Capitol Hill." That's good because it [gives] just the 5 W's.

Good subject lines also stress the time frame that we're dealing with. For example, "Labor Day Fashion" works because it has a timely element so the reporter knows he/she has to look at it quickly. Also, that implies that you know lead times and deadlines.

2. Carefully consider using humor in subject lines. Another way to keep from [being deleted] is to try something funny. Many time, if your pitch has a fun subject line, curiosity will be piqued. "Teach Your Dog to Meditate" is an example of a catchy subject line that worked (in a pitch) for a book on behavioral tips for animals. But this type of approach is not going to work for everyone.

3. Include surprising numbers or factoids to grab attention. Using numbers, statistics and facts is another good way to make sure an email stands out. For example, the National Housing Conference sent me an email pitch, "U.S. Housing Prices Rise 20% Nationwide." It got the reporter's attention."

4. Work e-mail pitches in tandem with phone calls. E-mails can make a phone call not a cold call and vice versa. A great thing to do is to call in advance and say you're going to send me an email later. Include something like "Maria, per our phone call" in the subject line so the reporter knows it's not a blanket pitch or cold call.

5. Be prepared to answer questions via e-mail or phone.
A lot of PR people aren't that prepared to answer questioned when following up on emails or phone pitches. That's not good. When good reporters have a PR person on the phone, they'll ask questions right then while pulling up the e-mail pitch so they can see if they are interested right at that moment. If you don't have answers, it's a waste of time.

6. Stay flexible — play off your target's comments for greater buy-in. Equally important: Flexibility is key because it may be that the story you're pitching isn't the one that's going to get published. Maybe a different story will come out — one that still highlights your client, but in a different way than you expected. In other words, reporters can feel it when a PR person is reading from a script. They don't want to get off the scripted pitch — and so they don't give the reporter a chance to get into it. Don't be one of those PR "people."

Here is some advice: "Listen to the reporter's reaction. At least, consider where we may be coming from on an idea. Listen and then consider sharing (the reporter's) ideas with the client. Be open to expanding upon the ideas you pitched. For example, I might grab onto a phrase you say in passing that seems to have real news value — and then ask you to pursue that in more detail. If you allow for it and practice (active listening), then these pitches can become (collaborative)."

Maria Stainer - Assistant Managing Editor - *The Washington Times*

on wheels. It allows consumers to view advertising messages in three-dimensional form. Research shows it creates a high retention rate among those who see it. Auto wraps are semi-permanent graphics that can be removed without harm to the vehicle. Auto wrapped vehicles are low-cost mobile billboards. Auto wrapping companies offer a number of services. They can assist in finding drivers who will allow the auto wrap advertising to be placed on their vehicle in exchange for some form of payment. For this, they may offer barter – placing the auto wrap advertising in exchange for providing a free vehicle to drivers. Many partner with trucking companies, bus transportation agencies, taxi companies and other businesses engaged in transit or transportation. It is already accepted that auto wrap advertising provides an excellent venue for increased brand exposure. See *building wraps*.

automatic merchandising – The selling of goods by use of vending machines.

availability – Advertising time on radio or television that is available for purchase, at a specific time. Often referred to as *inventory*.

available market – That part of the total market which has an interest in a product or service, can afford to purchase it and is not prevented from making the purchase.

Average Audience (AA) – The number of homes or people tuned to a television program during an average minute or the number of people who viewed an average issue of a print publication.

average cost – The average cost per unit of production of a set or group of products. The total cost of production divided by the total number produced. Also, called unit cost. See *long-run average cost*; *short-run average cost*.

average cost trends – A history of changes in the average unit (per message) process for each medium that is used in cost forecasting.

aversive factors – Qualities about people that turn others against them and may prevent the development of successful working relationships.

awareness – Brands with which a consumer is familiar.

b-roll – Film or videotape used as background footage for a TV news story that plays while an announcer speaks over it.

baby boomer – A person born between 1946 and 1964 – a period of explosive population growth. Baby boomers make up a large majority of today's work force, wealth component and have significant buying power. They are not afraid of spending money – free spenders – and are often credited with keeping the economy afloat. They tend to use professional contractors while *Gen-Xers* (born 1965-1974) like to "do it" themselves.

baby boomer marketing – Campaigns designed to target individuals born between 1946 and 1959 (77 million). Many strategies and campaigns aim for the wallets of free spenders.

baby bouncers – The generation of people who are the children of baby boomers. (Also called *yuppies* – a young upwardly mobile professional person under 40.)

back channel – The use of an unconventional, but ethical, approach to get something accomplished. Sometimes referred to as "back dooring it." Term used when editors or news directors leap over their own reporter to make a call to an organization's CEO – leaping over that firm's public relations practitioner or spokesperson, who may have been stonewalling the reporter/news outlet. Theory here is – top management may be more willing to talk to a perceived equal. Also used when news editors refer to: what we know; what we think we know; what we'll never know (used in brainstorming).

back checking – Much like fact checking. Looking back to make certain the information (quotes, etc.) contained in a document is accurate.

16 Techniques to Succeed: Budgeting – beyond the basics

1. Budgets are a necessary evil.
They're the only practical way to get a grip on your spending so you can make sure your money is being used the way you want it to be used.

2. Creating a budget generally requires three steps.
• Identify how you spend money now.

• Evaluate your current spending and set goals that take into account your financial objectives.

• Track your spending to make sure it stays within those guide-lines.

3. Use software to save grief
• Quicken®

• Microsoft Money®

4. Don't drive yourself nuts.
Once you determine which categories of spending can and should be cut (or expanded), concentrate on those categories and worry less about other aspects of your spending.

5. Watch out for cash leakage.
If withdrawals from the ATM machine evaporate from your pocket without apparent explanation, it's time to keep better records.

6. Spending beyond your limits is dangerous.
But if you do, you've got plenty of company – but it's definitely a sign you need to make some serious spending cuts.

7. Beware of luxuries dressed up as necessities.
If your income doesn't cover your costs, then some of your spend-ing is probably for luxuries – even if you've been considering them to be filling a real need.

8. Tithe yourself.
Aim to spend no more than 90 percent of your income. That way, you'll have the other 10 percent left to save for your big-picture items.

9. Don't count on windfalls.
When projecting the amount of money you can live on, don't include dollars that you can't be sure you'll receive, such as year-end bonuses, tax refunds or investment gains.

> **10. Beware of spending creep.**
> As your annual income climbs from raises, promotions and smart investing, don't start spending for luxuries until you're sure that you're staying ahead of inflation.
>
> www.money.cnn.com/pf/101/lessons/2/

back end – Marketing technique involving the use of a non-direct marketing vehicles to promote products or services through referrals. For example viral marketing, paid buzz or even carrying a brief message as a "butt print" on workout shorts or sweatpants. Read more at www.small-businessnewz.com/smallbusinessnewz-13-20031006HowToUseYourBackEndForMarketing.html.

back end marketing – Ads or other messages printed on the back side of your shorts and walking seductively though town so that you draw everyone's attention. Obviously, bikinis rate better results than flower print polyester cut-offs, but you have to be pretty "brief" with your message.

back matter – Items placed after the main body of a document. Examples of back matter include appendices and indices. Also called *end matter*.

back of story – In both print and broadcast journalism, it is the copy or information toward the end of the story.

back shop people – Stems from the days when getting the news out through the print media took typesetters, compositors, proofreaders and others.

back to back – Running more than one commercial, with one following immediately after another. Many times on radio, commercials are separated by a time check or weather forecast – known as *cluster busters*.

backbone – A central computer network connecting other networks together.

backed the right horse – Supported the right (winning) candidate or the right cause.

background (on background) – Information is just that – for *background only* – not to be used and not to be attributed until such a time (if ever) that the *newsmaker* gives the go ahead. It is purely an act of educating a journalist about the subject without saying anything that can be used in a specific story until it is released. (Chapter 9 – *The Public Relations Practitioner's Playbook* – Kendall/Hunt – 2008.) See *not for attribution; off the record.*

backgrounder – An in-depth document explaining a product, service, organization or company in the context of its need, position in the marketplace and place in history. Many times it supports and explains an accompanying news release. Also, an informal written or oral briefing for reporters about a specific issue, event, individual or company.

backsliding – To revert to a bad habit.

backward integration – Acquiring ownership of a firm or company's supply chain, usually in the hope of reducing supplier power and thus reducing costs.

backward marketing channel – A marketing channel in which goods – to be recycled or reprocessed – flow backward from consumer to intermediaries to producer; also called a *reverse marketing channel.*

bait and switch advertising – An alluring but insincere (and illegal, as deemed by the Federal Trade Commission) offer to sell a product or service which the advertiser in truth does not intend or want to sell. Its purpose is to switch consumers from buying the advertised merchandise, to buy something else, usually at a higher price. The FTC has ruled (Sec. 238.1 Bait advertisement) that no advertisement containing an offer to sell a product should be published when the offer is not a bona fide effort to sell the advertised product.

balanced scorecard – Technique allowing an organization to monitor and manage performance against defined objectives. Measurements might typically cover financial performance, customer value, internal business process, innovation performance and employee performance.

bandwagon effect – The observation that people often do (or believe) things because many other people do (or believe) the same. The effect is "herding" Without examining the merits of the particular thing, people tend to "follow the crowd."

banner – A rectangular graphic image (usually 469 x 60 pixels) on a Web site displaying an advertisement with a clickable link. Read more at *www.iab.net* for voluntary guidelines defining specifications of banner ads. Also, a newsletter's title, subtitle or mission statement, volume and issue, date of publication and logo. It covers about one-fifth of the front page. It can run at the top of the page or down the side. See *flag*; *nameplate*. In research, a question or demographic factor used as the basis for cross-tabulation.

banner ad – See *banner* above.

banner headline – A (newspaper) headline written in large letters (display type) across the width of the page.

bar back – Servers who wait on patrons sitting or standing at a bar rather than those at tables.

17 Technique to Succeed: Business dining: Dos and don'ts

Some tips to help make your business dinner successful:
• Have fun, but remain professional.

• Dress appropriately.

• Pick the right restaurant for your affair, making sure the atmosphere fits the tone of your business outing. If you are looking to have a quiet business dinner, and don't want to be disturbed by other diners, look for a place with private rooms or a very quiet environment.

• Go to a restaurant with which you are familiar. It's not the best idea to go somewhere that you have never been before.

• Make reservations in advance – not the day of a business dinner. You're usually safe on the same day during the week, but if you have a larger party you may be out of luck.

• Limit the alcohol.

• Order food you like. Don't order because of someone else.

• Make sure you have enough credit on your credit card if you are paying the bill.

• Always take care of your server.

Jim Haney - General Manager - Palm Restaurant - Atlantic City NJ
Courier-Post – Monday, April 4, 2005

18 Technique to Succeed:
Business angels – bearing cash for business

Business angels are private funders of start-up or growing businesses. They fill the role venture capitalists filled 20 years ago. Now venture capitalists generally will only fund companies that can grow huge, investing a minimum of a few million dollars. That leaves a big gap in funding for early-stage companies, the type needing $200,000, not $20 million. Angels fill that gap.

In 2004, angels actually invested more money in new companies than venture capitalists – a whopping $22.5 billion in angel funds, compared with $18 billion in venture capital. According to the Center for Venture Research at the University of New Hampshire, 48,000 companies received funding from 225,000 active angel investors.

The primary distinction between angels and venture capitalists is that angels invest their own money. They don't have to justify their investments to others, so they invest in a broader variety of businesses. They can have more patience in getting a return on their money, and they can invest in ideas that are just plain interesting, exciting or fun. Most are successful entrepreneurs themselves, so they understand and appreciate what business people are going through.

Why would a private foundation spend money to organize groups of private investors?

To find out or to find your own angel, check the directory on the Angel Capital Association Web site, www.angelcapitalassociation.org. For assistance in forming an angel group in your community, contact the Kauffman Foundation, www.kauffman.org.

Courier-Post - Tuesday, May 3, 2005

bar code – The nine-digit ZIP code translated into a coding structure of vertical and half bars used to speed mail sorting and enabling mailers to take a discount on postage. Similar technology is used to price and trade merchandise and inventory from manufacturer to retailer.

bar code (UPC) – An arrangement of lines and spaces in code form used to identify a product by style, size, price, quality, quantity, etc. The code, read by a scanning device, is used in marketing decision-making, including stock control and inventory level adjustment.

bargaining power – The strength or influence one party has in a business negotiation. The capacity of one party to dominate by virtue of its size or position or by a combination of personality and negotiating tactics.

barhead – A person addicted to the prescription drug Xanax®.

bartering – The trading of goods and services for advertising time or space. Also called *trade out*. See *exchange*.

barter syndication – Programs that are offered to a radio or television station at a reduced price or for a fee, with pre-sold commercial spots.

base line – Established during benchmarking as a "starting point."

base-point pricing – This pricing method charges clients freight costs based on their distance from the shipping location. These costs are different from general shipping cost.

bastard pop – Also called *mash up*. *Bastard pops* involve blending samples from two songs – generally, one song's vocals atop another's instrumental or rhythm track. Experts say the blending achieves a certain *synergy* not otherwise achieved with individual songs. The sum of the parts often surpasses the originals. The more disparate the genre-blending, the better. Experts say the best mash-ups blend punk with funk or Top 40 with heavy metal, boosting the tension between slick and raw. The finished product is called mash. This is now being done for jingles. Read more at http://www.mashups.com/.

battered (type) – When a letter in a printed document is defective – not fully printed (see *bump*).

battle of the brands – A term used in reference to the often intense competition between manufacturers' brands, wholesalers' brands and retailers' brands.

battleground state – A swing state in an election – a state that could go either way and help to decide an election's outcome. In municipalities, they would be referred to as battleground districts.

beacon – A snippet of code placed in an advertisement, on a Web site or in an e-mail, which helps measure whether the ad, page or e-mail was delivered to the browser and tracks actions.

bean counter – An accountant or bureaucrat who is believed to place undue emphasis on the control of expenditures.

beat – A specific topic that a reporter usually covers (e.g. business, education, police, a municipality, a sports team, etc.).

beauty shop journalism – Used in television news to describe the staged setting (many times, artificial) or backdrop for a standup or an important speech given by a major official, politician or other key newsmaker.

before and after survey – Survey is taken of the target audience before communication is put into effect and repeated after the audience has been exposed to the communication.

behavior analysis – Used heavily in public relations and advertising to determine why individuals make the choices they do and how to maintain, reinforce or change that behavior.

behaviorist segmentation – The division of a market into groups according to their knowledge of, and behavior towards, a particular product.

believability – The public's perception of whether an individual, organization or company is telling the truth. See *credibility*.

19 Techniques to Succeed:
When you think branding – think:

• Positioning – Where your company or product stands in the marketplace compared to the competition. It might be better to be different than to be better. To be a leader in the marketplace, you have to deliver.

• Promise – States expectations - contract – a simple strategic statement. Promise less, deliver more.

• Pipeline – Delivery systems, interaction – employees, advertising, public relations, communication, suppliers, vendors – from conception to customer service.

• Presentation – Name, logo, slogan, office space, employees, image (if the company is high-tech, it must be using the latest in technology).

• Personality – Emotional values, connecting with the customer – the characteristics of the firm or organization. Much like image – how your audiences perceive you, your products and/or company.

• Propositions – Rational values, claims, results, testimonials, deliverables.

Atlantic City (N.J.)
Public Relations Council

20 Techniques to Succeed:

The basics of budgeting – for business or personal

Crafting a budget is a must, especially if it is part of a business plan. But it is also important on a personal level. Here are some steps and categories that should be included:

- List all anticipated expenses starting with fixed expenses.
- Review previous years and estimate accordingly.
- Track your spending for a month. That means everything from rent to such incidentals as a pack of gum (include cash, check and credit card purchases).
- Divide by 12 to get a monthly average of your expenses.
- See where you may have gone over and cut accordingly.
- Some categories or line items would include:
  - RentCar
  - Gas
  - Loans
  - Home phone
  - Cell phone
  - Utilities
  - Food
  - Dry cleaning
  - Newspapers
  - Personal items
  - Entertainment
  - Insurance
  - Savings/401K

bells and whistles – The optional features built into a basic product to satisfy or impress as large a number of buyers as possible.

below the (Web) fold – The fold is jargon for how much of a Web page a person sees without having to scroll down. Fewer than 35 percent of computer users scroll *below the fold*. See *above the fold*.

below-the-line public relations – Employs non-traditional (direct) media such as direct mail, point of sales and free samples – often using highly targeted lists of names (*relationship marketing*) to maximize response rates. See *above-the-line public relations* (which focuses on TV, radio, print and Web sites.)

belt and suspenders – Term meaning always having a back up. For example, radio reporters having a second tape recorder or a photographer having a second camera with them in case the first fails. Many times, television anchors and/or newsmakers wear two lapel microphones plugged into two different amplifiers – one serving as a back up.

benchmark – A standard measure for comparison or a point of reference (*baseline*).

Many times, one organization will refer to another as "the benchmark" it wants to emulate or surpass.

benchmark statement – A declarative sentence or short paragraph that establishes a framework, blueprint or standard by which something can be measured or judged.

benchmark survey – Survey is taken of the target audience before communication is put into effect and repeated after the audience has been exposed to the communication. Also call *before and after survey*.

benday process – Used in the printing process, it is a shading or dot pattern on a drawing. Also called a ben day screen.

benefit – How the audience perceives a product or service's feature.

benefits – Statements about what a product can do for the user. See *features*.

Bernays, Edward – Regarded by many as the father of public relations. He is considered the first public relations counselor who relied on research and evaluation to help achieve persuasion or behavior change.

beta – A test version of a product prior to launch. Also, an experimental (beta) group.

Better Business Bureau (BBB) – A nonprofit organization offering consumers information on the business practices of certain companies. The BBB is *not* a government regulatory agency. Read more at *www.bbb.org*.

better for you snacks – Strategic tactic taken by snack manufacturers in which they reduce sugar content to make their products healthier.

bidding – A pricing method in which organizations bid for a buyer's business. The bid is the seller's price offer. Often in government, the purchase goes to the lowest bidder unless the agency can justify not doing so.

bidders' conference – A gathering of individuals or agency representatives – who may eventually bid or quote on a "job" – so all can have an equal opportunity to review a request for proposal (RFP) and ask questions before submitting the bid or quote. Bidders' conferences help to eliminate complaints about misinformation or that one potential bidder may be receiving preferential treatment.

big box stores – Warehouse size retailers who encourage selling in bulk – usually through club memberships. Examples would include BJ's® Wholesale Club, Costco® and Sam's Club®.

billboard – In print, a large outdoor sign or poster. In radio or television, sponsor identification at the beginning or end of a program.

billings – The total amount of money spent on media buying by agencies on behalf of clients.

binding – Various methods used to secure pages of a book or other publication. Examples would include side stitch (staples on the side), saddle stitching (staples in a folded spine – through the center of publication) and perfect binding (multiple sets of folded pages (signatures) sewn or glued into a flat spine.

bingo card – A card inserted into a publication that allows readers to request information from one or more of a group of companies listed on the card.

bio (biography/biographical sketch) – Short for biography. A brief synopsis of a person's credentials – an individual's education and career experience.

bio feedback – A technique whereby organizations and companies use their own resources to improve productivity, image and reputation. *See mindshare.*

bio-politicians – Congressmen/senators and other politicians who try to legislate "miracles" – e.g. Terri Schiavo case; stem cell research.

biometrics – Known as biometric technology – the study of methods for uniquely recognizing humans based on one or more physical (fingerprints or iris) or behavioral traits (voice or signature). An example, fingerprint readers on laptop computers that serve as security devices. Fingerprint sensors are far superior to passwords for protection.

bird dogs – Individuals who seek out sales leads and prospects for organization, companies or independent sales reps.

bird walking – A technique used by some workshop participants to distract the team or meeting leader (CEO) from the intended subject. The leader should not succumb to those who try, although it is tempting.

black box – A term for an electronic TV audience measurement system. Also called an audiometer or people meter. Read more at *www.nielsen-media.com*.

Black Friday – The day after Thanksgiving when retailers go from being "in the red"– that is, in debt – to "in the black" – as in making a profit.

black list – A list of e-mail addresses, generally of known or suspected spam sources, that are automatically blocked from an e-mail inbox by a spam filter.

---

21 Techniques to Succeed: Establishing a consistent image – building a brand

Brand (v.) = A mental mark of ownership; to impress upon one's memory

• Reinforces the focus of the strategic plan

• Valuable asset (brand equity)

• Personal (brand loyalty and brand insistence)

• Experience (brand familiarity)

• Brand power

Atlantic City (N.J.) Public Relations Council
The Public Relations Practitioner's Playbook
(Kendall/Hunt – 2008) - M. Larry Litwin, APR, Fellow PRSA

BlackBerry® – A wireless handheld device (resembling a personal data assistant) that is an integrated phone, wireless e-mail and data retriever for people who prefer a smaller handset design. It allows users to exchange data with others or retrieve information from the Internet – communicating in a multitude of ways using one single device.

Blackberry® thumb – Syndrome developed from thumbing BlackBerry®, Trio® or other PDA device. Syndrome is pain in the thumb or thumbs. The American Physical Therapy Association in Alexandria, Va., among other occupational organizations, warn that improper use and overuse of personal digital assistants can lead to hand throbbing, tendonitis and swelling, a condition known as BlackBerry thumb.

blanket branding – A brand name used for a number of products in the same line (many times the corporate name), such as Revlon®

cosmetics or Campbell's® canned foods. Also called *family brand* or *brand family*.

blanket purchase order – A purchase arrangement in which a buyer contracts with a supplier to take delivery of an agreed quantity of goods at a specified price over a fixed period of time. Also called a blanket contract.

bleed – An advertisement, illustration or other image printed to run off the edge of the page. To achieve a bleed, a product must be printed on oversized paper and trimmed.

blind ad – An advertisement that does not identify the advertiser, but elicits a response for a product or service. An example would be an ad asking a computer user to "click here" for a chance to win a vacation.

Bling® water – "Designer" water targeted at 21- to 35-year olds. Term has become a brand. It is geared for the luxury marketplace and is bottled close to the mountain spring source in the hills of Tennessee.

blink – One or two second commercial that uses one word or a familiar voice or slogan to serve as a quick recall of a product, brand or television program. For example, an audio clip of Homer Simpson saying "Doh!" The theory being to be as short as possible and use these reminders that don't interfere, but give those who are already aware of the brand a reminder.

block and tackle – Early steps or discussion in public relations brain storming session when basics are discussed. The thought behind is that a plan can work only through practice – whether it be in football or public relations. A goal (winning) can be achieved only when the blocking and tackling are executed according to the "game" plan.

blog – A Web log, online diary or journal. Derived from Weblog and evolved into "we blog." A blog is citizen-created content – unfiltered opinion. Bloggers use their expert knowledge based on categories. Blogs can act as a stimulus to traditional journalism. Podcasts and Vodcasts are blogs.

blogcasting (podcasting) – Personal on demand broadcasting. A method of publishing (digital download) audio broadcasts via the Internet, allowing users to subscribe to a feed of new files (usually MP3s). It became popular in late 2004, largely due to automatic downloading audio onto portable players or personal computers. The word "podcasting" combines the words "broadcasting" and "iPod®." The term can be misleading since neither podcasting nor listening to podcasts requires an iPod® or any portable music player.

blogger – An individual who blogs.

blogosphere – A non-mainstream media. The collection of all bloggers, blog sites, blog readers, and blog text. Considered citizen dialog in action using the Internet. Bloggers are watchdogs who may make main stream journalists more careful. They remind mainstreamers that speed without accuracy is no good.

blogstorm – When a large amount of activity, information and opinion erupts around a particular subject or controversy in the blogosphere – on a Web log – it is sometimes called a *blogstorm* or *blog swarm*.

blogware – Tools for editing, organizing and publishing Web logs are variously referred to as *content management systems*, *publishing platforms*, *weblog software* and simply *blogware*.

blog swarm – When a large amount of activity, information and opinion erupts around a particular subject or controversy in the blogosphere – on a Web log – it is sometimes called a *blogstorm* or *blog swarm*.

blow-in card – A printed card placed inside a publication – loose rather than bound to the publication.

blow it (the story) out– Editorial decision not to run a news story – to *bump it* or drop it from the newspaper, a magazine, radio or television newscast. The reason might be space or time, or new information that changed the story's contents.

blue screen – Known in television as *chroma key*. It is a term for the filmmaking technique of using an evenly-lit monochromatic background for the purpose of replacing it with a different image or scene. The term also refers to the visual effect resulting from this technique as well as the colored screen itself (although it is often a *green screen*). It is commonly used for TV weather forecasts, wherein the presenter appears to be standing in front of a large map, but in the studio it is actually a large blue or green background.

blue screen of death – Blue screen that emerges on computer when there is a glitch. Many times, it signals "bad" news.

blue skying – Suggestions made during public relations planning and brainstorming sessions that might be ideal and/or out of reach – quite possibly too expensive to implement as a *tactic*.

blue line (proof) or dylux – A printer's proof, blue (ink) in color and made from an off-set negative. This is typically the final step before publications (jobs) are plated. Many printers now make laser proofs available. Laser proofs can be provided in full color although the colors may not be the exact **PMS** (Pantone Matching System) colors that will be used for the completed publication.

blurb – A quote or other important point made in a copy block pulled out to gain attention and/or serve as a copy-breaking device. Many times, it is set off with a line rule above and below the blurb. Also called *pull quote.*

BMP file – A type of computer file used for graphic images or photos. BMP stands for Bitmap. BMP files are not compressed and are generally of higher quality than compressed files (like **JPG**). A BMP file uses the extension ".bmp".

body – The consistency of a printing ink.

body copy – The main text of (a message) any communication vehicle.

The ABCs of Strategic Communication

22 Techniques to Succeed: Healthier business travel by car

• Instead of buying roadside meals, pack and take along healthy, travel friendly foods available for take out at many super markets. They would include whole-grain crackers, fruit, vegetables (baby carrots, plum tomatoes) and lean sandwiches.

• To avoid overeating, plan designated eating times and don't skip meals. Stop at a rest area to sit and eat your meals even if you have brought your own food.

• Curb boredom snacking by listening to audio books and making frequent stops to stretch.

• Drink bottled water or sugar-free beverages. Coffee and tea drinkers should add their own creamer and sweetener instead of purchasing such high-calorie specialty drinks as lattes and blender drinks.

• At restaurants, order salads and grilled chicken rather than burgers, French fries and fried chicken. Ask for low-fat dressings.

Nikki and David Goldbeck - Healthy Highways - Ceres Press-2004

body language – A nonverbal form of communication in which posture, facial expressions (*facial coding*), hand movements, etc., convey a message from sender to receiver. Body language is often called physical editorializing.

boiler room – Used at national political conventions to direct verbal cheering and demonstrations. Each state delegation has a designated person (director) who is in direct contact to that delegation from a control room or boiler room. Directors are needed because many times state delegations cannot hear speakers. See *orchestrating*.

boilerplate – A short piece of text, usually no more than a single short paragraph, describing a company, person, product, service or event. It is standard wording about an organization that usually appears near the end of organization or company-issued news releases. Here is a sample boilerplate:

The Atlantic City Convention & Visitors Authority serves as the destination's principal marketing arm, stimulating economic growth through convention, business and leisure tourism development. The Authority oversees the management of the Atlantic City Convention Center and Boardwalk Hall on behalf of its parent agency, the New Jersey Sports and Exposition Authority.

boldface – A heavier, darker version of a type font.

bond – A kind of writing paper used for stationery that contains a certain amount of rag or cotton content.

bonus – Something given or paid in addition to what is usual or expected.

boomerang generation – College graduates moving back home after living away for several years. (One in five children move back home.) *Gen Xers* and *Gen Yers* are doing it in greater numbers – especially to save money.

23 Techniques to Succeed:

Helpful budgeting guidelines

1. Know the cost of what you propose to buy.
2. Communicate the budget in terms of what it costs to achieve specific results.
3. Use the power of your computer to manage the program.

boomerang method – A method used by sales people to respond to consumer objections by turning the objection into a reason for acting immediately. When people object, turn them around by using what *they* say to prove that they are wrong. Use their own arguments like a boomerang, so they go around in a circle and come back to persuade them.

boosting – The practice of moving from a lower-paying

24 Tips to Succeed: Belt and suspenders

Always have a back up. For example, radio reporters having a second tape recorder or a photographer having a second camera with them in case the first fails. Many times, television anchors and/or newsmakers wear two lapel microphones plugged into two different amplifiers – one serving as a back up.

job to a higher-paying job shortly before retirement. The higher salary has the effect of boosting an employee's final pension payment. For example, in New Jersey, state pensions are based on a formula that considers the average of the highest three salaried years and number of years of service.

Boston Consulting Group (BCG) advantage matrix – A marketing planning tool devised by the Harvard-based Boston Consulting Group. Among its findings and recommendations: when competing brands can no longer increase their market share, market expansion is recommended to attract new consumers (possibly by using product or institutional advertising). As the market expands, organizations should continue to use optimal competitive strategy to maintain or increase their market share.

Boston Consulting Group (BCG) model – A product portfolio analysis in which products can be classified as: Stars – high growth and market share; Cash Cows – high market share and low growth rate; Question marks – low market share in high growth rate markets; or Dogs – low market share and low growth rate. Read more at *www.bcg.com/offices/office_boston.jsp*.

bottom line – A colloquial term meaning costs or profits. It is also used as part of the *double bottom line theory* – first bottom line is developing, enhancing, building or maintaining relationship with the second bottom line being increased revenue leading to profits. Pat Jackson, a public relations counselor, coined the term.

bottom of story – The last paragraph or a paragraph near the end of a news story – the least important information. See *inverted pyramid*.

bottom-up approach to planning – A planning approach in which there is involvement at all levels. Plans (specifically tactics and tools) developed at the lower levels of an organization and funneled up through consecutive levels until they reach top management. See *top–down approach to planning*.

bounce (back) – Term used for what happens when e-mail messages are returned to the e-mail server as undeliverable. Or, the immediate increase in popularity for a political candidate or product after a major announcement or media exposure. An example would be a political convention or product launch.

bounce back card – See *blow-in card* and *business reply card*.

bounce factor – More of a political term when referring to a candidate's popularity that increases soon after a major announcement. For example, a presidential candidate may see his poll numbers increase soon after choosing a running mate or just after his speech at a political convention. Bounce factors are usually short-lived.

boutique agency – An agency that specializes in just one product or one service. Also called a *niche agency* or *pigeonhole agency*.

brag-and-boast copy – Advertising text that is written from the company's point of view to extol its virtues, feature, benefits and accomplishments.

brain dump – Sitting down at a computer, or with a note pad, and writing everything that comes to your mind. It is the earliest stage of crafting the message. It is only the first draft of what could be many. It is during this first draft that little attention is paid to the proper elements of excellent writing – spelling, grammar, syntax, punctuation, sentence construction, etc..

brainstorming – An idea-generating process that encourages open communication and full participation by group members. Evaluation takes place after all ideas have been expressed. A technique used by editors and news directors: what we know; what we think we know; what we'll never know (used in brainstorming). See *mind share*.

brand – One of the 11 basic types of advertising (*The Public Relations Practitioner's Playbook* – Kendall/Hunt – Chapter 11). A name, sign, symbol or design, or some combination of these, used to identify a product and to differentiate it from competitors' products. A brand is a product from a known source (manufacturer, product or service). It is the most used type of advertising.

brand acceptance – Positive opinions held by consumers about a manufacturer's product or service that encourages a consumer to repeat their purchase of the brand. See *brand loyalty*.

brand advertising – The featuring of a particular brand in media vehicles to build strong, long–term consumer attitudes toward it.

brand authorization – Obtaining the right of distribution and display, usually of a consumer-packaged good (brand), by a retail outlet.

brand awareness – The knowledge consumers have of a particular brand. See *brand familiarity*.

brand champion – A brand that possesses true power with consumer. The number one brand in the category. See *power brands*.

brand competitors – Competing brands of products which can satisfy a consumer's wants almost equally as well as each other. See *competitors*.

brand concept – The image that the brand sponsor wants a particular brand to have – the desired positioning of the brand in the market and in the minds of consumers.

brand conviction – The strong attitude or attachment consumers have towards a particular brand.

brand development index (BDI) – A comparison of the percent of a brand's sales in a market to the percent of the national population in that same market.

brand equity – The value of a well-known brand or service. Brand equity can greatly affect the buyout price of a company and mergers.

brand establishment – The building–up of a brand in the introductory stage of the product's life cycle. Brand establishment involves developing an effective distribution network for the product and convincing consumers to buy it. See *introductory stage of the product life cycle*.

brand expansion – Technique used for growing a brand. Example – Toyota® entering its cars in NASCAR® competition.

brand experience – The process of exposing consumers to the various features associated with a particular brand – a successful brand experience creates an environment where the consumer will be surrounded by the positive elements attached to the brand. Examples include Disney®, Starbucks® and General Motors®. For those who cannot travel to a Disney theme park, Disney brings to them the total brand experience through their specialty stores located worldwide. Starbucks transformed the mere activity of drinking coffee into a total lifestyle experience.

General Motors not only manufactures automobiles – it has opened the doors to Europe's first automotive theme park, based in Germany.

brand extension – The use of a well-known brand name to launch a new product of an unrelated category, into the market. Also called *franchise extension* and *line extension.*

brand extension strategy – The practice of using a current brand name to enter a new or different product class.

brand familiarity – The awareness consumers have of a particular brand.

brand family – A brand name used for a number of products in the same line, such as Revlon® cosmetics or Campbell's® canned foods. Also called *blanket branding* and *family brand.*

brand favorability – Much like *brand loyalty.* Consumers liking a brand and asking for it if they do not see it on the shelves.

brand franchise – The loyalty that attaches to a well–managed brand. See *brand extension.*

brand harvesting – Decreasing marketing expenditure on a brand to zero, or to a minimal level, when sales and profits begin to decline, relying on its purchase by loyal customers to sustain it. Brand harvesting, which often precedes total elimination of the brand – withdrawal from the marketplace – is usually undertaken to free up cash to pursue new market opportunities.

brand identity – How a manufacturer wants its brand to be perceived.

brand image – Perception of a product or brand by the consumer.

brand insistence – The stage of brand loyalty where the buyer will accept no alternative and will search extensively for the required brand.

brand label – A label that prominently includes the brand name of the product – usually on the front of a product. Labels on the back or sides of a product are not usually referred to as the brand label.

brand leveraging – Broadening a company's product range by introducing additional forms or types of products under a brand name, which is already successful in another category.

brand licensing – The leasing of the use of a brand to another company. For example, Spalding® and Puma® lease or license their names to shoe manufacturers rather than produce the brand of shoes itself.

25 Tips to Succeed:

The benefits of hiring a public relations or advertising agency

The agency-client partnership is the dominant organizational arrangement in public relations and advertising.

Full service or niche agencies:
• Offer objective advice.

• Draw on the collective experience and training of its staff.

• Provide people and management skills to accomplish advertising objectives.

• Provide supportive environment for professional advertising people.

In-house agencies:
• Handle most, if not all, of the functions of an outside agency.

• Provide more control for the advertiser over the costs and time schedule.

• Available for quick response and turn-around.

• Receive standard agency discounts

• May have a greater awareness of the company, products and services.

William Wells - John Burnett - Sandra Moriarty - Advertising Principles and Practice - (Prentice Hall)

brand life cycle – A concept, building on the *product life cycle* concept, which states that brands also have a life cycle – introduction, growth, maturity, decline, withdrawal – and that particular brand management strategies are appropriate at each stage. See *product life cycle.*

brand loyalty – A measure of the degree to which a buyer recognizes, prefers and insists on a particular brand. Brand loyalty results from continued satisfaction with a product considered important and generates repeat purchases of products with little thought but high–involvement. See *high-involvement products; low-involvement products.*

brand management – The process by which marketers attempt to optimize the marketing mix, the integrated marketing communication or synergy for a specific brand.

brand manager – An individual given responsibility for planning and coordinating the firm's marketing activities related to a single brand.

brand mark – The part of a brand that can be seen but not spoken – the logo, symbol or design that forms part of the brand. See *brand name.*

brand monopoly – A circumstance where a particular brand dominates a market.

brand name – The part of a brand that is spoken. It may include words, letters or
numbers.

brand personality – The feeling that people have about a brand – not really considering what the product can actually do.

brand power – The force a particular brand has to dominate its market category through its recognition.

brand preference – The stage of brand loyalty when a buyer will select a particular brand – but will readily choose a competitor's brand if the preferred brand is unavailable.

brand promiscuity – Consumer buying behavior marked by an absence of brand loyalty. See *brand loyalty*.

brand protection – Legislation forbidding other firms from using a company's registered brand names or brand marks without permission.

brand recognition – A buyer's awareness of a particular brand but with no preference for it.

brand reinforcement – Activity associated with getting consumers who have tried a particular brand to become repeat purchasers and with attracting new users. Brand reinforcement is a key objective of the growth stage of the product's life cycle. See *growth stage of the product life cycle*.

brand repositioning – Changing the appeal of a brand so that it attracts new market segments. Brand repositioning may or may not involve modifying the product.

brand revitalization – A strategy employed when a brand has reached maturity and profits begin to decline. Approaches to revitalization may include market expansion, product modification and/or brand repositioning.

brand revival – The resurrection of a brand that is being harvested (moving toward withdrawal stage of the life cycle) or which has previously been eliminated. Brand revival, where the brand name is still strong, is often a less costly strategy than the creation of a new brand and may provide a firm with a significant advantage in a mature market.

Examples would include: the canned meat product Spam® and Campbell's® placing its name over Franco America® on its canned Italian sauces and other products.

brand sponsor – The manufacturer, wholesaler or retailer who owns the brand.

brand strategies – Decision-making for the effective handling of brands. Three general branding strategies are available – a single brand for all of the organization's products, family branding or the use of individual brand names for all products.

brand switching – The changing of support and conviction for one brand to a competing brand. See *brand loyalty*.

brand value – The value, which a brand would be given if represented on a company balance sheet.

brand within a brand (sub-brand) – Dual brand. For example, Fairfield Inn®, which is part of Marriott® or Buick®, which is General Motors®.

branded entertainment – See *advertainment*.

branding – The process of establishing the elements of a brand, including its name, identifying symbols and related marketing messages. It is a manufacturer's promise to its customers.

breadth of product line – Measured by the number of product lines carried by a distributor, retailer or other outlet. See *width of product line*.

break (in a story) – Also called *story break*. An interruption in copy when a story is being sent – usually by a wire service – or e-mail.

break-even point – A point at which total revenue equals the total cost.

breakage – The salary difference between a retiring employee and a new one being hired – younger, with less experience and a lower salary.

---

26 Techniques to Succeed:

A lasting behavioral change

One of PR's most effective approaches is to accomplish change by having members of the public persuade themselves after considering the issues and hearing the arguments (strategic messages).

27

Technique to Succeed:
Annual Reports – Reading ease

Many company annual reports are difficult to read – and now we know why.

A study by suggests that annual reports of firms with lower earnings are harder to read – on purpose.

A study of more than 50,000 annual reports used two measures of readability:

• The Fog Index, which indicates the number of years of formal education a reader of average intelligence would need to read and understand a text.

• The Flesch-Kincaid Index, which rates text on a U.S. grade-school level.

The average Fog Index for all annual reports was a deplorable 19.4 (a score of 12-14 is ideal and higher than 18 is unreadable). In the same way, the annual report readability score on the Kincaid Index was 15.2 – about twice as high as the optimal score of 7 to 8.

Feng Li - Assistant professor of accounting - University of Michigan

breaking news – A major event or issue covered by the media as it is happening. News that is happening "right now."

bricks and mortar – A retail store. When major manufacturers open a retail location, it is referred to as bricks and mortar (Sony®, BOSE®, COACH®).

bridge – Transition from one scene to another in a commercial or program. Also, attribution used in the middle of a long quote. See *broken-back quote*.

bridge builder – A public relations counselor who serves as a peace-maker as he/she brings opposing sides together.

bridge loan – A short-term loan that is used until a person or company secures permanent financing or removes an existing obligation. This type of financing allows the user to meet current obligations by providing immediate cash flow. The loans are short-term (usually up to one year) with relatively high interest rates and are backed by some form of collateral such as real estate or inventory. Also known as interim financing, gap financing or a *swing loan*.

bridging – One of the most effective techniques that interviewees can use to help retain control of an interview. Verbal bridges allow an interviewee: to steer a reporter back to relevant topics and key messages if he or she loses focus or seems off on an unimportant tangent; to move away from controversial, uncomfortable or unflattering topics and back on to key messages; to end every answer to every question with a prepared, strategic message.

28 Techniques to Succeed: Bad with names?

Listen. Make sure you hear a name clearly and can pronounce it correctly. Never proceed past an initial introduction unless you are certain you can pronounce their name correctly. If necessary, ask the person to repeat his or her name. If the name is an unusual one, ask the person how to spell it. Uncertainty over a name will become an instant distraction.

Repeat their name. If you did not hear their name clearly, simply ask them to repeat his or her name to you. After hearing the name correctly, use it in a sentence a few times – especially early in a meeting. You can also repeat the person's name to yourself several times to get it fixed in your mind. Not only will this help you retain their name, it will also inspire confidence and reassure the other person that you're interested and paying attention to the conversation.

Relate their name to physical characteristics. Get a distinct impression of the person. Note physical characteristics. Listen to the person's voice. Try to "visualize" the personality. Start noting characteristics that formulate the first impression. Make an association based on any unique physical characteristics. "Visualize" their personality and form a mental picture based on sight, sound and the impression you get from them.

Attach their name with something or somebody famous. Associate the person's name with a word picture that's colorful, action-oriented and possibly even exaggerated. Any image that instantly triggers the recall of a person's name will be of valuable assistance. You can also think of a famous person too.

Anita Zinmeister - President - Dale Carnegie Training of
Central and Southern N.J. - Dale Carnegie Training -
ww.southjersey.dalecarnegie.com

bridging (pensions) – Working at a public sector job for a salary at or near the minimum salary allowed by law ($1,500 in New Jersey). Some public workers continue doing small amounts of work for the minimum so they can earn the required number of years of service needed to enter the state's pension plan.

briefing book – A book compiled in anticipation of a visit by a VIP or for media members. A briefing book typically contains summaries; fact sheets; news releases; short biographies with pictures of key people in the organization; brief descriptions of an organization, company or other entity; a brief history of the organization; as many demographics as possible including surrounding community; staff make–up; names of key staff members, awards won, etc..; anyone of note living in community or associated with organization; controversies or issues that should be known; possible questions that might be asked during any Q&A with staff or media; and a list of possible surprises (because there should be absolutely no surprises – every possible scenario must be anticipated). Include copies of brochures and other publications and pronunciations for unusual names.

brinkmanship – A term used in contract negotiations in which one party bluffs (takes a chance) or pushes the other on price, terms or conditions and refuses to concede further.

broadband – An Internet connection delivering a high bit rate – any bit rate at or above 100 kilobytes per second. Cable modems, DSL and ISDN all offer broadband connections.

broadcast – The dissemination of programs or messages through the radio, television or Internet – to transmit a radio or television signal over the public airwaves.

broadcast media – The news media that use the public airwaves. Includes local radio and television stations as well as the national networks (ABC, CBS, FOX, NBC, PBS) whose programs are carried on local TV stations.

broadening concept – The extension of marketing as a business philosophy to encompass the marketing activities of nonprofit organizations. See *positive association* and *cause related marketing.*

broadsheet – Term used to describe a full or standard size newspaper such as the *New York Times* and *Los Angeles Times*. Typically, a broadsheet newspaper is six, seven or eight columns wide by 20-22 inches high (300 lines deep). See *tabloid.*

29 Tips to Succeed: Be a better manager

Reward good work: Appreciate employees for a job well done to encourage continued good work. Make sure your compliments are spontaneous to avoid predictability. More specific comments mean more than a generic "good job."

Make everyday heroes: For those who've consistently performed well, make sure to spread the word throughout the company about their good work. Make them examples for other employees.

Avoid negativity: Don't indulge in office gossip or negative conversations. It's hard to create a positive environment if you're bashing others.

Find solutions, not problems: Rather than blaming employees for mistakes or problems, motivate them to seek out solutions.

Dr. Noelle Nelson - Author - The Power of Appreciation in Business

broadside – A promotion printed on a single folded sheet of paper with printing on one or both sides that opens up to a single, large advertisement or poster.

brochure – A printed piece created for informational purposes or promotion.

broken-back quote – A lengthy direct quote that is broken up with attribution. For example, "The new Cherry Hill Public Library is beyond state of the art," says Stephen C. Barbell, president of the library Board of Trustees. "Patrons have access to more than 500 computers, MAC® and PCs, and another 90 wireless laptops, which may be checked out."

broker – A marketing intermediary or middleman between buyer and seller.

brownfield – Abandoned industrial sites eligible for redevelopment under certain government programs.

browser – A software program that can request, download cache and display documents available on the Internet. Browsers can be either text–based or graphical.

bubble – The technical definition is a speculative market or stock where prices rise very rapidly and then fall sharply. Examples include: Years ago it was talk of the dot.com bubble and from time to time there is talk of the real estate bubble. These stocks and markets are likened to a bubble because of people's fears that the inflated stock or market will suddenly "burst" – or deflate – like a bubble.

bubble (on the bubble) – An irrepressible activity – or, speculative plan, some might call a scheme, that depends on unstable factors that the planner cannot control. Also, an idea or person who is described as being "on the bubble" – might be good enough to assume a task/responsibility/job or might not be. Also during the printing process where water-based inks are used, a blotch – possibly from a splash – will appear on the page. Sometimes referred to as a *hickey*.

bubbling (wireless) – Building a wireless (protocol network) network over such large areas as cities and/or towns and college or business campuses. Also known as *wireless bubble*.

buddy lists – The list of people that users of AOL Instant Messaging® commonly communicate with.

buddy system – an arrangement in which people are paired, for mutual safety or assistance. Many agencies use this approach when new employees join the firm. They are paired with more experienced personnel.

budget – Allocation of space for stories in a publication. Also an estimate, often itemized, of expected income and expense for a given period in the future.

budget determination – Decisions pertaining to the amount to be allocated to public relations (advertising) expenditure in a given period; common approaches to budget determination include arbitrary allocation, percent of sales, competitive parity, objective and task and budgeting models.

budgeting – The process of financial planning of income and expenditures for a firm's marketing mix activities – marketing, promotion, advertising, personal selling, etc. Budgeting is also the allocation of space or time for stories in a publication or on a radio or television news program.

bug – On TV screen, the network or station logo usually on the lower right. Also, a union logo or seal known as a *Union Bug* (printed very small) signifying that a publication has been printed by a union shop.

30 Tips to Succeed: Know your etiquette in business settings

Dining out with your boss or a client is your chance to make a good impression.

• Can I drink soda or beer from the bottle?

No. Use a glass.

• What if I am served something that I don't know how to eat?

Watch your host and do what he or she does. You may not be right, but you won't be wrong. And when you do have a choice of foods, don't order anything that you don't know how to eat.

• Is it OK to kiss colleagues in business social situations?

The handshake is the proper business greeting in most business and business social situations. Yet there can be situations where kissing may be OK, depending upon:

A. Your relationship with the person. If people know each other well, they may kiss at business social events.

B. The type of company you work for. Large, formal, or conservative companies usually have less kissing than smaller, creative or informal types of companies.

C. The type of business functions you attend. Company picnics may be more relaxed and informal than business dinners at a fancy restaurant.

D. When in doubt, shake hands.

Barbara Pachter - Author -When The Little Things
Count . . .And They Always Count

build-up (budgeting) method – Sometimes referred to as a "grass roots budget." Based on the previous year's budget. New programs and activities, as well as PPI (producer price index), must be factored in. Many times, this is a wish list. As with other methods, all line items must be justified. Previous budget history within the department should also be considered. Estimate how much each activity will cost and then add them up. (This is more of a micro-budgeting approach.)

building wrap – An advertisement which fully or partially covers a building. It is, an advertising technique using silk-screened vinyl tightly wrapped around a building or part of a building much as an *auto wrap* is adhered to a car, truck, bus or just about any other vehicle on wheels. It allows consumers to view advertising messages in three-dimensional form. Research shows it creates a high retention rate among those who see it. *Building wraps* are semi-permanent graphics that can be removed without harm to the building. See *auto wrap, bus wrap, car wrap* and *truck wrap*.

bulk mail – A large quantity of identical mail rated for postage by weight and number of pieces. Bulk mail rates are significantly less expensive than first class mail. Bulk mail sent as e-mail is considered *spam*.

bulk mail house – A highly mechanized commercial mail-processing center that organizes (sorts, folds, stuffs) bulk mail prior to it going to the post office. Also called a *fulfillment house.*

bulldog edition – An edition of a print publication that is available earlier than regular editions. Usually, this is the early edition of a large circulation newspaper – many Sunday editions become available in stores and on newsstands on Saturday evening.

bullet (dingbat) – Dot or small graphic used as ornamental device.

bullet point list – The use of *bullet points* rather than a narrative.

bullet points – Brief strategic messages or *key message points* set off with bullets or large dots or some other type of *dingbat*.

bullet proof – Fabric that doesn't breathe.

bullet proof reliability – Individuals, organizations and companies that resist or deflect criticism, verbal assault or attack by competitors or members of the public. See *fire proof.*

bully pulpit – A platform from which to persuasively advocate an agenda.

bum's rush – Getting the *bum's rush* means getting forcibly ejected, like a bum would be by a bouncer or a store owner. The phrase comes from the "shiftless beggar" meaning of bum.

bump – Term used by printers when referring to the intensity of ink on a finished product – "The reds and blues got a good bump" – meaning they thoroughly cover the intended surface. See *battered.*

bump fashion – Clothes designed for pregnant women to keep them fashionable.

bump it – To drop a story from an edition of a newspaper, magazine or a television or radio newscast. See *blow it out.*

bumper – A brief (usually two to 15 seconds) transition announcement – many times including high intensity graphics and sound – placed just before a television news story to gain the viewers' attention. Also called *separator*. See *attentioner*.

bundle –A consumer sales promotion in which two related product items are banded together and sold at a special price. Also called a banded offer.

bundling products – Selling two or more products together whether or not related (digital camera/printer or cable companies such as Comcast® and Verizon® offering special pricing for broadband, cable TV and home phone service). Similar to tie in.

bunker mentality – A fear of making suggestions or recommendation because they might not be accepted (you might get your head blown off). An insecurity or a lack of confidence.

BUPPIE – Black Urban Professional – a demographic grouping.

buried ad – An advertisement surrounded by other ads, making it less likely to be seen by the reader. Also called *clutter*.

burning your reputation – Any action that tarnishes or ruins an individual's public perception.

burst advertising expenditure – A major advertising expenditure over a short time period.

bus card – An advertisement placed in a bus or subway.

business angel – Someone who invests money in a new business. Unlike a *venture capitalist*, this is an individual who decides to "back a business" – in its early stages. Also referred to as *angel*. Read more at *www.angelcapitalassociation.org*.

business cycles – Historical patterns of prevailing economic conditions – prosperity, recession, depression and recovery.

business development – Techniques designed to grow an economic enterprise. Techniques include taking advantage of marketing opportunities by targeting markets and customers, generating sales leads and the constant evaluation of the business enterprise.

business list – A list of individuals or organizations based on a business-related interest, inquiry, membership, subscription or purchase. These lists must be kept updated and are integral in relationship marketing.

31

Tips to Succeed: Boost a small firm's image

Small companies have the same goals as larger companies: more sales, greater productivity, higher profit, enhanced image and widespread recognition. Small businesses, however, have the disadvantage when it comes to image. Below are some ways to increase the image and success of your small business.

Maximize person-to-person communications. Clients will feel more important when they talk to a real person rather than an answering service. Your prospect's image of you becomes very different when a live person answers your phone.

Get an 800 number. A toll-free number communicates success. Callers like your willingness to pay for them to reach you.

Get a Web site. Even if it starts out very basic, get a Web site set up and list the address on your business cards and letterhead.

Kill your larger competition by responding to a client automatically.

Be personable with your prospects and clients.

Do not use regular stamps. Established businesses use postage machines.

Get out of the house. Conduct business in an environment that allows you to collaborate, socialize and exchange ideas and business opportunities. Even solo entrepreneurs must get out there and be with other business people.

Roger Kahn - President - Intelligent Office - New York, N.Y.

business mix – Various businesses in which a firm is engaged. Also, the variety of businesses (stores) located in a retail district (mall or strip center). Having similar stores in the same center is not always a negative – many times they help attract customers. (It is not unusual to see a McDonald's®, Burger King® and Wendy's® within a short distance of each other.)

Business Newswire® – A distribution service that delivers business news to traditional and online newsrooms and to targeted journalists and other subscribers.

business plan – A blueprint for building an organization, containing its *mission*, *goals*, *objectives*, *strategies*, *tactics*, tools and evaluation measures.

business reply card – A card distributed with an advertising piece. The card is preprinted with the address of advertiser or its fulfillment house. Return postage is prepaid by the advertiser.

business-to-business (B2B) advertising – Advertising directed to other businesses, rather than to individual consumers.

business-to-business marketing – One business entity marketing to another. For example, a company offering cash registers to a retailer.

buy in – Those who get turned on to your proposal – positive behavioral change, or at the very least, maintaining positive behavior. See *push back*.

buyer – The individual who makes the actual purchase in a buying decision.

buyer behavior – The study of consumers and organizations in relation to their purchase decisions.

buyer intention forecast – A method of predicting future demand for a product by asking potential buyers for their likely requirements.

buyer involvement – A measure of the time and effort a buyer is prepared to devote to the purchase of a particular item. See *high-involvement products; low-involvement products*.

buyer readiness stage – The state of preparedness or willingness of an individual consumer in regard to the purchase of a particular product. The stages are commonly listed as awareness, knowledge, liking, preference, conviction and purchase.

buyer resolution theory – The idea that a buyer decides to purchase only after mentally resolving five specific issues – need, product, source, price and timing.

buyer's market – A market where there is an abundance of a particular good or service for sale. Opposite of a *seller's market*.

buying agency – A boutique (niche agency) primarily engaged in buying media space or time for advertising purposes. See *media planning/buying*.

buying allowance – A trade sales promotion where buyers are offered a price reduction for each carton, case, etc. purchased during the period of the promotion.

buying behavior – The process buyers go through when deciding whether or not to purchase goods or services. Buying behavior can be influenced by a number of external factors and motivations.

buying cycle – The time taken by an organization to complete its decision to buy. Individuals go through a similar process: need recognition; information search, evaluation of alternatives; purchase decision; and post–purchase evaluation.

buying Power – The resources, especially financial, that customers have at a given time.

buying signals – Signs or indications, verbal or nonverbal, that tell a salesperson the buyer is ready to buy.

buzz – A strategic message that gets media and public attention for an organization, company, product or service. Word-of-mouth is an integral part of buzz because the message is being communicated in an unsolicited manner. See *viral marketing*.

buzz marketing – Paying someone to recommend (different from endorse) a product without revealing they are doing so. Using real people (referred to a *connectors)* to create a *buzz* (manufactured buzz) for products or services – paid or otherwise, but most times paid (to recommend [word of mouth] a product or service). Also called *Viral Marketing* and *Word of Mouth Marketing*. If the endorser is not being paid, the word marketing is dropped and the term is simply *Word of Mouth* (the most effective form of "advertising.")

by-product – A secondary product produced during the process of manufacturing another.

byline – Name of the writer positioned under the headline at the beginning of a story.

byline strike – Journalists withholding their names from stories in protest of working conditions. **B**

c-type response – A response to an advertisement or an advertising campaign which is immediately obvious. Opposite of an *S-type Response.*

cable media – Media such as CNN, CNBC and FOX News that are accessible only to the public who pay a monthly fee to a company providing the service.

cable modem – A device that permits one- or two-way high-speed data communication over a cable television system for purposes such as Internet access. Also called *broadband.*

cable television – A form of subscription television where signals are carried to households and businesses via cable.

cache – Memory (on a computer) used to temporarily store the most frequently requested content/files/pages to speed its delivery to the user. A cache file can be saved locally on the user's hard drive or on the user's network.

caching – The process of copying (or storing in a user's favorites) a Web site or advertisement for later reuse. On the Internet, this copying is normally done in two places: in the user's hard drive and on proxy servers. Caching is done to speed up retrieval and/or to reduce network traffic, resulting in increased overall efficiency of the Internet.

café (corporate average fuel economy) standard – Commonly used corporate average for a product. Its origin is the corporate average fuel economy (CAFE) standards for new passenger cars.

caging – The opening and sorting of orders and the handling of checks and cash. What goes around comes around – in the early years, people worked in cages for security purposes. Caging has returned to many businesses including some retail stores and banking.

calculated (approach) – A deliberate approach with every word, phrase and message carefully crafted and sent or delivered.

calendar listings – A list of upcoming events that appears in many newspapers and magazines. Entries are brief and usually contain only the name of the sponsoring organization and a very short description of the event.

call – A visit to a client or prospective client by a public relations agency representative to gather information, make a pitch or secure a contract.

call center – The staging area for a telemarketing operation.

call chain or tree – A list of names and contact information that should be notified immediately in a crisis. The process might involve the first person initiating the action to a second who would call two or three people and each of those would in turn call a few.

call report – A written record of calls made by a representative for submission to a supervisor. See *call*.

call to action – A statement, usually at the end of a public relations plan or marketing piece, encouraging the client/reader/viewer/listener to respond to the objective of the piece.

callback – A follow-up call to a client or perspective client to present ideas and information.

calling card – Also known as a business card. It would contain such vital information as name, address, telephone and e-mail. Effective business cards also contain a company logo. Calling card is also the term used when referring to someone leaving their calling card – or an impression – favorable or otherwise. The latter is an intangible calling card.

callout – A line of text beside, above or below a photograph or illustration. It typically highlights a detail in the graphic, verbalizes the analogy implied by the graphic or emphasizes the message delivered through the graphic. See *blurb*.

32 Techniques to Succeed:
The communication audit

1. What is a communication audit?

It is a complete analysis of an organization's communication program – a picture of its goal, objectives, strategies, tactics and evaluations.

2. What is the scope of an audit?

The scope of an audit may be as broad and as deep as the size and complexity of the organization's demands. The audit can measure the effectiveness of communication programs throughout an entire organization, in a single division or department, or within a specific employee group.

3. What does the communication audit provide?

It provides meaningful information to members of management concerned with efficiency, credibility, and economy of their communications policies, practices, and programs. It also provides valuable data for developing or restructuring communications functions, guidelines, and budgets, as well as recommendations for action tailored to an organization's particular situation as uncovered by an analysis of the collected data.

4. When should an audit be conducted?

Generally, an extensive audit should be conducted every five to seven years. In the interim, reliable feedback techniques should be obtained periodically through the organization's routine communication function.

5. What subjects are covered?

Typically an audit covers such areas as:

• Communication philosophy

• Objectives and goals

• Existing communication programs

• Existing vehicles and their uses

• Personal communications

• Meetings

• Attitudes toward existing communications

• Needs and expectations

Joseph A. Kopec - Kopec Associates Inc., Chicago, Illinois
Read more at www.prsa.org/_Resources/resources/commaudit.asp?ident=rsrc3

33 Tips to Succeed:

Cell phone etiquette

The cell phone etiquette guide:

Lights off, phone off!
No one should take a call at a theater or in the movies.

Off means off!
Respect the rules and when asked by an establishment or airline to refrain from using a cell phone, do so.

Don't cross the personal space boundary!
Everyone should be mindful of how close they are to others when using a cell phone in a public place.

Stop noise pollution!
Remember to keep conversations private and not shout into the phone.

Heads up!
Act responsibly when walking or driving while on a cell phone. Many states now have laws for cell phone use in or on motor vehicles.

www.letstalk.com/promo/
unclecell/unclecell2.htm

camera-ready art – A photo, graphic or publication in finished form – ready to be processed into a negative, then plated and printed. It is printed, as is, with no changes. Also called *ad slick; laser; matte; repro; slick* and *velox.*

campaign – A planned selection and execution of integrated marketing communication (synergistic) activities to achieve communication objectives. Campaigns are premeditated.

canned approach – The same approach can be used with similar target audiences.

cannibalization (opposite of synergy) – The notion of an organization making a conscious business decision that will have a negative impact on either a current product or member of a distribution channel (or entire channel, via disintermediation). Removing one or more ingredients used to achieve synergy – either because of poor planning or lack of resources (financial or human).

capital – Assets of a company or organization – tangible, human resources or intellectual property. Following the 2004 election, President George W. Bush often referred to the public's support as "political capital."

caption – Short, but full, descriptive copy accompanying a picture or illustration. A line or block of type providing descriptive information about a picture. Headline or text accompanying a picture or illustration; also called a *cutline*. Also, an advertisement's headline – or major display type across the top.

captive audience – A group of people whom, because of their location, have a limited choice of products and services and might be more easily convinced by a persuasive strategic message. Or, a group of people who listen to or watch someone or something because they cannot leave.

captive product – A product made specifically to be used with another, such as a blade with a razor, batteries with a flashlight, etc.

car card – A poster placed in buses, subways, etc. Also called a bus card.

carbon footprint – A person's impact on the environment. For example, the average American household produces more than 35,000 pounds of carbon dioxide each year.

card deck – A pack of postcards, usually mailed in a clear package, used in both consumer and business-to-business direct marketing – many times to elicit a direct response. The postcard, which either orders the product or asks for more information, can be mailed back to the individual advertiser. The card deck is usually a co-op package put together by individual advertisers who share the cost or is sold by an independent company to individual advertisers who are encouraged, through incentives, to share cost.

card rate – Media rates published by a broadcast station or print publication on a rate card.

career path – The road an individual follows – or the jobs they hold – from the time they enter the professional world to their current position.

carrier route presort mail – U.S. mail sorted by carrier route to qualify for discount postage rates. Firms that rely on direct mail or occasional mass mailings should consider experienced fulfillment or mail order houses, which could save money because of their expertise in dealing with the U.S. Postal Service.

carrying costs – Costs associated with maintaining inventory, such as financing, storage and insurance.

carryover effect in advertising – The recall rate of an advertising campaign diminishes with the passing of time. For example, an advertising campaign or slogan this month may have a carryover effect of 60

The ABCs of Strategic Communication

C

34 Tips to Succeed: Credit Card Act protects you

Have you ever purchased a product only to find it is damaged or poorly made and the merchant refuses to replace it or give you a refund? If you paid with a credit card, you may be in luck.

The Fair Credit Billing Act gives consumers the right to withhold payment on poor-quality or damaged merchandise purchased with a credit card.

What you need to do:

• First, try to resolve the problem with the merchant. Try to take the merchandise back.

• Put your complaint in writing and send via certified mail to the merchant. Keep two copies.

• Contact the credit card company and alert them to the disputed purchase amount.

• Send a letter to the credit card company explaining the disputed purchase.
   – Enclose a copy of your complaint letter to the merchant and any other documentation you may have. Send your letter by certified mail, return receipt requested, to the address for "billing inquiries" and not the one for payments.

• Follow up.

The caveats? The sale must be for more than $50 and have taken place in your home state or within 100 miles of your home address. While few issuers enforce the criteria, they are all free to do so.

Also, you need to act within 60 days after a disputed charge was billed.

If the card company sides with the merchant, you'll have to pay for the disputed item, plus any finance charges. If they side with you, you're not out a dime.

www.bankrate.com

percent next month. Normally, unless an advertiser resumes or increases advertising and public relations, the carryover effect will continue to decrease.

cartel – An association of independent businesses formed to monopolize and control production, distribution and prices. Cartels are illegal in the United States.

cartography – The art or technique of making maps or charts.

case allowance – Discounts given to retailers to encourage them to purchase products in *case lots.*

case lots – Product sold by the case. For example, paper is traditionally sold with 10 reams (5,000 sheets) to a case. Other goods might have a quantity count of 12, 24 or 48. Case lots are less expensive than purchasing smaller quantities. Such larger stores – like BJ's® Wholesale Club, Sam's Club® and Costco® – became popular by selling in case lots to individual consumers.

cash cow – A product or a business unit that generates unusually high profit margins – so high that it is responsible for a large amount of a company's operating profit. This profit can be used by the business for other purposes. The expression is a metaphor for a dairy cow, which after being acquired can be milked on an ongoing basis with little expense.

cash discount – A reduction in price offered to a client in return for prompt payment of account. One of the five common types of discounts *allowances*; *cash discount*; *quantity discount*; *seasonal discount*; *trade discount.*

cash flow – The money required by a company to meet expenses in a given period.

cash-and-carry wholesalers – Wholesale distributors who require cash for goods sold. Traditionally, retailers pay for the goods (in bulk or by the case), and then take immediate possession of goods and provide their own transport.

casual survey – Also known as *self-selected survey.* Respondents volunteer themselves. The Internet, newspapers, radio and television stations and magazines that encourage or allow listeners, viewers or readers to respond fall into this sampling technique.

casual worker – Term used to describe part-time or daily worker at a radio or television news operation, or other media outlets. Similar to a *freelancer.*

cat walk – Term used for the runway on which models strut.

catalog marketing – A form of direct marketing where consumers order from catalogs, eliminating the middleman or distributor.

catalog retailer – Retailers who also mail catalogs to their customers.

catch and release – Illegal immigrants caught crossing the border or later and then sent back to their country of origin. Also, fishermen who catch fish and then turn them loose rather than keep them for a meal or other reason.

category development index (CDI) – An index that identifies the demand for the category (product or service) within a region.

caterer – Provider of food and service (as for a party and/or event).
cattle call – An open casting call for a movie television show.

cause-related marketing (CRM) – The public association of a for-profit company with a non-profit organization, intended to promote the company's product or service and to raise money for the non-profit (both parties benefit). *CRM* is generally considered to be distinct from corporate philanthropy because the corporate dollars involved in CRM are not outright gifts to a non-profit organization – therefore not tax-deductible. Also called *positive association; partnering; sponsorship marketing.*

caveat emptor – A Latin term meaning, "let the buyer beware." The term implies that it is the consumer's responsibility rather than the seller's to ensure the goods or services offered for sale are able to deliver the desired satisfactions.

CD-Rom – A device used to store hundreds of MB of data. Files are permanently stored on the circular device and can be copied to other disks.

cease-and-desist order – An order by the Federal Trade Commission requiring an advertiser to stop running a deceptive, misleading or unfair advertisement, campaign or claim. A cease-and-desist order is the second of three remedies for deceptive or unfair advertising. A *consent decree* is the first step. *Corrective advertising* is the third step.

35 Tips to Succeed:
Credit cards – Read those notices

Most people just throw them away. But those annoying mailers you receive about "important changes" to your credit card are actually valuable. You don't want to be surprised when your interest rate suddenly rises.

When you get such a notice, read it carefully, looking for:

• New or increased penalties for paying off your balance .

• Cutbacks in rebate programs, etc.

• Shorter waiting period before payments are late.

• Higher late charges.

• Penalty interest rate if you're late making payments.

www.checklists.com

celebradrek – Celebrity (gossip) news – which has become an obsession for many media readers, viewers and the publishers and networks that carry it. Their argument – *celebradrek* "sells. "

celebrity pounding – Seen on television and at live events when celebrities – and now "regular people" – bump their chests or pound the backs of their fists to celebrate or just say hello (a greeting).

celebrosphere – Celebrities going on such talk shows as "Larry King Live" serving as experts. For example, during the Scott Peterson trial, in addition to showing "perp walks" and interviews with tearful relatives, the peppy talk-show chatter of unemployed prosecutors, defense attorneys, jury consultants and public relations practitioners took center stage. As the *Philadelphia Inquirer* reported on Nov. 15, 2004, "… all glad to grab their 15 minutes by dissecting the latest eruption of human evil and pain in the celebrosphere."

cell phone picture in a classroom – High tech method of note taking during a class (picture of instructor's notes written on a board or shown on a screen rather than writing or typing notes on a laptop).

cellphonography – Short videos recorded and transmitted by cell phone.

census – The collection of data from an entire population.

center package – The major (lead) story in the center of a main page of a newspaper. Also called the *center piece story*. *USA Today* commonly uses this technique. See *cover story*.

center piece story – The major (lead) story in the center of a main page of a newspaper. Also called the *center package* or *cover story*. *USA Today* commonly uses this technique.

center spread – An advertisement appearing as a single printed sheet running across both facing pages at the center of a publication. This is considered favorable placement because it is a single, unbroken sheet flowing across two pages and because the publication tends to naturally fall open at the center spread. See *double truck*.

central business district (CBD) – The region of a city where retail and other businesses are concentrated – with a high volume of traffic.

36 Tips to Succeed:
Understanding your credit report

A credit report is basically divided into four sections:

- Identifying information. Simply, this is information used to identi-fy you. Besides your name and Social Security number, the report may include your current and previous addresses, date of birth, telephone number, driver's license number, employer and spouse's name.

- Credit history. Each account will include the name of the creditor and the account number, which may be scrambled for security purposes. Each entry will include account history, payment detail, balance and limit detail, and how well you've paid the account.

- Public records. This section, ideally, should be blank. It lists bank-ruptcies, judgments and tax liens, which all can damage your credit faster than anything else.

- Inquiries. A list of everyone who asked to see your credit report. Most inquiries are ignored by FICO scoring models and do not damage a credit score.

www.crediteducation.org

central processing unit (CPU) – The main part of a computer that routes all of the system information.

chain break – A pause for station identification and commercials, during a network broadcast. Also called a *cutaway*.

chain store – A group of retail stores, centrally owned and managed, generally carrying the same kind of merchandise.

chance survey – A sample where each member of the population has an equal chance of being chosen. Also referred to as a *scientific random sample*; or *simple random sample*. See *random sample*.

change agent – A public relations practitioner or other individual who leads a change project or business-wide effort by defining, researching, planning, building business support and carefully selecting volunteers (employees or outsiders willing to serve) to be part of a change team. Change agents must have the conviction to state the facts based on data, even if the consequences are associated with unpleasantness.

channel – One of the Seven Cs of Communication. Vehicles that the public respects and depends on, used to communicate a message. Different channels have different effects and serve effectively in different stages of the *diffusion process*. Different channels are called for in reaching target audiences. (Read more in *The Public Relations Practitioner's Playbook* – Kendall/Hunt – Page 200.)

channel distribution – The vehicles and people used to link advertisers with consumers to sell their product.

channel power – Circumstances, economic or social, that allow one communication vehicle to overpower another.

channel strategy – Decision-making related to the selection of the most appropriate method of controlling the flow of goods or services from producer to end-user. Also called *marketing strategy*.

channels of distribution – Routes used by a company to distribute its products. For example, through wholesalers, retailers, mail order, etc. The length of the channel of distribution affects the cost of the product.

character count – The number of letters, figures, signs or spaces – known as characters – in a selected block of copy.

chartoon – Colorful charts carried in such newspapers as USA today. When they are black and white they are referred to as *graytoons*.

37

Tips to Succeed:
'Credit Killers' – 5 common mistakes that can ruin a credit score

- Staying out of debt: Having no credit history is nearly as bad as having a poor credit history, because creditors have no way to judge how the person will handle a loan.

- Rate shopping: Too many inquiries can damage a credit score. Generally, six or more inquiries within six months will scare a lender. Transferring balances on credit cards can negatively affect a score for the same reason.

- Assuming there's a grace period: If a payment is even one day overdue, it's late, and even one late payment can lower a credit score.

- Closing old accounts: It seems smart to close unused accounts, but it can actually shorten a person's credit history by lowering the credit score.

- Cosigning on a loan: Cosigning has many risks and little reward, because the primary borrower's mistakes will end up on both signers' credit reports. Just say no every time.

Centers for Financial Education, a division of
Consumer Credit Counseling Services of New Jersey www.crediteducation.org

chat – Online interactive communication between two or more people on the Internet. One can "talk" in *real time* with other people in a chat room, but the words are typed instead of spoken.

chat room – An area online where you can chat with other people in *real time*.

cherry-pick – To choose the best items from a selection for oneself, often in an unfair manner.

Cheshire label – Paper specially designed to allow name and address labels to be mechanically affixed to individual mailing pieces, allowing the process to be automated. Technology, such as ink jet printing of addresses directly onto mailing pieces, has reduced the need for Cheshire labels and can reduce the cost of mailings.

chief communication officer (CCO) – A relatively new term given to the person whose principal function is to oversee all internal and external communications of an organization. The CCO should report directly to the CEO or an organization's board – with a seat at the corporate table.

chief executive officer (CEO) – Responsible for all aspects of a company or organization.

chief integrity officer (CIO) – A term used for public relations director/strategic counselor who is considered a company or organization's "truth teller."

chief operating officer (COO) – Responsible for operation of a company or organization.

Children's Advertising Review Unit (CARU) – Division of the Council of Better Business Bureaus that reviews advertising and promotional material directed at children in all media. Read more at *www.caru.org*.

choice fatigue – The stress of having too many options from which to choose. Sometimes referred to as American abundance, because Americans have so many choices of product and product variation.

choke (or shrink) and spread – Use of color in printing, particularly in areas without type.

Christmas credo – The trend of shopping earlier and earlier for the winter holidays. The Wharton School – University of Pennsylvania claims the Christmas season – with advertising – not begins earlier than ever. In some cases, just after Halloween rather than just before Thanksgiving.

chroma key – It is a term for the filmmaking technique of using an evenly-lit monochromatic background for the purpose of replacing it with a different image or scene. The term also refers to the visual effect resulting from this technique as well as the colored screen itself (*blue screen* or *green screen*). It is commonly used for TV weather forecasts, wherein the presenter appears to be standing in front of a large map, but in the studio it is actually a large blue or green background.

chrome – A color photographic transparency.

chunk survey – Often used on intercept surveys and Internet surveys. Chunking information — the process of breaking down large amounts of information, which is often very complex, into small manageable pieces. Responses can be derived from a combination of the overall number of questions, the average length of the questions, and how closely the questions relate to one another. The survey architect must group the questions in a way that is meaningful to the user, both in the order they are presented and in their proximity to one another. If possible, related questions should be located on the same page of a multi-paged survey. Also, survey pages should require little if any scrolling (on the Internet).

chunking – Breaking up long body copy.

chunks of information – Copy presented in short segments.

38 Techniques to Succeed: Convince vs. persuade

A person is *convinced* by evidence or argument made to the intellect (head). A person is *persuaded* by appeals made to the will, moral sense, or emotions (heart).

Convincing is long term – *persuading* is (for now) short term.

When you *convince* someone, you actually get them to believe something else.

When you *persuade* someone, you get them to act without convincing them.

churning of account – The act of a public relations or advertising client moving from one agency to another.

circulation – The average number of copies of a print publication sold or distributed through subscriptions and newsstand sales. For outdoor advertising, this refers to the total number of people who have an opportunity to observe a billboard or poster. Read more at *www.accessabc.com/*.

citizen action public – A group within a community, which may exert pressure on an organization to act in a certain way.

citizen journalism – Citizens playing an active role in the process of gathering and reporting news and information – using still and video cameras, other recorders, cell phones and blogs. Also called *participatory journalism*.

citizen soldier – National Guardsman.

39 Techniques To Succeed:
Increase business by cold calling

A "cold call" is a sales call – on the phone or in person – when the person you're calling has not approached you or expressed interest in your products or services.

"Cold calls" can be effective, especially if potential leads are found through effective, unbiased research. If a business is stagnant, or is developing a new product or service line, cold calls can be a relatively inexpensive way to attract new customers.

What's the secret of cold call success?

• Change your perspective. "Cold calls" can help someone rather than be a "bother."

• "Qualify" your leads. Narrow your target list.

• Listen: Find out what your prospect wants and needs.

• Develop a great pitch. Be clear about what you are offering and the benefits to the customer.

• Take people literally. If a prospect says, "I'm not interested right now," believe they mean right NOW. Perhaps they'll be interested another time.

• Don't be obnoxious: Take "No" for an answer. If someone is not interested, why waste your time or theirs?

• Mind your manners: If you walk in on someone and they're on the phone, wait until they are free. If you're phoning, and the person says "Now's not a good time," ask when a good time would be to call back, and get off the phone.

• Give yourself a quota. Set a minimum – but realistic – number of calls you have to make before you can call it quits for the day. Stick to it.

• Stay in practice. Cold calling is difficult, and it's easy to forget how to do it well.

Don't take rejection personally and don't get discouraged. Remember, you've got to kiss a lot of frogs before you find a prince.

Rhonda Abrams - www.rhondaworks.com/

civic journalism – Stories about the critical issues on readers' minds. Stories that reflect the community. Also known as public journalism.

claim – A statement about the product's performance.

clarity – One of the Seven Cs of Communication. Communicating the strategic message in simple terms to help assure it will be received exactly as intended – clearly, concisely, calculatingly, consistently and completely (specifically and simply). (Read more in *The Public Relations Practitioner's Playbook* – Kendall/Hunt – Chapter 5.)

class rate – The standard charge for the shipment of goods by a carrier.

classical conditioning – A stimulus that leads to a response. It could involve the "transfer effect." For example, Michael Jordan is associated with basketball and Nike, and Babe Ruth, the Yankees and baseball. Jingles are used for classical conditioning and serve as a *locking device.*

classes of type – General groups of fonts – serif, sans serif, script and novelty.

classification or demographic questions – Questions designed to generate data about the respondent such as age, education, income and gender.

classified advertising – Print advertising where similar goods and services are grouped together in categories under appropriate headings – sometimes referred to as *directory advertising.* In many newspapers, classified advertising brings in the most revenue.

claymation – An animation method that uses clay figurines.

clearance – The process where someone at an advertising vehicle reviews an advertisement's copy for legal, ethical and taste standards, before accepting the ad for use.

cliché – A trite expression – an overused idea.

click – The action of a user pressing the mouse button. Used to measure impressions of an Internet advertisement.

click-and-mortar – Retail or other type of store that has an online ordering capabilities as well as an actual building.

click fraud – Merchants are billed for fruitless traffic generated by scam artists and mischief makers who repeatedly click on an advertiser's Web link with no intention of buying anything. *Click fraud* or fraud has been identified as a sham aimed at a perceived weakness in Google's® (the Internet search leader) lucrative advertising network.

click rate – Ratio of advertisement clicks to ad impressions.

click-stream – The electronic path a computer user takes while navigating from site to site on a computer.

click-through (CT) – The action of a computer user clicking on an ad, banner or link transferring the user to a new page.

40 Tips to Succeed: Cover letters: Get to the point

Whether pitching an account or applying for a job, an effective cover letter is a must.

• Immediate attention is given to pitches and resumes with good cover letters

• First paragraph must be a grabber (reader will spend, on average, 15-30 seconds on first glance)

• Say what you mean

• Mean what you say

• Keep it short – but specific

• Keep it conversational

• Ask for what you want

• If applying for job
  – The job posting or vacancy reference number, if one is given in the advertisement
  – Your precise areas of relevance and expertise (bullet points are fine)
  – Your full contact information - including telephone numbers

Never forget this rule:
If you wouldn't say it in normal speech, don't write it.

Maury Z. Levy - www.levywarren.com
David Carter - www.job-hunting-tips.com

click-through ratio (CTR) – The ratio of click-throughs to impressions for a given ad run. *Per inquiry* advertising rates are based on impressions.

client – An agency term for an organization or person it represents.

client-initiated ad impression – One of the two methods used for advertisement counting. Ad content is delivered to the user via two methods – server-initiated and client-initiated. Server-initiated ad counting uses the publisher's Web content server for making requests, formatting and re-directing content. For organizations using a server-initiated ad counting method, counting should occur following the response to the ad on the publisher's ad server or the Web content server, or later in the process. This is important because Web ad rates may be determined by server-initiated ad impressions. See *server-initiated ad impression.*

client list – A list of a firm's key clients – often includes contact information, which is the foundation for relationship marketing.

Cliff Notes version – A summary of a report or a condensed version.

clincher – An additional incentive offered to a potential client to win the account.

clip (clipping) – A newspaper or magazine article cut out – many times to justify to client that a story ran or to illustrate a competitor's activities. Also, a short extract from a film, videotape, or radio or television news program.

clip retrospective – technique employed by television producers and network executives designed to introduce first-time viewers to a program's various plotlines (from earlier first year programs or a review retrospective of the entire first year). It was used with great success on ABC for "Grey's Anatomy."

clipart – Illustrations, pictures and designs that can be bought on a CD or copied from Web sites.

cloak and dagger – Operating in a way so as to ensure complete concealment and confidentiality. A clandestine – or stealth – approach.

close – The critical stage in the pitching process when the agency attempts to obtain a potential client's commitment for its services – usually comes toward the end of the pitch.

closed-end or forced-choice question – A question on a survey instrument that allows a respondent to choose an answer from a given list. See *open-end question*.

closed promotion – A sales promotion available only to a specific, high-potential target. A customized marketing mix to effectively reach a specific target market effectively.

closing date – The final date copy and other materials must be at the media outlet to assure it appears in a specific issue or time slot.

cluster – In research, a cluster is a universe or public with similar demographic characteristics. Also, two or more radio or television commercials airing either back-to-back or separated by time checks, weather or a brief promotional announcement.

cluster analysis – A multivariate (multiple variables) statistical technique used to identify entities with similar characteristics from those without them.

cluster buster – The tactic used to separate radio commercials that otherwise would be running *back to back* – a time check, jingle or weather forecast.

cluster sample – A form of probability (scientific or chance) sample where respondents are drawn from a random sample of mutually exclusive groups (usually geographic areas) within a total population – also called an area sample. Identifying these groups in advance could save costs. See *stratified sample*.

clutter – Ads surrounded by other ads all competing for reader, viewer or listener attention. This is a term usually reserved for print (newspapers, magazines, billboards, etc.), but can also be used when too many radio or television commercials air simultaneously.

CMYK – Acronym for Cyan-Magenta-Yellow-Black, and pronounced as separate letters C-M-Y-K. *CMYK* is a color model where all colors are described as a mixture of these four process colors. CMYK is the standard color model used in offset printing for full-color documents. Because such printing uses inks of these four basic colors, it is often called four-color printing. In contrast, display devices (monitors) generally use a different color model called *RGB*, which stands for Red-Green-Blue. One of the most difficult aspects of desktop publishing in color is color matching – properly converting the RGB colors into CMYK colors so that what gets printed looks the same as what appears on the monitor. Read more at *www.webopedia.com/TERM/C/CMYK.html.*

co-authoring advertising – Two brands sharing the same TV commercial sell their products – either related or unrelated. For example, Maytag repairmen riding around in a Chevrolet; a young man puts money in a vending machine to purchase a Pepsi and out come keys to a Mercedes Benz, which is then shown on the screen.

co-branding advertising – An ad or commercial for one product that has two distinct brand names (e.g. Kellogg's® Rice Krispies®; McDonald's® Big Mac®; Burger King® Whopper®.) See *sub-brand.*

co-branding code phrase – Catch phrase or buzz word used in a speech to launch an audience action. In political conventions, such a phrase might be: "Hope is on the way!" – the audience starts waving signs that had been given to them earlier in the evening.

co-op database – Two or more list owners combine their lists to gain access to each other's names.

co-shopping – Young people (usually tween girls), shopping with their mothers – who are advising them and vice versa.

coalition building – A tactic that emphasizes broad based support for an issue or candidate. Coalitions encourage groups to coordinate their efforts and prevent duplication.

coastout – An employee who merely does an adequate job but in a sense rests on his or her laurels until retirement – sometimes many years away.

coated stock – Paper with a slick and smooth finish (usually gives off sheen).

Coding Accuracy Support System (CASS) – A system created by the U.S. Postal Service to ensure the accuracy of software programs used by fulfillment or mailing services to check addresses and code mailings for delivery.

cognitive dissonance – Buyer's remorse – a doubt that surfaces after a purchase – second thoughts.

coincidental survey – A non-scientific survey asking viewers or listeners to respond to a question or issue during a television or radio program, or over the Internet. Non-scientific research gathered in an informal manner to elicit opinions. Coincidental surveys are neither random

41

Techniques to Succeed: Knowing how to correspond

Whether you have just met someone, or have known the person for some time, it is important to follow-up meetings with written correspondence.

A. Write a follow-up letter/thank you note within 48 hours.

1. Whether a handwritten note or formal letter always follow guidelines for writing effective business letters.

   1. Women should be addressed as "Ms." no matter what their marital status.

   2. Do not forget to sign your letter.

   3. Always proof for typos and misspellings.

2. Letters usually contain the following elements:

   1. Opener – the opener should be friendly and tells the reader why you are writing.

   2. Justification – the second paragraph reinforces or justifies what you are looking for and why you should get it.

   3. Closing – close the letter by seeking the person to act on your behalf or request.

Email etiquette has some specific guidelines.

1. Email is appropriate to use, but never use all caps and watch for typos.

2. Always include a subject line in your message.

3. Make the subject line meaningful.

4. Use correct grammar and spelling.

5. Always use a signature if you can; make sure it identifies who you are and includes alternate means of contacting you (phone and fax are useful).

6. Use active words instead of passive.

7. Do not ask to recall a message.

8. Use proper structure and layout

9. Avoid long sentences.

10. Be concise and to the point.

nor scientific. They don't tell the researcher very much except that people did respond and do have an opinion which may or may not reflect the universe as a whole.

cold calling – Making a call on a client without an appointment. Also, periodic, unscheduled proactive telephone calls or visits to members of the media. (While some may think this is unacceptable, others, including editors, welcome brief calls and personal visits – schedules permitting).

cold type – Refers to today's typesetting methods, such as photo or computer typesetting, because they do not involve pouring hot molten metal into molds for different type fonts – used in offset printing. Laser copies are cold type.

collate – To gather together separate sections or pages of a publication in the correct order for binding.

collateral – Additional documents or other materials that accompany or support a public relations plan.

collective thinking – The result of intellectual property, mind share, the thoughts of a committee or team. When all take equal credit, credit is giving to "the room."

collusion – The unlawful practice of two or more parties sharing information to gain an unfair advantage over a third party or manipulate prices. See *cartel*.

color matching – The process of assuring that a color on one medium remains the same when converted to another medium. This is extremely difficult because different media use different color models. Color monitors, for example, use the RGB model, whereas process printing uses the CMYK model. As color desktop publishing matures, color matching is gaining more and more attention. The most recent Windows® and Apple® operating systems include a color management system (CMS) to assist in color matching.

color proof – A full-color print of an unfinished advertisement, shown to a client for approval.

color proofing – Various steps necessary, up to final printing, to examine printed colors and compare shades and registration to original (anticipated colors) copy and the artwork being reproduced. It is important that colors be tested on the paper stock that will be used for the finished product because weight, shades and coating (matte, glossy, etc.) can affect the colors. See *pre-press services*.

42 Techniques to Succeed: In front of the camera

Unless you are an expert in front of the camera, DO NOT look directly into the camera. Look at the interviewer or if the interviewer is remote, pick a spot that is slightly off-camera.

If there is a TV monitor within view, ask that it be removed out of view. If that cannot be done, DO NOT look at the monitor at all.

If you must look into the lens of the camera, pretend that the person who you most want to convince is behind that lens. If that makes you uncomfortable, then pretend that your mother, best friend, daughter or son, or anyone else you feel comfortable with is behind that lens.

color registration – The alignment of colors on a printed product (newspaper, magazine, billboard, etc.). It's the alignment of successive colors and/or images as witnessed by register marks. The three uses of registration marks are to identify: the position/location of the image on the substrate, the color-to-color registration and whether the image is square to the lead edge of the substrate. Proper registration is necessary for an image to prevent unwanted colors and misalignments – many times causing the ad or other product to appear blurred.

color separation – Separating a full-color or spot-color advertisement or other printing job into the four separate colors: cyan, yellow, magenta and black. Traditionally, negatives and plates are needed for each of the four colors to complete the printing process.

column – Vertical spaces on a page to place text boxes within.

column inch – A common unit of measure for newspapers, where advertising space is purchased by the width, in columns (vertical spaces), and depth, in inches. For example, an ad that is three columns wide and five inches tall (or deep) would be 15 column inches.

combination branding – Emphasizing a corporate or family name as well as an individual brand name in product marketing. Example: Hershey Chocolate®, Campbell's® Soup. See *corporate branding*; *family brand.*

combination of (budgeting) methods – Process of combining various budgeting techniques to adopt the final workable budget.

combination rate – A special media pricing arrangement that involves purchasing space or time from more than one vehicle, owned by the same media corporation. Also known as a package deal.

comfort level – Readers feel comfortable with material written two or three levels below their actual reading level.

comfortable sinicism – The concept that two or more parties do not agree, but it's all right – they will get along.

commercial – A television or radio advertisement.

commission – A payment made to a salesperson based on a percentage of the value of the goods sold.

commission override – A commission paid to a sales manager based on a percentage of his or her salespeople's commissions.

commodity markets – Markets consisting of similar products, regardless of the brand name. These markets employ *institutional advertising* to create product demand. Example: milk (Got Milk? ®), pork (The other white meat.®) and beef (Beef – it's what for dinner. ®).

commodity product – A product that cannot be significantly differentiated from competitors' products. Examples include milk, sugar and salt.

commodity rate – A rate applied in any situation where freight is product specific (paid for per product) rather than based on volume or weight. Also called a *special rate.*

common carrier – Regular scheduled transportation services such as railways, airlines and trucking lines, available to all users.

common market (countries) – A group of geographically associated countries limiting trade barriers among member nations and applying common tariffs to products from non-members. Also known as regional trading blocks, such as the European Common Market.

communicability – The extent to which the features and benefits of a new product or service are likely to be noticed and discussed by consumers. Also known as *buzz*.

communication – The process of delivering and sending messages through various channels. The transfer of information from a sender (encoder) to a receiver (decoder). Effective two-way communication includes gathering feedback. Both the sender and the receiver are actively involved in a communication process.

communication audit – A systematic survey, by an independent third party, of members of a target audience (often members of the media or publics) to determine awareness of, or reaction to, vehicles used in an organization or company's overall awareness (communication) campaign. Audits validate measurement counts, reinforce accountability and help public relations practitioners maintain credibility and believability. It is a complete analysis of an organization's communications – internal and/or external – designed to "take a picture" of the communication

43 Techniques to Succeed: Dollar Bill Test

The *Dollar Bill Test* is simple: take a dollar bill and turn it on a page of copy. To pass the *Dollar Bill Test*, it must touch at least one copy-breaker. If it does, your publication passes. If not, you fail.

Rowan (N.J.) University Professor Claudia Cuddy has her own list of copybreakers to assure publications pass the *Dollar Bill Test*:
- Heads
- Subheads
- Pull quotes (Blurbs)
- Rules
- Initial (or drop) caps
- Shaded (screened) boxes
- Pictures
- Art (line art)
- Bullet lists

goal, objectives, strategies, tactics, accomplishments, needs, policies, practices and capabilities, and to uncover necessary data to allow top management to make informed, economical decisions about future objectives of the organization and its communication plan. According to PRSA's (Public Relations Society of America) Joseph Kopec, "The scope of an audit may be as broad and as deep as the size and complexity of the organization's demands. The audit can measure the effectiveness of communication programs throughout an entire organization, in a single division or department, or within a specific employee group. It can examine communications on a particular subject or communications via individual media, it can uncover misunderstandings, information barriers and bottlenecks, as well as opportunities. It can help measure cost effectiveness, evaluate ongoing programs, confirm hunches, clarify questions, and, in some instances, reorient concepts among senior management." A well done audit should also lead to a series of recommendations. A *communication audit* covers all aspects, not just public relations. (See *public relations audit*.)

44 Tips to Succeed: Communicating with older people

Communicating with older people often requires extra time and patience because of physical, psychological and social changes.
Some suggestions:
• Reduce background noises.
• Talk about familiar subjects.
• Keep your sentences short.
• Give the person a chance to reminisce.
• Allow extra time for a response.

communication conveyance – One employee carrying the organization's philosophy and message to another.

communication effect of advertising – The influence that an advertisement or some other form of promotional activity might have, is having or has had, on consumers or on the usage of a product advertised. See *advertising effectiveness*.

communication error – The failure of a Web browser/Web server to successfully bring up (request) or transfer a document.

communication mix – One of the Seven Cs of Communication. Used to help accomplish *consistency* and *continuity*. Repetition and consistency in an organization's publications – can include letterhead, brochure, business card, newsletter, flier, etc. used for to create an identity or to deliver a campaign. (Read more in *The Public Relations Practitioner's Playbook* Kendall/Hunt – 2008).

communication model – A theory that explains the foundations of all communication – including sender, message, receiver, channel, noise and feedback.

communication process – Two-way communication where a message transmitted by the sender (encoder) is sent through a channel to a receiver (decoder) who provides feedback.

communitarian spirit – Started with Ben Franklin. The establish of services for members of a community. For example, public libraries and parks. That has now grown to include such other institutions as museums and service organizations.

comp – Comprehensive artwork used to present the general color and layout of a page – often used by agencies in their design of advertisements and commercials (storyboards).

companioning – Assuming full responsibility (of an event) for a client – relieving the client of pressure. The client pays an agency or agent, steps back and observes and enjoys as their vendor researches, plans, implements and evaluates the tactic or activity.

company mission – The answer to the question "What business are we in?" (This is who we are; what we think about ourselves; why we need your support.) It is the corporate mission statement, with a broad focus and a customer orientation. It provides management with a sense of purpose. See *corporate mission statement*.

company specific training – Training programs specially tailored to meet company requirements for groups of people from the same company or organization.

comparative (competitive) advertising – Advertising in which a firm names a competitor's product and compares it with its own. Messages that compare brands, stores or service companies. This type of advertising is considered product-centered and must be based on fact. Also called comparison advertising.

comparative influence – Occurs when a niche audience compares their attitudes, beliefs and behavior – the more similarity there is between a consumer's opinions and those of the niche, the greater the comparative influence of that group. Comparisons are achieved through either scientific sampling or focus groups.

compare – Similarities or differences in "like items." See *contrast*.

comparison pricing – A pricing method where the price for a new product is set by comparing the features and benefits it offers to those of other (established) products in the same category.

compassion – A major ingredient during crisis communication – a deep awareness of and sympathy for another's suffering; the humane quality of understanding the suffering of others and wanting to do something about it. *Compassion* must be exhibited during a crisis in which there was a tragedy.

compartmentalize – To separate into distinct parts, categories or compartments – especially when thinking through, crafting or designing a *strategic plan*.

compatibility – A consumer's adjustment to a new product's features and benefits – a major determinant of the rate of new product adoption.

compensation – Payment for work done on behalf of another.

compensation systems – Payment options to salespeople for tasks performed. Commonly used systems include straight salary, straight commission and a combination of salary and incentives.

compensatory time – In broadcasting, air time given for "make goods" – commercials to be aired because they either didn't play because of some type of malfunction or because the promised audience (number of viewers or listeners) was not delivered.

competition – Organizations or firms vying for the same audience. See *competitors*.

competition-oriented pricing – A pricing strategy based on what the competition does.

competitions – Sales promotions that allow the consumer the chance of winning a prize. Many times, these are federally regulated.

competitive (product) advantage – The product, message, feature or benefit that puts a company ahead of its competitors.

competitive advertising – See *comparative advertising*.

competitive analysis – The assessment of the strengths and weaknesses of competing firms or brands.

competitive attack strategies – Options available for attacking a competitor through advertising techniques which include: frontal attack (head-on), a flanking attack (attack at a point of weakness), an encirclement attack (attack on several fronts at once), a by-pass attack (attack by diversifying into new territories, products or technologies) and a guerilla attack (attack by waging small, intermittent skirmishes).

competitive bidding – A process where buyers request potential suppliers to submit quotations for a proposed purchase or contract. Many times in government, bids must be submitted in sealed envelopes and are opened together at a designated time in a designated place.

competitive budgeting – A method of allocating a promotion budget based on matching the activity of a major competitor. Used when factoring in the competition. If a firm must increase its activities to develop more aggressive campaigns in their respective market, then it must employ this method. The competition must be analyzed to justify budget requests. The public relations practitioner should coordinate with a research and development team to gather support data on the competition and its resources.

competitive depositioning – Changing buyers' beliefs about the attributes of a competitor's product.

competitive environment – The atmosphere of a market where companies compete for the same audience.

competitive equilibrium – A relatively stable market.

competitive myopia – A company not recognizing the features and benefits of its competitors.

competitive niche – A narrowly-defined market in which a company can compete.

competitive position – An organization or company's ranking in comparison to others in the industry based on size and business strength.

competitive scope – The diversification of an organization's focus as measured by the range of industries, market segments or geographical regions it targets.

competitive set – Organizations or companies that offer the same product and/or service (brand or product line) in the same market(s).

competitive strategy – Planning intended to give a company a competitive advantage over its competitors.

competitor advertising – Messages that compare brands, stores or service companies. This type of advertising must be based on fact.

competitors – Organization or firms vying for the same audience.

compiled list – A list gathered from directories, newspapers, public records, etc. identifying people or organizations with common characteristics – used for identifying niche audiences and targeting.

complementary product pricing – The pricing of one product at a reasonable level, to increase the demand for another product that could be used with it – to maximize the profits of both products. Examples: cereal and milk; peanut butter and jelly.

complete segmentation/fragmentation – The division of a market into demographic and psychographic groups and to tailor products and marketing programs for each.

complexity – The degree of difficulty which a purchaser of a new product has in understanding the features and benefits of a new product or service. For example, a new microwave or new computer.

composer – Person who writes music.

composite proof – A version of an illustration or page where the process colors appear together to represent full color. When reproduced in one color – usually just black – colors are represented as shades of gray. If reproduced as a *blue line*, colors would be represented in various shades.

composition – The process of arranging the elements in a photograph or an illustration.

comprehensive approach – Public relations approach that includes all – or at least many – audiences – so that no one is excluded. It is an *intensive approach*. (Opposite of *targeting*.)

comprehensive layout – A rough layout of an advertisement designed for presentation only, but so detailed as to appear very much like the finished ad will look. Sometimes called a finished rough.

computer forensics – A technological, systematic inspection of the computer system and its contents for evidence or supportive evidence of a crime or other computer use that is being inspected – known as e-discovery. It is nearly impossible to permanently delete a document (or file) from a computer hard drive. It is forever embedded. On the Internet, there should be no expectations of privacy.

computer modeling – Constructing and manipulating computer-based simulations of public relations and other marketing situations to examine the consequences of alternative courses of action. Computer models, often developed from an analysis of historical data, may be used

45 Tips to Succeed: When a crisis strikes – communicate early and often

- Contact the media before they contact you
- Communicate internally – then externally
- Put the public first
- Take responsibility
- Be honest
- Never say "*No comment*"
- Designate a single spokesperson
- Set up a central information center (staging area)
- Provide a constant flow of information
- Be familiar with media needs and deadlines
- Be accessible
- Monitor news coverage and telephone inquiries
- Communicate with key publics
- Be accessible

to determine the optimum levels of advertising and other promotional expenditure, etc.

computer service bureaus – A company maintains lists for list owners. Services could include: updating the list, merge/purge, data overlays and preparing the list for mailing or rentals.

concentrated marketing – A marketing segmentation strategy where a firm concentrates its entire efforts and resources on serving one segment of the market. Also called *niche marketing* – becomes a *target market* when the marketer decides to sell to it.

concentrated target marketing – When a single market is pursued.

concept development and testing – A two-phase stage in the development of a new product where potential buyers are presented first with the idea or description of the new product (concept testing) and later with the product itself in final or prototype form (product testing), to obtain their reaction. See *product testing; new product development.*

concept to consumer – The evolution of a product or service from the thought process to the drawing board and finally into the marketplace.

conceptual plagiarism – Appropriation of research, ideas and concepts from another person (person's research) that eventually develops into such published material as a book, article or written or oral reports (speeches).

conduit theory – In public relations and advertising, the agency or consultant may be held liable for fraud if it passes along misleading information provided by the client. The understanding is that the agency or counselor should have done ample research. (He who acts for his client, acts for himself.) In investing, it is the idea that qualifying investment companies should be allowed to avoid double taxation by passing interest, dividend

46 Tips to Succeed: When a crisis strikes – learn from the best

- Don't duck the issue
- Take responsibility
- Offer to make good on broken promises
- Cover all the bases
- Measure results

Delahaye Medialink Worldwide

income and capital gains directly to shareholders, without also incurring a tax liability. (See *SEC v. Pig 'n Whistle Corp.* [1972] in *The Public Relations Practitioner's Playbook* – Kendall/Hunt – 2008.)

conference calls – Calls made between multiple parties using a phone or other equipment designed for communicating with multiple parties in multiple locations. See *video conferencing*.

confidence level-95 in 100 – In an infinite number of similarly designed and executed surveys, the percentage results would fall within a given margin of error in 95 percent of these surveys.

configuration – The shape of words based on the combination of uppercase and lowercase letters. When learning to read, people recognize words by their configurations – those words are called "sight" words.

conflict analysis – Another term for force field analysis. A useful technique for looking at all the forces for and against a decision – a specialized method for weighing the pros and cons. (See example of force field analysis in *The Public Relations Practitioners Playbook* – Kendall/Hunt – 2008.)

conflict of interest – An agency dilemma of having two competing clients.

conflict resolution – The process of attempting to resolve a dispute or a conflict.

confusion marketing – A controversial strategy where an organization or firm's message is designed to deliberately confuse the consumer.

conglomerize – The act of organizations joining to form conglomerates.

conjunctive model (of brand evaluation) – The theory that consumers establish minimum attribute levels which acceptable brands must possess. When about to make a purchase, consumers will consider only those brands that meet all their minimum requirements.

connections – Individuals who assist with networking – word-of-mouth to find clients and jobs.

connectivity – or connectivity effect (CE) – The ability of network TV to interact with the Internet. All of the major television networks are now practicing CE. In many ways, it is pure electronic "convergence." Also, a computer term for the unbiased transport of packets between two end points. This is also the essential definition of "IP" (*internet protocol*).

connector – See *buzz marketing; consumption pioneer; key communicator*.

consensus – Shared agreement (not necessarily a majority).

consent decree – An order by the Federal Trade Commission. The first step in the regulation process after the FTC determines that an ad is deceptive or unfair. Also called a consent order. The second step is a *cease- and-desist order* requiring an advertiser to stop running a deceptive, misleading or unfair advertisement, campaign or claim. *Corrective advertising* is the third step.

consequence probes – Verbal tactics used by a salesperson to illustrate the disadvantages to a buyer of *not* making a particular purchase.

47 Tips to Succeed: Bill Jones' 10 Commandments of Crisis Communication

1. *Perception is reality.* If your audience thinks it is, it is.
2. *Response is control.* The community wants access to information, and no crisis is unmanageable if you give clear, cool facts.
3. Information is power.
4. Credibility is survival.
5. Body language is crucial. If you behave like you have something to hide, people will think that you do.
6. Calmness is essential. Unflappability is your best asset. Always act knowledgeable and calm.
7. Give a confession. The public and the media want a confession; so don't be afraid to admit mistakes.
8. Tell the franchise what happened. It is in the best interest of the community to keep them informed.
9. Preparation is 99% of success.
10. *Out of every crisis comes the chance to "build a better mousetrap."* From every crisis there are major lessons to be learned.
11. Pray like hell that you never have to handle numbers 1 through 10!

J. William Jones - Former School Information Services Director
Philadelphia School District

consistency – One of the Seven Cs of Communication. Also referred to as continuity. Communication is an unending process, requiring repetition to achieve penetration. The strategic message must be consistent (simple, relevant and repetitious). (Read more in *The Public Relations Practitioner's Playbook* – Kendall/Hunt – Page 200.)

consolidation – The appointment of one public relations or advertising agency to handle all the advertising and PR of a client's divisions and brands.

consolidator – Works in tandem with fulfillment or mailing house to save clients money. A consolidator accepts processed mail for distribution through a particular type of delivery service – U.S. Postal Service, UPS®, FedEx®, etc. By grouping together mail from more than one company, consolidators are often able to obtain higher volume discounts than an independent mailer.

conspiracy theorists – Small, but powerful, and often hidden, elite *key communicators* (opinion leaders) who are able to use the mass media to condition and persuade passive audiences into conforming to the their wishes. It depends heavily on the notion of a powerful media and easily duped audiences.

constituency newsletter – A type of newsletter that communicates with a common interest group to influence its readership and foster a sense of community – hospitals, alumni associations, etc. would send their newsletters to a limited target audience and occasionally solicit donations.

constituency of one – Yourself or your client. When you are "speaking for a *constituency of one*," you are speaking for *yourself* or *your client*.

consultative selling – An approach to personal selling emphasizing the role of the salesperson as a consultant and an expert. The salesperson assists the buyer to identify needs and find need-satisfactions in the product range, seeking to build long-term customer relationships leading to repeat business. See *relationship marketing*.

consumer – Individual who buys and uses a product or service.

consumer advertising – Advertising directed at individuals, rather than businesses or dealers (a majority of newspaper ads and radio and television commercials).

consumer behavior – The buying habits and patterns of consumers when purchasing goods and services.

consumer credit – Finance made available to consumers with arrangements that the loan be repaid with or without interest.

consumer durables – A classification of consumer products consisting of goods with a long life – cars, electrical appliances and furniture.

consumer franchise – The understanding consumers have of a brand – which helps in their decision making.

consumer goods – Items purchased by consumers for personal and household use – toilet tissue, soap, toothpaste, etc.

consumer jury test – The testing of advertisements that involves asking consumers to compare, rank and evaluate the ads.

consumer list – Any list of individuals' home addresses who have bought merchandise, subscriptions, given to a non-profit, etc. Computer software can easily niche and target audiences based on tracking, buying or just inquiry habits.

consumer loyalty (reward) programs – Retailers reward customers for purchases by giving them points for dollars spent. While service is still the "bottom line," *loyalty programs* attract customers in droves and keep them loyal. Such programs can be traced to programs like Gold Bond Stamps®, which started in 1938. Grocery stores gave out stamps based on how much customers spent. Customers redeemed the stamps for free "stuff." Among the most successful Loyalty Programs are those sponsored by Marriott®, Staples® and Visa® Air Tran®.

consumer market – Buyers and potential buyers of products and services for personal and household use.

consumer need – The motive that initiates the design, manufacture and distribution of new products.

consumer non-durables – A classification of frequently purchased products consisting of goods that are consumed in one or a few uses. Also called expendables – paper products, cleaning supplies, paper clips, soap.

consumer publication – A newspaper or magazine intended for the general reader.

consumer research – Marketing research focusing on the needs, opinions, attitudes and behaviors of consumers.

consumer rights – What consumers should reasonably expect when purchasing a product or service.

consumer stimulants – Promotional efforts designed to evoke short-term purchasing behavior. Examples would include coupons, premiums and samples.

consumer wearout – A drop in the effectiveness of an advertisement or promotional campaign due to boredom and familiarity.

consumerism – A social movement to safeguard the rights of consumers.

consummatory advertising – Advertising that stresses the benefits of taking immediate action to purchase.

consumption pioneer – See *connector*; *key communicator*.

contact information – The name, telephone numbers, fax information, e-mail, etc. included on a news release should the recipient want to confirm or gather more information.

contactual reference group – A group with which an individual has contact and which influences the individual's purchase decisions.

container premium – Special product packaging where the package itself acts as a premium of value to the consumer – decorative coffee can, reusable bottle or a resealable plastic bag.

content – One of the Seven Cs of Communication. Information, the subject matter (strategic message) of what is being communicated, and it must have meaning to the receiver. The target audience determines the content. (Read more in *The Public Relations Practitioner's Playbook* – Kendall/Hunt – Chapter 15.) Also material in a publication or document.

content analysis – The technique of reading publications, advertisements or other messages to find references to an organization or an idea, then coding and analyzing the content to determine trends and opinions. Results are often compared with a different set channels or vehicles (print, radio, television, Internet). Often used for graduate and other research projects to compare categories listed or determine the success of channels, vehicles or media. For example, comparison of school district Web sites to determine content and effectiveness or law journals to determine why some might be more popular or effective than others. Comparisons include common and unique categories, frequency of use and effectiveness. The results are reported through a narrative analysis with illustrations.

content integration – Advertising woven into editorial content. Also called *advertorial* or web advertorial.

content management systems (CMSs) –Tools for editing, organizing and publishing Web logs are variously referred to as *content management systems*, *publishing platforms*, *weblog software* and simply *blogware*.

content on demand – Usually newsfeed services, which offer full-text newsfeeds to content redistributors or directly to the public customers. Content sources include branded newswires, newspapers, magazines, financial and business sources, official government feeds, and Web logs. The Internet providers offer reliable, fast and flexible service. Publishers for Content On Demand include The Associated Press, BBC Monitoring, Business Wire, Knight Ridder/Tribune Business News, EDGAR Online, M2 Communications, Market Wire, PR Newswire, PrimeZone Media Network, Xinhua News Agency, United Press International and others. The full-text content is available in standardized format, with stock ticker symbols, people tickers, taxonomy-based categorization and meta-tagging, all as XML or RSS newsfeeds—but without an end-user application or interface.

contents page – The page that lists articles, features, departments and chapters and their locations in a publication.

contests – A form of sales promotion where consumers are persuaded to buy earlier, or in greater quantity, by the offer of prizes of cash or merchandise to be won in a competition. Many contests are now federally regulated. See *sales promotion*.

contingent method – A closing technique where the salesperson attempts to isolate the last remaining objection or obstacle to the sale and closes it contingent upon being able to remove the obstacle. See *"What if..." method* (of handling sales objections).

continuation – An order from a mailer who has previously tested or used the list within 12 months and is using it again.

continuation line – Helps readers locate the continuation of an article from a previous page (the page from which it was "jumped").

continuity – One of the Seven Cs of Communication. Scheduling advertisements to appear at regular intervals over a period of time. Communication is an unending process, requiring repetition to achieve penetration. The strategic message must be consistent (simple, relevant and repetitious). (Read more in *The Public Relations Practitioner's Playbook* – Kendall/Hunt – 2008.) See *flighting; pulsing*. Also, script for commercial copy.

continuity program – An offer of a series of products to be received in timely intervals. Most often used for books, CDs, collectible plates and sports figurines.

continuous advertising – Scheduling advertisements to appear regularly, even during times when consumers are not likely to purchase the product or service, so that consumers are constantly reminded of the brand. Also called *saturation advertising*.

continuous marketing research – On-going marketing research (as opposed to that conducted for a specific purpose).

continuous tone art – Where a photograph or other art depicts smooth gradations from one level of gray (screen) to another – 10 percent to 20, 30, 40 and eventually 50 percent.

continuum of planning – The idea that planning is a multi-level process, beginning at the top with corporate planning and going downwards through all divisions of the firm, with each subsequent level linked to the one above it by the over-riding mission and objectives of the corporation.

continuum of sales jobs – The idea that all kinds of sales jobs are similar in some respects but vary in the degree of difficulty involved. The difficulty is linked to the amount of creativity required in finding new customers and persuading them to buy, and to the tangibility and complexity of the product.

contract – A formal agreement made between the service provider (public relations agency, for example) and the client, covering agreed objectives, timing and price.

contract carrier – A transportation firm operating exclusively in one industry and contracted to particular firms. For example, a carrier that hauls only produce may have an available trailer, which it contracts to another industry, such as canned foods.

contract law – The body of law relating to contracts.

contract manufacturing – The production and marketing by agreement of a company's product by an overseas firm.

contract rate – A charge negotiated between carrier and shipper for the transportation of a commodity. Sometimes called a *negotiated rate*.

contractual sales force – Salespeople who are not full or part-time paid representatives of a company but who sell for it on a commission basis.

contractual vertical marketing system – A form of vertical marketing system where independent firms at different levels of distribution are tied together by contract to achieve economies of scale (maintain competitive prices) and greater sales impact.

contrarian – A person who takes an opposing or contrary view or action – especially an investor who makes decisions that contradict prevailing wisdom, as in buying securities that are unpopular at the time.

contrarian effect – An investor who behaves in opposition to the prevailing wisdom. For example, buying when others are pessimistic and selling when they're optimistic, or buying out-of-favor stocks. In public relations, it would be someone who goes against the results of opinion surveys and other research. Public relations practitioners do not believe in "what you see is *not* always what you get."

contrast – Using design aspects of different sizes, shapes, shades and colors in a publication to keep the reader's attention. Also to compare in order to show unlikeness or differences – opposite natures. See *compare*.

contribution – The amount of money left over to contribute to overhead expenses after deducting for customer returns, cost of goods sold, direct selling expenses and variable order-processing costs.

control group – Used during scientific research and experiments to determine whether treatment really has an effect. Tester regulates and controls the testing.

controlled allocation system – A type of economy where some central authority makes a wide range of decisions pertaining to production and wages (e.g., Communist nations). Also called a command system. See *planned economy*.

controlled (qualified) circulation – Publications, generally business-oriented, that are delivered only to readers who have some special qualifications rather than through paid subscriptions. Generally, publications are free to the qualified recipients – e.g., retailers who sell sporting goods, pharmaceuticals and electronics. Revenue is raised through advertising.

controlled sampling – A form of non-probability sampling where the researcher selects the respondents in a marketing research study. It may result in researcher bias.

control-oriented pricing – A system of pricing where a product's price is controlled by the government or by some other regulating body. This practice is rare in the United States.

convenience goods (products) – A category of consumer goods which are bought frequently, quickly and with a minimum of emotional involvement or thought. Examples include snacks, sandwiches, *impulse goods* and *emergency goods*.

convenience sample – In research, a form of non-probability sample where the researcher selects readily available respondents. An example would be selecting a college class at random because it happened to be meeting at a particular time in a particular building. The survey results may or may not reflect the universe as a whole.

convenience store – A neighborhood store which stocks frequently purchased items such as milk, bread and cigarettes. Examples would be 7-Eleven® and Wawa®.

convergence news – Television news departments and newspapers – whether or not they are owned by the same corporation – partnering by combining forces and resources and cross promoting to deliver their products. For example, ABC-TV News and *USA* Today. *The Philadelphia Inquirer* and WCAU-TV (NBC10) in Philadelphia.

convergent diversification – Diversification into related businesses. See *divergent acquisition; diversification*.

convergent journalism – Allowing anyone to record life's events and share them with the world. Became popular with the growth of technologically sophisticated cell phones as cell users began to exchange photos over their phones – they no longer had to rely on the Internet for such transmissions.

convergent thinking – Thinking that uses logic to arrive at the "right" answer.

conversional marketing – Marketing activity intended to get people to change their ideas and attitudes about something they dislike. Making the use of third-party endorsers or credible endorsers – individuals not associated with a company who say good things about a product or brand – without getting paid.

convince – Change an attitude for a longer period. See *persuade*.

cookie – A file on the computer user's hard drive that uniquely identi-fies that user. There are two types of cookies: persistent cookies and ses-sion cookies. Session cookies are temporary and are erased when the user exits or disconnects for the source – usually the Internet. Persistent cookies remain embedded on the user's hard drive until the user erases them or until they expire. See *cookies*.

cookie buster – Software that blocks the placement of cookies on a user's hard drive.

cookie-cutter – Appearing to be mass-produced – identical in appear-ance. Tract housing in suburbia uses the *cookie-cutter* approach.

cookie-cutter approach – Within boundaries and little or no *outside-the-box* thinking.

cookies – Software tools designed to save passwords and other data on someone's computer. Cookies allow data to be called up automatically when the user shops online or revisits a Web site they've been to previ-ously. On the plus side, time can be saved because information might not have to be downloaded. The negative is that information remains stored or embedded in the computer's memory even though it may have been deleted. See *cookie*.

cooling-off period – A short period of time, usually a few days, during which purchasers of a product or service – including agreeing to hire a public relations agency or consultant – may void a sale contract if they change their minds about purchasing the goods offered.

cooperative (co-op) advertising – Form of advertising where a national manufacturer reimburses the retailer for part or all of the retail-er's advertising expenditures. Also, advertising (including direct mail, inserts, stuffers, card decks) where offers from several different mailers are included. It is an arrangement between manufacturer and retailer to reimburse the retailer in full or in part for local placement of manufac-turer-produced ads and commercials. These ads would include the addi-tion of the retailer's name in the copy. *Co-op advertising* might also mean a joint effort between two or more businesses to pool advertising money for more buying power. The ads would feature both company names and benefits. (See *The Public Relations Practitioner's Playbook* – Kendall/Hunt – Chapter 11.)

cooperative branding – Municipalities accepting sponsorships from corporations to advertise brands on city signs, police cars, buildings, etc.

cooperative broker – A person/company who recommends and takes orders for marketers who want to be part of a cooperative effort.

cooperative manager – A person/company who sells space in the co-op for the cooperative owner.

48 Tips to Succeed:
David Ogilvy's Advertising Tenets

- "Never write an advertisement you wouldn't want your own family to read"
- "The most important decision is how to position your product."
- If nobody reads or looks at the ads, "it doesn't do much good to have the right positioning."
- "Big ideas are usually simple ideas."
- Every word in the copy must "count"

David Ogilvy - Founder - Ogilvy and Mather

cooperative owner – A company that brings different marketers together into a co-op effort. Services may include: printing the individual inserts, combining them and mailing them to reselected lists.

cooperative (co-op) program – A system where advertising costs are divided between two or more parties. Usually, such programs are offered by manufacturers to their wholesalers or retailers to encourage them to advertise the product. See *cooperative advertising*.

coordinated universal time (UTC) – Replaced Greenwich Mean Time (GMT) as the world standard for time in 1986. UTC uses atomic clock measurements to add or omit leap seconds each year to compensate for changes in the rotation of the earth.

coordinates – A set of numbers that describes your location on or above the earth. Coordinates are typically based on latitude/longitude lines of reference or a global/regional grid projection (e.g., UTM, MGRS, Maidenhead).

cop shop – Police headquarters.

copy – Editorial content (text) or words printed in advertisements or a news story.

copy desk – The desk where copy is edited, headlined and placed on the page it will appear in the newspaper.

copy editor – The person who reviews the editorial content or text submitted by the reporter and makes changes to emphasize important facts or delete less significant material.

copy platform – Also called *creative strategy*. The basic issues or selling points an organization wishes to include in an advertising or public relations campaign. It is the strategic message. An outline of what message should be conveyed, to whom and with what tone. It provides a framework and guiding principles for copywriters and art directors who are assigned to develop the advertisement or commercial. Within the context of that assignment, any ad that is created should conform to that strategy.

copy strategy statement – A document prepared by advertising agency executives as a guide for their creative staff in the preparation and execution of an advertisement or an ad campaign. The copy strategy statement usually describes the goal, objectives, content, support and tone of the desired advertisement.

copy testing – Research to determine an advertisement's effectiveness, based on consumer responses to the ad. It could include the pretesting of advertising copy for print advertisements, usually by giving respondents a portfolio of dummy ads in a magazine format and asking them to recall copy points. It could also be the post-testing of advertising copy – usually by asking respondents to look through an actual magazine and then comment on advertisements they remember.

copybreaker – Different elements that break copy on a page of text – subheads, rules, pull quotes (blurbs), pictures, illustrations, captions, shaded boxes, sidebars, large initial caps, drop caps, etc.

copycat effect – Also referred to as contagion effect or imitation effect. It is the supposed power of the media to create an "epidemic" of behavior based on what consumers see, hear and read in the media – *buzz*.

copycat product – A product designed, branded and/or packaged to look exactly like that of a well-established competitor – a cheap imitation. Examples would include nonlicensed (counterfeit) products to resemble such brands as Coach®, Nike®, Rolex®, etc

copyright – Legal protection provided by the laws of the United States (title 17, U.S. Code) to the authors of "original works of authorship," including literary, dramatic, musical, artistic and certain other intellectual works. This protection is available to both published and unpublished works. Section 106 of the 1976 Copyright Act generally gives the owner of copyright the exclusive right to do and to authorize others to do the following: *To reproduce* the work in copies or records/CDs; To prepare *derivative works* based upon the work; *To distribute copies or records/CDs* of the work to the public by sale or other transfer of ownership, or by rental, lease or lending; *To perform the work publicly,* in the case of literary, musical, dramatic and choreographic works, pantomimes and motion pictures and other audiovisual works; *To display the copyrighted work publicly*, in the case of literary, musical, dramatic and choreographic works, pantomimes, and pictorial, graphic or sculptural works, including the individual images of a motion picture or other audiovisual work; and *In the case of sound recordings, to perform the work publicly by means of a digital audio transmission.* Read more at *www.copyright.gov/.*

copywriter – Someone who writes text for advertisements, commercials or other marketing communications material.

copywriting – Creative process where written content is prepared for advertisements, commercials or other marketing communications material.

cord-cutter – The telephone industry term for the thousands of Americans who have a cellular phone but no traditional phone with a cord.

core product – The intangible benefit or service offered by a product. For example, the core product (benefit) offered to a purchaser of shampoo is clean, healthy hair.

cornucopia (of stuff) – Huge number and variety of brands and brand extensions offered by manufacturers to attract target audiences across the many demographics.

corporate (identity) advertising – Strategic message used to enhance the image or identity of an entire corporation (e.g. Kellogg's®, which would include many of its individual cereal brands or General Motors®, which would include its car brands). This type of advertising is also used to communicate a particular point of view that a corporation has about an issue or cause. Sometimes confused with institutional (product) advertising. A form of institutional advertising focusing not on a particular product or product range but on the organization itself. The purpose of corporate advertising may be image or issue. See *institutional advertising.*

corporate advertising campaign – A campaign that promotes a corporation, rather than a product or service sold by that corporation. See *image advertising.*

corporate branding – Associating the name of a corporation with the individual brand name in product marketing, usually to ensure that new product introductions will be more readily accepted (Hershey's Kisses®, Dell's Latitude D600®). It differs from family branding in that corporate branding is used for all products of the company or division rather than merely for a family of brands. See *family brand; individual brand; individual brand name; product line brand name; single brand name; combination branding.*

corporate communications – Public relations for a corporation, integrated as part of the firm or company's overall strategic objectives, rather than activities designed for its individual segments.

corporate culture – The particular strategies, style, systems, environment and shared values within an organization which contribute to its individuality – and helps create its identity.

corporate espionage – The practice of obtaining **information** about an organization or a **society** that is considered **secret** or confidential (spying) without the permission of the holder of the information. What differentiates espionage from other forms of **intelligence work** is that espionage involves obtaining the information by accessing the place where the information is stored or accessing the people who know the information and will divulge it through some kind of subterfuge. Not all *corporate espionage* is illegal. Some employees of one company will share proprietary information with an employee of another company. While not illegal, it is more than likely, unethical.

corporate external newsletter – A type of newsletter that builds external support for a company or organization. Serves as a continual reminder to customers and clients that a company's services are available and promotes new products and new services.

corporate footprint – Business, store (retail) office, outlet, etc. locations illustrated on a map (sometimes looking like a footprint). An example would be the consistency of Commerce Bank® and/or McDonald's® buildings and their locations. A building's concept (image) must fit into company's footprint is another one to say it. This would be far more figurative than literal.

corporate identity – The character a company seeks to establish for itself in the mind of the public, reinforced by consistent use of logos, colors, typefaces and so on. *Identity* is how the corporation views itself. *Image* is how the public perceives it. See *corporate image*; *corporate reputation*.

corporate image – The perception of an organization as perceived by the public. See *corporate identity*.

corporate image advertising – Advertising aimed at establishing an identity for a firm in the public mind. See *corporate advertising*; *corporate image*.

corporate internal newsletter – A type of newsletter circulated throughout the staff of a company, organization or faculty to promote goodwill, teamwork and a sense of pride. Focuses on the achievements, goals and personal lives of employees. Serves as a continual reminder to customers and clients that a company's services are available and promotes new products and new services.

corporate issue advertising – Advertising where an organization states publicly its position on an issue – controversial or otherwise. See *advocacy advertising*; *corporate advertising*.

corporate logo – A mark, design, symbol, etc. used to identify and reflect an appropriate image of a company or organization. It is not a trademark or servicemark unless it is properly registered with the U.S. Patent and Trademark Office. Read more at *www.uspto.gov*.

corporate mission statement – mission or purpose – A clear and succinct reason the organization came into existence – its purpose. It answers the question: "Why we are here to serve you – why we are in business?" (This is who we are; what we think about ourselves; what we want to do; and why we deserve your support.) The corporate mission statement, with a broad focus and a customer orientation, provides management with a sense of purpose. A brief statement defines "What business are we in?" It should have a broad focus and a customer orientation.

corporate objectives – Specific, realistic and measurable steps (accomplished over a given period) taken as an organization attempts to achieve its goal using a strategic plan.

corporate patronage advertising – Advertising which encourages customers to patronize the firm. See *corporate advertising.*

corporate planning – Strategic planning at the highest level in an organization, involving an analysis of the current situation, the setting of objectives, the formulation of strategies and tactics, implementation and evaluation. See *strategic planning.*

corporate reputation – A complex mix of characteristics, such as credibility, identity and image, that go into making up a company's image (how public views it). Corporate reputation hinges more on investor confidence, unlike brand reputation, which is contingent on customer confidence and reflected in sales. See *corporate identity.*

corporate social responsibility (CSR) – How companies manage their business processes to produce an overall positive impact on society and communicate that identity.

corporate sponsorship – A form of advertising where a corporation offers funding to a group, association, sporting body, etc. in return for a range of promotional opportunities. Could be considered *below-the-line advertising or public relations.*

corporate strategy – A firm or company's plan of action – communicated to the public through commercial and such noncommercial messages as mission and vision statements. It would include the policies of a company with regard to its choice of businesses and customer groups.

corporate umbrella – Use of the corporate name and corporate image to enhance the introduction of a new product(s) or service – particularly if the corporate name has equity.

corporate vertical marketing system – A system of product distribution where the orderly flow of products from producer to end-user is controlled by common ownership of the different levels of the system. An example would be the auto industry where Ford®, General Motors®, Honda® and others, control design, manufacturing through assembly line, delivery to franchised dealerships and finally sales to the end-user.

corprocrat – A high earning and high achieving individual.

corrective advertising – Ordered by the Federal Trade Commission for the purpose of correcting consumers' mistaken impressions created by prior advertising. Corrective advertising is ordered when consumer research determines that an ad is false and/or misleading. Under this remedy, the FTC orders the offending party to produce messages for consumers that correct the false impressions the ad made. The FTC may require a party to run corrective advertising even if the campaign in question has been discontinued. Corrective advertising is traditionally the third step in a three-step regulation process. The first step in the process after the FTC determines that an ad is deceptive or unfair is a *consent decree* or consent order. The second step is a *cease-and-desist order* requiring an advertiser to stop running a deceptive, misleading or unfair advertisement, campaign or claim. *Corrective advertising* is the third step.

correlation techniques – A range of statistical techniques used to determine relationships – or comparisons – between diverse elements in a marketing situation.

cost advantage – The competitive edge which can be gained by one company over another by reducing production or marketing costs or both so that it can offer cheaper prices or use excess profits to bolster promotion or distribution.

cost certainty – Salary cap in such sports as professional hockey (National Hockey League). It gives team owners a "handle" on their maximum annual expenses and a better projection on break even.

cost efficiency – For a media advertising schedule, refers to the relative balance of effectively meeting reach and frequency goals at the lowest price.

cost-insurance-freight pricing – A pricing approach common in exporting. The price quoted to the buyer includes "cost, insurance and freight."

cost leadership – The strategy of producing goods at a lower cost than one's competitors. See *cost leadership advantage*.

cost leadership advantage – Producing goods at a lower cost than competitors and communicating that advantage through public relations and advertising strategic messages.

cost of goods sold (COGs) – The price paid by a company for the goods it sells to its customers - materials and production.

cost per action (CPA) – Cost of advertising based on a visitor taking some specifically defined action in response to an ad. "Actions" include time spent on a sales transaction, a customer acquisition, or a computer click – filling out a form (on computer or hard copy), downloading software or viewing a series of pages.

cost per click (CPC) – Applicable only to Web advertising. Similar to *per inquiry* advertising. The fee paid to the Web publisher each time a visitor clicks on an advertisement. This contrasts with a campaign that is bought at a set rate based on the number of impressions delivered and previously agreed to. Media outlet can and does determine the cost-per-thousand (CPM).

---

49 Tips to Succeed:
Credit Report vs. Consumer Report

Credit Report – Summarizes historical financial information collected to determine an individual's or an entity's credit worthiness – the means and willingness to repay an indebtedness.

Consumer Report – Information on a consumer's character, general reputation, personal characteristics, or mode of living obtained through personal interviews with neighbors, friends, or associates of the consumer reported on or with others with whom he is acquainted or who may have knowledge concerning any such items of information. The information does not, necessarily, include specific factual information on a consumer's credit record.

---

cost per customer – The cost an advertiser pays to acquire a customer.

cost per inquiry – The cost of getting one person to inquire about your product or service. It is a standard used in direct response advertising. See *per inquiry*.

cost per lead – Cost of advertising based on the number of database files (leads) received.

cost per order (CPO) – Cost of advertising based on the number of orders received. Also called *cost-per-transaction*.

cost per point – CPPs represent how much it would cost to deliver one target rating point, or 1 percent of the target audience. Primarily used in television and radio buying as a comparison and planning tool to determine how much media can be afforded at a given budget level. For example, a unit that costs $1,000 and delivers a rating of 10 men (in its target of 25-34) has a CPP of $100 (1000 divided by 10 = $100).

cost per rating point (CPRP) – A method of comparing media vehicles by relating the cost of the message unit to the audience rating. Also, the cost, per 1 percent of a specified audience, of buying advertising space in a given media vehicle.

cost per sale (CPS) – The advertiser's cost to generate one sales transaction.

cost per targeted thousand impressions (CPTM) – Based on targeted audience – audience advertiser is trying to reach – defined by particular demographics or other specific characteristics, such as female joggers ages 18-25. The difference between CPM and CPTM is that CPM is for gross impressions, while CPTM is for targeted impressions.

cost per thousand (CPM) – The cost to reach 1,000 television viewers, radio listeners, newspaper or magazine readers or direct mail households. Used as a comparison tool to determine the efficiency of different media vehicles. (Media term describing the cost of 1,000 impressions.) Cost of a media vehicle divided by the targeted impressions expressed in thousands. For example: a media vehicle that costs $10,000 and has an audience of 500,000 men 18-34 has a CPM of $50. Another example would be a Web site that charges $1,500 per ad and reports 100,000 visits has a CPM of $15 ($1,500 divided by 100).

cost per thousand criterion – A measure for comparing the cost effectiveness of media vehicles, calculated by dividing the cost of an advertisement in a particular medium by the number of thousands of its circulation, listeners or viewers.

cost per transaction (CPT) – Total cost to complete a sale or transfer of goods. See *cost per order*.

cost per visit (CPV) – In sales, all expenses related to having a company representative call on a client or prospective client.

cost per year of usage – A method for determining what items or services cost over a 12 month period.

cost/profit analysis – A sales management control measure involving the calculation of expenditure incurred in making sales. Also called a profitability analysis.

cost-plus pricing – A simple method of pricing where a specified amount or percentage, known as the standard mark-up, is added to the unit cost of production of an item to determine its selling price. See *competition-oriented pricing; target return pricing; value pricing.*

cottage industry – An industry – primarily manufacturing – usually on a small-scale industry carried on at home by family members using their own equipment.

counseling memo – Prepared by public relations practitioner for upper management. Broken into five major sections, it should contain: 1) Background; 2) Issues; 3) Criteria (to help management make an effective decision; 4) Analysis of Options; 5) Recommendation.

counselor approach – Advice given by public relations practitioner to client(s). Public relations is a management function where many top executives depend on the practitioner for counseling and include the practitioner at the board table to participate in strategic planning and decision making.

count audit – Now called an *activity audit*. It is an independent verification of measured activity for a specified time period. Some of the key components validated are advertisement impressions, page impressions, Web site clicks, total Web site visits and unique users. An *activity audit* results in a report verifying data and serves as a success measure of public relations or other type of communication or business plan.

counter advertising – Advertising sponsored by pressure groups in opposition to certain products. It might take a position contrary to an advertising message that preceded it. Such advertising may be used to take an opposing position on a controversial topic or to counter an impression that might be made by another's advertising.

counterfeiting – The copying of a competitor's well-known products. Some counterfeit products are intended to look as much like the original as possible, including the brand name. Others are close, but not exact, copies. Counterfeiting is generally illegal. Also, a product designed, branded or packaged to look exactly like that of a well-established competitor – a cheap imitation. Examples would include nonlicensed (counterfeit) products to resemble such brands as Coach®, Nike®, Rolex®, etc.

countermarketing – Marketing activity intended to reduce interest and demand for a product.

countertrade – A system of international trade based on bartering. Such transactions may or may not involve cash payments.

coupon – A promotional technique used by marketers to increase sales or store traffic by offering a discount when the coupon is redeemed. A popular form of sales promotion, distributed on the package of the product, by direct mail or in newspaper and magazine advertisements. The consumer is usually offered "cents off" the next purchase upon presentation of the coupon.

cover – The four pages that make up the outside wrap of a magazine or book. Referred to as cover 1, cover 2, cover 3 and cover 4.

cover call – Magazine editors' decision on photo or other artwork chosen for an issue's cover.

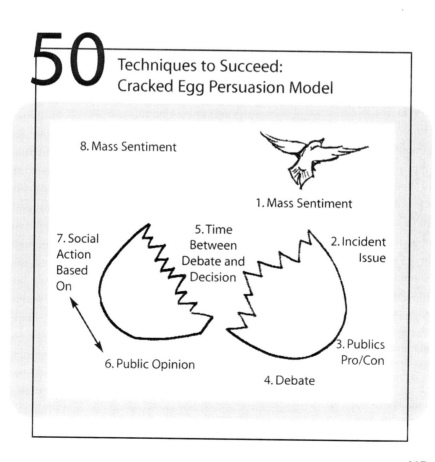

50 Techniques to Succeed: Cracked Egg Persuasion Model

8. Mass Sentiment

1. Mass Sentiment

7. Social Action Based On

5. Time Between Debate and Decision

2. Incident Issue

6. Public Opinion

4. Debate

3. Publics Pro/Con

cover line (mention) – A line or two about an inside story on a magazine's cover. The line is just type. The use of a picture makes it a mention.

cover page – The first page in a section. Also called *section front*.

cover song – A song closely associated with a singer, musician or band. See *signature song*.

cover story – See *center package* and *center piece story*.

coverage – A measure of a media outlet's reach, within a specific geographic area. Also, printed and electronically transmitted reports by the news media about a particular event or topic.

coverage area – Geographic area reached by a radio or television station or newspaper – usually indicated on a coverage map.

CPM pricing model (cost per thousand) – A model based on the cost of delivering ad impressions. The cost of exposing each 1,000 members of the target audience to the advertising message.

Cracked Egg (Persuasion) Model – Also known as Public Opinion Formation Model. It is an eight-step process whose purpose is to shape or change public opinion: 1) Mass Sentiment - morals/values; 2) Incident/Issue - interrupts morals; 3) Publics Pro/Con; 4) Debate - PR people and advertisers come in and try to change peoples' attitudes to agree with theirs; 5) Time (opinions marinate) - very important or you do not have a true public opinion; 6) Public Opinion - the accumulated opinion of many individuals on an important topic in public debate affecting the lives of people (need all these elements or you do not have public opinion); 7) Social Action - new law, or action, is taken against people. Society could be so traumatized that it goes overboard; 8) Mass Sentiment - Society gets a certain attitude/moral/values due to the social action. Society becomes very sensitized.

crafting a message – Skillfully, systematically, methodically and logically choosing words for a news release or other public relations product. It is broadly accepted that the first draft should come from the heart – while the second and further drafts come from the head (David Trotter – The Screenwriting Center – See *The Public Relations Practitioner's Playbook* – Kendall/Hunt – Chapter 5).

cramming – Slipping a monthly charge onto recurring monthly bills without a customer's knowing it.

Crayola® theory – Choosing colors (for a project) based on longstanding tradition. For example, racial groupings runs very deep in our culture, and when small children – and even some adults – sit down at the play table, or crafts bench, those are crayons they reach for. (Indians are redskins, Asians have yellow skin, African Americans are black, caucasians are white, etc.)

crawl – Superimposed messages that run slowly across the bottom or top of a television screen. The messages – used for visual efficiency – may be news content, promotional or advertising. Some Web pages also use crawls.

crawler – A software program which visits virtually all pages of the Web to create indexes for search engines. They are more interested in text files than graphic files. Referred to as spider, bot (a software robot) and intelligent agent (or just agent). Read more at *www.alicebot.org*.

51 Technique to Succeed: Stretching your cash

Here are some tips for stretching the cash from your first real job.

• Create a budget. Know what's coming in and what's going out.

• Match your company's 401(k) contribution.

• Pay down your credit card debt.

• Create an emergency fund to cover at least three months of living expenses. One idea: Start with the cash gifts from graduation.

• Automatically deposit a portion of your paycheck into a savings account.

• Repay your student loans on time.

• Be thrifty. Make your lunch. Watch for sales. Monitoring your cell phone bill.

Courier-Post - Camden, N.J. - July 7, 2005

crawlers – Web search engine sites (e.g. Google®, Excite®, Infoseek®) also called search engine spiders.

credit line – Appears with the explanation of a photo or illustration and gives credit to the photographer or artist. Also used to attribute text – such as the *Tips* and *Techniques* in *The ABCs of Strategic Communication*.

creative – Public relations or advertising agency department responsible for the activities involved in the creation of marketing materials. It may include copy writing, design, photography, illustration, music, etc.

creative brief – A document or script containing the *creative strategy* and the key execution details. A planning tool widely used by advertising agencies and marketing personnel when designing or implementing a marketing program. It can be used when creating communications directed at clients, employees, shareholders, potential investors, the media or any other target group. The *creative brief* is a cooperative tool by which those involved in a project focus their thoughts and analyze the best method(s) of approaching a program. When used properly it can also reduce the time and cost associated with marketing projects, as it requires all the key participants to agree on important factors at the beginning of the project.

creative director – The public relations or advertising agency employee responsible for supervising the work of all people involved in the creative aspects of producing advertising, including art directors, graphic designers, copywriters, etc.

creative platform – A document that outlines the message strategy decisions behind an individual advertisement or commercial.

creative selling – An approach to selling where salespeople aggressively seek out customers and use well-planned strategies to secure orders.

creative strategy – Also called *copy platform*. The basic issues or selling points an organization wishes to include in an advertising or public relations campaign. It is the *strategic message*. An outline of what message should be conveyed, to whom and with what tone. It provides a framework and guiding principles for copywriters and art directors who are assigned to develop the advertisement or commercial. Within the context of that assignment, any ad that is created should conform to that strategy.

creatives – The art directors and copywriters in a public relations or an ad agency.

creativity – The thought process used in public relations - changing our minds about what's possible – being imaginative.

credibility – One of the Seven Cs of Communication. A climate of belief built on the institution's performance. Receiver must have confidence in the sender and high regard for the source's competence on the subject. Credibility deals more with trust while believability deals more with truth. Once credibility is tarnished, it is very difficult to bring back the shine. (Read more in *The Public Relations Practitioner's Playbook* – Kendall/Hunt – Chapter 15.)

credit – The allowance of time or an arrangement for deferred payment for a purchase.

credit card – A small card, usually of plastic, used to obtain consumer products without immediate payment. The card is issued by a financial institution on the understanding that the consumer repays sums spent against the card with interest.

credit terms – Conditions negotiated between seller and buyer relating to the time within which the buyer is obliged to pay for the products purchased and any discounts to be allowed by the seller for earlier payment or additional services performed.

crime deterrent feature – Feature available on such portable devices as a cell phone that might help prevent a crime.

crisis communication – The effective use of communicating a systematic, well thought out, planned strategic message when dealing with a situation or issue that could adversely affect a company or organization.

crisis management – The practice of preparing a communication plan that can be effectively put into action in the event of a potentially negative issue for a company or organization.

critical-path analysis – A planning technique used to keep projects on schedule. A *Gantt chart* or other type of flow chart shows time allotments and priorities for each activity.

crop – To eliminate or cut out specific portions of a photograph or illustration. Trimming extraneous areas on the sides or top and bottom of photographs to help focus on the most important part of the scene.

crop marks – Marks to indicate which portions a photograph or illustration are to be used, and which are to be eliminated. With the advent of computers and such programs as Adobe Photoshop®, conventional photo cropping is not as prevalent as in the past.

cropping – Trimming extraneous areas on the sides or top and bottom of a photograph to put focus on the most important part of the scene – or – changing the shape or size of a photo or illustration to make it fit in a designated space or to cut out excess or undesirable elements.

cross elasticity of demand – A measure of how changing the price of one product affects the demand for a substitute or complementary product. See *elasticity of demand*.

cross headline – Headline copy or display type that stretches across more than one panel or one page of a brochure or other publication.

52

Tips to Succeed:
Get yourself ready for a career move

The average American stays at a job for only four years

Here are important steps to take while you're not job hunting to further your career.

• Develop your career plan and goals.

• Make a list of 40 to 60 contacts you would like to keep in touch with or meet. Some of these people can help you in years to come.

• Attend meetings of professional organizations to boost net working. Accept leadership roles within these organizations.

• Build your reputation by public speaking and writing for publications.

• Take courses or teach them - continue learning.

• Review your resume and try to add new accomplishments every six months.

• Every year, assess where you are in your career and set new goals in writing.

• Do an annual checkup with a career coach and revise your long-term plan. Using the coach as a sounding board can help you achieve perspective in your career.

The Five O'Clock Club – A career coaching network – New York, N.Y.

cross merchandising – Displaying a variety of products together to create a comprehensive visual story to drive sales of the products – displaying neck ties with shirts; belts with slacks, etc. This type of merchandising communicates breadth of product and educates your customer about merchandise they may be unaware that you carry.

cross platforming – The convergence of distribution – print, radio, television, broadband, wireless and digital signage. Originally, *cross platform* was a term referring to computer programs, operating systems, programming language and computer software. The term now refers to using the media available to carry a strategic message. Included are mainstream and alternative print, radio, television, Internet (and Interactive – Blogs), iPod®, (Podcasts, etc.), Vcasts®, cell phone, iPhone®, digital signage, aroma marketing, WOMM (word of mouth marketing) and silent publicity. (An example would be shifting music, movies, photos and other content easily from computer to television to cell phone to the latest gadget.)

cross-over selling – See *cross selling*.

cross reading – *Back checking* copy with another person – reading to each other. Comparing the information in one document to that in another. For example, if a news release contains a number of facts, two people should work together to check the release against the original data.

cross-reference – An in-text notation that directs the reader's attention to an attached illustration or to another section of the publication.

cross selling – Encouraging customers to buy other products (known as "hook ups") and services related to the ones they have purchased or are about to purchase. Also selling by a salesperson of some part of the company's total product range for which another salesperson (or division) has prime responsibility.

cross-tabulation – Statistical analysis of subset of data created from within the data. For example, how did all the men in the sample respond to the question?

crosshairs – As in "caught in the crosshairs." Crosshairs are seen in a gun's sight to zero in on a target. When one is caught in the crosshairs, they are being targeted or being put under extreme pressure. Also indicators on film used to align individual color separations or layers of film *negatives* when items using color are being printed. It is the precise alignment of different films or printing plates (color separations) to produce a final printed image. See *registration marks*.

crossover SUV – A car that is a cross between a sport utility vehicle, sedan and a station wagon and offers front-wheel and all-wheel drive.

crossover (utility) vehicles – Sport utility vehicles built to look more like station wagons. They are popular among consumers because of fuel economy, smooth handling and easy-to-manage size. Unlike SUVs, they're built on the underlying architecture of a car rather than a truck. SUVs are built on truck platforms. *Crossovers* ride lower to the ground than SUVs, but offer similar interior comfort.

crowding out – An economic term describing a situation where the government is borrowing heavily at the same time businesses and individuals also want to borrow. The government can always pay the market interest rate, but businesses and individuals cannot and are *crowded out*. An example would be the government going into an area to develop a road or construct an office building, which might increase demand for real estate – thus driving up the cost of money. While the government has the resources to pay the higher interest rates, private investors do not and are crowded out. When government invokes eminent domain to accomplish its goal, the taking and destruction of otherwise "good" homes, businesses and other property is referred to as economic displacement.

cue – To prepare a tape for playback or to alert talent they are about to go on the "air" in radio or television.

cue light – Red light on television studio camera to alert "talent" he/she is "on the air." Sometimes referred to as a *tally light*.

53 Tips to Succeed: Cell phone guidelines

Cell phone use at work can be annoying to co-workers and inappropriate. Here are guidelines every professional with a cell phone needs to know:

• Do not use inappropriate songs as your ring, such as TV theme songs or current pop songs.

• Avoid making sensitive or confidential business calls or mention the names of clients in trains, restaurants or any public setting.

• Don't use your cell phone to send messages or surf the Web during meetings.

• Don't wear more than one wireless device on your body.

• Avoid walking around work while talking on your cell phone. You need to be meeting and greeting people.

• Do not answer your cell phone when you're having a conversation.

Barbara Pachter - Pachter & Associates Business
Communications Training - Cherry Hill, N.J.

cue sheet – A piece of written material containing messages about the client or its products, or an extract from a paper or magazine. Also referred to as *clipping*.

cues – An environmental entity within a store, office, mall, etc. (advertisement, sign, store display, etc.) which results in a specific response to satisfy a drive – getting someone to a destination or to make a purchase. See *learning*.

cultural and social influence – The forces that other people exert on your behavior.

cultural anthropology – Important to the practice of public relations – the demographic, psychographic and geodemographic make up of a society - its thoughts, world view, rules of moral and ethical conduct and patterns of social interactions (e.g. social structure, family).

cultural diversity – Psychographic term. The range of different value systems existing in a multicultural society.

cultural marketing – Marketing to a segmented or fragmented demographic.

cultural values – Psychographic term. Ideas, beliefs, attitudes, opinions, principles, etc. embraced and cherished by members of a society.

culture – Psychographic term. The basic beliefs and values cherished by a society as a whole and handed down from one generation to the next. Also, the philosophy of a company, reflected in aims such as the maximization of customer satisfaction.

cumes – An abbreviation for net cumulative audience. Refers to the number of unduplicated people or homes in a broadcast program's audience within a specified time period. This term is used by A.C. Nielsen. It also is used by many advertising practitioners to refer to the unduplicated audience of a print vehicle, or an entire media schedule. Read more at *www.nielsenmedia.com*.

cumulative quantity discount – A price reduction offered to a purchaser where the amount of the discount increases over time with the volume purchased. See *non-cumulative quantity discount*.

curbside sales training – Informal coaching or training of a sales representative by a supervisor in the field. See *buddy system*; *formal training*; *on-the-job training*.

curling – The buckling of paper due to excess moisture.

currency exchange – A service that changes money from one currency to another.

current ratio – The most common of three financial ratios used to evaluate a firm's liquidity – current assets are expressed as a percentage of current liabilities. The others are *acid-test ratio* and *quick ratio.*

curve fitting – A method of analyzing associated research data where a number of possible curve shapes – straight lines, concave, convex, s-shaped etc. – are used with historical data to discover trends or relationships to simplify its interpretation.

custom marketing – Marketing activity where a company attempts to satisfy the unique needs of every customer. Also called *market atomization strategy.*

custom publisher – Any publisher who (for a fee) creates a publication for a direct marketer that is often used for self-promotion or as a premium.

custom publishing – The publishing of a magazine by an organization trying to strengthen its bonds with its customers and to exercise greater control over the editorial environment in which its advertisements appear. Custom published magazines usually carry outside advertisements to defray the cost of the launch and lend an air of legitimacy. Jenny Craig International®, Mary Kay Cosmetics®, the Benetton® Group and IBM® Corp. have all launched magazines.

customary price – A single, well-known price for a long period of time. Movie theatres and candy manufacturers employ this pricing strategy in the hope that the customer will become less sensitive to price. Also known as traditional price. It's the price that consumers expect to pay for a certain product.

customer – A person or company who purchases goods or services – not necessarily the end user.

customer attitude – A customer's beliefs and feelings about a product, its attributes, the brand associated with it and all aspects of the marketing mix applied to its promotion.

customer-driven distribution systems – A system of distribution designed with customer requirements rather than a company's convenience in mind.

54

Techniques to Succeed:
Businesses can learn through osmosis

Jonathan Tisch, chairman and CEO of Loews Hotels, believes the lessons he has learned in the luxury hotel business can be translated to other industries.

The most basic: Turn customers into guests.

At the core of all thriving businesses is a meaningful, long-lasting customer connection.

In the hotel business, for example, he says, "Over the years, I've learned a lot about the art of welcome. Chocolates on the Pillow Aren't Enough."

"It's something all successful hoteliers must master ... a skill that virtually every organizational leader must learn, since nowadays, we're all in the business of attracting and keeping customers."

The major stresses facing many kinds of business that are making it harder to retain customers:

• Shrinking brand loyalty.

• Increased price sensitivity.

• More competition.

• Increasing customer knowledge, skepticism and power.

In the spirit of thinking we can all learn from each other. A variety of consumer-driven businesses seem to be getting it right.

The aim is to illustrate how a bank, for instance, might be able to learn good practices from a retailer.

Don't be afraid to learn from seemingly unrelated businesses.

These mini-profiles include Commerce Bank, Cherry Hill, N.J.; clothing retailer Urban Outfitters; In-N-Out Burger, Irvine, Calif.; and Duke University Medical Center.

From each vignette, Tisch pulls a series of tips or lessons, called "Your Big Aha's."

Some of the tips are obvious, but worth noting. They include:

• Don't be afraid to stand for something.

• When you find a formula that works, stick with it.

• Adopt the outsider's view of their company.

> • Visit your organization's retail outlets, sales offices, or service departments in an unfamiliar town without identifying yourself.
> • Call the customer hotline with a complaint, concern or question.
> • Visit the Web site, and try ordering a product or asking a question.
>
> Tisch salutes retailer Urban Outfitters for harnessing "the power of welcome to attract customers."
>
> Jonathan M. Tisch - Chairman and CEO of Loews Hotels and Co-Author
> (with Karl Weber) - Chocolates on the Pillow Aren't Enough:
> Reinventing the Customer Experience

customer lifetime value (CLV) – The profitability of a customer during the lifetime of the relationship, as opposed to profitability on one transaction.

customer loyalty – Feelings or attitudes that incline a customer either to return to a public relations or an advertising agency, company, shop or outlet to purchase goods or services – or to re-purchase a particular product, service or brand. Some say there is no such thing as *customer loyalty*. However, public relations research is clear – *customer loyalty* does exist.

customer-need management – Supervising or directing the planning, researching and development of determining product or service need and demand before investing in its manufacture.

customer orientation – Business designed to serve its customers or clients. Sometimes referred to as *customer-oriented management*.

customer-oriented management – A management philosophy or state-of-mind that recognizes the effective and efficient satisfaction of customer needs and wants and provides the surest means and methods of achieving the organization's own goals.

customer panels – A qualitative public relations/marketing research technique where an independent facilitator interviews (leads discussion) a small group of consumers (nine to 12) from the target audience in an informal setting to get a reaction to an issue, a new product, brand name, advertising or other communication efforts, etc. Also referred to as a *focus group*. See *qualitative marketing research*.

customer record – A card, slip or computer file that contains facts and other information about a prospect, client or customer (name, address, account history, etc.) as an aid to making a sale when next contacted by a salesperson. It is an important aspect of *relationship marketing*.

customer relations department – A division of an organization with responsibility for ensuring that customers are satisfied with the goods or services they have purchased and with the way the organization has served them.

customer relationship management (CRM) – Providing better communication, offers and services to a firm's customers by evaluating their previous interactions with them. Data bases play a key role in *CRM* and *relationship marketing*.

customer retention – Maintaining the existing customer base by establishing good relations with all who buy the company's product. Research is clear – it costs far less to retain a customer than to attract a new one.

customer satisfaction – The provision of goods or services which fulfill the customer's expectations in terms of quality and service, in relation to price paid.

customer service – A wide variety of activities intended to ensure that customers receive the goods and services they require to satisfy their needs or wants in the most effective and efficient manner possible.

customer service program – Strategy for assuring customers a positive buying experience to improve customer loyalty, increase cross selling and promote advertising by word-of-mouth. See *customer satisfaction*.

customer training – Training in the proper and efficient use of equipment given by a vendor to its customers after the equipment purchase. Making training a provision of the sale adds value to the product and also separates the vendor from competitors selling the same or similar equipment. It helps with competitive *positioning*.

customer value analysis – An organization's rating of the value it provides to its customers relative to that provided by its competitors.

customized marketing mix – A marketing program uniquely designed for a particular client, niche or target audience.

cut – A (antiquated) term that refers to a photograph or illustration. Also, an abrupt transition from one shot or scene to another. Also, a segment of recorded sound on a CD or tape.

cut the head off – When police arrest the leader of a crime organization (e.g. a drug kingpin).

cut to the chase – Meaning to get to the point. A movie term from the 1920s – it originally meant to cut from a dramatic scene to an action scene (like a chase).

cutaway – When used in reference to television or other form of moving video, it is a brief shot that interrupts the main action of a film (showing reporter's face while newsmaker is answering a question or showing the reporter asking the question – usually edited in after the interview has been completed), often to depict related matter or supposedly concurrent action. In graphics and publication layout, a model or diagram of an object with part of the outer layer removed so as to reveal the interior. Also, when a television or radio network allows local advertisers to run their own commercials in their local area.

cutline – A name and title under a picture – briefer than a *caption*. Also called a name line. (Some publications use the terms cutline and caption synonymously.)

cutouts – Irregularly shaped extensions added to the top, bottom or sides of standard outdoor billboards. Also used in publications when, for example, a head and shoulders protrude through the top of a box or border.

cutting – A film editing technique that creates a quick transition from one scene to another.

cutting edge – A company or product that enjoys the leading position – for one reason or another. It could be innovative or just different. When flash drives, also known as thumb drives and USB drives, hit the market, they were referred to as *cutting edge*.

cyber café – A place which contains computers with access to the Internet and which is available to the public. They usually serve beverages and snacks.

cyberbullying – The sending or posting of harmful text or images using the Internet or other communication devices.

cybersquatting – Registering, trafficking in or using a domain name with bad-faith intent to profit from the goodwill of a trademark belonging to someone else. The cybersquatter then offers to sell the domain to the person or company who owns a trademark contained within the name at an inflated price.

cybertips – Snippets of information provided by firms and organization through their Web sites either free or through paid subscriptions. **C**

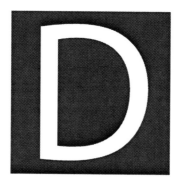

DAGMAR – Stands for *defining advertising goals for measured advertising results*. It is a process of establishing goals for an ad campaign that makes it possible to determine whether or not the goals have been met.

DAGMAR approach – An approach that measures advertising effectiveness in which advertising objectives are turned into specific measurable goals. See *DAGMAR*.

dailies – Refers to unedited film. They are called *dailies* because the film typically is viewed from a single day's shooting, even if the final commercial or program takes many days or weeks of shooting. Also called rushes. Daily newspapers are also referred to as dailies.

daily activities report – A record of a salesperson's activities on a day-by-day basis, showing clients visited, products presented and results. It might also include reasons for not closing on the deal.

daily effective circulation (DEC) – Used in outdoor advertising. It is the gross number of exposure opportunities, per unit, per day toward a target audience. Provides basis of all outdoor measurement.

daily sales plan – A record of a salesperson's intended sales calls on a day-by-day basis, listing clients to be visited, objectives of each call and anticipated outcomes.

daily 10 – A 10-minute exercise some agencies and other organizations use at the end of the work day to review the day's activities and to brainstorm – referred to as "the daily 10."

dais – A raised platform, as in a lecture hall, for speakers or honored guests – a raised head table. See *lectern; podium*.

damage control – To reduce or prevent the spread of misinformation – particularly during a crisis. Crisis communication is, for the most part, damage control.

dash – A short horizontal rule or varying lengths used to indicate a pause or clause in a sentence. See *em dash; en dash.*

data – Facts or information gathered in a marketing research study. See *primary research; secondary research.*

data analysis – The processing of *marketing research* findings to summarize a situation, discover relationships between elements of the information, or to draw conclusions from them. See *marketing research.*

data collection – The activity of gathering facts or information about a subject in a *marketing research* study. See *marketing research.*

data documentation initiative (DDI) – An international effort to establish a standard for technical documentation describing social science data.

data entry – The entering of names, addresses and other information into a data storage and retrieval system. Data can be entered via manual keying, electronic data transfer or by scanning.

data mining – Gathering and using (personal) data for purposes other than for their intended use (e.g. census data retrieved and used for commercial purposes). Also using data to establish certain patterns and behaviors.

data overlays – See *list services.*

data processing – Obtaining, recording and holding of information, which can then be retrieved, used, disseminated or deleted. The term tends to be used in connection with computer systems, and today is often used interchangeably with information technology.

data sheet – Advertising that provides detailed technical information.

database – List of consumers with information that helps target and segment those who are highly likely to be in the market for a certain product or service. Also, a file that is maintained on a computer comprised of such information as a company's prospects or customers. The file can serve multiple applications and be manipulated for various purposes. The following definitions apply to databases used for direct marketing purposes. Using the data can help predict future customer behavior. True *relationship marketing* depends on databases. Many states now ban collecting such information as Social Security numbers, home addresses and telephone numbers. See *database marketing*.

55 Techniques to Succeed: One expert's 'New 4 Ps of Marketing'

According to Lior Arussy, president of Strativity Group, Parsippany, N.J. and London, the traditional four Ps are being replaced.

The original four Ps are Product, Placement, Price and Promotion, but any new product that hits the market today faces significant competition. Arussy suggests that companies who still practice the traditional four Ps are usually at-par with their competitors – holding but gaining little ground.

HERE ARE ARUSSY'S FOUR PS OF MARKETING:

Premium price – If the customers perceive your product as superior, differentiated and worth their business, this will affect your ability to charge a higher or "premium" price for your product. Companies that cannot command price are losing ground and heading towards cost cutting, value depreciation and reduced margins.

Preference of company (or product) – It involves public support and a willingness to refer friends and peers. Thus, customers lend personal credibility to and actually assist the company in selling it. This is measured by how often and how many referrals you receive.

Portion of overall customer budget – When a customer gives more of their budget to your product and/or service than they do to your competitors, it's a sign of commitment.

Permanence of relationship longevity – Based on a personal relationship. It is the ultimate measure of marketing success. The longer a customer stays with a vendor, the deeper and more invested a relationship becomes.

Newstrack Executive Information Service
www.news-track.com - 800-334-5771

56 Tips to Succeed: Getting a handle on debt

According to the Federal Reserve, outstanding consumer credit is at $2.09 trillion, a record high.

Here are a few tips to improve your personal debt.

• Concentrate on paying off the debt with the smallest balance first.

• Move, then, to repaying debts with the highest interest rate. This will allow you to save a significant amount of money in frivolous interest charges over time.

• Be persistent, and responsible. If you find that you are unable to meet your basic financial obligations, contact your creditors immediately to advise them of your situation.

Most will offer an individual short-term solution, but be careful to consider the benefits of a long-term payoff strategy.

www.crediteducation.org

database marketing – The use of large collections of computer-based information to better target marketing communications and more finely tune marketing (strategic) messages for individual prospects at specific points in their lives and buying cycles. The database listings may be reference databases containing information on specific topics, full databases which contain full transcripts of documents or articles being sought or source databases, which contain listings of names and addresses, etc. of prospective customers. See *customer relationship management (CRM)*.

database retrieval systems – Information compiled from print, broadcast and other sources stored in computer memories and made available online for random access and retrieval and subsequent print-outs.

date code – A date on a package indicating either the date by which the product should be used or the date the product was packaged. See *date stamping*.

date stamping – See *open dating, dating code*.

dateline – Place and date of an article's (news story) origin that appears at the beginning of the first paragraph of an article. Also used in public relations news releases. Include a state abbreviation if the city does not frequently appear in the news or would be confused with another city. Dateline looks like this:

PHILADELPHIA, Jan. 1, 2009 – (text of story follows)

Include a state abbreviation if the city does not frequently appear in the news or would be confused with another city. For example, FAIRFIELD, Iowa, Dec. 28, 2008 – (see *The Associated Press Stylebook*).

daughter window – An advertisement that runs in a separate window associated with a concurrently displayed banner. In normal practice, the content and banner are first and the daughter window appears thereafter.

day and date system – Release of a motion picture, its DVD and the television pay-per-view "first show" are coordinated so all occur on the same day. This is controversial because theatre owners believe they will suffer losses at the box office. See *death spiral*.

day-after recall test – A research method that tests consumers' memories the day after they have seen or heard an advertisement, to assess the ad's effectiveness.

daybook – Daily schedules of upcoming news events, published by the *Associated Press*, other wire services and used internally at newspapers, radio and television stations.

daypart – Broadcast media divide the day into several standard time periods, each of which is called a *daypart*. Cost of purchasing advertising time on a vehicle varies by the *daypart* selected.

dayparts (television) – How the day is broken down for buying purposes:

Early Morning (EM): 5 a.m. - 9 a.m.

Day: 9 a.m. - 4 p.m.

Early Fringe (EF)/ Early News (EN): 4 p.m. - 6 p.m.

Prime Access (PA): 6 p.m. - 7 p.m.

Prime: 7 p.m. - 11 p.m.

Late News (LN): 10 p.m. or 11 p.m. depending on the market

Late Fringe (LF): 10:30 p.m. or 11:30 p.m. - 1 a.m.

Overnight: 1 a.m. - 5 a.m.

dayparts (radio) – How the day is broken down for buying purposes:

> **Morning Drive:** 5 a.m. (or 6 a.m.) - 10 a.m.
>
> **Day (or Mid Day):** 10 a.m. - 3 p.m. (or 4 p.m.)
>
> **Afternoon Drive:** 3 p.m. (or 4 p.m.) - 7 p.m.
>
> **Evening:** 7 p.m. - 12-midnight
>
> **Overnight:** 12-midnight - 5 a.m.

deadline (deadline driven) – Time when an article or other assignment must be completed by a reporter or other contributor.

deadhead – An empty truck.

dealer listing – The naming in a product advertisement of certain retailers who carry the product. The naming of dealers is done as a convenience to consumers and to encourage the retailers to carry higher stock levels. Also referred to as *tagging*.

dealer loader – A gift given to a retailer who purchases a specified quantity of a product during a trade sales promotion. See *trade sales promotion*.

dealer tag – Time left at the end of a broadcast advertisement that permits identification of the local store.

death (five stages) – Five stages of grief – denial, anger, bargaining, depression and acceptance, from Dr. Elisabeth Kubler-Ross, author "On Death and Dying."

death spiral – Lower attendance in movie theatres which means lower profits for studios – so studios move up the release dates for DVDs. When consumers hear the motion picture/movie is soon to be released on DVD, they no longer go to theater. That begins the spiral. It is only a small percentage, but it does drive theaters out of business. It also relates to other industries. For example, bowling alleys in New Jersey are suffering the same fate since a smoking ban in all publicly used common areas. See *video window*.

debit card – A payment card linked directly to a customer's bank account. When a purchase is made, money is immediately withdrawn from checking or savings.

debt – Money, goods or services that a person or company is obligated to pay to another according to a previous agreement.

57 Tips to Succeed: Business dining etiquette

You're having dinner with a prospective client. Do you know which fork to use?

OK, so you might not lose a potential deal because you grabbed the wrong utensil to eat your salad, but bad table manners can affect your overall professionalism.

Business etiquette is more than dining. It's also about professional presence and image. Manners and etiquette are not usually taught in school, but necessary to give workers extra "polish." Many of the things are little, but when you put them together they create an impression of you in the workplace, which can work for or against you.

Here are some sample dining etiquette tips:

• No grooming at the table – Don't reapply your lipstick, comb your hair or use your napkin as a tissue.

• Don't lick your utensils or fingers.

• Know your distance – in the United States, average distance between two people in business is about three feet or arm's length. Don't stand too close.

• Never tell ethnic, sexist, religious or racial jokes.

• When dining out, don't launch into a business conversation immediately. Make small talk first. It might be wise to follow the lead of others – unless you are the host.

Barbara Pachter - Pachter & Associates -
Author - *When Little Things Count* - 856-751-6141
Courier-Post - April 29, 2005

decay constant – An estimate of the decline in product sales if advertising were discontinued.

deceptive advertising – Federal Trade Commission definition: A representation, omission, act or practice that is likely to mislead consumers acting reasonably under the circumstances. Advertising intended to deceive consumers with false or misleading claims. See *Federal Trade Commission*.

deceptive packaging – Packaging intended to deceive the purchaser; excessive *ullage* creates the impression that the volume of the contents is greater than it actually is. See *ullage*.

deceptive pricing – The pricing of goods and services in such a way as to cause a customer to be misled. See *bait-and-switch pricing*.

deciders – Those who actually make the decision in the organizational buying process. Deciders are often difficult to identify because they may not necessarily have the formal authority to buy.

decision making – Choosing between alternative courses of action using cognitive processes – memory, thinking, evaluation, etc. Also called problem solving.

decision making unit (DMU) – The team of people in an organization who make the final buying decision.

decision matrix – A tool used in decision making in which the various dimensions of a problem are listed and rated to determine the most appropriate alternative in a particular situation. See *force field* or *conflict analysis*.

decision support system – Computerized system of changing raw data (sales, stock levels, etc.) into information that can be used by management in decision making.

deck head – Similar to a *subhead*. An introductory line that offers supplementary information not included in the headline. See *Subhead*.

decline stage – The next to final stage of the product life cycle (after *introductory stage*, *growth stage* and *maturity stage*) when sales are dropping because the original "need" and "want" have diminished or because another product innovation has been introduced. See *product life cycle*; *introductory stage*; *growth stage*; *maturity stage*; *withdrawal stage*.

decoding – The step in the two-way communication process in which the receiver accepts and interprets the message. See *communication process*; *encoding*.

decoy – A name in a mail, telephone or e-mail list placed solely for the purpose of tracking the use of the list to ensure that the list purchaser or renter does not break the sales or rental contract. The decoy person, household or organization either works for the list owner/broker or otherwise agrees to help by reporting any misuse. A similar term, "dummy," is a fictitious name included for this purpose. The process of including decoys or dummies is called seeding or salting.

de-dupe – Eliminate any duplicate (dupe) listings in a mail, telephone or e-mail list. This can be difficult because listings may not be perfect duplicates. For example, one may carry a first initial while another carries full first and middle names, or one may contain an old address while another contains the new one.

deejay – Disc jockey. Associated Press style is now DJ.

deep assortment – An assortment strategy in which a reseller carries many variations of each product in the range (could be good, better and best to offer a number of price ranges). See *exclusive assortment*; *scrambled assortment*.

defensive advertising – Advertising intended to combat the effects of a competitor's promotion.

defined pension benefit plans – After the death of a participant in an employer sponsored-retirement plan, his or her beneficiary is required to take required minimum distributions in accordance with IRS rules. Some plans permit beneficiaries to leave the inherited funds in the plan and to stretch out the distributions over a number of years. However, a large number of plan sponsors do not wish to assume the burden or the cost of administering distributions in this manner, so they require lump-sum distributions upon the death of a participant.

definition of terms – Defining jargon when addressing audiences that may not be familiar with topic, but might have, at least, a passing interest.

deflation – A slowing of the economy characterized by falling prices and wages. It is the reverse of *inflation*.

delayed lead – A writing style where the specific subject of a story doesn't come into clear focus until some time after the first paragraph(s), usually in an attempt to set the background and tone before getting to the main point. Sometimes called a multi-paragraph lead.

delayed quotation pricing – An industrial pricing method in which the seller delays quoting a price until delivery. This method protects the seller against cost over-runs and production delays.

delegate – A participant at a professional training course, workshop or seminar.

delinquent – Failure to deliver even the minimum payment on a loan or debt on or before the time agreed. Accounts often are referred to as

30, 60, 90 or 120 days delinquent because most lenders have monthly payment cycles.

deliver information – PR practitioners craft the strategic message and must be certain it gets to the target audience – even if they hand carry it themselves (the first step in multi-step or three-step flow).

delivered pricing – A pricing method in which the final price to the buyer is adjusted to include transportation costs. The seller takes responsibility for arranging delivery but adds the cost to the quoted price.

demand – The desire for a product or service at market price.

demand and supply – Demand is the desire for a product or service at market price, while supply is the quantity available at that price.

demand backward pricing – A pricing method that estimates the price consumers are willing to pay for a particular product. This price is then compared to the per-unit cost to determine if it meets the firm's profit objectives.

demand curve – A line drawn on a graph representing the number of units of a product, which will be purchased at any particular price point.

demand elasticity – see *elasticity of demand.*

demand inelasticity – see *inelasticity of demand.*

demand-pull approach – Developing new products on the basis of market demand rather than on that of company-generated ideas. See *product-push approach.*

de-marketing – Marketing aimed at limiting growth; practiced, for example, by governments to conserve natural resources, or by companies unable to serve adequately the needs of all potential customers.

democratic leadership style – A style of leadership or management characterized by group participation in decision-making.

demographic data – Characteristics describing and segmenting a population in terms of age, sex, income, marital status, ethnic origin and education level and so on. Can be used to target marketing campaigns. See *demographics.*

demographic segmentation – Dividing the total population into relatively homogeneous (niche) groups, or selected demographics, on the basis of variables within the population mix – so that different groups can be treated differently – sometimes called *state-of-being segmentation*. For example, two advertisements might be developed, one for adults and one for teenagers, because the two groups are expected to be attracted to different types of advertising appeal.

demographics – The vital statistics (common characteristics) about the human population, its distribution and its characteristics (age, gender, income, education, etc.). Used for audience segmentation and fragmentation. See *demographic data*.

58 Tips to Succeed: Help your employees get the most from their doctor visits

Most people use doctor appointments to confirm that they're sick, but many would benefit if they took them as an opportunity to ensure they're actually well

Here is a blueprint for getting the most out of any doctor visit:

• Provide family history: Raise your family's health issues with your doctor as they can provide important red flags for preventative treatment.

• Do your homework: Keep a log of your health, including the frequency, duration and intensity of symptoms, and bring it to your visit.

• Define success for drug prescriptions: When prescribed medication ask the following:
  1. Is it OK to drive after I've taken it?
  2. What are the side effects?
  3. How will I know if it's working or not working?
  4. At what point will we re-evaluate its effectiveness and determine whether or not to stay on it?

• Ask questions: Solicit your doctor's opinion of your overall fitness. Most physicians don't offer lifestyle advice such as "lose weight, exercise more," unless the patient has an active medical condition or asks.

Dr. Alan Muney - Pediatrician - Former Chief Medical Officer -
Oxford Health Plans LLC - www.oxhp.com/

demography – The study of the range of physical, social and economic and other non-psychological or attitudinal characteristics that exist within a population.

demon customers – Customers considered unprofitable by retailers and other sellers because they cost money, either because they return too many items, are too labor intensive or buy merchandise, submit rebates and then return the items. Also called *evil customers*.

De novo – Latin term for "from new" as in "De novos" banks (with s is plural for De novo). Used in business conversations.

department store – A large retail store offering a wide variety of goods and services in different departments.

deployment – The arranging and sending of a sales force into territories on some logical basis.

depreciation – An allowance made in a balance sheet for wear and tear of an item or piece of equipment. It is a measure of the loss of value of a fixed asset because of use or obsolescence.

depth interview – A qualitative marketing research method, whereby a trained interviewer meets with consumers individually (face-to-face) rather than in groups, and asks a series of questions designed to detect attitudes, opinions and thoughts that might be missed when using other methods. If those interviewed are chosen through a scientific, random method, the research becomes quantitative.

depth of product line – See *product line length.*

depth selling – See *problem-solving approach.*

deregulation – Complete or partial removal of government control and restrictions relating to a specific business activity or industry.

derived demand – Demand for raw materials based on the demand for consumer products. See *primary demand.*

descender – The part of a printed letter (character) that passes below the baseline.

descriptive label – *Label* on a product showing the size, net weight, ingredients, composition, nutritional value, calories per serving, etc. See *label.*

design-build method (firm) – Architectural firms that not only design buildings, but also "handle" construction. They are generally considered more efficient and less stressful for clients. *design-build firms* are expensive to run because they have a large stable of professionals on staff. They are also excluded from many, if not most, public sector projects, which generally require separate bids for the design and construction.

designated market area (DMA) – A geographic designation, used by A.C. Nielsen, which specifies which geographic areas fall into a specific television market. See *area of influence; area of dominant influence*. Also the area reached by television stations in a particular market.

desire competitors – All companies, firms and organizations offering a product that the consumer desires immediately. See *competitors*.

desk research – Research used that had already been compiled. See *secondary research*.

desk-to-desk direct marketing – A form of business-to-business selling in which firms purchase and use computer databases to locate potential customers. Many times, the databases are compiled by list brokers and are organized according to business type, sales revenue, number of employees, location and telephone area code. See *list services*.

detailer – A salesperson, whose primary responsibility is to inform clients about new products. See *academic detail; foot solder; missionary selling; sales calls*.

determinance model (of brand evaluation) – A model used in the study of consumer decision processes to evaluate alternative brands. The idea that consumers, about to make a purchase, will not be swayed in their product choice by any one product attribute, no matter how important, if all products possess the same amount of the attribute. Therefore, it is believed, the decision is made based on a less important attribute.

deterministic models – A statistical tool in sales forecasting where such marketing variables as price levels, advertising expenditures and sales promotion expenses are used to predict market share or sales.

developmental marketing – Marketing activity intended to increase demand for a product or service once it is determined there is a need for the product or service in the market.

The ABCs of Strategic Communication

59

Techniques to Succeed: Address the mess: A clean desk clears the working mind *and* the working area

Still looking for last Wednesday's lunch? Before the health department breaks down the door to your office, you might want to think about cleaning your desk.

After all, if, as they say, cleanliness is next to godliness, how does that translate at work? A sloppy desk can stifle your creativity and thinking, make a bad impression on your co-workers, and even make you sick.

To help tackle the mess, we've put together a four-step method that will make cleaning your cube no sweat.

Step 1: Garbage time
First, tackle the mounds of paper littering your desktop. File what you want and toss what's obsolete. Then empty overflowing wastebaskets and recycle those old newspapers.

Step 2: Farewell, germs
Scientists say desktops typically contain more bacteria than a toilet seat. Buy some wipes labeled "disinfecting" or "sanitizing" and clean everything you touch, including your mouse, phone and desk surface.

Step 3: Desk re-org
Place only the bare necessities on your desktop and put away things you only use once or twice a week. Try to reserve at least one drawer for personal items like breath mints and contact solution.

Step 4: Personal touch
Try making a few enhancements to your workspace. Bring in some tasteful pictures of your friends and family or put up a colorful calendar. Bringing some of your personality to work can inspire creativity and demonstrate your commitment to the boss.

Philadelphia Inquirer - May 15, 2005 - www.philly.com/careerbuilder

devils advocate – Someone who takes a position for the sake of argument. This practice is generally an instructional technique in which one person argues a position that another is less familiar with, thereby teaching proper argument. Pope John Paul II called it Promoter of Justice.

diagnostic research – Research used to identify the best approach from among a number of alternatives.

diary – Method of surveying radio or television audience where a person fills in the time he listens to radio or watches TV.

dichotomous question (simple) – A closed-ended question in a (quantitative) marketing research questionnaire in which the respondent chooses one of only two possible responses. Also survey question that provides two contradictory response options. Choices can include yes or no, approve or disapprove, like and dislike. See *multichotomous question.*

die cut – A mechanical process for cutting, scoring and/or creasing a finished print product.

differential advantage – The element or factor in a firm's product or strategy, which stresses its superiority over that of a competitor.

differential pricing – A pricing strategy in which a company sets different prices for the same product on the basis of differing customer type, time of purchase, etc. (not always legal). It is also called *discriminatory pricing, flexible pricing, multiple pricing* or *variable pricing*. See *one-price policy.*

differentiated segmentation strategy – One of four approaches (the others being concentrated segmentation strategy, market segment expansion strategy and product line expansion strategy) available to a firm in relation to the market segment or segments it wishes to target. In a differentiated segmentation approach, a firm operates in a number of markets where it attempts to sell different products to each (target) market.

differentiated (target) marketing – A segmented approach to marketing that divides a heterogeneous market into relatively homogeneous segments (niche audiences) so that the needs and wants of the segments may be served more effectively. It becomes Differentiated Target Marketing when an organization simultaneously pursues several different market segments – usually with a different strategy for each.

differentiation – A firm or organization with products and/or services that have a unique element, which allows them to stand out from the rest.

The ABCs of Strategic Communication

diffusion of innovation – The thought that some groups within a market are more ready and willing than others to adopt a new product that the product is diffused through a society in waves. The groups, in order of their readiness to adopt are innovators (2.5 percent of the population), early adopters (13.5 percent), early majority (34 percent), late majority (34 percent) and laggards (16 percent).

diffusion process – The manner in which an innovative technology, product or service spreads across a market awaiting the readiness of consumer acceptance or adoption. The five steps are: awareness, interest, trial, evaluation and adoption (or rejection). It is also known as the *adoption process.*

digital color proofing – See *pre-press services.*

digital advertising – Use of virtual advertising technique. Banners or billboards electronically appear on the television screen. Viewers at home see the ads while spectators inside the sports venue do not. Virtual ads can actually cover a billboard that has been erected inside a sports stadium or arena. (The yellow first-down line and direction arrows on football fields use the same technology to help entertain home audiences by making it easier to follow the game.) See *digital billboard.*

digital archiving – Scanning and storing documents on computer chips or using other technologies.

digital backpack – *Flash drive* (or *TravelDrive®*). Computer memory, which connects to a computer's *USB port* – also called pen, thumb, jump, smart or key drive. It is an enormously powerful tool that has changed the concept of "personal" computer. It is an inexpensive digital storehouse.

digital (advertising) billboard – Electronic billboard that shows changeable ads (messages) on huge high definition plasma-like billboard (screen). Messages change every eight seconds. Municipal governments have embraced *digital billboard* technology because of its ability to instantly post such important public safety messages as severe weather conditions, highway delays or closures due to traffic accidents, and "Amber Alerts" for missing children.

digital democracy – Use of the Internet – much like the radio, television, cable and online revolutions of the past – to provide information about political campaigns. It is considered an opportunity to make the media more democratic, more diverse and more participatory.

60

Tips to Succeed: How to safeguard your debit card – from 'phishing' & 'skimming'

Don't respond to unsolicited e-mails seeking account numbers and passwords: E-mails can be disguised as customer-service messages from banks to trick victims into giving up personal financial information. Debit cards are a prime target for these "phishing" scams.

In a typical "phishing" scam, the e-mail will ask you to type your account number and your password or PIN into an official-looking Web site. With that information, crooks can embed your account number in a phony debit card. Armed with your PIN, they can use the card to withdraw money from your account.

Legitimate financial institutions don't e-mail requests for personal information.

• Be on the lookout for "card skimmers" when using automated teller machines: In these schemes, criminals place scanners over ATM card slots to lift account information from debit cards. They use hidden cameras or old-fashioned shoulder surfing to get PINs. Avoid suspicious ATMs and shield your transactions from prying eyes. If the ATM eats your card, contact your bank immediately.

• Don't keep your PIN anywhere near your debit card: If someone steals your wallet or purse, he has the keys to the kingdom.

• Practice vigilance: Set up online accounts with your financial institutions and monitor them regularly. You'll be able to see fraudulent charges early on, rather than waiting 30 days for your bank statement.

USA Today - May 20, 2005
Jordana Beebe - spokeswoman for the Privacy Rights Clearinghouse

digital distribution – Release of motion pictures on DVDs and through Video on Demand.

digital (LCD) signage – An up-and-coming wave of advertising that's basically plasma screen TVs in retail stores, on the walls of malls, at train stations, in airports – any place people gather. Rather than having a poster/billboard, it shows moving video. Digital signage is also used for the public relations/human resources worlds where companies use it for training, their own in-house news and information channel that can be seen in a lunch room or meeting rooms. It is a growing industry that is already widely used in China and Japan.

digital signatures – Signatures for electronic documents. They establish identity and therefore can be used to establish legal responsibility and the complete authenticity of whatever they are affixed to – in effect, a tamper-proof seal has been created.

digital subscriber line (DSL) – offered as a high-speed dedicated digital circuit to computer users. DSLs are faster than modem dial-up, but not quite as fast as some broadband connections.

digital video recorder (DVR) – A high capacity hard drive (rather than tape) that is embedded in a video recorder, which records video programming from a television set. (An example would be the Tivoli® brand.) These DVDs are operated by personal video recording software, which enables the viewer to pause, fast forward and manage all sorts of other functions and special applications.

digital video server – A dedicated computer at a central location that receives command requests from the television viewer through a video-on-demand application. Once it receives the request, it instantly broadcasts specific digital video streams back to that viewer.

dingbat – Another term for *bullet* (dots or other symbol used to help set off typed line – to make it stand out. Also a *bullet* or symbol used as an end sign.

DINKY (double income no kids yet) – A demographic grouping.

DINS (double income no sex) – Couples (married or significant others) who, for the most part, work so many hours they don't have time for and don't miss having sex. It has become a way of life.

direct accounts – Large accounts serviced by head office personnel or company executives rather than by an individual salesperson. Sometimes called *house accounts* or *national accounts*.

direct close – The most straight-forward closing approach – the salesperson simply asks the buyer for an order. See *close*.

direct competition – Products or brands, which compete in the same product category. See *indirect competition*.

direct competitive advertising – Advertising meant to stimulate immediate purchase of a particular brand or service. See *indirect competitive advertising.*

direct costs – Costs which can be attributed directly to the production of a particular product. See *indirect costs.*

direct entry/injection – Process of entering mail directly into another area's mail stream. Mail that is sent *direct injection* goes directly to the designated postal area and receives a local indicia and return address.

direct house – An advertising specialties company that manufactures and sells its goods directly with its own sales force, rather than through retailers.

direct mail – Marketing communications delivered directly to a prospective purchaser (targeted audience) via the U.S. Postal Service, a private delivery company or e-mail. It promotes a specific product, idea or service.

direct mail advertising – Advertising directly to end-users by sending catalogues or other sales literature or materials through the mail.

direct marketing channel – A distribution channel in which no intermediaries or "middlemen" are used. A manufacturer sells direct to an end-user. Also called a *zero level channel.*

direct marketing – Selling to end-users using catalogues, direct-mail advertisements, etc. to sell merchandise and services. Also all activities that make it possible to offer goods and/or services or to transmit other messages to a targeted audience by mail, telephone, e-mail or other direct means rather than through a mass media. The targeting of marketing communications directly to individuals (typically a large number at a time) rather than through a mass media. Includes methods such as *direct mail* and *telemarketing.* See *direct selling.*

direct premium – A premium provided to the consumer at the same time as the purchase.

direct response – Promotions that permit or encourage consumers to directly respond to the advertiser by mail, telephone, e-mail or some other means of communication. Some practitioners use this as a synonym for *direct marketing.* See *response card.*

direct response advertising (DRA) – Advertising incorporating a contact method such as a phone number, address and inquiry form, Web site or e-mail address, to encourage the consumer to respond directly to the advertiser by requesting more information or placing an order.

direct-response marketing – A type of non-store retailing in which consumers order merchandise by mail, telephone or the Internet. Goods are shipped directly to their homes. It is also referred to as *direct-response selling*. See *at-home TV shopping*.

direct-response selling – A type of non-store retailing in which consumers order merchandise by mail, telephone or the Internet. Goods are shipped directly to their homes. See *at-home TV shopping*.

direct response television (DRTV) – The liveliest medium in that it can show products actually in use (Home Shopping Network; QVC). Unlike *brand advertising* or general advertising on TV – which is designed to create awareness – *DRTV* attempts to change behavior by getting people to react by calling a toll-free number or logging onto a Web site.

direct selling – Selling directly to consumer (end-users) by means of a sales force, catalog or the Internet. See *direct marketing*.

direct selling expenses – All of the marketing expenses, including labor and out of pocket costs, associated with producing, printing and mailing catalogues or other printed matter.

direct to consumer (DTC) – Products sold directly to consumers or end users without the use of middleman.

direct-to-home retailing – See *direct-response selling*.

direct traffic – Influencers, opinion leaders, connectors or key communicators serving as carriers of a strategic message.

director – The person in charge of the actual filming or taping of a commercial, television show or movie.

directories – Alphabetized lists of names and addresses of individuals and organizations. Used in selling or prospecting for new accounts and in marketing research as sources of secondary data.

director's cut – Movie scenes not included in the final version distributed to theatres – but included on a DVD version or at the end of the "final cut," which is shown in the theater. See *outtake*.

directory advertising – One of the 11 basic types of advertising. People refer to it to find out how to purchase a product or service – many times listed alphabetically. (e.g. Yellow Pages advertising or classifieds.)

directive probes – Questions asked to prospective buyers to gain a better understanding of the consumer /customer's business.

disaggregated market – A market in which separate products must be made for each consumer because each has different (custom) needs. It is also referred to as *complete segmentation*. See *customized marketing mix; market atomization strategy*.

disclaimer – Use of material in way makes user responsible – a repudiation or denial of responsibility or connection.

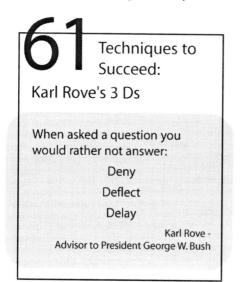

61 Techniques to Succeed:

Karl Rove's 3 Ds

When asked a question you would rather not answer:

Deny

Deflect

Delay

Karl Rove -
Advisor to President George W. Bush

discontinuous innovation – A completely new product made to perform a function for which no product has existed previously.

discount – A reduction off the (list) price offered by a producer to a buyer. There are five common types of *discounts*: *Allowances; Cash Discount; Quantity Discount; Seasonal Discount and Trade Discount.*

discount house – A retailer that attracts consumers by offering low prices. Typically, discount houses operate on low mark-ups and offer a minimal customer service.

discount store – See *discount house.*

discredit – Technique used by newsmakers to downplay, distract or deflect questions asked by a reporter or other interviewer.

discretionary income – Also called *disposable income.* It's the balance of a person's income, which is available for spending after paying such fixed costs as taxes, mortgages, rent and other basic necessities of life (e.g. food, car, etc.).

discriminatory pricing – See *differential pricing.*

62 Techniques to Succeed:
Drip-Drip-Drip

The steady output of information from the time it is decided an event is going to take place. As the event draws closer, the release of information intensifies. The heaviest barrage of information is released shortly before the actual event or launch.

Nike uses this technique "to build anticipation and demand."

M. Larry Litwin, APR, Fellow PRSA - The Public Relations Practitioner's Playbook (Kendall/Hunt – 2008)

disjunctive model (of brand evaluation) – A model used in the study of consumer decision making to evaluate alternative brands. It follows the idea that consumers, about to make a purchase, evaluate competing brands on the basis of one or a number of features or attributes – ignoring their feelings about features that are less important to them.

Disneyfied – A special event where members of the public or media react spontaneously, but every step is methodically, logically planned and calculated (at such Disney properties as Disneyland®).

display – The showing or exhibiting of merchandise so that it attracts the attention of consumers. This is a popular technique in retail stores.

display advertisement – In print media, any advertisement other than a classified ad. Also includes any stand-alone ad, such as a window sign or billboard. It can appear anywhere in a newspaper except on the editorial page. They usually have a border; e.g. three columns by 6 inches (equals 18 column inches).

display aids – Posters, pictures, scale models, videos, etc. that present information visually to help communicate a product or service's image.

display allowance – A type of sales promotion in which manufacturers or sellers are given incentives in the form of price reductions or merchandise to encourage them to display the items prominently to attract consumer attention. See *allowances.*

display copy – Type set in larger sizes that is used to attract the reader's attention.

display type – Type or hand lettering for headlines; usually larger than 14 points.

disposable income – Also called *discretionary income*.

disrupt (blow up or explode) – Term police use when firing or shooting into a device (a bomb or other explosive) containing water or other element.

DISS (double income some sex) – Couples (married or significant others) who, for the most part, work so many hours they have time limited time to have sex and don't miss having it. It has become a way of life.

dissocialize groups – Groups (cliques) with whom an individual does not wish to be associated. Many times, they might be groups whose use of a product will deter other buyers. For example, the Toyota Scion® is targeted toward the *echo generation*. That could deter "older" consumers from purchasing that brand. See *aspirational groups*.

dissolve – Fading from one scene to another in a videotape or film production. The alternative would be abrupt scene changes.

dissonance – A discrepancy between what a consumer received and what they expected to receive. See *cognitive dissonance*.

distance learning – Studying at home or some other remote location through teleconferencing, DVD, CD-ROM and/or workbooks.

distortion – A misrepresentation. See *selective distortion*.

distribution – The process of getting goods from the manufacturer or supplier to the retailer or consumer.

distribution center – A short-term storage center (terminal) located close to a major market to facilitate rapid order processing and shipment of goods to retailers or directly to consumers. Unlike a warehouse, the emphasis is on the moving of goods rather than on long-term storage.

distribution channels – The path or route taken by goods and services as they move from producer to retailer and eventually to the consumer. See *marketing channels*.

distribution costs – Costs associated with the holding of inventory and the shipment of goods to retailers or consumers.

distribution intensity – This is a retail price controlling method. The level of availability selected for a particular product by the marketer determines price. The level of intensity chosen will depend upon factors such as production capacity, size of the target market, pricing and pro-

63

Techniques to Succeed:
Call it 'reverse psychology'

Philadelphia advertising executive Steve Schulman takes a reverse approach to educating communicators about the importance and effectiveness of advertising. He offers *10 easy steps on why **NOT** to advertise*:

1. DON'T ADVERTISE. Just pretend everybody knows what you have to offer.

2. DON'T ADVERTISE. Tell yourself you just don't have the time to spend thinking about promoting your business.

3. DON'T ADVERTISE. Just assume everyone knows what you sell.

4. DON'T ADVERTISE. Convince yourself that you've been in business so long customers automatically come to you.

5. DON'T ADVERTISE. Forget that you have competition trying to attract your customers away from you.

6. DON'T ADVERTISE. Forget that there are new potential customers who would do business with you if they were urged to do so.

7. DON'T ADVERTISE. Tell yourself that it costs too much to advertise and that you don't get enough out of it.

8. DON'T ADVERTISE. Overlook the fact that advertising is an investment - not an expense.

9. DON'T ADVERTISE. Be sure not to provide an adequate advertising budget for your business.

10. DON'T ADVERTISE. Forget that you have to keep reminding your establishment (customers/clients) that you appreciate their business.

motion policies and the amount of product service required by the end-user. See *exclusive distribution; intensive distribution; selective distribution*.

distribution management – See *physical distribution management*.

distribution strategy – See *place strategy*.

distribution-based pricing strategies – Pricing methods designed to recover or offset costs associated with the shipment of goods to customers. See *geographic pricing*.

distributor – A company or middle person that distributes a manufacturer's goods to retailers. Distributors are sometimes called wholesalers and/or jobbers.

distributor's brand – Also known as private brand, house brand or manufacturer's brand. It is a brand owned or controlled by an organization. A manufacturer makes the product for the retailer under the retailer's private label. Examples would include Kenmore® by Sears®, Berkley® and Jensen® at BJ's Wholesale Club® and Sonoma lifestyle® by Kohl's®.

64 Techniques to Succeed: The Double Bottom Line Public Relations Theory

Public relations has evolved from products (newsletters, brochures, etc.) to counseling, strategizing and training. Two-way communication is imperative.

First Bottom Line:

• An organization's successful efforts to please its publics before and during doing business with it.

• Who knows what's in the public interest better than the public relations professional?

• Who knows if a public is satisfied with an organization's image, management and motive toward the public better than the public relations professional?

• Once this essential relationship is established, the company can do business with its publics.

Second Bottom Line:

• The actual acceptance of the products or services by the public.

• The sale from the fruit of the relationship in the first bottom line leads to profits.

Who better to strategize the Double Bottom Line Theory – reputation leading to profits – than the public relations practitioner or relationship manager? In fact, Bank of America has an executive staff position – vice president for relationship marketing – responsible for achieving the first bottom line.

Patrick Jackson - Jackson, Jackson & Wagner - Exeter, N.H.

divergent acquisition – Diversification into new or unrelated businesses. An example would be Cendant, which had been in the mortgage business, but also owns hotels and motels. Another might be Warren Buffet whose investments are diversified among many different companies. See *diversification*.

diversification – A growth strategy where an organization takes on new products and new markets. An increase in the variety of goods and services produced by an organization or firm or a conglomerate that includes a number of manufacturers and brands (e.g. Beatrice Foods®, Campbell's®). It may be encouraged, either by business owners or by governments, to reduce the risk of relying on a narrow range of products. Also in investing, it is the spreading of risk by putting assets in several categories of investments – including stocks, bonds, money market accounts, mutual funds, precious metals and real estate. See *horizontal diversification*.

diversification risk model – It is widely accepted that the more diversified or spread out a firm or organization, the less overall risk it faces. See *diversification*.

divest strategy – A strategically planned decision to get out of a particular business or product line (sell it off).

dividend – A cash payout a company gives stockholders. It's a method for companies to reward stockholders' loyalty and to distribute profits.

divisional marketing manager – A marketing manager with responsibility for the marketing activities of one of the operating divisions of a company.

divisional sales manager – A sales manager with responsibility for the sales activities of one or more of the operating divisions of a company.

document – A computer file containing text and/or graphics.

documentary – A work, such as a film or television program, presenting political, social, or historical subject matter in a factual and informative manner and often consisting of actual news films or interviews accompanied by narration. Facts should be presented objectively without editorializing or inserting fictional material.

documented – A government term for aliens who receive proper papers to remain in the U.S.

Technique to Succeed:
Be alert for workplace problems

Supervisors and employees should be aware of the people around them, and be able to identify those who are at risk for workplace violence. Here are some behavior indicators that may be present in at-risk employees:

• Attendance problems

• Decreased productivity

• Inconsistent work patterns

• Lingering depression

• Poor on-the-job relationships

• Inability to concentrate

• Fascination with weapons

• Chronic excuses or blaming

• Evidence of substance abuse

FirstCALL - An Employee Assistance Program -
www.courierpostonline.com - July 12, 2005

dodge – Manipulating the exposure in a photographic print. See *ink bump*.

dodging – Use of excuses – not always truthful – to avoiding answering a reporter's question(s). One of the 10 Ds of Crisis Communication. A spokesperson making a conscious effort to avoid a direct question by a reporter. It is never a successful approach – a reporter will lose trust and respect for the spokesperson because he/she is not being direct with the media. If you don't have an answer to a question, simply say, "I can't discuss it (or details) on that at this time, but I will get back to you on that." And make sure to follow up with the reporter. It is all about preparation and anticipation. If you aren't prepared and anticipate a reporter's questions you will make yourself look even more foolish by trying to dodge a question. Other Ds are: direct, distance, deflect, distract, divert, diffuse, defuse, dilute and dissolve.

dog whistle message – Strategic messages crafted so that ideally, only targeted audiences hear or see it.

dogs – A term used as a product classification by the Boston Consulting Portfolio Analysis Matrix. Dogs are products with a relatively low market share in a slow-growth market. See *Boston Consulting Group advantage matrix*; *cash cows*; *question marks*; *stars*. Read more at *www.bcg.com/home.jsp*.

dollar bill test – A test to help determine whether a publication's layout is pleasing to the eye. The *dollar bill test* is simple: Take a dollar bill and turn it on a page of copy. To pass the *dollar bill test*, it must touch at least one *copybreaker*. If it does, your publication passes. If not, you fail. (See Technique 43.)

dollar volume quota – A common form of sales assignment, goal or target used to measure a salesperson's performance. For example, a salesper-

66 Tips to Succeed: Choosing the correct coach

Business coaches are becoming a common part of executive development and are assisting in career transition in companies reducing ranks.

Here are tips for choosing an executive coach:

• Most executive coaches work by phone. Schedule a half-hour get-acquainted session with potential coaches to learn about their backgrounds and experience. Discuss your goals, the process the coach follows and their costs.

• Look for chemistry. Is this a person who you will be comfortable working with on a regular basis? Will you be able to listen to both positive and negative feedback from the coach?

• Check some references.

• Be prepared to commit to a minimum of three months — this is the amount of time it normally takes for a solid coaching relationship to develop.

• Check the coach's flexibility. Sometimes it is critical for the coach to come to your location to meet, to observe you and others in group settings.

Courier-Post - Camden, N.J. - Nov. 21, 2005

son may be told that his or her sales must total $400,000 during the coming year. Other common forms of sales quotas are unit volume quotas, gross margin quotas, net profit quotas and activity quotas. See *sales quota.*

domain name – The unique name that identifies an Internet site.

dominant photo – The largest photo on a page that attracts a reader's attention.

domino effect –Events linked by time. A subsequent event requires a preceding event to happen. A sequence of events, stages, phases, life cycles, actions and outcomes that require a preceding event to happen.

doughnut – Type of commercial spot where live copy runs between a musical open and close. Also a recorded news report where a reporter opens it – either on camera or voice on tape – inserts a Soundbite and returns on camera or on tape. See *sandwich spot; wrap.*

doorhanger –A flier distributed in a neighborhood canvassing campaign.

dooh nibor economics – Robin Hood in reverse. Economist Paul Krugman defines it as stealing from the poor to give to the wealthy.

door-opener – A product or advertising specialty given by a sales person to retailers or consumers to persuade them to listen to a sales pitch.

door-to-door selling – Direct selling in which a salesperson calls on prospective buyers at their homes with or without appointments. If it is without an appointment, it is referred to as a *cold calling.*

dot whack – A sticker, usually round, that's affixed to a catalog cover (or printed directly on the cover) that touts a special offer or message to customers. Many newspapers now use Post-it® type stickers (sticky notes) on the front page to attract readers' attention. Also called a *popper.*

dots pr inch (DPI) – The measurement of resolution for (computer) printers, phototypesetting machines and graphics screens. The more DPI, the better the product. Standard personal laser printers produce at 600 DPI.

double-barreled question – An item on a survey questionnaire that asks about more than one topic.

Double Bottom Line (public relations) Theory – The late Patrick Jackson of Jackson, Jackson & Wagner (Exeter, N.H.) was among the first to state that public relations had evolved from *products* (newsletters, brochures, etc.) to counseling, strategizing and training. Two-way communication is imperative. Jackson created this theory – *First Bottom Line*: An organization's successful efforts to please its publics before and during doing business with it. A) Who knows what's in the public interest better than the public relations professional? B) Who knows if a public is satisfied with an organization's image, management and motive toward the public better than the public relations professional? C) Once this essential relationship is established, the company can do business with its publics. *Second Bottom Line*: A) The actual acceptance of the products or services by the public. B) The sale from the fruit of the relationship in the first bottom line leads to profits. Jackson asked, "Who better to strategize the double bottom line theory – reputation leading to profits – than the public relations practitioner or relationship manager?" (Bank of America has an executive staff position – vice president for relationship marketing – responsible for achieving the first bottom line.) See *Triple Bottom Line*.

double space – Placing one line of blank space after every line of text. Double space all submissions to media, as it leaves editors room to edit or make comments.

double truck – A two-page spread in a print publication, where the ad (editorial copy) runs across the middle gutter. It could be the center fold ("center spread") or any two full side-by-side pages (facing each other). If it prints across the gutter between the two pages, and if the pages are on the same sheet, rather than two adjacent sheets, it might be called a "true" *double truck*. This name comes from the days when the heavy forms for newspaper pages, largely filled with lead type, were rolled around the composing room floor on heavy carts called trucks. Two pages for one project meant a double truck.

down page – Editors assigning a story toward the bottom of a newspaper page – particularly on a broadsheet page. See *broadsheet*.

down-market consumers – Consumers who habitually search for, and purchase, low-priced rather than more expensive products. They are commonly called "bargain hunters." See *up-market consumers*.

downlink – A transmission path for the communication of signals and data from a communications satellite or other space vehicle to the earth.

download –Transfer of data from a computer server to a computer's hard drive.

downside elasticity – The demand for a product increases significantly as the price falls. Used in reference to the sensitivity of consumers to a

Tips to Succeed: College seniors preparing to jump into the job market

- Prepare a 2-3 minute response that best highlights your achievements and skills, especially moments during an internship or school assignment that pertain to the job. (Recruiters will often ask the question, "Tell me about yourself.")
- Show enthusiasm for the job.
- When talking to the recruiter, use language common to the field.
- Dress appropriately. "Dressing inappropriately is the biggest no-no," she said. "Make the change from collegiate appearance to professional. If you look like a professional, the recruiter will have an easier time seeing you fit in at the company."

Lizziel Sullivan-Williams – Director of Career and Academic Planning - Rowan University – Glassboro, N.J

decrease in the price of a particular product. See *downside inelasticity*; *upside elasticity.*

downside inelasticity – There is no significant increase in demand as the price falls. See *downside elasticity*; *upside elasticity*.

downstyle – A headline type where the first letter is capitalized and all others are lowercase.

downward stretching – The introduction of a new product into a product line at the lower priced end of the market. An example might be car manufacturers, which offer several brands (General Motors, Ford, Chrysler) and a number of price points (models) within each of those brands.

downzoning – Reducing the number of units (houses) that may be built on a parcel (acre) of land.

doyenne – A woman who is the eldest or senior member of a group.

drag and drop –Computer term for transferring data. User would (double) click the mouse on the file to be transferred (highlighting it) and drag it to a different file before releasing the mouse. For example, files can be copied or moved by dragging them from one folder to another. Programs can be executed by dragging and dropping. To print a document, an icon of the document is dragged on top of the icon for the printer. Drag and drop is essential for graphics applications where you need to position text and images on the page or on top of each other. However, there are drag and drop options for copying and moving files, which can be just as easily accomplished with the standard Copy, Cut and Paste functions in the Edit menu. Read more at *http://en.wikipedia.org/wiki/drag-and-drop*.

dramatization of presentation – The enthusiasm given to a presentation or demonstration of a product by a salesperson to a buyer, especially during a product launch. Presentations can be dramatized by using such audiovisual aids as PowerPoint or physical demonstrations.

drill down – When an online user accesses more and more pages of the Web site – the user is going deeper into the content of the site. It is the term used to describe the accessing of numerous links of a Web site.

68 Tips to Succeed: Improve your credit score

- Sign up for automatic bill payment. A late bill can make your credit score drop by as much as 100 points.
- Watch the timing of your spending, especially if you plan to apply for a loan. The lower the balance, the better the credit rating.
- Limit credit-card applications. Each time a lender inquires to view a credit report, it gets noted and can reduce the score.
- Think twice before canceling cards. Consumers gain points if they are tapping only a small percentage of the total credit available to them.
- Make sure credit limits are posted.

Consumer Reports

drip advertising – Limited expenditure on advertising over a relatively long period of time. See *burst advertising expenditure*.

drip-drip-drip method – A public relations/advertising technique in which information is released slowly – almost as a tease – and builds to a crescendo. This method is usually used for a product launch or a change in a strategic approach.

drive – A motivating force or need sufficiently strong enough to impel a person to seek its satisfaction.

69 Tips to Succeed: Store-brand goods rival national names

Store-brand products have the same quality as brand name products.

Comparison tests were conducted on 65 grocery products in six categories – peaches, yogurt, plastic bags, facial tissues, paper towels and french fries.

Consider this when buying:

- A national-brand manufacturer might make several formulations of the same product to appeal to consumers with different needs - and snatch valuable shelf space from competitors.

- Most store brands come in several tiers to dispel the notion that store brands are strictly for penny pinchers.

Consumer Reports

drive time – Used in radio, this refers to morning and afternoon times when consumers are driving to and from work. These are considered prime times for radio listeners. See *daypart*.

driver (social style) – One of the four social styles (with *amiable, analytical* and *expressive*) used to classify salespeople and their customers. Drivers are characterized by high assertiveness and low responsiveness. See *amiable, analytical* and *expressive*. .

drop and run – Used by caterers when they prepare buffet style lunches or dinners and drop off the food at site in disposable containers. Much like take-out except it is delivered.

drop cap – A large initial capital that drops down a few lines into the text. It usually begins the paragraph at the top of the story.

drop error – A mistake made by a company when it decides to abandon a new product idea that, in hindsight, might have been successful if developed.

drop shipper – A sales person who receives orders from consumers and forwards them to a manufacturer for shipment direct to the consumer.

drug mule – A person who transports drugs for a fee – from dealer to dealer or end user – but is not considered a dealer. They serve only as intermediaries.

drummers – A 19th century term of American origin for a traveling salesperson.

DSL (digital subscriber line) – offered as a high-speed dedicated digital circuit to computer users. *DSLs* are faster than modem dial-up, but not quite as fast as some broadband connections.

dual brand – Brand within a brand. For example, Fairfield Inn®, which is part of Marriott® or Buick®, which is General Motors®. (Different from *co-authoring advertising* or *co-brand advertising*.) See *sub-brand*.

dual distribution – When a manufacturer uses two approaches simultaneously to get products to end-users. Usually, one approach is to use marketing intermediaries, while the other is to sell direct to consumers.

dubbing – Recording sound from one source to another.

due diligence – The verification of all information given to a company by any prospective business associate. The process (research and analysis that takes place in advance of an investment, takeover or business partnership) includes: an in-depth credibility assessment of the company and its key executives; a check of county and federal civil, criminal, and bankruptcy records to uncover suits, liens, judgments, convictions and bankruptcy filings; database searches for any information printed publicly, (e.g., books, magazines, newspapers, congressional hearings, crime commission reports), about the company or officers. Read more at *www.researchassociatesinc.com/articles/duedil.pdf.*

dummy – A mock-up of a print piece (brochure, advertisement, magazine, newspaper, etc.) or even blank sheets of paper, provided to a printer or artist as an example of the size, color or other aspect of the project to be produced. Also a fictitious name in a mail, telephone or e-mail list placed solely for the purpose of tracking the use of the list to ensure that the list purchaser or renter does not break the sales or rental contract. A similar term, "decoy," is a real name included for this purpose. The decoy person, household or organization either works for the list owner/broker or otherwise agrees to help by reporting any misuse. The process of including decoys or dummies is called seeding or salting.

dummy media vehicle – A mock-up of a media vehicle (newspaper, magazine, etc) used to test advertising effectiveness with a representative group of the target market – or to sell advertising.

dumping – A practice in which a firm sells its product cheaply into a foreign market undercutting the domestic price.

dumpster diver – Someone who looks through trash for valuables or others' identities.

duopoly – One corporation owns two TV stations in same market.

dupe – A duplicate listing of the same person, household or organization in a mail, telephone or e-mail list. The listing may not be a complete duplicate to be considered a dupe. For example, a name may carry a first initial while another carries full first and middle names. Dupes are important to be aware of because they could cost list subscribers additional fees – one may contain an old address while another contains the new one. See *de-dupe.*

duplicate elimination – Eliminate any duplicate listings in a mail, telephone, e-mail list. This is not easily accomplished since the listings may not be perfect duplicates. For example, one may carry a first initial while another carries full first and middle names. One may contain an old address while another contains the new one, etc. Also called *de-dupe.*

duplicated audience – That portion of an audience that is reached by more than one media vehicle – or members of a radio/TV audience that are reached multiple times during a given period by the same station.

durables – A classification of consumer products consisting of goods with a long useful life, such as cars, electrical appliances and furniture. See *consumer non-durable;, consumer durables.*

dylux – A printer's proof, blue or brown (ink) in color and made from an off–set negative. This is typically the final step before publications (jobs) are plated. Many printers now make laser proofs available. Laser proofs can be provided in full color although the colors may not be the exact **PMS** (Pantone Matching System) colors that will be used on for the completed publication.

dynamic ad placement – Inserting advertisements (banner, display, pop-ups, etc.) into an Internet web page in response to a user's request. *Dynamic ad placement* allows alteration of specific ads placed on a page based on data available to the placement program. At its simplest, *dynamic ad placement* allows for multiple ads to be rotated through one or more spaces. In more sophisticated examples, the ad placement could be affected by demographic data or usage history for the computer's current user.

dynamic ad rotation – Delivery of advertisements (banner, display, pop-ups, etc.) on a rotating, random basis so that users are exposed to different ads, and ads are served in different pages of the site. **D**

80/20 principle or rule – See *eighty-twenty principle or rule* below.

e-bates – Rebates offered via the Internet. Many retailers offer and even encourage purchasers to apply for their rebates on line. There is a company called Ebates® which assists rebate application n behalf of retailers. One drawback is that not all retailers subscribe to Ebates®.

e-commerce – Also called e-marketing. Marketing conducted electronically, usually over the Internet – includes on-line shopping, on-line banking, on-line bartering, etc.

e-hybrid – Hydrogen vehicles that also carry a larger battery that can be charged while parked. Standard hybrids' batteries are smaller and charge while driving.

e-learning – Interactive online tutorials, accessed via the Internet.

e-mail (electronic mail) – Text files sent from one person to another over the Internet. *Associated Press style* calls for "e" in e-mail to be lower case.

e-mail campaign – Advertising campaign distributed via e-mail.

e-mail pitch – A pitch sent via e-mail instead of presented to the media by phone, mail or fax.

e-mail trail – An e-mail reply (replies) that contains all of the previous mails – a chain of sorts – pertaining to the subject.

e-marketing – Also called e-commerce. Marketing conducted electronically, usually over the Internet.

e-tailer – Online retailer.

e-world – The Internet or Web.

e-zine – Online newsletter or magazine.

ear worm – Words and phrases woven into the mind – the name for a song that you hear once and can't get out of your head all day. One of the reasons behind advertisers paying for the use of certain songs as jingles (a major locking device).

earbud – "Headphone" for iPod®-type devices.

early adopters – The group in a market second only to innovators in the speed with which they adopt a new product. See *diffusion of innovation; early majority; innovators; laggards; late majority*.

early majority – The group in a market who are more deliberate than the innovators and the early adopters in making purchase decisions, but less conservative than the late majority and laggards. See *diffusion of innovation; early adopters; innovators; laggards; late majority*.

earmark (political) – Line items "sneaked" into legislative bills as "porkbarrels" so that congressmen reap the benefits for their districts. According to Sen. John McCain (R-Arizona), most times these *earmarks* go unnoticed, costing taxpayers millions of dollars.

earned rate – A discounted media rate, based on the number of advertisements or commercials placed.

ears – Space at the top of the front page of a newspaper on each side of the newspaper's name where weather news, index to pages or announcement of special features appears. *Ears* are now being sold for advertising.

eat your peas journalism – News that people do not want to see or hear at dinnertime but must because of its magnitude – war stories or such catastrophic disasters as Katrina when it hit the Gulf Coast in 2005.

echo boomers – Born after 1980. They are big spenders who don't understand the value of money. They are not used to doing anything on their own. According to CBS' "60 Minutes" (Oct. 3, 2004) they are awarded for participation and not achievement. They expect a lot of feedback and be told they are wonderful. *Echo boomers* are not used to hearing they are not THAT good, can't think long range and are not methodical. They have difficulty making decisions for themselves.

echo lead – In radio or television reporting, when an anchor uses exactly the same words to introduce a piece of tape (*sound bite, actuality* or reporter's report) as the first few words on the tape.

economic development – The strategic pursuit of business growth to benefit the public and sustain the community.

economic dislocation – Government gets what it wants because of its power and security of seemingly endless funds (money). An economic term describing a situation where the government is borrowing heavily

70 Tips to Succeed: Renew your workplace enthusiasm

Many professionals, whether in business, sports or just in life, lose their zest and enthusiasm. At times, energy is elevated, enabling you to maintain enthusiasm for years. Other times, you can be lackadaisical about work – and that can continue for weeks – or even months.

Dale Carnegie Training and others offer these tips to help you overcome that lack of enthusiasm – especially if you own a small business or manage a larger one:

• **Connect with other managers to gain new perspectives.** For example, join a local chamber of commerce or get involved in a trade association.

• **Assess your business life.** Have you deviated too far from the areas of your job that you love? Have you lost sight of your goals? Have you forgotten what makes you happy?

• **Discover your legacy.** Ask yourself whether you've lost site of where you are going. Reassess your vision and the company's mission and then rewrite them so they reflect your new mindset. (Remember, the mission and vision statements are not the same.)

• **Set concrete short-term goals.** Sometimes we just have to get through a "funk." Set specific goals for each day, each week and each month – some people even set goals for each hour.

Ensure that you are on the right path – you will rediscover your enthusiasm along the way.

www.dalecarnegie.com

at the same time businesses and individuals also want to borrow. The government can always pay the market interest rate, but businesses and individuals cannot are crowded out. An example would be the government going into an area to develop a road or construct an office building, which might increase demand for real estate – thus driving up the cost of money. While the government has the resources to pay the higher interest rates, private investors do not and are crowded out. When government invokes eminent domain to accomplish its goal, the taking and destruction of otherwise "good" homes, businesses and other property is referred to as economic displacement.

economic environment – Factors in the economy, such as inflation, unemployment, interest rates, etc., that influence buying decisions of consumers and organizations.

economic forecast – A prediction of the likely impact on the business environment of factors such as inflation, interest rates, unemployment, government, consumer spending, etc. Particular interest is paid to the Board of Commissioners at the Federal Reserve.

economic order quantity (EOQ) – The amount, in dollars, of orders that minimizes or reduces the total (variable) costs required to market and inventory products.

economic utility – The ability of a good or service to satisfy a customer's needs or wants.

economies of scale – Reductions in the price per unit of marketing or manufacturing a product as the quantity marketed or produced increases. In other words, manufacturing costs decrease as volume increases.

eddress – E-mail address.

editing block – A plastic or metal block used to align tape properly for cutting and splicing.

edition – A press run of a newspaper. A daily newspaper generally has more than one edition a day – for example, "City Edition," "Lakeshore Edition," "Early Edition," "Late Edition."

71 Tips to Succeed:

PR practitioners don't make excuses

Don't make excuses – make it happen.

Losers make excuses.

Winners make it happen!

editor – The supervisor of a department of a newspaper, magazine, etc. An editor selects the information that will run, assigns writing tasks and determines its placement in the publication or broadcast.

editorial – Opinion, as opposed to an objective news article, appearing in a newspaper, magazine, on an Internet site, radio or television. Also the department of the newspaper where news is gathered, written, edited and readied for publication.

editorial calendar – A schedule of topics a magazine, newspaper or other media vehicle plans to cover in future issues or on future newscasts.

edu-tainment (edutainment) – Appearances dubbed as entertainment that are also educational. For example, in Philadelphia, impersonators of Benjamin Franklin incorporate show business in their lectures about the founding fathers. One such lecture markets Philadelphia as a historic destination city, with a determined sales pitch to visitors. The lecture stresses scholarship about Franklin's life, along with a sense of fun in the spirit of *edu-tainment*.

effectancy – Regularly used in the public relations profession to mean effective and efficient.

effective buying income – An individual's disposable or discretionary income, consisting of salary and wages, dividends, interest, profits, etc., less taxes. See *disposable income*; *discretionary income*.

efficient consumer response (ECR) – Having the right product in the right place at the right price with the right promotions. Product appearance and displays are integral parts of achieving ECR.

ego-drive – A psychological term meaning the need of one individual to persuade another to a particular point of view and feel satisfaction in having done so.

ego phoniac – One who cannot get along without grabbing the cell phone – much like craving a cigarette or having some other habit.

eight-sheet poster – A poster, the size of eight, 8-1/2 x 11 inch sheets of paper, used on poles, located mainly on secondary arteries and in urban neighborhoods.

eighty-twenty principle or rule – Also known as *Pareto's principle*. A rule-of-thumb that, for the typical product category, 80 percent of the products sold will be consumed by 20 percent of the customers. Others have been known to say, 80 percent of the work is done by 20 percent of the staff.

elaboration probes – Questions raised by salespeople when positively encouraging prospects that help to provide additional information about their needs.

elasticity of demand – A measure of the degree to which any change in the price of a product or service will affect the demand for it. See *inelasticity of demand.*

electric spectacular – Outdoor signs or billboards composed largely of lighting or other electrical components. A criticism of electric spectacular is that, often, the production overwhelms the message causing *vampire creativity.*

electronic funds transfer at point of sale (EFTPOS) – A system commonly used in retailing in which a consumer pays for purchases by using a debit card – which electronically transfers funds from his or her bank account to the store's.

electronic point of sale (EPOS) system – A relatively new system whereby electronic tills are used to process customer transactions in a retail outlet. Local EPOS systems are usually connected to a central computer system, so that financial and inventory-related data can be exchanged between the store and head office, allowing automatic accounting and replenishment.

electronic programming guide (EPG) – An application that allows a viewer to interactively select his/her television programming.

electronic retailing – The use by customers of computer terminals in conveniently located shopping kiosks and elsewhere to call up product information and then to place orders using credit cards.

electronic shelf-talkers/shelf screamers – An electronic (video or audio) advertising message triggered to operate when a customer walks in the vicinity of a product usually in a retail store. It might be touting "on special" or "sale item" or just the product name itself. See *shelf-talkers.*

electronic transcription (ET) – A recorded program or message on a vinyl disc, tape or CD.

elevator speech – A strategic message (about 30 seconds) with two or three *key message points* – that can be delivered quickly – even during an elevator ride.

ellipse – In print, the use of three dots (periods) to signify some words have been skipped over in a direct quote. In broadcasting, the three dots (periods) signify that a pause should be taken.

em – A unit of type measurement in printing, based on the (width of the) "M" character.

em dash – An elongated dash (–) that indicates the separation of elements of a sentence or clause – or to show that the next phrase should be emphasized. See *dash; en dash*.

embargo – The total restriction on the release of information before a given date. It is also a restriction on a particular good leaving or entering a country. See *hold for release*.

embargo date – Part of the heading on a news release indicating that the news is not to be reported before that (particular) date.

embedding – Also known as *product placement*. It is a form of subliminal advertising – sometimes showing the product fully (at a cost to the advertiser) or concealing the imagery in various products and advertisements to appeal to the subconscious drives of potential customers. Also see *subliminal advertising*.

embedded advertisement – A form of *subliminal advertising* – sometimes showing the product fully (at a cost to the advertiser) or concealing the imagery in various products and advertisements to appeal to the

72 Techniques to Succeed: Getting on the air

The National Association of Broadcasters (NAB) suggests that if your appeal is to be effective, you should have the answer to some key questions before contacting local stations: (Some refer to it as the MAC Triad - message, audience, channel.)

• What is your message? [message] Are you sure of the basic idea you want to communicate?

• Who should receive your message? [audience] Is it of general interest to a large segment of the audience? Can it be tailored to reach a specific audience?

• How can you best put your message across? [channel] Does it have enough general interest for a special program? Would a PSA serve just as well?

Your answers to these questions should help you determine in advance whether your pitch will achieve the desired result – coverage.

National Association of Broadcasters - Washington, D.C.

subconscious drives of potential customers. Also see *product placement*; subliminal *advertising*.

Emergency Alert System (EAS) – A network used for broadcasting emergency information to the public.

emergency goods – A category of consumer goods consisting of items purchased quickly in necessity. See *consumer goods*; *convenience goods*.

emergent worker – A relatively new breed of worker. One who takes charge of his/her career, wants to learn new skills and embraces change. Based on a 2005 by the outsourcing group, Spheroid Corp., emergents have been growing in numbers and now make up 31 percent of the work force, 18 and older. They feel it is the only way to have peace of mind, security and satisfaction.

eminent domain – The power of the federal government, a state or municipality to take private property for public use. It most cases, the property's owner is compensated.

---

73 Techniques to Succeed: For those who commit industrial or corporate espionage

Sometimes illegal. Almost always unethical. None the less, many use it in this competitive environment.

1. Gather the information – use a camera

2. Transmit the information – use a fax

3. Destroy the information after getting out of it what you want – use a shredder

---

emoticon (smiley) – Little text-based faces and objects often seen in e-mail and online chat. They help give the reader a sense of the writer's feelings behind the text. For example, the classic =) face shows that the writer is happy about something or that his message in good humor. Mike Jones, who works in the systems and networking research group at Microsoft's headquarters in Redmond, Washington, has determined that the **first smiley** was posted on Sept. 19, 1982.

emotional appeals in advertising – Advertising messages, usually based on imagery rather than information, which attempt to achieve the advertiser's objectives by evoking strong emotional feelings (fear, anger, passion, etc.) rather than by a rational appeal. See *fear appeals in advertising*; *rational appeals in advertising.*

emotional close – A technique a salesperson uses in closing a deal. It attempts to get a favorable response from a buyer by appealing to his or her fear, pride or similar emotion. See *close.*

emotional containment – A conscious choice to temporarily isolate certain emotions from the interactions and decision-making processes at hand. Containment enables emergency responders to function adequately even when they are feeling fear or horror.

emotional risk – The concern or uncertainty felt by a prospective buyer that he or she would feel bad about the purchase afterwards; also called *dissonance*; *psychological risk.* Also see *risk.*

74 Tips to Succeed: Shaping *your* life

"Define yourselves not by what you do, but by what you believe in, not by how much money you make, but by how you live your life, not by how many hours you work, but by how well you love and are loved. That is the most important charge."

Dr. Donald Farish - President - Rowan (N.J.) University
Commencement - May 13, 2005

emotional selling preposition (ESP) – The unique associations established by consumers with particular products. For example, the emotional response to a certain brand of car ensures their continual success, even though other makers may offer superior performance at the same price.

empathy – The ability of an individual to project his or her own personality into a situation and understand it. Successful salespeople possess this quality, because they see the product from the buyer's point of view.

empirical research – Any activity that uses direct or indirect observation to gather information.

employee poaching – The practice of "stealing" key employees from a competing firm.

employee publics – Also referred to as *internal audience*. It's the part of a company's public consisting of its employees.

empower – To give authority (to an audience) to act – when responsibilities have been delegated (because the audience has been educated).

empty nesters – A *demographic* characteristic identifying those in the stage of the family life cycle where the children have all grown up and left home. Research indicates that, typically, empty nesters are at the peak of their earning potential, and are an excellent market for travel, leisure and sporting goods, and home improvement merchandise. See *family life cycle*.

75 Techniques to Succeed: Reducing stress at work

Stress has a tendency to build up or snowball. The best way to reduce stress is to handle it when it's small and take advantage of relaxing moments.

- The way to reduce stress early on is by breaking the momentum of the snowball rolling down the hill by taking breaks.

- Allow yourself to relax, refuel and regroup throughout the day. Do not do too much, feel guilty for relaxing, or think about your "to do" list.

- Force yourself to take several mental breaks throughout the day. Even if they are only five minutes each, they will make a huge difference in your stress level. Anytime you do something other than relax during your 5 minutes, start the time over.

- Do something that feels relaxing, like listening to music, going for a brief walk, talking with a friend or co-worker. Try different activities to see what helps you feel less stressed and more focused on your work afterward.

Larina Kase - Doctor of Psychology, career coach and former counselor at the University of Pennsylvania - www.extremecommunicator.com

en dash – A dash (-), hyphen, half the width of an em dash, that often replaces the word "to" or "through," such as 10-6 or Monday-Friday. See *em dash*.

encirclement attack – A competitive tactic (sometimes thought of as a strategy) used by a strong market challenger to attack the market leader. The market challenger launches an attack on several fronts at once (known as *guerilla marketing*) in an attempt to break the leader's grip on the market.

encoder – The sender of a message. The translation of a message into code by a sender (*encoder*) so that it can be relayed through a medium to a receiver (*decoder*). Also, a hardware or software application that compresses audio and video signals for the purpose of streaming, or other files into packets that can be delivered over a network.

encouragement probes – Questions posed by salespeople to get additional information from a prospective buyer.

encryption – The scrambling of digital information to make it unreadable without the use of digital keys and/or passwords.

end matter – Also called back matter. Items placed after the main body of a document. Examples of *end matter* include appendices, epilogues, indices and *boilerplates*.

end user – The person who actually uses a product, whether or not they are the one who purchases the product.

endless chain method – A *prospecting* method in which a salesperson asks each customer called upon to suggest the names of other likely purchasers of the same product. This method is successful in establishing a key communicator's network. See *prospecting*.

endorsement – Affirmation or recommendation to purchase a particular brand of product made in advertisements by well-known personalities or experts. These third party endorsers need not have used the product. If they have, their endorsements become *testimonials*.

engage audience – To attract and hold onto an audience.

enterprise competitors – Similar firms, organizations or manufacturers competing for a consumer's business. See *competitors*.

enterprise reporting – Self-generated stories. Invent (not fabricate) the news by digging and exploring deeper.

entertainment marketing – Promotion of a product by means of movie tie-ins, endorsements by entertainment industry celebrities, or similar entertainment-related activities.

entitlement – One's belief that he/she is deserving of some particular reward or benefit.

entrepreneur – Someone who sees an opportunity and risks their own money and other resources to establish a business organization.

entry barrier – A circumstance or feature of a market, which inhibits or deters a firm from entering it. Among the greatest market entry barrier is the presence of a firmly established competitor with a significant competitive advantage. See *market entry barrier.*

entry level product – A product introduced by a manufacturer at a lower price point to attract first-time buyers. For example, Toyota® introduced the Scion®; Dell® has lower priced computers.

envelope stuffer – A direct mail advertisement or other advertising piece included with another mailed message (such as a bill). Many employers include envelope stuffers with paychecks.

envelopes and stubby pencil (ESP) – An old term for a rough method of calculating the size of the market for a particular product, based on the market's known size, geographic or population.

environmental assessment (EA) – A public document that analyzes a proposed federal action for the possibility of significant environmental impact required by The National Environmental Policy Act. If the environmental impact will be significant, the federal agency must then prepare an environmental impact statement.

environmental forecasting – Attempting to predict the nature and intensity of the microenvironmental and macroenvironmental forces likely to affect a firm's decision-making and have an impact on its performance in a given period.

environmental management – A term coined by U.S. marketing guru Philip Kotler, to describe the type of marketing activity required when it is necessary to manage elements of the firm's external environment (governments, media, pressure groups, etc) as well as the marketing variables. Kotler suggests that two more Ps must be added to the marketing mix – public relations and power. See *megamarketing.*

environmental print – Excellent technique or "entry points" for young children to begin learning to read, write and do math. Environmental print is the print of everyday life – it is everywhere: The symbols, signs, numbers and colors found in McDonald's®, Target®, Macy's®, Pizza Hut®, Wawa® on Web sites. They offer excellent entry points for young children to begin to learn to read, write, and do math.

environmental scanning – The process of examining the internal and external factors that influence a firm's operations and decision-making to help identify market opportunities and threats.

EPS file – A type of computer file. *EPS* stands for Encapsulated Post Script. EPS files are usually of high quality and are often used to send complex documents, like newsletters, to professional printing shops. (An *EPS* file uses the extension .eps).

equal time – A Federal Communications Commission requirement – when a broadcaster allows a political candidate to broadcast a paid message, opposing candidates must be offered equal paid broadcast time.

equipment-based services – Services that rely on machinery or equipment to play a significant role for delivery of that service. For example, automatic telling machines play a significant role in the delivery of banking services. See *people-based services*.

equity – Ownership interest in an asset, such as a house.

eros – Physical love – is romantic.

error rate – The percentage of mistakes (wrong items, wrong quantity, wrong address, etc.) made in shipping merchandise to customers.

escalator clause – A clause in a contract which allows adjustments to the final amount charged, taking into account price increases in component parts between acceptance of the bid and completion of the delivery, installation, etc. of the product or service.

Eskimo – A complimentary term meaning someone who comes to the aid of someone in need – there when you need him/her.

esteem needs – The desire to feel important in the eyes of others. See *Maslow's hierarchy of needs*.

estimated time enroute (ETE) – The time it will take to reach you destination based upon your present position, speed and course.

Ethernet – A networking technology that links computers together.

ethical marketing – Marketing that takes account of the moral aspects of decisions, as opposed to legal aspects.

ethics – Moral principles or beliefs governing the communication pro- fessions. See *laws*; *marketing ethics*; *morals*.

76 Tips to Succeed: Work etiquette

- Be timely. Arrive to work and meetings on time. Complete work assignments on time.
- Be polite, pleasant and courteous.
- Learn office politics – use effective listening skills to discover appropriate office behavior. Pay attention to the way things are done.
- Understand the unwritten rules of business.
  - The Boss is the Boss – right or wrong, the boss always has the last word.
  - Keep the boss informed. Good or bad, you don't want the boss to hear information mentioned from an inappropri- ate source.
  - Never go over the boss' head, without telling him/her first.
  - Make your boss look good. Promotion and opportunities will arise when you help to reach the organization's goals.
  - Appear as professional as possible. Being well groomed and clean is essential. Dress for your next job/promotion.
  - Adopt a can-do attitude. Those who accept challenges and display creativity are valuable.
  - Be flexible. By remaining flexible and implementing change you gain a reputation as a cooperative employee.
  - Give credit to everyone who made a contribution to a project or event.
  - Don't differentiate people by position or standing in a company.

The Career Center - Florida State University

ethnic marketing – Focusing marketing activities toward members of a specific minority or nationality group (a niche marketing technique). These various ethnic groups create new demand for numerous consumer items that appeal to these groups. Ethnic-specific marketing requires expertise from marketing professionals who understand the target audience, their language and their culture.

ethos – The art of speaking or writing effectively using a message that makes appeals. An *ethos*-driven documents relies on the reputation of the author.

Euro – The relatively new (during the '90s) single currency of 12 of the 15 European Union member states that make up the Economic and Monetary Union.

> # 77
> ## Techniques to Succeed:
> ### How to improve *your* customer relations
>
> • If nothing else, improve customer service.
> • Offer value: a solid balance of quality, price and selection.
> • Make it easy to get there and get around.
> • Welcome the children.
> • Don't add entertainment unless the shopping experience is already a good one.
> • Give back to the community.
> • Provide a positive and memorable experience.
> • Acknowledge that mom's influence stretches far and wide and make sure she knows you know.
>
> Nora Lee - Author - The Mom Factor - www.momfactor.com/

European economic community – A group of European nations acting as a trading block, limiting trade barriers among members and applying common tariffs to products from non-members.

evaluation – The final step in the public relations process *PR-pie – purpose, research, planning, information, evaluation* – an examination of the plan to determine if *objectives* have been met (*The Public Relations Practitioner's Playbook* – Kendall/Hunt – 2008 Chapter 7).

evaluative criteria – Features of a product, brand, supplier, service provider, etc. considered by a buyer when choosing between alternatives. Evaluative criteria may be objective or subjective.

78 Techniques to Succeed:

Customer satisfaction – Make it an experience

"Customers want to bank with you not because you give them a better rate but because you give them a better retail experience."

Vernon Hill - CEO - Commerce Bancorp - Cherry Hill, N.J.

evaluative probes – Questions asked by salespeople to increase their understanding of a prospective customer's feelings on a subject.

evaluative research – Research intended to measure the effectiveness of finished or nearly finished advertisements.

event planning – Planning of a significant occurrence or happening, or social gathering or activity for individuals, businesses or government offices.

evergreen – When used to describe a feature type news release, it means the content will not become outdated – it will last forever or at least for a very long period of time.

evil customer – Larry Seldon, professor emeritus at Columbia University, says they are customers out to cheat retailers/banks/etc. Best Buy ® calls them *demon customers*.

evoked set – Brands that a buyer is aware of, and thinks well of, when considering a purchase. Also called the consideration set.

exchange – The transfer of an object, idea, service, etc. from one person or organization to another in return for something desired. Or, when two mailers agree to share their lists via a trade rather than charging the regular fee. See *bartering*.

executive summary – Two-to three-page summary of the contents of a lengthier report.

exclusive – An interview or story opportunity presented solely to one reporter or publication and not to others. Public relations practitioners must be careful about showing favoritism. A rule of thumb is that stories are offered generally to those covering an organization. If the reporter approaches the public relations practitioner with an idea, then that story would be his or hers.

exclusive agreements – Agreements between manufacturers and middlemen in which the middlemen are granted sole rights to distribute a product within a defined territory.

exclusive assortment – An (assortment) strategy in which a reseller decides to carry the product line of only one manufacturer. See *deep assortment*; *scrambled assortment*.

exclusive dealing agreement – An arrangement in which a manufacturer prohibits a marketing intermediary from carrying competitors' products. (In some cases, this has been deemed illegal.)

exclusive distribution – Restricting the availability of a product to one particular outlet. See *distribution intensity*; *intensive distribution*; *selective distribution*.

exclusive sales territory – A region in which a distributor has been given sole rights to a manufacturer's product.

79 Technique to Succeed: Achieving goals takes planning

To maximize productivity, either in the office or at home:

- Carefully plan your day to achieve your goals. Look at your goals and estimate how long it will take to accomplish each one. Plan for some "buffer" time to allow for an unexpected interruption. This will help in setting up your schedule correctly.

- Start your day by planning out exactly what it is you want to accomplish. Be realistic, not overly ambitious. Remain aware of time and schedules and watch out for pitfalls or time traps. Another key is sorting your list by projects and then the steps that need to be worked on.

- Develop a plan that will enable you to achieve that day's goals. This can include a calendar book, a personal digital assistant or just a piece of paper. This will allow you stay on track with you goals for that day and keep your goals achievable.

- Remember to stick to your plan. A certain amount of flexibility and dexterity will always be necessary, but avoid tangents that will distract and cause a shift in focus. Keep to your plan and remember that unforeseen circumstances will no doubt arise. The key is to adapt your plan to achieve the goals without rendering it unrecognizable.

Dale Carnegie Training of Central and Southern New Jersey

exclusivity – See *exclusive agreements; exclusive distribution.*

exercise bulimia – A subset of the psychological disorder called bulimia in which a person is compelled to exercise in an effort aimed at burning calories and fat reserves to an excessive level that negatively affects their health.

expandable banners – A banner advertisement that can be expanded on a Web site after a user clicks on it or after a user moves his/her cursor over the banner.

expectancy –Value Model (of Brand Evaluation) – A model used in the study of consumer decision processes to evaluate alternative brands. This model is based on the weighting of brand attributes. In this complex approach, a consumer's beliefs about each brand's attributes are multiplied by the respective weights to produce a preference ranking of the alternatives.

expense account – A budgeted amount of money allocated to a salesperson for food, travel, accommodations, client entertainment and other items considered necessary to making sales.

expense quota – The amount budgeted for a salesperson for expenses associated with making sales. Sales managers use expense quotas as a cost control measure.

experience curve – A graphical representation of the way in which average unit cost of production decreases as output rises. It's the plotted relationship between the number of products produced and the cost per unit over time from launch. As more units are produced, the cost per unit usually declines, an effect that is partially attributable to the accumulation of experience. Also called a *learning curve.*

experience curve pricing – The pricing of a product at a lower than average cost level on the basis that costs will decrease as production and sales increase.

experiment – A research method or technique that manipulates a set of variables to test an assumption or hypotheses.

experimental diversity – Willing to try many of the disciplines that comprise a profession. In the communication profession it would include the disciplines checked off on the cover of *this* book.

experimental group – A test version of a product prior to launch. See *beta.*

experimental research method – A systematic and scientific approach to marketing research in which the researcher manipulates one or a number of variables and measures any change in other variables.

experimental variables – The variables a researcher manipulates in conducting an experiment.

expert forecasting survey – A sales forecasting method in which outside specialists or industry experts – economists, academics, management consultants, advertising executives, etc. – are asked to assist in the preparation of the sales forecast.

explanatory variables – See *experimental variables*.

exploratory research – Research conducted even before primary research is started in a marketing research study, including an informal search for material from internal, external and secondary sources, interviews and discussions with informed sources, etc. Also called informal intelligence gathering – backgrounding. See *marketing research*; *primary research*; *secondary research*.

exponential smoothing – A quantitative technique for sales forecasting using historical data weighted more heavily toward the most recent information.

export-import agent – An independent marketing intermediary bringing together buyers and sellers (marketers) from different countries and taking a commission on sales.

export marketing – The marketing of goods or services to customers overseas.

exposure – Consumers who have seen (or heard) a media vehicle, whether or not they paid attention to it (radio, television, newspapers, billboards, etc.). Also, the extent to which the target audience becomes aware of a person, activity, theme or organization from the efforts of public relations or advertising.

express warranty – A manufacturer's guarantee, stated in written or spoken words, that the product offered for sale would satisfactorily perform as intended and to the buyer's reasonable expectations.

expressive (social style) – One of four social styles (with Amiable, Analytical and Driver) commonly used to classify salespeople and their customers. *Expressives* are characterized by high assertiveness, forcefulness and high responsiveness.

80 Technique to Succeed: Retaining talented employees

Looking for ways to keep employees on board? The following tips can help to retain talented employees:

• Provide a competitive compensation and benefits package to show employees you place a fair value on their work.

• Promote activities that build rapport among staff members.

• Lend a hand and be willing to make concessions when employees encounter personal difficulties.

• Acknowledge staff contributions during a meeting or with a personal note.

• Give them a break. Consider closing early on Friday.

Tracey Fuller - Executive director of The Creative Group, a national staffing firm - www.creativegroup.com

eXtensible Markup Language (XML) – A richer, more dynamic successor to HTML utilizing HTML-type tags to structure information. XML is used for transferring data and creating applications on the Web. See *hyper-text markup language (HTML)*.

extension approach to pricing – An approach to global pricing in which a firm sets the same price for its product around the world and expects purchasers to pay whatever additional freight and import costs apply. See *adaptation approach to pricing; geocentric approach to pricing*.

extensive decision-making – See *extensive problem solving*.

extensive problem solving – Buying situations, which require considerable effort because the buyer has had no previous experience with the product or suppliers. Also called *extensive decision-making*. See *limited problem solving; routine problem solving*.

external analysis – Study of the external marketing environment, including such factors as customers, competition and social change.

external factors – Elements of the problem situation that are found outside the organization (often addressed in the limitations section of a project).

external marketing environment – Relatively uncontrollable factors outside the firm that influence its decision-making. See *internal marketing environment*.

external stimuli – Advertisements, posters, coupons, point-of-purchase materials, store displays, etc. which give rise to a drive - a motivating force sufficiently strong enough to impel a person to act. See *learning process*; *drive*.

exterior transit advertising – Advertising posters that are mounted on the sides, front, rear and top of vehicles. See *auto (car) wraps*.

extrinsic rewards – Rewards for doing a job which are external to the individual, such as wages, bonuses, incentives, fringe benefits, job promotions, etc. See *intrinsic rewards*.

extraivity – Convergence of the words extra and activity. Used when describing an extra marital affair.

extraordinary rendition – The euphemism used for sending terrorism suspects to foreign countries that practice torture for interrogation. See *renditioning*.

extreme commuter – A person who lives in one suburb and works in another suburb. The "traditional" commuter is a person who lives in a suburb and commutes to the "city" as portrayed in the early television programs "The Adventures of Ozzie & Harriet" and "Leave it to Beaver."

eye candy – Something appealing to look at. For example, depending on gender – a good looking male to a female or vice versa.

eye pupil dilation test – A physiological method of objectively pre-testing advertisements (video or print) in which involuntary eye pupil dilation is used to measure the level of interest shown by a particular consumer.

eye tracking – A research method that determines what part of an advertisement (video or print) consumers look at, by tracking the pattern of their eye movements.

eyeballs – Reference to the number of people who view, or "lay their eyes on" a certain advertisement. **E**

fabricate (fabrication) – Claiming something is true when it is false (fiction) – writing a "piece" of fiction and passing it off as if it were "real." *Plagiarize (plagiarizing)*, on the other hand, is representing someone else's work as your own.

face-to-face selling – Selling situations where the salesperson and buyer meet together (rather than use telephone, mail or the Internet) to conduct their business.

face validity – Apparent plausibility of the results of marketing research, which on the basis of logic and common sense seems to be correct.

facial challenge – The challenge of a law before it goes into effect.

facial coding – Using video of people's faces to infer things about them – like whether they want assistance, whether they are in pain, etc. Many times, *facial coding* reveals one's inner thoughts. See *body language*.

facilitating channel institution – An agency or organization, such as a bank, transport company or insurance agency, which provides specialized assistance to members of a marketing channel. The *facilitating channel institution* does not take title to the goods.

facilitating functions – One of the three kinds of functions performed by intermediaries in a marketing channel. *Facilitating functions* refer to any activity that makes it easier to complete a task. See *logistical functions*; *transactional functions*.

facings – The number of billboards used for a particular advertisement.

fact checker – The editor responsible for authenticating facts in an article or book.

81 Tips to Succeed: From the late Frank Perdue – 'Not all chickens are alike' – or *fronting* your brand

By establishing Perdue® as the brand of chickens that was different from all others, Frank Perdue's Perdue Farms Inc. increased sales from $56 million in 1970 to $1.2 billion in 1991. At one point in time, telephone surveys showed that 97 percent of people asked to name a brand of chicken came up with Perdue. By putting a brand name on an inseparable product like chickens (Chiquita® did it with bananas and Morton's® did with salt) it set the product apart and made Perdue a household name.

Ed McCabe, a copywriter at Scali, McCabe & Stoves believed that chickens could be "hawked" but that the spots had to be funny. Frank Perdue was skeptical that a man with a deadpan expression and a funny-sounding voice, a balding, big-nosed man who looked a bit like a chicken himself, could make his brand into a household name. He not only did that, but he started a trend that continues today – having a CEO or some other company "face" or "voice" front a product or service.

Philadelphia Inquirer, April 2, 2005

fact checking (back checking) – Much more than verification. Comparing with the record. It is being certain that even though secondary research may be confirmed, at times, it is important and even imperative that fact checkers go deeper to be certain primary research numbers are correct – comparing with the record. *Back checking* is making certain that quotes and information other than numerical facts are correct.

fact Sheet – Usually a page that provides a list of facts or statistics about a particular topic that allows media to quickly grasp a particular issue, situation or "snapshot" look at a company, product or service. Many times, fact sheets are included in a media or press kit.

factory outlet – A retail store that sells the products of one manufacturer, usually at very low prices.

factory pack – A premium (giveaway) attached to a product, in or on the packaging.

factually based – What is said is the truth, based on actual numbers and results.

fad – A product or *fashion* that comes quickly to the attention of an eager public, achieves peak sales in a relatively short time, and then rapidly declines in popularity. It is a popular product with a particularly short life cycle. See *fashion*.

fail-safe – Guaranteed not to fail. Capable of compensating automatically and safely for a failure – a mechanism or power source programmed to kick in, should a failure occur.

fair use – Using copyrighted work without obtaining permission or consent from the copyright holder for purposes of critique, education or research.

fair use in commentary – Quoting a relatively few lines from a copyrighted work such as in a music review, summarizing and quoting from a medical article on an ailment, copying a few paragraphs from a news article for use by a teacher or student in a lesson, or copying a portion of a magazine article for use in a related court case.

fairness doctrine – Until the mid-1980s, a Federal Communications Commission policy that required broadcasters to provide time for opposing viewpoints any time they broadcast an opinion supporting one side of a controversial issue. This ended during the Reagan administration.

fake interview – A job interview held when a company advertises a non-existent position in its firm hoping to attract personnel from competing firms. The aim of this unethical tactic is usually to obtain information about competitors.

familiarity scale – A scaling device for measuring a target audience's awareness and knowledge on an opinion survey. Responses are commonly recorded on a five-stage scale: 1. Never Heard of It 2. Heard of It 3. Know a Little 4. Know a Fair Amount 5. Know It Well. See *favorability scale*.

family/ad family – Also called advertisement campaign. A collection of one or more ad creatives.

family brand – A brand name that is used for more than one product in the same line – a family of products. Examples would be the Ford® family of cars and Revlon® cosmetics.

family life cycle – A series of stages through which the typical family passes, including bachelor stage, young marrieds (relatively newlyweds, *full nest*, *empty nest* and sole survivor.

fashion – A product that is popular at the moment. *Fashions* tend to follow recurring life cycles. See *fad*.

fashion marketing – Developing, analyzing and implementing sales strategies focused on current *fashion* trends. *Fashion marketing* requires an eye for style and a head for business that can move *fashions* from the designers' showrooms to retail sales floors. *Fashion marketing* requires a degree of *cultural diversity*, which is important to developing marketing campaigns that span across divergent cultures. Successful professionals in *fashion marketing* understand the importance of strong *branding* and creating a desirable product image, as well as recognizing the patterns of *consumers* and their unique shopping behavior.

FAST marketing – Focused Advertising Sampling Technique – an approach concentrating promotions into a short space of time to saturate the market.

fast moving consumer goods (FMCG) – such as snacks and other packaged food, beverages, toiletries and tobacco.

fast-tracking – Many aspects of a project worked on simultaneously rather than in an articulated, systematic order. This, if properly done, can help complete the project quicker – once all the "parts" are put together.

favorability scale – A scaling device for measuring a target audience's attitudes and opinions towards an issue, a company, products, etc. Responses are commonly recorded on a five-stage (Likert) scale: 1. Very Unfavorable 2. Somewhat Unfavorable 3. Indifferent 4. Somewhat Favorable 5. Very Favorable. Also called *image analysis*. See *familiarity scale*.

fax preference service (FPS) – A database of businesses and others who have elected not to receive unsolicited direct marketing faxes.

fear appeals in advertising – Advertising messages, which use fear as their focus. This strategic technique is used in public service announcements, such as those seeking to discourage smoking, drinking and driving, etc. See *emotional appeals in advertising*; *rational appeals in advertising*.

"fear, uncertainty and doubt" (FUD) – Using positioning of one's own products or services to cast fear, uncertainty and doubt on the

82 Tips to Succeed: If you think you'll be fired

The writing is on the wall: You're getting fired.

Maybe you've done your darnedest to keep it from happening, but there's no denying it – the pink slip is coming.

You're mad. You're devastated. You're depressed. You think of just quitting. Maybe you should snoop in computer files to see what is being said about you.

Here are some important rules of an "imminent termination," including:

- **Documenting performance:** It's always a good idea to keep personal hard copies of memos, e-mail or reports showing the work you did for a company. When facing termination, however, it may be against the employer's rules for you to take home any-thing pertaining to your employment, and that includes your work records. Showing great care in this area – taking anything that you do not have the authority to have "could jeopardize your ability to recover full damages at trial" should you decide to sue your former employer.

In case you are not allowed to take anything home, make a log of key documents relating to your employment, especially those showing a good performance. Make sure you note date, parties, subject, content and location.

Do not make illegal tape recordings, which will be thrown out of court anyway. Do not go near the boss's written or computer files – any such action is grounds for instant termination.

- **Keeping an events diary:** As soon as you feel your job is threat-ened, begin keeping a written chronological account of your time at a company, with lots of detail. At the top of the page, write "to my attorney," which will make it privileged information. Write down when you were hired, how you performed, when things started to sour, why you think it happened and significant dates that led to the problems.

- **Listing witnesses:** These are people you believe could help your case. Get full names, addresses and telephone numbers.

- **Starting a job search:** Don't wait until you have the pink slip in hand. Start making contacts and sending out resumes.

- **Doing your job:** Don't slack off or sulk. Perform to the best of your

The ABCs of Strategic Communication

ability, and don't give the boss any more reasons to let you go.

- **Schmoozing:** Now is the time to get along as best you can with those around you. You want to leave the company with a good reputation. Don't leave co-workers holding the bag.

- **Never quitting:** Those who quit not only lose income, but put unemployment benefits or future legal action in jeopardy.

Anita Bruzzese - Gannett News Service - April 4, 2005
From: Richard C. Busse, Esq. - Portland, Ore. - *Fired, Laid-off or Forced Out* (Sphinx)

competitor's. An example might be a Toyota® commercial that begins with a dad shopping for a safe car for his daughter. The salesman whispers, "You might want to go up the street to buy her a Toyota."

feature – A product's prominent or distinctive aspect, quality or characteristic.

feature article (story) – A human-interest story. Features can amplify a news story or stand alone. A newspaper or magazine article that discusses and interprets an event or trend, as opposed to spot reporting. Many times, features are softer news, sidebars (related to a main story) and might not be as objective as a news story.

feature modification – A change made to any feature of a product to make it safer, more useful, more efficient or more valuable to a purchaser. Also called *functional modification*.

features – Prominent or distinctive characteristics of a product's use, construction or design. Also referred to as attributes.

features, advantages and benefits analysis – Marketing plans need to understand these concepts to develop effective marketing programs. People often confuse features and benefits. For example, in an automobile, air bags are features that produce the benefit of greater safety. Advantages fall in between. Features, whose advantages are communicated properly, are recognized as benefits to the end user.

features and benefits selling – A selling style in which a salesperson relates each feature of the product being presented to a particular benefit that the feature will deliver to the buyer.

Federal Communications Commission (FCC) – The federal agency responsible for regulating the broadcast industry.

Federal Educational Rights and Privacy Act (FERPA) – A Federal law that protects the privacy of student education records. The law applies to all schools that receive funds under an applicable program of the U.S. Department of Education. *FERPA* gives parents certain rights with respect to their children's education records. These rights transfer to the student when he or she reaches the age of 18 or attends a school beyond the high school level. Students to whom the rights have transferred are "eligible students."

Federal Trade Commission (FTC) – The federal agency primarily responsible for regulating advertising.

Fedspeak – Coined by Alan Greenspan, former Federal Reserve chairman, meaning – that "certain answers – no matter how you phrase them, no matter what you do – have (stock) market effects."

feedback – The mechanism in the communication process, which allows the sender to monitor and evaluate the receiver's response to a message. See *communication process*.

fees – A negotiated price, usually based on hourly billable rates, for the time a staff works on client projects, generally invoiced in regular monthly installments and monitored through daily time records. Out of pocket expenses are billed separately.

fiber screeching reporters – When television (or radio) reporters allow themselves to become part of the story they are reporting rather than allowing the pictures or sounds to tell the story. They allow emotionalism and outrage to takeover. Some say it is an aggressiveness – manipulative gimmickry – unlike the days of Edward R. Murrow. For example, during Hurricane Katrina in 2005, media personally took exception with response and rather than just reporting it, gave their personal observations rather than using a *third party validator*. See *hectoring*.

fiber-to-the-premises (FTTP) – Technology that replaces traditional copper telephone wires – to deliver voice, data and video applications to users. Verizon® calls their fiber optic network technology Fios®. It is between three and 20 times faster than DSL.

F-I-C-A – (Researcher Earl) Newsome's Principles of Persuasion – Familiarity (audience, message, surrogates); Identification (rewards/benefits); Clarity (avoid jargon/passive verbs); Action (ask for behavior/what you want) try! buy! sell! (relate).

fictitious pricing – The unethical, deceptive and possibly illegal practice of announcing a price reduction (e.g. "now $19.99, formerly $39.99") when, in fact, there has been no reduction at all.

field marketing –The practice of sending representatives to retail outlets to build brand and supporting sales. *Field marketing* might include in-store promotions, set up point-of-sale displays, and ensuring that products are displayed to best advantage.

field research – Research gathered personally by firm or organization representatives. See *primary research.*

field sales manager – A sales manager whose prime responsibility is for the supervision of the sales force in its outside selling activities. *Field sales managers* usually have only minimal involvement in the internal, administrative sales management operations.

field selling – Face-to-face sales calls made by company representatives on consumers and other customers in their homes or places of business.

fighting brand – A low-priced manufacturer's brand sold with minimal advertising and promotional dollars. The low-priced brand is used to compete with other brands, dealers' own brands and generics. Also called a *price brand.*

figurehead – A head or chief in name only – a leader with no real power.

filesharing – refers to peer-to-peer technology that allows one Internet user to access files of another Internet user through a public or company directory. Napster pioneered filesharing, providing a place for peers to share files.

fill (filler) – Short news stories used by newspaper editors and broadcast news directors to fill in available space on an editorial content page or in a newscast. Television and radio consider them ready-to-run segments.

fill-in – Information inserted into a form letter to personalize it. Examples may include the recipient's name, address or information about past purchases. This can be done through a digital mail merge.

financial leverage – A measure of the extent to which a firm uses debt in its total capital structure. The higher the debt, the more leveraged is the firm. Leverage is calculated by dividing total assets by equity.

financial resources – The availability of money by an organization in the form of cash, securities, loans, etc.

83

Tips to Succeed:
The right way to get a favor

Many people, when they need a favor, frantically call long forgotten contacts and ask for, or even demand, help. Asking for favors, if done wrong, can strain or even break a relationship. Effective networking is the proactive solution.

If you think ahead and network well, asking for a favor can be an easy, natural thing to do. Sometimes you may find that you don't even need to ask! Here are a few easy ways to maintain your relationships so that favors come easily:

1. Get organized
   - Keep track of your contacts whichever way works best for you. You can use computer databases, Pads or even index cards
   - Keep track of birthdays, anniversaries and other miscellaneous information
   - Know your contacts' needs, such as information, jobs and other contacts

2. Keep in touch
   - Review your contact list regularly and make a follow up plan
   - Send notes and cards on occasions such as birthdays and holidays
   - Regularly call and set up lunch meetings or dinner appointments

3. Nurture mutually beneficial relationships
   - Send any helpful information to your contacts
   - Connect your contacts with others who can help them
   - Use your skills to help others

If you care for your network of friends, colleagues and acquaintances, it will be your best resource. Whether the favor you need is information, a job referral, technical help or even more clients, the best solution is a strong network. Most importantly, always remember to say thank you with an e-mail, a hand-written note or a gift.

March 2005
420 E. 51st Street · Suite 12D · New York, NY 10022
e-mail: info@mybusinessrelationships.com

The ABCs of Strategic Communication

F

financial risk – Concern in the buyer's mind that the product being considered for purchase is too expensive, or will be a waste of money. See *risk*.

fine bore – Used in describing one's virtues. For example, presidential candidate John Kerry has the virtues of a *fine bore*. He is steady, persevering, deliberate, unflappable and safe. (David Brooks – New York Times – July 27, 2004).

fire in the belly –A slang term meaning passion. A powerful desire or emotion.

fire wall – Computer program used to prevent hackers from embedding a hard drive. Also, in broadcasting, preventing broadcast mega owners from dictating what topics talk show hosts may discuss. Fire walls allow host certain freedom unless previously agreed to.

fire proof – Fact checking to assure there is no possibility of legal action over possible libel or slander proof.

First Amendment – The first article of the American Bill of Rights, guaranteeing Americans freedom of religion, speech, press, assembly and petition.

first bottom line – Part of Pat Jackson's *Double Bottom Line (Public Relations) Theory*. First *Bottom Line*: An organization's successful efforts to please its publics before and during doing business with it. A) Who knows what's in the public interest better than the public relations professional? B) Who knows if a public is satisfied with an organization's image, management and motive toward the public better than the public relations professional? C) Once this essential relationship is established, the company can do business with its publics. *Second Bottom Line*: A) The actual acceptance of the products or services by the public. B) The sale from the fruit of the relationship in the first bottom line leads to profits. See *Double Bottom Line Theory*.

first-day story – A story published for the first time and dealing with something that has just happened, as distinguished from a "follow-up" story.

first mover advantage – The advantage gained by the first company that enters a certain market. It's an accepted belief that a company that enters a particular market first is able to increase sales quickly and can reduce the average cost of the product, over other competitors. This allows the first company to have more flexibility with pricing, either reducing the price to make it less attractive for new entrants (increasing barriers to entry) or increasing the margin and therefore profit while prices remain fixed. The additional profit can then be used for further innovation. Unless competitors move quickly, it can be difficult to attract those customers away from the first marketer.

first mover disadvantage – Factors that can turn first mover advantages into weaknesses. They include resolution of technological uncertainty; resolution of strategic uncertainty and the free-rider effect (others try to duplicate based on the leader's success).

first reader – Term used for the first person, other than a document's (usually a book or lengthy magazine article) writer to read the first draft.

first responder – Designee to be first on the scene, whether emergency personnel, media crews, public relations counselors, etc.

fiscal year – Standard accounting practice allows the accounting year to begin in any month. Fiscal years are numbered according to the year in which they end. For example, a fiscal year ending in February of 2009 is fiscal 2009 or FY 2009, even though most of the year takes place in 2008.

fishyback – A term used in the distribution of goods to refer to a system of transportation when goods are shipped by transferring the containers from truck to ship. See *piggyback*.

five Ws – The five essential elements of a story: Who, What, When, Where and Why. Often a sixth element is added: "How."

fixed cost – Running costs that take time to wind down – usually taxes, rent, overhead, salaries, etc. Technically, *fixed costs* are those that the business would continue to pay even if it went bankrupt. In practice, *fixed costs* are usually considered the running costs and are an important assumption for developing a break-even analysis. The standard break-even formula estimates a break-even point of sales based on per-unit cost, profit margin and the number of units that must be sold to break even.

fixed position – A radio or television commercial or print advertisement aired at a specific time or placed on a particular page and location.

fixed pricing – A traditional method of media pricing where rates are published and are applied equally to all advertisers.

fixed rate – An interest rate that does not fluctuate with general market conditions.

fixed-sum-per-unit method – A method of determining an advertising budget, based directly on the number of units sold.

flack – Commonly used term for public relations representatives – slang, not to be taken so seriously. A homage to publicist Gene Flack.

84 Tips to Succeed: View your failures as a learning experience – or – turning a stumbling block into a stepping stone

"What's the key to being a successful entrepreneur?" Change how you think about failure.

Failure is the "F word" of business – It's not polite to mention it. After all, failure is what happens to other people, right? But what happens when we ourselves fail? We either try to quickly forget the experience, or we wallow in self-doubt and recrimination.

If you're in business, sooner or later, you're going to have failures. But sometimes, these "failures" can turn out to be fortunate. They force you to re-examine your goals, decisions, methods. Then, you can choose to take a different – better – path.

Here's how the best entrepreneurs deal with failure:

• Redefine it. Experienced entrepreneurs make a failure a learning experience.

• Analyze it. If – when – you fail, take a close look at the causes. After each and every setback, big or small, take a clear cold look at what happened.

• Depersonalize it. Stop kicking yourself; everybody fails. While you must analyze your mistakes, you won't learn anything if you're too busy beating up on yourself.

• Change it. Remind yourself of what you learned and actively try to change your behavior. Be patient and forgiving because change takes time.

• Get over it. Move on. Don't dwell on your successes or on your failures. You've got a life to live, and each day is precious. So, like the old song says, "Pick yourself up, brush yourself off, and start all over again."

Rhonda Abrams - www.rhondaworks.com/

flag – The banner across the top of the front page and some sections of a newspaper announcing the newspaper's name, volume and number, date, and section number. Also, an area on a product label, which interrupts the design to announce a special offer or similar promotion. See *banner*; *masthead*; *nameplate*.

flame – An inflammatory opinion or criticism distributed by e-mail or posted on an Internet newsgroup.

flanker brand – A brand introduced into a market by a company which already has an established place to increase competition and, following the Harvard University model, expand the overall market in a product category.

flanking attack – A competitive marketing strategy where one company attacks another in a weak spot, commonly by paying maximum attention to either a geographic region or a market segment where the rival or competition might be under-performing.

flanking defense – A competitive marketing strategy in which the market leader attempts to identify and strengthen its own weak points - commonly geographic areas or market segments where it is under-performing. They take this strategy to prevent a smaller rival from mounting an attack against it.

flanking strategy – See *flanking attack*; *flanking defense*.

flash – Animation technology used on the Internet.

flash drive – Computer memory, which connects to a computer's *USB port* – also called pen, *thumb, jump, smart* or *key drive*. It is an enormously powerful tool that has changed the concept of "personal" computer. It is an inexpensive digital storehouse. Also known as a *digital backpack* and *TravelDrive®*.

flash mob – A large group of people who gather in a usually predetermined location, perform some brief action, and then quickly disperse. Many times, individuals are contacted via e-mail or text message, told what to do, do it and disperse soon after.

flat rate – A media rate that allows for no discounts.

Flesch-Kincaid – Designed to indicate how difficult a reading passage is to understand. There are two *Flesch-Kincaid* tests: the Flesch Reading Ease, and the *Flesch-Kincaid* Grade Level. Both these systems were devised by Rudolf Flesch. See *Gunning Fog Index* (See Technique 100).

flexible method (flexible budget) – Not necessarily an accepted method by most finance people. However, some organizations do allow use of this method. Example: As time passes, the department head may decide to increase or a decrease projected line items in the budget to accomplish the best possible job of managing the public relations function in light of the current events. However, some organizations are allowing (projected) bottom lines in budgets (based on some of the above techniques) to be adjusted during the fiscal year. Those (projected) budgets are evaluated periodically and adjusted according to a number of criteria set forth by upper management. It should be noted that public (government) agencies may not unilaterally alter a budget once it is approved.

flexible pricing (multiple pricing) – A pricing method where the price charged for some consumer shopping goods and specialty goods, and for many industrial products, is open to negotiation between buyer and seller. It is also known as multiple pricing and variable pricing.

flier – *Associated Press* style for a one-sided publication that presents a single message. See *flyer*.

flighting – A media schedule that involves more advertising at certain times and less advertising during other time periods. Or, the scheduling pattern of an advertising schedule.

flimsies – News and other material printed on paper products and enclosed with such items as bank statements, pay checks, etc. See *insert*.

flip – Purchase a business or other property, keep for a "short" time and resell it at a profit – turn it over.

floating ads – An advertisement or ads on top of the Web page's normal content, appearing to float over the top of the page.

floor price – A price, usually imposed by law, below which market prices are not permitted to fall under. See *price ceiling*.

flop – Printing a picture backwards to enhance the layout. For example, a headshot that may be "looking" off the page is flopped to drive the reader onto the page.

flow chart – A *flow chart* (also spelled flow-chart and flowchart) is a schematic representation of a process. Commonly used in business/economic presentations to help the audience visualize the content better, or to find flaws in the process. Examples include instructions for a bicycle's assembly, an attorney outlining a case's timeline, diagram of an automobile plant's work flow, the decisions to be taken on a tax form, etc.

fluctuating demand – Demand that rises and falls sharply in response to changing economic conditions and consumer spending patterns.

flyer – A promotional leaflet or mailing piece. See flier.

focal point – The first element in a layout that the eye sees.

85 Tips to Succeed: Family businesses need to have rules, too

Here are some tips for working with family members:

- Write a business plan describing your mission, documenting assets and defining roles. It should contain:
  - Goal
  - Objectives
  - Strategies
  - Tactics
- Agree upon succession.
- Establish exit options for family members wanting to leave the business.
- When hiring your child, be clear about expectations, give feedback, expect mistakes and allow time for learning and growth.
- Encourage different points of view and make an effort to discuss and understand them.
- Remember the shared family bond and the shared commitment to success.
- Don't use sarcasm or belittle family members.
- Institute "rules of behavior" for meetings.
- When a solution has not been agreed upon within an established time, table that item for later discussion. If that fails, seek outside help and advice.
- Leave work at the office.

Family Business Institute
www.Entrepreneur.com
Family Business magazine

focus group (discussion) –
Sometimes referred to as focus
panel. A qualitative public
relations/marketing research
technique where an independent facilitator interviews (leads
discussion) of a small group of
consumers (six to 12) from the
target audience in an informal
setting to get a reaction to an
issue, new product, brand
name, advertising or other
communication efforts. The
objective is to get the group
talking in a conversational format so researchers can observe
the dialogue and interactions
among participants. Also
referred to as a *customer panel*.
See q*ualitative marketing
research*.

focus group interview –
A qualitative, non-scientific
research method that brings
together a small group of consumers who are asked questions about a product, service
or advertising, under the guidance of a trained facilitator -
whose job is to stimulate
group members to talk candidly about the topics at hand.
Also referred to as a *customer
panel*.

FOIA – Freedom of
Information Act.

fold – An advertisement or
other content that is viewable as soon as the Web page loads. One does
not have to scroll down (or sideways) to see it.

folio – The page number on a publication (top or bottom). It could contain such other information as a title (name of newspaper) and date.

follow-the-leader strategy – Decisions and actions taken by a firm, which chooses to follow the market leader as an alternative to challenging it. This is a reactive approach also known as a "me-too" strategy. It minimizes the risk of retaliation, which could result from an attack, direct or indirect, on the market leader's share.

follow up – To contact a journalist after an initial phone call, e-mail, fax or news release to ask if the reporter needs additional information.

follow-up – A news article or news story that results directly from a previous article or story. Also, the vital final stage in the selling process. It's when a salesperson calls a client after the ordered goods have been supplied to check that everything is satisfactory – a key to *relationship marketing*.

follower role – A company satisfied to maintain its existing market share behind an established market leader. See *market challenger*; *market leader*; *market nicher*.

font – A typeface style, such as Helvetica, Times New Roman, Comic Sans, **Cooper Black**, etc., in a single size. A single font includes all 26 letters, along with punctuation, numbers and other characters. Also, computer or Internet typeface (though it's technically interchangeable with "typeface," font actually means a specific instance of a typeface including point size, pitch (width) and spacing. A type family would include all variables of the font: normal, **bold**, *italics*, etc.).

food embossing – Stamping an advertising message on a morsel of food (candy, pizza, potato, etc.). Hershey® Bars are embossed.

food stylist – A person who prepares food products for photo shoots, advertising and commercials.

foot soldier – A salesperson, whose primary responsibility is to inform clients about new products. See *academic detailer; detailer; sales calls.*

footer – The type located at the very bottom of a page. Could include chapter title, newsletter name, page number, etc.

foothold firm – A company whose products serve market segments too small to be of interest to firms with larger shares of the market. Also a small but profitable segment of a market unlikely to attract competitors.

Also called market specialists, threshold firms or foothold firms. See *market challenger*; *market nicher*.

footprint – Retail store buildings that have a similar "look." For example, McDonald's® and Commerce Bank® buildings have a "logo look." Concept must fit into company's footprint is another one to say it.

force field (conflict) analysis – A useful technique for looking at all the forces for and against a decision – a specialized method for weighing the pros and cons. Also called *conflict analysis*. (See example of force field analysis in *The Public Relations Practitioners Playbook* – Kendall/Hunt – 2008)

forecasting – Calculation of future events and performance including predicting future variables, such as the level of sales in a given period, environmental factors that will influence the firm's performance, etc.

foreground radio – A term used in reference to pre-recorded or live radio programs featuring music and commercial announcements broadcast direct to stores where the advertised merchandise is available. Also called specialty radio.

foreign currency exchange rate – The price of one country's currency expressed in terms of the currency of another country. Many newspaper business pages print this daily. It is always available via the Internet.

foreign market entry – A firm or company's expansion by entering an overseas market. Four possible methods of entry into an overseas market are by exporting, licensing, joint venturing or direct ownership.

foreseeability doctrine – The notion under product liability laws that a manufacturer has the responsibility to foresee how a product might be misused and warn consumers accordingly.

form utility – The value given to a product considering the materials and components, which comprise it to make the finished product. See *synergy*; *utility*.

formal product – A product's features, including styling, quality level, features, brand name and packaging. Also called the *tangible product*.

formal (scientific or quantitative) research methods – Rigorous use of the principles of scientific investigation such as the rules of empirical observation, random sampling in surveys, comparison of results against statistical standards and provision for replication of results. Research that provides objective and systematic data gathered from scientifically representative samples. (Employs the scientific method.)

formal training – Training given in a classroom setting as opposed to that given in the field. See *on-the-job training*.

formative research – Usually not scientific. Formative research such as focus groups and mall-intercept interviews with consumers are used to help test messages and materials designed to motivate target audiences. Considered a critical step in crafting research questions.

formula approach – Either the *diffusion process* (awareness, interest, trial, evaluation, adoption or rejection) or *AIDA* concept (awareness, interest, desire, action) used by public relations practitioners and other communicators as a guide to taking targeted audiences from one stage of the acceptance or buying process to the next; also called the *mental states approach*. See *AIDA*.

"formula" businesses – Retail stores, restaurants, hotels and other establishments that are required by contract to adopt standardized services, methods of operation, decor, uniforms, architecture or other features virtually identical to businesses located in other communities. Examples include McDonalds®, Burger King®, Wendy's® and such independent super markets as Shop Rite®.

formula marketing – A public relations or marketing approach that relies heavily on conventional wisdom rather than researching and trying anything innovative.

forward buy (futures) – The placement of an inventory purchase order earlier than required, in order to take advantage of a special price offer, or similar opportunity.

forward integration – Growth strategy firms use for seeking ownership of, or some measure of control over, its distribution systems. See *backward integration*; *horizontal integration*.

four As (American Association of Advertising Agencies) – A non-profit trade association dedicated to improving and strengthening the advertising agency business. Read more at *www.aaaa.org*. Also, accountability, accreditation, assessment and articulation.

four-color process – A printing process that combines differing amounts of each of the four colors (red, yellow, blue and black) to provide a full-color print. See *spot color*.

four Ms (Money, Material, Machine and Manpower) – traditional framework for viewing resources available to a business, which can be useful when designing a public relations or marketing plan.

four Ps – Originally stands for Product, Price, Place (i.e., distribution), and Promotion. This is also known as the marketing mix. Rowan University's M. Larry Litwin, APR, Fellow PRSA, has expanded that to Litwin's Nine Ps – the original four plus Public Relations, Policy, Politics, Positioning and Packaging (last opportunity to change consumer behavior and persuade consumer or client to make the purchase).

fourth estate – The term is used to refer to the fourth branch of government, mass media – particularly those covering and reporting the news. Historically, the fourth estate has been viewed as the public's watchdogs.

fractional ad – A display advertisement that occupies less than a full page in a publication.

fragment (fragmentation) – Segmenting audiences is no longer enough. Audiences must be fragmented – *demographically, psychographically* and *geodemographically* – niched or narrowly defined and identified as an audience to be persuaded or convinced. Known for years as *ISPR* – identify, segment, profile, rank – the accepted audience identification and ranking method has now become *IFPR* – identify, fragment, profile, rank.

frame – A specific marked area in a publication that surrounds text or an image. It is also called a border.

frame-by-frame tests – Tests that evaluate consumers' reactions to the individual scenes that unfold in the course of a television commercial.

frame rate – The number of frames of video displayed during a given time. The higher the frame rate, the higher the image quality.

franchise-building sales promotions – (Consumer) Sales promotions that include a selling message along with a give away such as free samples or premiums related to the product. (Consumer) Sales promotions, which are not "franchise-building," include price-off (cents or dollars) packs, contests and sweepstakes, and premiums not related to the product. See *consumer franchise.*

franchise extension – The use of a well-known brand name to launch a new product of an unrelated category, into the market. Also called *brand extension* and *line extension.*

87 Techniques to Succeed:
Try a charette design

Charettes began as an intense effort to solve any architectural problem within a limited time. However, there is no rule stating public relations counselors can't use them. In fact, charettes strongly resemble focus panels and in many cases – town meetings. From a creative standpoint, a charette can be divided into three portions:

1. LISTEN. Listen to what the financial backers, realtors, owners, and other specialists have to suggest. Work together with them to come to an understanding about the project, what their goals and limitations are, and how these might fit with your ideas.

2. ENVISION. Imagine together all of these various considerations to come up with a realistic and creative proposal which will be interesting while at the same time financially, environmentally, and otherwise feasible.

3. DRAW FAST! The ability to work with creative team who can bring ideas to a tangible design sketch quickly, allows for instant communication ... a picture is worth a thousand words!

How a charette facilitates the process – much like focus panels, which are a tactic of a public relations plan. There are two main advantages to working in the context of a charette.

1. A charette operates in a highly collaborative atmosphere. Instead of an architect (or PR practitioner) taking ideas and plans and going away to develop them on his or her own (one-way), a charette allows for the participation of everyone involved with the project, resulting in a highly charged and creative atmosphere. The inclusion of many points of view results in well-rounded and realistic proposals, with everyone satisfied that they were able to contribute.

2. Charettes are fast, and relatively inexpensive. In the initial stages of a project, the venture is necessarily highly speculative. It is important to keep costs at bay, while also moving forward quickly to take advantage of changing situations and often critical deadlines.

www.masterplanning.com/masterplanning/charette.html
www.doverkohl.com/writings_images/charrettes_for_NU_in_FL.htm

The ABCs of Strategic Communication

franchised position – An advertisement position in a periodic publication (e.g., centerfold) to which an advertiser is given a permanent or long-term right of use or exclusivity.

franchising – The selling of a license by the owner (franchiser) to a third party (franchisee) permitting the sale of a product or service for a specified period. The agreement usually involves a common brand and marketing plan and format. The supplier grants the franchisee the right to sell a product in return for some percentage of the total sales. The franchiser, typically, designs and provides buildings and equipment, management advice and marketing assistance to the franchisee, who agrees to operate according to the franchiser's general rules.

88 Tips to Succeed: You are hired for a reason

Your public relations approach should contain *your* fingerprint.

CBS Sunday Morning

free-alongside-ship pricing – A pricing approach in which the manufacturer pays the freight cost to the docks. Other costs associated with loading and shipping are paid by the purchaser. See *geographical pricing*.

free associations – A data collection method in which respondents are asked to supply the word or idea that first comes to mind in response to a word or phrase given by the researcher. The technique is used to further understand and plan branding, shopping, advertising, etc. Also, called *open-ended method*.

free dispersal of knowledge – Benjamin Franklin's belief that information should be shared and often. He often gave only humorous acknowledgement of his sources. Franklin constantly attacked the notion of the ownership of authorship. See *plagiarism*.

free-form presentation – A selling approach that does not rely upon any set formula or method. See *formula approach*.

free-in-store pricing – A pricing method in which the producer is responsible for all freight and delivery costs. Ordered goods are delivered freight free to the customer. See *geographical pricing*.

free-in-the-mail premium – A type of sales promotion where consumers are offered a gift (e.g., rebate) which is sent to them by mail in return for proof of purchase of the product.

free market – A market place with minimum government involvement.

free merchandise – A type of trade sales promotion in which resellers are given a quantity of merchandise free of charge in return for an order of a specified size. See *trade sales promotion*.

free on board (FOB) pricing – A pricing method in which a producer bears only the costs involved of delivery of goods "free-on-board" to a local carrier's dispatch point. It's at that time the title for the goods passes to the purchaser, who is responsible for the remainder of the freight charge. See *geographical pricing*.

free samples – Products distributed free of charge to prospective buyers to promote future purchases. See *samples*.

free-standing insert (FSI) – An advertisement or group of ads loosely inserted – not bound – in a newspaper or other print publication, on pages that contain only the ads and are separate from any editorial or entertainment matter. They are called FSIs because they can be freely removed from the publication.

free-standing retailer – A retail store, not located in a shopping complex with other retailers, having its own premises and parking area. Also called a stand alone.

freelance writer – A person who sells his or her articles to a publication without a long-term commitment – usually on a per project basis.

freelancer – A self-employed or contracted service provider to public relations departments and agencies. A person who sells his or her articles to a publication without a long-term commitment – usually on a per project basis. Also called a *vendor*.

freight absorption pricing – A pricing method in which the manufacturer bears some or all of the freight costs involved in transporting goods to the customer. See *delivered pricing*.

freight charges – Transportation costs for shipping goods from producer to customer.

89 Tips to Succeed: Workplace relationships

A leader, whether in or outside of the office, must be able to understand the different types of personalities on his or her team.

Here are some tips to help strengthen professional and personal relationships:

- Don't criticize, condemn or complain. Avoid being negative and offer only honest and sincere appreciation when warranted.

- Always show you're happy to see someone. A pleasant or warm greeting, especially after some length of time, is a particularly effective approach.

- Be a good listener. Encourage others to talk more about themselves, reaffirming your sincere interest. When you do speak, always try to talk in terms of the other person's interests. This is an excellent way to redirect a conversation should you want to move on to a different subject.

- Never forget that people are always impressed when you remember their name. Nothing can strengthen a relationship like showing you are interested enough in a person to recollect his or her name. It adds an effective personal dimension to any relationship. And saying the person's name when you meet them is exactly what they want to hear.

- Make the other person feel important. Use a sincere and honest manner to establish a sense of worth and importance. Remember that everyone has some quality or skill that makes him or her important. When you recognize this in others, point it out in a proactive manner – like catching them doing something good.

Dale Carnegie Training of Central and Southern New Jersey

freight forwarders (FFs) – Firms specializing in supplying transportation services for goods. The larger FFs (UPS, DTS, cross-country haulers), buy large volumes of land, sea, air and pipeline transportation at low rates, which enable them to offer attractive rates to small businesses whose products they combine into large shipments.

frequency – Number of times an average person or home is exposed (sees or hears an advertisement) to a media vehicle (or group of vehicles) within a given time period. It is also the position of a television or radio station's broadcast signal within the electromagnetic spectrum.

90

Tips to Succeed:Dressing for work

TIPS FOR MEN

If you're looking for a classic suit:

Gray, blue or black suit with a white dress shirt.

Do not experiment with the color of the shirt; you can add color through the tie.

Ties can have a simple pattern with basic colors like blue, gold or red. Do not wear pastels or try the monochromatic shirt and tie look if you're meeting someone, like a hiring manager or a client, for the first time.

Stay away from tan-colored suits or bold pin stripes.

TIPS FOR WOMEN

Women have more options when dressing for work than men. Pay attention to four key items: fit, accessories, color and style.

Fit – Do your clothes fit properly? It doesn't matter how expensive an item is – if it is too tight or too big, it isn't going to look good on you.

Accessories – Are your accessories too big, too bold or too bright? Your accessories should be good-quality items that add to your outfit without overpowering it.

Color – Are you wearing clothing that is noticed because of its color? Darker colors convey more authority than lighter ones. Bright colors can "shout," and you should decide whether you want to shout or not.

Style – Are your clothes very stylish or part of the latest fashion trend? If so, they will be noticed. This may be appropriate for your social life but less so for work.

Neil Rosenthal - Owner - Executive Clothiers
Barbara Pachter - Pachter & Associates - Cherry Hill, N.J

frequency marketing – Activities that encourage repeat purchasing through a formal program enrollment process (BJ's®, Barnes and Noble®, Costco®, Sam's Club®) to develop loyalty and commitment from the customer base. Frequency marketing is also referred to as loyalty programs.

frequently asked questions (FAQ's) – A list of questions and answers for the media pertaining to a news release or other hot topic. Many times, FAQs are included in a media or press kit or on a Web site.

freshman churn – Students who transfer from one college to another before their sophomore year.

Freudian motivation theory – Employed in public relations to help reinforce behavior. It's a theory that believes a consumer's buying preferences are dictated by unconscious motives and that visual, auditory and tactile elements of a product or service may evoke emotions that stimulate or inhibit purchase. See *motivation; Maslow's hierarchy of needs; Herzberg's theory of motivation.*

Friday night dump – Government releasing bad news on Friday afternoons and evenings. Other organizations do it, too. It's commonly referred to as "throwing out the trash."

fringe benefits – Benefits given to employees as part of a total pay or compensation package.

fringe time – A time period directly preceding and directly following prime time on television.

front matter – Introductory and organizational material that comes before the main content of a document. Examples of front matter include title page, table of contents, copyright information, publication data, foreword, acknowledgements, etc.

front-of-counter (FOC) – The prime and most sought after position for impulse goods.

front page notes – Use of Post-it® type note for page one advertising in newspaper. Also called a *tab-on*, *dot whack* and *note advertising*.

frontrunner – One who is in a leading position in a race or other competition. A competitor who performs best when in the lead. Someone looked at as a future leader (of an organization).

fulfillment – All activities involved in the processing and servicing of mail, fax and telephone orders and reimbursements through rebates and other promotions. Public relations *fulfillment* refers to sending news releases and pitches to news organizations, many of which subscribe to the service on their end. Subscription *fulfillment* is a specialized service for periodical publishers. Those services include maintaining a subscriber

91

Tips to Succeed:Dress up to move up

A woman who wants to climb the ladder of success might have to do it in tasteful, mid-height pumps.

A man intent on getting ahead might invest in a few new ties — and keep them straightened.

In fact, a recent survey (Office Team, a subsidiary of Robert Half International) reports 93 percent of managers said an employee's work dress influences his or her odds of winning a promotion; 33 percent said wardrobe plays a "significant" role in moving up.

KEY QUESTIONS

• Would my manager wear this?

• Could my outfit be a distraction for others?

• Does my attire make me feel self-assured and confident?

• Are my clothes clean, pressed and in good condition?

• Is my outfit comfortable and well-fitting?

It's not about wearing expensive clothes, it's about being appropriate

It is suggested professionals maintain business attire, suits with trousers or skirts for women and suits and ties for men.

Our business casual should be sweater sets and dress slacks. It's important for workers starting out at a company to know the corporate culture regarding dress.

In building a career wardrobe, stock your closet with the basics:

• A navy blazer is a good staple for a man or a woman

• A black suit is versatile because you can throw on different shirts to change the look.

• Keep clothes clean and pressed, with hair neatly groomed.

• Women to use a light hand in applying makeup and to avoid flashy jewelry.

Another suggestion: before you go for that promotion, visualize yourself in the job.

Ask yourself, "would my manager wear this?" If there are two candidates with equal skill sets, the person who presents himself more professionally has the edge.

www.courierpostonline.com

F

The ABCs of Strategic Communication

92

Techniques to Succeed: Sculpt e-mail to make it stand out

It pays to spend a little time thinking about an e-mail before you send it. Paying more attention to what you write can make your messages more effective and guard against workplace catastrophes.

There are numerous ways to make e-mails stronger and more likely to be read faster.

• To get your message recognized, read and acted upon, strengthen the subject, sculpt the body.

• The way to get fewer e-mails is to send fewer e-mails.

• Cut down on your use of the "cc" and "reply to all" functions, as well as group distribution lists, he said.

• A better e-mail starts with a better subject line. Instead of writing "Meeting," be more specific, like "Sales team meeting from April 3rd."

• If you're confirming a meeting, write back in the subject line, "Confirmed." And when you're sending information the recipient requested, use the word "Delivery" before describing what you're sending.

Like the title of *this* book, have an *ABC* structure:

A stands for "action summary." In the first line should be the "summary point.," It should leave no room for guesswork. An example might be: "Action: Please submit business plan by 5 p.m. on April 3rd." It's important to list a deadline or time element, he said.

B stands for "background." This second part should be a series of bullet points, with information the recipient needs to know. This avoids a "wall of words" that no one will want to read, or an e-mail that, conversely, doesn't provide enough detail.

And C stands for "close." This final portion should speak to the next steps that need to be taken, or perhaps a personal message to lighten the e-mail. Finish it with an auto signature with contact information, such as:

M. Larry Litwin, APR, Fellow PRSA
Associate Professor – Public Relations/Advertising
"Loyalty, Judgment, Trust, Ethics, Integrity" = PR
Counselor/Strategic Advisor
Rowan University
201 Mullica Hill Road
Glassboro NJ 08028
856-256-4224
856-673-0717 (Fax)
www.larrylitwin.com

Mike Song - Co-author - *The Hamster Revolution:*
How to Manage Your E-Mail Before it Manages You

list, generating invoices and renewals, and recording payments. Product *fulfillment* is the storage and shipping of samples and merchandise.

fulfillment house – A coupon or rebate-clearing house. A company that receives coupons and manages their accounting, verification and redemption.

fulfillment piece – Any marketing material sent in response to a reader, viewer or listener's request for more information.

full-cost pricing (strategy) – A pricing strategy that includes all variable and fixed costs (total costs) directly attributed to the product or service. This information is used in setting a product's selling price or a public relations agency's fees. See *incremental-cost pricing*.

full disclosure – In public relations and other areas of business – an obligation to disclose all the facts relevant to a news story, business transaction or to a security, as required by the SEC or another government entity.

full-function merchant wholesaler – A wholesaler offering a complete range of services including buying, selling, storage, transporting, sorting, financing, providing market feedback and risk-taking. Also called a full-function wholesaler.

full Ginsburg – Someone who makes the rounds on all of the Sunday morning news/talk programs – ABC's "This Week," CBS's "Face the Nation," NBC's "Meet the Press" "FOX News Sunday," etc. Coined by media after attorney William Ginsburg had client Monica Lewinsky on all of the Sunday shows in one day during the "Lewinsky-(President Bill) Clinton scandal."

full-line department store – A department store that offers many different lines of products, including clothing, sporting goods, food, furniture, electrical goods, etc., and many different services, including wrapping, delivery and credit. See *limited-line department store.*

full-line strategy – A producer's decision to offer a large number of product variations (features) in a product line – establishing various price points. See *limited-line strategy.*

full nesters – A term used to describe the stage in the typical family life cycle in which the household consists of parents and growing children. Marketers use three sub-stages of *full nesters* in targeting their products: Full Nest 1, where the youngest child is under six years of age; Full Nest 2, where the youngest child is over six; and Full Nest 3, where the household consists of parents and older dependent children. See *family life cycle.*

full position – An advertisement that is surrounded by articles in a newspaper, making it more likely consumers will read the ad. This is a highly desirable location for an ad.

full service – See *full-service public relations agency.*

full-service advertising agency – An *advertising agency* offering a complete range of services including overall planning, marketing research, media planning, creative design (of packaging and advertisements), production, placement (media buying), etc. A *full-service agency* will have its own accounting department, a traffic department to internally track projects toward completion, departments for broadcast and print production (usually re[port to creative director), and a human resources department.

full-service public relations agency – A public relations agency offering all aspects of the public relations process – planning, research, budgeting, account management, creative services, media relations, publication and other graphic design, media planning, buying and placement. Today, full-service generally suggests that the agency also handles other aspects of marketing communication, such as sales promotion and direct marketing.

93

Tips to Succeed:
Fashion choices for workplace

When temperatures climb, workers wrestle with finding the middle ground between cool summer clothing and appropriate work attire. Here is a summer fashion refresher for women:

- Show respect with how you dress at the office. Social skills are 75 percent of what determines a person's success in business. Those skills include knowing how to dress.

- Business casual should be a mix of both. Pressed khakis and a crisp shirt are a better choice than a T-shirt and jeans.

- Beachwear such as flip-flops, tank tops, short skirts and shorts are not appropriate for the office.

- Women should choose sandals with straps over the flip-flops. Shoes should be closed-toed and beware of backless shoes that make an annoying clap-clap-clap sound when you walk.

- Do not wear sleeveless shirts, but if you have to wear one, pick a nice-looking sleeveless shell that can be worn under a jacket in case you need to look formal, fast.

- Other shirts that should be banned on most professionals: Shirts with spaghetti straps and anything that shows cleavage or bare midriffs.

- Your skirt should not be more than a dollar bill's width above your knee.

Leah Ingram - Author - The Everything Etiquette Book: A Modern Day Guide to Good Manners and Gannett News Service

full-service research supplier – A marketing research firm, which offers clients a complete range of services, including problem definition or conceptualization, research design (protocol), data collection and analysis and reporting. See *limited-service research supplier*.

full-service wholesaler – A wholesaler offering a complete range of services including buying, selling, storage, transporting, sorting, financing, providing market feedback and risk-taking. Also called a full-function wholesaler.

functional costs – Costs associated with a specific business activity, such as research, news release writing, selling, advertising, marketing research, etc.

functional discount – A price allowance given to a firm performing some part of the public relations or marketing function for other members of the channel of distribution. Also called trade discount.

functional middlemen – See *functional wholesalers*.

functional modification – A change made to any feature of a product to make it safer, more useful, more efficient or more valuable to a purchaser. Also called *feature modification*.

functional organization – The organization of a firm's business activities so that a separate division is responsible for each business function – planning, research, production, new product development, sales, finance, personnel, advertising, marketing, distribution, etc. See *organizational structure*.

functional risk – Concern in the buyer's mind that the product being considered for purchase will not work efficiently. See *risk*; *performance risk*.

functional wholesalers – Brokers, "reps" or agents who sell for manufacturers and producers to retailers or directly to consumers and receive commissions for their services. See *functional middlemen*.

fundamental application theory – Best defined with examples: If you know that a particular person is always going to be late, tell him an earlier time. The theory is – you already know he'll be late. Used is sports – if a batter just can't lay off a fastball that's what the pitcher throws.

fundamental freedom – Not without reason. As Alexander Hamilton pointed out in *The Federalist, Number 84*, "arbitrary imprisonments have been, in all ages, the favorite and most formidable instrument of tyranny." Freedom of speech and religion and all the rest are mere rhetoric if the powers-that-be can lock you up for breathing—or, worse, without naming any charge at all. The protections of *habeas corpus* are designed to prevent this sort of tyranny by providing a judicial check on the government's power to imprison. Directly translated, "habeas corpus" means "you have the body." In use, it means something like "show us the body you've got." A writ of *habeas corpus* amounts to a command from a court that the keeper of a body (a jailor) produce that body (a prisoner) at a particular time for a particular purpose – generally to show just cause for limiting that body's liberty. **F**

gallery tributes – Popular tactic used by U.S. presidents during States of the Union and other key speeches. Pointing out significant audience members as they relate to speech. Also called the *transfer effect*.

galley proof – A typeset copy of an advertisement or editorial material, before it is made into pages for final production. Galley proofs are not as prominent today as in the past, because of desktop publishing. Laser prints generate camera-ready copy (CRC), repros, slicks (if printed on glossy paper) or a matte (if printed on non-coated off-set paper). For all intents and purposes, CRC, repros, slicks and mattes are synonymous.

game day – Sports term used generally in public relations on the day of a long-planned *special event*.

galvanic skin response (GSR) – A physiological testing technique where electrical conductivity of the skin is measured to check the level of arousal caused by an advertisement, commercial or other strategic message. See *galvanometer*.

galvanometer – A scientific instrument used in marketing research to measure the reaction of a subject in a study of an advertisement, commercial or other strategic message. A *galvanometer* measures the perspiration that accompanies the subject's interest or arousal. See *galvanic skin response*.

galvanometer test – A research method that measures physiological changes in consumers when asked a question or shown some stimulus material (such as an advertisement, commercial or some other strategic message).

game – A type of sweepstakes that requires the player to return to play several times.

Gantt Chart – A time-task matrix to keep projects on schedule – with vertical (tactics/tasks) and horizontal axes (calendar) used to integrate implementation of the strategic plan. The calendar should be organized by public and strategy, scheduling each tactic. See *critical-path analysis* (See Chapter 7 – *The Public Relations Practitioner's Playbook* – Kendall/Hunt – 2008.)

gap analysis – The determination of the methods and techniques used to fill the "gap" between financial objectives and agency billing (or corporate sales) taking into account yearly or even long-range revenue forecasts.

94 Tips to Succeed: Advice from Google®

"Anything you don't develop is a garden left unattended ."

Google founders

Garden of Eden effect – Using a woman as the front person or spokesperson because they have more credibility, which assists in maintaining, reinforcing or changing behavior.

gatefold – Double or triple-size pages, generally in magazines, that fold out into a large advertisement. Gatefolds have become more popular in recent years.

gatekeeper – People within an organization who "protects" the decision maker – screens phone calls and/or e-mails. Many times, public relations practitioners must get past the *gatekeeper* when pitching stories to assignment editors, news editors or news directors. *Gatekeepers* can control the flow of information. Research is clear – the most effective method for getting past the *gatekeeper* is through relationship building.

gatekeeper's gatekeeper – The protector of the *gatekeeper*. The (first) contact person within an organization who answers the phone or greets visitors. Like *gatekeepers*, the initial contact can control or even stifle the flow of information.

gatekeeping – The selection or rejection of events. For example, an editor decides on what's going to be covered, an organizer briefs the camera crews, the reporter decides what "angle" the story will be covered from, etc. These people are all *gatekeepers*. Public relations practitioners should never take the concept of *gatekeeping* for granted.

gender convergence – Men's and women's lives becoming similar – at work and *at* home.

general assignment – A reporter who covers a variety of stories rather than a single "beat."

general election – Election to choose candidates for office. See *primary election*.

General Electric strategic business portfolio planning grid – A portfolio analysis and planning grid developed by General Electric®; it uses a two-dimensional matrix based on industry attractiveness and business strength.

general public – All of the people (audiences) in the society receiving a message whether or not they are being targeted. Each of the narrowly defined audiences is a niche audience. They become target audiences when the sender or encoder is aiming its message at them. Some practitioners believe there is no such thing as a "general" public.

generation – A society or peer group born over a period of time (20 year segments) – roughly that same length as the passage from youth to adulthood who collectively possess a common persona. In education, a generation of students who share a common persona seems to change every five years.

Generation Debt – Ages 17-31 who are deeply in debt from college loans and out-of-control credit card bills.

Generation Next – Ages 16-25, generally born from 1977 and 1991. Also known as *Generation Y*.

Generation P (Plastic) – Born in the 1980s who use plastic (credit cards) for most of their purchases. They are the leading edge of a generation that is shunning cash ("paper") payments. See *Generation Debt*.

Generation X – These members of society born from 1965 and 1976. In the U.S., *Gen X*ers number 55 million or between 15 and 20 percent of the population. *Gen X*ers spend more than $125 billion annually on consumer goods in the United States. Author Douglas Coupland was the first to use the term Generation X. He says Generation X is characterized by a propensity for technology, skepticism to advertising claims and attraction to personal style rather than designer price tags. *Generation X* members spend a lot of time in front of the computer and are comfortable with e-commerce, high impact internet marketing techniques and take full advantage of online purchasing.

Generation Y – These members of society were born from 1977 and 1991. In the U.S., *Gen Y*ers number nearly 80 million. The *Y Generation* is the largest consumer group in the history of the U.S. Other names for *Generation Y* are Echo Boomers and the Millennium Generation. Gen Yers have annual incomes in excess of $210 billion, according to a study from Harris Interactive. They spend $172 billion per year, but place nearly $40 billion per year in savings and other accounts. Their input drives many adult-purchasing decisions. Consequently, the *Y Generation* represents the future market for most consumer brands. Also known as *General Next*.

Generation Z – Also known as the "New Silent Generation." It constitutes the break up of *Generation Y (Generation Next)* into subcategories in order to recognize the generation being sent overseas to defend the United States and its "War on Terror."

generic advertising – Also called institutional or product advertising, it is a category or class of product rather than a particular brand, as in "Pork, the other white meat! " or "Got Milk?" These messages enhance a product rather than a brand or corporation. The thinking behind product advertising is manufacturers and farmers must convince consumers to use a particular product before they can convince them to purchase their brand.

generic brand – Products not associated with a private or national brand name. Also called a "no-name" brand.

generic competitors – Products which are all different in type but are capable of satisfying the same basic want and/or need of a prospective purchaser. For example, the consumer may want to buy new furniture, but must choose between a sofa, love seat, lounge chair, coffee table, end tables, etc.

generic products – Unbranded products identified only by product category. Also called a "no-name" brand.

generics – see *generic brand*.

geocentric approach to pricing – Also know as pricing what the market will bear. It's an approach in which local market conditions are

95

Tips to Succeed:
Chicken soup for the investor

Relationships between investors and the ever-changing financial markets can be complex.

These principles have withstood the test of time.

• People don't invest to become rich. They invest so they don't become poor. Individuals invest in stocks to keep up with the rate of inflation. Bonds and cash will not allow you to keep up.

• Don't constantly look up your account balance. You wouldn't pull up your plants every day to check on the roots, would you?

• Most people underestimate how long they will live after retiring and how much money they will need. Living longer has had a major impact on retirement planning. You don't want to run out of money before running out of time.

• Your investment decisions should be based on careful analysis of your time horizon, risk tolerance, expected return and asset allocation preference. If a salesman starts fishing around and talks about investments before addressing these issues with you, don't take the bait.

• It is never too late to start saving and planning for retirement. The key is to get started and have a plan.

Joseph M. Johnson - Vice President
Main Street Financial Group - Pitman, N.J. - 856- 218-0080

supplied to public relations agencies or retailers who then set prices accordingly to maximize profits in each national market. See *extension approach to pricing.*

geocentrism – The view that the whole world is one single market.

geodemographics – A contraction of geography and demographics. A method of combining geographic and demographic variables. The demographics of individuals or groups who reside in the same geographic area.

geographic market concentration – A distinctive characteristic of the industrial market; which tends to be more geographically concentrated than the consumer market.

96

Tips to Succeed:
Doing business with government

The U.S. Government is the world's largest customer, and it routinely does business with small businesses. There is a procedure to follow when doing business with the "feds."

• Educate yourself extremely well on the process.

• Make sure you meet the basic requirements for doing business with the government, such as accepting electronic funds transfer and credit cards.

• Determine your NAICS code (North American Industry Classification System – www.census.gov/epcd/www/naics.html) and make sure you qualify as a small business.

• Determine who in the government purchases your products or services.

• Determine if there are any special programs for which you may qualify.

• Obtain a DUNS (Data Universal Numbering System) number for free from Dun & Bradstreet.

• Register with the Small Business Administration (SBA) and the agency with which you wish to do business.

• Subscribe to the Commerce Business Daily, which lists notices of proposed government procurement actions, contract awards, sales of government property and other procurement information.

• Respond to the bids effectively and get awarded contracts!

• For more information, get in touch with the local Small Business Administration office. Go to www.sba.gov.

Scott Allen - www.about.com

geographic organization – The organization of a firm's marketing activities so that a separate division is responsible for each of its major geographic markets.

geographic segmentation – The division of a total, heterogeneous market into relatively homogeneous groups on the basis of area, district, region, state, etc. See *segmentation bases*.

geographic variables – Area or regional differences used to segment a market.

geographical pricing – A pricing method where customers bear the freight costs from the producer's location to their own. See *free on board pricing*; *base-point pricing*; *zone pricing*.

get – When a reporter or talk show hosts "gets" a well-known (big name) guest.

get out the vote (GOTV) – Considered integral in winning elections and referenda – tactics used to encourage registered voters to go to the polls.

ghostwriting – Writing generated without published credit to its author and is often credited to another.

graphics interchange format (GIF) – A graphics file format used on the Internet. It uses compression to store and display images. GIFs are the image format commonly used for ad banners. See *GIF file*.

GIF file – A type of computer file used for graphic images or photos. GIF files are often used on the Internet to display graphics. The extension ".gif" is used for a GIF file. See *graphics interchange format*.

gigabyte – One gigabyte equals 1000 megabytes.

gimmick – An innovative approach or tactic.

gist – A summary that focuses on the central idea.

global brands – Brands sold throughout the world using essentially the same promotion. Coca-Cola®, Pepsi®, IBM® and Apple® are examples of global brands.

global dialogue – Listening as well as sending messages.

Global Generation X – Those born from 1965 to 1980 – a bit longer than *Generation X* which runs from 1965 to 1975.

global marketing – Marketing the same or similar products to world markets using essentially the same promotion. It is also referred to as *international marketing*.

global prospective – A corporate philosophy that directs products, services, advertising and public relations functions toward a worldwide rather than a local, regional or national market.

glossary box – Highlighted illustration in a book or other publication to help readers understand publication's terms. Find a way to indicate which words are defined by putting them in color or in a different type-face or underlining them. Also, show pronouncers (in parenthesis) for difficult words. Readers will better remember them.

go error – A failure at any stage (but especially at the screening stage) in product development when a decision is made to proceed with a product that should have been abandoned. See *drop error; new product development.*

97

Techniques to Succeed: Stress and anxiety

It's important to understand the difference between stress and anxiety because the strategies to deal with each are actually the opposite of one another.

STRESS

• Stress is the feeling of being overburdened and overwhelmed. This is having a desk full of papers in front of you, 100 unread emails in your inbox and a tight deadline quickly approaching.

• Stress makes you feel pressures with physical symptoms such as muscle tension, headaches and backaches.

• The way to deal with stress is to decrease it. You want to find ways to relax in and outside of work.

• Improving your time management or assertiveness skills can help you decrease the burden of your workload.

ANXIETY

• Anxiety is an internal, fear-based response to difficult situations.

• It is the trembling, heart-palpating, short-of-breath feeling you get when you are singled out in front of everyone or the adrenaline rush before doing a major presentation.

• The way to deal with anxiety is to increase it. It sounds crazy, but the way to get over a fear is to confront it over and over. For instance, if you're afraid of public speaking, find as many opportunities to do it so that over time it will become easier and your confidence will grow.

Larina Kase - Doctor of Psychology, career coach and former counselor at the University of Pennsylvania - www.extremecommunicator.com

goal – The primary result an organization is attempting to achieve through its public relations efforts. Where the organization wants to be sometime in the future. See *objective*; *strategy*; *tactic*.

goldbricking – Employees wasting time on the job (they are being paid to perform).

golden hours – The first few hours after a crisis – used for fact gathering and other research, planning and crafting the strategic message.

gone to bed (put to bed) – Refers to newspapers or other print media – meaning that the publication's deadline has passed and it is now ready for the press or is on the press – being printed.

goodwill – The difference between the value of a business as a going concern and the sum of the value of its assets if taken separately. In layman's terms, *goodwill* deals with *relationship marketing* and the value of its customer base.

Googling – Searching the Internet.

gotcha journalism – A technique by which an article or broadcast story shocks readers or listeners by making a charge that shatters a commonly held perception. For example, some outlets might target a person by showing him not to be as humanitarian, free or generous as his supporters claim. The problem with *gotcha journalism* is that sometimes it's wrong.

GOTV (get out the vote) – Considered integral in winning elections and referenda – tactics used to encourage registered voters to go to the polls.

government markets – Federal, state and local government departments and agencies that buy goods and services needed to conduct their operations.

grace period – Interest-free time a credit-card company allows between a purchase and the billing date. The standard grace period is usually 20 to 30 days. People who carry a balance on their credit cards (usually) have no *grace period*.

grade label – A tag, sticker, label, letter, mark or symbol which identifies the quality or grade of a product offered for sale. See *label*.

gradient – In printing, a series of progressively increasing or decreasing shades of a color – from lighter to darker or vice versa. See *dodge*.

Gramm-Leach-Bliley Act (GLB) – Signed into law in 1999. *GLB* regulates how financial institutions can disclose consumers' personal information to non-affiliated third parties. *GLB* also requires financial institutions to provide privacy notices to consumers and customers.

graph – Professionals (journalists and public relations practitioners) use the words *graph* or *graf* when referring to a paragraph. Newsroom slang for paragraph. Also known as graf.

graphic noise – Too many type fonts, poor layout and/or poor quality illustrations.

98 Techniques to Succeed: Beware of office gossip – it will come back to 'getcha'

If you want to be trusted, never gossip. When you talk negatively about others – especially in business – to people you just met, or even to people you have known for some time, but don't know well, you may have been seen as a gossiper. And, many times, it is not what you say, but how you say it.

Be nice to people on your way up because you never know who you will meet on the way down. Never treat anyone poorly. You never know when someone will become your boss.

The dos and don'ts of office gossip

• If you must gossip make sure your indiscretion won't get either you or your colleague into trouble with the boss.

• An incredible 70 per cent of workers are shocked that their secrets are common knowledge in the office. Don't be. If you gossip about your workmates the chances are they will gossip about you.

• If you are uncomfortable with a situation at work go straight to one of your superiors.

• If you're bored, find something other than gossiping to fill your time.

Keith Ferrazzi and Tahl Raz - Authors - *Never Eat Alone: And Other Secrets to Success, One at a Time* (Currency - 2005)
http://www.ivillage.co.uk/print/0,,164246,00.html

grassroots marketing – Also called word-of-mouth and face-to-face. It's connecting with existing and prospective customers through non-mainstream media methods. *Grassroots marketing* relies on *relationship marketing*, which is proven to survive the test of time. Advantages to *grassroots* and *relationship marketing* include gaining customer loyalty and involvement, consistent repeat business, increased sales and a potentially positive effect on the community. By engaging in *grassroots marketing*, a company focuses more on nurturing relationships and developing higher quality market share that makes them less vulnerable to competitive attacks and external economic factors. It has been said that those who practice *grassroots marketing* "do well by doing good."

gravitas – Behaving with dignity and a certain chemistry and charisma. An attractiveness. A dignified demeanor. *Gravitas* can be found in one's personality or charisma.

gravure – A printing process that uses an etched printing cylinder.

gray page – A publication that does not use copybreaking devices and bores the reader rather than catch his/her attention.

green advertising – Advertising that promotes a product or service's ability to help or, more likely, not hurt the environment.

green bars – Slang used for fanfold computer printout paper. Alternate bars are green and another color – usually white – to make it easier to compare numbers and other information.

99 Tips to Succeed: Know the branches of government

They are known as the "three powers." In a Democratic society, power is in principle divided between the three branches of government:

- **Legislative** – makes the laws (e.g. the US Congress)
- **Executive** – Makes executive decisions on a day-to-day basis (e.g. the US President)
- **Judiciary** – Interpret the laws (e.g. the US Supreme Court).

The powers/branches are designed to counterbalance one another. This system of "checks and balances" works to ensure that none of the three powers becomes too strong. Thus, for example, the President can send troops to war, but the Congress can refuse to vote the budget to sustain the war. Congress can pass a law, but the Supreme Court can rule it unconstitutional.

green marketing – The marketing of "environmentally-friendly" products. It is marketing that takes into account environmental issues such as wastefulness of the earth's resources, pollution and the release of toxins into the atmosphere. Green marketing began in Europe in the early 1980s when specific products were identified as being harmful to the earth's atmosphere. As a result, new "green" products were introduced that were less damaging to the environment. The concept caught on in the United States and has been gaining popularity ever since.

green screen – Known in television as *chroma key*. It is a term for the filmmaking technique of using an evenly-lit monochromatic back-

100 Techniques to Succeed: Gunning Fog Index

The Gunning Fog Index, developed by Robert Gunning in *Technique of Clear Writing* is the easiest of the readability indexes to use, most popular and considered the most effective. Here is how it works:

STEPS IN APPLYING GUNNING

1. Select a sample

2. Count 100 words (continue counting until you finish a sentence)

3. Determine the average number of words per sentence

4. Divide the number of sentences into the number of words. (Remember, an average sentence should not exceed 17 words.)

5. Determine the percentage of hard words
   a. Count all words containing three or more syllables.
   Do NOT count:
   • proper nouns
   • verbs made into three syllables such as excited, persuasive or devoted
   • words of three or more syllables that are combinations of easy words such as butterfly, lawmaker, bumblebee.

6. Add the two factors (Steps 4 and 5) and multiply by 0.4

The result is the minimum grade level at which the writing is easily read.

M. Larry Litwin, APR, Fellow PRSA
The Public Relations Practitioner's Playbook (Kendall/Hunt – 2008)

ground for the purpose of replacing it with a different image or scene. The term also refers to the visual effect resulting from this technique as well as the colored screen itself (although it is often a *blue screen*). It is commonly used for TV weather forecasts, wherein the presenter appears to be standing in front of a large map, but in the studio it is actually a large blue or green background.

Greenwich Mean Time (GMT) – The mean solar time for Greenwich, England, which is located on the Prime Meridian (zero longitude). Based on the rotation of the earth, *GMT* is used as the basis for calculating standard time throughout most of the world.

greeters – Dating back to the mid-19th century, salespeople were called *greeters*. Today, they have taken on a new meaning – *greeters* welcome shoppers at retail stores and they meet patrons in hotel lobbies as they arrive on business or vacation visits.

grey market – The importing of goods by firms that are not official distributors of the product. For example, car dealers that sell particular brands legally, but are not authorized dealers of such manufacturers as General Motors®, Ford® or Chrysler®. *Grey marketing* is also called

101 Tips to Succeed: De-clutter your space

Does your office contain two filing systems: the desk and the floor? Here are some tips for de-cluttering a messy work space:

- Keep only the items on your desk that relate to your current projects.

- Clean out your files, but before you go through the expense of buying more file cabinets and folders, purge all unnecessary paperwork and materials.

- Don't waste time searching for papers. Keep all paperwork that pertains to a certain project together in one large folder.

- Don't overstuff file cabinets. Leave enough room so you're not using all your energy to get a piece of paper in and out.

- Add shelving for reference books and manuals. Add space extenders in desk drawers. Use stacking bins.

www.courierpostonline.com - Oct. 17, 2005

parallel importing when referring to the illicit sale of imported products contrary to the interests of a holder of a trademark, patent or copyright in the country of sale. It is also a term used to describe the demographic (population) of 65 and over market. It is also referred to at the "silver market" or "white hair group."

Greying, Leisured, Affluent, Middle-aged (GLAM) – Demographic grouping.

grid – A pattern of regularly spaced horizontal and vertical lines forming square zones on a map used as a reference for establishing points.

grid card – A broadcast media rate card that lists rates on a grid, according to the time periods that might be selected for the advertisement. Television listings in newspapers and magazines use the *grid card* approach.

grip 'n grin – A picture showing two people shaking hands and smiling (obviously posed). For example, award winners, association officers, etc.

gross audience – The audiences of all vehicles or media in a campaign, combined. Some of the *gross audience* may actually represent duplicated audience members.

gross cost – The total cost of a media vehicle or media schedule that includes the discount typically offered by a media supplier as commission to the agency placing the "buy."

gross exposures – The total number of times an advertisement is seen by a single person. It does not take into account the effectiveness of those exposures.

gross impressions – Total number of unduplicated people (readers, listeners or viewers) or households represented by a given media schedule.

gross margin – See *gross profit*.

gross margin quota – A common form of sales assignment, goal or target used to measure a salesperson's performance. A gross margin quota is used to urge a salesperson to sell a healthy portion of higher-profit items which are usually higher in price and often harder to sell. Other commonly used types of sales quotas are unit volume quotas, dollar volume quotas, net profit quotas and activity quotas. See *sales quota*.

gross national product –Total dollar value of all final goods and services produced for consumption in society during a particular time

102

Tips to Succeed: Demand attention in cover letter

- **Make yourself stand out.** Get the competitive edge by writing a cover letter that focuses on your unique and exceptional qualities.

- **Target the right person.** Sending your letter to the proper person can make all the difference.

- **Stay simple.** Keep your cover letter brief. Never send a letter that is more than a page in length; half a page is ideal. Be sure to use clear, professional language while steering away from buzzwords, acronyms, jargon, or anything overly personal.

- **Make it shine.** The overall visual impression of your cover letter can be just as important as what's written upon it.

- **Be an attention getter.** Don't waste your first paragraph by writing a dull introduction.

www.allbusiness.com

period. Its rise or fall measures economic activity based on the labor and production output within a country.

gross profit – The amount left after selling costs and operating expenses are deducted from total revenue. Also called *gross margin.*

Gross Rating Points (GRPS) – The total number of homes that can be reached through a media buy at a particular radio or TV station or through the entire buy. A ratio measuring the value of a media schedule in advertising, calculated by multiplying reach by frequency. It's the sum of reach of a media schedule. See *frequency*; *rating points, reach.*

gross sales – The total revenue from all sales to customers in a specified period.

Ground Zero – Most Americans and many others around the word associate this term with the terrorist attacks on New York City's World Trade Center on September 11, 2001. The actual definition (ground zero [lower case]) of the term is: the point closest to any exploding bomb.

group influences – Members of a family, peers, opinion leaders, key communicators, etc. who have an effect on a consumer's behavior.

103 Techniques to Succeed: Bookkeeping – Don't get overwhelmed

Small-business owners can be overwhelmed by all the different tasks they perform. If you are a small-business owner and you can't perform these duties, it might be time to outsource:

- Maintain accounting records after working 10- to 15-hour days.
- Set up, select and computerize an accounting system.
- Deal with filing and processing payroll.
- Reconcile bank accounts and actively monitor cash balances.
- Possess the expertise to code expenses, assets and other income to provide a CPA with information to prepare tax returns at year's end.
- Prepare financial information to monitor trends, profitability, cash balances and accounts receivable.
- Hire and train a bookkeeper to run the financial aspects of the business.

www.osyb.com - Outsource Your Books

group prospecting – Finding new clients/customers by displaying and demonstrating merchandise at seminars, conventions, functions, clubs, home parties, etc. See *prospecting*.

group sales training – The training of sales representatives, usually in formal sessions, as a group. See *formal training*.

group selling – A selling situation where a salesperson presents a product or product range to a group of buyers from one company or to a buying committee. See *team selling*.

growth rate – The rate, commonly expressed as a percentage per year, at which a market is increasing (or decreasing) in size. See *market growth rate*.

growth stage of product life cycle – The second stage (after the *introductory stage*) in the life cycle of a successful product. Sales revenues increase steadily as the product finds market acceptance, prices generally remain high despite increasing competitive threats and profit margins are at peak level. The other three stages are *maturity*, *decline* and *withdrawal*.

growth strategies – The means by which an organization plans to achieve its objective to grow in volume and turnover. Four broad growth

104

Tips to Succeed:
Make your e-mail effective

Use the technology of e-mail to your professional advantage. E-mails must give the right impression.

• **Get to the point fast.** Make sure the important information is within the first couple sentences.

• **Make your subject line like the headline of a newspaper article.** The subject line should give the reader a reason to open the message.

• **Avoid constantly checking your e-mail and responding right away.** This can take your focus off work. Instead, turn off your computer's "you've got mail" signal and give one succinct reply to several messages from the same person.

• **Keep e-mail professional, even if you're writing to a work buddy.** Keep in mind that every e-mail you send is subject to forwarding.

• **Use active instead of passive language.** It sets a professional image and gets the point across quickly. Active language is energetic and clear while passive language weakens your writing.

Janis Fisher Chan - Author - *E-mail: A Write It Well Guide*

strategies are - market penetration, product development, market development and diversification.

Global System for Mobile (GSM) – The wireless telephone standard in Europe.

guarantee – A written assurance by a manufacturer its product will be replaced or repaired to the customer's satisfaction if it is found to be defective or does not perform as intended. See *warranty*.

guaranteed circulation – A media rate that comes with a guarantee that the publication will achieve a certain circulation.

guaranteed price – An assurance given by a manufacturer to a marketing intermediary that if the wholesale price of a product is lowered while the intermediary is still holding stocks, the difference will be refunded. The theory being that such a guarantee encourages the intermediary to order a large quantity of the product with confidence they would not be financially hurt.

105

Techniques to Succeed: Burnout busters

To prevent burnout:

• Start your day with powerful high-energy music. Whether it's rock or country or jazz or pop, listen to music that "pumps you up" and makes you feel great about yourself.

• Set aside blocks of time to complete various tasks. During those blocks of time, do not allow yourself to be interrupted for other things. (For example, the hour from 2 to 3 p.m. might be set aside for reading and responding to e-mails.)

• Make "Fix it, then forget it" your mistake mantra. Do not allow mistakes to ruin you. Do everything you can to fix a problem with a client or associate in order to make them happy. After that, do not dwell on what went wrong.

• Get an accountability partner to help you stay focused. Ask someone other than your spouse or romantic partner to fill this role. Make sure it's someone you trust and feel comfortable with to just be yourself. You should meet with this person at least once a week to talk about your goals, progress, setbacks, and thoughts on your personal and professional life.

• Use "comic memos" to ease anxiety at work. The comic memo technique involves attaching a funny cartoon to routine, boring paperwork that has to be distributed at the office.

The Staver Group - 914 Atlantic Avenue - Suite 1E - Fernandina Beach, FL 32034

guarantees and warranties – Legal documents committing a company to deal with faulty goods or services by a variety of methods including repair, replacement or compensation.

guerilla marketing – First used by Jay Conrad Levinson, *guerilla marketing* usually refers to using innovative and aggressive tactics to market on a very small or even non-existent budget. The idea is to use creative methods to reach people where they live, work and socialize to create a personal connection and a high level of impact. It targets niche and specialized audiences in such a way that bigger companies will not find it worthwhile to retaliate.

guided dreams – A method of collecting *qualitative marketing research* data (many times through focus panels) where participants are asked to imagine they are dreaming or fantasizing. While in this state, a facilitator/ researcher seeks their emotional reactions to issues, particular products, brands, services, etc. See *qualitative marketing research*.

Gunning Fog Index – A readability formula created by Robert Gunning that approximates the grade level at which a person must read to understand the material in a publication. See *Flesch-Kincaid*. (See Technique 100.)

GUPPIE – Acronym for Grossly Under-Performing Person. A Green YUPPIE is also a term to describe a lifestyle-based market segment consisting of "young, urban professionals" who might be grossly under-performers. Used to describe the majority of the people who work for corporations. A formal definition is difficult to construct because of the diversity of the workforce. For a list of *GUPPIE* characteristics, read more at *http://rdeen.tripod.com/GUPDEF.HTM*. See *yuppie*.

gutter – In bound documents, the gutter is the margin space closest to the binding (most times toward or in the center of a publication). Also, the inside margins of two pages that face each other in a print publication. **G**

habeas corpus – A fundamental freedom of the founding fathers. In legal terms, it means something like "show us the body you've got." A writ of habeas corpus amounts to a command from a court that the keeper of a body (a jailor) produce that body (a prisoner) at a particular time for a particular purpose.

habitual decision making – Consumer decision making, or problem solving, requiring only minimal search for, and evaluation of, alternatives before purchasing. Also referred to as automatic response behavior, routine response behavior and routinized problem solving. See *extensive problem solving*; *limited problem solving*.

hack – Slang for "breaking into" a computer's hard drive. Also, writer of computer programs.

hairline – The thinnest line (border) in a publication that can be made within a font.

halftone – A method of reproducing a black and white photograph or illustration, by representing various shades of gray as a series of black and white dots. Pictures that appear in print, for the most part, have been made into halftones.

halo effect – The transfer of goodwill from one product in a company's line to another. The attribution, by association, of the qualities of one item to others in the group.

hamster – An employee who is constantly spinning his/her wheels.

Hancock – A signature.

handbill – A flier distributed by hand.

handler – A manager (advisor) who coordinates the activities of a supervisor or client – movie star, sports star, etc.

handout – A press (news) release – prepared material given to news people in the hope that it will be printed without change or that it will be helpful in preparing news stories hard news – important news – straight news reporting without interpretation or background material. Also called *takeaway*.

handraiser – A consumer who contacts a company with a question or comment about its products. Many times, handraisers' comments and possible endorsements are turned into strategic messages or leads to help generate sales.

hard bounce – An e-mail that has been sent back to the sender undelivered without having been accepted by the recipient's e-mail server.

hard break – When a television or radio network program cuts away (leaves the program) to identify the station viewers or watching or listening to. It differs from a *soft break* in that during a *soft break* the identification is made by the host or anchor.

hard copy – Term for the research you have in hand from a news story, or it can refer to the actual print out of the story (rather than what is seen on a computer monitor or screen).

hard news – A story that is truly newsworthy, presented factually and objectively. Many times, it is breaking news. It is information that is timely and relevant to or affects a large number of people.

hard opening – A grand opening celebration of a retail store or other business. See *soft opening*.

hard sell approach – An approach to selling where the salesperson puts pressure on the buyer to make a commitment to purchase.

hardscape – Bricks, concrete and other materials used in *landscaping* projects – decorative items that don't grow. See *landscape*.

harvest strategy – A deliberate decision to cut back expenditure of all kinds on a particular product (usually in the decline stage of its life cycle) to maximize profit from it, even if in doing so it continues to lose market share. See *hold strategy*.

has legs – When a news story gets sustained coverage over a period of time because of its interest to viewers, listeners and readers. Hurricane Katrina, in 2005, is one of those stories editors referred to as "*has legs.*"

hatriol – A lethal combination of hate (to dislike intensely) and vitriol (severe criticism). Coined by Philadelphia-based talk show host Michael Smerconish. Read more at www.mastalk.com.

106 Techniques to Succeed: Home entertaining for business

Entertaining successfully at home can add to your personal image – if done well.

Some techniques for business entertaining at home:

• Make the invitation specific
  – Dress code
  – Time the party starts and ends
  – Whether spouses or dates are invited
  – If a meal will be served

• Check dietary requirements ahead of time and plan simple, easy food to eat

• Prepare your spouse or partner.
  – Try to share something about each person so that they can make conversation with all of your guests

• Make sure children are well-behaved or have a baby sitter available.

• Be cautious with alcoholic beverages

• As the host, make sure you mingle with everyone.
  – Help others mingle, also.
  – If everyone doesn't know everyone, make the introduction.

• Don't just talk about business.
  – This is an opportunity to get to know others outside of the business environment. (Just don't get too personal.)

• Offer a brief speech or toast to welcome your guests

Barbara Pachter - Business Coach
When The Little Things Count - And They Always Count - (Marlowe & Company)
856-751-6141

The ABCs of Strategic Communication

H

hawk – To sell. See *hawker* below.

hawker – Someone who travels around selling products or wares (street vendors) much like a peddler, pitchperson or huckster (a seller who yells a message to potential buyers).

head end – The site in a cable system or broadband coaxial network where the programming originates and the distribution network starts. Signals are usually received off the air from satellites, microwave relays or fiber-optic cables at the head end for distribution. Used in video conferencing.

107 Tips to Succeed: Update HR policies to avoid lawsuits

In August 2003, two Caucasian plaintiffs sued Ricoh Electronics Inc., headquartered in West Caldwell, alleging they had been passed over for promotion based on their race or national origin. They claimed the firm had a practice of promoting Japanese and other Asians ahead of Caucasians.

In March 2005, a jury unanimously found that the company did not discriminate on the basis of race or national origin.

Employers should consider these practices to minimize their exposure to a similar claim:

• Maintain good human resources policies, including harassment and discrimination policies, and communicate those policies to all employees.

• Ensure that management and employees adhere to the company's policies.

• Maintain and enforce policies for handling a complaint of harassment or discrimination.

• Provide training for all management on harassment and discrimi-nation awareness and on what to do if management receives a complaint.

• Conduct regular employee performance reviews to document employee performance; and provide clear written feedback to employees.

Dan Callahan - Partner with law firm Callahan & Blaine (represented Ricoh®)
714-241-4444

head-to-head competition – A competitive situation where the second or third leading company decides to challenge the leader.

header (head) – Element or elements repeated at the top of each page. It can include the chapter title, newsletter title, date, page number, etc. Also called *standing head*. See *footer*.

headline – The title or heading of a newspaper or magazine article, broadcast news report or news release (not to be confused with a *slug*) that indicates the subject matter of the story.

headshot – A picture of a person's shoulders and above – sometimes referred to as a "thumbnail" picture or cut.

Health Insurance Portability and Accountability Act (HIPPA) – Under HIPPA, healthcare entities must take specific steps to protect the privacy and personally identifiable information of their patients, including names, Social Security numbers and diagnoses. The Act is federally enforced by the U.S. Department of Health and Human Services' Office of Civil Rights.

healthcare PR –Specialty public relations discipline that communicates about healthcare products or issues to medical groups, interested third parties, specialist media and the general public.

hectoring – Television reporters allowing the pictures or sounds to tell the story. The more dramatic the story, the less a reporter should say. The reporter should allow the pictures to tell the story. Ron Nessen, President Gerald Ford's press secretary and Brookings Institution vice president of communications, used the term on National Public Radio. See *fiber screeching reporters*.

hedge and wedge – Technique used by public relations practitioner whereby they conduct research to determine where a public may be vulnerable to a change in behavior. Once the opening (See *aperture*) is found, a strategic message is delivered with behavior change as its goal.

hedonists – Individuals who habitually seek pleasurable experiences. Consumers, who, by nature, seek products which provide them with the most pleasure, without regard to calories, sugar content, salt content, cholesterol levels, coloring or preservative additives, etc. Research shows *hedonists* are above-average consumers of chocolates, soft drinks, beer, etc.

hegemony – The dominance of one social class over others.

The ABCs of Strategic Communication

108 Techniques to Succeed: The proper business handshake

There are five basic types of handshakes most of us have experienced – none is correct.

Try *this* for success:

PROPER HANDSHAKING

The protocol for handshaking is simple to learn: Walk up to the person you want to meet. Look into their eyes, smile and extend you hand. Offer a warm, firm, palm-to-palm handshake.

When you proffer your hand to a stranger or a distant acquaintance, simultaneously say, "My name is......(use both first and last names). This way you eliminate the awkward moment of the forgotten name. The person being greeted is often relieved at being reminded, and will usually respond with their full name, which will in turn relieve you.

Both men and women should rise to shake hands. Rising is a compliment – it shows energy and eagerness to connect.

Initiating a proper handshake will make an incredibly positive impression. You will be perceived as a person who is knowledgeable, possesses excellent social skills and has leadership capabilities.

An excellent handshake shows your charm and self-confidence. It becomes an integral part of your style.

DON'T BE ONE OF THESE:

• **Knuckle Cruncher**

This type of person is earnest but nervous. While meaning to convey warmth through a tight grip of your hand, the person only causes you pain. The impression created is definitely that of a person who lacks sensitivity.

• **Dead Fish Handshaker**

This type of person, who places a limp, lifeless hand in yours, is sending a negative message. While the knuckle cruncher hurts you, at least there is a desire to express a real feeling. You are left with the impression of this person having a lackluster personality.

• **Pumper**

This handshake is overly eager but also insecure. This person doesn't know when to quit, almost as if stalling because of not knowing what to do next. They keep on vigorously pumping your hand up and down – and with it your entire arm. You may not feel pain but you certainly feel foolish.

- **Sanitary Handshaker**
  This person will barely put three or four fingers in your hand-and then withdraw them quickly, almost as if afraid of catching a dread disease. They appear timid and sheepish.

- **Condolence Handshaker**
  This is the person who comes across as too familiar, clasping your right arm or hand, and perhaps attempting to hug you. This behavior may be appreciated at a funeral, but it comes across as condescending and inappropriate.

The Canadian Progress Club - Bob Lockhart - National President Elect
www.progressclub.ca/Whats_New/Progression/2005_03/04Features_01.htm

helicopter bosses – Those who watch closely over their employees.

helicopter parents – Those who watch closely over their children.

hell and high water – Saying used by people caught between "a rock and the hard place." In other words, two difficult situations. Also surviving or overcoming nearly insuperable obstacles. An example, "I will graduate from college *come hell or high water*." In 1939, Paul Wellman published a book with the title *Trampling Herd: the Story of the Cattle Range in America* in which he wrote: "'In spite of hell and high water' is a legacy of the cattle trail when the cowboys drove their horn-spiked masses of long-horns through high water at every river and continuous hell between."

herd journalism – Much like lemming journalism – when a pack of reporters rush to cover the same story. See *lemming journalism*.

Herzberg's theory of motivation – A theory of motivation, used in public relations, developed by Henry Herzberg where satisfiers (factors that cause satisfaction) are distinguished from dissatisfiers (factors which cause dissatisfaction). The theory proves consumers will compare the number and degree of satisfiers to the number and degree of dissatisfiers before making purchase decisions. See *Freudian motivation theory*; *Maslow's hierarchy of needs*.

heterogeneity – One of the four characteristics (with *inseparability*, *intangibility* and *perishability*) which distinguish a service. It expresses the notion that a service may vary in standard or quality from one provider to the next or from occasion to the next. Also referred to as *variability*.

heterogeneous shopping goods – Products perceived by consumers as considerably different in quality and attributes – price is less important. See *homogeneous shopping goods; shopping goods.*

hiatus – A period of time during which advertising is not run. *Hiatus* is referred to when an advertiser purchases several flights (advertising schedules) and then takes time off before continuing its ad campaign – or abandoning it all together.

hibernate – The process of a computer going into a "sleep mode" – powering off. *Hibernation* does not damage computer and does not the shorten lifespan. *Hibernation* makes a snapshot of a PC's state, records it on the hard drive, then sends the PC into a truly deep, power-saving sleep. When the PC is roused or awakened, you start working where you left off.

hibernating – The process a computer goes through as it powers off or shuts down. See *hibernate.*

hickey – In printing, a spot or imperfection in the printing, commonly caused by dirt on the film or flakes in the ink.

hidden objection – An unstated objection which a prospective buyer has to a product offered by a salesperson. See objection; invalid objection; stated objection; valid objection.

hierarchy of effects models – Illustrations of the notion that marketing and other types of promotion induce consumers to move from one mental state to the next before eventually deciding to purchase a particular product or service. For example, in the *AIDA model* the steps are awareness, interest, desire and action. In the Lavidge and Steiner's expanded model (1962) they are ignorance, awareness, knowledge, liking, preference, conviction and

109 Tips to Succeed:

Impress the boss – know the difference between *home in* and *hone*

Home in – Direct onto a point or target. For example: *The firm homed in on the public relations plan's goal.*

Hone – To sharpen or perfect. For example: *A speaker who honed her delivery by long practice. Hone your skills before asking for a raise.*

purchase. The diffusion model's steps are awareness, interest, trial evaluation and adoption (or rejection).

hierarchy-of-effects theory – A series of steps where consumers receive and use information in reaching decisions about whether or not to buy a product. A set of consumer responses that moves from the least serious, least involved or least complex up through the most serious, involved or complex.

110 Tips to Succeed:
Look for errors in handbooks

Even small firms – with just one employee – should have an employee handbook. But often employers forget to include key elements in their manuals.

Employers should review their manuals to make certain these five top errors are avoided and the issues have been addressed:

• Lack of acknowledgment. Employers forget to have the employee sign an acknowledgment page stating they have received the manual and are responsible for reading it. The paper should be filed in the employee's personnel file.

• Employers are still using the term "probationary" for their introductory period of employment, which is usually 90 days. Probationary implies that at the end of the 90 days they will become a permanent employee. This in turn implies an employment contract.

• Employers might have a harassment policy, but often they don't spell out clearly and plainly how to and whom to see to file a complaint. Too many policies are too vague.

• Employers often use the term "salaried" instead of defining employment categories as regular full time with exempt and nonexempt categories, and regular part time.

• Forgetting to update. Most employers don't update their handbooks often enough. Manuals should be reviewed regularly and updated every two to three years or as necessary to reflect law and employment regulation changes.

Christine Mazza Schaefer - President of CEM HR Strategies, Inc. - Woodbury, N.J. - 856-845-0060

111

Tips to Succeed:
Avoiding holiday office party overload

How to get in, get out, and stay in line

According to a recent survey of nearly 3,000 adults conducted by New York based market research firm Harris Interactive, the average American will attend 2.7 office parties during a holiday season and spend 2 hours and 36 minutes at each. Now that you know you'll be spending at least a few wonderful evenings this December wearing funny hats, eating crazy cracker creations and avoiding those darned mistletoed doorposts, how can you make the most of this season's merry making?

Here are a few tips on how to tackle office parties:

1. **Appropriate Dress is Essential** – If in doubt, leave it out. Save your party clothes for personal gatherings.

2. **Limit Libations** – Keep any type of a drink other than eggnog to a minimum. Holiday party '"disasters" follow you back into the office for the whole year.

3. **Ho, Ho, Ho, It's Almost Review Time** – Make sure you say hello to your boss, his or her boss and other co-workers that you haven't seen recently.

4. **Bring Your "Ball and Chain"** – If your work allows it, bring your spouse. He or she can be helpful when conversing with co-workers you really don't know, can help you remember others and help keep the conversation flowing.

Look at the holiday office party as an opportunity to see and be seen. Make the most of it, enjoy your co-workers, indulge in a piece of fruitcake and have your exit strategy when you've made all of your holiday connections. Remember, you will see them at work again very soon!

www.selfmarketing.com

hierarchy of needs – See *Maslow's hierarchy of needs*.

high-contact retailing – A relatively new trend in retailing where some retailers attempt to position themselves by emphasizing some aspects of their products rather than the products themselves.

high–definition television (HDTV) – A higher quality signal resolution using a digital format for the transmission and reception of TV signals. *HDTV* provides about five times more picture information (picture elements or pixels) than conventional television, creating clarity and wider aspect ratio as well as digital quality sound.

high-involvement products – Products for which the buyer is prepared to spend considerable time and effort researching – because of its long-term importance. Examples might include a refrigerator, television or some other appliance. See *low-involvement products.*

high Murrow/low Murrow – Referring to legendary broadcast journalist Edward R. Murrow. High Murrow is serious, non nonsense journalism. Low Murrow refers to more human interest type stories. CBS News is proud to say that its perennially top-rated program "60 Minutes" is both.

high-price strategy – A planned approach to pricing – sometimes called *prestige pricing* – (appropriate in situations of inelastic demand) where a manufacturer decides to keep its prices high. Some reasons given for such a strategy include a growing segment of the market, overcrowding at the bottom-end of the market or the desire to create a prestige image for the product. Also called *premium pricing.*

high scalers – Workers who dangle from sides of mountains, bridges, buildings or other high places during the construction process.

high-touch service – Customer service that is characterized by a high level of personal contact with customers, as opposed to *low-touch* customer service which is provided by vending machines, self-service counters, etc. See *low-touch service.*

Hispanic marketing – Advertising and promotional activity aimed at the 41 million (and growing) Hispanic members of the U.S. Hispanic consumer market. Its goal is to capture part of the hundreds of billions in buying power this powerful market represents. Public relations and advertising practitioners recognize that effective Hispanic marketing goes far beyond just language translation. It's important to develop culturally appropriate materials to appeal to this target audience. A critical element of any Hispanic public relations or marketing campaign is to successfully convey the intended strategic message. Manufacturers and businesses across the nation are closing the gap on the language barrier by including product information, labeling and instructions in both English and Spanish. Hispanic marketing niche agencies or boutiques may also be able to give businesses an advantage by implementing their expertise of culture and language into the marketing mix to achieve synergy. Successful *channels* may include Hispanic radio, television and print publications.

historical analogy – An approach to sales forecasting where past sales results of a similar product are used to predict the likely sales of a similar new product.

historical budgeting method – A relatively simplistic version of budgeting. It is based on previous budgets (several years). A budget may simply be based on last year's budget with a percentage increase for inflation or *some other marketplace factor.*

history lists – A drop-down menu on a computer which displays the sites you've recently visited so you can return to the site instantly or view your latest session. The same mechanism makes it possible for servers to track where you were before visiting a particular site.

hit – Each time a news story appears in or on a different media vehicle. In an Internet sense, it is a visit to a particular page on a Web site by a Web visitor. See *ad value* and *impression.*

ho-hum products – A colloquial term used in reference to common, everyday items (such as paper clips, thumb tacks, staples and scribble pads) which cannot be differentiated significantly from those of competitors. Purchasers of "ho–hum" products generally favor the cheapest available.

hoisting the flag – An approach to product introduction or launching – useful when product features are "improved."

hold (Hold For Release [HFR]) – A date indicating when a news release may be published. See *embargo.*

hold strategy – A course of action appropriate for a product (usually in the decline stage of its life cycle) when a company decides to hold by keeping expenditures on it to a minimum to maximize the return before having to delete it from the line. See *harvest strategy.*

holdbacks – A term used by car manufacturers and new car dealers. It is a percentage of either the manufacturer's suggested retail price (MSRP) or invoice price of a new vehicle (depending on the manufacturer) that is repaid to the dealer by the manufacturer. The holdback is designed to supplement the dealer's cash flow and indirectly reduce "variable sales expenses" (code words for sales commissions) by artificially elevating the dealership's paper cost. For example, many times when a dealer shows a prospective customer the paper invoice, it does not include the *holdback*, which the dealer eventually receives.

112

Tips to Succeed:
Hosting a business dinner

When you host a business dinner, remember one crucial point: You are in charge.

Doing business over dinner is a good way to introduce yourself to clients, build relationships and seal the deal. Get it right, and it's duck soup. Get it wrong, and you're dead in the water.

HELPFUL HINT NO. 1: Be sure the date works for you. This seems obvious, but if you have to postpone or cancel, you'll look disorganized and will have wasted your clients' time.

• Always call ahead and make it clear to the maitre d' that you will be hosting an important business dinner. Stress that everything must be perfect and that you'll pay the bill. Make arrangements with the restaurant to pay the bill prior to the dinner.

• Be sure to call your clients the day before to confirm the dinner. If there's a mix up on their end, be gracious and reschedule.

• When preparing for the event, dress in appropriate business attire, and kick it up a notch. This underscores your seriousness about the clients and their business. It's better to be a little over-dressed than woefully under-dressed.

• On the day of the meal, get to the restaurant ahead of time so you'll have a chance to attend to any last-minute details. A tip in advance never hurts.

HELPFUL HINT NO. 2: Don't forget seating strategy. Work out the seating before your guests arrive.

• Make sure the guests have the best seats – those with a view of the water or skyline, for example. You don't want your guests facing the wall, kitchen or restrooms. If the table isn't suitable, don't be bashful about asking for a better one.

• This is a business dinner, and you don't want to shout across the table. If you have one client, sit next to each other. If you have two clients, seat one across from you and the other to your side.

HELPFUL HINT NO. 3: Limit the amount of alcohol you and your guests consume at dinner.

• The meal is about business. It might be wise to stick with wine.

• If you must excuse yourself, do so only between courses.

The ABCs of Strategic Communication

holding audience (holdover audience) – The percent of a program's audience that watched or listened to the immediately preceding program on the same station. Also called inherited audience.

holding company – A company that owns stock in other corporations.

holding costs – Costs associated with keeping inventory, including warehousing, spoilage, obsolescence, interest and taxes. Also called *inventory carrying costs*.

holding power – The ability to keep an audience throughout a broadcast, rather than having them change channels. It is represented as a percent of the total audience.

hologram – A three-dimensional photograph or illustration created with an optical process that uses lasers.

holography – A technique that produces a projected three-dimensional image.

home delivery model – Used by e-commerce and original catalog houses such as Montgomery Ward®, Sears®, JCPenny® and others. It is direct-to-home delivery. First used by the dairy industry, which discovered housewives enjoyed the convenience of fresh milk being delivered to their homes early in the morning.

home page – The page designated as the main point of entry of a Web site (or main page) or the starting point when a browser first connects to the Internet. Typically, it welcomes you and introduces the purpose of the site, or the organization sponsoring it, and then provides links to other pages within the site.

home shopping – Forms of non-store retailing which include television home shopping (in which articles are demonstrated on TV so that consumers can place telephone orders for direct-to-home delivery), videotext or electronic catalogue shopping, etc.

113

Technique to Succeed: Customer Service – Practice the 'Customer Delight Principle'

Turning regular customers into loyal customers assures repeat business. Determine what they need, want and expect – and give them more. It's achievable through relationship marketing – learning as much as you can demographically, psychographically and geodemographically.

Smiling at clientele, promptly responding to requests or complaints, and honoring warranties isn't enough to make the rigorous customer service grade any longer. Many experts would argue that standard amenities don't represent customer service at all because they are expected as a matter of course.

• Ask for customers' e-mail addresses and send them special offers.

• Empower your employees to handle customer disputes.

• Meet daily with employees to discuss customer issues and invite input from your staff on how each should be handled.

• Keep an eye on the competition.

Do as Nordstrom's does:
Start with the Basics

1. Make customer service a core value.

2. Hire the right people.

3. Empower your employees.

4. Solicit and use feedback.

5. Target your customers

Get Your Creativity Flowing

Once the basics are in place, you and your employee team can unleash your collective creativity to develop ways to further enhance customer service.

Here are some ways to get that process moving.

1. *Order pizza* and have a freewheeling brainstorming session. Create an atmosphere that encourages everyone to share their "wild and crazy" ideas. Be open to any suggestions – reject nothing at this stage.

2. *Make it fun.*

3. *Bring in professional trainers* to conduct a seminar on a particular aspect of customer service.

4. *Give everyone on your staff* a copy of a popular customer service book and hold a round-table discussion to see if any of the suggestions might be applicable to your business.

5. *Start a rewards program* for the best customer service idea, making it something significant and enticing that employees will strive to achieve.

Examples of Innovative Ideas

1. **Give your customers something unexpected** – a special treat.

2. **Extend the warrant on your product**. This communicates both a quality statement and a commitment to customer satisfaction.

3. **Add value through information**. Provide your customers with new ways to use your products or increase their efficiency. This can include newsletters, special seminars or face-to-face consultations.

4. **Use the Internet**. Improve the frequency of your customer communications via e-mail. Brief notes with tips on product usage, coupons and special offers – even just a seasonal greeting – can keep your firm top of mind. One caveat: always give your customers an easy way to be deleted from your e-mail list if they so desire.

5. **Celebrate with your customers**. Sending birthday cards and congratulatory notes on new babies and job promotions may seem "old hat," but in today's depersonalized world, it's appreciated once again. Add a coupon for a special gift or discount on the customer's next visit. (Hello, Sports Fans! – Cherry Hill, N.J. found great success from this relationship marketing technique.)

6. **Expand your services or product line**. In today's harried environment people prize convenience and time savings. Ask your clientele how you can serve them better – subsequently extending your product and service offerings to provide additional benefits for your customers and additional profits for you.

7. **Employ mass customization**. Offer your clients options that result in products that are "tailor-made" to their needs. As Burger King has said for years, "Have it you way!"

The ultimate key is to put yourself in the position of your customers. Give them what they want—and a little bit more. They will be delighted and, in turn, will delight you with a prosperous and rewarding business.

Bill Kalmar - Former Malcolm Baldrige National Quality Award examiner (judged firms for annual U.S. Commerce Department awards) - Lake. Orion, Mich.
Gannett News Service

114 Tips to Succeed: The elevator 'speech'

The "elevator pitch" is a short description about your company that you can convey in the time it takes to ride an elevator. And not an elevator in a skyscraper, either. Your elevator pitch must be clear and concise and show that you understand the core aspects of your business.

Because it must be short, you have to decide what facets of your company to leave out. Often, these can be the things you're most excited about – a new technology, a great location, outstanding customer service, etc.

But if they're not central to the core or success of your business, they don't belong in an elevator pitch.

You should touch – very briefly – on the products or services you sell, what market you serve, and your competitive advantage.

You must be brief and clear. Unless you're in a highly technical field, your neighbor or grandmother should be able to understand your business well enough to describe it to someone else. After all, you want grandma marketing for you too, don't you? People you meet need to quickly understand the nature of your business if you want them to send business your way.

Make sure your employees, investors, even vendors know your company's elevator pitch. Have your employees practice your company's elevator pitch so they're able to network for you as well.

It's often a good idea to use an analogy, especially if you're in a new or difficult-to-grasp field. "We're the Google for car buyers" is a good shorthand way to say that you're trying to create a search engine for people wanting to purchase an automobile.

Think in these terms (sort of like a mission statement):

• This is who we are;

• What we think about ourselves;

• What we want to do;

• Why we deserve your support

You'll find you use your elevator pitch often – in e-mails to prospective customers and investors, to introduce yourself at organizational meetings or when running into an old friend at a

The ABCs of Strategic Communication

ballgame. Who knows? You may even use it if you meet a potential customer in an elevator.

So go out and find a three-story building with an elevator, ride up and down and practice your pitch. That way, you'll be prepared the next time some one asks you, "What do you do?"

Rhonda Abrams - Gannett News Service
M. Larry Litwin, APR, Fellow PRSA - Author - *The Public Relations Practitioner's Playbook*

homogeneous shopping goods – Shopping goods perceived by consumers to be essentially the same in quality and attributes. It turns out that price becomes the deciding factor. See *heterogeneous shopping goods*; *shopping goods*.

hook – The stylistic device used by a reporter to draw a reader into the story.

hook-ups – Much like *tie-ins*. Two products that complement each other, but sold as separates in retail stores – a dress shirts and tie; blouse and slacks.

horizontal channel conflict – Discord among members at the same level of a marketing channel, e.g. wholesaler-wholesaler discord or retailer-retailer discord. See *inter-type channel conflict; vertical channel conflict*.

horizontal cooperative advertising – Shared advertising by two or more members at the same level of a distribution channel, each paying part of the total cost – partnering or co-authoring. This is different from normal co-op advertising where retailers and manufacturers share the cost for advertising a particular brand.

horizontal discount – A discount on a media purchase resulting from a promise to advertise over an extended period of time.

horizontal diversification – A growth strategy where a company seeks to add new products (line extensions) to its existing lines that will appeal to existing customers.

horizontal integration – A strategy for growth where a company develops by seeking ownership of, or some measure of control over, some of its competitors. See *forward integration*.

115

Techniques to Succeed:

Internet security: Password creation takes homework and creativity

Develop different strong passwords for every system or program you log into.

If an attacker does guess it, he would have access to all of your accounts. You should use these techniques to develop unique passwords for each of your accounts:

- Don't use passwords that are based on personal information that can be easily accessed or guessed.
- Don't use words that can be found in any dictionary of any language.
- Develop a mnemonic for remembering complex passwords.
- Use both lowercase and capital letters.
- Use a combination of letters, numbers and special characters.
- Use different passwords on different systems.

U.S. Department of Homeland Security

horizontal market – A market for a product, which is bought by many industries. See *vertical market*.

horizontal marketing management – Independent firms on the same level in a marketing channel work closely together in buying, promotion, etc. to save money and achieve other economies of scale to remain competitive.

horizontal price fixing – The practice, usually unlawful, of sellers of different brands of the same product making agreements to charge the same price to consumers. See *collusion*; *price fixing*; *vertical price fixing*.

horizontal publications – Publications directed to consumers who hold similar jobs in different companies across different industries. Also, business publications designed to appeal to people of similar interests or responsibilities in a variety of companies or industries. Examples would include magazines directed at business managers, sales, truckers, etc.

host – Any computer on a network that offers services or connectivity to other computers on the network. A host has an *IP (Internet Protocol)* address associated with it.

host/hostess gift – A gift to a consumer who sponsors a sales demonstration party or meeting.

host selling – A show's primary host or children's show characters who "pitch" a product. There are federal regulations pertaining to children's television advertising. Also advertising contained on Web site *home pages*.

hot – A label given to an important story.

hot composition – A method of typesetting that uses molten metal to form the letters for a typeface. Also called hot type. See *cold type*.

hot plugging –The ability to remove and replace components of a computer, while it is operating. Once the appropriate software is installed, a user can plug and unplug the component – such as a *flash drive, key drive, thumb drive*, etc. without rebooting. Any of the *Universal Serial Bus (USB)* devices have changed the way computer files are transported. Also called *hot swapping*.

hot spot – see *hyperlink*.

hot swapping – See *hot plugging*.

hotline names – Most recent buyers on a mailing or other "customer list."

hotspots – Areas outside in many communities or inside buildings (offices, colleges, coffee shops, hotel lobbies, etc.) that offer wireless connection to the Internet if laptops and other types of devices are equipped with a special card.

house accounts – Large accounts serviced by head office personnel or company executives rather than by an individual salesperson. Sometimes called *direct accounts* or *national accounts*.

house ads – Advertisements by the publication for the publication in which it appears – or by the organization sponsoring the publication. They are also called promos –

116 Techniques to Succeed:

Perfecting business letters

The ability to write a perfect business letter is an important skill. Here are some ways to improve your letter writing:

• Map out your thinking and go to others for suggestions.

• Make a bold statement in the beginning of the letter to grab the reader's attention.

• Write simply.

• Be specific.

• Accentuate the positive things your company has done.

• Edit your work.

• End with a catchy statement.

Gannett News Service

newspapers, magazines, radio or television stations running ads or commercials about themselves, their sections or programs. Revenues from house ads, if there are any, should not be included in reported revenues.

house agency – An advertising agency owned and operated by an advertiser, which handles the advertiser's own account.

house list – A mail, telephone or e-mail list compiled and therefore owned by a company rather than being purchased or rented from a third party. (A list bought with a contract that allows unlimited use would, after purchase, become part of the purchaser's house list.)

house organ – A company-published newsletter, magazine or other publication used to promote the advertiser's products or services.

house style guide – A style sheet or guide adopted by companies and organizations – many time to supplement the *AP Style Book*. Organization style may differ from *AP style* or common practice.

house to house distribution – Delivery of goods or literature to the consumer's front door or mailbox.

housefile – Commonly referred to as a customer list. A housefile is a consolidated database containing each customer's name, address and summarized order information. Some information is now being challenged by individual states' Open Public Records Acts.

household – All those people who occupy one living unit – whether or not they are related.

households using television (HUT) – The number of households in a given market watching television at a certain time. This term is used by A.C. Nielsen.

huckster – A retailer – usually one who sells goods from the back of a truck or van – and yells to his potential buyers. Also a person who writes radio or television commercials. See *hawker*.

human interest – Emotional appeal in the news. A "human interest" story, as compared with a "straight news" story, bases its appeal more on the unusual than on consequence.

hybrid pricing – Pricing model based on a combination of a cost per thousand CPM pricing model and a performance-based pricing model. See *CPM pricing model*.

hydrogen sippers – Cars that use hydrogen for fuel.

hype/hyperbole – Exaggerated or extravagant claims made especially in advertising or promotional material. A figure of speech in which exaggeration is used for emphasis or effect, as in "I could sleep for a year" or "This book weighs a ton."

Hyper-Text Markup Language (HTML) – A set of codes called markup tags in a plain text file (*.txt) that determine what information is retrieved and how it is rendered by a web browser. There are two kinds of markup tags – anchor and format. Anchor tags determine what is retrieved, and format tags determine how it is rendered.

Hyper-Text Transfer Protocol (HTTP) – The format most commonly used to transfer information on the World Wide Web.

hyperlink – An element in an electronic document that when clicked on, links to another place in the same document or to an entirely different document. A hyperlink can bring you to a Web site, Web page or link you to an e-mail address.

117 Tips to Succeed: Product placement

A growing number of advertisers are using technology that makes their products appear in places they weren't before.

It's called digital product integration, and it's the new frontier for paid product placements – embedded advertising.

Advertisers such as Chevrolet® and Dannon® yogurt are among the marketers using technology to digitally insert their products into scenes of popular prime-time TV episodes after the episode has been filmed.

In general, product placements – in which products are strategically placed in TV shows, movies, video games, songs and books – are booming as advertisers try to grab the attention of consumers who have video recording devices to dodge the traditional 30-second commercial.

www.courierpostonline.com
M. Larry Litwin, APR, Fellow PRSA - Author - *The Public Relations Practitioner's Playbook*

hyperbuild – Use of prefabricated or preconstructed "finished" sections – not just materials – of roads, bridges, buildings, etc. The secret of the efficiency is building larger components offsite and storing tem at near-by locations. *Hyperbuild* also involves more and better planning (mind-share) before beginning a project, tighter deadlines and adhering to those deadlines. Products must be tested and deemed safe and reliable. *Hyperbuild* products are being used in *fast-tracking*.

hypermarket – A giant, one-stop shopping facility offering a wide choice of grocery and general merchandise at discount prices. Examples would include B-J's®, Costco® and Sam's Club®.

hypermiler – People who try to get the most mileage possible out of their car's gas.

hyphenator – a woman who marries and chooses to retain her maiden (*nee*) name when she marries by joining it with her husband's last name using a hyphen.

hypothesis – A theory that allows itself to be disproved by experiment.

i-Coach – Online support service for marketing students and delegates, offering online tutorials, case studies and exercises.

iceberg principle – A theory that suggests that aggregated data can hide information that is important for the proper evaluation of a situation.

iconography – Study of icons, pictures and/or images. Also the study or analysis of subject matter and its meaning in the visual arts.

ID – Station identification during a commercial break in a television or radio program. Station IDs must include call letters and city of license.

idea – A mental representation. Also, a concept created by combining thoughts. See *mind share*.

idea generation – The first stage in the new product development process – the sourcing of ideas for new products. Important sources include the firm's own R & D (research and development) work, focus groups, competitor's products and suggestions from customers, distributors and salespeople. See *new product development*.

idea marketing – Activities associated with the marketing of a cause or idea. See *broadening concept*.

idea screening – An early stage in the new product development process when ideas for new products are sifted or screened to identify those that the firm might profitably develop; two broad approaches to idea screening are possible: managerial judgment and customer evaluation. See *drop error*; *go error*; *new product development*; *screening*.

ideal brand model – A model used to study consumer evaluation of alternative products. In this model, the consumer compares actual brands to a hypothetical ideal brand. Among other models used for this purpose are the expectancy-value model, conjunctive model, disjunctive model, lexicographic model and determinance model.

identity – How an organization or firm wants to be perceived – what you are.

identifier – Information superimposed on the television screen identifying the person and/or story. It is stationary rather than a *crawl* (moving across the screen).

identify, personalize, solve the problem (IPS) – When a member of the public answers questions about challenges or problem, the public relations practitioner attempts to make the individual or group relate so that it becomes personal and familiar. As the audience solves the problem or meets the challenge, they persuade themselves to change their behavior.

identify segment (fragment), profile, rank (ISPR or IFPR) – Audience identification and ranking method.

identifiability – One of the four major requirements for useful market segmentation; *identifiability*, sometimes referred to as *measurability*, expresses the notion that the size and purchasing power of the segment must be able to be measured. See *accessibility*; *actionability*; *substantiality*.

identity – How an organization or firm wants to be perceived.

---

118 Tips to Succeed:
Just what does *APR* stand for?

When it comes to communication professions, it has nothing to do with interest rates.

APR is Accreditation in Public Relations, a designation for public relations professionals who are selected based on broad knowledge, strategic perspective and sound professional judgment.

The APR program is administered by the Universal Accreditation Board, which was created in 1998. It is a consortium of 10 professional communication organizations.

www.praccreditation.org

---

ideology – A system of ideas and beliefs. In communication studies, the term is often used to refer to a "dominant ideology." The idea derives Karl Marx's use of the term to apply to any system of thought which upholds the position of the dominant class – "In every historical epoch the dominant ideas are those of the ruling classes."

illustration – An original drawing. Usually done by hand, but sometimes done on a computer.

image – Much like reputation – how the public perceives an organization or firm. It is the opinion or concept of something that is held by the public and/or interpreted by the mass media.

image advertising – Rather than promoting a product, brand or service's specific attributes, *image advertising* promotes a general perception of a company, product or service. *Image advertising* is generally used to position a product relative to the competition. For example, to create an *image* of it as producer of a luxury product (Mercedes Benz® cars or Coach® bags) or macho product (Timberland® boots). See *corporate advertising campaign*.

image analysis – A scaling device for measuring a target audience's attitudes and opinions of an issue, a company, products, etc. Responses are commonly recorded on a five-stage (Likert) scale: 1. Very Unfavorable 2. Somewhat Unfavorable 3. Indifferent 4. Somewhat Favorable 5. Very Favorable. See *familiarity scale*.

image differentiation – As a source of competitive advantage, a company may differentiate itself from its competitors by *image*. The particular *image*, perception or "personality" it acquires is created by its logo and other symbols, its advertising, its atmosphere, its events and personalities. Other sources of differentiation for competitive advantage include product differentiation, services differentiation and personnel differentiation.

image manipulation – Used both by professional printers and desktop publishers. Printers can make changes in *illustrations* manually or by computer. Desktop publishing takes advantage of such programs as Photoshop. *Image manipulation* calls for accurate calibration and a keen eye.

image-oriented change strategy – An *advertising plan* or tactic intended to change a *brand's* image (rather than to maintain it over time) which relies on imagery and symbolism (rather than on printed or spoken information) to achieve its objective. See *image-oriented mainte-*

nance strategy; *information-oriented change strategy*; *information-oriented maintenance strategy*.

image-oriented maintenance strategy – An *advertising plan* or tactic intended to maintain a *brand's* position over time (rather than to change its position) which relies on imagery and symbolism (rather than on printed or spoken information) to achieve its objective. See *image-oriented change strategy*; *information-oriented change strategy*; *information-oriented maintenance strategy*.

image persistence – The idea that images may persist long after an organization has changed. For example, many years ago, Sears Roebuck and Company attempted to move toward a more upscale-type department store. It changed its logo to just the name Sears. The approach never reached the success aimed for.

image pricing – A pricing strategy where prices are set at a high level, recognizing that lower prices will inhibit sales rather than encourage them and that buyers will associate a high price for the product with superior quality. Also called *prestige pricing*. See *psychological pricing*.

image utility – The value given to a product because it brings satisfaction to the user in creating prestige and esteem. See *utility*.

imagery – Symbols, images or graphic representations used in advertising to suggest a particular mood or feeling.

imagesetter – A typesetting device that produces very high-resolution output on paper or film. Imagesetters are too expensive for homes or most offices, but can be obtained by taking or sending files to a printer or franchise location such as Kinko's®. Also called *pre-press services*.

immediate audience – The people responsible for evaluating a report and getting it to the appropriate decision makers.

immeasurable bonus impressions – Silent publicity – impressions shown or heard through residual media.

impact – Force that an advertisement or message will have on a target consumer. Television advertising should have a greater impact than print media or *billboards* because it evokes greater excitment and emotion.

impact evaluation – Determining to what extent a campaign informed, persuaded, influenced or changed public opinion and/or behavior in the desired direction.

impingement points – Also called hash marks. Incremental deadline dates for the completion of certain tactics in a public relations or other communication plan. When planning backwards – from the deadline – *impingement* (dates) *points* are clearly marked on a *Gantt chart.*

implementation – The stage in the marketing management process when plans are put into action. See *marketing management.*

implied warranty – The notion that manufacturers are liable for injury caused by a product even if there has been no negligence in manufacturing. Implied warranty has been upheld by courts in recent years in response to mounting consumer complaints that a product is covered by

119 Tips to Succeed:
Be proactive to keep identity secure

- Centralize your banking – Keep credit cards, mortgages, bank accounts, all in one place.
- Ask your bank or credit organization about its policy for selling customer information.
- Request your information not be sold to brokers.
- Reconcile bank statements, credit card statements and other accounts monthly.
- Check your credit report at least once a year.
- If you think you've been a victim of fraud, ask about a fraud alert.

Web sites worth checking:

✓ The Identity Theft Resource Center: www.idtheftcenter.org

✓ Federal Trade Commission's identity theft unit: www.consumer.gov/idtheft or (877) 438-4338. Its TTY line is (866) 653-4261.

✓ Equifax: www.equifax.com or (800) 525-6285

✓ Experian: www.experian.com or (888) 397-3742

✓ TransUnion: www.transunion.com or (800) 680-7289

Jim Walsh - Co-author - *Identity Theft: How to Protect Your Name, Your Credit and Your Vital Information . . . and What to Do When Someone Hijacks Any of These*

warranty even if not expressly stated. The term caveat vendor or "let the seller beware" has never been more relevant. See *warranty*; *express warranty*; *promotional warranty*; *protective warranty*. Also see *caveat emptor*.

import quota – A government-imposed limit on the number, quantity or value of a product to be imported, usually to protect local industry.

imposition – The arrangement of pages that will appear in proper sequence after press sheets are folded and found. Varies according to number of pages, sheet size, printing technique and binding method.

impression – The number of potential readers, listeners or viewers who could see a printed or broadcast story, ad or commercial or number of visitors to a Web site. *Impressions* are based on a publication's circulation or a radio or television program's unduplicated audience. Some consider an *impression* the number of pairs of eyes or ears that will be exposed to a media vehicle. See *hit*.

impression management – Deliberately managing the *impressions* that others form of us. Techniques include self-enhancement to make firms,

120 Techniques to Succeed: Audience Segmentation (ISPR)/ Audience Fragmentation (IFPR)

- Identify
- Segment/Fragment (demographically, psychographically, geodemographically, behavioristically, benefits)
- Profile
- Rank
  - Audience Power Structure
    - Elite (Key Communicators)
    - Pluralistic or Diffused
    - Amorphous/Latent

Audiences are I(S)FPRd as matters of understanding and economics. Public relations practitioners and their clients may have limited resources. Audiences must be I(S)FPRd to help determine which are most important and how much time and money will be allocated trying to reach them to either change, maintain or reinforce behavior. All four steps (I[S]FPR) are imperative to a successful PR plan.

organizations, products, brands and individuals seem good – for example, through smart dress, careful language, etc.

imprinted product – A promotional product. This is a product with a company logo or advertising message printed on it.

improved services strategy – Applying sound management practices to all aspects of the business that touch consumers and clients. Giving consumers the impression that services are getting better.

improvised explosive device (IED) – Booby traps. It is a "homemade" device that is designed to cause death or injury by using explosives alone or in combination with toxic chemicals, biological toxins or radiological material. IEDs can be produced in varying sizes, functioning methods, containers and delivery methods. IEDs can utilize commercial or military explosives, homemade explosives, or military ordnance and ordnance components.

impulse buying – Unplanned consumer buying. It helps if products are attractively presented or conveniently located.

impulse goods – Goods that are purchased quickly because of a sudden urge to have them. See *convenience goods*.

in-company training – Training programs specially tailored to meet company requirements. Researchers believe such programs don't become effective until the audience to be trained (groups) numbers at least six (from the same company).

in-home shopping – Forms of non-store retailing which include television home shopping (where articles are demonstrated on TV so that consumers can place telephone orders for direct-to-home delivery), videotext or electronic catalogue shopping, etc. See *home shopping*.

in-house – All publishing tasks are performed in the company. For example, a staff newsletter published and photocopied within the company to cut down on expensive costs.

in-house agency – An advertising or public relations department within a firm or company (advertiser) that handles most, if not all, of the functions of an outside agency. Many times, *in-house agencies* are viewed as bona fide agencies and receive "agency discounts" from advertising/media outlets.

in kind – A manufacturer, retailer or other type of business donates goods or services to a charity or a nonprofit event in exchange for a mention(s) verbally, on a sign or in event advertising.

in-line producer – TV newscast producer.

in-magazine recognition tests – To test the effectiveness of advertising, individuals selected from the target market are asked to look through a magazine and then to recall advertisements they have seen. See *recognition tests*.

in-market tests – Tests that measure the effectiveness of advertisements by measuring actual sales results in the marketplace.

in-pack premium – A sales promotion where a premium is included in the packaging of another product. For example, you buy a can of shaving cream and get a free razor in the same package or attached to it – a method to encourage consumers to purchased the tied-in product. See *tie-in advertising*.

in register – A precise matching of colors in images.

in-service training sessions – Updating employees during the work day to keep them current. Also called in-service workshops.

in-store media – Media and other techniques and methods used inside department or variety stores, food markets and *big box stores* (warehouse size retailers) to encourage foot traffic and generate more sales. Examples would include specialty TV or radio networks owned and operated by the store, which might include music and news, as well as commercials and promotion.

in-suppliers – Suppliers who are already well known to an organization and from whom they will purchase with confidence. See *out-suppliers*.

in the can – Feature or news stories written and/or recorded by print or broadcast journalists and held for some future publication or air date. Many times, obituaries of well-know people are pre-written. Term derived from the early days of film journalism when photographers would shoot and develop celluloid and place it back in the film can until a future air date.

inbound telemarketing – Telemarketing where a company receives telephone orders and inquiries from consumers. Most times, toll free telephone lines are used. See *outbound telemarketing*.

121

Techniques to Succeed: Keeping sane when stressed by *client* or *co-worker*

It doesn't matter what you do, you're likely to have at least one difficult co-worker or customer. Staying sane during chaos doesn't have to be difficult.

• Draw in as few people as possible. Try to address the situation with the individual without bringing in other people like supervisors. You never know how the situation can be turned around to make *you* look like the problem. Show yourself and the other person that you have the confidence and competence to handle it yourself.

• Don't make it personal. Realize that the reason the person is being difficult might have nothing to do with you. Try to empathize with them and recognize that they need to learn how to manage stress.

• Take control. Ask yourself what you have control over in the situation. It may be that you can control how you choose to respond or that you choose not to discuss the situation at that moment.

• Turn the situation into a challenge or a game. Try to make the best of difficult interpersonal situations by seeing the humor in them or by creating opportunities to learn. For instance, an irate customer lets you practice your poise and assertive communication skills.

• Take a look at *yourself*. We may be fostering annoying behavior by others based on how we respond to it. Try out a different response and see what happens.

Larina Kase - Doctor of Psychology, career coach and former counselor at the University of Pennsylvania - www.extremecommunicator.com

incentive – An inducement to buy. *Incentives* include special price deals, premiums, contests, etc.

incentive catalog company – A company that creates *incentive* programs for agencies, organizations, firms and/or sales people and provides them with a catalog from which to select their prize or premium.

incentive marketing – The offering of gifts, rewards, premiums, etc. to motivate the sales team, to get bigger or more frequent orders from dealers, or to induce consumers to buy.

incentivize – Getting people to act or behave in a certain way. When public relations practitioners (and such sales-people as car dealers) attempt to change behavior, they are *incentiving* their audience.

incremental approach (to calculating sales force size) – An approach used in determining the ideal size of a sales force (or other staff) based on the difference between the expected gross profit that will be earned by the addition of an extra salesperson (or other staff member) and the cost of hiring, training and maintaining that salesperson. A number (point of no return) could be reached where it is no longer profitable to add members to a staff.

incremental-cost pricing (strategy) – A pricing strategy where by the cost of a product continually increases with the addition of ingredients or features. For example, a new house or new car might have a base price, but each option adds to the final cost (price). See *full-cost pricing (strategy)*.

incremental product – A product added to a manufacturer's line to give consumers another price-point choice. For example, General Motors® offers car brands ranging from Chevrolet® to Cadillac®.

incremental sales – Increase in revenue from sales (using established baselines) over a given period. Also the measurement of sales or sales revenue for a particular period.

incremental-cost pricing – An approach where the price of all additional units produced after the fixed costs of production have been met are based on variable cost rather than on total cost. The cost of each additional item once initial break-even has been met.

122 Tips to Succeed:
Tips to make investing work

Investing is a way to make money – but before you invest:

- Pay off consumer loans
- Keep no more than a percentage approximately equal to your age in fixed-income investments
- Don't invest in anything you don't understand
- Don't invest in anything quickly
- Don't hold onto an investment for sentimental reasons
- Get professional advice

www.checklist.com

123

Tips to Succeed: Looking for a job: These tips should help

In addition to Handout No. 29 on www.larrylitwin.com, these tips should come in handy – especially for women:

THE DAY BEFORE THE INTERVIEW

• Make your travel plans for getting to the interview; know exactly where you are going and to whom you will be speaking.

• Buy your ticket of fare for transportation, fill your car with gas, or re-confirm other transportation plans.

• Make sure that you have several clean copies of your resume to take with you.

• Decide what you will wear and check that it is clean, pressed, no missing buttons, etc.

• Check that you have at least two pairs of new or as-good-as-new hosiery – sheer, off black or nude; no opaque or white!

• Confirm child care plans and any other plans which leave you depending on someone else. Have a back-up in mind in case you need it.

• Try to learn two or three facts about the company and/or its products, so you will sound well-informed at the interview (visit their Web site).

THE NIGHT BEFORE THE INTERVIEW

• Check the weather forecast! Will you need an umbrella? Should you wear a coat?

• Decide what you will be taking in your handbag and set it aside. Be sure to include a pen and paper as well as an extra pair of hosiery.

• Plan how you will wear your hair and make-up. (You shouldn't try anything new in the morning.) Make-up should be appropriate for daytime, not Saturday night. No glimmer or shimmer and keep eye makeup to a minimum or wear none at all.

• Check your nails! They should be conservative in length and color; no chipped polish.

• Do as much of your morning preparation for both yourself and your family as you can.

• Do something to relax: take a warm bath, exercise, etc.

• Have a light dinner (no alcohol) and get to bed early.

The ABCs of Strategic Communication

indemnity statement – A document in which a public relations practitioner seeks legal exemption from penalties attaching to unconstitutional or illegal actions – similar to those granted to public officers and other persons. Under the *conduit theory* (Pig 'n Whistle case), in public relations and advertising, the agency or consultant may be held liable for fraud if it passes along misleading information provided by the client. The understanding is that the agency or counselor should have done ample research. For more, see *The Public Relations Practitioner's Playbook* – Kendall/Hunt – 2008).

independent contractor – A person who is hired by a company, but works for himself/herself. The company is a client, rather than an employer. Many times this is done as a cost-saving measure (no need to provide fringe benefits). Taxes are the responsibility of the contractor.

independent station – A broadcast station that is not affiliated with a national network of stations.

index – Table of contents of the newspaper, usually found on page one.

indicia – Imprinted designation on mail that denotes postage payment (e.g., permit imprint). Bulk mail usually contains an *indicia*, but other forms of U.S. mail do, as well.

indirect competition – A product that is in a different category but functions as an alternative purchase choice. For example, a soda or juice drinker may purchase bottled water – just one of the reasons behind such companies as Coke® and Pepsi® purchasing bottled water and juice manufacturers. See *direct competition*.

indirect competitive advertising – Advertising intended to stimulate purchase of a particular brand at some future time. See *direct competitive advertising*.

indirect costs – Costs that cannot be traced directly to a particular product. Also called overhead. See *direct costs*.

indirect denial method – Handling a buyer's objection by initially admitting the validity of the objection to maintain rapport, but then offering evidence to rebut the objection. It is sometimes referred to as the *"Yes, but ... Method."* See *objections*.

individual brand – A brand name used for a single product within a product line. Examples would be Reese's Peanut Butter Cup® and Kellogg's Rice Krispies®. See *corporate branding; family brand*.

individual brand name – The part of the brand name which identifies a particular product when it follows a family brand name. For example, in the brand name "Courtyard by Marriott®," Marriott® is the family brand name, while Courtyard is the individual brand name. See *corporate branding; family brand; product line brand name; single brand name*.

individual product – A product with its own distinctive attributes (price, packaging, etc.). Also called a *stock-keeping unit* and a *stock-taking unit*. See *product item*.

indoor advertising – A form of advertising used indoors in high-traffic locations. *Indoor advertising* is recognized as being effective in reaching potential customers in relatively captive locations. Research shows that when a captive audience is presented with information it may retain it longer than any other audience – depending on how well it stands out and the amount of clutter.

Inducements – *Incentives* offered to overcome resistance to buy. For example, special offers or money-back guarantees.

industrial advertising – A form of business-to-business advertising aimed at manufacturers. It typically promotes such industrial goods and services as parts, equipment and raw materials used in the manufacturing process. Also advertising directed at businesses that buy products to incorporate into other products or to facilitate the operation of their businesses.

industrial buyer behavior – The study of the motives and actions of, and the influences on, industrial buyers engaged in the purchasing of goods and services. See *organizational buying behavior*.

industrial buyers – Individuals who buy goods and services on behalf of the clients who employ them – purchasing officers. See *organizational buyer*.

industrial distributor – A marketing intermediary – wholesalers in consumer markets – who purchases industrial products in bulk from manufacturers for resale to small industrial users.

industrial goods – Goods and services purchased by industrial buyers for use in the production of their own goods and services or in the conduct of their business. Industrial goods would include equipment, raw materials and services. See *industrial product classes*.

industrial marketing – The marketing of goods and services to business organizations for use in the manufacture of their products or in the operation of their businesses. Also called *business-to-business marketing*.

industrial packaging – The protective wrapping and boxing of finished industrial goods for shipment.

industrial product classes – Categories of goods and services bought by organizations for use in production or in the operation of their business. They would include installation, accessories, raw materials, component parts, supplies and services.

industrial selling – All forms of personal selling to organizational and industrial buyers of products for resale, or for use in manufacture, or for use in the operation of their businesses.

inelasticity of demand – Demand which is not greatly effected by a change in the price of the product. See *elasticity of demand*.

inelimantalism – Not deciding more than you have to.

inelimentalist – A person who will not decide more than he/she has to.

inept set – Brands a buyer is aware of when considering a purchase, may not have any interest in or thinks poorly of, but still uses in some way as a source of information. See *inert set; evoked set*.

inert set – Brands that a buyer is aware of when considering a purchase but has no interest in. See *evoked set; inept set*.

124

Tips to Succeed:
The telephone: Friend or foe?

Here are 10 Steps to assure the phone is your company's friend:

1. **Preparation** – You can actually prepare to take a phone call. Taking certain preparation steps will help you listen better and concentrate more fully on what the customer is saying.

2. **A Strong Start** – If a phone call gets off to an awkward start, it can go downhill quickly from there.

3. **Building Rapport** – Whether the caller's a high-powered businessman or a soft-spoken elderly person, there are appropriate and effective ways to build rapport.

4. **Effective On-Hold Techniques** – There's a right way and as wrong way to put a caller on hold. For example, when's the last time a receptionist politely asked you if you were able to hold?

5. **Effective Call-Transferring** – Be polite. Alert the caller they are being transferred. Offer a direct number should the caller be disconnected.

6. **Speaking Clearly** – Anyone who wants to succeed in business today should be able to enunciate and speak clearly.

7. **Proper Tone of Voice** – Tone of voice is the nonverbal component of your telephone personality. Learn how to treat each phone call as a separate "performance".

8. **Positive Speech** – Your use of language can make or break a call. There are certain words and phrases that can quickly turn off a caller; conversely, there are words and phrases that are music to a caller's ears.

9. **Effective Listening** – Don't just hear the caller, listen to what is being said. That will help you form a response.

10. **Practice the Golden Rule** – Wouldn't it be a better world if we all treated each other the way we wish to be treated? When you're on the telephone with a client, you should treat the caller with the same dignity and respect you extend to the owner of your company.

www.thephonecoach.com/products-TPC-G10.htm#TenSteps

inertia buying – Consumer buying of unimportant items. Done frequently with the buyer choosing the same brand over and over again without consideration of other brands.

inertia selling – A selling practice where unsolicited goods and services are sent to consumers in expectation that many will prefer to purchase rather than to return them (music and book clubs). In some cases, the practice is considered undesirable and legislation protecting consumers has been enacted.

inference – An assumption.

inflation – An economic situation where rising prices result in a fall in the purchasing value of money. *Inflation* can affect public relations and advertising – depending on the state of the economy.

info crawl – Same as *crawl* but another name for when it runs across the screen carrying news info or headlines.

infomercial – A commercial (television or radio) that is very similar in appearance to a news program, talk show or other non-advertising program content. The broadcast equivalent of an *advertorial* – ads which appear to be editorial copy. The advertiser pays to promote its product under the guise of a 15- or 30-minute program. It usually offers information, advice and useful techniques showing a product's features and how they benefit the consumer. Entrepreneur Ron Popeil is known as the "father of the *infomercial.*"

informal marketing organization – The part of a marketing organization made up of the many working relationships that develop over time, outside the formal lines of authority, among departmental managers.

informal methods – Exploratory research that is not gathered from scientifically representative samples. Includes personal contact, informants, community forums, advisory committees, phone and mail analysis and field reports.

informal (or nonscientific) research – investigation without use of the scientific method (usually undertaken as exploratory and/or preliminary to more rigorous methods).

information box (info box) – The small boxes that accompany news stories that are not quite sidebars, but yet snippets of information. Often with headline of "For more information" and a list of contacts, references, etc., or "If you go..." with a list of the 5 Ws.

information flow – Information about products, potential customers, consumer needs and wants, etc., that is passed forward and backward (two way) along a channel of distribution. See *marketing channels*.

Information Technology Industry Council (ITIC) – Represents the leading U.S. providers of information technology products and services. It advocates growing the economy through innovation and supports free-market policies. Read more at *www.itic.org*.

information-oriented change strategy – An advertising plan or tactic within the plan intended to change a brand's image (rather than to maintain it over time) and which relies on the provision of information (rather than imagery and symbolism) to achieve its effect. See *image-oriented maintenance strategy*; *information-oriented change strategy*; *information-oriented maintenance strategy*.

information-oriented maintenance strategy – An advertising plan or tactic within the plan intended to maintain a brand's image over time (rather than to change its image) and which relies on the provision of information (rather than imagery or symbolism) for its effect. See *image-oriented change strategy*; *image-oriented maintenance strategy*; *information-oriented change strategy*.

information utility – Value given to a product because it can provide the user with information that is useful. See *utility*.

informational advertising – A message that contains a great deal of information (pharmaceutical display ads). *Advertorials*, for the most part, are information ads, but corporations have been known to run *display advertisements* explaining or taking a stand on an issue – such as a strike or labor negotiations.

informational influence – One of three types of influence (with comparative influence and normative influence) exerted on consumers by reference groups. Informational influence occurs when the group is the source of information about products and brands. See *reference group*; *comparative influence*; *normative influence*.

informational label – A label that carries information including use instructions, nutrition information, precautions, warnings, etc. See *label*.

informed judgment techniques – The use of the opinions of knowledgeable people (*key communicators*) to forecast demand and sales.

informization – Disseminating information (*message*) to target an *audience* through the proper *channel* at the best possible *time*. To achieve *informization*, PR practitioners rely on the *MAC Triad – Plus*.

infosnacking – Webster's New World College Dictionary named *infosnacking* the 2005 word of the year. Checking e-mail, Googling, shopping online or reading headlines on the Internet are what employees are doing and in "snack" fashion. It is a time-robbing practice.

inherited audience – The percent of a program's audience that watched or listened to the immediately preceding program on the same station. Also called *holdover audience*.

initial public offering (IPO) – A corporation's initial efforts of raising capital through the sale of securities on the public stock market.

125 Techniques to Succeed: Just what is *integrated marketing communication – synergy?*

Like many practitioners, you may spend much of your life trying to get friends and relatives to understand what you do for a living. Try this example:

• You see a gorgeous girl at a party. You go up to her and say, "I'm fantastic in bed." That's **Direct Marketing**.

• You're at a party with a bunch of friends and see a gorgeous girl. One of your friends goes up to her and pointing at you says, "He's fantastic in bed." That's **Advertising**.

• You see a gorgeous girl at a party. You go up to her and get her telephone number. The next day you call and say, "Hi, I'm fantastic in bed." That's **Telemarketing**.

• You're at a party and see a gorgeous girl. You get up and straighten your tie, you walk up to her and pour her a drink. You open the door for her, pick up her bag after she drops it, offer her a ride, and then say, "By the way, I'm fantastic in bed." That's **Public Relations**.

• You're at a party and see a gorgeous girl. She walks up to you and says, "I hear you're fantastic in bed." That's **Brand Recognition**.

ink affinity – Speed in which ink dries on a paper or other type of surface.

ink bump – During the printing process, when the spread of ink becomes uneven – some areas appear lighter than others – because ink is running low or a roller is uneven, technicians will call for "*ink bump*." See *dodge*.

ink jet printing – Dots of ink sprayed from an ink reservoir on a printer's printhead to form full characters. Resolution is much better than that of a dot matrix printer.

inner-directed consumers – Members of the population, universe or public motivated by a desire for self awareness.

innovation – Introduction of a product new to both the company and its customers. Development of new products, services or ways of working. See *product extension; new product duplication*.

innovators – The small group of alert people who are the earliest to adopt a new product. They are the first to purchase a product. See *diffusion of innovation; early adopters; early majority; laggards; late majority*.

inquiries – Consumer response to a company's advertising or other promotional activities, such as coupons. It is used for measuring the effectiveness of some promotions. See *per inquiry*.

inseparability – One of the four characteristics which distinguish a service. Inseparability expresses the notion that a service can not be separated from the service provider. See *services marketing; intangibility; perishability; variability*.

insert – An advertisement, collection of advertisements or other promotional matter published by an advertiser or group of advertisers, to be inserted in a magazine or newspaper. It may be bound into the publication, or be inserted without binding. *See free-standing insert; flimsies*.

insertion – Actual placement of an advertisement in a vehicle (newspaper, magazine, radio or television).

insertion order – Purchase order between a seller of advertising (vehicle) and a buyer (usually an advertiser or its agency). Many times, the insertion order becomes a contract. It is an advertiser's authorization (often through the advertiser's ad agency) for a publisher, radio or TV station to run an ad at the agreed upon rate or a particular date (and time).

inside order-taker – A salesperson who simply writes up sales orders at a sales counter, or those forwarded to the company by telephone, but is not required to sell persuasively to customers. See *outside order-taker*.

inside-the-box-thinking – Not taking advantage of options and opportunities – concerned with results from taking a risk.

inside-the-circle-thinking – A package of templates developed to help achieve and maintain consistency – one of PRSA's Seven Cs of Communication. The package helps every office, department and branch (school), follow the same look and style in accordance with the company or organization's identity. Also called *public relations in a box*. See *template*.

instant messaging (IMing) – A method of users communicating one-to-one or in groups over the standard IP protocol on a computer. Users can assemble "buddy lists" and chat with friends, family and colleagues.

instant poll – Much like a *snap poll*. A survey taken immediately after an action such as a corporate statement or event – containing only a few questions to determine the opinions of a specific audience or a representative sample of the audience.

Institute of Professional Sales (IPS) – Sister institute to the Chartered Institute of Marketing. *IPS* offers in-depth training and development at every stage of the sales career.

institutional advertising – Advertising intended to promote a product rather than a company or its brands. Among its objectives is to create public support and goodwill, which manufacturers hope will lead to the purchase of their brand. Also called *product advertising*.

institutional loyalty – Devotion, attachment or affection to the organization a person works for and/or represents.

institutional market – A market consisting of schools, universities, hospitals, charities, clubs and similar organizations, which buy goods and services for use in the production of their own goods and services (business).

intaglio – A form of printing – a raised or engraved surface.

intangible product attributes – Characteristics that a product possesses that appear to be identical no matter the brand. For example, flour, sugar or milk. See *tangible product attributes*.

126 Techniques to Succeed:

Why information campaigns fail

- The voter is generally uninformed.

- There are large groups in the population who admit to having little or no interest in public issues.

- People tend to expose themselves to material that is compatible with their attitudes and beliefs and to avoid exposure to issues, candidates and products that do not match their beliefs *(selective perception)*.

- *Selective perception* and interpretation of content follows exposure: individuals perceive, absorb and remember content differently.

- Changes in attitudes (even following exposure to a message), are difficult to achieve. It may be a mistake to take too much time or spend too many resources in an effort to lead to a more favorable behavior. (Concentration should be placed on getting out the vote of those in agreement with your candidate or issue.)

intangibility – One of the four which distinguish a service. Intangibility expresses the notion that a service has no physical substance. It is something you just can't put your fingers on. For example, the difference between brands of flour or sugar. See *services marketing*; *inseparability*; *perishability*; *variability.*

intangible product attributes – A product's characteristics – style, quality, strength, beauty, etc. – perception *(image)* rather than actual ingredients, which might be measurable. See *tangible product attributes.*

intangibles – A service that might have characteristics, but they cannot be detected by the senses.

integrated agency – a public relations or advertising agency that provides all or nearly all services – account management, research, planning, writing, graphic design, printing, radio/television production, online, media planning and buying, etc.

integrated campaign – A multidisciplinary approach that uses a number of marketing communications techniques to deliver a consistent set of strategic messages. When those messages achieve their objectives, which lead to achieving a plan's goal, *synergy* has been achieved.

integrated entertainment – Connecting many entertainment appliances and devices so they provide video, audio, computers and interactive entertainment. Home entertainment centers would fall into this category.

integrated marketing communication (IMC) – A management concept designed to make all aspects of marketing communication (e.g., advertising, sales promotion, public relations and direct marketing) work together as a unified force, rather than permitting each to work in isolation. When those messages achieve their objectives, which lead to achieving a plan's goal, *synergy* has been achieved.

Integrated Services Digital Network (ISDN) – High-speed dial-up connections to the Internet over ordinary phone wires. DSL (*digital subscriber line*) has, in large part, replaced ISDN except in broadcast media, which still uses it primarily for sending live voice or taped transmissions from remote locations.

integrative growth – A strategy for growth where a firm acquires some other element of the chain of distribution of which it is a member. See *backward integration*; *forward integration*; *horizontal integration*.

integrity – Defined as honesty, sincerity, character and "doing the right thing when no one is looking."

intellectual property (IP) – Any product of human intelligence – a product of the mind – that is unique, novel, not obvious and carries value (such as a logo, trademark, servicemark, literary work, idea or invention).

Intellectual Property Rights (IPR) Center – A group that coordinates the U.S. government's efforts to protect intellectual property rights by cracking down on brand counterfeiters. Its work is appreciated by such brands as Coach®, The North Face®, Nike®, etc.

intensive approach – Public relations approach that includes all – or at least many – audiences – so that no one is excluded. It is also called *comprehensive approach*. (Opposite of *targeting*.)

intensive distribution – Distributing a product through a wide variety of outlets.

intensive growth – Growth opportunities related to a company's current operations. Intensive growth opportunities are *market penetration*, *product development* and *market development*.

inter-type channel conflict – Disagreement among members of the marketing chain – whether it be from manufacturer to consumer or manufacturer, public relations practitioner or media.

interactive advertising – Advertising designed to draw an "online" consumer response (two-way communication). Forms of online, wireless and interactive television advertising include *banners* (click throughs), e-mail, keyword searches, referrals, slotting fees, classified ads and interactive television commercials.

Interactive Advertising Bureau (IAB) – *IAB* is a non-profit trade association devoted exclusively to maximizing the use and effectiveness of *interactive advertising* and marketing. Read more at *www.iab.net*.

interactive advertising revenues – Revenues realized from the sale of *interactive advertising*.

interactive commerce – Shopping *online*. Or, what you buy, you buy online.

Interactive Marketing Unit (IMU) – The standard ad unit sizes endorsed by IAB (Internet Advertising Bureau). Read more at *www.iab.net* for more information.

interactive television (iTV) – Any technology that allows for two-way communication between the audience and the service provider (such as the broadcaster, cable operator, set-top box manufacturer) via standard or enhanced television appliance.

interactive voice response (IVR) system – Prompts programmed into a firm or organization's telephone system to answer preprogrammed questions of callers. Newer technology allows callers to respond verbally as well as using touch tones. See *telemarketing services*.

interactive voice response (IVR) systems – Automated answering devices many firms use rather than "real" people. They offer a protocol of steps and numbers to tap (touch tone) or say in order to reach your desired party.

intercept interviews – A random, but unscientific, consumer research method – often used at shopping malls and other areas (stadiums, college campuses, resorts) where large numbers of people congregate – where interviewers randomly stop passersby to ask questions and gather data. This method yields rich data on preferences, attitudes and needs – useful for screening a large number of concepts or issues quickly and at reasonable cost. *Intercept surveys* can provide a quick, inexpensive method to pretest advertising campaign themes, headlines and value propositions.

127 Techniques to Succeed: The on-camera interview

DO
- Use first names
- Speak to the interviewer and not to the camera
- Stand up for your rights
- Deliver your message early
- Be prepared from the time you leave your office/home
- Couch your position as necessary (avoid specifics)
- Speak only the truth; be ready with facts
- Be aware of and sensitive to time
- Know what the interviewer wants
- Be big enough to learn from your mistakes
- Thank the interviewer and crew for their time

DON'T
- Let the topic/subject drift
- Assume anything
- Be afraid to take a compliment (but keep your guard up)
- Consider the interviewer a friend…or an enemy
- Gossip, criticize or speculate
- Use *YES* and *NO* answers
- Put the interviewer on defensive without good cause
- Forget the importance of body language
- Speak too fast or too slow
- Go into any situation without preparation
- Be too hard on yourself
- Never say "*NO COMMENT*"
- Ask for a copy of the final interview

intercept survey – Also known as *chunk survey*. A random, but unscientific, consumer research method – often used at shopping malls and other areas (stadiums, college campuses, resorts) where large numbers of people congregate – where interviewers randomly stop passersby to ask questions and gather data. This method yields rich data on preferences, attitudes and needs – useful for screening a large number of concepts quickly and at reasonable cost. *Intercept surveys* can provide a quick, inexpensive method to pretest advertising campaign themes, headlines and value propositions.

interconnects – A special cable technology that allows local advertisers to run their commercials in small geographical areas through the interconnection of a number of cable systems. They are much like "local cutaways" taken by network affiliates and made available for local advertising on network television and radio programs.

interest group – A person or political organization established to influence governmental policy or legislators in a specific area of policy. Companies and organizations may also be affected by *interest groups.*

intergovernmental discussions – Discussions or talks among groups.

interior transit advertising – Advertising on posters mounted inside such vehicles as buses, transit cars and taxis.

interlocal services – General term based on 1972 Interlocal Services Act. It means any service that can be performed by a single entity can be done in partnership.

interlock – A version of a commercial with the audio and video times together, although the two are recorded separately.

intermediate sellers – Independent firms which assist in the flow of goods and services from producers to end-users. They include brokers, agents, wholesalers, retailers, marketing services and public relations agencies, physical distribution companies and financial institutions. Also referred to as middlemen. See *marketing channel; marketing intermediaries.*

intermodal transportation – A shipping method where two or more modes of transport are used. For example, where containerized goods are loaded from truck to ship and back to truck again and then delivered to distributors, retailers, etc.

internal analysis – The study of a company's internal marketing resources to assess opportunities, strengths or weaknesses. See *SWOT analysis.*

internal audience – Also referred to as *employee publics*. It's the part of a company's public consisting of its employees.

internal communications – Communicating, using various vehicles, with employees and shareholders.

internal customers – Employees within an organization viewed as consumers of a product or service provided by the organization – products or services which the employees need to do their own work. For example, the marketing department could be internal customers of the information technology department.

internal data – Information recorded and stored by an organization as it completes normal transactions and activities.

internal factors – Perceptions and actions of key actors in the organization, structure and process of organizational units somehow related to the problem, and history of the organization's involvement.

internal information search – A stage in the consumer buying process for a low-involvement product. Experiences with items in this product class are considered. See *low-involvement products*.

internal marketing – The process of eliciting support for a company and its activities among its own employees to encourage them to promote company goals and its mission. This process can happen at a number of levels, from increasing awareness of individual products or marketing campaigns, to explaining overall business strategy.

internalized – A message that is memorized so well, it is spoken naturally as if it were extemporaneous.

international advertising – Advertising a product or service in a country other than where it originates.

international brand – A brand of product that is available in most parts of the world.

international marketing – Marketing activities that facilitate the exchange or transfer of goods between nations. Also, the coordination of marketing activities in more than one country.

International Priority Airmail (IPA) – A volume-based, lower-cost First-Class Airmail service provided by the U.S. Postal Service.

International Surface Airlift (ISAL) – A bulk service from the U.S. Postal Service for printed matter and small packets. Mail sent by *ISAL* travels from the United States to the destination country by air. It then enters into the domestic postal stream of that country and travels by surface to its final destination.

Internet – A global system of interconnected computers. Also the worldwide system of computer networks providing reliable and redundant connectivity between different kinds of computers and systems by using common transport and data protocols. It is a global network connecting more than 100 countries and millions of computers.

Internet generation – Those born since the explosion of the home computer market – in the mid to late 90s.

Internet Protocol (IP) – A standard procedure telling a computer network how messages are addressed and routed. It is a standard procedure for regulating data transmission between computers.

Internet Protocol address (IPA) – *Internet Protocol* numerical address assigned to each computer on the network so its location and activities can be distinguished from other computers.

Internet Protocol TV (IPTV) – Allows users to download and record TV shows.

Internet Relay Chat (IRC) – Much like *IMing*, it is a technique that allows computer users to chat in real time. The chats, or forums, are typed remarks, and they can be either public or private. Also, a procedure that allows users to hold computer conversations with others in real time. *IRC* is structured as a network of servers, each of which accepts connections from client programs.

Internet service provider (ISP) – An organization or company that provides access to the Internet. An ISP can be a commercial provider, a corporate computer network, a school, college, university or the government. Examples would include Comcast® and Verizon®.

interstitial – An advertisement that appears in between two pages of a Web site. When the user clicks on a link, the ad displays for a short time, before allowing the user to proceed.

interstitial ads – Advertisements that appear between two editorial content pages. Also known as transition ads, intermercial ads, splash pages and Flash pages. Many times, newspapers and magazines charge extra for the ads – if the publications consider the placement to be preferred.

129 Tips to Succeed: Prepare for interview with questions

Before going to a job interview, it is important to practice describing yourself. As a starting point, respond out loud to the following questions:

- Tell me about a time you worked as part of a team?
- Why should I select you over other applicants?
- What are your greatest strengths and weaknesses?
- Tell me more about the project you described on your resume.
- Describe a work or school-related problem and how you solved it.
- What are your short-term goals?
- Why do you want to work in this occupation and for this company?

U.S. Department of Labor

interview alert – Similar to a *media alert*. It is a method of presenting an expert source willing to comment on a timely issue, including contact information to set up an interview.

interview study – A common technique for gathering primary data in marketing research. Respondents in an interview study complete a questionnaire delivered to them by face-to-face interview, telephone or mail.

interviewer bias – Intentional or unintentional prompting by a marketing researcher, which affects the interviewee's response.

intranet – A computer network that belongs to an organization and is accessible only by the organization's members, employees or others with authorization. Also a network dedicated to information and resources about and for the corporation or organization that maintains it, enabling a company and its employees to share resources without the information – confidential or otherwise – being made available across the Internet.

intraorganizational environment – An organization's internal computer environment. It affects public relations, advertising and marketing operations.

intrapreneur – A person within a large corporation who takes direct responsibility for turning an idea into a profitable finished product through risk-taking and *innovation*.

130 Tips to Succeed:
Slash your phone bills

• Switch to Internet phoning. Voice over Internet Protocol, or VoIP, transmits phone calls via a high-speed Internet connection. VoIP providers include phone and cable-TV companies and some, such as Packet8 and Vonage, that specialize in the service.

• Use your cell phone for everything. Drop your landline and use wireless at home and on the go.

• Trade down to a cheaper cell plan. Some providers have less-costly plans than the ones they tend to push, but you might have to ask or poke around their Web sites.

• Take a local/long-distance bundle.

• Buy a phone card for long-distance. A prepaid long-distance card can cut costs if you don't make many long-distance landline calls.

Consumer Reports

intrinsic rewards – *Employees* doing a job for personal reward (feeling good) rather than for wages, bonuses, incentives, fringe benefits, job promotions, etc. See *extrinsic rewards*.

introductory allowance – Fees paid by a manufacturer to a retailer for the retailer's shelf space for products whether new or established. See *slotting allowance*.

introductory stage of product life cycle – The first stage in the life cycle of a successful product. The product wins acceptance relatively slowly, there are limited versions of it, there is no competition, distribution is patchy, promotion is designed to inform the market (awareness rather than to persuade or remind) and a pricing strategy may be offered to get a foothold in the market. See *product life cycle*; *growth stage*; *maturity stage*; *decline stage*; *withdrawal stage*.

invalid objection – An excuse offered by a prospective buyer to cover some hidden objection to the product or brand. See *hidden objection*; *valid objection*.

inventory – The number of commercial minutes available for sale by a radio or television station, column inches available in newspapers or magazines or the number of ads available for sale on a Web site.

inventory carrying costs – Costs associated with keeping inventory, including warehousing, spoilage, obsolescence, interest and taxes. Also called *holding costs*.

inventory management – Activities involved in maintaining the appropriate level of stock in a warehouse. Also, the traffic manager at a radio or television station who monitors the number of minutes sold.

inventory remarketing – An innovative strategy for reducing the risks of introducing a new product. Prior to the launch of the new product, a firm may negotiate with an inventory remarketing company for the sale of any unused stock of the new product in the event it fails to sell as well as expected. Inventory remarketing companies agree to buy the balance of the stock, at the previously agreed price, and resell it, usually in a different market and through different distribution channels.

inventory turnover – The ratio of dollar or unit sales or gross profit to average inventory; used in inventory control where the average number of times a company sells the value of its inventory in a year is measured.

inverted pyramid – Style of writing – the standard news writing structure – where the most important information is put in the lead, followed by less and less important information (descending order of importance). Designed so an editor can cut after any paragraph and have a complete story that meets space limitations. Traditionally, stories are cut from bottom up, depending on space, because the least important information is on the bottom. Thanks to computers and cutting and pasting, an editor has the option of eliminating an internal paragraph without the story losing continuity or syntax.

invitation to cover – A brief summary of an upcoming news event, which could include the background and credentials of an expert willing to discuss it. Also known as a *news and photo memo, media alert* and *interview alert*. The format includes either "Event; Date; Time; Place; Details" or "What; When; Where; Why; Details" – or a combination of both.

involvement – The intensity of the consumer's interest in a product.

island display – A point-of-purchase in-store display away from competing products, typically in the middle or at the end of an aisle.

island position – A print advertisement that is completely surrounded by editorial material, or a broadcast ad surrounded by program content, with no adjoining advertisements to compete for audience attention. If a publication or broadcast outlet considers it to be a preferred location, a premium or surcharge is applied to the basic rate.

isolation effect – The notion that a price will appear more attractive if the product is placed in the store next to an alternative product which is more expensive.

issue – A point or matter of discussion, debate or dispute – legal and moral issues. A matter of public concern – debated economic issues. Anything that affects someone or some thing.

italic – A type variation that uses letters that slant to the right.

item runaround – Text around a picture is set around the borders of the picture box.

itemize – A budgeting term – financial or otherwise – for a list of "particulars." Line item budgets are an itemized list, each containing a anticipated revenue and projected cost. **I**

jargon – Language known only to members of a specific group, company, trade or industry. Language of a profession – such as educational *jargon* or medical *jargon*.

Java® – A programming language designed for building applications on the Internet. It allows for advanced features, increased animation detail and real-time updates. Small applications called Java® applets can be downloaded from a server and executed by Java®-compatible browsers like Microsoft Internet Explorer® and Netscape Navigator®.

jimmy legs – Originated on the "Seinfeld Show" as did the terms "regift" and "sponge worthy." It means a disorder where a person moves limbs involuntarily and has symptoms or problems related to the movement – many times from anxiety or nerves. If a person moves his/her limbs during sleep but there are no consequences, it is simply called periodic limb movements of sleep (PLMS).

jingle – A short song, usually mentioning a brand or product benefit, used in a *commercial. Jingles* are considered locking devices – techniques used to help consumers remember a product or *brand*.

jobspill – The time-robbing practice for hours of work performed off the clock (and many times without extra compensation).

joint demand – A situation where demand for a product or service rises and falls with demand for another product or service it is tied to. For example, if a consumer enjoys milk and brownies, but the bakery is out of brownies, then demand for milk is also likely to decline.

131

Tips to Succeed: New rules: Have right goals and strategy for job hunt

The average job seeker commits two drastic sins: having the wrong goal and having no strategy. Now do you know why you're not getting anywhere?

To change from a getting-nowhere-fast direction to one where you're making headway, here are your new rules.

NEW RULE NO. 1: CHANGE YOUR GOAL FROM GETTING A JOB TO GETTING INTERVIEWS.
When your goal is to "get a job," you're fixated on selling yourself. If you do get interviews, you go in thinking, "I gotta get this job" and "What do they want to hear?" You sound desperate. Remember, a job interview is a conversation, not a sales call.

Once you do get the interview, you should have the same objective as the interviewer: to explore whether this is a good fit while making a positive impression. If you've done that well, you're more apt to get to what you want – an offer.

NEW RULE NO. 2: CREATE A STRATEGY.
Plopping yourself in front of your computer and sending your resume to job sites is not a strategy. It's one activity that's part of an overall strategy. To create a strategy, look at your objective.

Then work your strategy:

• Focus on what it is you want to do.

• Conduct a search of the companies that make those products or provide the service (public relations, advertising or manufacturing).

• Figure out the best way to approach them. Going through your list, write down names of people you might know at each company. Write down those you know who might steer you to a decision maker. Research hiring managers.

• With your goal being to get an interview, "practice" what you want to say in a phone call, letter or e-mail to entice them.

• Check out the companies' Web sites for posted positions, apply online and follow up by mail.

• Talk to other people you know who could suggest companies you didn't know about or are starting up or know of other openings that fit your criteria.

• Through Web site and elsewhere, learn as much as you can about

Joint Photographic Experts Group (JPEG/JPG) – A type of computer file used for images or photos. *JPG* files are commonly used on Web pages. Commonly used for pictures taken digitally and placed on a computer hard drive. It is also an image file format commonly used for ad banners. The information in these files is compressed for smaller file size. In the process, some information may be lost and the result is distortion of the image. ".jpg" is the extension for a *JPG* file.

joint venture – A risk-reducing method of market entry where two firms combine forces to manufacture or market the same product. Also, a method of entry into a foreign market where a U.S. firm joins with an overseas company to establish a partnership for the production and marketing of its product abroad.

journalism – Reporting, writing, editing, photographing or broadcasting news. It is a process of verification.

journalist – A writer for newspapers and magazines. Viewed as vigilant, critical and objective – a "truth teller."

JPEG – A digital photo format. When saved on a computer, it would appear as filename.jpg. *JPEG* is derived from joint photographic experts group. See *Joint Photographic Experts Group.*

judgment sample – A type of *non-probability sample* used in gathering primary data in marketing research. The sample is drawn from respondents the market researcher judges to be knowledgeable about the subject. See *probability sample; non-probability sample.*

judgmental or purposive sample – A sample based on the investigator's best judgment to determine what would be representative. Should be used only when the consequences of possible errors from bias would not be serious, and when other sampling is impractical.

J

The ABCs of Strategic Communication

jumble display – A mixture of products or brands on a single display, such as a clearance table.

jump – To continue a story from one page of a publication to another. (Continued on page 10; Continued from page 1).

jump the couch – Similar to *jumping the shark* – A defining moment when you know someone has gone off the deep end.

jump line – Usually begins with "continued on" – telling the reading which page a story is continued on when it won't fit on the original page. (Continued on page 10; Continued from page 1).

132 Tips to Succeed:
Getting a job after graduation

- **Be nice to nerds**: The friendships you develop in college can be some of the richest relationships you ever have. They might also be your ticket to the top and your way to help your friends. You never know, that computer whiz you were nice to in freshman English might need a right-hand person when he takes over a multimillion-dollar media corporation.

- **Make noise**: Look for opportunities to let people know who you are and what you offer. Tell people that you're graduating and create a way for them to ask you what you want to do with your life. And remember to always say and send a thank you.

- **Keep on talking**: Start conversations at sporting events, while you're eating out or even at the park where you're enjoying the spring weather. Find a positive way to follow up so that you collect their contact information and stay in touch. You just might run into someone who needs you on their team.

- **Call your hero**: Find successful people in your field of interest and take them to lunch. Let them know your aspirations and ask for advice.

- **Turn obstacles into opportunities**: Challenges are inevitable in searching for a career. Keep a positive perspective and figure out how to improve and convince the next person you meet to make you CEO of their company.

Andrea Nierenberg - Author
Nonstop Networking: How to Improve Your Life, Luck and Career
www.mybusinessrelationships.com/

133

Tips to Succeed: Call it – 'An applicant statement'

Polish your resume by including a summary paragraph stating what you bring to the table, qualifications, experience and examples of a job well done. It should be succinct and contain buzzwords human resource managers look for – containing many of the same key message points you would include in an elevator speech.

Here is an example:

Applicant Statement: My supervisors describe me as "mature beyond her years, articulate, well tailored and polished, loyal, has a passion for the profession, outstanding writer, and a skilled organizer and strategic thinker." It is my dream to bring those qualities, passion and dedication to ELLE's readers – just as I do the residents of Cherry Hill. My zest for knowledge and new challenges is contagious and should appeal to ELLE magazine's staff and target audience.

Nina Ebert - President - A Word's Worth - Plumsted, N.J.
M. Larry Litwin, APR, Fellow PRSA - Author -
The Public Relations Practitioner's Playbook

jump page ad – Microsite (a computer page) reached by a click-through from a button advertisement or *banner ad* on a *home page* or original page. The jump page itself can list several topics, which are linked to either the advertiser's site or the publisher's site.

jumping the shark – A defining moment. It's the instant that you know from then on – it's all downhill – things will simply never be the same. Expression was first used during the television series "Happy Days" – when Fonzie actually jumps over a shark. The rest is history – and so was the show.

jury of executive opinion – A forecasting method based on the opinions of senior management.

134

Tips to Succeed: Choosing good restaurants

- Take a look inside.
- Study the menu.
- Keep it affordable.
- Ask someone leaving who just ate there.

just-in-time inventory system – An inventory control method, first used in Japan, for keeping inventory costs to a minimum. Supplies are ordered frequently, but in relatively small quantities. Also known as *kanban*.

just-in-time purchasing – See *just-in-time inventory system*.

justify – Spacing the type so the left and right margins are aligned.

justified – A form of typeset copy where the edges of the lines in a column of type are forced to align by adding space between words in a line. Also horizontal alignment of copy from side to side. **J**

kanban – An inventory control method, first used in Japan, for keeping inventory costs to a minimum. Supplies are ordered frequently, but in relatively small quantities. See *just-in-time inventory system*.

kangaroo out – Used in sports for players who opt to jump from one team to another. First used when players jumped from the National League in baseball to the "new" American League at the turn of the 20th century. Used again when the American Football League was formed to compete with the National Football League (NFL) and the American Basketball Association organized to take on the National Basketball Association (NBA). Term has become prevalent with the advent of free agency in sports.

keep-out pricing – A pricing practice where large companies maintain very low prices to discourage smaller competitors and thus protect their own market shares. See *umbrella pricing*.

keeper – A premium (giveaway) used to encourage a consumer to take some action, such as completing a survey or trying a product.

keeper success factors – The factors necessary for success in a given market.

kelly grids – A technique for representing the attitudes and perceptions of individuals. The technique can be useful in developing market research (and other) questionnaires. Also known as personal construct technique.

kennel-keeper – Used to refer to marketers whose products are largely "dogs" – those with a relatively small share of a slow-growth market. See *Boston Consulting Group advantage matrix*; *dogs*.

kerning – Spacing between the letters of a word. Or adjusting the space between the letters within a word (not the space between words).

key account management – Account management that deals with an organization or firm's most important customers. See *account management*.

key communicator – Influential resident and/or business person in a community. Influential person such as an opinion leader, consultant, expert, etc. who can carry a strategic message or report audience opinion. Also known as a *connector* or *consumption pioneer*. His/her early and enthusiastic endorsement of an issue or new product is sought by public relations practitioners or salespeople. See *opinion leader*.

key drive – A *flash, jump or thumb drive* – used to transport computer files – which connects to computers through a USB port. They are inexpensive digital storehouses.

136 Techniques to Succeed: Pre-business plan for the small business

Thinking about starting or expanding your own small business?

- Start at the beginning. Establish a company goal, objectives, strategies and tactics.
- Determine your company's name: Make sure the name you want isn't taken.
- Decide your location: Can you work at home? Do you need office or manufacturing space? Local Realtors have listings for commercial space to lease or buy.
- List the equipment you will need: Make a list of everything – from office paper and computers to company cars and machinery. You will get a feeling for start-up costs and be able to start thinking about how you are going to pay for it all.
- Calculate your compensation: Some business owners forgo a salary when getting started. Others pay themselves too much. Sit down with the other pieces of your pre-business plan and calculate a practical salary for yourself.

Andrew Glatz - Sun National Bank - www.sunnb.com

key frame – A single frame of a commercial that summarizes the heart of the message.

key messages – The most important fact(s) or statement(s) about your organization, service, product or event you wish to convey through media to inform, influence or persuade your target audience. *Key messages* are elaborated upon by *talking points*. See *talking points*.

key message points – Much like *talking points*, but fewer and more brief – deliverable in quick fashion. For political candidates they might focus on taxes, education and social security; for a chief executive officer they be about wages, fringe benefits and working condition. See *elevator speech*; *talking points*.

key newsmaker – Term commonly used by police and attorneys when dealing with someone with notoriety.

key visual – Dominant image around which a television commercial's message is planned.

key word(s) – Specific word(s) entered into a search engine (for example Google® or Yahoo!®) by the user that result(s) in a list of Web sites related to the *key word(s)*. The *key word(s)* can be purchased by advertisers to direct the user to the advertiser's site or to serve an advertisement related to the user's search.

keystone – Retail price that is double the cost. Double *keystone* is triple the cost. For example, if a retailer pays $50 for an item, it would sell for $100 if *keystoned* or $150 *if* double *keystoned*. See *mark up*.

keyword search revenues – Fees advertisers pay to link computer users (searchers) to a Web site or information about an organization or firm.

kicker – A small headline above the main headline in a newspaper or other publication. Usually, one line. Also, the last line of a radio commercial. Also called a stinger. See *tag line*.

kickback – A bribe or illegal payment offered to an organization's buyer to obtain the business.

kicks – Slang word for athletic shoes.

kidults – Adults who buy products predominantly aimed at children. When it comes to technology, the *kidult* and adult markets have great cross-over.

The ABCs of Strategic Communication

137

Techniques to Succeed: Meeting people

When meeting people both your nonverbal and verbal behavior help to define your social skills. Using effective handshakes, good eye contact, and making the proper introductions show proper etiquette.

A. Handshakes are vital in social situations.

1. Develop a comfortable handshake and keep it consistent.

2. Handshakes should not be too hard; or too soft.

3. Make a solid connection of the web skin between the thumb and forefinger.

4. The host or person with the most authority usually initiates the handshake.

B. Eye contact is another critical factor when meeting people.

1. Eye contact increases trust.

2. It shows confidence and good interpersonal skills.

3. Eye contact shows respect for the person and business situation.

Proper introductions help to establish rapport when meeting people.

1. Authority defines whose name is said first. Say the name of the most important person first and then the name of the person being introduced.

2. Introduce people in the following order:

   1. younger to older

   2. non-official to official

   3. junior executive to senior executive

   4. colleague to customer

3. Keep the introduction basic.

4. Remember names for future reference.

5. Provide some information about the people you are introducing to clarify your relationship with that person.

6. Always carry business cards.

7. Keep notes on people in order to follow-up both personally and professionally.

The Career Center - Florida State University

kill – "Kill" the story is the term used when an editor and reporter decide to no longer pursue a story, or it gets axed from the daily budget list of stories going into the paper or on the air due to space/time constraints, relevancy, etc. To eliminate all or part of a story.

kill date – The date that an ad or commercial or public service announcement should no longer run in a publication or on radio, television or the Internet.

kinesic communication – *Body language.* Communication by body movement – posture, stance, hand movements, winking, head nodding, etc. See *non-verbal communication*; *proxemic communication*; *tactile communication.*

kinetic boards – Outdoor advertising that uses moving elements.

kinked demand curve – The shape of a demand curve when any rise in price above the customary level will result in a sharp decline in demand.

kiosks – Multisided bulletin board structures designed for the public posting of messages. Also, free standing retail location in the center aisles of malls and concourses.

KISS principle – "Keep It Simple and Straightforward."

knock and talk – Law enforcement practice in which police (*pox*) visit someone to ask questions then request permission to conduct a search of that person's residence.

knocking copy – Advertising copy in which one manufacturer compares its product to the product of another. The Federal Trade Commission has ruled that *comparison advertising*, if it disparages the competition or uses negatives, must be based on fact. See *comparison advertising.*

knockoffs – A term used in reference to new product innovations which are almost identical, look-alike copies of competitors' items. Knockoffs are common where the item copied fits nicely with the manufacturing and marketing strengths of the company which copies it, and are intended to take overall market share from the competitor. If the knockoff uses the brand name of another, it is an illegal federal offense. Many times sports, entertainment and other licensed products are victims of knockoffs.

The ABCs of Strategic Communication

knock on – Handbags, jewelry and other items (without a brand name) that are as good or better than the original that carry a designer's label.

knockout – same as *reverse*.

knockout and fill – Same as overprint (fill in reverse with colored ink).

knowledge gap – Theorists have found that as the information is pumped into society by the mass media, segments of the population with higher socio-economic status tend to acquire this information at a faster rate than the lower status segments, so that the gap in knowledge between these segments tends to increase rather than decrease.

knowledge leaders – Experts in a specific field (medicine, politics, business, etc.) who serve to add credibility to a *message* in public relations.

knowledge management – The collection, organization and distribution of information in a form that audiences can understand. Public relations practitioners work to boil down information so that consumers find it easier to understand. It's known as the "effort/benefit ratio." The less effort it takes to read (hear) and understand a message, the greater the return. Effort/benefit ratio lends itself to practical application. Knowledge management often relies on information technology to facilitate the storage and retrieval of information.

knowledges, skills and abilities (KSAs) — That list of special qualifications and personal attributes that someone has decided you should have to fill a particular job. It's not enough that you meet the basic qualifications for the position and have the specialized experience that's required. It's not enough that you have a polished up-to-date applications package that clearly lays out all your experience and expertise. Now you have to put more time and effort into developing a "supplemental statement" set of responses to these additional evaluation factors that may be relevant only to this job vacancy. And you have to do it in time to meet an incredibly short application deadline. Federal government commonly uses KSAs to fill job openings.

Kotler's black box model – A model devised by U.S. marketing academic, Philip Kotler, to explain the hidden nature of consumer decision-making. Kotler uses the analogy of the "black box" to represent the human mind. He describes the marketer's task as that of trying to understand why, how, when, and from whom, consumers buy. See *consumer behavior.* **K**

label – The part of a package that carries information about the product it contains. Legally, a *label* may be a permanent part of the primary package or tag, sticker, band, etc.

labeling – All activities associated with the design and content of the wording on a product or package which identifies it and provides instructions for its handling and use. Also a term that identifies groups whose behavior lies outside the domain of what is normal or acceptable to the rest of society.

labels – Paper printed with a name and address that is affixed to a mailing piece and serves as the mailing address vehicle. Different types of labels include peel-off or pressure-sensitive labels, gummed labels and paper (or *Cheshire*) labels.

laboratory test market – Market testing of consumer goods using a simulated store technique rather than an actual test market. It is also referred to as purchase laboratories. See *accelerated test marketing*.

laddering – Buying a series of investments with a range of maturities. As one investment matures, the proceeds can be used to buy another at the prevailing interest rate.

lag – The amount of time between making a request and receiving a response. See *latency*.

laggards – Those in a community who are slowest to adopt a new product. Generally, laggards are not interested in new technology and are the last group of consumers to buy. See *diffusion of innovation*; *early adopters*; *early majority*; *innovators*; *late majority*.

lagged effect – See *lagged response*.

lagged response – A delayed (latent) response by consumers to an advertising campaign. Measuring the effectiveness of a current advertising campaign is made more difficult by a lagged response to an earlier one because it might be difficult to clearly separate the two. Also called *lagged effect*.

lame duck advantage – A public official not running for re-election – doesn't have to worry about how a decision might affect a future election (votes).

landscape – to improve the appearance of an area – surrounding a house or other building - by planting trees, shrubs or grass, or altering the contours of the ground. See *hardscape*.

Lanham Act – Federal trademark law. It defines the statutory and common law boundaries to trademarks and service marks. *Trademarks* (and *service marks*) are words or designs used in the advertising of goods and services. Rights to use a trademark are defined by the class(es) for which the trademark is used. Therefore, it is possible for different parties to use the same trademark in different classes. The *Lanham Act* defines the scope of a trademark, the process by which a federal registration can be obtained from the Patent and Trademark Office for a *trademark* and penalties for trademark infringement. The Legal Information Institute provides Title 15 of the US Code, which encompasses the *Lanham Act*. Read more at *http://legal.web.aol.com/resources/legislation/tradeact.html*.

lapdog journalism – The opposite of *watchdog journalism* – those in authority control a reporter or entity.

large voice – Much like a third-party endorser – usually well known, like Oprah Winfrey, especially when she "pushes" a book or other product. See *third party endorse*.

laser print – A high-quality proof of an advertisement printed on glossy paper (using a laser printer), which is suited for reproduction. In many cases, laser prints have replaced blue lines as the final step before a printing job is shot and plated before printing. Laser proofs can be provided in full color although the colors may not be the exact *PMS* (Pantone Matching System) colors that will be used on the completed publication. Also referred to as *ad slick, blue line; camera-ready art; matte; repro; velox*.

laser printing – The output of a laser printer, which uses a laser beam, toner and fuser to "etch" the image onto a photoelectric drum. Results are similar to a photocopy machine.

last-chance close – A closing technique where a salesperson tries to get a quick commitment to a purchase by telling the buyer that the demand for the product is heavy and that only a limited quantity is left. See *standing room only*.

last eyes – The final editor before a publication goes to press.

late majority – The large, conservative group in a community slower than all except the *laggards* to adopt a new product. See *diffusion of innovation*; *early adopters*; *early majority*; *innovators*.

latency – The time it takes for a data packet to move across a computer network connection. Also, the visible delay between request and display of computer content.

138 Tips to Succeed: PRSA's Code of Ethics

PRSA lists the following 10 principles of behavior for the practice of public relations:

1. Conduct in accord with the *public interest*.
2. Exemplify high standards of *honesty and integrity*.
3. *Deal fairly* with the public.
4. Adhere to highest standards of *accuracy and truth*.
5. Do not knowingly disseminate *false or misleading information*.
6. Do not engage in any practice that *corrupts the channels of communication* or processes of government.
7. *Identify publicly* the name of the client or employer on whose behalf any public communication is made.
8. Do not make use of any individual or organization professing to be independent or unbiased but actually serving another or *undisclosed interest*.
9. Do not *guarantee the achievement* of specified results beyond member's control.
10. Do not represent conflicting or competing interests.

The ABCs of Strategic Communication

latent demand – Demand for a product which can satisfy a want not currently available by any existing product.

lateral capacity building – Investing in leaders so they can be better leaders. *Lateral capacity building* works best when it has a clear purpose, a means of measuring whether progress is being made in achieving the purpose and a clear evidence-based definition of best practice to inform action. The key is not to enforce collaboration but to offer incentives which reward it. Read more at *http://home.oise.utoronto.ca/~change-forces/Articles_05/Tri-Level%20Dev't.htm*

launch – Releasing a product to the consumer market for the first time. The new product is launched when service, sales and distribution channels are ready.

laws – Piece of enacted legislation – a rule of conduct or procedure established by custom, agreement, or authority. See *ethics; morals.*

layout – A (rough or finished) drawing indicating the relative positions of the elements (e.g., *headline*, photo, *logo*, *body copy*, etc.) of an advertisement or other publication.

lazy lockout – A radio or television reporter who signs off of his/her *package* or *wrap* immediately after a voice cut or sound bite without adding any additional information (e.g. Sandy Starobin, KYW Newsradio, Harrisburg – although Starobin would never be accused of using a *lazy lockout*).

LBO (leveraged buyout) Lane – Also called Buyout Boulevard. Slang term for New York City's Times Square – "crossroads of the world" now that so many private equity firms have been buying up large slices of corporate America. For example, Burger King®, Dave & Buster's®, Dunkin' Donuts®, The Limited®, Toys R Us® and many more stores, outdoor advertising and parking lots now have private equity owners.

lead – The *lead* is the introductory portion (paragraph or two or even three, at times) of a news story that includes the most pertinent information. It is pronounced "leed" and sometimes spelled "lede" – generally containing the (summary) who, what, when, where and why, although a *lead* could be a tease, quotation or question.

lead amplifier – Such information as quotes, statistics or other pertinent information that expands the information first presented in the lead paragraph.

lead generation – The activity of identifying potential clients or customers.

lead in – In television and radio, one program that precedes another to serve as a draw to attract viewers or listeners to the subsequent program, which may be considered more important to the station or network.

lead story – Dominant article that is given primary attention and prominent placement on the first page of a publication. It is generally accepted that a newspaper's most important story runs down the right side of page one.

lead time – The amount of time in advance that a publication or broadcast outlet needs to receive information, such as a news release or calendar listing. The deadline for submission of articles, set by reporters or publications, which allows enough time for a piece to be written, edited and sent to press.

leader pricing – See *loss leader pricing*.

leading – The amount of space that appears between the lines within a paragraph (as opposed to the space between paragraphs) in a printed document. The space between lines of type. (Pronounced "ledding".)

leading question – A question that is worded so as to lead a respondent to answer in a particular way. For example, "You don't like this competitive product, do you?"

leads – Telephone inquiries, letters, responses to advertising, direct mail or word-of-mouth tips etc. that direct a salesperson to a prospective client or customer. See *sales leads*.

leaflet – A printed, usually folded, flier intended for free distribution. A *leaflet* could be a booklet, brochure, folder or pamphlet.

leak plumbing – Preventing *journalists* from protecting their sources. A term coined by journalist William Saffire.

learning – Behavioral changes resulting from an individual's experiences.

learning curve – A graphical representation of the way average unit cost of production decreases as output rises. Also called an *experience curve*.

learning curve effect – The learning curve represents the outcome of a company's experience when developing a product. Traditionally, as the

The ABCs of Strategic Communication

139

Tips to Succeed:
Make your customers your friends

Are you a friend to your customers? If not, you should be.

At least 50 percent of all the sales made in America on any given day are made on the basis of friendship.

If you and your company are looking for more sales, then you ought to be developing more friendships. Successful salespeople and relationship builders don't just give customers and clients free tickets to attend a sporting event, a concert or some other entertainment event. They attend with the client.

Why would any salesperson pass up the opportunity to spend time with a customer away from the work environment? This is when many friendships begin. By spending quality time with people, you get to know them, and if they're people who spend money with your company, the time spent is beyond price.

Some "place" to go with customers and potential clients:

• ball games
• theater
• concert
• gallery
• Chamber of Commerce event
• community-help project
• breakfast
• lunch
• dinner
• seminar given by your company
• I-Max theater with your customer and all your children.

While you and your sales people should all be well-versed in all the best selling techniques, sales is still about relationships, and friendships. You can only earn a commission using a sales technique, but you can earn a fortune building friendships and relationships.

Jeffrey Gitomer - Author - *The Sales Bible and Customer Satisfaction is Worthless, Customer Loyalty is Priceless* - www.salesman@gitomer.com
njbiz - Feb. 7, 2005
Newstrack Executive Information Service - www.news-track.com - 800-334-5771

L

The ABCs of Strategic Communication

company becomes more experienced, it is able to develop a better product, or develop products more efficiently at reduced cost. The *learning curve effect* plays a significant role in helping companies benefit from first-mover advantage (first to market a product). Later entrants into the marketplace have a difficult time overcoming the experience advantage established of first-movers especially as they release additional versions of the product.

learning log – Charts that assess an individual's progress during a specified period of time.

learning process – The way an individual's behavior changes as a result of personal experiences. The *learning process* consists of four basic components – a stimulus, or cue, which creates a drive; the drive that motivates the individual to make a response; the response or action undertaken by the individual; and reinforcement by means of reward or punishment which determines whether the individual will act in that way again.

leasing – The granting, under contract, of use of a product or brand name for an agreed upon period of time in return for a rental payment. Examples of brand names leased to manufacturers include Spalding®, Wilson® and Puma®.

leave-behind – A premium left with prospective customers by a sales person to remind them of the product or service being sold. *Leave-behinds* are intended to jog the prospect's memory about the sales call and the product or service being sold.

lectern – A stand with a slanted top, used to hold a book, speech, manuscript, etc., at the proper height for a reader or speaker. See *dais; podium.*

legacy cost – Retirees costing firms and corporations a great deal of money through pensions, health care, etc.

legal and political environment – Factors in government, the law and the regulatory system which affect the way an organization operates.

legibility – The clarity of a publication (layout, artwork, use of *copybreaking* devices, etc.). How pleasing the layout is to the eye.

legislative liaison – See *lobbyist.*

lemming journalism – Much like herd journalism – reporters who hear about a story and follow a reporter from another news outlet. See *herd journalism.*

less-than-carload freight rate – The freight rate charged by a railroad company when a producer's shipment is less in volume than one full carload.

letter to the editor – Letter written and submitted by a non-publication staff member, complimenting or criticizing the coverage of an issue or editorial stand by the publication or an expression of a personal or organization's opinion. Publications have guidelines for submission – most limit such letters to 250-300 words. A general approach to writing a letter to the editor might include stating the problem (why the letter is being written), listing issues, taking a position, explaining why and listing some benefits of why.

letterpress – A printing method that stamps ink onto paper, using raised lettering and, depending on the quality of the press and the paper stock, may leave an impression in the paper.

lettershop – A firm that assembles and inserts printed products of a direct mail piece, and labels, sorts, tags and delivers the mailings to the post office for mailing. The *lettershop* provides the mailer with written proof of delivery to the U.S. Postal Service.

lexicographic model (of brand evaluation) – A model used in the study of the consumer decision processes to evaluate alternatives. The theory behind this model is based on the idea that if two products are equal on the most important attribute, the consumer moves to the next most important, and, if still equal, to the next most important, etc. The purchase decision is made when one of the brands possesses more of an attribute, looked at in order of importance, than its rival. Other

141

Tips to Succeed: Leadership

What is *leadership*?

It's a title

It's charisma

It's expertise

Dr. Philip Tumminia - Special Assistant to President for University Advancement - Rowan University - Glassboro, N.J.

models of brand evaluation include the *ideal brand model*, *conjunctive model*, *disjunctive model* and *determinance model*.

lexicon – Knowledge base about some subset of words in the vocabulary of a natural language. The *lexicon* may also contain additional information about the syntax, spelling, pronunciation and usage of the words.

liability – The responsibility imposed by legislation on a manufacturer to appropriately warn consumers about possible harmful effects of a product, to foresee how it might be misused, etc. Also, a claim on the assets of an individual or company, excluding any portion previously paid. See *product liability*.

libel – Broadcasting false or defamatory statements that injure a person's reputation. There must be intent and it must be proven. In many, though not all, legal systems, for statements to be defamatory, they must be untrue. Truth is often the best defense against a prosecution for libel. In some systems, however, truth alone is not a defense. It is also necessary in some cases to show that there is a well-founded public interest in the specific information being widely known, and this may be the case even for public figures.

licensed characters – Figures from fiction, television, movies, etc., used, under license from their creators, in the marketing of consumer goods such as breakfast cereals, chocolate bars, ice creams, etc.

licensed product strategy – Marketing plans and actions based on the use of licensed characters. See *licensed characters*.

licensing – The granting of permission by one manufacturing organization to another to use a registered brand, symbol, process, patent, etc.

life cycle – A model showing the sales volume cycle of a single product, brand, service or a class of products or services over time described in terms of five stages – *introductory, growth, maturity, decline* and *withdrawal*.

The ABCs of Strategic Communication

life cycle cost – The costs associated with the use and maintenance of a product over its expected life span.

life stage buying power segmentation – The division of a total heterogeneous market into relatively homogeneous groups on the basis of their ability to afford a product at their particular stage in the *family life cycle* – bachelor stage, young marrieds, full nest, empty nest and sole survivor. See *family life cycle*.

lifestyle – An individual's way of life as shaped by his or her interests, attitudes and opinions.

lifestyle marketing – Promotional activity shaped around the interests, attitudes, opinions and way of life of consumers. *Lifestyle marketing* works best when companies are able to identify and connect with how their potential customers live. Consumers are consistently changing their perceptions, attitudes and consumption patterns, which results in considerable effort and research to keep track of these changes. A major factor complicating the lifestyle marketing equation is the Internet, which has major effects on consumer buying patterns. Companies must now target consumers online based on their activity and shopping habits, which can change rapidly. Constant research and investigation is the key to tapping into consumers' needs and wants.

142 Tips to Succeed:
Often-made loan mistakes – beware

- Agreeing to co-sign. Some studies have found that of co-signed loans that go into default, as many as three out of four co-signers are asked to repay the loan.

- Not reading the fine print. When you obtain a line of credit or loan, you are entering into a legally binding agreement. Read everything to understand why and how often interest rates could change and what will cause the account to default.

- Borrowing your way out of debt. The only real way to get out of debt is to pay it off. "Moving money" has as many risks as rewards and will never work unless you are committed to a lifestyle change.

www.crediteducation.org.

lifestyle segmentation – Separating consumers into (homogeneous) groups, based on their hobbies, interests and other aspects of their lifestyles. Key components are consumers' interests, attitudes and opinions. See *psychographic segmentation.*

lifetime value – The net present value of all future purchases expected from a customer. ("Net present value" means that future sales are discounted to take into account the fact that a dollar received tomorrow is worth less than a dollar received today.)

lift – A process used by many publications (newspapers, magazines, etc.) or television network news programs (ABC, CBS, NBC) where one story is replaced by another or the same size or length. Reasons for *lifts* might be to update a story from an earlier edition of a newspaper or a news program. National magazines that publish regional editions *lift* stories depending on where the magazine is sold.

liftout quote – A quotation or statement that is separated from the rest of a news story and sometimes set off with borders above and below – for emphasis. The quote is usually taken from the story it accompanies. Also called a *blurb* or *pull quote.*

lightening rod – Controversial issue or person.

Likert scale – A rating device frequently used in marketing research questionnaires where respondents indicate their level of agreement with a statement by choosing the appropriate response from a scale (strongly disagree, disagree, undecided, agree, strongly agree).

limited decision making – See *limited problem solving.*

limited-line department store – A department store that carries a narrower range of merchandise than a full-line department store. *Limited-line department stores* usually carry high-quality merchandise at higher (prestige) prices and stress customer service.

limited-line retailer – A retailer carrying only one line, or a few related lines, but a large assortment of the product. An example would be a neck tie store, women's lingerie, perfume shop, etc. Mall *kiosks* also fall under the category of *limited-line retailer.*

limited-line strategy – The decision by a producer to offer fewer product variations – possibly to maintain price levels or to control costs. See *full–line strategy.*

The ABCs of Strategic Communication

limited problem solving – Buying situations where a purchaser has had some previous experience but is unfamiliar with suppliers, product options, prices, etc. Also referred to as *limited decision making*. See *extensive problem solving*.

limited-service advertising agency – A firm specializing in one or some of the following (but not all): creation, design, planning, execution of promotional campaign and/or media placement of advertisements. See *advertising agency; boutique agency; full-service advertising agency; niche agency*.

limited-service research supplier – A marketing research firm, which offers clients fewer services than a full-service research supplier. A limited-service research supplier might concentrate in only focus panels or taste testing rather than conducting research through multiple techniques. See *full-service research supplier*.

linage – A print advertising term that refers to the size of an advertisement, based on the number of lines of type used in the ad.

line – A group of products manufactured or distributed by a firm or organization. Examples would include Campbell's® soups, Gillette® razors and blades and Bic® pens. See *product line*.

line art – Artwork used in publications and video where all elements are solid with no intermediate shades or tones.

line conversion – A high contrast reproduction of an illustration, with no shading. It is purely reduced to a stark black or white.

line extension – Adding depth to an existing product line by introducing new products in the same product category (another car model, beverage flavor, dip chip). Research shows that *product line extensions* give customers greater choice and help protect firms from attack by competitors. See *product line; product line depth; product line extension; product line stretching; sub-brand*.

line manager – The person responsible for the marketing strategies of all the *brands* in a product line. Also called a product line manager or category manager.

line organization – An organizational structure where authority moves down in a line from the *chief executive officer (CEO)*. At one time, it was the *CEO* who had complete authority over decision-making. Today's

143

Want to advance in the workplace? Here are some strong suggestions. They are characteristics of a strong and successful leader:

Strong leaders spend most of their day:

• consensus-building

• offering recognition and reward

• negotiating

• planning

• organizing

• collaborating

• helping others reach their potential

• stressing ethics

• giving feedback (both positive *and* negative)

Leaders show greater respect on the job for others by:

• Meeting with employees a level below for ideas and feedback.

• Using cross-training and job swapping to develop employee understanding for other workers' duties and perspectives.

• Moving front-line supervisors to other departments for an entire year to fully experience the challenges of that position.

• Putting fun and creative rewards into place to recognize outstanding employee effort and achievement.

The bottom line – do the right thing.

Anita Bruzzese - Author of *Take This Job and Thrive*
(Impact Publications) - Gannett News Service

L

The ABCs of Strategic Communication

successful chief executive accepts counseling from his public relations specialists and other subordinates. See *organizational structure*.

line pricing – All products sell for same price. For example, Southwest® Airlines charges the same for all seats on a flight – unlike other airlines.

line pruning – Reducing the depth of a product line by eliminating less profitable offerings in a particular product category (Coke®, Diet Coke®,

Cherry Coke®, Diet Cherry Coke®, Lemon Coke®, Diet Lemon Coke®, etc.). See *product line pruning.*

line retrenchment – Reducing the width of a product mix by decreasing the diversity of items offered across product categories. An example would be General Motors® eliminating the Oldsmobile® brand and Campbell's® dropping the Franco American® brand in favor of carrying the same line under the Campbell's® brand. See *product line*; *product line retrenchment; product mix width.*

link – An electronic connection (or portal) between two Web sites. Also called a hot link or a hyperlink.

liquid crystal display (LCD) – A display circuit characterized by a liquid crystal element sandwiched between two glass panels. Characters are produced by applying an electric field to liquid crystal molecules and arranging them to act as light filters.

liquid library – Online availability of royalty-free pictures, clip art, articles and books. Controversial, because many may have been posted in violation of copyright laws.

liquidity – Current assets of a firm or organization that can be readily turned into cash. *Liquidity* represents a company's ability to meet its immediate liabilities.

liquor quicker® – a carousel where six different bottles (of liquor) can be hooked up to deposit a shot with the push of a button. The bottles can be straight liquor or mixed drinks.

list broker – A firm or individual who sells or rents mail, telephone or e-mail lists. The lists may have been assembled by the broker or, more likely, by a third-party organization that uses the broker as its sales agent.

list cleaning – The process of updating a mail, telephone or e-list to remove any undeliverable addresses. The process includes removing duplicates and names of the deceased.

list maintenance – The ongoing process of keeping a mailing list up-to-date by adding, editing or deleting data.

list manager – While a list broker works for a mailer, the *list manager* works for the list owner. The primary function is to promote the list to mailers and list brokers for list rental. *List managers* might be an internal employee of the list owner, or work for an outside list management company paid a commission by the list owner. Management services include marketing of the list, coordinating and controlling rental activity and accounting.

list of callbacks – People executives will return phone calls to. Often used in the phrase, "not on his/her list of callbacks."

list services – Computerized records containing addresses and in many cases ZIP+4, U.S. Postal Service carrier routes and other delivery information. Many lists contain such additional data as *demographics* or *geodemographics*. As assurance that a client is getting its money's worth, seeding is used – false or "dummy" names added to a mailing list as a way to check delivery and to uncover any unauthorized list usage. See *listserv*.

144

Techniques to Succeed: Leadership development

There are five areas that define the success of an executive training program:

- Satisfaction (were the participants happy?)
- Learning (did knowledge increase?)
- Application (did on-the-job behavior change?)
- Business impact (were there changes in business outcomes?)
- Return on investment (did the company make more money resulting from the training than it spent on the training?)

Newstrack Executive Information Service
www.news-track.com
800-334-5771

list price – The regular price of a product before any *discount* is given or allowances made. See *discount*.

list rental – Rather than being purchased, mail, telephone and e-mail lists are often rented for one-time use or a limited number of uses. Mailing, calling or e-mailing people on the list more than the specified number of times is a breach of contract. (If someone on the list responds to the initial campaign, the list renter is then considered to "own" that name and can then conduct unlimited communications with the person or organization.)

listserv – A mailing list comprised of e-mail addresses. Individual states are coping with the question, are names and addresses on a *listserv* public information?

The ABCs of Strategic Communication

listserver – A program that automatically sends e-mail to a list of subscribers or *listserv*.

lithography – The first fundamentally new printing technology since the invention of relief printing in the 15th century. It is a mechanical planographic process in which the printing and non-printing areas of the plate are all at the same level, as opposed to processes where the design is cut into the printing block. It is now commonly referred to as *offset printing*.

Litwin's 9 Ps of marketing – In addition to the original four Ps of Marketing (product, price, place, promotion), *The ABCs of Strategic*

145 Techniques to Succeed: Communication and leadership

A coach's 10-point game plan:

• Have a concrete vision – in other words, be clear about your vision for the group's future.

• Be your own messenger – direct communication is important not just on major issues, but on the day-to-day matters, as well.

• Build a team ego – it is the difference between mediocrity and being something special.

• Act with integrity – don't cut corners or bend rules; it will only undermine your effort.

• Act decisively – you won't always be right, but you must be willing to put your ideas and yourself on the line.

• Be adaptable – you must change, and so must those around you or everyone gets behind.

• Be consistent – have a strategy for when things go wrong to get through it quickly without panic.

• Maintain focus – this is a discipline, so you must train yourself at it, learning from the tough times.

• Live for the future, not in the past – "short-term goals to manage the present, long-term goals for the future," he writes.

• Act selflessly – "leaders are judged by the successes of the people they lead."

Rick Pitino - Author - *Lead to Succeed*

Communication author, M. Larry Litwin, APR, Fellow PRSA, includes five more Ps to help achieve synergy – public relations, policy, politics (mind share/intellect), personal selling and packaging.

live shot – An on-scene television or radio news story reported as it is happening.

lizard look – Stares of boredom (deer in the headlights) when an audience doesn't understand or is not interested.

load – Usually used as upload or *download*. It means to transfer files or software from one computer or server to another computer or server. Quite simply, it is the movement of information online.

loading objective – One of three possible objectives of a consumer sales promotion. Purchasers are offered incentives to buy a greater quantity of the product than they would otherwise have done. Incentives could include additional product or promotional gifts. See *loyalty objective*; *trial objective*.

lobbyist – Legislative liaison.

lobby journalism – News stories that carry only one point of view by quoting just one person or source.

lobbying – Direct attempt to influence legislative and regulatory decisions in government. For some, *lobbying* is a negative term signifying the manipulation of government for selfish means or ends.

local advertising – Advertising rates available to local (spot) advertisers as opposed to national advertisers. Local rates are usually less. Also, advertising in a national or regional publication or on a national television or radio program that uses a lift (print) or cutaway (TV/radio) that features a local advertiser. See *local buy*.

local area network (LAN) – A group of computers connected together (a network) at one location.

local brand – A brand marketed in one specific country.

local buy – The buying of media (print, newspapers, television, radio and outdoor advertising) serving a local region only.

local rate – An advertising rate charged to a local advertiser, typically a retailer or local agency, by local media and publications, as distinguished from a national rate that is charged to a national advertiser.

The ABCs of Strategic Communication

localize – To emphasize the local angle in an out-of- town story.

locator – Information (titles) superimposed on a television screen during a news report identifying the location of the report (video) being shown.

lock box – A service offered by banks to individuals and companies where they receive payments by mail to a post office or other type of box and the bank picks up the payments several times a day, deposits them into the individual's or company's account, and notifies the receiver of the deposit. This enables the individual or company to put the money to work as soon as it's received. Also any of several legislative mechanisms that attempt to isolate or "lock away" funds of the federal government for purposes such as reducing federal spending, preserving surpluses, or protecting the solvency of trust funds.

lockdown – Used to protect people inside a facility from a dangerous external or internal event. It helps control the movement of people.

locking device – A *tactic* used to assure that an advertising message is not forgotten. Examples would include *jingles, signatures, slogans, endorsers* and *taglines*.

locking power – Creative approach that captures the attention of the consumer and assists with their recall. Locking devices include *jingles, slogans, taglines (kicker), signatures, logos,* celebrity *endorsers* and repetition. An example would be the Aflac® duck.

log meeting – Editorial planning sessions at newspapers and radio and television news departments.

login – The identification or name used to access a computer, network or Web site.

logistical costs – Costs involved in the acquisition and transportation of materials required for production, and for the storage, handling and shipment of finished goods to customers.

logistical functions – One of the three kinds of functions performed by intermediaries in a marketing channel. Logistical functions include the assembling of a variety of products, storing them, sorting them into categories and sizes and arranging them on retail store shelves. See *facilitating functions; transactional functions.*

logistics – Activities involved with the orderly and timely acquisition and transportation of materials required for production, and with the storage, handling and distribution of finished goods to customers.

logo (logotype) – A distinctive or unique mark, sign or symbol, group of letters, or a graphic version of a company's name or, used to identify and promote the company, its product or brand. For a *logo* to become a trademark, it must be registered with the United States Patent and Trademark Office.

logo merchandise – A product (such as a t–shirt, baseball cap, pen or paper weight) displaying a *logo* or other promotional image. Sometimes jocularly (or occasionally disparagingly) referred to as "trinkets and trash." Advertising specialty items would fall under this category.

long-range planning – Strategic planning over an extended period. Long–range is commonly thought to be at least three years into the future.

long-run average cost – The average cost to produce each unit of an item or a set or group of products in the long term. Over a period of time (in the short term), the *average cost* may be reduced through experience of producing the product(s). See *average cost.*

loss leader– A retail item advertised at an invitingly low price (many times below dealer cost) to attract customers for the purchase of other, more profitable merchandise.

loss leader pricing – The pricing of a product at below cost to attract purchasers to a store in the hope they will buy additional items at normal prices. See *loss leader.*

L

147 Techniques to Succeed:

The plan is nothing – planning is everything

Some of the things your business plan needs to do:

- **Define your strategy.** Figure out what you're really selling, who wants it, why they want it and how your business provides something different from the competition.

- **Control your destiny.** Determine where you want to go and break that down into specific, concrete steps with dates, deadlines and budgets.

- **Plan your cash.** You've got to make a good, educated guess, then manage your planned cash flow vs. actual cash flow very carefully.

- **Allocate resources realistically.** This doesn't just have to do with cash, but also with know-how and responsibility. Who's in charge?

- **Communicate your plan.** The business plan is the standard tool for communicating the main points of a business to a spouse, partner, boss, banker, investor, manager or other interested person.

Careerbuilder.com

lost account ratio – A measure used to evaluate salespeople in which the salesperson's ability to keep prior accounts as active customers is calculated.

lottery – A form of consumer sales promotion (also called *sweepstakes*) where purchasers are offered a chance to win prizes if their names are selected – usually electronically. Sweepstakes are federally regulated.

low cost carrier (LCC) – Airline industry acronym for low-cost carrier (includes AirTran®, JetBlue® and Southwest®).

low involvement communication – Text messaging rather than talking on phone or face to face.

low-involvement products – Products bought frequently and with a minimum of thought and effort – low risk – because they are not of vital concern and do not have any great impact on the consumer's lifestyle. See *high-involvement products*.

low-touch service – A customer service approach characterized by a low level of personal contact with the consumer, which include service provided by vending machines, automatic telling machines at banks, self-service gasoline pumps, etc. See *high-touch service*.

lowercase – Words in all small letters (no caps).

loyalty cards – Preferred shopping cards used by super markets and other retailers – offering deep discounts to holders but they also gather a great deal of person data.

loyalty index – Frequency of viewership or listenership of a particular television or radio station. With the advent of cable television (large variety of program channels) and increase in radio formats, viewer and listener loyalty has greatly decreased.

loyalty marketing – The practice of using existing customers as a client or consumer base by enticing them through such incentive programs as cash back or *discounts* (Staples®, CVS® Pharmacies, super markets, etc.). Loyalty marketing programs are based on the concept that the more a customer spends, the more he/she gets back. Now, technological advances have allowed *loyalty marketing* companies to expand on this concept, allowing every company selling almost any product to enroll their customers in a loyalty marketing program. However, for a program

148 Tips to Succeed:
Keep holiday cards professional

- Holiday greeting cards should be more tailored and formal than cards for family and friends. Keep messages brief and secular unless you are certain of the recipient's religious faith.

- Sign each card personally – even if your name is preprinted on the card.

- An e-mail greeting is a poor substitute for a real greeting card.

- Mailing holiday greeting cards first class will ensure they are delivered to a forwarding address or returned if the address cannot be located.

- Include your return address in the upper left-hand corner or on the back flap of the envelope.

- Use an office address when mailing holiday greeting cards to business associates.

- Take the extra step to verify how recipients' names are spelled.

Marc Wagenheim - Hallmark®

to be successful, companies must practice *relationship marketing* – understand their customers, know them demographically and psychographically. Research is clear, it is a waste of assets to try to turn a bad customer into a loyal customer, while turning a good customer into a loyal customer can reap profits for the company.

loyalty objective – One of three possible aims or objectives of a consumer sales promotion. Purchasers are offered incentives to stay loyal to a particular brand. See *loading objective*; *trial objective*.

loyalty (consumer) (reward) programs – Activities designed to encourage repeat purchasing through a formal program enrollment process and the distribution of benefits. Loyalty programs may also be referred to as frequency marketing. Retailers reward customers for purchases by giving them points for dollars spent. While service is still the "bottom line," Loyalty programs attract customers in droves and keep them loyal. Such programs can be traced to programs like Gold Bond Stamps®, which started in 1938. Grocery stores gave out stamps based on how much customers spent. Customers redeemed the stamps for free "stuff." Among the most successful Loyalty programs are those sponsored by Marriott®, Staples® and Visa® AirTran®. See *loyalty marketing*.

luck – When preparation meets opportunity. **L**

m-commerce (mobile commerce) – The ability to conduct transactions involving money via the Internet using a wireless device, such as a cell phone or a PDA. *M-commerce* is much more popular in Europe and Japan than in the United States. Predictions are that *WAPs (web access phones)* will soon become necessities rather than luxuries. See *interactive commerce*.

MAC Triad – *Message, audience* and *channel* (plus *purpose* and *timing*). Once the target *audience* is determined, a *message* is crafted and a delivery *channel* (media vehicle) chosen. The message's delivery must be at a time when the target audience is available and listening. To be successful, all four (*message, audience, channel* and *timing*) must be correct. For example, the correct *message* delivered on the wrong *channel* is failure; the wrong *message* on the correct *channel* is a failure. When *synergy* is achieved and *goals* are met it is called *informization*. When the *Mac Triad* is broken the message is lost.

macro-environment – External factors, beyond an organization's control, that affect a company's planning, performance and decision making. Examples would include economic, *demographic*, technological, natural, social and cultural, legal and political. See *micro-environment*.

macromarketing – A type of marketing where a company or organization must be resilient as it adapts itself to uncontrollable factors within the industry or an entire market.

macrosegmentation – The division of a market into broadly defined groups, each with its particular needs and wants, prior to further division or segmentation on the basis of more narrowly defined needs and wants (also called *niche* markets). See *market segmentation*; *microsegmentation*.

magalogues – Ad-driven publications. Catalogues designed to look like magazines where the articles are actually *advertorials*. An example would be *LUCKY – The Magazine About Shopping*.

mail-in premium – A premium obtained by mailing in a suitable response to a manufacturer or distributor, with or without money.

mail jail – E-mail messages that get monitored by employers from a remote location using key words. Also used to describe the screening of phone calls using voicemail messages, blocked e-mail addresses and packages that are undeliverable because of incomplete addresses that often consist of just a name.

mail monitoring – Mailers track their mail to verify content within the direct mail package (packaged by a *vendor*) and to determine the length of delivery time.

mail-order advertising – Advertising that provides paperwork for the consumer to make a purchase through the mail.

mail-order house – A retailing organization that uses catalogues rather than a sales force to promote its goods to customers. Also called a *catalogue retailer*.

mail-order selling – A system of retailing where customers order merchandise, usually from a catalogue, by mail. Orders are shipped direct to the customer's home.

> # 149
>
> ## Techniques to Succeed:
> ## Litwin's 9 Ps of Marketing
>
> • Public Relations
> • (Sales) Promotion
> • Positioning (Place)
> • Price
> • Personal Selling
> • Product (itself)
> • Politics (in the workplace Brainstorming)
> • Policy
> • Packaging
>
> Litwin's 9 Ps of Marketing
> M. Larry Litwin, APR, Fellow PRSA - *The Public Relations Practitioner's Playbook*
> (Kendall/Hunt – 2008)

mail-order wholesalers – Wholesalers who use catalogues to sell to certain retailers considered too small to call on in the traditional profitable way.

150

Tips to Succeed:
Some reasons to earn an MBA degree

Here are some reasons Rowan (N.J.) University and other graduate students pursue an MBA:

- To improve management/leadership knowledge and skills.
- To increase opportunities for obtaining a new job or finding a better job.
- To increase earnings opportunities.
- To improve knowledge in areas of finance and accounting.
- To improve personal skills, quantitative, oral, writing, critical thinking.
- To increase job opportunities in current workplace.

Robert Lynch - Professor, College of Business - Rowan (N.J.) University
www.rowan.edu/mba

mail surveys – Research conducted by mailing *questionnaires* to the sample and tabulating the responses that are completed and mailed back. It is a relatively inexpensive method of obtaining data in a marketing research study. Mail surveys keep interviewer bias to a minimum, but they require considerable time to conduct and response rates are generally low. Another disadvantage is that the targeted respondent may not be the person who answers the questions.

mailer – A flier distributed by mail.

mailing area – Required on a self-mailer newsletter. Takes up one-third or one-half of the page. Post offices prefer the mailing label at the top of page.

mailing list – A series of names and addresses – either postal or e-mail – available to firms or organizations who want to reach targeted audiences.

Mailing Preference Service (MPS) – A database of individual home addresses where the occupiers have elected not to receive unsolicited direct (marketing) mail.

mainstream media (MSM) – The *mainstream media* consist of outlets that cover a larger territory than your own neighborhood. For instance, a city's daily newspaper would be a *mainstream media* outlet. So would a local television and radio stations. *Mainstream media* outlets can also be national and even international.

maintenance marketing – A marketing activity aimed at maintaining the current sales level in a highly competitive situation.

maintenance selling – Generating sales volume from existing customers.

maintenance strategy – Seen in business, marketing and public relations plans as a decision-making tactic appropriate for organizations with low growth opportunities. These organizations have relatively strong positions in their market. They continue to invest in their business, in a limited way, just to maintain the current volume of business.

major equipment – Long-lived (business) assets that must be depreciated over time. These can also be called capital items.

majority fallacy – An erroneous belief that the biggest segment of a market will be the most profitable for a firm or organization to enter. Research shows that competition will usually be keenest in the biggest segment. See *market segmentation*.

make good – The free repeat of an ad or commercial to compensate for the publication or broadcast vehicle's error in the original insertion. Many times the mistakes are blamed on technical difficulties.

make or buy decision – A choice sometimes faced by a manufacturing company when considering the acquisition of a new product – to lease or purchase a product or brand name or to manufacture it internally using its own (new) brand. Costs are a major factor.

making the rounds – The activity of reporters using the telephone to conduct periodic (several times a day) checks of police department activities and hospital information (has become much more difficult because of the federal HIPPA (Health Insurance Portability and Accountability Act) – National Standards to Protect the Privacy of Personal Health Information. Checking the police blotters – or crime logs.

malapropism – Words or phrases used out of the context in which they are expected – misuse of words.

mall intercept – A type of marketing research interview where respondents are chosen randomly – for example, walking through shopping centers, in stores, on college campuses, etc.

MAN (money, authority, need) – Acronym used in selling for qualifying new prospects. Does the prospect have the money to pay? Does the prospect have the authority to buy? Does the prospect have a need for the product? Also referred to as PAN – Pay, Authority, Need.

man on the street (MOS) – Term used in print and broadcast journalism for intercept-type interviews with ordinary people walking the streets or in malls, etc.

management by objectives – A long-accepted evaluation and control system where administrative and salespeople set goals and objectives for themselves that are acceptable to management. Progress towards these goals and objectives is reviewed periodically to judge an employee's accountability – did he or she deliver the promised results?

managerial judgment – A forecasting method where predictions about the likely level of sales for a specified future period are made by experienced senior managers.

manipulate – Influence by getting into one's mind with persuasive, strategic messages. Sometimes considered shrew or devious – but when messages are open, honest, thorough and valid, they are ethical.

manipulation – To control by skilled use. Getting into one's mind with persuasive, strategic messages. Sometimes considered shrewd or devious – but when messages are open, honest, through and valid they are ethical.

manipulative selling techniques – Selling practices where attempts are made to overwhelm the prospective buyer – high-pressure methods. Many consider these unethical. See *non-manipulative selling techniques*.

mannequinism – A "condition" caused by political inactivity. Sufferers experience a hardening of the skin and firmness of all joints until ultimately the body is transformed into a plastic hollow shell. It is a "disease" of the mind that ultimately affects the person's whole being – and community.

manufacturers' agent – An agent or representative used by manufacturers to put in place their own sales staff. See *outside sales facilities*.

manufacturer's brand – A brand owned or controlled by a particular company or organization. Also called a *national brand*.

manufacturers' representative –See *manufacturers' agent*.

manuscript – Typed copy before layout begins. Magazine and book publishers accept with revisions or rejects a manuscript. After editorial work is completed on the accepted manuscript, it is sent to the art department for layout – which turns it into an article.

marcom – Term used for marketing communications.

The ABCs of Strategic Communication

margin –The white space left on the outer edges of the page – to frame the ad content.

margin of error – The range, plus or minus, within which results can be expected to vary with repeated random samplings, under exactly similar conditions. There is an inverse correlation between sample size and margin of error.

marginal analysis – Used in setting the advertising budget by assuming the point at which an additional dollar spent on advertising equals additional profit. Also, the price-breaking point where the manufacture and sale of additional units reduces the cost of producing and delivering the product.

marginal cost – The change in total cost that results from producing an additional unit.

marginal profit – The change in the total profit that results from the sale of an additional unit.

marginal revenue – The change in total revenue that results from selling an additional unit.

marital status – Used for *demographic* purposes - whether an individual is married, single, divorced or widowed. Considered an important variable. See *demographics*.

mark-down – When a firm reduces an item to sell it below its original retail price, the difference between the original price and the reduced price is called the *mark-down*.

mark-down ratio – The difference between the original selling price of an item and the reduced price needed to sell it. It is expressed as a percentage of the reduced price. For example, if a firm sells an item originally priced at $100 for a reduced price of $75, the *mark-down* is $25 and the *mark-down ratio* is 33.3 percent – $25 being one third of $75.

mark-up – The amount added by a wholesaler or retailer to the cost of a product to determine the selling price to the customer. The increase in the price of goods to create a profit margin for a business. Profits are dependent on a carefully calculated *mark-up*. See *keystone*.

mark-up ratio – The difference between the buying price of an article and its selling price, normally expressed as a percentage of the selling price. For example, if a firm buys a product at $80 and sells it for $100, the mark-up is $20, and the *mark-up ratio* is 20 per cent, $20 being one-fifth of $100.

market – A geographic area of the country or a group of buyers and potential buyers of a product or service – or the overall demand for a product.

market accessibility – One of the four major requirements, with *actionability*, *measurability* and *substantiality*, for useful market segmentation. *Accessibility* expresses the notion that the audience segment targeted must be able to be reached and served adequately by the firm's promotion and distribution system. See *accessibility*.

market allocation system – A market place with minimum government involvement.

151

Tips to Succeed: Think twice before challenging the media

Have your facts straight before arguing with the person who buys ink by the barrel and paper by the ton.

Many newspaper editors

market atomization strategy – The division of a market into audience segments consisting of individual customers and tailoring a product service for each. See *complete segmentation*; *custom marketing*.

market attractiveness – The degree to which a market offers opportunities to a firm or organization, taking into account market size, growth rate and the level of competition (and other constraints).

market-based marketing organization – A marketing structure of an organization where specialists have responsibility for particular markets (rather than for particular products of the organization). Companies use this structure if they believe the needs of each market it serves differ widely. See *market segmentation organization*; *product-based marketing organization*.

market-driven economy – An economy controlled by market forces rather than by government action. See *market allocation system*.

market broadening – A major research strategy where a company looks beyond its existing product line to the needs or wants of the consumers who buy it. For example, a company that makes or markets jelly, knowing that consumers like and want PB&J sandwiches, might expand its operations to manufacturing a line of peanut butter.

market challenger – A company holding a major market share and competing vigorously (through marketing efforts) with the market leader for outright leadership. Examples would include beverage, computer and car manufacturers. See *market follower; market leader; market nicher.*

market development – A strategy where a company attempts to grow by taking its existing products into new markets. Also, increasing sales by offering existing products (or new versions of them) to new customer groups (as opposed to simply attempting to increase the company's share of current markets). See *market expansion.*

market diversification – A strategy where a company seeks growth by adding products and markets currently unrelated to its existing products and markets.

market dynamics – Changes that occur within the market that a company may have no control over, but influence its decision-making and impact its performance.

market entry – The launch of a new product into a new or existing market. A different strategy is required depending on whether the product is an early or late entrant to the market. Research is clear – the first entrant usually has an advantage, while later entrants must demonstrate that their products are better quality and a better buy.

152 Techniques to Succeed: Key elements of a mission statement

- This is who we are
- What we think about ourselves
- What we want to do
- Why we deserve your support

Larry Litwin and Ralph Burgio © 1971; © 1999
www.larrylitwin.com

market entry barrier – Any circumstance or feature of a market which could prevent a company, firm or organization from entering it. Research shows that the greatest *market entry barrier* is the presence of a firmly entrenched competitor with a significant competitive advantage. An example would be Virgin Cola® attempting to break into the soft drink market dominated by Coca-Cola® and Pepsi®.

market expansion – A growth strategy where an organization targets existing products toward new markets. *Market development* is used to target new geographic markets, new *demographic* or *psychographic* segments or totally new users.

market factor – Any external variable affecting a company's sales.

market follower – A firm satisfied with following the leaders in a market place without challenging them – happy with moving a product when the *market leader's* product is not available. The firm is satisfied with its existing *market share*. *Market followers* rely on the *market leader's* marketing efforts to sell their product, as well. See also *market challenger* and *market leader*.

market forecast – The anticipated sales for a particular time period. All internal and external circumstances must be considered.

market growth – The increase in revenue raised (total sales) in a particular market for a particular product, brand or for all products combined.

market growth rate – The rate of increase in market sales – commonly expressed as a percentage.

market index – A combination of *market factors* used to predict future sales levels.

market leader – The company whose products or brand hold the largest market share. See *market challenger*; *market follower*; *market nicher*.

market minimum – The level of sales that a company can expect to achieve in a market without promotional or advertising efforts of any kind.

market niche – A small but profitable segment of a market – one that is narrowly focused and unlikely to attract competitors.

market nicher – A company whose products serve segments too small to be of interest to firms with larger shares of the market. They are also

The ABCs of Strategic Communication

called *market specialists, threshold firms* or *foothold firms.* See *market challenger; market follower; market leader.*

market opportunity – A newly-identified market or a market offering an opportunity for a company to move into with its product – a product gap.

market opportunity evaluation – The matching of an identified market opportunity to an organization or company's objectives and resources.

market penetration – A growth strategy where a company concentrates its efforts on its target market or an existing market to attract a higher percentage of (sales) users of its product. See *market share; market development.*

market penetration pricing – An approach to pricing where a company sets a relatively low price for a product in the introductory stage of its life cycle with the intention of building market share. See *market skimming pricing.*

market philosophy – The general attitude of the marketer toward the customer.

market positioning – A marketing activity intended to place a product into a desired competitive position in a market and to have the target audience perceive it as intended. See *real positioning; repositioning.*

market potential – The size or value in dollars of a total market should everyone interested in that product or brand buy it. Potential consumers must be able to afford the product.

market profile – A summary of the *demographic* and *psychographic* characteristics of a market, including information of typical purchasers and competitors, and often general information on the economy and retailing patterns of an area.

market research – The systematic gathering of information about a market through surveys, observation or experimentation. Any research that leads to more market knowledge and better-informed decision-making.

market segment – Groups or *niche* audiences (narrowly defined) within a market consisting of consumers or organizations with relatively similar needs and wants. It is not unusual for various audiences to respond to a given set of marketing stimuli (promotion/advertising) in a particular way. See *market segmentation.*

153

Tips to Succeed: 14 ways public relations practitioners should *deal* with the media

1. Make the CEO responsible for media relations.
2. Face the facts.
3. Consider the public interest in every operating decision.
4. Be a source before you are a subject.
5. If you want your views represented, you have to talk.
6. Respond quickly.
7. Cage your lawyers.
8. Tell the truth – or nothing.
9. Don't expect to bat 1.000 (to be perfect).
10. Don't take it personally.
11. Control what you can.
12. Know with whom you are dealing.
13. Avoid TV unless you feel you can speak candidly.
14. Be human.

M. Larry Litwin, APR, Fellow PRSA - *The Public Relations Practitioner's Playbook* Kendall/Hunt - 2008

market segment expansion strategy – One of four possible *market segmentation* approaches available to a firm in relation to the segment or segments it wishes to target. In a *market segment expansion approach*, a company targets one product to several segments of the market – expanding the market for one product. See *segmentation strategies; concentrated segmentation strategy; product line expansion strategy; differentiated segmentation strategy.*

market segmentation – The division of a total market into groups, subgroups or sectors (*demographically* and *psychographically*) with relatively similar needs and wants. It's important that the proper message and channel be used to communicate to *market segments* at a time when the segments are available to receive the message.

market segmentation organization – The organization of a firm's marketing activities so that a separate division is responsible for each of its major market segments. One of the four major requirements of useful *market segmentation* with *accessibility, actionability, measurability* and *substantiality*. *Accessibility* expresses the notion that the segment targeted must be able to be reached and served adequately by the firm's promotion and distribution system. See *actionability; measurability; organizational structure; substantiality.*

M

The ABCs of Strategic Communication

market share – A company's sales expressed as a percentage of the sales for the total industry – a piece of the total (100 percent) pie.

market share protection strategy – Marketing decisions and actions taken by a company or organization to protect its *market share* from competitors.

market skimming pricing – A pricing approach where the producer sets a high introductory price to attract buyers with a strong desire for the product and the resources to buy it, and then gradually reduces the price to attract the next and subsequent layers of the market. See *market penetration pricing.*

market specialist – A company whose products serve segments too small to be of interest to firms with larger shares of the market. Also called a *threshold firm* or *foothold firm.* See *market challenger; market follower; market leader; market nicher.*

market testing – Introducing a new product and marketing program into a market on a limited basis to evaluate projected success before a full launch. See *new product development.*

marketing – Determining what people need and giving it to them. Business activities that direct the exchange of goods and services between producers and consumers. It focuses on developing, expanding and facilitating the profitable introduction and promotion of a company's products and/or services. Traditionally, this is taken to include the original *4Ps* – *Product, Price, Place* and *Promotion. Product* refers to market requirements and ensuring that those requirements are seen in the products and/or services offered by the company. *Price* is determining and setting the most appropriate prices for the products/services. *Place* is determining the best geographic areas to sell in – taking into account the competition (positioning) and also the best "channels" for distributing to those markets. *Promotion* refers to all activities involved in making potential customers aware of the company, its products and services and their features and how the features benefit the consumer and encourages them to buy the product or serve. *Marketing* stresses product or brand differences than similarities.

marketing acronyms – Usually, abbreviations such as *YUPPIE, BUPPIE,* and *GLAM.* There are many. Successful communicators should learn them, and never hesitate to ask what one stands for if it is unknown.

154

Techniques to Succeed: Top 10 list of media relations mistakes

BEST EVIDENCE

10. Lack of preparation/plan
9. Failure to identify audience
8. Reluctance to accept responsibility
7. Inability to show compassion
6. Failure to focus
5. Natural bias against reporters
4. Inability to shut mouth
3. Natural tendency to want to sound more intelligent than we really are
2. Fear & loathing
1. Panic

Best Evidence, Inc.
Executive Communications Counsel
Crisis Communications Management
Cherry Hill, N.J.
bestevidence911@aol.com

marketing advantage – The competitive edge that can be gained – through research – by accurately identifying customer needs and wants and by developing products that deliver what customers ask for. Effective public relations, advertising and other marketing efforts can help companies achieve a *marketing advantage*. See *cost advantage*.

marketing analysis – See *marketing audit*.

marketing audit – The periodic, systematic, *objective* review, analysis and evaluation of an organization's marketing structure, *goals*, *objectives*, *strategies*, *tactics* and other action plans, performance and results. Some contain recommendations for the future.

marketing budget – The amount allocated for spending on marketing activities in a specified period.

marketing channel – Often used interchangeably with *sales channel* or *distribution channel*. People and organizations used to help move a product from producer to consumer. Also, any individuals or organization that uses communication efforts to help market a product or service. In addition to the products and services themselves, *brand name*, information, promotion and payment also move along the *marketing channels*.

marketing communications – All strategies, tactics and activities involved in getting the desired marketing messages to intended target audiences regardless of the media (*channels*) used. The formal and informal messages that sellers communicate to buyers and potential buyers.

marketing concept – A business philosophy that holds that organizational success depends on the efficient identification of the needs and wants of target markets and audiences and effectively satisfying them.

marketing consultants – Independent marketing specialists hired by companies, usually on a short-term contract basis, to advise on a wide range of marketing matters – marketing planning and management, marketing research, marketing communications, etc. See *marketing intermediaries*.

marketing control – Activities involved in checking that marketing action plans are producing the desired results and taking corrective action if they are not.

marketing controller – An individual – usually with training in finance and marketing – responsible for analyzing and evaluating a company's marketing expenditures.

marketing cost analysis – A tool used in marketing planning where the costs associated with selling, billing, warehousing, promoting and distributing of certain products or product groups, or to certain customers or market segments, are examined to assess their profitability.

marketing database – Data brought into an organization through marketing research projects or a marketing information system and used to help decision making. See *database marketing*.

marketing definition – Identifying unmet needs, then producing products and services to meet those needs – and pricing, distributing and promoting those products and services to earn a profit.

marketing department – A division within a company responsible for the planning and coordination of all marketing activities.

marketing differentiation – A brand or product's unique elements, which separates it from the competition.

marketing environment – The internal and external influences which affect marketing decision-making and have an impact on its performance. See *macro-environment*; *micro-environment*.

marketing era – The period following the end of World War II, which saw marketing emerge for the first time as the prevailing trend in business.

marketing ethics – The standards or moral (beliefs) principles governing the marketing profession.

marketing expense-to-sales ratio – A marketing control measure used to determine whether the cost of the marketing activities for a particular product or service in a given period is excessive. Total marketing expenses are expressed as a percentage of total sales revenue.

marketing firm – A business that carries out the distribution and sales of goods and services from producer to consumer – including product or service development, pricing, packaging, advertising, merchandising and distribution and aspects that can help a firm achieve synergy and reach its goal.

marketing implementation – The activities involved in putting marketing strategies into action to achieve marketing objectives. See *marketing management.*

marketing information – Information used or required to support marketing decisions – often drawn from a computerized *marketing information system.*

marketing information system – The department of a firm or organization responsible for gathering, organizing, storing, retrieving and analyzing data relevant to a firm's past, present and future operations. It is done on an on-going basis to continually provide support for management's marketing decisions.

marketing intelligence – Information gathered from sources external to the firm for use in decision-making. See *marketing information system.*

marketing intermediaries – Independent firms that assist in the flow of goods and services from producers to consumers. These include *agents*, *wholesalers* and *retailers*, marketing services agencies, physical distribution companies and financial institutions. Also referred to as *middlemen.* See *marketing channel.*

marketing management – The analysis, planning, organization, implementation and control of the firm's marketing activities.

marketing metrics – Measurements that help with the quantification of marketing performance, such as market share, advertising budgets for a product or brand, and response rates elicited by advertising and direct marketing.

marketing mix – The combination of marketing inputs that affect customer motivation and behavior. These inputs traditionally encompass four controllable variables, the *4 Ps*– product, price, place and promotion. The list has subsequently been extended to *Litwin's 9 Ps of Marketing* – including public relations, politics (people interaction or as Ogilvy and Mather® refers to it – *mind share*), personal selling, policy and packaging. It is a blend of designing, pricing, distributing and communicating about the product or service.

marketing myopia – A term coined by academic Theodore Levitt, in an article published in *Harvard Business Review* in 1960. Levitt described companies' lack of vision – a failure of management to adequately "see down the road." He said because of a lack of research, management suffers from short sightedness.

marketing objectives – Goal broken down into subsets. They are specific milestones that measure predicted progress toward the achievement of a goal. They must address the desired result in terms of behavioral

155 Tips to Succeed: Understanding reporters and editors

Generally, journalists strive for:
• Accuracy

• Balance

• Fairness

• Memorable (what will the reader get out of the story?)

When pitching a story, the public relations practitioner must answer two questions:
• What is news?

• What is the point (to the story)?

A goal of editors is to:
• Educate

• Inform

• Inspire

• Motivate (staff)

…to help the public make intelligent decisions.

Ev Landers - News Coach - Gannett

change, designate the target audience(s), specify the expected level of accomplishment and identify the time frame (given period) in which the accomplishments are to occur.

marketing opportunities – Circumstances that offer an organization the chance to satisfy particular consumer needs and wants at a profit.

marketing opportunity analysis – The systematic examination and evaluation of a firm's external environment used to identify market needs and wants which it can satisfy profitably.

marketing organization – The structure of the marketing function within the firm or organization. The two most commonly used approaches to organizing the marketing effort are a *product-based organization* and a *market-based organization*. See *market-based marketing organization*; *product-based marketing organization*.

marketing orientation – A business philosophy or strategy that helps organizations achieve success through the efficient identification of the needs and wants of target markets and audiences and effectively satisfy them. See *marketing concept*.

marketing-oriented company – A company that subscribes to the philosophy that survival and prosperity depend on satisfying the needs and wants of its target markets more effectively and efficiently than its competitors.

marketing performance assessment – The periodic, systematic, objective review, analysis and evaluation of an organization's marketing structure, goals, objectives, strategies, tactics and other action plans, performance and results. Some contain recommendations for the future. See *marketing audit*.

marketing plan – A detailed, written account and timetable of the *objectives*, *strategies*, *tactics* and tools (methods) to be used by a firm to achieve its marketing goal(s). Plans may include product pricing, *promotion*, messaging, *channel strategies* and an analysis of the competitive environment.

marketing planning process – A systematic approach to the achievement of marketing goals. Steps in the process include providing a situation analysis, establishing *objectives* and *strategies*, developing action programs (*tactics*), implementing carry-out tactics and evaluating the plan.

marketing program – The combination of all of a firm or organization's marketing plans.

marketing research – A formal, systematic, planned approach to the collection, analysis, evaluation, interpretation and reporting of information required for marketing decision-making. Data, conclusions and recommendations are used in the transfer and sale of goods and services from producer to consumer.

marketing research brief – A document prepared by a firm or organization for an independent market researcher which provides background to help the researcher establish *goals, objectives, strategies, tactics*, tools, budget, timing, etc.

marketing research objectives – The purpose of a marketing research study. Many times, purpose becomes the first step in the public relations process – even before research (research, planning, implementation, evaluation – known as *PR-PIE* when purpose is included).

marketing research-to-sales ratio – A marketing control measure used to determine whether the amount spent on marketing research in a given period was excessive in relation to its sales. The total marketing research expenditure is expressed as a percentage of total sales revenue.

marketing services – Services produced or purchased by a marketing organization for use in the *production, pricing, promotion* and *distribution* of products which they themselves market. Services commonly produced or purchased by organizations for use by their own marketing departments include *market research, advertising* and *promotion*.

marketing services agencies – Independent companies providing assistance to firms in getting products to their target markets (from producer to consumer). They include public relations agencies, marketing research agencies, advertising agencies, sales promotions specialists, marketing consultants, etc.

marketing strategy – Includes public relations and advertising plans to assist a firm or organization in determining *goals, objectives, strategies, tactics*, its *target audiences* and an appropriate marketing mix (*integrated marketing communication*) to achieve its goals.

marketing synergy – The principle in public relations and marketing that the whole is greater than the sum of the parts. Using as many of the marketing mix variables together in a way that achieves maximum effect.

marketplace factor – Supply and demand are considered when product or service prices are set. This is in addition to manufacturing,

156 Techniques to Succeed: Media interviews: Dos and don'ts

Executives faced with a news media interview should seize the opportunity to deliver a positive message on behalf of their company.

Keep these tips in mind when preparing for news media interviews:

• Return calls promptly. Reporters are usually on deadline, and if they don't hear from you quickly, they will move on to someone else – possibly your competitor.

• Be candid. If a reporter thinks you're misleading them or trying to hide something, the story they write may not present you in the best light.

• Help them understand your business. Reporters are a proxy for your audience, the readers, and you need them to communicate your messages accurately.

• Be proactive – Cultivate relationships with reporters. Drop them a note commenting on a story that interested you; offer to be an expert or to refer them to other experts. Every story doesn't need to be about you or your company, but if reporters know you are a reliable, helpful source, they will call you again.

Steve Lubetkin - Lubetkin & Co. Communications,
Public Relations and Technology Counsel, LLC - www.lubetkin.net

distribution and other costs, inherent to getting the product to market. Profit margin must also be factored in.

marquee – Highlighted or activated items similar to a neon sign. Also, a roof-like structure, often bearing a signboard, projecting over an entrance – on a theater or hotel.

married partners – Not considered husband and wife in such states as Texas. In public relations copy, it is strongly recommended that it be clearly stated that the married partners are, in fact, a man and a woman (a husband and wife) as tradition defines. If the married partners are not a man and a woman, that, too, should be stated in the most politically correct way possible.

mash up – Also called *bastard pop*. *Mash ups* involve blending samples from two songs – generally, one song's vocals atop another's instrumental or rhythm track. Experts say the blending achieves a certain *synergy* not otherwise achieved with individual songs. The sum of the parts often surpasses the originals. The more disparate the genre-blending, the better. Also the blending of any two or more computer applications. The finished product is called mash. This is now being done for jingles. Read more at http://www.mashups.com/.

Maslow's Hierarchy of Needs – Also known as Maslow's Theory of Motivation. A theory first used in 1954 by Abraham Maslow, a U.S. psychologist, who hypothesized that some innate human needs are more pressing than others, and must be satisfied before any less pressing ones can be attended to. He arranged human needs into five categories in ascending order – physiological needs, safety needs, belongingness and love needs, esteem needs and self-actualization needs.

mass marketing – A marketing philosophy in which the seller views the market as a homogeneous whole, and, therefore, has only one marketing program (the same product, the same price, the same promotion and the same distribution system) for everyone. Also, the distribution of marketing communications through *mass media* (print, radio and television and in some respects, the Internet). The seller views the market as homogeneous – offering the same product at the same price through the same distribution system. Also referred to as *unsegmented marketing* or *undifferentiated marketing*. See *differentiated marketing*; *product-differentiated marketing*; *target marketing*.

mass media – Print, radio and television and in some respects, the Internet.

mass media advertising – Advertising in a non-selective way by means of the popular media to reach the widest possible audience. Advertising that reaches non-targeted audiences is referred to as *wasted coverage*.

mass merchandisers – Retail stores which sell finished, non-food items Best Buy®, Circuit City®, Staples®, etc. Typically, there are four types of *merchandisers* (categorized on the basis of service, price and product line) – *specialty stores* (full-service, high-price, limited product line); *department stores*; *merchandisers*; and *discount stores* (limited-service, low-price, wide product line).

mass society theory – The view that the *mass media* address a mass audience who pay attention or are dependent on receiving information from the media.

master tape – An edited audio tape or video tape used to record mass quantities for distribution. The copies are referred to as prints. See *dubbing*.

masthead – Statement of ownership, place of publication, executive personnel and other information about the newspaper, generally placed on the editorial page. Usually found on the editorial page of newspapers, but elsewhere in magazines and other publications (in newsletters, either on page 2 or the back page). Includes the names of the editorial staff, the publisher's address, copyright information, subscription rates, phone and fax numbers, e-mail and Web site.

masstige – A retail category that includes relatively low priced goods that come with a relatively prestigious *brand name* – goods and services priced between low-end, mass market items and high-end, prestigious items. Also, prestige items affordable to the masses. Examples include products marketed by Bath & Body Works®, Coach® and a number of car brands.

mastigious items – Prestigious products, but still available to the masses (new luxury items fall into this category). Examples include products marketed by Bath & Body Works®, Coach® and a number of car brands. See *masstige*. Read more at *www.wordspy.com/words/masstige.asp*.

material event (moment) – A corporate change, an action or significant event at a publicly held company that could affect stock prices – an acquisition, merger, bankruptcy, resignation of directors/officers, a change in the fiscal year, etc. When announcement of *material event* is made, it must be released to all audiences simultaneously. Annual and quarterly financial filings are *material events*.

material management – An organizational trend in purchasing in which some companies combine several functions – purchasing, inventory control, production scheduling, traffic, etc. – into one high-level function under the control of a materials manager.

materiality – The *FTC* theoretically will not regulate deceptive advertising unless the deceptive claim is also material – meaning, in simple terms, that the claim must be important to consumers, rather than trivial. The *FTC* requires that the deception be likely to affect consumers' "choice of, or conduct, regarding a product or service."

materials closing – The final date by which a publication must receive the advertising materials to be printed. Sometimes referred to as the drop dead date.

materials handling – Activities involved in the physical handling and moving of inventory.

mathematical forecasting techniques – Mathematically stated relationships or models used to arrive at forecasts – or predict trends and sales - from historical data. Often used in financial budgeting.

157 Techniques to Succeed: Ways to meet on the job

New on the job and not sure how to meet people? Just get out of your cubicle and start talking with new colleagues or managers to build your network.

Here's what to do:

• Start slowly by attending different functions at a company. Choose your seating. Don't sit down next to an empty chair. Try to sit next to someone new and introduce yourself - don't expect someone to come over to you.

• Are you shy? Try an ice-breaker like "did you hear what the speaker said?" to initiate a conversation.

• While waiting for a speaker, maximize the time and exchange numbers with the person sitting next to you.

• Use the elevator as talk time (known as 30-second elevator conversation or message).

• After leaving a meeting, use the time to chat up colleagues or meet someone new.

• Compliments are key – an easy way to make an introduction is to comment on an article of clothing or jewelry.

• Plan a lunch – follow up with new contacts by setting up one-on-one meetings to foster the relationship.

Stacey Sweet-Belle - Chubb Insurance - wwww.chubb.com/

matrix – A illustration or other type of visual shows in rectangular form with the information set out by rows and columns.

matte – In printing, the term precedes desktop publishing. It is camera-ready copy sent to a printer, which is shot with a printer's camera, as is. The *negative* is made into a plate. Using desktop publishing, it would be called a final laser print. Other terms include *ad slick, camera-ready, repro, slick* and *velox. Matte* is also defined as a dull, often rough finish, as in textured paint, glass, metal or paper. In printing, it would be the opposite of a glossy finish.

matte shot– A printing term where a camera shot is made with a *matte* (rubbery material) or mask in part of the frame to allow another shot to be printed in the opaque area. This technique preceded desktop publishing which accomplishes the same result, electronically.

matures (mature generation) – Members of society born before 1946.

maturity stage of product life cycle – The third stage (after introduction and growth) in the life of a typical product. In maturity, the product is well-known, has some loyal customers and strong competition. The final two stages are decline and withdrawal. See *product life cycle; introductory stage; growth stage; decline stage.*

McKinsey 7- S framework (model) or Seven Ss of Management – A framework or model, developed by the McKinsey Company, a leading consulting firm, for maximizing an organization's effectiveness. The framework or model, which McKinsey considers an essential business strategy, refers to seven interrelated aspects of the organization – systems, structure, skills, style, staff, strategy and shared values.

me-too competitive strategy – See *follow-the-leader strategy.*

me-too products – Risk-avoiding products not significantly different from those of competitors.

measurability – One of the four major requirements (with *actionability, accessibility* and *substantiality*) for useful market segmentation. *Measurability,* sometimes referred to as *identifiability,* expresses the notion that the size and purchasing power of the segment must be able to be measured. See *accessibility; actionability; substantiality.*

measurement – Measurements that help with the quantification of marketing performance, such as market share, advertising budgets for a

The ABCs of Strategic Communication

product or brand and response rates elicited by advertising and direct marketing. See *marketing metrics.*

mechanical – Also called a (finished) paste up. A finished layout that is photographed for offset printing. With desktop publishing, the *Mechanical* stage is skipped, because the laser print *is* the *mechanical*, which can be e-mailed.

media – Plural of *medium.* Any form of communication that carries a message to the public. Most carry advertising. *Media* include newspapers, magazines, radio, television, Internet, billboards, transit advertising and direct mail. Also, unbiased third parties (press representatives) who report information for public consumption.

media advisory – A brief summary of an upcoming news event, which could include the background and credentials of an expert willing to discuss it. Also known as a *news and photo memo; media alert; invitation to cover; interview alert.* The format includes either "Event; Date; Time; Place; Details" or "What; When; Where; Why; Details" – or a combination of both.

media alert – A brief summary of an upcoming news event, which could include the background and credentials of an expert willing to discuss it. Also known as a *news and photo memo; media advisory; invitation to cover; interview alert.* The format includes either "Event; Date; Time; Place; Details" or "What; When; Where; Why; Details" – or a combination of both.

media buying service – Agency that specializes in the services of media buying by purchasing time and space for the delivery of advertising messages through *mainstream (MSM) media.* Media buyers either conduct their own planning or contract with a *media planning* service to conduct research that determines the amount and combination of advertising "buys" needed to achieve objectives. Media buyers recommend the right audiences to advertise to, negotiate rates and monitor the performance of the advertising. See *media planning.*

media call report – A log that keeps track of media contacts whether written or verbal. It includes topic or client, when the contact was made, with whom and the results.

media concentration theory – Technique of scheduling media that involves buying time or space in one medium only and developing strength through concentration.

media convergence – Also known as convergence of distribution and *convergence news*. Newspapers, magazines, radio and TV news, and the Web – podcasts, videocasts and blogs – *cross platforming* techniques playing a role in news distribution.

media coverage – Mention in the media of a company, its products or services. Also called a *hit*.

media dominance theory – The technique of scheduling media that involves buying a large amount of space in one medium (print or radio or television), and shifting to another medium after achieving desired results.

media evaluation – The assessment of the effectiveness of media use – channels and individual vehicles.

media kit – A package of information distributed through a firm or organization's public relations office to media outlets. Kits typically include *news releases*, features, fact sheets, biographies, *backgrounders*, histories, photos, *captions*, quote sheets, *op-ed* pieces and any other information deemed important to the media. (See Chapter 5 in *The Public Relations Practitioner's Playbook* – Kendall/Hunt – 2008.)

media (advertising) kit – A package of information distributed by *media vehicle* outlets to sell its advertising space. The kit typically includes information about the *media vehicle*, advertising rates, information about the audience it can deliver, mechanical specifications for ads or commercials, closing dates, etc.

media list – A list of reporters, editors and news directors strategically chosen to reach a specific audience relevant to the firm, organization, person or story being pitched.

media mix – The combination of *media vehicles* and *channels* used to carry the advertiser's message.

media minions – Public relations and/or media relations practitioners who carry a message to the media on behalf of an organization or its leader.

media neutral planning – *Media planning*, whether advertising or public relations, approached in a totally objective and unbiased manner. Recommendations are based solely on research, analysis, insight and objective conclusions of the data.

media plan – Using extensive research, a plan designed to select various media for news release distribution, story pitches, an advertising campaign schedule and placements, etc. *Demographics* and *psychographics* are integral in selecting target audiences. The plan may be for a specific campaign or for all campaigns within a year. It may be a plan for a single product or service or for an entire firm, manufacturer or organization.

media planning – The process of developing media goals, objectives, strategies, tactics, tools, budget, etc. which help determine the selection of specific media that will effectively and efficiently reach target audiences for a specific product or service. *Media planning* requires matching the target audience to the appropriate media. Successful *media planning* requires the ability to identify, plan and act upon the best mix for the business.

media policy – A strategically written organizational directive that describes how a firm or organization's representatives will communicate with the media (newspapers, magazines, radio, television, etc.).

media pool – See *pool coverage.*

Media Rating Council (MRC) – A non-profit trade association dedicated to assuring valid, reliable and effective syndicated audience research. The MRC performs audits of Internet measurements as well as traditional media measurements. Read more at *www.mrc.htsp.com.*

media rehearsal – Preparing for an actual media event by practicing for the types of questions which might be asked by a reporter or reporters during a *news conference, news availability* or *one-on-one interview.* (See Chapter 10 in *The Public Relations Practitioner's Playbook* – Kendall/Hunt – 2008.)

158

Tips to Succeed: A 5th 'P' of marketing

Jonathan Byrnes, a senior lecturer at MIT, has joined others in expanding the original four "Ps" of marketing - product, place, price and promotion.

Dr. Byrnes' fifth "P" is *profitability*, which can be improved through:

• Control of internal knowledge

• Selectivity

• Coordination

• A shift from mass marketing to precision (more focused or niche) marketing

Jonathan Byrnes - Harvard Business School's *Working Knowledge* Newstrack Executive Information Service www.news-track.com 800-334-5771

media relations – Developing positive working relationships with editors, news directors and reporters. An objective is for the firm or organization to gain positive coverage. Reporters and their superiors now point to relationships as the number one criterion in their dealing with public relations practitioners or company spokespeople to help them do their reporting jobs. Others include knowing what news is, always telling the truth, understanding deadlines, providing the latest facts (rather than outdated information), being available – especially when bad news breaks – and always returning phone calls.

media (news) release – Information written by an organization and distributed to media outlets for publication. Also referred to as *news release* or *press release*.

media schedule – A plan listing when and how often a firm or organization will advertise or distribute *news releases*.

media script – A story line that shapes news coverage. For example, the theme of a movie that becomes of interest to a newspaper editor or broadcast news director, which then generates a news or feature story. Examples would be "Bad News Bears" and "The Rookie." Reporters are sent out to do stories on "real" people who may be involved in similar circumstances. Often used during *sweeps*.

media strategy – A plan of action by a public relations practitioner or an advertiser for sending messages to consumers through selected media.

media tour – Used in public relations. PR practitioners and media relations specialists take their strategic messages directly to such news vehicles as newspapers, radio, television station, etc. These are face-to-face. They may involve a particular pitch a product launch or may simply establish or reinforce a relationship.

media training – Providing coaching to individuals specifically targeted to dealing with the news media. Participants are taught guidelines, strategies and skills to work effectively with media for public relations purposes. (See Chapter 10 in *The Public Relations Practitioner's Playbook* – Kendall/Hunt – 2008.)

media vehicle – A specific medium for the transmission of a firm or organization's public relations (strategic) or advertising message.

medical marketing – Promotion (public relations) or advertising efforts focusing on the exclusive needs of the medical profession and/or

M

industry, healthcare, pharmaceutical and managed care companies. The target audience in medical marketing activities includes registered nurses, pharmacists, diagnostic professionals and other medical personnel who have been trained to communicate with doctors, patients and other medical providers.

medium – Plural is media. A vehicle or group of vehicles (*channel* is an umbrella term for print or radio, etc.) used to carry information, news, entertainment and advertising messages to an audience. These include such individual media as newspapers, radio, television, cable television, magazines, radio, billboards, etc.

medium is the message – Coined in the 1960s by media guru Marshall McLuhan. McLuhan argues that no medium is neutral and what is said is profoundly affected by the medium in which it is said. The saying may also be taken to imply, in a sense, that the *medium* is "more important" than the *message* (based on the power of medium, the market in which it is carried, the intermediary carrying the message, such as a major, well-respected newspaper or a powerful TV anchor, or strong video production etc.).

meet and greet – A public relations tactic where a celebrity or someone seeking public office meets with members of the public in either an official or social capacity.

megabyte – A computer term meaning one million bytes.

megachurch – A church – or other house of worship – with more than 2,000 members.

megamarketing – A term coined by U.S. marketing academic, Philip Kotler, to describe the type of marketing activity required when it is necessary to manage elements of a firm or organization's external environment (governments, the media, pressure groups, etc.) as well as the marketing variables. Kotler suggests adding two more Ps to the original four (product, place, price, promotion) to the marketing mix – public relations and power. *Litwin's 9 Ps* already include public relations. See *four Ps*.

megamergers – Combinations of large international public relations and/or agencies under a central holding company.

megatrend – A major movement, pattern or trend emerging in society. An emerging force likely to have a significant impact on the kinds of products consumers will want to buy in the foreseeable future. Examples of *megatrends* evident today include a growing interest in health, leisure, lifestyle and environmental issues.

membership group – A reference group to which an individual belongs. For example, environmentalist, pro-life advocate, anti-smoking, etc.

memorized presentations – Information about products and/or services that presenters know and can communicate naturally. It is said that they know the information as well as their own names. Sometimes called canned presentations.

mental states approach – Either the *diffusion process* (awareness, interest, trial, evaluation, adoption or rejection) or *AIDA* concept (awareness, interest, desire, action) used by public relations practitioners and other communicators as a guide to taking targeted audiences from one stage of the acceptance or buying process to the next. See *formula approach*.

merchandise allowance – A trade sales promotion where manufacturers offer payments or a quantity of free merchandise to buyers for in-store promotion of their products or for purchasing a certain quantity of their product.

merchandisers – Retail stores which sell finished, non-food items. Typically, there are four types of *merchandisers* (categorized on the basis of service, price and product line) – *specialty stores* (full-service, high-price, limited product line); *department stores*; *mass merchandisers*; and *discount stores* (limited-service, low-price, wide product line).

merchandising – Anything intended to make the product more saleable (sellable) – like promotional materials, licensed sports team merchandise or other saleable products (caps and other clothing, mugs, athletic-type bags, novelties, etc.). The list is limited only to one's imagination and good taste. *Merchandising* also applies to the use of a brand name on other merchantable (saleable) materials. For example, Coach®, Nike® Guess®, etc. all use their brand name and/or logo on items other for which they are best known.

merchandising conglomerates – A system where a producer uses more than one channel of distribution. Some producers who use multi-channel marketing systems operate their own retail stores as well as sell through other wholesalers and retailers. Also called multi-channel retailers. See *multi-channel marketing system*.

merchant – An independent marketing intermediary – an individual who runs a retail business – a shopkeeper.

merchant wholesaler – An independent marketing middleman buying and taking title to goods and reselling them to retailers or industrial users. See *full-service wholesaler; limited-service wholesaler.*

merchantable – Saleable. See *merchandising.*

merge-purge – The process of combining two or more lists into one and identifying and removing any duplicates and "dead" data. See *list services.*

merger/acquisition-merger – The formation of one company from two existing companies. An acquisition is one company acquiring control of another by purchase of a majority shareholding.

merging – The process of combining two or more lists of prospects.

message – What is being communicated – verbal, written or using *facial coding.*

message action points (MAPs) – Strategic messages, many times crafted by public relations counselors, used by CEOS and political candidates to help achieve their objectives, which will eventually help them reach their goal.

message boxes – Set up like a *matrix.* The paradigm might contain boxes for message, audience, channel, timing and spokesperson. They are filled in with relevant (strategic) information for each, which would eventually be carried into a public relations or other type of communication plan.

message discipline – staying on message. Not straying from key message or other talking points.

messages – Agreed words or statements that a client wants to convey to third parties, such as the media, consumers or shareholders.

metaphor – A figure of speech where a word or phrase that ordinarily designates one thing is used to designate another, making an implicit comparison – as in *"a sea of troubles"* or "All the world's a stage" (Shakespeare).

Metcalfe's law – The value of a network increases proportionately with the number of people who use it.

metropolitan statistical area (MSA) – An urban area with a population of at least 50,000 that is designated by the Office of Management and Budget for statistical reporting purposes and used in audience measurement studies. This is generally synonymous with the former term standard metropolitan statistical area.

mezzanine marketing – Seen in many major department stores. They carry the better brand names and some lower price brands. Their house (store/private) brands fall in between. Examples would include Kenmore® by Sears®, Berkley® and Jensen® at BJ's Wholesale Club® and Sonoma Lifestyle® or Chaps® by Kohl's®. See *private brand; sub-brand.*

mezzo (economics) – Between macro and micro economics.

micro-environment – Factors or elements in a firm's immediate environment which affect its performance and decision-making. These elements include the firm's suppliers, competitors, marketing intermediaries, customers and publics. See *macro-environment.*

micro-sites – Multi-page computer ads accessed by a click-through from the initial ad. The user typically stays on the publisher's Web site, but has access to more information from the advertiser than a standard ad format allows.

micromarketing – The study of marketing decision-making from the perspective of an individual firm or organization. Activities a firm practices to react controllably to external forces, e.g., setting objectives and selecting target markets. See *macromarketing.*

micromarkets – Markets where demand is relatively small because of the fragmentation or splintering of mass markets. Markets where there is great diversity in the needs and wants of customers. See *mass marketing.*

microsales analysis – Analysis of the sales performance of an organization during a particular accounting period by close examination of the work of individual representatives, or of specific products, regions, territories, etc, paying particular attention to areas that failed to achieve the expected results.

microscheduling (of advertising expenditure) – The allocating of the total expenditure on advertising within a short period of time to obtain maximum impact.

microsegmentation – The division of a market into smaller groups of customers on the basis of more narrowly-defined needs (*niche markets*) and wants, after having already divided or segmented it on the basis of broadly defined needs and wants. See *market segmentation.*

M

The ABCs of Strategic Communication

middle of the road (MOR) – Radio station format that plays music once considered between classical and hard rock.

middle-of-the-roaders – Firms in a market which do not pursue their own clear marketing strategy.

middleman – An independent *marketing intermediary* who sells a product to a retailer after purchasing it from a manufacturer. It could be an agent, wholesaler, retailer, distributor, etc. See *marketing channels*; *marketing intermediaries*.

middleman's brand – Brand packaged expressly for the wholesaler or distributor. For example, at one time, the Unity Frankford wholesale grocery distributor (now Shop 'n Bag®) carried most "famous" brand names, but also marketed its own brands – Unity, the higher cost brand and Frankford, the economy brand. Both sold for less than the "famous" brands but for more than generic or no-name items. See *private brand*.

Migo®-enabled device – Software that allows removable storage devices such as USB drives and iPods® essentially function as portable computers. They work like this: Plug a *Migo-enabled device* into a computer and enter your password, and a secure session launches where you can send and receive e-mail and work on documents, with the background desktop and icons from your own PC rather than the ones on the host computer. When you are finished and remove the drive, all traces of what you did are removed from that computer. The next time you plug the drive into your home computer, data on each are synchronized – similar to a Palm Pilot® or other *personal data assistant* (PDA).

milieu – An environment or setting.

millenials (millennial generation) – Born after 1991.

milline rate – Used to determine the cost effectiveness of advertising in a newspaper. It is reached by multiplying the cost per *agate line* by one million, then dividing by the circulation. Also referred to as milline.

mind share – Coined by the public relations firm Ogilvy and Mather. It is the amount of thinking an individual or group does about a particular product, service or company. Also, the employees' mental resources, capabilities and talents (intellectual property).

mini-bios – A collection of abbreviated (summaries) biographies of key individuals that highlight only the information relevant to the subject of a media kit in which they are included. Each *mini-bio* is usually a paragraph or two.

mini niche – While a *niche market* is a narrowly defined market, a *mini niche* is even more refined – for example, 18-25 year old, dark-haired, left-handed women with a shoe size smaller than a 5.

minimalism – Used to allow the audience reaction to tell a story (let crowd reaction speak for itself) – such as asking a question – always anticipating the questions so that the answer is prepared in advance – and generates interaction between the speaker and the audience.

159

Tips to Succeed: Don't blame the reporter

Never hold a reporter responsible for an editorial stand his newspaper may have taken even if you believe the reporter had input in the action. Unfortunately, a paper has the right to take any stand it wishes and usually has an editorial board that establishes the opinion.

minimalist – An individual who achieves the highest performance with the least effort. A speaker who allows the audience reaction to tell a story (let crowd reaction speak for itself) – applause, chants, types of questions asked – always anticipating answer. Also, a speaker interacting with an audience to successfully communicate the intended message.

minimum payment – The lowest amount a consumer is required to reimburse on a charge account to keep that account in good standing. If the *minimum payment* is not made, late payment penalties will be charged. If a consumer pays only the minimum due, interest continues to accrue on all outstanding balances.

minor decisions close – See *minor points close.*

minor points close – A closing technique where an agency representative or salesperson attempts to get the client or buyer to agree to the value or usefulness of various smaller attributes and features of a product so that it will be easier to get a favorable response to the bigger decision – purchasing the product or service.

minority marketing – *Niche marketing* that specifically addresses minority groups (not necessarily visible minorities – many times determined through *demographics* and *psychographics*) within a larger population.

minstrel – Slang term for NBA and Division One basketball – composed mostly of black players who provide entertainment for spectators who are mostly middle and upper income whites. Term coined by author Harvey Araton in his book *Crashing The Borders: How Basketball Won The World And Lost Its Soul At Home.*

mission – A brief statement defining "What business are we in?" It should have a broad focus and a customer orientation. See *corporate mission.*

mission statement – A company's summary of its business philosophy and direction. A succinct statement defining "This is who we are, what we think about ourselves, what we are trying to do and why we need your support." In 100 words or less, it should provide management and employees with a sense of purpose. See *corporate mission statement.*

missionary selling – Selling where a salesperson's role is to inform an individual with the power to influence others to buy a product, rather than to make a direct sale to that person. A missionary salesperson is also known as an *academic detailer.* See *detailer; sales calls.*

mixing – Combining different tasks of music, voices and *sound effects (SFX)* to create a final commercial.

mobile advertising – An advertising method or technique using trailers or cars (*auto wraps*) to serve as mobile billboards, advertising a business, products and/or services in a high-traffic location.

Mobile Internet Provider (MIP) – *Internet service provider (ISP)* dedicated to providing wireless service.

mock purchase – A tactic where a person poses as a customer, usually to obtain information about a competitor's product, service or plans.

mockumentary – Spoof on a *documentary.* A satirical look at producing a *documentary.* Producer Michael Moore has become famous for producing what have become known as *mockumentaries.*

model – A set of variables and their interrelationships designed to represent some real system or process. The *MAC triad plus P and T* is a communication model originally used by newspaper editor Walter Lippmann and modified by public relations practitioner and *The ABCs'* author M. Larry Litwin, APR, Fellow PRSA.

model bank – A variety of mathematic models used in a marketing information system to simulate real-life situations to assist in decision making.

models (or marketing models) – Graphical representations of a process designed to aid in understanding and/or forecasting. Computerized models allow the simulation of scenarios based on different assumptions about changes to the *macro-environment* and *micro-environment*. See *macro-environment*; *micro-environment*.

modem – A device that transfers digital signals to analog signals and vice versa, suitable for sending information across phone or cable lines.

160 Tips to Succeed: The basics of conducting a scientific survey

HOW-TO-DO-IT

1. Decide what *you* want to learn from the survey.

2. Ask why *you* want to learn this.

3. Ask *yourself* whether *you* could get this information without doing a survey.

4. Decide whom your public or audience is going to be.

5. Determine the type of survey method you will use.

6. Establish confidence levels for your survey.

7. Develop a timeline from start to finish for your survey.

8. Decide how the information will be analyzed and disseminated to your publics or audience (especially those surveyed).

modem speeds – The speed at which one connects to the Internet through a computer's modem. There are dial-up, *DSL* and *cable modems*. Dial-up modem speeds include 14.4, 28.8, 33.6, 56K and *ISDN (Integrated Services Digital Network)*. *Cable modem* speeds range between 500 K and 2.5 Mbps. T1 and T3 are high-speed connections that do not require a modem. See *digital subscriber line (DSL)*.

modes of transportation – The range of methods available for the shipment of goods – air, rail, road, sea, pipeline, etc.

161

Tips to Succeed: iPod® etiquette

Assuming your company allows iPods:

• Let your colleagues know you're turning it on to work.

• If anyone in your workplace approaches you, always take out the earbuds from both ears, even if your iPod is off. Anyone you have a conversation with deserves respect.

• No singing, head popping or taking your iPod to meetings.

• Be aware of your iPod's volume.

Robin Craig - Scottsdale, Ariz.

modified rebuy – A buying situation where an individual, firm or organization buys goods that have been purchased previously but changes either the supplier or some other element of the previous order. See *new task buying*; *straight rebuy*.

modular training – A training program that is studied over a period of time, delivered in modules and then linked together to complete the process.

modulation – The electrical imprint of a sound signal on a radio wave – audio levels used in radio broadcasting.

mommy track – Women who continue their professional careers – balancing work with raising a family and home life. It is a route more likely to be taken by women in high-powered careers than men, according to Gayle Porter, associate professor of management at Rutgers-Camden. As of fall 2005 19,000 women who never married earned $100,000 (in 2004); 12,000 had attained professional degrees. Some prominent women who fit the demographic are Condoleezza Rice (Secretary of State for George W. Bush), Janet Reno (Attorney General during the Clinton administration) and Harriet Miers (a failed Supreme Court Associate Justice nominee).

mompreneurs – Mothers who run their household as if it were a business. They have a plan. Some use paper organizers and some use *PDAs (personal digital assistants)*, but all of them use some sort of planner to balance their work life with their family life. They work with the family,

162 Tips to Succeed:

Be specific when giving presentations

If you're nervous about making the next big presentation, keep the following tips in mind:

- Don't wing it. Prepare an outline of what you want to say and practice it.

- Be specific and talk about the things you know best. Don't try to teach people everything you do.

- Use handouts, visuals or PowerPoint® slides to support your presentation.

- Remember you're the expert. Think about ways that help show that and are not threatening for you.

Ivan Misner - Business Networking International - Claremont, Calif.

not against them. When their children are young, they make sure their office or other adult-type rooms are kid-proof. *Mompreneurs* are noted for starting their day before their family wakes up, continuing during nap times and going on into the late hours of the night (from *www.CareerBuilder.com*).

monadic rating – A method for measuring consumer preferences where potential purchasers are asked to rate their liking for each of a certain number of products on a one to 10 scale. Product A may be rated as 9, Product B as 5, and Product C as 2. The method allows researchers to derive the individual's preference order and to know the qualitative levels of their preferences and the approximate distance between their preferences.

money-based competitors – Organizations other than yours, offering products that your potential customers might spend their money on. See *competitors*: *product-based competitors*.

money shock –In entertainment, it is a "frenzy of the visible" – using shocking visuals or shocking verbal strategic messages, considered out of the mainstream, to persuade consumers to purchase a product or support an issue. An example would be Carl's® Hamburgers using Paris Hilton who appeared in a sleek bathing suit, holding a hamburger while "getting it on with a car." Also, a surprise increase in an economy's money supply which drives the interest rate down and economic activity up, at least in the short run.

monitor – Any speaker or television-like screen used to listen to an audio source or view a video source – in a radio or TV station.

M

The ABCs of Strategic Communication

monitoring time – Part of the non-monetary price a consumer pays for a product. What it costs the consumer, other than money, to buy a product. For example, the time devoted to shopping for it and the risk taken that it will deliver the expected benefits. See *non-monetary price*; *time prices*.

monopolistic competition – A market situation where there are many sellers and many buyers of products which can be differentiated by price and other features.

monopoly – A market situation where there is only one seller.

monopsony – A market situation where there is only one buyer – or the buyer is such a "strong player" in the market that he/she controls it and drives the price down. Sometimes referred to as buyer's monopoly.

mood mapping – Research on how people react to certain scents.

Moore's law – A theory that the speed of computing (computers) doubles every 18 months.

moral compass – A person's direction is determined by his/her values, character, principles, ethics, integrity, judgment and trust.

moral pricing – A pricing method used where the product is socially or politically sensitive and costs are difficult to identify. Examples would include "sex toys" and certain types of lingerie.

morals – Rules or habits of conduct. See *ethics*.

morph – Combining two words to become one. Governor and terminator = governator (Arnold Schwarzenegger).

motivation – An inner feeling that drives a person to act.

motivation research – Research, often used by advertising and public relations practitioners to investigate the psychological reasons why individuals buy specific types of merchandise, or why they respond to specific advertising appeals, to determine the base of brand choices and product preferences.

motive – An inner state directing a person towards the satisfaction of a need. See *learning process*.

mouth marketing – Another term for *viral marketing* – paying "ordinary" people to say good things about a product or service.

moves the needle on ratings – An individual who appears on a radio or TV program or the individual him/herself who increases (or decreases) ratings. Some individuals are considered lightening rides and will attract viewers just their very presence. For example, *The Philadelphia Inquirer* columnist Stephen A. Smith, who went on to get his own television program on ESPN.

movie advertising – Designed to reach as many targeted consumers as possible at the lowest cost (not unlike other advertising types and techniques). Effective *movie advertising* goes beyond traditional media and reaches consumers in unique and creative ways - including alternative advertising (partnering with brands or tie-ins [see *movie marketing*] with products), one-on-one promotions, partnering with events, sponsorships, etc. Movie theater advertising can be handled at the venues themselves, with marketing teams promoting a variety of products to consumers as they are waiting in line or approaching the theater.

movie marketing – Creating and implementing advertising and promotional efforts designed to make a film stand out in a competitive

163 Techniques to Succeed: Recovering from a crisis

Executives believe it takes companies slightly more than three years – 3.2 years – to recover from a crisis that damages their reputation.

The top 10 crisis turnaround strategies are:

1. Quickly disclose details of the scandal/misstep (69 percent)
2. Make progress/recovery visible (59 percent)
3. Analyze what went wrong (58 percent)
4. Improve governance structure (38 percent)
5. Make leaders accessible to media (34 percent)
6. Fire employees involved in the problem (32 percent)
7. Commit to high corporate citizenship standards (23 percent)
8. Carefully review ethics policies (19 percent)
9. Hire an outside auditor (18 percent)
10. Issue an apology from the CEO (18 percent)

Burson-Marsteller - New York, N.Y.

market environment. Film marketing typically uses the same methods other products do. *Movie marketing* is often a significant part of the entire movie cost.

movie tie-ins – A promotional strategy where a motion picture may be featured along with a tangible product, which offers a discount to the movie if the product is purchased. In some cases, the product is shown (embedded or product placement) in the movie. In some cases, money does change hands. In other cases, it could be a *barter*. See *entertainment marketing; promotional partnership*.

moving average – A *forecasting* method using the average volume achieved in a number of recent sales periods to predict the volume likely to be sold in the next period.

mp3 – A computer file format used to compress and transmit audio files online.

MPEG – Pronounced M-peg. It stands for **Moving Picture Experts Group** – refers to the family of digital video compression standards and file formats used for coding audio-visual information (e.g., movies, video, music) in a digital compressed format. The major advantage of MPEG compared to other video and audio coding formats is that MPEG files are much smaller for the same quality. (From www.mpeg.org.)

MRO supplies – Abbreviation for maintenance, repair and operating supplies.

MTV generation - Individuals born in the late 1970s and early 1980s, at times identified as an overlap group of both Generation X and Generation Y.

multi-camera angle or individualized television – A technology (not yet readily available) that allows viewers to control camera angles during live events, select which commercials they want to watch, and generally control a selection of choices content producers provide as part of the broadcast. *E-commerce* and interaction with those commercials is possible. In the backend, servers collect choice information and offer viewers further selections based on those choices.

multi-channel marketing system – A system where a producer uses more than one channel of distribution. Some producers who use *multi-channel marketing systems* operate their own retail stores as well as sell through other wholesalers and retailers. Also called *merchandising conglomerates; multichannel retailers*.

Multi-channel retailers – Producers or manufacturers who use several channels to distribute their products

multi-level marketing (MLM) – Plans designed to sell goods and services through distributors. Other names for *MLM* are network and matrix marketing. The *MLM* concept is based on a promise from a company that if a person signs up to sell their products, they will pay a commission on all sales generated by that person as well as other distributors the person recruits. *MLM* plans typically guarantee commissions through two or more levels of recruits that make up a downline. There are federal laws governing *MLM* activity where individuals are paid to recruit distributors. This unfavorable and illegal activity is known as pyramiding. *MLM* laws allow companies to pay commissions only on the sales of goods and services. The *Federal Trade Commission* cautions anyone thinking of joining a *MLM* opportunity to exercise good common sense before signing up and always investigate the company, its products and services.

multibrand strategy – A manufacturer has more than one brand of product in the same category competing with each other, in a given market (Hershey's® and Reese's®; Campbell's® and V8®; Kellogg's®, General Mills®, General Motors®, Ford®, etc.). This contrasts with the strategy of *family brands* where separate items are given a common line identity and are usually each directed to one segment within the market. Under *multibrand strategy* there may not be manufacturer identification, unless required by law. The use of more than one brand within a product category limits brand switching.

multichotomous question – A closed-ended question in a research questionnaire where a respondent must choose one response from multiple alternatives. See *dichotomous question*.

multicultural marketing – Advertising and public relations combined to promote brands and other products to specific audiences based on ethnic or racial makeup. In 1947, the Pepsi-Cola® Co., as it was then known, is considered among the first mainstream companies to market to a specific cultural demographic. At the time, the purchasing power of black Americans, estimated at $10 billion, went largely ignored by mainstream marketers. Pepsi® made a conscious effort to aim its advertising's strategic messages at black Americans.

multifactor authentication – Verifying a retail customer's identity online. Many banks employ this type of authentication.

multiform corporations – Highly diversified conglomerates with many unrelated businesses. For example, Berkshire Hathaway Inc. ®, Comcast® and Cendant®.

multilevel in-depth selling – Used by many selling organizations. They concentrate on the buying center of a large and important company attempting to reach as many buyers as possible at all levels in the shortest time period.

multiminding – Process of simultaneously thinking about various things. Different from multitasking in that these are only thoughts and not acts.

multimodal transportation – A combination of rail, sea, road, air and pipeline services for the shipment of goods.

multinational corporation – An organization operating in several countries.

multiple channel system – The use of more than one *distribution channel* to sell a product. For example, catalogues or other direct mail, retail stores and use of home shopping on television.

multiple choice questions – Questions that offer three or more alternatives. Often a three-point, or five-point, rating scale.

multiple exchanges – A term used in non-profit marketing in reference to the fact that non-profit organizations must deal with donors in receiving funds and with their clients in allocating them.

multiple marketing channels – A system where a producer uses more than one channel of distribution. Some producers who use *multi-channel marketing systems* operate their own retail stores (NIKE, SONY, SAS Shoes) as well as sell through other wholesalers and retailers. Also called *merchandising conglomerates*; *multichannel retailers*.

multiple niching – A strategy adopted to reach more than one narrowly-defined audience at a time. See *market niche*; *single niching*.

multiple packaging – The practice of placing several units of a product (energy bars, bottled water, yogurt, etc) in one container when offering them for sale in order to increase total sales, to help introduce a new product or to win consumer acceptance.

multiple pricing – A pricing method where the price charged for some consumer shopping goods, specialty goods and for many industrial products is open to negotiation between buyer and seller. It is also known as *flexible pricing* and *variable pricing*.

multiple publics – A term used in non-profit marketing in reference to the fact that non-profit organizations must market themselves to their donors as well as to their clients. As with many other types of marketing, non-profits must implement different marketing approaches for each target.

multiple segmentation approach – Targeting a number of different segments in the same market and developing a separate marketing mix for each.

164 Techniques to Succeed:

Wanted: A strategic advisor (communicator) with a deep understanding of the process

Strategic advisors must have credibility throughout the professions (see cover of *this* book) and the ability to deal deftly with challenges anytime, anywhere. The strategic advisor must be politically adept, a consensus builder, be unflappable and have – at least some – business experience.

multiple sourcing – Buying supplies from several vendors so that the risk of any one source being unable to supply items is minimized.

multiple unit pricing – Offering a lower price per unit for the purchase of two or more products of similar type (tee shirts and shorts; innerwear/underwear tops and bottoms) when bought together than when units are bought individually.

multiple zone pricing – A pricing method where all customers within a number of defined markets or regions are charged the same price. A theory is that customers (retailers) more distant from the company pay a higher price than those closer to the company's dispatch point. Also called *geographic pricing*.

Multi-Purpose Internet Mail Extensions (MIME) – A method of encoding a file for delivery over the Internet.

multi-step flow – Once referred to as *two-step flow*, it is now called multi-step flow because of the influence of mass media. In multi-step flow, the message is created by the public relations or communication counselor/practitioner (step one), given to the CEO or other spokesperson, who sends it (step two) to influential intermediary audiences – such as *key communicators*, but not to the mass media – who then (step three) carry the message to the general public. In the *two-step flow theory*, message goes from spokesperson (step one) to the mass media which skips *key communicators* and delivers the message directly (step two) to the general public.

mummy dust – A slang term referring to the ingredients, parts or accessories that manufacturers sometimes add to their products to enhance them, but for which no scientific basis can be found. Federal agencies regulate the use of *mummy dust*. Also referred to as *whiffle dust*.

murderabelia – Personal items of convicted serial killers being sold online.

Murphy's law – "If it could be done wrong, in all probability it would." *Murphy's law* took root at Edwards Air Base in California in 1949. Read more at *www.murphys-laws.com/murphy/murphy-true.html*.

mutual aid agreement – A shared service that involves a contractual agreement between two or more municipalities, usually adjoined, to provide emergency services under certain circumstances. Usually based on capability or availability of municipality being served.

mystery shopper – An individual, hired by a retailer, or other business owner, to "act" as a customer with one goal in mind – improving service quality. The anonymous "resources" – as they are referred, resemble real customers in every aspect as they determine customer service efficiency, business environment (face-to-face approach, phone etiquette), product/service quality, etc. **M**

name line – Name under a head shot or thumbnail in a newspaper, magazine, newsletter or other publication.

nameplate – The printed title (i.e., name and *logo*) of a newspaper at the top of the front page. Also called a *flag*. Includes a newsletter's title, subtitle or mission statement, volume and issue, date of publication and *logo*. It covers about one-fifth of the front page. It can run at the top of the page or down the side. See *banner; flag*.

namenesia – "Disease" of forgetting names.

nanny – A woman who cares for a child (on a regular basis).

narrowcast radio – Radio stations that target niche audiences. For example, "Radio Disney."

narrowcast television – Cable television "networks" that target specific interests and niche audiences – for example, "The Cooking Network" and "The Golf Channel."

narrowcasting – The use of broadcast media to target very narrow interests. For example, a cable channel dedicated exclusively to food, golf, shopping or fishing. Programming is designed to appeal to special interest audiences. *Narrowcasting* allows advertisers great selectivity in targeting their message to certain audiences. Also used in political campaigning – "one door bell – one vote."

nat sound (natural sound) – Audio that's part of a television or radio news story but is not the sound of someone speaking directly into a microphone or to the camera (background sound).

national account marketing (NAM) – The creation of marketing teams or groups (*NAM* teams) within a company specifically to meet the needs of major client organizations. Teams or groups usually consist of marketing, public relations and sales personnel, as well as such other specialists as engineers, production specialists, etc.

national accounts — Major accounts, which are sometimes served by a separate sales force because of their importance. Using various research techniques, account specialists try to meet clients' special needs and develop close relationships with key personnel. Also referred to as *direct accounts* and *house accounts.*

national advertising – Advertising aimed at a national market, as compared to local advertising. Traditionally, *national advertising* commands higher rates in newspapers and on local radio and televisions. When national advertisers buy radio and TV locally, it is referred to as spot advertising.

National Advertising Division of the Council of Better Business Bureaus (NAD) – This organization serves as a major self-regulatory mechanism for advertising. Read more at *www.nadreview.org.*

National Advertising Review Board of the Council of Better Business Bureaus (NARB) – When an alleged problem arises with an advertisement, and a satisfactory solution is not obtained via the *NAD* (see above), the *NARB* acts in the capacity of an appeals board. It reviews the decision of the NAD, and passes judgment on it. Read more at *www.narcpartners.org.*

National Association of Broadcasters (NAB) – An association whose membership is largely composed of radio and television stations. Read more at *www.nab.org.*

national brand – A nationally distributed product *brand* name. May also be distributed regionally or locally.

national introduction – The launch of a new product on a nationwide scale. Because of the risk and the substantial investment in production and marketing that a national introduction requires, many organizations choose *rollout* approach instead. See *rollout.*

national marketing manager – A marketing manager with the responsibility for the nationwide operations of a marketing division.

national sales manager – A sales manager with responsibility for the nationwide operations of a sale division.

165 Techniques to Succeed: The right way to get a favor – networking

Effective networking is the proactive solution. If you think ahead and network well, asking for a favor can be an easy, natural thing to do. Sometimes you may find that you don't even need to ask! Here are a few easy ways to maintain your relationships so that favors come easily:

1. Get organized
   - Keep track of your contacts whichever way works best for you. You can use computer databases, PDAs or even index cards.
   - Keep track of birthdays, anniversaries and other miscellaneous information.
   - Know your contacts' needs, such as information, jobs and other contacts.

2. Keep in touch
   - Review your contact list regularly and make a follow up plan.
   - Send notes and cards on occasions such as birthdays and holidays.
   - Regularly call and set up lunch meetings or dinner appointments.

3. Nurture mutually beneficial relationships
   - Send any helpful information to your contacts.
   - Connect your contacts with others who can help them.
   - Use your skills to help others.

If you care for your network of friends, colleagues and acquaintances, it will be your best resource. Whether the favor you need is information, a job referral, technical help or even more clients, the best solution is a strong network. Most importantly, always remember to say thank you with an E-mail, a hand-written note, or a gift.

Andrea Nierenberg - The Nierenberg Group
420 E. 51st Street Suite 12D New York, NY 10022 -
www.mybusinessrelationships.com/

166

Tips to Succeed: Hiring an accountant takes research

Choosing an accountant for any size business - even a small one - would be a smart move, but it does have its challenges. These tops could help avoid mistakes:

- Determine what services you'll need (tax preparation, filing monthly local and state taxes, payroll).

- Ask with whom you will be working. Hiring a big firm doesn't necessarily mean you'll be working with the most experienced people.

- Inquire about fees. Hourly rates can range from $150 to $300 an hour for a larger firm, and between $75 and $100 an hour for a smaller one.

- Find a firm with your general philosophy and approach. They should be as aggressive as you are about tax strategies.

- Obtain recommendations and work with someone you trust.

Tony Lee - www.startupjournal.com

N

natural sound (nat sound) – The audio portion of a broadcast tape that is recorded naturally by the camera or microphone. Also called background sound or *noise*.

nautical mile – A unit of length used in sea and air navigation, based on the length of one minute of arc of a great circle, especially an international and U.S. unit equal to 1,852 meters (about 6,076 feet).

naval gazing – Stuck in one place and not being able to think outside the box.

navigation message – The message transmitted by each GPS satellite containing system time, clock correction parameters, ionospheric delay model parameters, and the satellite's ephemeris data and health. The information is used to process GPS signals to give the user time, position, and velocity. Also known as the data message.

NAVSTAR – The official U.S. Government name given to the GPS satellite system. *NAVSTAR* is an acronym for NAVigation Satellite Timing and Ranging.

near-pack premium – An item offered free or at a discount with the purchase of another product. The item is usually positioned close to but neither touches nor is attached to the purchased product. It is a type of product promotion.

nee – Born with or maiden name.

need-directed consumers – One of three broad groups of consumers (with *outer-directed consumers* and *inner-directed consumers*) identified in the Stanford Research Institute's survey of American lifestyles. *Need-directed consumers*, representing about 10 percent of consumers in the U.S., are motivated by need rather than by choice. See *outer-directed consumers*; *inner-directed consumers*.

need-gap analysis – An approach to identifying the unmet needs of consumers, where respondents are asked to describe what they believe to be the ideal brand or product and then to compare or rate various existing brands or products on those key feature. If no existing brand or product measures up to the ideal, a "gap" exists, which could be filled by a new brand or product.

need-satisfaction approach – An approach to selling based on researching information to uncover a buyer's need. It follows the public relations term *anticipate*, because it provides the seller with information that could help close a deal by knowing in advance what the buyer needs and wants.

need objection – An objection by a prospective buyer that he/she has no need for the product offered by a salesperson. See *objections*.

needle artist – One who does work with a needle – needlepoint, embroidery, etc.

needs – Something an individual requires – an inner feeling of deprivation. Manufacturers believe that as part of research and development, they will determine whether a product or service is needed before further resources are spent in manufacturing it or following through with further development of a service. See *wants*.

negative – Developed film that contains an image that has reversed shadows and light areas. Used in printing as an intermediary step between camera-ready matte and transferring images to a plate.

negative demand – Demand for products which consumers dislike and would prefer not to have to purchase. Negative demand for a particular product exists when consumers, generally, would be prepared to pay more than the price of the product to avoid having to buy it. Examples would include purchasing a fungus ointment for the skin or having to undertake a colonoscopy or some other unpleasant and painful medical treatment.

negotiated contract – A formal arrangement for the supply of goods or services at a price agreed upon between both the buyer and seller and any other parties involved.

negotiated price – A price agreed upon for the supply of goods or services by both the buyer and seller.

negotiated rate – Typically, a non-standard charge for the shipping of goods – agreed to by both the manufacturer and transport company.

negotiated selling – A selling approach where a salesperson attempts to produce a "win-win" outcome for both parties. The approach involves the assumption of a partnership between buyer and seller. Trust and a relationship are prerequisites because the salesperson acts as a counselor to assist the buyer in finding the best solution to a problem.

nesting – Embedding one enclosure inside another before inserting it into an envelope. (Derived from the ancient art of nesting dolls.)

net cost – The cost of advertising in or on a media vehicle after all discounts are deducted. For example, gross charges minus all commissions. Also, the costs associated with services rendered by an advertising agency excluding the agency commission.

net names – See *list services.*

net neutrality – An Internet service provider must treat all data equally – not speed its own and slow or block others'. "It's crucial to the free flow of information and commerce" – Jeff Gelles, *The Philadelphia Inquirer* – Jan. 16, 2006.

net TV – Relatively new technology – televisions which have the ability to dial up to the Internet (Web TV®). Often, a manufacturer has integrated the Internet into the TV or offers a special "box" which permits the viewer to connect online via broadband or telephone wires.

net unduplicated audience – The combined cumulative audience exposed to an advertisement – each consumer or individual who sees or hears an ad or commercial at last once.

net worth – Assets, including bank accounts, retirement savings, investments, pensions, real estate, vehicles, jewelry and tools, minus such liabilities as bills, credit-card debt, taxes, mortgages, loans and deferred payments.

netiquette – A term is used to describe the informal rules of conduct ("dos and don'ts") of online behavior.

network – In broadcasting, a network exists when two or more stations (*affiliates*) are able to broadcast the same program that originates from a single source. The programming may be transported by hard wire or satellite. Examples of networks include ABC, CBS, FOX, NBC and PBS. *Affiliates* are contractually bound to distribute radio or television programs for simultaneous transmission. Network also refers to two or more computer systems that are linked together.

Network Advertising Initiative (NAI) – A cooperative group of network advertisers which has developed a set of privacy principles in cooperation with the Federal Trade Commission. The *NAI* provides consumers with explanations of Internet advertising practices and how they affect both consumers and the Internet. Read more at *www.networkadvertising.org*.

network option time – Programming time the network controls on each of its *affiliate* stations. Also referred to as network time. *Affiliates* are expected to, and in many cases required to, carry network programming.

networking – Establishing an informal set of contacts among people with common social and business interests as a source of prospects, for the exchange of information, and for support. Research is clear, the most successful method for finding a job is through networking.

new account-conversion ratio – A measure used to evaluate salespeople on their success in converting prospects to customers.

New Americans – Indians, Asians and others who have moved to the United States. Term has become more popular when referring to businesses now owned and operated by *"New" Americans* – gasoline stations, news stands, convenience stores, etc.

new-brand strategy – The messages used in the development of a new brand and or new offering for a product class that has not been previously served by a firm or organization.

167

Techniques to Succeed: Meet the new boss with an open mind

Just when you feel you've got a good relationship going with the boss, she leaves. Now a new person is coming in, and you have no idea what to expect.

Will the new boss be as receptive to your ideas? Do you have to start all over, proving yourself? How will you let the new boss know of your past achievements without sounding like a braggart?

Many may look at a new boss as a curse when it actually may be a blessing. Remember, just as the new boss can't know of your past successes, he can't know of your failures. So in a way, it's like starting over with a new chance at impressing the boss with your abilities.

• One of the first lessons is not to assume anything about a new boss.

• Next, do your homework. Review your achievements, how you participated in various projects, the role you play both officially – and unofficially – on the job.

• If you're looking to get out from under work the old boss dumped on you, now will be the time to make the case that the work can be done more efficiently in another way.

Some other things to keep in mind when the new boss shows up:

• Listen and watch carefully: You should be able to get clues imme- diately as to what the boss likes and doesn't like.

• Don't gossip: It's going to be tempting to dissect with co-workers everything the new boss says and does. Don't! Give the new boss every benefit of the doubt, and don't offer an opinion that may come back to haunt you.

• Be helpful: You don't want to schmooze the new boss too much, because it looks false and may tick off co-workers.

• Ask questions: Don't assume you know how the new boss wants things done. Always ask when you're not sure, and especially don't say anything like "Well, Mary (the old boss) always liked it done this way."

• Be open to change: It's not always easy to accept change, but fighting it will only hurt you in the long run.

Anita Bruzzese - Gannett News Service

new luxury – Spending money (you might not have – credit) on items that may be better than you are used too.

new product committee – A group within a company responsible for new product policies, including the assignment of priorities to options and ideas for new products. The final decision on whether or not to manufacture and market the product is up to them.

new product department – A permanent department within a company responsible for overseeing the development of all new products.

new product development (NPD) – The creation of new products, from evaluation of proposals through to launch. The creation of new products needed for growth or to replace those in the decline stage of their life-cycle (fourth of five stages in *product life-cycle*). The stages in the new product development process are commonly listed as idea generation, screening, concept development and testing. Also taken into account are the formulation of marketing strategies, business analysis, production, market testing and commercialization.

new product duplication – When a firm or organization introduces a product known to the market but new to the company. See *innovation*; *product extension*.

new products – Products new to a firm or organization or new to a market. They could include existing products which have been improved or revised, brand extensions, additions to an existing line, repositioned products targeted to new markets, and new-to-the-world products. See *innovation*; *new product development*; *new-to-the-world products*; *product extension*.

new qualitative technologies (NQT) – New methods for separating and counting data – using computer software, media and digital hardware to analyze and visualize research results.

new task buying – An organizational (or personal) buying situation where the organization has had no previous experience with the purchase of that type of product.

new-to-business (N-2-B) – Used to describe someone new to a business or profession.

new-to-the-world products – Products designed with a combination of features different from any other product. This product serves a purpose for which no product has previously existed. See *new products*.

N

news – Information of interest to a large number of people. Information that might be new, unusual, unexpected, controversial, or of wide significance or interest to the audience of a publication or program. When dealing with the media, *news* is anything the *gatekeeper* (editor or news director) says is news.

news and photo memo – A brief summary of an upcoming news event, which could include the background and credentials of an expert willing to discuss it. Also known as a *media alert; invitation to cover; interview alert*. The format includes either "Event; Date; Time; Place; Details" or "What; When; Where; Why; Details" – or a combination of both.

news angle – The *hook*. Something an editor, news director or reporter believes is new, important, different or unusual about a specific event, situation or person.

news availability – A newsmaker being accessible to the media for an interview – possibly one-on-one – rather than through a *news conference*. Sometimes called a "stand-up news conference."

news conference – A scheduled presentation to a group of media representatives. Most times, a *news conference* is a prearranged gathering of media representatives to answer questions, announce and/or explain a significant and newsworthy subject or event. *News conferences* are considered special events by public relations practitioners.

news feed – Electronically transmitted broadcast information – sound bites, voice cuts, actuality, *b-roll* (background footage), etc.

news hole – Space reserved for material other than advertising. Also the amount of space left for news after advertisements have been arranged on the page.

news judgment – Determining whether an event would be of interest to a large number of people (see *news*), covering it and then reporting it in an open, honest, thorough and valid (relevant) manner – objectively and ethically. Determining reader, viewer or listening interest is a major component of decision making. Some stories are "no brainers." Others may take a strong pitch from a public relations practitioner.

news management – Normally used to describe the way individuals (public relations practitioners) or organizations attempt to control the flow of news to the media and attempt to **set the agenda** for the media. This might involve issuing a *news release* (usually embargoed to be released by all outlets simultaneously), holding *news conferences* timed to make a particular news program (noon show or evening show) or staging an event (special event) which is big enough or unusual enough to grab the media's attention.

news peg – A particular angle of a story that ties in with current events or something newsworthy. The better the *news peg* or *hook*, the better the chance of getting it in print or on radio or television.

168 Techniques to Succeed: Organize better for networking

Organize your contacts to make the most of your efforts. Author Andrea Nierenberg, a nonstop networker, divides her list into three different categories: A, B and C, and follows up accordingly.

Here's how you can make it work for you.

The "C" list consists of "touch base" people – acquaintances whom you want in your network. However, you're not involved with them on a business or personal level. Keep in touch by sending:

• A quarterly newsletter with a short personal note.

• A card or note once or twice a year.

• A holiday card in December.

The "B" list consists of "associates" – people you're actively involved with, either professionally or personally and you would keep in touch by:

• Meeting them for a meal, tea, or coffee at least two times a year.

• Sending at least six personal notes in a year.

• Giving them holiday and premium gifts.

The "A" list is for "close friends and associates" – people you keep in touch with often.

If you effectively follow up with everyone on your list, from your closest friends to the person you see only on rare occasions, your network will continue to thrive.

Andrea Nierenberg - Author - *Nonstop Networking* (Capital Books)
www.mybusinessrelationships.com

news planner – The staff member who chooses which stories are covered by a TV station and sends it to assignment editor who chooses reporter and crew.

news release – *News* information written by an organization and distributed to media outlets, with the hope that they will use it as the basis

169 Techniques to Succeed: Networking at non-networking events

Nonstop networkers find places and times to network outside of scheduled meetings and business events. Whether in an elevator, at a sporting event, or waiting in line, networkers are always looking for ways to connect with others. This kind of networking is a great way to meet contacts that could become good friends or associates.

However, networking inappropriately can be destructive to possible relationships. It is important to be considerate both of the person you are talking to and to those around you. Here are a few ways to avoid embarrassment for yourself and your potential contact.

• Recognize where you are and what you are there for.

• Be prepared to graciously suggest that you talk about business at a more appropriate time and place. You could say, "Perhaps this is not a good time to discuss business, so may I give you a call on (date) and we could discuss this further, (consider some options), (I could help you out)?"

• Ask permission before exchanging business cards, and do so discreetly

• Remember that some establishments, such as private clubs, simply do not allow the conducting of business. Be aware of this and follow the prescribed behavior.

Successful networkers care about the person they are speaking with as well as those around them. Showing respect is one of the best ways to make and keep contacts. Network whenever and wherever you can, just do so with discretion, so that you will avoid embarrassment and build a strong, reliable network.

Andrea Nierenberg - author of *Nonstop Networking* (Capital Books)
www.mybusinessrelationships.com

170

Tips to Succeed: Talk and drive? How to survive

The Harvard Center for Risk Analysis estimates that the use of cell phones while driving causes about 2,600 deaths and 330,000 injuries each year in the United States.

The safest approach is to never use the phone in a car, except in an emergency. But if you absolutely must talk and drive at the same time, here are some tips to improve the chances that you and your car will make it home in one piece.

• Preprogram frequently dialed numbers. Speed dialing and voice-activated dialing help to keep you from taking your eyes off the road.

• Memorize your keypad. If you insist on dialing while you drive, learn how to operate your phone without looking at it.

• Use a hands-free device. Studies show that hands-free users react to trouble no quicker than do drivers with hand-held phones. But when you are forced to respond to trouble, two hands are definitely better than one.

• Avoid long, emotional or complex calls. They make you even more distracted.

• Use voice mail. More than 40 percent of cell phone-related accidents occur when drivers take an incoming call.

• Secure your phone. Loose phones can become projectiles in a crash.

• Be a wireless Samaritan. Cell phones are ideal for promptly reporting crimes, emergencies or drunken drivers.

AAA, the University of Delaware and the Cellular
Telecommunications & Internet Association - www.udel.edu/

of a written *news* story. The term is essentially synonymous with *press release*. It is the most common written form used in public relations, announcing a client's news and information.

news reporter – Truth teller who paints reality as it is. (Defined by James Smart, Pulitzer Prize-winning author, on "Imus in the Morning" – Feb. 16, 2005.)

news services – News-gathering agencies such as Associated Press, or United Press International, that distribute news to subscribing newspapers.

news values – The criteria which journalists and editors use to determine whether or not an event is newsworthy.

newser – A news conference.

newsgroup – An electronic bulletin board devoted to information about a specific topic and open to anyone who wants to participate. Some permit advertising but most do not.

newsletter – A publication used to communicate correct information to a specific audience. It can be in various sizes (commonly the finished product is 8 1/2x11), has a centerfold and is usually more than one typed page. One-page newsletters and Web newsletters (*e-zines*) have become marketing tools. See *e-zines*.

Newsome's Principles of Persuasion – F-I-C-A – Researcher Earl Newsome is credited with: Familiarity – audience, message, surrogates; Identification – rewards/benefits; Clarity – avoid jargon/passive verbs; Action – ask for behavior (what you want) – try! buy! sell! (relate). See *F-I-C-A*.

newsprint – A soft, course wood pulp paper used in printing newspapers.

newswire – An electronic service providing news stories or other up-to-the-minute information. Most newswires are provided by such commercial organizations as Associated Press®, Reuters®, Business Wire® or PR Newswire®.

niche – A narrowly defined market.

niche agency – An agency that specializes in just one product or one service. Also called a *boutique agency* or *pigeonhole agency*.

niche channel – A narrowly focused cable channel (network). For example, the "Food Channel®" and "Golf Channel®" devote nearly all programming to one topic.

niche marketing – Communicating a strategic message to a narrowly defined market for the purpose of changing behavior and ultimately gaining support for an issue or sale of a product or service. The marketing of a product to a small and well-defined segment of the market place. See *concentrated marketing*.

171

Techniques to Succeed:
20 Ways to Rate Your Web site©

1. Is your content segmented for specific audiences?
2. Does the site encourage interaction between end-users and your company?
3. Does the Web site meet your visitors' expectations?
4. Is the site content-focused, rather than design or technology-focused?
5. Is the site easy to maintain?
6. Is the site search engine friendly?
7. Is your content timely, relevant, concise, consistent and honest?
8. Does your content reinforce your company's mission and business objectives?
9. Is the navigation intuitive?
10. Does your site contain dead links or dated content?
11. Does your site contain a site map and search capability?
12. Does the site reflect your organization's brand standards?
13. Is your site visually appealing?
14. Is the typography, spacing, headline treatment, graphics and copy consistent?
15. Do employees, customers, prospects, media and others view your site as a valued source of company news?
16. Is the site consistent with your offline PR, marketing and sales materials?
17. Is the URL short and easy to remember?
18. Does the site employ gratuitous use of Flash?
19. Is your site user-focused rather than company-centric?
20. Is contact information easy to find?

Bonus: Is the site jargon-laden and acronym heavy?

Rick Alcantara - Tara Communications LLC,
Strategic Public Relations, Marketing and Internet - www.tarapr.com

nichemanship – A term used to refer to the art of skillful selection of market segments in which a firm can compete effectively.

Nielsen (A.C.) rating – A measurement of the percentage of U.S. television households tuned to a network program for a minute of its telecast. Read more at *www.nielsenmedia.com.*

nighttime silhouettes – A logo projector that displays ads on the side of a building.

NILKIE – No Income, Lots of Kids – A demographic group.

nixies – Pieces of mail returned as "undeliverable as addressed."

no-name brand – See *generic brand.*

no-need objection – An objection raised by a prospective buyer on the ground that the product offered by a salesperson is not needed.

noise – Any influence external to the sender or receiver, which distorts the message in the communication process from *encoder* to *decoder.* Confusion caused by too many messages trying to be delivered at one time. If production is overwhelmed by noise or production, it is referred to as vampire creativity. See *communication process.*

non-business marketing – See *non-profit marketing* below.

non-commercial advertising – Radio and television advertising that is designed to educate and promote ideas or institutions. The use of the words "free advertising" is an oxymoron. However, it is generally accepted that public service announcements are free advertising.

non-cumulative quantity discount – A one-time reduction in list price for a quantity purchased. See *cumulative quantity discount.*

non-durable goods – See *consumer non-durables.*

non-family households – Households where singles and non-related individuals live together.

non-guested confrontation – When a talk show caller with an opposing point of view gets through and an argument ensues.

non-manipulative selling techniques – Selling techniques where a salesperson, rather than trying to force an unwanted product on a customer by high-pressure means, works with the customer to identify a genuine need and to provide a satisfying solution. See *manipulative selling techniques.*

non-monetary price – Consumer costs, other than money, to buy a product. Non-monetary costs of a product or service include the time devoted to shopping for it and the risk taken that it will deliver the expected benefits.

non-packaged goods – These are a sub-category of *consumer non-durables*. Candy products by the pound are an example of *non-packaged goods*. See *consumer non-durables*; *packaged goods*.

non-price competition – Competition where something other than price (location, convenience, taste, style, prestige, etc.) is the major element of differentiating the product of one company from that of another or rival. See *competitors*; *price competition*.

non-probability sample – Used in polling (survey public opinion). Does not involve random selection. A sample in which the chance of an individual within the total population being chosen is not known. The selection of a sampling unit is by arbitrary methods, such as convenience and judgment. It is a non-scientific sample. The results do not necessarily reflect those of the entire universe.

non-profit marketing – Marketing activity undertaken by a firm whose primary objective is one other than profit. Examples would be the United Way, Catholic Charities or the Jewish Federation. Sometimes called *non-business marketing*.

non-profit organizations – Organizations that buy and distribute goods and services for reasons other than the return of profit to their owners. (Examples would include Goodwill Industries and other similar thrift shops run by certain charities.)

non-registered user – Someone who visits a Web site and elects not to, or is not required to, provide certain information. By not providing the information, they may be denied access to advance through the site.

non-selling activities – Tasks other than selling activities which form part of a salesperson's duties and responsibilities – paperwork, reports and sales meetings, etc.

non-store retailing – The merchandising of goods by means other than retail shops or stores. It could be merchandising by mail order, vending machines, telephone, door-to-door, etc.

non-traditional delivery – Delivery of magazines to readers through such methods as door hangers or inserted in newspapers.

non-verbal communication – The transmission of a message from sender to receiver without using words – possibly using *body language*. See *body language*; *kinesics communication*; *proxemic communication*; *tactile communication*.

normative influence – The influence exerted on an individual by a reference group (group of individuals who support a particular issue) to conform to its norms or join in supporting their opinion and behavior.

norms – The rules of behavior that are part of the ideas or philosophy of a group. *Norms* tend to reflect the values of the group which specifies those it agrees with and those it doesn't.

not for attribution – Information a newsmaker (source) gives to a reporter with the stipulation that it not be attributed to the newsmaker. (Chapter 9 – *The Public Relations Practitioner's Playbook* – Kendall/Hunt – 2008). See *background*; *off the record*.

note advertising – Advertising technique using Post-It® type notes for page one advertising in newspaper. Also called *front page notes* and *poppers*.

novelty (type) – A type of font that does not fit into the categories of serif, sans serif or *script* (cursive). Should be used only when it matches the tone of the publication.

Nth number of systematic sampling – A method of drawing a sample by dividing the sample size into the universe to obtain an interval to be used to select respondents. For example, if the universe were 1,000 and the sample size were 100 the interval would be 10. Consequently, every nth name from a directory could be the 9th, 19th, 29th, etc. A random method must be employed to select the starting point in the universe from which each nth name is to be drawn.

nuclear option - Congressional term meaning eliminating the Senate filibuster.

number pad – A grouping of numbers that look like a calculator on the right side of a computer keyboard. The *number pad* differs from the keyboard numbers, which are found above the letters on the keyboard.

nut graph – The explanation paragraph that generally follows the lead *graph*. It explains the significance of the story and gives its news "peg." Some public relations practitioners also refer to *boilerplates* as *nut graphs*.

nutritional labeling – The requirement, either by law or under voluntary industry codes, that certain products be marked with the nutritional value of their ingredients. Labeling is regulated by the Food and Drug administration. See *label*. **N**

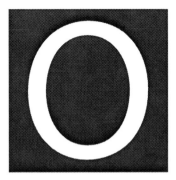

O & O station – Radio and television stations owned and operated by a network.

O dark hundred – Time check for those who work well into the night, overnight or early morning. In military time, reference might be 0-300 for 3 a.m. In public relations time, it would be *O dark hundred*.

obit or obituary – A biography of a dead person. Sometimes "canned obits" are kept on file in the newspaper's library to be used at the time of a prominent person's death.

offset press – A printing press in which the inked image is transferred from a plate to a rubber roller, which in turn puts the ink onto the paper.

objections – Any form of sales resistance offered by a buyer to a sales-person.

objective and task method of budgeting – A budgeting method where the amount to be spent on public relations, advertising, sales promotion, personal selling, etc. is determined by the desired result of the activity and the nature of the tasks needed to achieve it.

objectives – Single goals broken into subsets. Specific milestones that measure progress toward the achievement of a goal. *Objectives* must: address the desired result in terms of behavioral change; designate the target public(s); specify the expected level of accomplishment; identify the time frame in which the accomplishments are to occur; explain the desired or needed result to be achieved by a specific time. An *objective* is broader than a *goal*, and one objective can be broken into a number of specific *goals* – but all criteria must be addressed.

observation – A method of data collection in which the subject(s) of interest is/are watched and the relevant facts, actions and behaviors are recorded.

observation method – A method of obtaining marketing research data by watching human behavior. Mechanical monitoring devices are now being used to assist with the visual and tactile methods.

octothorp – The real word for the # (pound) sign.

odd pricing – Pricing so that all prices end in an odd number, as in $5.95, $19.99; sometimes referred to as *odd-even pricing*. See *psychological pricing*.

odd-even pricing – See *odd pricing*.

off-card – Refers to advertising time sold at a rate that does not appear on the rate card.

off-invoice allowance – A reduction in price allowed to a retailer in return for purchasing specific quantities of goods within a specified time. Its purpose is to sell slow-moving merchandise, to counter competitive programs or to introduce new products or line extensions. Also referred to as a *purchase allowance*.

172

Tips to Succeed: Practice organizational learning

Organizational learning requires:

• A clear understanding of recurring problems

• The willingness to allocate resources to address the root cause of those problems

• Cultural values that foster learning – which means encouraging workers to find, fix and report mistakes rather than heroically patching over recurring failures

Jeffrey Pfeffer - Professor of Organizational Behavior-Stanford University Graduate School of Business - Business 2.0, January/February 2005
Newstrack Executive Information Service
www.news-track.com - 800-334-5771

off-premise buying – Buying done by wholesalers and retailers through buying offices located overseas or in distant locations.

off-price retailer – A retail store specializing in buying leading brand items in bulk for resale at discount prices.

off-site measurement – When a Web site sends its log files to an off-site Web research service for analysis, which counts hits, impressions, time on various pages, etc.

173

Tips to Succeed:
On and off the record

When talking with reporters you are always on the record – even during informal or chance meetings. Avoid casual comments or "off the record" remarks unless you specify first that what you are about to say is not for publication or air. And be sure the reporter will accept "off the record" information before volunteering it. **Background** information is just that – for *background only* – not to be used and not to be attributed until such a time (if ever) that the *newsmaker* gives the go ahead.

M. Larry Litwin, APR, Fellow PRSA
The Public Relations Practitioner's Playbook - Kendall/Hunt - 2008

off the record – Information a newsmaker gives to a reporter, but may not to be used (Chapter 9 – *The Public Relations Practitioner's Playbook* – Kendall/Hunt – 2008). When talking with reporters you are always on the record – even during informal or chance meetings. Avoid casual comments or "off the record" remarks unless you specify first that what you are about to say is not for publication or air. And be sure the reporter will accept "off the record" information before volunteering it. See *background; not for attribution*.

offensive marketing – A competitive marketing strategy designed with one goal in mind – to win market share away from other competitors in the market.

offer – The proposal to accept.

official statement – A written comment prepared for the purpose of responding consistently to any question from the media regarding a particular controversial issue. Many times, *official statements* contain message action points or key action points, which are simple, relevant and repeated often.

offset lithography – A planographic printing process. A photographic image from a printing plate is transferred to a rubber blanket, which, in turn, transfers or prints the image onto the paper. Result looks much like the finished product of a home laser printer.

offset printing – Using a metal or paper plate, ink is first transferred to an offset drum and then passed to the paper.

offsetting – when (wet) ink during the printing process transfers from a previously printed sheet to the next one as they come off the press or out of the printer.

OINK (one income, no kids) – a demographic group.

oligopolistic competition – A competitive situation, where there are only a few sellers of products that can be differentiated but not to any great extent. Each seller has a high percentage of the market and cannot afford to ignore the actions of the others. See *monopolistic competition*; *pure competition*; *pure monopoly*.

oligopoly – A market situation where there are only a few sellers – with one firm's marketing strategies usually having a direct effect on the others.

oligopsony – A market situation where there are only a few buyers.

omnibus survey – Also called a *piggyback survey*. A type of public relations or marketing research survey usually administered for one main organization, but may contain a question or questions from other firms or organizations for a fee. Some information, such as *demographics* and *psychographics*, may be shared. Organizations buy into other surveys either to save money or because they do not need a survey on their own. *Omnibus surveys*, like other polling, is commonly organized by a major professional marketing research company, where different cross sections of the community are interviewed by *probability* (scientific) *sampling* at regular intervals about attitudes and opinions toward issues, buying habits, product and brand preferences, etc. They are called *omnibus surveys* because any marketer can join in for a fee to add questions.

on-air tests – A research method that tests recall among viewers of a commercial or program during a real broadcast of the tested communication.

on-pack (on-pace premium) – Discount *coupons* or gifts that are attached or banded to, or accompany, the product to be purchased – used to promote sales of a product. See *premiums*; *in-pack premium*; *near-pack premium*; *with-pack premium*.

on-site measurement – A computer term meaning when a server has an appropriate software program to measure and analyze traffic on its own site.

on the bubble – A competitive term meaning, one more loss and you or your team is eliminated – a win and you advance.

174

Techniques to Succeed:
Getting *you* out there!

How often do you tell your clients and your prospects what's going on in your company or organization? Probably not enough. Try a basic communication technique (not just "fancy" newsletters):

• Write a letter

• Write one every few months

• Don't make it a pitch piece
 – Be honest
 – Be straight forward
 – Be conversational
   • Something like: "It's been a while since I told you about what's happening here. We've been growing nicely. I just want to share some of those successes with you."

 – Tell them what you've been up to
   • Without breaking any confidences, talk about the successful work you've done for your clients and customers.

   • Offer a little behind-the-scenes strategy and talk about results - the bottom lines – relationships and finances.

Be certain not to overstate the message. The truth works. And the truth will get *you* and your *client* and/or *firm* out there.

Maury Z. Levy - Levy Warren Marketing and Media
Jenkintown PA - www.levywarren.com

on-the-job training – Sales training given in the field rather than in a formal classroom setting. See *curbside sales training*; *formal training*.

on the line – Used in political campaigning when candidates greet crowds of people. Many times, the campaign plants "someone" on the line to gain favorable shots for television and still photographers.

on the wires – News, now transmitted via the *Internet*, was once transmitted by Associated Press, Reuters and United Press International (UPI) using teletype (teleprinter) machines (resembling typewriters). See *wire*; *wire services*.

one level channel – A marketing channel where there is only one intermediary (for example, a retailer) between manufacturer and end-user or consumer. See *multiple marketing channels*.

one man band – TV reporter who carries his/her own camera, tapes him/herself and the interviews, self edits, and many times sends those completed "packages" back to station's control room either by microwave or fiber optics. See *package*.

one-price policy – A policy of offering the same price to every customer. See *differential pricing*.

one sheet – Also called a *one up*. A summary used for public relations planning, advertising sales, promotion, executive briefing. The summary is no longer than one page.

175 Tips to Succeed: Encourage thinking outside of the box

Creativity and innovation are essential to healthy businesses, corporations, and their business and public relations plans. Encourage creativity in the workplace, by:

• Setting aside chunks of time to concentrate on creative projects

• Brainstorming (getting the most out of mind share)

• Envisioning multiple futures.

• Looking in other worlds and outside of your organization.

• Restructuring your problem or challenge.

• Making new associations.

Jo Anne White - Therapist and Temple University Professor
www.drjoannewhite.com

one-three-six workshops – A communication technique or approach to give employees a chance to be heard. It is used to gather feedback from employees (anonymously). All employees meet in a large group. Each employee is asked to list anonymously all his or her likes and concerns about the employer. Each employee then joins two other employees, and the three combine their lists. Those three, in turn, join another group of three employees, and they, too, combine their lists. Without using names, the coordinator of the session lists on a flipchart, overhead projector or smartboard all the likes and concerns. Employees then vote to identify the top 10 likes or concerns. The employees can be grouped to develop strategies for maintaining the strengths and eliminating the concerns.

one-to-one marketing – Promotional activities aimed directly at the consumer. *One-to-one marketing* includes *door-to-door selling*, shop-at-home parties, *telemarketing*, product sampling, etc. It offers consumers the advantage of convenient and personal attention – establishing relationships based on trust, reliability and loyalty that can extend far into the future.

one-way freeways – During times of such crises are hurricanes, major roads are converted to one-way to get traffic out of endangered areas. Such cities as Saint Louis go to *one-way freeways* following major sports or other entertainment events. It helps unclog downtown areas of traffic.

onesies – Products or items that are custom made, e.g. dolls or toys with a child's name on it or an outfit specially designed and fitted for an individual such as an exquisite evening gown – one of a kind that doesn't have to be expensive just because it is unique.

online focus groups – A cost-effective alternative to

176

Tips to Succeed: Take stock when traveling

If you're preparing to travel here are thoughts on how to avoid lost luggage stress.

• Remember to keep valuables, such as prescriptions, electronics or jewelry, on you or in a carry-on bag.

• Have with you, in a carry-on, whatever you might need to get through a 24-hour period if your bags are lost.

• Make a list of what you pack so if your luggage is lost you can file a claim more effectively. Include a good description of the items.

• Wear clothing suitable for your trip.

• If traveling on business, dress appropriately in case the rest of your items are lost.

• Check to be certain that you have an ID tag on the outside and also put identification inside your bag.

• If you check luggage, confirm that the three-letter destination tags attached to your bags are actually for your location.

Diana Dratch - www.bankrate.com

The ABCs of Strategic Communication

O

face-to-face *focus groups*. Paid online focus groups offer participants the opportunity to meet at a designated time in an online chat room. The controlled environment of *online focus groups* enables the participants to view text, graphics, video and other forms of multimedia for testing and evaluation. They may also engage in question and answer sessions, providing their input to various product/service concepts. Online focus groups are directed by moderators who are skilled in motivating participants by presenting them with a list of questions geared to achieve maximum results. *Online focus groups* are often more cost-effective than in-person focus groups and many times generate more immediate reports. Research shows that participants in paid *online focus groups* tend to speak more freely because of the uninhibited environment.

online handle – E-mail name used so that it cannot be traced back to the "sender."

online learning – Course material accessed via the internet or a company Intranet. Many colleges and universities now offer for-credit courses online – *distance learning* – via teleconferencing.

online media – Media outlets accessible on the Internet, including online newsletters, online newspapers and Web sites. Though newspapers, magazines, and radio and television stations frequently offer online versions of their news coverage on the World Wide Web, content on these sites may differ from the original media source.

Online Privacy Alliance (OPA) – A group of corporations and associations who have come together to introduce and promote business-wide actions that create an environment of trust and foster the protection of individuals' privacy online. Read more at *www.privacyalliance.org*.

online producer – Producer in charge of Web content for TV news show or all-news radio station

177 Tips to Succeed:
A personal *Code of Ethics*

Every strategic message must be *Open, Honest, Thorough, Valid* (relevant).

M. Larry Litwin, APR, Fellow PRSA
The Public Relations Practitioner's Playbook (Kendall/Hunt – 2008)

178

Tips to Succeed: Making the best impression on your audience

1. **Always be prepared** – Audiences quickly detect lack of preparation.

2. **Make others comfortable** – If you are comfortable, your audience will be, too. Comfort, on your part as the sender, exudes confidence.

3. **Be committed** – Commitment is crucial. Audiences can detect lack of commitment or sincerity.

4. **Be interesting** – An interested audience is more apt to receive your message as it was intended to be received.

Roger Ailes and John Kraushar - Authors - *You Are The Message*

Online Publishers' Association (OPA) – Trade association representing a segment of online publishers. Read more at *www.publishers.org.*

OPAL (older people with active lifestyles) – A demographic group.

op-ed – Opinion and column page usually opposite the editorial page that features by-lined articles (commentaries) expressing personal or organizational viewpoints, or which take exception to a media outlet's editorial stand.

open bid – A system, commonly used by local, state and federal government, calling for (sealed) bids from selected suppliers.

open dating – An aspect of labeling where certain products are required, either by law or under voluntary industry codes, to be marked with a "use by" date to indicate their expected shelf life (regulated by the Food and Drug Administration.) Also called *date stamping.*

open end – Time left at the end of a commercial or program for the use as a local tagline (local advertiser) or station tagline. Also, a radio or television program with no specific time to end.

open-ended question – A question on a survey that allows the respondent the opportunity to express an opinion in his or her own words rather than choosing from among the best of multiple answers. See *closed-end question.*

open pricing – A method of media pricing where prices are negotiated on a contract-by-contract basis for each unit of media space (print) or time (broadcast).

open promotion – A sales promotion which is advertised widely and available to anyone who wishes to enter. See *closed promotion*.

Open Public Meetings Act (Sunshine Law) – In most states, it establishes the right of all citizens to have adequate advance notice of all public meetings and the right to attend meetings at which any business affecting the public is discussed or acted upon.

Open Public Records Act (OPRA) – Many states, such as New Jersey, have enacted legislation adopting the following philosophy: government records, with certain exceptions, should be readily accessible to the public for inspection, examination and copying. While limitations on the public's right of access should be decided in the public's favor, a public agency is required to keep a citizen's personal information from public access when that access would violate the citizen's reasonable expectation of privacy.

open system – Any firm, company, organization or government body affected by external forces (weather conditions, road construction, economy, environment, etc.).

open-to-buy – The amount of money a reseller has available to spend on purchasing (inventory) for a given period of time.

operating expenses – All the costs incurred by a firm in carrying out its day-to-day activities.

operating statement – A statement of the financial results of a company's operations during an accounting period.

opinion – Expression of an *attitude* (inner feeling) – the behavioral act or action that is carried out. For example, feeling positive about a political candidate is the *attitude* – voting for the candidate is the *opinion*.

opinion leader – An individual who actively provides opinions about products to others or from whom views, opinions and advice is sought. Also called *connector* and consumption pioneer. See *key communicator*.

opportunity analysis – See *marketing opportunity analysis*.

opportunity cost – The value of the benefit forfeited by choosing one alternative over another. It could be the increased cost of purchasing one product over another because of the convenience of its availability, or the purchase of advertising in one media outlet over another, because of the relationship established with the account executive.

opportunity matrix – A diagnostic marketing tool (used in some forms of research) providing a systematic means (paradigm) of appraising environmental attributes to alert managers to the benefits associated

179 Tips to Succeed: Take the time for workspace spring cleaning

Everyone thinks their stuff is important and other people's stuff is just clutter.

There are a few rules to take into consideration when doing an office overhaul. A checklist can serve as a handy guide for "cleaning up."

• Is this a duplicate? Does the information exist somewhere else?

• What is the worst that can happen if it is thrown away?

• Is it a legal document that needs to be retained? If it is, is there a better place for its safekeeping?

• Do I need to take some kind of action on this information?

• Is it out of date?

• Do I know exactly how the information can be used?

• Am I sure the person I plan to refer this to really wants it?

• Where will I keep this information? Do I have a place labeled for it, or does a new file need to be created? Does one already exist that would suffice?

• To retain it, are the supplies available? Would it be best suited for hanging files, manila envelopes or the "immediate action" box?

• Being careful: It's easy to get caught up in the cleaning frenzy and overdo it. Workers should be cautioned to avoid heavy loads, and lift with their knees, not their backs.

• Organizing the piles: Boxes should be labeled with "to be filed" or "discuss with …" or "move to …"

Anita Bruzzese - Author - *Take This Job and Thrive* (Impact Publications)

180

Tips to Succeed: Reaching the desired outcome

EDUCATION - Providing knowledge or training to employees or other targeted audiences.

KNOWLEDGE -What employees know about the organization or company for whom they work.

ATTITUDE - Beliefs, a state of mind or inner feelings acquired through education and observation.

BEHAVIOR - What employees say about their employer and how employees act. (Expression of attitude.)

OUTPUT - Is affected by *education, knowledge* and *behavior.*

OUTCOME - Determined by *output.* The firm or organization that achieves its desired *outcome* has been successful in educating and bringing about the desired behavioral changes.

Education > Knowledge > Attitude > Behavioral Change > Output=Desired Outcome

(When output = desired outcome, *synergy* has been achieved.)

Ed Ziegler - Director of Marketing
Rowan University

with changing environmental conditions and to impending dangers. See *SWOT analysis.*

opportunity to see (OTS) – This is a computer term which is the same as *page display* – when a page is successfully displayed on the user's computer screen.

opportunity zone – Sections of cities set aside for development and offered to prospective developers with huge tax breaks. In Philadelphia, for example, a major corporation leased space in a proposed 57-story office tower that exempted its tenants from most city and state taxes (*Philadelphia Inquirer,* Jan. 5, 2005).

opt-in – Refers to an individual giving a company permission to use data collected from or about the individual for a particular reason, in public relations, advertising or in other aspects of its marketing. Also an ad campaign targeted to individuals who have requested to receive offers and information on specific products or services. See *permission marketing.*

opt-in e-mail – Lists of Internet users who have voluntarily signed up to receive commercial e-mail about topics of interest. *Opt-in e-mail* *marketing* campaigns send bulk or blast e-mail messages, but only to lists of people who ask to join the list. (Some mailings that do not use *opt-in e-mail* are categorized as "spam"—the mass mailing of unsolicited e-mail. If spam becomes illegal, *opt-in e-mail* would be the only legal form of bulk e-mail marketing.)

opt-out – When a company states it plans to market its products and services to an individual unless the individual asks to be removed from the company's mailing list.

optical center – A point slightly above the mathematical center of a page.

181 Techniques to Succeed: Big 12 Dining Etiquette Rules

1. Always wear your nametag on your right.
2. Allow the Host to point out where the guests should sit.
3. Follow the Host's lead. Once the Host begins to eat – you eat.
4. Once seated, immediately place the napkin in your lap.
5. Utensils: eat from the outside in – NEVER pick up dropped silverware.
6. Your bread is to the right, water is to the left.
7. Elbows should never rest on the table while eating.
8. Use the silverware to signal you're finished (the 4:00-10:00 position on a clock).
9. Take out food the same way it went in. (If you put a piece of food in your mouth with your fork and the food is unpleasant (tough or not tasty), you should remove the piece of food with your fork. Don't spit the food into a napkin or use your fingers to remove it.)
10. If you have to pick or clean your teeth – excuse yourself from the table.
11. Never order alcohol – even if the Host does.
12. Whoever invited the guest will be paying unless discussed.

Elon University - Public Relations Student Society of America - Professor Jessica Gisclair, Esq. - Advisor

opticals – Visual effects used to attract a lasting interest as well as portray mood and continuity to a commercial. Could be used to assure locking power (recall). They include dissolves, gross fades, fast moving cuts and montages.

optimal reorder frequency – See *economic order quantity*; *just-in-time inventory system.*

optimizing – An approach to planning where a firm or organization expresses its intention to do things to their fullest in the future.

orchestrating – To arrange or control the elements. To achieve a desired overall effect, goal or synergy. For example, used by some events planners – planting people or groups in an audience to create what appears to be a spontaneous reaction to portions of a speech or an action. See *boiler room.*

order cycle time – The time between placement of the order by the customer and the receipt of the merchandise.

order filling costs – Costs associated with filling orders – warehousing, transportation or shipping, order processing, billing and collection of payments.

order generation costs – Costs associated with obtaining orders – advertising, personal selling and sales promotion.

order getter – A salesperson responsible for actively persuading customers to buy rather than simply collecting orders that the customers wish to place. See *order taker.*

order processing – All activities related to filling a customer's order – pricing, credit checking, establishing terms, checking the order, maintaining inventory, producing an invoice, picking the goods from the warehouse or shelves, packing and shipping them, and collecting payment.

order taker – A salesperson who writes up orders but is not involved in persuading customers to buy. See *order getter.*

organic growth/development – A company's expansion by the growth of its activities and reinvesting profits to assure company stability and growth, rather than grow by mergers/acquisitions. Companies that grow from within by opening new stores and offices rater than acquiring other companies. Examples would include McDonald's® and Home Depot®. Examples of two companies that to the merger/acquisition route are Rite Aid® and Walgreens®., Rite Aid® bought 1,854 Brooks®

182

Techniques to Succeed:
It's all about preparation

Here's how you can use the time before your next sales call to maximize your chances of advancing the sale by preparing thoroughly:

Learn about your prospect: Visiting your prospect's Web site is a good start. Try "Googling" the company name or product names to get information about their marketplace. Learn about challenges that might be facing your prospect's industry.

Ask intelligent questions: Use the info you gathered to help prepare intelligent questions. With your product and service in mind, prepare questions that uncover challenges you can help them solve. Be ready to ask follow-up questions.

Polish your presentation: Never prepare a canned, memorized presentation. Your prospect will see right through it and feel like the 100th person this week to hear that pitch from you. Instead, prepare talking points that are flexible enough to be interwoven into a sales discussion.

Use your sales tools: In the classic Batman television show, the one starring Adam West, it was impressive that the superhero always had exactly what he needed within easy reach on his utility belt. Before facing off with the dastardly Mr. Freeze, Batman made sure that he had ice-thawing Batspray on his hip. When you're selling, anticipate the tools you'll need in each upcoming encounter so that, like Batman, you can pull out the right tool at the right time. Have the right samples,
literature and other resources readily available.

Handling objections: Sales managers tell you to anticipate the objections you might hear from customers. That's fine, but anticipating is not enough. You need a well-thought-out plan for responding effectively to the objections you anticipate. What are the five most popular objections you encounter? What are the five toughest objections you hear? Invest a
couple of hours in developing great responses to those objections and watch your sales success rates rise.

There aren't too many volunteer salespeople around. By default, that makes the rest of us professional salespeople.
As professionals we must be prepared to demonstrate the professional level of service and preparedness that will help us succeed.

The ABCs of Strategic Communication

and Eckerd® stores, and six distribution centers in 18 states, making it the largest drugstore chain on the East Coast. Walgreens® with nearly 6,000 stores quickly expanded by purchasing the regional "drug store" chain Happy Harry's® with 76 stores. Walgreens' goal is 7,000 stores before the next decade. See *merger/acquisition*.

organization marketing – Activity related to the marketing of an association, school, college, hospital, sporting or social group, club, charitable body, etc.

organizational buyer – The individual responsible for the firm or company's purchasing.

organizational buying – Purchasing by organizations for resale purposes, for use in the manufacture of other goods and services, or for the operation of their businesses.

organizational buying behavior – The study of the motives and actions of, and the influences on, organizations while they are involved in purchasing goods and services.

organizational goals – An organization's broad, longer-term aims (often more than three years) or performance expectations as opposed to its organizational *objectives*, which are of a more specific nature and generally cover a shorter, specified period of time (often three years or less).

organizational markets – The sum of all industrial, institutional, reseller and government markets whose buyers purchase products for use in making other products, for resale, or in the operation of their businesses.

organizational structure – The way a firm has arranged its lines of authority and communication and allocates duties and responsibilities.

original – One of a kind. In advertising, unusual and unexpected.

orphan – One line of type at the end of a column or page that begins the next paragraph. Also a business account (or retailer) whose account executive or sales representative has left the company and the company no longer has a representative for the client to deal with.

orphan film – A documentary produced and shot by an independent film maker which cannot be sold to a studio or distributor because of a lack of interest.

out in front (of the story) – Taking a news story to the media before they come to you.

out-of-home (OOH) – Any form of visual communication outside a consumer's place of residence.

out-of-home advertising – Exposure to advertising and mass media away from one's home – includes *billboards*, transit bus shelters, point-of-purchase, sides of buildings, business signs, etc.

out-of-pocket (expenses) – Money spent by public relations, advertising and other agencies on a client's behalf, which is reimbursable. Examples might be production costs, travel expenses, etc. – and would be in addition to routine agency fees and commissions.

out-of-stock costs – Cost of sales lost when a particular item is not available when ordered by a customer.

out-suppliers – Suppliers, or agencies, never used before by the buying organization or client. Some therefore consider it risky business until relationships are established. See *in-suppliers*.

outbound telemarketing – Telemarketing where a company uses trained salespeople to sell to customers by telephone. See *inbound telemarketing*.

outdoor advertising – Advertising by means of posters and signs (*billboards*) that are stationary or mobile. Any outdoor sign that publicly promotes a product or service, such as *billboards*, movie *kiosks*, etc.

outer-directed consumers – One of three broad groups of consumers identified in the Stanford Research Institute's (SRI) survey of American lifestyles. According to the study, outer-directed consumers buy "with an eye to appearances and to what other people think." SRI says this group represents about two-thirds of consumers in the U.S. See *value and life style system (VALS)*; *inner-directed consumers*; *need-directed consumers*.

outside order-taker – A salesperson who visits customers to write up orders but is not responsible for persuading them to buy. See *inside order-taker*.

183

Tips to Succeed:
You are what you wear

When dressing for work, what you wear can dictate how others act toward you. Here are four key items to keep in mind:

Fit – Do your clothes fit properly? It doesn't matter how expensive an item is — if it is too tight or too big, it isn't going to look good on you.

Accessories – Are your accessories too big, too bold or too bright? Your accessories should be good-quality items that add to your outfit without overpowering it.

Color – Are you wearing clothing that is noticed because of its color? Darker colors convey more authority than lighter ones. Bright colors can "shout," and you should decide about whether you want to shout or not.

Style – Are your clothes very stylish or part of the latest fashion trend? If so, they will be noticed. This may be appropriate for your social life but less so for work.

Barbara Pachter - Pachter & Associates Business
Communications Training - Cherry Hill, N.J.

outside sales facilities – Manufacturers' agents and representatives, sales agents, dealers, distributors, etc., available to supplement or replace a firm's own sales force.

outside-the-box thinking – *Out-of-the-box thinking* requires an openness to new ways of seeing the world and a willingness to explore. *Out-of-the-box thinkers* know that new ideas need nurturing and support. They also know that having an idea is good but acting on it is more important. Results are what count. Read more at *www.canadaone.com/ezine/april02/out_of_the_box_thinking.html*.

outsourcing – Using an outside service or vendor rather than performing the work in-house with staff. *Freelancers* are often used when *outsourcing*.

outtake – A section or scene, as of a movie, filmed but not used in the final version. See *director's cut*.

overlay – A transparent or opaque covering used to protect designs or layouts. Also, separate transparent prints placed on top of one another (combined) to form a finished design or graphic.

overline – The caption above a photograph. Also a subhead that leads into the headline.

overprint – Same as *knockout and fill* – fill in reverse with colored ink.

overrun (or underrun) – Printed copies in excess of the specified quantity. *Overruns* may take place to meet unexpected needs or demands, or could be extra copies printed inadvertently. **O**

package – There are a number of definitions for a *package*. A merchandise enclosure or container. The last opportunity for a manufacturer to influence the consumer. It is one of *Litwin's Nine Ps of Marketing*. Also a combination of programs or commercials offered by a network available for purchase by advertisers either individually or as a discounted package deal. In a news broadcast, a *package* is the finished news report – a prerecorded television news story voiced by a reporter. It usually consists of standup or bridge, sound bites and *b-roll* – anchor introduces the reporter, either live or on tape who narrates the story, which contains sound bites, background video and a sign off or lockout (reporter saying his/her name and location).

package enclosure – See *in-pack premium*.

package insert – Separate advertising material included in another product's *package* that advertises goods or services. It could be a tie-in or a totally unrelated product. Any promotional offer included with the shipment of a customer's order (not necessarily on the product's *package*, but rather in the shipping box). Offers may be from the same mailer shipping the product or other vendors who pay to be included. Also referred to as a *package* stuffer.

package modification – Making any change to the attributes (size, shape, color, graphics, lettering, etc.) of a *package*.

packaged goods – A sub-category of consumer non-durable goods – toothpaste, shaving cream and soap are packaged *consumer non-durables*. See *consumer non-durables*; *non-packaged goods*.

package plan – A combination of advertisements or commercial spots devised by an advertising outlet and offered by advertisers at a special price (rate). They are usually weekly or monthly buys.

packaging – The materials (bubblewrap, cardboard, Styrofoam, etc.) originally intended to protect a product. More recently, the role of *packaging* has been broadened so that, in addition to protection, its purpose is to attract attention, provide additional product information and assist in promotion.

packet sniffer – A computer program used to monitor and record activity and to detect problems with Web transactions on a network.

pad and pencil interview – When a newsmaker talks on the record, but will not consent to a taped interview.

page display – When a page is successfully displayed on the user's computer screen.

page impression/hit – A measurement of responses from a Web server. Each time a computer is directed to a Web page, it registers as an *impression* or *hit*. In other forms of media, *impressions* are the total number of people who could see or hear the ad – for example, a newspaper's circulation.

page layout – Arranging the type and elements on a page.

page one (or page 1A) – The first page of the newspaper or the importance of a story – as in "page one news."

page slugs – Symbols located at the bottom and/or top of each page that indicate if the copy continues by using "MORE" or concludes by using "30," "###" or "END."

PageMaker® – Layout and design program.

pagination – The electronic (computerized) design, laying out (make up) of a page – commonly used by newspapers and magazines. Also, using a design program to layout pages electronically.

paginator – The person who lays out publication pages using *pagination*.

paid circulation – Distribution of a magazine or other publication to people, households or organizations that have paid a subscription fee. See *controlled circulation*.

painted bulletin – A freestanding steel or wooden structure, approximately 50' wide by 15' high, with molding around the outer edges similar to a poster panel and including a hand-painted copy message. Bulletins are generally found near highways or roofs of buildings in high traffic areas. Also called *billboards*.

pallet – A range of colors. A painter's pallet holds a range of oils or other types of paint.

palletisation – The packing of goods onto small wooden or strong plastic platforms, or *pallets*, for ease of handling in shipment.

pamphlet – An unbound booklet (that is, without a hard cover or binding).

pander – Never telling anyone what they don't want to hear – talking a lot without really ruling anything out so you can draw your own conclusions. Good public relations counseling advice would be – "Don't tell the boss what he/she wants to hear, tell him/her what /she needs to hear." In other words, don't *pander*.

184 Tips to Succeed: Staying positive: Smile

We all know we should appreciate who we are and what we have. But sometimes it's so much easier for many of us to believe the negative things we hear and think about ourselves than it is to listen to, and believe, the best.

Here are some tips on what you can do to become more aware of the positive things in life right now, feel better and be more productive.

• Send yourself an e-mail or call your voice mail and say something positive about yourself or note one thing you are happy about today. Make this a daily routine.

• Add an area to your things-to-do list where you can list at least one thing each day that makes you smile.

• Once an hour, stop, look around and find something or someone that you can say something positive about. The harder you have to look to find that silver lining, the better.

• Decide today that you will no longer compare yourself to others.

• Create a place where you can keep photos, positive letters, articles and other reminders of good things that you have accomplished and that are a part of your life.

Lee Silber - Organizational Expert and Author - www.creativelee.com

panel test – A technique used to pre-test advertising, new products, etc. A group of individuals selected from the target market are asked to evaluate alternative versions (of an advertisement, new product, etc.). Also called *focus panels*.

panels – Regular and illuminated types of *outdoor advertising*. Regular *panels* are seen only during the daytime. Illuminated *panels* are seen also from dusk until dawn.

Pantone Matching System® **(PMS)** – A system that precisely characterizes an ink color for printing, so that a color can be matched, even by different printers. By knowing the Pantone color specifications, a printer does not even need to see a sample of the color to match it. Much like a recipe, but much more exact.

paparazzi – Photographers who take pictures of celebrities during "unguarded or personal moments."

para-social relationship – Television viewers come to feel they know TV characters because they see them all the time. *Para-social relationships* developed in "Friends," "Cheers," "Desperate Housewives," etc. This is the same feeling people get when they associate a positive figure (character) with a product (transfer effect). Leads to *third party validation* through advertising *endorsements* and *testimonials*.

paradigm – A pattern or model.

paradigm shift – Something has changed so that everything changes. Outcomes are no longer what we can expect.

185

Tips to Succeed: ABCs of strategic public relations

• **Anticipate** = For every public relations action there is a reaction. Explore all possible reactions in advance. Successful practitioners are *never* surprised.

• **Be Prepared** = For that first call from the media. Don't go public until you are absolutely ready.

• **Communicate** = Clearly, Concisely, Calculatingly, Consistently and Completely (Specifically and Simply)

M. Larry Litwin, APR, Fellow PRSA - *The Public Relations Practitioner's Playbook* (Kendall/Hunt – 2008)

parallel importing – See *grey marketing*.

parasitic advertising – Advertising by one group which has an adverse effect upon another group. For example, the advertising of veal may reduce sales of beef, or the advertising of oranges may reduce sales of grapefruit.

paretopoly – A market situation where there are a few large sellers and many smaller ones.

paretopsony – A market situation where there are a few large buyers and many smaller ones.

Pareto's principle – The idea or notion in business, commonly known as the *80/20 rule*. It states that 80 percent of the revenue comes from 20 percent of the products, that 80 percent of the sales volume is derived from 20 percent of the customer accounts, etc. It is named for Vilfredo Pareto, a 19th century economist and sociologist.

parity products – Product categories where several *brands* within that category have the same or similar features, making one *brand* a satisfactory substitute for most other *brands* in that category.

participation – Commercial announcements made during a radio or television program. An arrangement where a television or radio advertiser buys commercial time from a network. More commonly used when a number of advertisers join together to sponsor a program. If there is only one or a major sponsor, the title of the program often carries the brand name as part of it. For example, "The Hallmark Hall of Fame." At one time, sponsored programs were the rule. Today, they are the exception because of the cost of producing most programs.

participatory journalism – Citizens playing an active role in the process of gathering and reporting news and information – using still and video cameras, other recorders and cell phones. Also called *citizen journalism*.

partnering – Also called *affinity marketing*. Marketing targeted at individuals sharing common interests that predispose them towards a product, (e.g. an auto accessories manufacturer targeting motoring magazine readers). Also, a campaign jointly sponsored by a number of different, possibly dissimilar organizations that are non-competitive but have a particular interest in common.

pass-along rate – The number of times a received document (article, newsletter, brochure, report, etc.) is shared with others.

pass-along readers – A reader who becomes familiar with a publication without purchasing it. These readers are taken into account when calculating the total number of readers of a publication.

pass-up method – Handling a buyer's *objection* by attempting to ignore or "pass off" the buyer's objection, especially if there is reason to believe that the objection is not made seriously and does not warrant a response. See *objections*.

passive audience – Uninterested. Will usually rely on surrogates (stand-ins) to gather information.

password – A group of letters and/or numbers which allow a unique computer user access to a secured Web site and/or a secure area of a Web site.

paste-up – A camera–ready or "rough" layout of graphic and typed material configured in the proper position on paperboard or as a laser print, which is to be used for reproductive purposes. If *camera-ready*, it could be called a *matte*, *repro* or *slick*.

pathos – The rhetorical principle based on the emotional persuasiveness of an argument. See *ethos*; *logos*.

patronage motives – The motives that drive an individual user to select a particular outlet, retailer or services supplier.

pay for non-performance – Huge salary and bonus packages given to chief executive officers of under-performing companies.

pay-per-click – An Internet advertising pricing method where advertisers pay agencies and/or media outlets based on how many users clicked on an online ad or e-mail message. Similar to *per-inquiry advertising*.

pay-per-impression – An advertising pricing method where advertisers pay based on how many users were served their ads. See *CPM pricing model*; *per-inquiry advertising*.

pay-per-lead – An advertising pricing method where advertisers pay for each "sales lead" generated. For example, an advertiser might pay for every visitor that clicked on an ad or Web site and successfully completed a form. See *CPL (cost per lead)*.

pay-per-sale – An advertising pricing method where advertisers pay agencies and/or media outlets based on the number of transactions generated as a direct result of the ad. See *CPS (cost per sale)*.

pay-to-play –The unethical process through which professionals and contractors donate to political candidates, and then are rewarded with hefty government contracts, sometimes without a bidding or quoting process. Taxpayers end up footing the bill (see Technique 195).

payback period – The time taken for a new product to recover its investment cost and to generate profits. It is used as an accepted measure of performance for new products.

payday loans – Small sums that consumers borrow and pay back in a short time, creating high annual interest rates.

payment by results (PBR) – A portion or all of a salary or pay to an employee or service provider is based on productivity (possibly sales or other output) or other measures of performance.

payment in lieu of taxes (PILOT) – A fee charged by some municipalities to businesses, colleges, hospitals and some other institutions as a discounted alternative to real estate taxes to attract them to the community. Also, a "contribution" that some nonprofits, exempt from real estate taxes, pay to municipalities to cover such services as police and fire protection, etc.

payout planning – Approach to advertising (and many times public relations) budgeting where the dollars spent to advertise are represented as an investment toward sales and profits.

PDF (portable document format) files – A translation format developed by Adobe® used primarily for distributing

186

Tips to Succeed:
Think first – then carry out CBAs of strategic public relations

• Conceive = Head

• Believe = Heart

• Achieve = Hands

Public relations practitioners conceive their plans through research and thought. A great majority have a strong belief, which helps them achieve it through hands on tactics (by doing or carrying out)…thus they achieve with their head, believe in the heart and achieve with their hands.

Anthony J. Fulginiti, APR, Fellow PRSA
Professor-Public Relations
Rowan (N.J.) University

P

files across a network or on a Web site. Files with a .pdf extension have been created in another application and then translated into .pdf files so they can be viewed by anyone, regardless of platform.

peer to peer (P2P) marketing – Technique of encouraging customers to promote their product to one another – particularly on the Internet. An example might be a Web site that offers users a discount on products in return for recruiting new customers for the site. See *word-of-mouth*; *viral marketing.*

peg (in a news story) – The hook and timeliness that make a story newsworthy.

penetrated market – The individuals or organizations in a particular market who have already purchased the product. Also, actual users consuming the product or service even if they didn't make the purchase.

penetration – The percentage of a market that a medium or an individual media vehicle reaches. Also, the percentage of the market that a particular marketing message reaches, regardless of the media vehicles used.

pension tacking – The legal practice of an employees and a private contractor (vendor) combining two or more part-time government salaries into one public paycheck. That one paycheck has the effect of boosting an employee's final pension payment.

people-based services – Services where people, rather than equipment or machinery, play the major role in delivery. For example, people play the major role in the delivery of financial planning services. See *equipment-based services.*

people (portable) meter (PPM) – Digital device attached to a listener much like a beeper – used to record all exposure to broadcast media. It replaces the unreliable, listener-kept paper diaries previously used to track listenership (of each radio station).

per capita income – Average income per person in a population.

per diem expense plan – The payment of travel and accommodation expenses to a salesperson at a fixed daily rate.

per inquiry– An advertising method or technique where the advertiser pays for print ads or commercials based on the number of responses – either phone calls, returned coupons or Web site clicks. (The Internet is

187

Tips to Succeed:
Know your audiences

AUDIENCE POWER STRUCTURE

Audiences within a community or organization can be segmented into *elite, diffused* and *amorphous* and illustrated by using a pyramid – *elite* is where the power is concentrated at the top (a few opinion leaders or key communicators who are actively involved); *diffused* or *pluralistic* is where the power is spread throughout (aware of issues, but not aware of effects on them) and *amorphous* or *latent* is where the power has yet to surface (probably not concerned or even aware of how issues affect them – e.g. a new condominium community).

M. Larry Litwin, APR, Fellow PRSA - *The Public Relations Practitioner's Playbook*
(Kendall/Hunt – 2008)

P

coping with click fraud where accusations have been made that outlets could falsely click on ads to drive up revenues).

perceived risk– A functional or psychosocial *risk* a consumer feels he or she is taking when purchasing a product. See *risk*.

perceived value – A product or service's worth in the mind of the consumer – could be more or less. Many times, the *perceived value* is much greater than the cost. For example, a bank that gives its business customers a golf putter with the bank's name and logo. Purchased in quantity, the bank gets the club for much less than those purchased by the customer. However, the customer perceives it at its regular retail price. For the bank, it's a club that will be used, and it's a great promotional tool. The *perceived value* is greater on both ends – the bank's and the customer's.

percentage-of-sales (budgeting) method – Method of setting a budget for public relations, advertising andpromotion where the amount to be spent during a given period is a fixed percentage of the sales

188 Techniques to Succeed: Grunig's *Four Models of Public Relations*

James Grunig and Todd Hunt developed *four models of public relations.* Each differs in the purpose and nature of communication.

Press Agentry/Publicity – one-way communication – uses persuasion and manipulation to influence audience to behave as the organization desires (One way with propaganda as its purpose.)

Public Information – one-way communication – use news releases and other one-way communication techniques to distribute organizational information. Public relations practitioner is often referred to as the "journalist in residence." (One way with dissemination of truthful information.)

Two-way asymmetrical – two way – Sometimes called "scientific persuasion" (short term rather than long term). Uses persuasion and manipulation to influence audience to behave as the organization desires – incorporates lots of feedback from target audiences and publics – used by an organization primarily interested in having its publics come around to its way of thinking rather changing the organization, its policies, or its views.

Two-way symmetrical – two way – Uses communication to negotiate with publics, resolve conflict, and promote mutual understanding and respect between the organization and its public(s). Research is used not only to gather information, but also to change the organization's behavior. Understanding, rather than persuasion, is the objective. (Every attempt is made for each side to understand the other's point of view. If your public agrees with you, then you must find a way to communicate with the public and motivate it to act.) Seems to be used more by non-profit organizations, government agencies and heavily regulated businesses (public utilities) rather than by competitive, profit driven companies.

James Grunig and Todd Hunt - University of Maryland - 1984

income for the previous period. To help justify increases, it is important, if not imperative, to show, that if your organization projects a 10 percent increase in sales, then your PR or advertising budget might be worthy of a 10 percent increase.

perception – The way an individual interprets information received by the five senses – and acknowledges and assigns meaning to the received information.

perceptual mapping – A tool or process used in marketing research for charting the way select individuals from the target market perceive various companies, products or brands. Also called *position mapping*.

peremptory challenge – An obscure legal term meaning the right of the plaintiff and the defendant in a jury trial to have a juror dismissed before trial without stating a reason.

perfect binding – A binding method where the spine is flat. Each page is glued to the spine and to the adjacent pages.

perfect competition – A marketing situation where there are a large number of sellers of a product or service, which cannot be differentiated and, therefore, no one firm has a significant influence on price. There are other conditions which might include ease of entry of new firms into the market and perfect market information. Referred to as atomistic competition. See *monopolistic competition*; *pure competition*.

performance allowance – A discount or price reduction given to a wholesaler or retailer who promises to perform some additional (promotional) activity (special display, etc) to sell a greater quantity of product.

performance appraisal – An evaluation of the activities and effectiveness of a salesperson, marketing officer, etc. during a given period.

performance price – The value to a consumer of the time saved by using a new product to complete a specified task. It follows the adage "time is money."

performance pricing model – An advertising model where advertisers pay based on a set of agreed upon performance criteria, such as a percentage of online revenues or delivery of new sales leads.

performance risk – Concern in the buyer's mind that the product being considered for purchase will not work efficiently. Also called *functional risk*. See *risk*.

P

periodical – Magazines, newsletters and journals. A publication with issues appearing on a regular schedule – daily, weekly or monthly.

perishability – One of the four characteristics (with *inseparability, intangibility* and *variability*) which distinguish a service. *Perishability* expresses the notion that a service cannot be made in advance and stored.

perks – Perquisites, also called employee benefits are various non-wage compensations provided to employees in addition to their normal wages or salaries. *Perks* can include, but are not limited to: group insurance (health, dental, life etc.), income protection, retirement benefits, daycare, tuition reimbursement, sick leave, vacation, retirement plans and other specialized benefits. The purpose *perks* are to increase the economic security of employees. The term *perks* is often used colloquially to refer to those benefits of a more discretionary nature. Common *perks* are company cars, hotel stays, free refreshments, leisure activities on work time (exercise room) etc.

permission-based marketing – Typically associated with e-mail marketing, although other forms of direct marketing also use *permission-based marketing*. It is when marketing messages are sent only to people who have opted to receive these messages. These targeted individuals have expressed an interest in receiving permission marketing information from specific advertisers.

permission marketing – When an individual has given company permission to market its products and services to the individual. See *opt-in*.

pernicious – The theory that women are more persuasive than men.

persistent cookie – A *cookie* which remains on a computer's hard drive until the user erases it.

person marketing – Marketing activity aimed at creating target market awareness, and a favorable opinion, of a particular person.

personal data – Data related to a living individual who can be identified from the information. It includes any expression of opinion about the individual. This is a major aspect of *relationship marketing*.

personal data (or digital) assistant (PDA) – Handheld computer-like device that stores and retrieves information. Among the brands that manufacture and sell *PDAs* are Dell® and Palm®.

Personal Identification Number (PIN) – A group of numbers which allow a unique user access to a secured Web site and/or a secure area of a Web site. See *password*.

personal improvement plan – A plan set forth by an employer or an individual that leads to self improvement. It contains personal *goals*, *objectives*, *strategies* and *tactics* to be used to achieve the objectives and eventual goal.

personal income – Wages, salary, etc. earned by an individual.

personal interview – A face-to-face meeting with a client, job applicant, buyer, marketing research respondent, etc. A survey technique – face-to-face questioning of the respondent by the researcher. Once the most common surveying method.

personal seat license (PSL) – A contractual agreement between a sports team (*PSL* licensor) and the purchaser (*PSL* licensee) in which the licensee (purchaser) pays the team a fee in exchange for the team guaranteeing the right to purchase season tickets at a specified seat location for a specified period of time (could be the life of the venue) so long as the licensee does not violate the terms of the agreement.

personal selling – Sales made through face-to-face communication, personal correspondence or personal telephone conversation, etc. Also, a form of promotion using the services of a sales team. One of the major controllable variables (with public relations, publicity, advertising and sales promotion) of the *promotion mix*. See *promotion mix*.

personal video recorder (PVR) – Set-top box that stores up to 30 hours of TV programming and works with cable and satellite systems. Viewers can pause or rewind live TV shows, record a season's worth of episodes and skip past commercials. TiVo® is one of the brands on the market. See *digital video recorder*.

personality – The distinctive character of an individual. It is used as a basis for the psychographic segmentation of a market in which individuals of relatively similar personality, with similar needs or wants, are grouped into one segment. See *psychographic segmentation*.

personality segmentation – The division of a heterogeneous market into homogeneous groups on the basis of personality characteristics and such behavior patterns as aggressiveness, compliance or compulsiveness. See *psychographic segmentation*.

P

personalization – Customizing a marketing communication vehicle (using any medium) for the individual who will see it. This can be inserting the individual's name (referred to as "ink jet") or as complex as producing a unique presentation of the printed or electronic (CD) vehicle for each recipient based on his or her needs, tastes or stated preferences.

personalize – To add a name or other personal information about the recipient on direct mail advertising.

personally identifiable information (PII) – Refers to information such as an individual's name, mailing address, phone number or e-mail address.

persons of opposite sex sharing living quarters – *Demographic* grouping known commonly as POSSLQ.

persons using television (PUT) – A percentage of all people in a certain viewing area that are viewing television during a specific period of time. Used by *A.C. Nielson*.

persons viewing television (PVT) – Same meaning as *PUT*, except this term is used by *Arbitron*.

persuade – Change the audience's behavior or getting someone to do something – even for a short time.

persuasion process – The process used by public relations practitioners and advertisers to influence audience or prospect attitudes, especially purchase intent and product perception, by appealing to reason or emotion. It is accepted that *attitudes* (inner feelings) must be reinforced, maintained or changed before sought-after behavior can be achieved.

persuasion test – A test that evaluates the effectiveness of an advertisement by measuring whether the ad affects consumers' intentions to buy a product or specific brand.

persuasive advertising – Advertising intended to persuade (rather than to inform or remind).

persuasive communication – Communication directed toward changing or altering another person's beliefs, attitudes and, ultimately, behaviors.

pester power – The influence children have over purchases by adults, an influence many advertisers may play to or try to stimulate.

pestering factor – Used by advertisers to reach children. It's the concept of designing commercials and other ads so that children bother their parents to purchase a product.

phantom – An illustration showing the exterior of an object as if it were transparent, while revealing interior detailing.

189

Tips to Succeed: Like artists, public relations practitioners should see the whole apple before painting it

Even before starting the formal research, PR practitioners should do as architects and artists do – develop their own blue print, look at situations with a painter's eye – view the scene from every angle and perspective. Gather as many "nuggets of knowledge" as possible – then research after determining why you are doing what you are doing (purpose), plan (goal and objectives), inform (strategies and tactics) and evaluate. That's why this public relations process is called *PR-Pie*. As the "nuggets of knowledge" take shape, you will move closer to the plan's goal and achieving *synergy*.

phantom freight – A freight charge imposed on a customer in excess of the true freight cost incurred by the supplier (this does, in fact, happen). For example, in the *base-point pricing* approach, a local customer will be charged a *phantom freight* when the freight charge is calculated from an arbitrarily-chosen, possibly distant, central point. See *base-point pricing*.

phishing – Internet scams – *logos* or *slogans* used fraudulently so victims take the bait. *Phishing* attacks use "spoofed" e-mails and fraudulent web sites designed to fool recipients into divulging such personal financial data as credit card numbers, account usernames and passwords, Social Security Numbers, etc. By hijacking the trusted brands of well-known banks, online retailers and credit card companies, phishers are able to convince up to five percent of recipients to respond to them.

phoner – An interview taped over the phone by either a radio or TV reporter.

photo – A picture.

photo caption – A brief description that identifies the event and the people or subjects included in a photograph sent to the news media. The *caption* should include the names and titles of the individuals pictured. Also include the name and telephone number of a person the reporter can contact for further information. Here is an example (provided by Anne Klein & Associates – public relations counselors):

(DATE OF PHOTO) John Doe, (left) registered representative of the Philadelphia office of Charles Schwab, and Susan Jones, (right of podium) personal financial advisor of 1st Union Bank, were the featured speakers at the May meeting of the Delaware Valley chapter of the National Association of Investors Corporation (NAIC). Jones stressed the importance of long-term investing while Doe reviewed the many ways individual investors and investment clubs can save money by using discount brokers and online services.

photo manipulation – A picture that is fabricated ("doctored") and has obviously been manipulated. See *photofiction*.

photo shoot – A session where a photographer takes shots (pictures) of an individual or group for individual or commercial purposes (for organizations, promotional materials, etc.)

photoanimation – A process (long before computer animation) of creating animation through the use of still photographs.

photoboards – A set of still photographs made from a video (television) commercial, accompanied with a script, to be kept as records by an agency or client. A type of rough commercial with frames that are actual photos rather than *sketches*.

photocomposition – A method of setting type by using film negatives of the characters which are projected onto aluminum plates used for *offset printing*. It is much like printing a document from a home computer onto a laser printer. The laser (camera-ready copy) print is photographed onto a negative and transferred onto an aluminum plate. It is referred to as *cold type*. The older method uses zinc plate made using hot type – also called *letterpress*.

photoengraving – The process of making *letterpress* printing plates by photochemical means. Also a picture printed from a plate made by this process.

photofiction – A picture that is fabricated and has obviously been manipulated. See *photo manipulation*.

190

Techniques to Succeed: Turning the 'green' handshake into the 'confident' handshake

Delivering a proper handshake can make or break your first impression on a person. A handshake that's too limp or weak can convey weakness or lack of self-confidence. A handshake that's too strong or crushing can convey hostility. A well-executed handshake is one that conveys self-confidence, trust, and a genuine interest in the other party.

Several factors contributing to a good handshake, from start to finish.

A handshake is generally common courtesy during most introductions, and when greeting a familiar person.

- **Eye contact**. Once your hands have met, you should make eye contact and maintain it throughout the handshake. If you're particularly coordinated, or gifted with great peripheral vision, make eye contact prior to the handshake, and maintain it for the duration.

- **Grip**. Grip with your whole hand, not just the fingertips or just the thumb. Make it firm, but not crushing. A good help for learning this would be asking a friend to help you practice your handshake grip. In most situations, you should only use one hand. Using both could convey hostility, or intent to overpower.

- **Position**. Your body should be approximately 12 to 20 inches away from the other party. Both parties' hands should be straight up-and-down, even with each other. The web of your hand (skin running between the forefinger and the thumb) should meet the web of theirs.

- **Shake**. Should be smooth, not limp or over-enthusiastic. Shake from the elbow, not the wrist or the shoulder.

- **Flow**. Before the handshake, establish eye contact. Break eye contact, if needed, to extend your hand to meet theirs. When the web of your hand meets the web of theirs, re-establish eye contact and engage your grip. Shake two or three times, for a duration of one to three seconds, breaking off cleanly and smoothly before the introduction is over.

To test your handshaking finesse, try shaking hands with a few close friends.

www.faqfarm.com/Q/How_does_one_give_a_proper_handshake

The ABCs of Strategic Communication

P

photoplatemaking – A process that converts original art material into printing plates required to print ads.

Photoshop® – Production tool developed by Adobe® that allows the operator to create original artwork, retouch photos, etc.

photostat – A type of high contrast photographic negative or positive in the form of paper. Also referred to as stat or *velox*.

physical distribution – The storage, handling and movement of goods within an organization and eventually their shipment to customers.

physical distribution management – Moving products from manufacturer to the consumer. The management and control of the activities involved in the storage, handling and movement of goods within an organization and in their shipment to customers. Also called *product-differentiated marketing*.

physical evidence – The elements of the marketing mix (*Litwin's 9 Ps of Marketing*) which customers can actually see or experience when they use a service, and which contribute to the perceived quality of the service. For example, the physical building that houses a department store, its entire chain and its reputation for customer service.

physical risk – Concern in the buyer's mind that the product being considered for purchase will be harmful, unhealthy or cause injury.

physiological needs – Anything a person needs to survive. Public relations practitioners who conduct research understand that most times, a person's *needs* must be recognized before a strategic message is developed. See *psychological needs*.

physiological tests – Measures emotional reactions to advertisements by monitoring reactions such as heart rate and pupil dilation.

pica – A unit of measurement for type specification and printing which measures width – six picas to one inch. A size of type – one pica = 12 points.

pick your own friends – When you have something that others want, they "all" become your friends. This means you get to pick who it is you want to choose.

pickups – Media outlets running news releases.

picture window – An ad layout where the picture is placed at the top of the page, and the copy is placed below.

piece – The general term applied to any newspaper article written by a reporter; also called *story*.

pigeonhole – A term for *niche agency* or *boutique agency* – a *pigeonhole* or a *pigeonhole* agency.

piggyback – A system of transportation requiring the transfer of containers from truck to rail. See *fishyback*. Also, a direct mail offer that is included free with another offer. Two radio commercials played back-to-back or two television commercials shown back-to-back by the same sponsor.

piggyback advertising – Two or more (not necessarily related) advertisers combine their resources to purchase large blocks of space or time which they divide among themselves. By *piggybacking* their resources, they should save money. (e.g. Four advertisers purchase a full newspaper page at the full-page rate. Each runs a quarter page ad. Dividing the full-page rate by four saves money over the cost of each advertiser buying a quarter of a page individually.) See *sandwich spot*.

piggyback survey – Also called an *omnibus survey*. A type of public relations or marketing research survey usually administered for one main organization, but may contain a question or questions from other firms or organizations for a fee. Some information, such as *demographics* and *psychographics*, may be shared. Organizations buy into other surveys either to save money or because they do not need a survey on their own. *Omnibus surveys*, like other polling, is commonly organized by a major

191 Techniques to Succeed:
Newsome's Principles of Persuasion

Familiarity (audience, message, surrogates)

Identification (rewards/benefits)

Clarity (avoid jargon/passive verbs)

Action (ask for behavior/what you want) try! buy! sell! (relate).

Earl Newsome - Researcher

professional marketing research company, where different cross sections of the community are interviewed by probability (scientific) sampling at regular intervals about attitudes and opinions toward issues, buying habits, product and brand preferences, etc. They are called *omnibus surveys* because any marketer can join in for a fee to add questions.

piggybacking – A low-cost market entry tactic where manufacturers of products arrange for manufacturers of complementary, non-competing products to represent their products in another country or region.

piney – Anyone whose life remains somehow entwined with the land – cranberry farming or fighting forest fires, for example – and whose lineage with the land goes back several generations. To outsiders, the word *piney* stirs unsettling images of people living marginal lifestyles in run-down shacks in the woods, hillbilly-like people to ridicule or even fear.

pioneering advertising – Advertising intended to create *primary demand* rather than *selective demand*. It is commonly used at the introductory stage of the product's life cycle. See *primary demand; selective demand.*

pipeline – The channel an article goes through from receipt of the manuscript to its publication in a magazine.

pipeline transportation – The carriage, delivery or shipment of a gas or liquid product by pipeline.

pitch – In public relations, it is generally an attempt to get positive coverage for a product, service, event, etc. using an angle of interest that might be unique to catch the media's attention. A prepared sales presentation, usually one-on-one. A story idea presented to the media in written or oral form. A sales letter.

pitching – The act of presenting your story to the news media.

pix – Abbreviation for pictures.

pixel – A single display element on an LCD screen. The more *pixels*, the higher the resolution and definition. Also picture element (single illuminated dot) on a computer monitor. The metric used to indicate the size of Internet ads.

place – One of the four controllable variables (with *product, price* and *promotion*) of the original marketing mix. The delivery of a good or service to a consumer. See *distribution; marketing mix.*

place holder – A person nominated ("used") by a political party as a "temporary" candidate until the party decides on a permanent candidate for that particular office. Laws for using a *place holder* vary from state to state and may not be legal in some jurisdictions.

place marketing – Marketing activity intended to promote an awareness, and favorable opinion, of a particular place or region.

place strategy – The element of a firm's decision-making concerned with developing an efficient and effective (efficacy) means of storing and handling finished products and of getting them efficiently to the target market.

192

Techniques to Succeed: Recency-Primacy – try it; it works

There are a number of approaches. Here are just a couple:

The last statement made (the most recent information received) is most recalled or remembered. That's why having the last word is better. It leaves the *most* lasting impression.

There is also the *primacy effect* – the greater impact of what we first learn about someone (first impressions). Remember, we get just one chance to make a first impression.

P

place utility – Making a product available so that it is easily accessible and purchasable for consumers who want it.

plagiarize – Claiming someone else's work as your own. Also, claiming or implying, original authorship or incorporating material from someone else's written or creative work, in whole or in part, into ones own without adequate acknowledgment. See *fabricate*.

plain vanilla – Slang term for a product with only the most basic features – no "bells and whistles."

PLANET code – A bar code that will allow mailers to track a mail piece, or an entire mail campaign, throughout the USPS delivery system.

planned cannibalization – The opposite of *synergy* – dismantling a public relations *IMC (integrated marketing communication)* campaign rather than planning and implementing one. Also, the expected loss of

193

Tips to Succeed: A picture is worth 1,000 words – scoring more coverage with newsworthy photo opps

Treat photographers like you would other journalists – and treat them equally.

• Don't try to micro manage the photo shoot.

• Incorporate newsworthy photo opps into your media relations efforts:

1. **Avoid logos and "CEO shots" in media photos.** Recognize that photographers want "real" photos. They want to capture natural moments with some "real emotion."

2. **Avoid photo opportunities that look staged.** Readers can tell when someone is smiling for the camera or when body language looks awkward. (Avoid the grip "n" grin shots.)

3. **Treat photographers like "back doors" to the front page.** Try to accommodate the photojournalist. Think about these things – human drama, emotion and reader interest – and try to provide them using real people when photographers show up.

4. **Be a good host – facilitate and foresee photojournalists' needs.** Another common mistake organizations make is they don't have things like parking passes available for photographers. They'll have one for the reporter, but not the photographer. Photojournalists have to lug a lot of equipment and gear. It can be a [real headache] when there's nowhere to park and we're not given access.

5. **If you must shoot your own photos – then hire qualified photojournalists.** The problem with most PR-provided photos is that they have no life or emotion. "They are very static, and usually feature a lot of logs and people looking right into the camera. These people tend to be important figures, but the reader doesn't care about your CEO or CFO. They want to be drawn to someone like them."

Other problems with PR photos include a lack of compelling composition, an [absence of] technical excellence – including things like focus, balance and proper exposure – and an overall sense that they were taken by an "amateur."

Marie Poirier Marzi - Photojournalist - Washington, D.C. - www.mariemarzi.com/

sales of a product in a line to a more recent product introduction. *Planned cannibalization* might occur when a company wants its customers to switch to another of its own products rather than to a product of a competitor.

planned economy – A type of economy where some central authority makes a wide range of decisions pertaining to production and wages (like Communist nations). Also called *controlled allocation system*; command system. See *free market*.

planned obsolescence – A tactic used by some manufacturers deliberately seeking to make earlier versions of its product appear undesirable in the eyes of consumers who have purchased them to expand the market for later versions by improving the characteristics of later versions – or by altering consumers' perceptions of the desirability of the models they have already purchased.

planning – A systematic, strategic, logical, methodical course of action to achieve a set of *objectives* and eventually to reach a *goal*. See *strategic planning; marketing planning; sales planning*.

planning editor – Person at television and radio stations responsible for scheduling reporters and crews for story coverage once the stories are selected by the *assignment editor*.

planning horizon – The total time span covered by a firm's marketing plans. The length of the *planning horizon* is commonly determined by the degree of uncertainty in the environment.

planning process – The steps or stages taken in planning a public relations or advertising campaign. The steps include identifying the target market, establishing a *goal, objectives*, developing the budget, strategies, selecting the appropriate media and evaluating the public relations effectiveness. See *planning*.

plastectomy – The act of chopping up (shredding) one's credit cards. Kenny from Mississippi used a blender to chop up his seven credit cards. Dave Ramsey, a national radio talk show host and debt-fighting crusader who's determined to beat the credit industry coined the term – "to save one debtor at a time.")

plastic bag memory – Durable items packed in plastic "refuse" to take on a different shape. For example, chords packed in plastic in a rolled up fashion are stubborn and want to return to the way they were packaged – making it difficult to adapt them for their given purpose.

platform – The type of computer or operating system on which a software application runs, e.g., Windows®, Macintosh®, WebTV®, etc.

Platform for Privacy Preferences Project (P3P) – Computer browser feature that analyzes privacy policies and allows users to control their privacy needs. It is a tool designed to help consumers better protect their online privacy.

PlayStation Portable® (PSP) – Manufactured by Sony®.

plug – A free and positive mention of a company, product, service and/or event in any media vehicle.

plug 'n play – Electronic devices designed so that installation is considered simple and seamless.

pluralism – In media studies, a view of the mass media as enjoying a considerable degree of independence from government and pressure groups. The independence of media outlets encourages competition. Broadly speaking, the media are seen as offering a wide selection of the views of various groups in society.

pluralist – The *pluralist* view of the mass media sees them as important agencies within a free and democratic society. Media institutions are seen as being free, by and large, of any government control and therefore free to present whatever point of view they want.

plurality – In a *plurality* voting system, each voter votes

194

Techniques to Succeed: Getting 'pinged'

Think war movies: A submarine is looking for an enemy ship. Sonar emitted by the hunter returns a "ping!" Everyone starts running around yelling, "Man the torpedoes!"

Hackers send out streams of small data packets to thousands of IP (e-mail) addresses. When the packet bounces back to the hacker, he knows he has "pinged" a computer that is currently online.

The ping, though, is nothing more than a probe and *cannot* affect your PC.

The hacker's version of a torpedo – a program that can infiltrate your PC and open it to the hacker – is of no use if you have a firewall protecting the PC.

John J. Fried - *Philadelphia Inquirer*
johnfriedfaq@phillynews.com

for one candidate, and the candidate with the *plurality* (most votes) wins, regardless of whether that candidate gets a majority or not.

podcast – Self-styled audio productions recorded in digital format and downloaded to computers, iPods® or other digital music players. A digital download.

podcasting – The process of creating an audio show available in mp3 format via an *RSS* 2.0 feed that supports enclosures. *Podcasts* are designed to include talk shows, tutorials, music or other audio content. Also a method of publishing (combines the words broadcasting and iPod®) sound files to the Internet, allowing users to subscribe to a feed and receive new audio files automatically. Also known as *blogcasting*.

podium – Much like a lectern – a stand for holding the notes of a public speaker – except that it is raised. A *lectern* is not. See *dais*; *lectern*.

point – A small unit of measurement for type, equal to 1/72 of an inch. Also, a small unit for measuring the thickness of paper, equaling 0.001 inch.

point of entry – The place where a person's eye enters a page and begins looking at the page's elements.

Point of Purchase (POP) advertising – A retail in-store presentation that displays product and communicates information to retail consumers at the place of purchase. See also *electronic point of sale (EPOS)*.

point size – A relative measure of the size of a type font – the higher the number, the larger the font.

point-of-purchase displays – A form of promotion used to support personal selling and advertising. *Displays*, consisting of packages, signs, display cartons, etc. (more common in the marketing of consumer goods) are used to provide additional product information and to encourage impulse or on-the-spot buying.

poison pill amendment – Item or items added to a proposed federal bill that might be distasteful enough to get the bill defeated in an up or down vote. There are no line item vetoes of federal bills.

poke – A method to get someone's attention on a social media Web site (MySpace® or Facebook®) without sending them a message. An alert, that someone *hit* the Web site.

P

polemic – A film or video produced to appear like a *documentary*, but in the truest sense, is not. Rather, it is written and produced as an opposing argument. It is much more a commentary than a *documentary*. Also, *polemic* is the art or practice of inciting disputation or causing controversy, for example in religious, philosophical, or political matters. A *polemic* text on a topic is written specifically to dispute or refute a topic that is widely viewed to be a "sacred cow" or beyond reproach, in an effort to "stir up trouble." The antonym of a *polemic* source is an apology. See *documentary*.

polemics – Politics of opportunism. Saying what you believe a client wants to hear rather than what he/she needs to hear.

Politically Active and Not Seeking Employment (PANSES) – A *demographic* grouping.

political advertising – Advertising used to persuade people to vote for politicians. *Political advertising's* requirements are different from all other types. The purpose of *political ads* is to persuade people to vote for a candidate, or in some cases, an issue. There is no consumer protection under political advertising. It is protected by the First Amendment. While the Federal Trade Commission and Federal Communication Commission view *political ads* liberally when it comes to "truth in advertising" and "deceptive" practices, there are certain guidelines that must be followed:

Political advertising does not have to adhere to truth in advertising as other types of ads do. They may use deception and misleading information.

If a printed piece is mailed, the name and address of the candidate or representative must be on the ad.

All printed pieces, brochures, fliers and newspaper and magazine ads must indicate who is paying for them.

Radio commercials must contain the candidate's voice and television commercials must show the candidate's face (even a still shot). They must also state who is paying for the commercial.

Candidates for federal office must disclaim their radio and television ad – either at the beginning or end – stating their name and saying "I approve this message." On TV, they must be shown saying it.

Generally, both print and electronic media charge the lowest rate on a rate card for a section or page in the newspaper or magazine, or "day part" in radio or TV. (Congress is considering legislation related to political pricing charged by TV stations.)

As a safety precaution, most media outlets require that payment is made at the time ads are placed.

political, economic, environmental, socio-cultural and technological (PESST) – A framework for viewing the *macroenvironment*.

political, economic and social trends (PEST analysis) – *PEST* is a popular framework for situation analysis, looking at political, economic and social trends. Analyzing these factors can help generate marketing ideas, product ideas, etc. – a framework for viewing the *macroenvironment*.

political, economic, socio-cultural, technological, legal and environmental (PESTLE) – A framework for viewing the *macroenvironment*. See *macroenvironment*.

poly bag – An outside mailing envelope made of polyethylene instead of paper.

polyopoly – A market situation where there are no large sellers but many small ones.

polyopsony – A market situation where there are no large buyers but many small ones.

polysemy – A word that has more than one meaning.

pool (media) coverage – When one news organization covers an event and distributes the information, audio and/or video to other news (media) organizations – including the competition. *Pool coverage* is used, usually, when space is limited.

pop-under ad – Computer ad that appears in a separate window beneath an open window. *Pop-under ads* are concealed until the top window is closed, moved, resized or minimized. See *superstituals*.

pop-up ad – A computer ad that suddenly appears in a separate window on top of content already on-screen. See *superstituals*.

pop-ups – Any computer window that pops-up over the original browser window. See *superstituals*.

popcorn entertainment – Watching a motion picture.

popper – An ad, usually on front page of newspaper attached as if it were a Post-it® – usually at the top on top of the *banner* (*flag*). Also called *dot whack; sticky note*.

population – In marketing research, the total group that a researcher wishes to study. The individuals whose opinions are sought in a survey. The *population* can be as broad as every adult in the United States or as focused as liberal Democrats who live in the Fifth Ward of Chicago and voted in the last election. The sample is drawn to reflect the population. Sometimes called the *universe*.

population characteristics – Variables including age, gender, income, marital status, education, nationality, race, religion, etc. upon which a *population* may be segmented.

porkchop – Half-column picture. Same as *thumbnail*.

195

Techniques to Succeed: How pay-to-play works

1. The politicians in power need money to get re-elected

2. They solicit donations from professional firms that do work for the town (lawyers, engineers, etc.).

3. Professionals feel obliged to contribute large sums to re-election campaigns to get municipal contracts.

4. The money funds expensive campaigns, overwhelming all challengers.

5. Re-elected officials reward contributors with no-bid contracts.

6. The result: Overpriced contracts and higher taxes for residents. Lack of diversity in contractors.

Cherry Hill, N.J. Pay-to-Play Reform Committee

portal – A Web site that often serves as a starting point for a computer user's session. It typically provides such services as search, directory of Web sites, news, weather, e–mail, homepage space, stock quotes, sports news, entertainment, telephone directory information, area maps and chat or message boards. Examples would include Yahoo!® and AOL® .

Porter's five forces – An analytic model developed by Michael E. Porter. The five forces in the analysis of business and industry are – buyers, suppliers, substitutes, new entrants and rivals.

portfolio – The set of products or services which a company decides to develop and market. Also, a collection of published and/or written materials stored and carried in a portable case. In financial circles, a group of investments held by an investor, investment company or financial institution.

portfolio analysis – The systematic evaluation or assessment of a company's businesses or products. Two variables frequently used in the evaluation are *market attractiveness* (including *market growth rate*) and business strength (including *relative market share*). Used to determine which products or services are the most promising and deserving of further investment, and which should be discontinued.

portfolio tests – A method of *pretesting* an advertisement. After looking through a portfolio of different versions of a particular advertisement, respondents, chosen from the target market, are asked to recall in detail those which they can remember.

portmanteau – A word or morpheme that blends two or more words to give a combined mean – for example, *podcast* or *podcasting*.

position charge – An additional fee, usually a percentage of the basic charge, charged to an advertiser that wants to specify where its ad will appear in a publication or at a particular time on radio or television.

position mapping – See *perceptual mapping.*

position paper – A document outlining a cause or an issue and explaining an organization's position on the issue and why – problem, issues (effects), organization's adopted position including the benefits to the audience. (See *The Public Relations Practitioner's Playbook* – Kendall/Hunt – 2008).

positioning – The placement of a company, its products or services in a market category or in relation to its competition. Also, the location a company's web page appears on a search engine after a searcher enters

P

key words to search. Also, the creation of an image for a product or service in the minds of customers, both specifically to that item and in relation to competitive offerings. See *market positioning.*

positioning system (GPS) – A global navigation system based on 24 or more satellites orbiting the earth at an altitude of 12,000 statue miles and providing very precise, worldwide positioning and navigation information 24 hours a day, in any weather. Also called the *NAVSTAR* system.

positive – A photographic image which appears as the original image, as opposed to a *negative* which reverses the black and white.

possession utility – The value given to a product by virtue of the fact that the purchaser has the legal right to own and use it freely.

196

Tips to Succeed: Punctuality – important in the U.S.

While being punctual is not important in other countries, it *is* in the United States. It has a number of definitions – but they all arrive at the same destination – and on time and or deadline – as should you when you have an appointment or other commitment.

Punctuality is exactness – arriving at or before the time of the appointment fully prepared for any eventuality.

post-purchase evaluation – The quick mental assessment of a *low-involvement product* by a consumer after purchase. See *low-involvement product.*

post-purchase satisfaction – The pleasure that a carefully selected *high-involvement product* gives to a consumer after purchase. See *high-involvement product.*

post-testing – Testing the effects of an ad after it has appeared in the media.

postage-paid reply service – A service allowing mailers to use a *lettershop's* postage-paid permit and have the business-reply mail sent there instead of opening their own account with the USPS.

postage stamp pricing – See *uniform delivered pricing.*

postal (going "postal") – Slang term meaning to suddenly become extremely and uncontrollably angry, possibly to the point of violence. The term derives from a series of incidents since 1986 in which United

States Postal Service (USPS) workers shot and killed managers, fellow workers, members of the police and the public.

postal customer local – A USPS approved method for bulk mailing from a government agency to all mail recipients in a municipality or region. Rather than address each piece of mail, mail is addressed: Postal Customer Local, City and State. This is cost saving, but comes with strict regulations. Check with your local U.S. Post Office.

postal walk – A geographical area defined by the post office based on letter carrier routes. When using the post office to distribute unaddressed mail, a *postal walk* is usually the narrowest level of specification you can use to geographically target distribution. (However if, for example, a *postal walk* contains both single family residences and apartment buildings, you can usually choose to have the piece be delivered to just one type of residence.)

poster – An outdoor advertising medium – a *billboard*.

poster panel – An outdoor *billboard* where advertising is displayed on printed paper sheets rather than being painted. The most widely used form of outdoor advertising. Its standard size is approximately 25' x 12' with the image printed on sections of 24 to 30 sheets.

postscript (P.S.) – A note that follows a letter's signature.

potential market – All the individuals and organizations in a particular market who have some level of interest in the product.

potential product – Research reveals a need for a product. It is conceived, designed, tested, etc. and eventually launched.

potentially dangerous taxpayer (PDT) – A classification established by the government to identify an individual who advocates violent

197

Tips to Succeed: Public relations practitioners

- Analyze conditions
- Assess policies
- Inform
- Develop programs
- Make recommendations
- Persuade
- Get people to act

P

protest against the United States or other tax systems. *PDTs* include persons who are active members of groups that advocate violence against IRS employees, or against other federal employees, where advocating such violence could reasonably be understood to threaten the safety of IRS employees and impede the performance of IRS.

Potter Model – An ethical decision-making paradigm first used by Dr. Ralph Potter of the Harvard Divinity School using a four-stage questioning process for making an ethical decision – definition, values, principles and loyalties.

pouring rights – An agreement restaurants and schools have with soft drink and other beverage companies to serve their products. Although the products are paid for, when *pouring rights* are exclusive, discounts and other premiums are given to the "establishments."

power brands – Such national brands as McDonald®, Kellogg's®, Coke®, etc. See *brand champion*.

power lunch – Much like "speed dating." Tables of small groups – six to 10 people – each taking three to five minutes to talk about themselves, their audiences and objectives. Its purpose is to help with *networking*.

pox – Police.

PR Newswire® – An electronic distribution service that provides communications services for public relations and investor relations professionals, such as information distribution and market intelligence. Read more at *www.prnewswire.com*.

PRain – Strategically analyzing the simplest situation as a public relations strategist would – in terms of a goal, objectives, strategies and tactics, which are the components of a PR plan. (Coined by Rowan University student Rosie Braude.)

pre-approach stage – The first stage in the selling process. The stage where a salesperson prospects for new accounts, qualifies them and prepares to make contact with the client.

pre-gaming – A public relations social event (socializing), usually by invitation only, held just before a main event (product launch, banquet, dinner, show, etc.). It could be a cocktail or other type of gathering.

pre-press services – Various steps necessary, up to final printing, to transform original copy and art into the form required for printing.

Services include type setting, galley preparation, negative preparation, cleaning negative, plating, press preparation, etc. Also, all work done between writing and printing – typesetting, layout, proofing, etc.

pre-ticketing – The practice by a *vendor* of placing a tag on each product sold listing its particular style, size, color, etc. *Pre-ticketing* is designed to make re-ordering easier for a reseller.

pre-visualization – Such great artists as Ansel Adams see (envision) the picture (or finished product) before picking up the camera. Talented TV shooters and movie producers use the same concept.

précis — Background information on the news that is being provided in a *video news release (VNR)* or an electronic press kit (EPK).

predatory pricing – A pricing practice where a company hopes to inhibit or eliminate competition by charging lower than normal prices for its products in certain geographic regions. This could be viewed as a risky strategy.

predictive dialing — See *telemarketing services.*

preemptible rate – A usually discounted rate for commercial time or ad space which is sold to an advertiser and is not guaranteed. Time or space may be sold to another advertiser who is willing to pay more for the "preferred time or location" – therefore, the advertiser buying this rate gambles to save money on the spot or space.

preferred position – A position in a printed publication that is thought to attract a higher level of reader attention and is sold at a higher rate; for example, the back cover of a magazine or page three in a newspaper.

preflight check — A final check of a page layout that verifies all fonts and linked graphics are available, that colors are properly defined and that all specs have been met.

premeditation – Carefully planned and executed integrated marketing communication (synergistic) activities to achieve communication objectives.

premium — A free gift offered to a prospect to induce a greater response to the main product or service that is being sold. A *premium* need not be related in any way to the product being offered. A type of sales promotion where merchandise is given free or at a reduced price to purchasers of products or visitors to a store.

P

premium pricing – See *high-price strategy*.

preprint – A reproduction of an advertisement which is viewed before actual publication and is created by an advertiser for special purposes, e.g., to serve as retail displays or to gain support from retailers.

presidential hangover – The residual effects that carry over after a president leaves office.

presorted mail – A form of mail preparation, required to bypass certain postal operations, where the mailer groups the pieces in a mailing by ZIP Code or by carrier route or carrier walk sequence (or other USPS-recommended separation).

press – Term commonly used when discussing members (reporters) or vehicles (newspapers, magazines, radio news or television news) of the media.

press (news) conference – A scheduled presentation to a group of media representatives. Most times, a prearranged gathering of media representatives to answer questions, announce and/or explain a significant and newsworthy subject or event. *News conferences* are considered by public relations practitioners as *special events*.

press (pack) kit (media kit) – A package of information distributed through a firm or organization's public relations office to media outlets. Kits typically include news releases, features, fact sheets, biographies, backgrounders, histories, photos, captions, quote sheets, op-ed pieces and any other information deemed important to the media.

198 Techniques to Succeed: An effective public relations planning rule

Generally, a campaign will have only one goal. That goal may have several objectives associated with it. Each objective could have a number of strategies, although experts believe the strategies (messages) should be limited so that audiences remember them. However, the number of tactics that can be developed for a given strategy is almost infinite [certainly, there are many ways to deliver the message(s)]. A campaign is a premeditation to act.

press office – Handles all media inquiries and distributes all strategic messages and news releases to the media on behalf of an organization. It is either an in-house function or outsourced to a PR firm.

press (media or news) release – Information written by an organization and distributed to media outlets for publication. News information written by an organization and distributed to the media, with the hope that they will use it as the basis of a news story. (The term is often used interchangeably with *media release*, however a *media release* can imply a wider distribution — to all media outlets. *Press release* and *news release* are virtually synonymous.)

press (media) tour– Often broader than a tour of just the press, it is a series of interviews held in the offices of publication editors, industry analysts and/or other industry influencers rather than in a firm or organization's office.

pressure group – Any group of individuals who work together to exert an influence upon the decision-making of a company to achieve some specific outcome.

pressure selling – Also called high pressure selling – a selling approach in which the salesperson attempts to control the sales interaction and pressure the customer to make a purchase.

prestige builder – The highest-priced item in a product line. See *product line*; *traffic builder.*

prestige pricing – A pricing strategy in which prices are set at a high level, recognizing that lower prices will inhibit sales rather than encourage them and that buyers will associate a high price for the product with superior quality. Also called *image pricing.* See *customary pricing*; *price lining*; *psychological pricing.*

prestige products – Items of superior quality – high status merchandise.

pretesting – A preliminary survey of a small sample to determine if the *questionnaire* is properly drawn. The testing of a *questionnaire*, advertisement, etc. on respondents selected from the target market before using it in a full-scale research study, campaign, etc. See *questionnaire pre-testing.*

pretexting – Individuals who may or may not know you personally calling firm for information about you on the pretext that they are you.

price – The value agreed on by the buyer and the seller in an exchange of products and/or services – one of the original four controllable variables (with *product, promotion* and *place*) of the *marketing mix*. See *marketing mix.*

price adjustments – *Allowances, discounts*, etc. granted by a seller to meet the requirements or circumstances of specific buyers.

price band – The range where a product can be priced as dictated by competitive intensity (and *supply and demand*) and the perceived value of the product to consumers.

price brand – See *fighting brand.*

price bundling – A pricing strategy where various products sold to a customer together are offered at a price less than the sum of the prices of the products sold individually. (For example, washer and dryer; computer and printer).

price ceiling – A price, usually imposed by law, above which market prices are not permitted to rise. Also called a ceiling price. See *price floor.*

price competition – A competitive situation where price is used as the major means of differentiating the product of one firm from that of a rival. See *non-price competition.*

price cycle – The regular, periodic fluctuation in the price of a product, especially of an agricultural product, owing to increase or decrease in its supply.

price deal – A temporary reduction in the price of a product.

price discounting – See *discount.*

price discrimination – A pricing strategy, generally illegal, where a seller charges different prices to marketing intermediaries for the same product. See *differential pricing.*

price-elastic segments – Segments of the market that are more responsive to price changes than other segments of the market. See *price elasticity.*

price elasticity (of demand) – Buyers' sensitivity to price. It is measured by the percentage change in quantity demanded that results from a percentage change in price. The change in demand relative to a change in price for a product or service. See *price inelasticity.*

199

"It's not the plan; it's the planning."

Gen. Dwight D. Eisenhower

price fixing – Generally illegal, it is the agreement or collusion between competitors to maintain certain fixed price levels to avoid competition. See *horizontal price fixing*; *vertical price fixing*.

price floor – A price, usually imposed by law, below which market prices are not permitted to go below. (Many states regulate minimum prices for milk.) Also called a *floor price*. See *price ceiling*.

price gouging – A monopolistic pricing technique where the seller takes advantage of the lack of competition by charging unusually high prices relative to a product's cost.

price incentives – A common form of sales promotion where price reductions are offered to consumers to encourage them to buy a particular product earlier or in larger quantity.

price inelasticity – Buyers' insensitivity to price. It is when the percentage change in quantity demanded is less than the percentage change in price that consumers are price-insensitive. See *price elasticity*.

price leader – A firm whose prices set a lead for other firms in the industry to follow.

price leadership – A situation which occurs when one or a few companies – usually larger companies – are consistently the first to institute price changes.

price lining – Pricing different products in a product line at various price points, depending on size and features, to make them affordable to a wider range of customers – good, better, best. (Sears has been using price lining for years.) See *customary pricing*; *line pricing*; *prestige pricing*; *psychological pricing*. Also, targeting a specific market segment based on price. A retailer that practices *price lining* only carries goods that sell within a defined price range.

The ABCs of Strategic Communication

P

price look up (PLU) – Tiny stickers (*PLUs*) placed on fruits and vegetables to assist with pricing at checkout. Being replaced with *tattoos*.

price objection – An objection raised by a prospective buyer on the grounds of price, credit terms, discounts, allowances, freight charges, etc. the seller (agency or retailer – it is that broad) realizes it is the most that can related to the cost of a product offered by a salesperson.

price packs – A type of sales promotion where consumers are offered a reduction in the regular price of a product. The amount of the reduction is usually marked, or "flagged," prominently on the label or package; also called a "cents-off" deal.

price point – A point where be charged for a product or service.

price sensitivity – See *price elasticity*.

price space – The price difference between items in a *product line*. Having the right amount of price space is often critical as too little space may confuse buyers and too much space may leave gaps which can be exploited by competitors. See *product line*.

price-taker – Any firm unable to influence the general level of product prices by altering the quantity of the product produced. *Price-takers* are sometimes also referred to as *quantity adjusters* as their chief decision is to adjust the amount they produce to a given price. See *perfect competition*. An example would be if a company sells water, which is supplied by hundreds of firms and utilities. If the firm decides to set the price of a gallon of your water at $8, your firm will likely sell far less because this product is readily available elsewhere for a much cheaper price.

price-value relationship – The connection that consumers make between price and quality. Products with a higher price are commonly perceived to be of better quality.

price wars – A conflict situation likely to occur in industries where products cannot be differentiated. A decrease in price by one company will attract a large number of customers to it, forcing other companies to retaliate by cutting the price even further.

pricing – Marketing activity concerned with the setting of prices for new products and the adjustment of prices for existing products.

pricing strategy – A firm's decision-making concerned with setting prices that will attract the *target market* and allow profit objectives to be met.

primacy/recency – The last thing said is the most remembered. In essence, "last in, first out." See *recency/primacy.*

200 Techniques to Succeed: Plan before you publish

- Save time and misunderstanding by creating a design brief or *thumbnail(s)*
  - Clarify your objectives
  - Provide designers (if you use them) with key organization points

A number of other considerations fall under *production*:
- Choosing the right paper
  - Weight, texture and size affects look and feel
  - Paper can account for up to half the job's cost
  - Seek printer's advice
  - Ask how printer purchases, uses and charges for paper
  - Use printer's advice to limit waste and save money

- Choosing colors
  - Increases readership
  - Adds cost
  - Spot color is less expensive than process color because the color separation work is less tedious.

- Folding
  - Publications should be designed with folding and binding in mind
  - Think in terms of "signatures" (a folded sheet containing 4, 8, 12, 16 and so on, pages that are folded to form a part of a book or pamphlet. Also called a "section.")

- Choosing the proper binding
  - Plan binding before printing
    - Saddle stitch
    - Side wire
    - Spiral
    - Perfect (book)

  - Consider margins, staples, etc.

  - Ask whether it will be done in-house

P

primary audience – The people who will use the information you are providing – public relations strategic message, advertisement, commercial, etc. – to make a decision.

primary advertising – Advertising intended to create demand for a class or category of product rather than for a brand. See *generic advertising; institutional advertising; pioneering advertising; product advertising.*

primary data – Information obtained directly from first-hand sources by means of such research as surveys, observation or experimentation. See *secondary data.*

primary definers – Powerful groups in society who have greater access to the media and therefore a greater influence over the media's decision to carry certain stories. For comment on politics, for example, the media will consult college political science or public relations professors, for comment on crime, law and justice professors, for comment on economic policy, they might consult business leaders or professors at such colleges and universities as the Wharton School. Such people are *primary definers.*

primary demand – Demand for a product class rather than for a particular *brand* within the class. For example, luxury cars or leather coats.

primary demand advertising – Advertising designed for the generic product category, as opposed to selective demand advertising. See *generic advertising; institutional advertising; pioneering advertising; product advertising.*

primary election – Held to choose a political party's candidates for office. Precedes the *general election.*

primary packaging – A product's immediate container or wrapper. See *secondary packaging; shipping packaging.*

primary research – New (original) research study. Research you do yourself.

prime time – The broadcast periods viewed or listened to by the greatest number of persons and for which a station charges the most for air time. In television, the hours are usually 8 to 11 p.m. E.S.T. (7 to 10 p.m. C.S.T.). In radio, morning drive is prime time and depending on the station and the market, it is usually 6 to 10 a.m. or 5 to 9 a.m.

principle of integrating interests – A technique used in selling where the salesperson, knowing the buyer's personal interests or buying motives, places emphasis on these in the presentation rather than on the features or benefits of the product. A major ingredient in *relationship marketing.*

print campaign – The use of newspapers, magazines and other publications to communicate strategic messages and/or create a strong brand, promote a product launch or reinforce what customers already believe to be true — both through advertising and promotion. An effective print campaign also reaches out to convince consumers who haven't yet used a product or service. All of ads and public relations *pieces* must be strategically designed to project a consistent corporate look and feel.

print media – Newspapers, magazines or other printed news publications.

Privacy Leadership Initiative (PLI) – A partnership of CEOs from 15 corporations and nine business associations using research to create a climate of trust that will accelerate acceptance of the Internet and the emerging information economy, both online and offline, as a safe and secure marketplace. Read more at *www.understandingprivacy.org.*

privacy policy – A statement about what information is being collected, how it will be used and how an individual can access his/her own data collected. It should also contain information on how the individual can opt-out and what security measures are being taken by the parties collecting the data.

private brand – A *brand* owned by a wholesaler, retailer, dealer or other merchant. Also called a *private label.* Many retail department store chains use private brands to accomplish mezzanine pricing – offering items in a product line that fall between higher and lower priced goods in the same product category. See *manufacturer's brand; mezzanine marketing; sub-brand.*

private carrier – Any form of transport operated by an independent organization and used for the shipment of goods. See *common carrier; contract carrier.*

private label – See *private brand.*

private treaty – A market agreement arranged by a buyer and seller in private negotiation.

privatization – The conversion of a publicly held (stock publicly sold) firm or organization to a private enterprise. Or, when a government-owned entity is sold to an individual or an investment group.

201

Techniques to Succeed: Maslow's Theory of Motivation

Human needs arranged into five categories in ascending order:

- Physiological needs
- Safety needs
- Belongingness and love needs
- Esteem needs
- Self-actualization needs.

Abraham Maslow - Human Psychologist -1954

P

prize – Barters of merchandise given as prizes on television or radio shows in exchange for mentions of the *brand* names of the merchandise donated.

pro bono — Services performed free of charge – usually by a public relations practitioner or other professional – for a charity or other nonprofit organization.

pro forma – Some activity performed as a formality or a document provided in advance of an action or activity.

proactive marketing strategies – Marketing activities, which anticipate competitive action and attempt to delay it. Also know as *offensive strategies*. See *reactive marketing strategies*.

proactive PR – Aggressive public relations strategies that strive to anticipate events, circumstances or situations, often through the execution of effective, well thought-out contingency plans.

probabilistic models – A statistical tool where the probability that an event will occur again is estimated using historical data. For example, in *sales forecasting*, past purchasing behavior is used to estimate the degree of probability with which consumers will purchase the same item again.

probability sample – A sample where each individual within a total population has exactly the same chance of being chosen. Also known as a scientific sample or a *chance survey*.

problem children – See *question marks*.

problem situation model – A model of a problem situation faced by a decision-maker, constructed (often by a marketing researcher) to get as clear a picture as possible of the problem. A *problem situation model* typically includes a description of the desired outcomes, the relevant variables and the relationships of each of the variables to the outcomes.

problem statement – A brief summary of the problem situation written in present tense describing the situation and the general goal(s) of the program.

problem-solving approach – An approach to selling where the salesperson works with the buyer to evaluate alternative solutions to a problem and to select the best solution. A major ingredient of *relationship marketing* because it is intended to build long-term relationships with clients. Also called *depth selling*.

process audit – *Third party validation* of internal control processes associated with measurement. *Audits* are commonly used to evaluate public relations programs and/or overall communication output and effectiveness of firms and organizations. See *audit*.

process colors – Four basic inks – cyan, magenta, yellow and black *(CMYK)* – mixed together to produce a full range of colors found in four-color printing. The use of all four colors primarily in photographs – a special printing process that enables you to employ high-quality photos and illustrations.

process evaluation – Measuring the effectiveness of media and non-media efforts to get the desired message out to the target audience.

process materials – A classification of goods bought by organizations for incorporation into a product. Usually, the *process materials* cannot be recognized or identified in the finished product.

procurement costs – The costs involved in reordering an inventory item. The costs include processing and transmitting the order as well as the cost of the item itself.

producer – The person in charge of all the arrangements for a commercial, including settings, casting, arranging for music and handling budgets and quotes (bids).

product – A bundle of need-satisfying tangible and intangible attributes offered to a buyer by a seller. It could also be the result of work or thought (a magazine article). The *product* is always primary whether it

P

be the original *4 Ps of Marketing* or *Litwin's 9 Ps of Marketing*. Delivering a *product* that fulfills the promise and more is an integral part of branding. See *core product*.

product advertising – Advertising where a company pays to promote a particular good or service.

product attributes – Distinctive tangible and intangible features of a *product* that convey its value to a user.

product audit – A systematic appraisal of a firm's product mix to evaluate its strengths and weaknesses and to assess the available opportunities.

product-based competitors – Firms or organizations that market the same or similar products and compete for market share. For example, Coke® and Pepsi®, Dell® and Gateway®.

202 Tips to Succeed: A dozen tips to produce top publications

1. Never lose sight of your audience
2. Know the purpose of your publication
3. Have your design enhance the message, not obscure it
4. Be judicious in use of color
5. Use photographs well
6. Don't print over designs unless you are certain it will enhance the product
7. Avoid using too many type faces in the same publication
8. Design your publication for different types of readers
9. Use informative headlines
10. Avoid large tinted or screened boxes
11. Avoid a layout that looks "busy"
12. Read your writing aloud and determine if it sounds conversational

product-based marketing organization – A marketing structure of an organization where staff specialists have responsibility for various products of the organization (rather than for particular markets). This is considered most appropriate when customer needs are differentiated by product rather than by geographic market. See *market-based marketing organization*.

product bundling – Attaching (literally or figuratively) more than one product for a sale. This is very common for digital *products*, books and other products where the profit margins are considered low.

product category – The specific generic attributes that place a good or service in a classification. For example, Fruit 2 O® is a brand name. The *product category* to which it belongs is bottled water.

product concept – See *product orientation*.

product definition – A stage in the new product development process where concepts are translated into actual products for additional testing based on interactions with customers.

product demo – A physical run-through of a product or service by a company representative (usually to analysts or members of the media). The objective is to get positive news coverage.

product depth (of line) – See *product line length*.

product development – A growth strategy where the firm develops new products for existing markets.

product-differentiated marketing – A marketing philosophy where the seller views the market as a homogeneous whole (a member possesses the same *demographic* or *psychographic* characteristics), and produces two or more products for it that are different from its competitors. The products, differing in attributes (price, style, quality, etc), are designed to offer variety rather than to satisfy the needs and wants of different market segments and appeal to the market as a whole. See *mass marketing*; *target marketing*.

product-differentiated marketing – Enhance product distribution by defining the *product*, including target markets, product concepts, features and benefits to be delivered, positioning strategy, price points, etc. before moving the product to consumers.

P

product differentiation – A strategy, which attempts (through innovative design, packaging, positioning, etc.) to make a clear distinction between products serving the same market segment.

product differentiation advantage – A strategy that shows why a firm or organization's products are unique or superior to a competitor's.

product elimination – The decision to drop a product (for example, in the *decline* or *withdrawal* stage of its *product life cycle*) to use the costs associated with it to enhance profits or to release resources that could be more effectively used in other ways.

product extension – The introduction of a product that is known to the company but which has features or dimensions that are new to consumers. Three types of product extensions are possible – revisions, additions and repositioning. For example, Coke-Cola® adding Cherry Coke®, Diet Coke®, etc. See *innovation*; *new product Duplication*.

product failure – A product that does not meet management expectations in the marketplace.

product flanking – A competitive marketing strategy where a company produces its brands in a variety of sizes and styles to gain shelf space and inhibit competitors.

product form competitors – Firms offering slightly different variants of the same basic product. For example, Vlasic Pickles® offering pickle products in different sizes and shapes; Dell® computer offering laptops with slightly different features.

product item – A product variant with its own distinctive attributes (price, packaging, etc.); also called a *stock-keeping unit* and a *stock-taking unit*.

product knowledge – Detailed knowledge of a product's features and benefits required by a salesperson to persuade a prospect to purchase.

product leveraging – See *brand leveraging*.

product liability – The responsibility imposed by legislation on a manufacturer to warn consumers appropriately about possible harmful effects of a product, to foresee how it might be misused, etc. For example, disclaimers that must be used by pharmaceutical companies to assure consumers are informed of effects or possible reaction.

product life cycle – A concept which draws an analogy between the span of a human life and that of a product, suggesting that, typically, a product's life consists of a sequence of five stages – *introductory*, *growth*, *maturity*, *decline* and *withdrawal*. The concept is used as a tool to form marketing strategies appropriate to each of the stages. Also, the history of a product from its introduction to its eventual decline and withdrawal. See *Techniques to Succeed* – No. 261

product line (or just line) – A group of products manufactured or distributed by a firm or organization. A group of closely related products with similar attributes or target markets. Examples would include Campbell's® soups, Gillette® razors and blades and Bic® pens. See *line*.

product line brand name – A brand name applied to several products within a product line (Campbell's® soups; Coke®). See *product line*; *individual brand name*; *family brand*; *corporate branding*.

203

Tips to Succeed:
Planning ahead

When planning…

!sdrawkcab kniht*

*Think backwards!

product line expansion segmentation strategy – One of four possible *segmentation strategies* available to a firm in relation to the segment or segments it aims to target. One strategy in a *product line expansion segmentation approach* is for a firm to offer a number of products to one segment. See *segmentation strategies*; *concentrated segmentation strategy*; *market segment expansion strategy*; *differentiated segmentation strategy*.

P

product line extension – Adding depth to an existing *product line* by introducing new products in the same product category (more flavors of a soft drink; Hershey's® Milk Chocolate and Hershey's® with Almonds). *Product line extensions* give customers greater choice and help to protect the firm from a flanking attack by a competitor. See *product line*; *product line depth*; *product line stretching*.

product line featuring – A strategy where certain items in a *product line* are given special promotional attention, either to boost interest (at the lower end of the line) or image (at the upper end). See *product line*.

product line filling – Introducing new products into a *product line* at about the same price as existing products. An example would be Dell® offering a variety of computers, closely priced, but with features that might appeal to one market segment and not another. See *product line*.

product line length – The number of different products in a product line. See *product line*.

product line manager – The person responsible for all aspects of a product once production begins through the advertising, public relations, promotion and other aspects of the marketing mix to help assure that *synergy* is achieved.

product line modernization – A strategy where items in a *product line* are modified to suit modern styling and tastes and re-launched. See *product line*.

product-line pricing (price lining) – The setting of prices for all items in a product line involving the lowest-priced product price, the highest price product and price differentials for all other products in the line. Similar to *price lining* – pricing different products in a product line at various price points, depending on size and features, to make them affordable to a wider range of customers – good, better, best. (Sears has been using price lining for years.) See *customary pricing; line pricing; prestige pricing; psychological pricing*.

product line pruning – Reducing the depth of a product line by deleting less profitable offerings in a particular product category. See *product line*.

product line retrenchment – Reducing the width of a product mix by decreasing the diversity of items offered across product categories. An example would be General Motors eliminating the Oldsmobile brand and Campbell's dropping the Franco American brand in favor of carrying the same line under the Campbell's brand. See *product line; product line retrenchment; product mix width*.

product line stretching – Introducing new products into a product line. See *product line; downward stretching; two-way stretching; upward stretching*.

product management – Assigning specific products or brands to be managed by single managers within a public relations or an advertising agency.

product management system – A system which ensures that total marketing control of a product line or brand rests with the person who has profit responsibility for it.

product manager – An individual given responsibility for the planning and coordinating of a firm or organization's marketing activities related to a single *product, product line* or *market.*

product mix – The variety of distinct *product lines* and items manufactured or distributed by a firm or organization. See *product item; product line.*

product mix consistency – The degree of how closely related (features and possible benefits) *product lines* are in the *product mix.* See *product line; product mix.*

product mix width – The number of distinct *product lines* manufactured or distributed by a firm or organization. See *product line; product mix.*

product modification – Any substantial change made to the attributes (size, shape, color, style, price, etc.) of a product. Modification of a product is usually done in an attempt to revitalize it to increase demand or reestablish its position among the competition.

product objection – An *objection* by a prospective buyer to the quality or characteristics of the goods offered by a salesperson. See *objections.*

product organization – The deployment of a firm's sales force or the organization of its public relations and/or marketing activities so that a separate division is responsible for each of its major products or product groups. See *organizational structure.*

product orientation – A management philosophy, concept, focus or state of mind which emphasizes the quality of the product rather than the needs and wants of the target market. It is telling consumers what they *need* to hear rather than what they *want* to hear. The orientation assumes that consumers will favor products that offer the most quality, performance and features and that the organization's objectives will be achieved by repetition of the strategic message.

product petrification – Used to describe the small but persistent demand by loyal customers for a declining product. See *product life cycle; decline stage.*

P

204

Techniques to Succeed: Fly with less 'turbulence'

KEY TRAVEL TIPS

• Fly early. The atmosphere needs time to heat up to produce the severe weather that tends to hit later in the day.

• Select nonstop flights. Consider connecting thru airports other than major hubs.

• Avoid flights that are chronically delayed.

• Confirm your reservation and flight status in advance.

Following these tips will help you reduce your wait time at the security checkpoint.

BEFORE THE AIRPORT

• Do not pack or take prohibited items to the airport.

• Place valuables such as jewelry, cash and laptop computers in **carry-on baggage only**. Tape your business card to the bottom of your laptop.

• Avoid wearing clothing, jewelry and accessories that contain metal. Metal items may set off the alarm on the metal detector.

• Avoid wearing shoes that contain metal or have thick soles or heels. Many types of footwear will require additional screening even if the metal detector does not alarm.

• Put all undeveloped film and cameras with film in your carry-on baggage. Checked baggage screening equipment will damage undeveloped film.

• Declare firearms & ammunition to your airline and place them in your checked baggage.

• Do not lock your baggage.

• Do not take lighters or prohibited matches to the airport.

• Do not pack wrapped gifts and do not take wrapped gifts to the checkpoint.

AT THE AIRPORT

Each adult traveler needs to keep available his/her airline boarding pass and government-issued photo ID until exiting the security checkpoint. Due to different airport configurations, at many airports you will be required to display these documents more than once.

- Place the following items *in* your carry-on baggage or in a plastic bag prior to entering the screening checkpoint:
  - Mobile phones
  - Keys
  - Loose change
  - Money clips
  - PDA's (personal data assistants)
  - Large amounts of jewelry
  - Metal hair decorations
  - Large belt buckles
- Take your laptop and video cameras with cassettes *out* of their cases and place them in a bin provided at the checkpoint.

Take *off* all outer coats, suit coats, jackets and blazers.

www.tsa.gov/public/interapp/editorial/editorial_1254.xml

P

product placement (embedded advertising) – Also referred to as *brand* (product) integration. Advertisers seamlessly blending their products with editorial content – both electronically and in print, which some view as a violation of "church and state" (so to speak). It is the paying for the use of a product or service (easily distinguishable) within a television or radio program, a film or in a magazine article. The placement may be visual or verbal. A most visible example was seen in the motion picture "Cast Away," which featured FedEx®.

product portfolio – The mix of products manufactured or distributed by a company. See *product mix; product mix width.*

product portfolio analysis – An examination of each of the products manufactured or distributed by the company to assess future marketing strategies. See *Boston Consulting Group Advantage Matrix.*

product position map – A tool (matrix or paradigm) used in comparing consumer perception of the differences between products or brands. Consumers are asked to mark the particular location of a product or brand on a two-dimensional "map" or grid, where the axes of the map are attributes felt by consumers to be important. See *perceptual mapping.*

product positioning – A marketing activity intended to place a product into a desired competitive position in a market and to have the target audience perceive it as intended. The consumer perception of a product or service as compared to its competition. See *market positioning.*

product positioning strategy – Marketing decisions and actions intended to create a particular place for a product in the market and in the minds of consumers. A *product positioning strategy* may attempt to differentiate a marketing offer from a competitor's or to appear similar to it.

product-push approach – An approach to the generation of new product ideas where a company's strengths rather than market needs are given prime emphasis. See *demand-pull approach.*

product recall – The advertised request by a company that a product be returned to it by those who have already purchased it. *Product recalls* may be voluntary or ordered by a federal agency when it is deemed a product may be unsafe or unreliable.

product-related segmentation – A method of identifying consumers by the amount of product usage, usually categorized *demographically* or *psychographically.*

product strategy – The element of a firm's decision-making concerned with developing the most appropriate products for its target market(s).

product testing – Exposing consumers to a new product, in final or prototype form, so they might compare it to their usual brand and rate it. The results of product testing will help the company decide whether further evaluation of the product in test markets is desirable – and eventually, whether the product should be marketed. See *concept development and testing; new product development.*

product variant – A product variant with its own distinctive attributes (price, packaging, etc.); also called a *stock-keeping unit* and a *stock-taking unit.* See *product item.*

product warranty – See *warranty; express warranty; implied warranty.*

production – In public relations and advertising, the process of physically preparing the advertising idea into a print or broadcast advertisement – creative conception to finished product.

production goods – A classification of industrial goods. Goods purchased by industrial firms for use in the manufacture of their finished products. See *industrial product classes.*

production orientation – A management philosophy, concept, focus or state of mind which emphasizes production techniques and unit-cost reduction rather than the needs and wants of the target market. It's a philosophy that assumes that consumers will favor products that are the most readily available and at the most affordable prices and that a concentration on efficient production and distribution will help achieve the firm's objectives.

professional advertising – Advertising directed toward professionals such as doctors, dentists, lawyers and pharmacists, etc., who are in a position to promote products to their patients, clients or customers.

professional services – The services of individuals or companies that are accredited by professional bodies, such as public relations practitioners (APR), accountants (CPA) and financial planners (CFP).

professionalize – Adhering to *key message points*. Used by political candidates, CEOs and corporate spokespeople. Points are repeated so often, that even if they aren't true, the sender believes it is true. David Brooks of the *New York Times* says, "some politicians say it so many times, they begin to believe it and even say the same things in off-the-record conversations."

profiling – Used in determining the importance of audiences. *Profiling* is a four-step process – identifying, profiling, segmenting/fragmenting and ranking audiences. *Profiling* is best accomplished through *demographics, psychographics* and *geodemographics. Profiling* is an important step, because it helps in determining where best to spend resources – both money and *mind share.*

profit – Profit is an accounting concept, normally the financial bottom line of the Income Statement, which is also called a *profit and loss statement.* Start with sales, subtract all costs of sales and all expenses, and that produces profit before tax. Taxes must be subtracted to determine net profit.

profit and loss statement – An accounting statement showing income, expenditure and profit over a given period.

profit center – A division of an organization with responsibility for generating its own income and with accountability for profits.

Profit Impact of Marketing Strategies (PIMS) – A U.S. database supplying such data as environment, strategy, competition and internal data with respect to 3000 business. This data can be used for benchmarking purposes. Read more at *www.cambridge.org/uk/catalogue/ catalogue.asp?isbn=0521840538.*

profit maximization – Earning the most profit possible, realizing that profit is the difference between a firm's total revenue and its total cost to produce a product – and that total revenue is the amount of income earned by selling products.

profit maximizers – Firms that minimize their costs to achieve a stronger bottom line. Not for profits and non-profit organizations are encouraged to emulate for profits considered to be *profit maximizers*.

profit objective in pricing – Setting prices with short-run profits rather than long-term market share in mind. Among the *objectives* is generating cash.

profit or loss – Also called a *profit and loss statement*. An income statement is a financial statement that shows sales, cost of sales, gross margin, operating expenses and profits or losses. Gross margin is sales less cost of sales, and profit (or loss) is gross margin less operating expenses and taxes. The result is profit if it's positive, loss if it's negative.

profit sharing – A compensation system where employees are awarded a share of the company's profits to encourage increased productivity.

profitability control – Marketing effort intended to assess the level of profitability of each product in the portfolio, of each market segment, of each marketing channel, etc. Related production, public relations and advertising expenses must be considered and monitored.

ProfNet – A service of *PR Newswire*® that distributes media queries to various audiences to connect writers and reporters with expert sources. Read more at *www.prnewswire.com*.

program delivery (rate) – Percentage of a sample group of people tuned in to a particular television or radio program at a particular time.

program evaluation and review technique (PERT) – A quantitative technique used as a managerial tool in planning and controlling complex programs. Common use has been made of *PERT*, originally introduced for use in the aerospace industry, in the coordinating, timing and scheduling of the many activities in the new product development process.

program preemptions – Interruptions in local or network programming usually caused by special events.

progressive commission – A sales commission system where the commission rate increases as the salesperson sells more goods. See *regressive commission*.

205

Techniques to Succeed:
The power of the personal note

The art of writing personal notes is sadly disappearing. A personal note is one of the best ways to connect and re-connect with others. There are several kinds of notes to let people know you're thinking of them.

1. Thank-You Notes are one of the least expensive and most effective networking tools. You can send them to acknowledge:
   • Compliments you receive
   • Gifts given to you
   • Referrals
   • Time and consideration

2. FYI Notes help you keep in touch at any time. You can send many things, such as clippings or articles. This lets them know that you:
   • Thought of them when you read it
   • Know what they are interested in
   • Care about their business

3. Congratulations notes are a perfect opportunity to let someone know you are cheering them on. You can give these out on many occasions:
   • Promotions
   • Awards or Honors
   • Anniversaries

4. Nice Talking to (or, Meeting) You Notes help a person to remember you fondly. You can send these out after several events:
   • Meetings
   • Chance encounters
   • Phone conversations

The post office reports that only four percent of mail is personal correspondence. This means that now, more than ever, a handwritten envelope will stand out among the piles of bills and advertisements. A note will get someone's attention, let them know you care about them, remind them of you, and, ultimately, strengthen your network to help you succeed.

Andrea Nierenberg - Author - *Nonstop Networking* (Capital Books)
www.mybusinessrelationships.com

progressive discipline – A process for dealing with job-related behavior that does not meet expected and communicated performance standards. The primary purpose for *progressive discipline* is to assist the employee to understand that a performance problem or opportunity for improvement exists.

progressive indexing – An economic term used to illustrate how some individuals will benefit from long-term changes while others will not.

206 Techniques to Succeed: Political Advertising

The purpose of *political* ads is to persuade people to vote for a candidate, or in some cases, an issue. While the Federal Trade Commission and Federal Communication Commission view *political* ads liberally when it comes to "truth in advertising" and "deceptive" practices, there are certain guidelines that must be followed:

• Political advertising does not have to adhere to truth in advertising as other types of ads do. They may use deception and misleading information.

• If a printed piece is mailed, the name and address of the candidate or representative must be on the ad.

• All printed pieces, brochures, fliers, and newspaper and magazine ads must indicate who is paying for them.

• Radio commercials must contain the candidate's voice and television commercials must show the candidate's face (even a still shot). They must also state who is paying for the commercial.

• Candidates for federal office must disclaim their radio and television ad – either at the beginning or end – stating their name and saying "I approve this message." On TV, they must be shown saying it.

• Generally, both print and electronic media charge the lowest rate on a rate card for a section or page in the newspaper or magazine, or "day part" in radio or TV. (Congress is considering legislation related to political pricing charged by TV stations.)

• As a safety precaution, most media outlets require that payment is made at the time ads are placed.

M. Larry Litwin, APR, Fellow PRSA - *The Public Relations Practitioner's Playbook*
(Kendall/Hunt – 2008)

President George W. Bush used *progressive indexing* to support proposed changes in Social Security. For example, in calling for Social Security reform, President Bush said he wanted to protect lower-income workers' benefits. To do so and improve the system's finances, he endorsed changing the way starting Social Security benefits are calculated for middle- and high-income workers. The *progressive indexing* would lower future benefits for middle- and high-income workers relative to what is currently promised. Low-income workers, meanwhile, would see no change in their promised benefits.

progressive proofs (progs) – Set of proofs made during the four-color printing process which shows each color plate separately and in combination. Used in color separation whether it be spot color or process color. Also referred to as color proofs.

project fee retainer – A flat fee that a client and public relations practitioner/agency agree on as a monthly or yearly payment for services or a particular project. If it is primarily for a project, it would be a project fee.

promise – A strategic message that uses a benefit statement that looks to the future.

promo – An eye-catching graphic element, usually on "page one" or section front, that promotes an item inside. Also called a *teaser*.

promoter of justice – Devil's advocate (according to Pope John Paul II).

promotion – One of the original four controllable variables (with *product*, *price* and *place*) of the *marketing mix*. All forms of communication other than advertising that call attention to products and services by adding extra values toward the purchase. Includes a number of public relations and *synergistic* techniques and temporary discounts, allowances, premium offers, coupons, contests, sweepstakes, etc. All marketing activities designed to persuade members of a target audience to take a specific action.

promotion manager – An individual within an organization responsible for promotional activities and campaigns. Would report to public relations, marketing director or chief communication officer (CCO).

promotion mix – The communication techniques available to an organization for communication with its *target market* – public relations, advertising, sales promotion, personal selling and publicity. See *Litwin's Nine Ps of Marketing*.

promotional adaptation – A strategy where the same product is sold in different geographic locations but with a unique promotional strategy for some or all of the different locations.

promotional allowance – A price reduction or discount granted by a manufacturer to a member of the marketing channel in return for some form of special promotion of a particular product.

promotional budget – The sum allocated in a particular accounting period for expenditure on promotion.

promotional campaign – A coordinated series of public relations efforts built around a single theme and designed to achieve a specific *objective*.

promotional (consideration) partnership – An alliance between a manufacturer of a product and another company – or television or radio program – for the purposes of promotion. For example, Dell® may form a promotional partnership with Disney Corp.®, agreeing to pay Disney® a fee to display the computer prominently in an upcoming film. See *advertainment; embedded ads; entertainment marketing; movie tie-ins*.

promotional pricing – The temporary pricing of goods and services at lower than normal levels for a special promotional effort.

promotional product – A product imprinted with, or otherwise carrying, a *logo* or promotional message.

promotional stock – Merchandise offered at a reduced price to a reseller for some special promotion.

promotional strategy – The element of a firm's decision-making concerned with choosing the most appropriate mix of public relations, advertising, sales promotion, personal selling and publicity for communication with its target market.

promotional warranty – A *warranty* designed to reduce the perceived financial or performance *risk* that a consumer might consider in purchasing an expensive product. See *warranty; express warranty; implied warranty; protective warranty*.

proof – An impression on paper of type, an engraving or printed copy (galley), for the purpose of checking the accuracy and content of the material to be printed. Copies of type and visuals that eventually become the finished printed product.

207

Techniques to Succeed:
Pricing Strategies

Customary or Traditional – A single, well-known price for a long period of time. Movie theaters and candy manufacturers employ this pricing strategy in the hope that the customer will become less sensitive to price. It's the price that consumers expect to pay for a certain product.

Odd – Strategy of having prices that end in an odd number, as in $5.95, $19.99; sometimes referred to as odd-even pricing.

Line – All products sell for same price. For example, Southwest® Airlines charges the same for all seats on a flight – unlike other airlines.

Psychological – Strategy intended to manipulate the customer's judgment process. Two common forms of psychological pricing are odd pricing ($9.97) and *Prestige Pricing*. There are also psychological price breaks such as – $9.99; $19.99; $24.99; $99.95; etc.

Price lining – The strategy of pricing different products in a product line at various price points, depending on size and features, to make them affordable to a wider range of customers – good, better, best. (Sears® has been using price lining for years; State Farm® Insurance has introduced this strategy.) Also, targeting a specific market segment based on price – a retailer who practices price lining only carries goods that sell within a defined price range.

Prestige or Image – A strategy where prices are set at a high level, recognizing that lower prices might inhibit sales rather than encourage them and that buyers will associate a high price for the product with superior quality – certain cars, appliances and clothing brands.

Value – A strategy where the selling price of a good or service is based on the company's assessment of the highest value of the product to the consumer – what the consumer is willing to pay for it; what the market will bear. Many times, it is predicated on supply and demand.

M. Larry Litwin, APR, Fellow PRSA - *The Public Relations Practitioner's Playbook*
(Kendall/Hunt – 2008)

P

proofread – Carefully reading a document to correct errors.

propaganda – One-sided argument – often used by public relations practitioners as part of their strategic message. Sometimes misunderstood as a negative – but it was originally intended as a positive, persuasive method. The use of ideas, information or opinion for the purpose of furthering or hindering a cause or promoting or denigrating an idea.

PropheSEE® – A research device that combs the Internet to pick up *buzz* about TV programs being developed. Such agencies as Initiative in New York sell their findings to networks, advertisers and ad agencies. The device serves in helping predictions.

proportional sampling – A sampling method used to ensure that a survey contains representatives of each subset in the *population* being studied, according to the proportion of their representation in the universe. For example, if a certain *population* contains 53 percent women, a *proportional sample* would contain 53 percent women.

proposal – Document outlining a proposed public relations or advertising campaign to an existing or potential client.

prospect – A potential customer. See *sales leads*; *suspect*.

prospecting – The first step in the selling process. The activity of seeking out potential customers. See *sales leads*.

prospecting plan – A systematic approach to finding new customers. It could involve the setting aside of time after allowing for calls on existing customers specifically for prospecting.

prostitot – A child who dresses in revealing, adult type fashion. May include hair and makeup styles that are not age appropriate.

protectionism – Trade policies of governments aimed at protecting domestic industries by limiting the volume of imports.

protective warranty – See *warranty*; *express warranty*; *implied warranty*; *promotional warranty*.

protocol – A uniform set of rules. A plan of action which follows a strict format to assure that objectives are met. Also sometimes referred to as research design. The controlling plan for a marketing research study where the methods and procedures for collecting and analyzing the information to be collected are specified. The plan of action follows a strict format to assure that objectives are met.

P

prototype – A sample or early version of a new product made or built specifically for trial and testing before being placed on the market.

prototype testing – The trialing of a sample of a newly developed product on selected consumers from the target market.

proxemic communication – A form of *nonverbal communication* or *body language* where messages are conveyed from one person to another by the changing space that separates them during a conversation. See *facial coding*; *kinesic communication*; *nonverbal communication*; *tactile communication*.

proximity – The distance between lines of type and other items and elements on a page – keeping related information close together.

PR-pie – A public relations process – purpose, research, planning, information, evaluation. First, establish a purpose, then conduct research, craft a plan, communicate with targeted publics, and conduct evaluative research of the process and plan.

prudential – Exercising good judgment or common sense.

psychodrama – A qualitative marketing research technique where respondents are asked to engage in impromptu role-playing exercises intended to have them reveal their feelings about certain products or brands. See *qualitative marketing research*.

psychodrawing – A nonverbal, qualitative marketing research technique where respondents use colors, shapes, symbols, etc. to express their feelings about certain products or brands. See *qualitative marketing research*.

psychographic segmentation – The division of a heterogeneous market into relatively homogeneous groups on the basis of their attitudes, beliefs, opinions, personalities and lifestyles. Sometimes called *state-of-mind segmentation*.

psychographics – A term that describes consumers or audience members on the basis of psychological characteristics initially determined by standardized tests. Psychological characteristics many times are determined by standardized tests. Used for audience segmentation and fragmentation. Any attributes relating to personality, values, attitudes, interests, or lifestyles. They are also called IAO variables (for Interests, Attitudes, and Opinions). Combined with *demographics and geodemographics*, *psychographics* play a key role in strategic planning.

P

psychography – The study of the attitudes, beliefs, opinions, personalities and lifestyles of individuals in a *population*. Includes all psychological variables that combine to share our inner selves and help explain consumer behavior.

psychological discounting – The advertising of a product at a heavily reduced price, as in "Was $39.95, now only $25.00." See *psychological pricing*.

psychological needs – Inner human feelings of deprivation related to an individual's mental well-being. See *needs*; *physiological needs*.

psychological pricing – Pricing techniques intended to manipulate the customer's judgment process. Two common forms of *psychological pricing* are odd pricing ($9.97) and *prestige pricing*. There are also psychological price breaks – $ 9.99; $19.99; $24.99; $99.95; etc. See *odd pricing*.

psychological repositioning – The attempt by a firm to alter the beliefs of prospective buyers about the key attributes of its product offering, especially where the buyers generally underestimate its quality. See *market positioning*; *real positioning*; *repositioning*; *competitive depositioning*.

---

208 Tips to Succeed: New managers: Being boss and friend – but be careful

- **Don't get too close too quickly.** The easiest way to gain approval from employees is to shower them with attention and approach them as friends. But with the right mix, it's possible to be a boss and friend.

- **Be in power with, not over.** When you are in power over them, they feel intimidated and defensive. This means erasing the title and remembering who you were before you walked in your first day as a manager.

- **Find sources of honest feedback. You** have to realize as the new boss that people might try to butter you up. So when you ask your favorite employee what she thinks of your leadership skills and she has nothing but glowing things to say, be skeptical. It can be lonely at the top if you don't latch on to mentors and subordinates who aren't afraid to tell you what they think – for real.

Gannett News Service

psychological risk – See *risk*; *emotional risk*.

psychological segmentation – The separation of consumers into psychological characteristic categories on the basis of standardized tests.

psychological set – A consumer's mind set – his or her positive or negative feelings or predispositions (attitudes) towards a particular brand or company. The consumer's mind set is formed by his or her *needs*, *perceptions* and *attitudes*.

pub – Short for publication.

pub-set – Ads designed and produced for the advertiser by the publication in which they will appear.

public affairs – The process of communicating an organization's point of view on issues or causes to political audiences. The public policy aspect of public relations. Many government agencies refer to public relations as *public affairs*.

public affairs programs – Programming that serves the public interest.

public discourse – Space where citizens gather to deliberate about common issues.

public domain – Any created work the public may copy and use without paying (royalty) fees.

public interest – Matters the media believes the public should be aware of and of which they should be concerned. Read more at *www.pcc.org.uk/index2.html*.

public language – What people are saying about you, your organization or product. See *buzz*.

public opinion – People's beliefs, based on their conceptions or evaluations of something rather than fact. An accumulation of individual opinion on an important matter in public debate affecting the lives of people.

public persona – A company (or personal) identity perceived in a manner that differentiates it from the competition.

public policy environment – That part of a firm's external environment which consists of controversial issues or matters of concern to governments, the media or influential pressure groups. Factors in this environment may have an influence on a firm's decision-making or an impact on its performance.

209

Tips to Succeed:
They call it – Workplace politics

Politics is among this book's author's Nine Ps of Marketing – as in office *politics*. Here are seven tactics for successfully navigating office politics:

1. **Over communicate**. Let people in on what you're working on, or planning to do. For example, if your project affects another department or someone else's responsibilities, it's smart to give those people a heads-up. Nobody likes to be surprised.

2. **Get a mentor**. Look for someone at a higher level, with experience in the organization and who knows the personalities of the "senior team."

3. **Ask open-ended questions**. A lot of business decisions, unfortunately, are made on assumptions. Using open-ended questions, really listening to people's answers and taking notes can help avert making misguided decisions.

4. **Review constantly**. Always compare notes with colleagues and others about what's going on at work – from discussing a new company policy to rehashing what the boss said in a staff meeting. Having everyone on the same page helps organizations move ahead more quickly.

5. **Get buy-in**. This goes hand-in-hand with over communicating. If you're working on a project, get the opinions of staffers it may affect.

6. **Give –and take – due credit**. Give people the credit they're due, and you'll garner the support of your peers. "Credit hogs" are setting themselves up to fail. (While men tend to do a good job of broadcasting their contributions, he said, women often don't give themselves enough credit. So women, acknowledge the work of your peers, but also let management know of your own contributions.)

7. **Keep style in mind**. How you dress influences how you're perceived. Appearance is often the first gauge someone uses to decide whether or not to help you. For women, dress is especially important. (It's an unfortunate fact of life that a man can get away with being pretty badly dressed ... it's more difficult for a woman. A common mistake in attire for both genders, especially among younger workers, is dressing too casually – that includes flip-flops, shorts and shirts that bare your belly.)

public relations (PR) – A management and counseling function that enables organizations to build and maintain relationships with their various audiences through an understanding of audience opinions, attitudes and value. It is planned, deliberate and two way. *Public relations* succeeds when it fills three key roles – as an organizational conscience, as an overseer of the corporate brand and/or reputation, and as a manager of relationships with internal and external audiences. Journalist's definition – the art or science of developing understanding and goodwill between a person, firm or institution and the public.

public relations advertising – Advertising by a corporation that focuses on public interest but maintains a relationship to the corporation's products or agencies. It could be an issue ad or other type of message that contains a great deal of information about an organization. Many times, *advertorials* and *infomercials* are public relations advertising.

public relations advisor – A person who provides public relations guidance (may work inside or outside a PR firm or for the firm or organization being advised.)

public relations audit – A research tool used specifically to describe, measure and assess an organization's public relations activities, and used to provide guidelines for future public relations programming. Can include public opinion surveys, content analysis, program evaluation and recommendations for the future. It is *third party validation* of log activity and/or measurement process associated with public relations activities, which measure results against the plan. Some *audits* evaluate Internet activity/advertising. Activity *audits* validate measurement counts. Process *audits* validate internal controls associated with measurement.

public relations consultant – Independent professional who provides public relations counsel, advice and recommendations.

public relations counsel – A person who provides public relations guidance (may work inside or outside a PR firm or for the firm or organization being advised.)

public relations firm – A company or organization made up of public relations advisors and their support staff.

public relations (PR) in a box – A package of templates developed to help achieve and maintain consistency – one of PRSA's Seven Cs of Communication. The package helps every office, department and branch (school) follow the same look and style in accordance with the company or organization's identity. Also called *inside-the-circle-thinking*. See *template*.

public relations plan – A document that details specific actions to achieve a public relations result. It contains a *goal, objectives, strategies, tactics, tools*, budget, research questions, research actions and a full *situation analysis*. Successful strategic advisors suggest: determine your destination and then plan the journey to get you there.

public relations practitioner – One who practices the public relations profession – a counselor, strategic advisor, strategic evaluator. PR practitioners assess, influence and then manage public opinion. They assess the effectiveness of accountability channels – content, strategy, development.

public relations-to-perception ratio – A control measure used to determine whether the public relations message in a given period was effective based on the perception of that brand, product or service in the marketplace.

public service [advertising] announcement (PSA) – Used to communicate a message on behalf of a cause or non-profit organization (many times in the public interest). The media once provided time and space free. Now, with competition keen for so-called available space and time, non-profits have been forced to turn to corporate dollars to help underwrite even reduced costs.

public service broadcasting – A term difficult to define because broadcast outlets, for the most part, are in business to make money. The term would mean that broadcasting's function is not simply to satisfy commercial interests by giving the public what they want in an attempt to maximize audience figures, but, rather, to inform, educate and entertain the public – the quality being most important. Examples would tie into the Communications Act of 1934, which states that radio and television stations should operate in "the public interest, convenience, or necessity." Coverage of news, current events and public affairs programming should be impartial and some should be during prime time.

publication – Body of information distributed to others – flier, newsletter, brochure, newspaper, magazine, etc.

publicity – Information about a product, service or idea supplied to a news medium without cost.

publicity/media tour – Scheduled publicity appearances in a series of cities or locations with the intent of getting a story in newspapers or on radio and/or television.

publicity photo – Picture and/or graphics that amplify a story.

publics – The various groups in a society which can influence or bring pressure to bear upon a firm's decision making and have an impact on its marketing performance. Groups include the financial *public*, media *public*, government *public*, citizen action *public*, local *public*, general *public* and international *public*.

publisher – The business head (chief executive) of a newspaper organization or publishing house – commonly the owner or the representative of the owner.

publishing platforms – Tools for editing, organizing and publishing Web logs are variously referred to as *content management systems*, *publishing platforms*, *weblog software*, and simply *blogware*.

puffery – A legal exaggeration of praise (using subjective opinions, superlatives and similar techniques not based on objective fact) lavished on a product that stops just short of deception.

puffing – The legitimate practice of making obviously exaggerated claims in advertising. An example would be the *strategic message* "cleaner than clean." The Federal Trade Commission does not find that a deceptive message, because it feels the public should recognize it as an advertising message and not necessarily fact.

pulchritude – Great physical beauty and appeal.

pull promotion – *Pull promotion*, in contrast to *push promotion*, addresses the customer directly with a view to getting them to demand the product, and hence "pull" it down through the distribution chain. It focuses on advertising. See *push promotion*.

pull quote – (*Blurb*) A quotation or statement that is separated (such as by placing it inside a box or between rules) from the rest of a document (brochure, article, white paper, etc). The quote or statement provides information that emphasizes a point in the rest of the document. The quote may be a repetition of one used in the document or it may not appear anywhere else in the document.

pull (communication) strategy – A promotional strategy designed to encourage consumers to ask for a product. The practice of creating interest among potential buyers, who then demand the offering from intermediaries, ultimately "pulling" the offering through the channel. See *push strategy*.

pulp fiction – A paperback book. Derived from paperback books from the earliest days of popularity – when they sold in corner drug stores for 25 cents.

pulsing – Scheduling advertising campaigns in fairly regular bursts followed by periods of relative or complete inactivity. See *continuity*; *flighting*.

pump and dump – A scam where con artists promote shares of a thinly traded company, claiming the price is about to soar. Once demand has driven up the stock price, the scammers dump their shares and pocket the profits. Then the price falls, leaving the investors with big losses.

punchlist – A list of tasks ("to-do" items). In the construction industry, a *punchlist* is the name of a contract document used to organize the completion of a construction project. Some contracts allow the owner to withhold (retain) the final payment to the general contractor as *retainage*.

punk (type) – Ultra condensed type used during the days of letterpress to get more characters into a document.

pupilometrics – A method of advertising research where a study is conducted on the relationship between a viewer's pupil dilation and the interest factor of visual stimuli.

puppy dog close – A closing technique where a salesperson urges an indecisive prospect to take a product home and try it for a short period of time believing that once the product is in the customer's hands, he or she will be unwilling to part with it.

purchase allowance – See *off-invoice allowance*.

purchase cycles – The time periods between purchases of a product, which is important in estimating product or service demand.

purchase intentions – The likelihood that a consumer will buy a particular product resulting from the interaction of his or her need for it, attitude towards it and perceptions of it and of the company which produces it.

purchase laboratory – See *accelerated test marketing.*

purchase probability scale – A tool used in marketing research surveys of buying intentions. Respondents are asked to rate the likelihood of their purchase of a particular product on a scale ranging, for example, from "definitely not" to "certain to buy."

purchasing officer – An individual within an organization responsible for purchasing the goods and services it requires.

purchasing performance evaluation – The establishment of criteria by which the performance of purchasing officers can be assessed and of incentive systems so that good purchasing can be rewarded.

pure competition – A marketing situation where there are a large number of sellers of a product or service, which cannot be differentiated and, therefore, no one firm has a significant influence on price. There are other conditions which might include ease of entry of new firms into the market and perfect market information. Also referred to as *perfect competition* and *atomistic competition*. See *monopolistic competition.*

pure monopoly – A marketing situation where there is only one seller of a product. See *pure competition.*

purging – The process of deleting repeated names when two or more lists are combined.

pursuit intervention technique (PIT) – A term that communication specialists who work with police agencies should be familiar with. Law enforcement officers are taught this technique, which should be used early (up to the first three minutes) in the pursuit of vehicles in high speed chases. Two police vehicles are needed. The first attempts to bump the vehicle being chased on the outside back fender forcing it to "fishtail." The second police vehicle then broadsides the vehicle in pursuit, bringing it to a stop. Police advocate for all chases that they be done at a safe speed and injury free with the goal being suspect apprehension. One of the first jurisdictions using this technique was the Los Angeles Police Department.

push advertising – A promotional (proactive) strategy directed to the trade in an attempt to move the product through the *distribution channel*.

push back – Potential voters being turned off (negative change in behavior) by being exposed to negative ads. See *buy in*.

push money – A direct payment of money offered to the sales force of a reseller by a manufacturer to encourage greater efforts with a particular product or range.

push poll – Considered unethical by most legitimate pollsters (such as Gallup Organization). It is the distribution of information as part of the polling process. It is a political campaign technique where an individual or organization attempts to influence or alter the view of respondents under the guise of conducting a poll. *Push polls* are generally viewed as a form of negative campaigning. *Push polling* has been condemned by the American Association of Political Consultants.

push promotion – Relies on the next link in the distribution chain – a wholesaler or retailer – to "push" out products to the consumer. It relies on sales promotions – such as price reductions and point of sale displays – and other marketing activities.

push-pull strategy – Promotion and/or advertising of a good or service to both resellers and to end-users. Such advertising could be carried by magazines, radio or television.

push strategy – In contrast to *pull strategy*, it is directed toward members of the marketing channel (mainly by means of personal selling) rather than promotion to end-users (mainly by means of advertising, sales promotion and publicity) to facilitate the flow of a good or service from producer to final consumer. Also, directs marketing efforts at resellers, and success depends greatly on the ability of these intermediaries to market the product, often with the help of advertising. The principal emphasis is on personal selling and trade promotions directed toward wholesalers and retailers. See *pull strategy*; *push-pull strategy*.

push survey – Opinion surveys designed to provide information at the same time data is being gathered – communicate a message while asking the questions.

pushing the goal posts back – Raising the bar or increasing the challenge.

put to bed – Printer's term meaning all the pages of an edition are completed and the presses are ready to roll.

pyramid selling – An illegal selling system where members of a sales organization derive their earnings by selling to newly introduced members of the distribution network (who pay a fee to enter). It is called a pyramid because it starts with one seller, who sells to another and then another and the original sellers each get a "cut" of the fee paid by others to join the "network." History shows that early sellers earn much more through selling membership than they do selling product to end-users. **P**

Q factor – A measure of celebrity based on surveys and other research.

Q methodology – Quantitative evaluation – for example, poetic interpretation, perceptions of organizational role, political attitudes, appraisals of health care, experiences of bereavement, perspectives on life and the cosmos, etc. Coined by British physicist/psychologist William Stephenson (1902-1989).

Q&A – An exchange of questions and answers, typically between a single newsmaker and a reporter or a number of members of the media. Also copy in question and answer form – as in verbatim reports of court proceedings.

Q&A/rude Q&A – A document that lists predictions of difficult questions that may be posed to a company spokesperson or other newsmaker, and the best answers the newsmaker can give to answer the questions and meet personal or company objectives.

quadrants – Four equal squares that divide a page.

qualified available market – The individuals and organizations in a particular market that are interested in a product, can afford it and who are not prevented from purchasing it by any access barrier or legal restriction.

qualifying the prospect – Asking questions to discover whether a prospective buyer has a need for the product, can afford it and has the authority to buy the product.

qualitative objectives – *Objectives* which cannot be expressed in quantifiable terms, because they were not established using scientific data. For example, a salesperson might set as an *objective* (in a specific period of time) to acquire certain product knowledge, or the form a close business relationship with the buyer from a major account. See *quantitative objectives*.

qualitative (data) research – Research that attempts to understand how and why people think and behave as they do – not scientifically gathered and usually involves one or only a few issues (unlike *quantitative [data] research*. *Qualitative research* techniques include *focus groups*, in-depth interviews and projection techniques such as free association, psycho-drawing and psychodrama. See *quantitative (data) marketing research*.

210

Tips to Succeed: Don't get caught – Quid Pro Quo

Quid Pro Quo = money exchanged for an official act – expecting something in return for a political donation. Not only is it unethical, but illegal.

Simply put – *someone* gives *something* expecting *something* in return. Politicians call it "pay to play." (See Technique 195.)

quality circles (QCs) – A management technique with its origin in Japanese industry and used in the United States by such corporations as Westinghouse® to increase productivity. *QCs* use groups of autonomous workers, responsible for their own output, who meet together voluntarily to plan their work so that a better-quality product results without delaying the work of other autonomous groups further down the production line.

quality control – An ongoing analysis of operations, to verify that goods or services meet specified standards, or to better answer customer and/or user complaints.

quality controls – Measures taken by organizations to ensure that all legal requirements and consumer expectations of their products are met. Most firms and organizations believe that good product performance, achieved by efficient quality control, helps to ensure that consumers will become repeat purchasers.

quality creep – A phenomenon which works in a counter-productive way – a manufacturer enhances a product over time, but increases its price (because of demand and popularity). Eventually its appeal diminishes and thereby demand drops and market share is lost.

quality modification – Any change made to the quality of a product.

quandary – Dilemma, uncertainty, perplexity.

quantitative objectives – Objectives which can be expressed in specific numerical terms based on scientific research sampling. For example, a salesperson might set as an objective for his or her territory "to increase sales revenue of product 'c' by 'x' percent in one year."

quantitative (data) research – Public relations and advertising research that uses statistics to describe audiences (consumers) – scientifically gathered. The collection of data that can be expressed in numerical terms. Although it usually involves a large number of issues, it concentrates on statistics and other numerical data, gathered through scientific sampling (opinion polls), *customer satisfaction* surveys, etc. See *qualitative research*.

211

Tips to Succeed:
Want to sit at the corporate table?

Don't tell your boss what he/she *wants* to hear – tell him/her what she *needs* to hear!

quantity adjuster – Any firm unable to influence the general level of product prices by altering the quantity of the product produced. Price-takers are sometimes also referred to as *quantity adjusters,* as their chief decision is to adjust the amount they produce to a given price For example, a company sells water, which is supplied by hundreds of firms and utilities. If the firm decides to set the price of a gallon of your water at $8, your firm will likely sell far less because this product is readily available elsewhere for a much cheaper price. See *price-taker*; *perfect competition*.

quantity discount – A price reduction made to encourage a purchaser to order a larger quantity than would otherwise have not been purchased.

quantum leap – Significant advance in method, information or knowledge.

QuarkXPress® – A computer program used to process type and design page layout. It allows the user to create high-quality publications – often referred to as the "industry standard" for publishing.

query – A request for information. It could be to pitch a news or magazine article, or, when using a computer, a key word asked of a search engine like Google® or Yahoo®. See *query letter*.

query letter – A letter sent to a publication asking whether the publication would be interested in receiving a bylined article.

question marks – A classification of products or strategic business units used in the *Boston Consulting Group advantage matrix*. *Question marks* are products characterized by low market share in a high growth market. An example would be the Beta format video launched by Sony® which was badly overshadowed by the VHS video format. Also called *problem children*.

question method – Handling a buyer by making the prospect answer his or her own objection. If, for example, the buyer objects that the item being considered for purchase is excellent but that the price of $100 is too high, the salesperson responds by asking, "Why do you feel that way?" or "Are you willing to invest $100 in an asset that will return you 100% per annum?"

questionable costs – Costs that may be considered as variable or as *fixed costs*, depending on the specifics of the situation.

questionnaire – An instrument used for soliciting responses in public relations, advertising or other marketing research survey. Also the introduction, explanation and questions posed – in person, on the phone or through the mail – by the researcher to the respondent. This tool contains a list of questions.

questionnaire pre-testing – The testing of a *questionnaire* to be used in a marketing research study on a small sample of respondents from the target group prior to its full-scale use in order to eliminate ambiguities and other design problems.

quick ratio – One of three financial ratios commonly used to evaluate a firm's *liquidity*. It is calculated by dividing current assets less stock on hand by current liabilities. See *current ratio*.

quintessential – Being the most typical, the purest and the very best.

quizjacking – Using ultra high speed Internet to look up answers to television quiz shows so you look smarter than you really are.

quota – Any restriction imposed by law on the quantity of a product which can be produced or imported. It is a form of *protectionism*. See *protectionism; sales quota*.

quota sample – A nonprobability research sample chosen from individuals who meet certain specified criteria. Selection of a group to be polled that matches the characteristics of the entire audience (e.g. Interviewers select respondents according to certain *demographics* such as age, gender, ethnic group, education, income, etc.).

quote – Estimate of costs.

quotes – Quotation marks. A *quote* is a portion of a story that consists of direct quotations. When punctuating, the period or comma always goes inside the "close" *quote*. **Q**

Q

Rs (three Rs) – Respect for yourself; respect for others; responsibility for all your actions.

racino – A horse or greyhound race track which also houses casinos. In some cases, the casino games are limited to slot machines or video lottery terminals (VLTs) only.

rack-jobber – A specialized form of merchant wholesaler who supplies products that generally go on rack-type shelving to supermarkets, pharmacies, hardware stores, etc.

radio frequency identification (RFID) – Technology replacing bar codes. An electronic reader receives and decodes data from *RFID* tags that transmit a weak radio signal (as far as about eight feet away.) Tags are attached to clothing and other products sold by retail stores, to library books, etc.

radio media – Media outlet that broadcasts news and other programming over AM or FM radio waves. Includes local radio stations and national or regional networks, or services that provide news or program content to the local stations.

rainmaker – A public relations or advertising agency employee who brings in new business (new accounts). When someone is referred to as a *rainmaker*, they are considered very successful in helping to contribute to their employer's financial bottom line.

raising the bar – setting a higher standard.

random-probability (scientific or chance) sample – A sample selected in such a manner that each element of the *universe* has an equal or known chance of being in the chosen sample.

random digit dialing – Computerized calling method used in opinion polling. Phone numbers are scientifically selected by a computer, which dials the phone.

random sample – A sample taken from any given population in which each person maintains an equal chance of being selected. This differs a bit from a scientific random sample in that a random sample may be taken from a predetermined audience such as students in a particular classroom or residents of a particular neighborhood. To be purely scientific, every member of the *universe* must have the exact same "chance" of being chosen as everyone else. See *scientific random sample.*

range – The maximum distance a consumer is ordinarily willing to travel for a product or service. This determines the outer limit of a market area.

rapid responder – Designee at a company or organization team responsible for quick reaction to negative news or accusations.

rapid response team – Group of campaign team members or company personnel responsible for responding to negative news.

RAPPIES (Retired Affluent Professionals) – A demographic grouping.

rapport – It means, relationship – especially one of mutual trust or emotional affinity. Important to public relations practitioners. Among the most misspelled words.

rate –The amount charged by a communications medium to an advertiser based on per unit of space or time purchased. The *rate* may vary from national to local campaigns, or may be a fixed rate. Also, to estimate a particular media's audience size based on a research sample.

rate card – An information card that lists the standard rates for a publication, radio station/network, television station/network, Web site or other advertising vehicle. It contains the various supplements, advertising products and/or programs offered by the media outlet. It would also contain information about mechanical and production requirements, issue dates, closing dates, cancellation dates, circulation data, etc.

rating point – *Rating points* represent the percent of the total available target audience impressions that are delivered by a media vehicle. One percent of all households viewing (television) or listeners listening (radio) to a particular station at a particular time. Ten percent of all households watching a station or program at a particular time would have a rating of 10. *Gross Rating Points (GRP)* – the sum of all the *rating*

212

Tips to Succeed:
How to make an editor angry

There are some PR practitioners who would try just about any trick in the book to make sure an editor takes a look at their news release. So here is a list of the top five ways to make an editor angry when presenting your news story.

1. Write a news release that is excessively long

Unless you're the President and have just proposed a new version of the Constitution, think brief. Your news should be short and sweet. Any additional information can be sent to the editor once you've obtained interest.

2. Get the editor's attention and then tell them they have to use the release word for word

Many news releases will get published verbatim, but don't test the editor's journalistic integrity by making it mandatory.

3. Send a huge photo e-mail attachment when emailing a release

Editors receive hundreds of unsolicited news releases emailed to them everyday. Why waste their time with a huge file unless they ask you for it?

4. Send your release in a fancy package so that it commands attention

Most editors will simply use your apparent disregard for the number of trees destroyed to make the unnecessary package as reason to disregard your release.

5. Call the editor and ask to read the entire release over the phone

If you have to read the release the editor will label you as a lightweight. Say goodbye to the credibility of your release.

The bottom line is that editors want to see the news in a news release. If you don't have news in your release don't try to tap dance your way to their hearts. Start over and send it to them when you have some real news to tell.

Rowan (N.J.) University PRSSA *Newsbriefs* - March 30, 2005

213

Tips to Succeed:
10 essential tips to ensure your news release makes the news

1. Make sure the information is newsworthy.
2. Tell the audience that the information is intended for them and why they should continue to read it.
3. Start with a brief description of the news, then distinguish who announced it, and not the other way around.
4. Ask yourself, "How are people going to relate to this and will they be able to connect?"
5. Make sure the first 10 words of your release are effective, as they are the most important.
6. Avoid excessive use of adjectives and fancy language.
7. Deal with the facts.
8. Provide as much Contact information as possible: Individual to Contact, address, phone, fax, email, Web site address.
9. Make sure you wait until you have something with enough substance to issue a release.
10. Make it as easy as possible for media representatives to do their jobs.

points for a specific time period. *Target Rating Points (TRP)* – the *rating points* delivered to a particular target audience for a specific time period.

rational appeals in advertising – Advertising messages, usually product-feature based, in which advertisers attempt to achieve their objectives by appealing to logic and reason rather than to the emotions. See *emotional appeals in advertising.*

rational buying motives – Reasons for buying based on logic or judgment rather than on emotion.

raw footage – Unedited or "uncut" video that has been recorded for a story. See *raw tape.*

raw materials – A classification of industrial goods that are basic materials which become part of the finished product in the manufacturing process.

raw tape – Unedited or "uncut" video that has been recorded for a story. See *raw footage.*

re-direct – When used in reference to computer online advertising, one server assigning an ad-serving or ad-targeting function to another server, often operated by a third company. For example, a Web publisher's ad management server might *re-direct* to a third party hired by an advertiser to distribute its ads to target customers. In some cases, the process of *re-directs* can slow down the sales process and might even discourage a purchase – if the navigation is difficult.

reach – The percentage of different homes or individuals exposed to a media outlet or vehicle(s) at least once during a specific time period. It is the percentage of *unduplicated audience*. Unique computer users that visited a Web site over the course of the reporting period, expressed as a percentage of the *universe* for the *demographic* category – also called *unduplicated audience*. Sometimes referred to as the total number of unique users who will be served a given advertisement. Specifically in broadcast media – the percentage of the target audience that will see or hear an ad at least one time.

reaching out – To make an effort to communicate with a segment or fragment of a (targeted) public – many times for the purpose of gaining that public's support.

react – Term used when *journalists* conduct interviews to get a response to a news story or other issues.

reaction (vs. response) – *Reaction* is an action caused by another action. *Response* is an answer.

reactive marketing control systems – Evaluation and control systems where management finds that marketing performance is not satisfactory and takes corrective action. Any action taken after the fact is reactive. See *steering control system*.

reactive marketing strategies – Marketing activities forced on an organization by competitive action – defensive strategies. See *proactive marketing strategies*.

reactive/defensive PR – A policy of responding to a given set of circumstances, situations or events after the fact.

readability – The ease with which a reader understands a printed message – the reading (grade) level of written material.

readability tests – Tests designed to measure the grade level of reading skills a particular piece of writing demands from its audience.

reader (talent reader) – A TV news story with no accompanying video.

R

readership – The total number of readers of a publication (includes primary and pass-along readers). Also, the percentage of people that can recall a particular advertisement, aided or unaided.

readership (listenership or viewership) studies – Research conducted periodically to determine patterns of readership of print media and television.

reading Z – A theory of eye direction. The eye is drawn to the upper left quadrant of a page and follows a "Z" pattern across the page.

ready-to-run segments – Short news stories used by radio and television stations to fill in available time in a newscast.

real positioning – The modification of a product offering so that it better delivers the benefits which buyers of this type of product desire. See *market positioning; repositioning*.

Real Simple Syndication (RSS) – Software code used to deliver news stories, *blogs* and other items via the Internet to computer screen on readers such as My Yahoo!® or NewsGator®. Eventually, *RSS* will become the primary method everyone uses to access "stuff" on the Web. *RSS* is a family of web feed formats. The initials *RSS* are variously used to refer to the following standards:

Really Simple Syndication (RSS 2.0)

Rich Site Summary (RSS 0.91, RSS 1.0)

RDF Site Summary (RSS 0.9 and 1.0)

According to Wikipedia®, *RSS* formats are specified in *XML* (a generic specification for data formats). *RSS* delivers its information as an *XML* file called an *RSS* feed, web feed, *RSS* stream, or *RSS* channel.

real time – Events that happen in *real time* are happening virtually at that particular moment. When a person chats in a chat room, or sends an instant message, one is interacting in *real time* since it is almost immediate.

reason why – A strategic statement that explains why a feature will benefit the user.

reasonable certainty – Many times, referred to as *reasonable certainty* of "no harm." Something that appears clearly established or assured based on research and other investigation. Public relations counselors often rely on *reasonable certainty* before making recommendations.

rebate – A temporary price reduction – an *incentive* to buy – to encourage immediate purchase. See *refund*.

rebranding – Attempting to get audiences to forget or dismiss current or earlier reputation or image by reidentifying or reshaping a brand. Democratic presidential candidate John Kerry tried *rebranding* America as he ran again President George W. Bush. Kerry felt America had lost its prestige and he and Democrats tried to regain it.

recall – The ability to remember specific information from an advertisement or commercial. Also, the advertised request by a company that a product be returned to it by those who have already purchased it. Product recalls may be voluntary or ordered by a federal agency when it is deemed a product may be unsafe or unreliable. See *product recall*.

recall tests – A method of evaluating the effectiveness of a recent advertisement by asking respondents to bring to mind advertisements they have read, heard or viewed. See *aided recall*; *unaided recall*.

receiver – The encoder or target of a message in the communication process.

recency/primacy – The last thing said is the most remembered. In essence, "last in, first out." See *primacy/recency*.

recency, frequency and monetary value (RFM) – A methodology used by marketers to determine appropriate circulation strategies.

reception analysis – Research that focuses on the way individuals draw conclusions or make meanings from strategic media messages. *Reception analysis* has some similarity with uses and gratifications research, but is much more likely to use an ethnographic approach involving in-depth interviews, participant observation, etc.

recession – An extended decline in general business activity. The National Bureau of Economic Research formally defines a *recession* as three consecutive quarters of falling real gross domestic product. A *recession* affects different securities in different ways.

reciprocity – A practice, which can be deemed illegal under the Trade Practices Act, where a firm gives purchasing preference to a firm to which it sells – favoritism. Most government agencies require sealed bids when the expected purchase price exceeds a certain amount. At the very least, government agencies should seek no fewer than three quotes when

R

making a purchase. Public relations and other private agencies have no restrictions. See *reverse reciprocity*.

recognition – Formal acknowledgment given by a communication medium to a public relations or an advertising agency to recognize that agency as being bona fide, competent and ethical, and therefore, entitled to agency discounts (or commissions). Also the ability of an individual to recall an advertisement or campaign when seeing or hearing it again or upon having it described to him or her.

recognition tests – A means of evaluating the effectiveness of a firm's recent advertising. Respondents are shown an ad, asked if they have seen it before, and, if so, is quizzed on its contents. The same type of tests are done for radio and television commercials.

recruiting – Seeking new employees for a public relations or an advertising agency and also seeking new accounts for an agency.

recycling – The collection and processing of used materials for reuse.

red flag – A term used send out or recognize a caution.

redact – To prepare for publication. When referring to public records in which certain information must be protected, it is the obliteration of such items as address, phone number, Social Security number, etc.

redemption – The conversion of a sales promotion coupon to a purchase.

redemption rate – The number of sales promotion *coupons* converted to purchases expressed as a percentage of the number distributed.

reduced price pack – A type of consumer sales promotion where two or more units of the same product are banded together and sold at a lower price.

reference group – A group of people that a researcher uses as a guide for behavior in a certain situation. Also a group of people or an organization that an individual respects, identifies with or aspires to join. A group with which a person identifies in some way and whose opinions and experiences influence that person's behavior. For example, a basketball fan might buy a brand of athletic shoe worn by a favorite player.

referral fees – Fees paid by public relations agencies or by advertisers for delivering a qualified (sales) lead, potential client or purchase inquiry. The person who supplies the lead is sometimes called a "bird dog."

214

Tips to Succeed:
Crafting your resume

Recruiters usually spend less than 20 seconds looking at your resume. Monster.com says most resumes don't get a second look. Only about three percent of candidates are called for an interview.

No one seems to be immune to a pathetic resume. Even seasoned professionals can improve their image on paper.

The most common offenses: being too generic and not convincing enough about your accomplishments.

For instance, if you say you doubled sales in a short amount of time, say so. But be specific. Which sounds better? "Worked diligently to surpass sales quota on an ongoing basis" or "exceeded $1 million quarterly sales quota by at least 25 percent for six consecutive quarters"?

Eleanor Farmer, resume writer and business coach from Merchantville, N.J. says, "Do not use a generic resume. Customize your resume to the company and job to which you are applying."

Let them know why they should hire you. Use an *applicant statement* on the top of page one just under your personal information. That statement should tell something about the value you would bring to the company. For example:

Applicant Statement: Rowan University Professor Anthony J. Fulginiti, APR, Fellow PRSA, describes me as: "Mature beyond her years, articulate, well tailored and polished, loyal, has a passion for the profession, outstanding writer, and a skilled organizer and strategic thinker." I promise to bring those features to Burwyn Associates to increase the firm's double bottom line.

If your resume is more than one page, use footer on right hand side. For example:

Alana Kramer
Resume, page 2
kramer@njtown.net

For Resume Writing Suggestions, contact:
M. Larry Litwin, APR, Fellow PRSA - larry@larrylitwin.com

referral link – A computer term where the referring Web page, or referral link, is a place from which the user clicked to get to the current page. Also known as the source of a visit.

referral premium – A premium (possibly a discount on a future purchase) offered to customers for helping sell a product or service to a friend or acquaintance.

215 Tips to Succeed: Maintaining a strong professional relationship

Life is about finding ways to get along with people, not ways to separate yourself. You really find out who your friends are when you are down.

Rep. Robert Andrews (D-N.J.)

referral selling – Selling to customers whose names have been suggested by previous satisfied customers.

reflective probes – A tactic of using neutral statements by an agency representative or a salesperson reaffirming or repeating a client's comment to stimulate the client to provide more information.

refund – An offer by a marketer to return a certain amount of money to the consumer who purchases the product. See *rebate*.

regional brands – Opposite of *power brands*. Manufacturers' brands sold only in certain regions. Examples would include Strawbridge's® and Genuardi's®. Strawbridge's® was a department store chain in the Philadelphia area purchased the May Company, which eventually was purchased by Macy's®. At the same time May Company operated Strawbridge's® it was also operating Hecht's®, Kaufmann's®, Foleys® and Marshal Fields®. Safeway Corporation operates Genuardi's® Supermarkets in the Philadelphia area and Safeway® stores, elsewhere. Since integrating nearly all of its stores under the Macy's® nameplate, it made Macy's a *power brand*. See *brand champion*.

regional marketing – The practice of using different marketing mixes to accommodate unique preferences and competitive conditions in different geographical areas.

R

regional shopping center – A major retail shopping complex serving a distinct geographic area of a city or state, housing at least one major full- line department store and a number of other retailers and service providers.

regionalization – A permissive cooperative agreement or arrangement by which a common service is provided.

register – Correct placement of printing on the sheet. In color printing, *register* means the correct placement of each plate so that the colors are laid down properly, without running "off-register." See *registration*.

register marks – Used in the printing process. Indicator symbols located in the margins of negatives to be used as guides for perfect *registration*.

registered design – A form of legal protection against the copying by a competitor of the external appearance of a product. Patents and trademarks are approved and registered through the U.S. Patent and Trademark Office. Copyrights are regulated through the Library of Congress. All are considered *intellectual property*.

registration – In publishing, the alignment of colors on a printed product (newspaper, magazine, *billboard*, etc.). It's the alignment of successive colors and/or images as witnessed by *register marks*. The three uses of *registration marks* are to identify: position/location of the image on the substrate, color-to-color *registration* and whether the image is square to the lead edge of the substrate. Proper *registration* is necessary for an image to prevent unwanted colors and misalignments – many times causing the ad or other product to appear blurred. In computer language, it is a process for Web site visitors to enter information about themselves. Sites use *registration* data to enable or enhance targeting of content and advertisements. *Registration* can be required or voluntary.

registration marks – Small "crosshairs" or indicators on film used to align individual color separations or layers of film *negatives* when items using color are being printed. It is the precise alignment of different films or printing plates (color separations) to produce a final printed image.

regressive commission – A sales commission system where the rate of commission paid decreases with the quantity of goods sold. See *progressive commission*.

regulatory environment – That part of the firm's external marketing environment where legal and political forces act to change regulations, which could affect the marketing effort. History and experience show that regulatory changes can pose threats or present opportunities.

reinforcement – The reward or punishment delivered by a particular response to a stimulus. Ivan Pavlov used what he called, "conditioned reflex" – rewarding his dog for good behavior, which reinforced further good behavior.

reinforcement advertising – Advertising intended to reassure purchasers, to tell them they have done the right thing in buying the particular product or service and to explain how to get the best results and most satisfaction from its use. A major purpose of *reinforcement advertising* is to maintain market share.

216

Techniques to Succeed: The power of the referral

Many salespeople are wondering about the best way to go after new business. The prevailing wisdom is that you have to develop a cold list, start from scratch and build your business that way. This is so far from the truth that it's laughable. An unqualified list will yield two to three appointments out of a hundred approaches. A referred list, when called by a professional salesperson, can yield initial appointments at the rate of 25 per 100 approaches – sometimes even more. That raises the question: Why don't we leverage referral prospecting as much as we should?

Warren Wechsler's Total Selling Times
Fairfield, Ia.

relationship marketing – The ongoing process of identifying and maintaining contact with high-value clients and customers. It is the strategy of establishing a relationship with the customer which continues well beyond the first purchase. Agencies and other businesses successful in *relationship marketing* continually gather demographic and psychographic information and keep their databases current. Also, when dealing with the media, it is developing sound relationships and loyalty by making media outlets and their reporters feel good about working with you – a mutually trusting relationship.

relationship selling – Selling where the primary objective is the building of long-term relationships with customers to assure a flow of repeat business.

relative advantage – The degree to which a new product is superior to an existing one. It is a major determinant of the rate of adoption of a new product.

relative market share – The size of a company's share of the market compared to that of its competitors.

release prints – Duplicate copies of a commercial or advertisement that are ready for distribution.

relevance – The quality of an advertising message that makes it important to the audience.

relevant costs – Expenditures that are expected to occur in the future as a result of some marketing action. Those costs differ among other potential marketing alternatives and external influences on the market.

reliability – The degree of accuracy with which data in a marketing research study has been collected. A *reliable* marketing research study should produce the same or similar results time after time. To ensure the integrity of any research, the researcher should consider it mandatory to state clearly and definitively the specifications of the measuring instrument.

religiosity – Enthusiasm for a religion.

remail – The process of preparing mail for deposit in the postal system of another country for delivery to its final destination. With A-B-C remail, mail travels as cargo from "Country A" to "Country B" where it

217

Techniques to Succeed: Using a boilerplate

A boilerplate is a short piece of text, usually no more than a single short paragraph, describing a company, person, product, service or event. It is standard wording about an organization that usually appears near the end of organization or company-issued news releases. Here is a sample boilerplate:

The Atlantic City Convention & Visitors Authority serves as the destination's principal marketing arm, stimulating economic growth through convention, business and leisure tourism development. The Authority oversees the management of the Atlantic City Convention Center and Boardwalk Hall on behalf of its parent agency, the New Jersey Sports and Exposition Authority.

The ABCs of Strategic Communication

R

enters the postal stream for delivery in "Country C." While the mail may not be *bulk mail* as we know it, it is shipped in bulk to expedite delivery.

remarketing – Marketing activity intended to encourage renewed use of a product where market interest has declined.

reminder advertising – Advertising aimed at reminding a target market that a product is available rather than informing or persuading it to buy a new product. This method or technique is usually associated with products in the mature stage of their life cycle. Also referred to as *retentive advertising*. See *advertising objectives*.

remnant space – Discounted magazine space, which is sold to help fill regional (or national) editions of the publication. Also unsold space in a print publication or unsold banner impressions on a Web site. *Remnant space* is typically sold at a discount to the publication or site's rate card.

remote broadcast – Production or broadcast location at a site other than in the studio.

renditioning – Interpreting in a way to suit our own needs. The euphemism we use for sending terrorism suspects to countries that practice torture for interrogation.

renewal rate – The percentage of individuals who renew their print media subscriptions to extend beyond the previous expiration date.

reorder frequency – The amount, in dollars, of orders that minimizes or reduces the total (variable) costs required to market and inventory products. See *economic order quantity*.

reorder level – The point where is it economically profitable to increase inventory levels. See *economic order quantity*.

rep or representative – A person who solicits advertising space on behalf of a particular medium.

rep firm – A company that represents independent radio and television stations – regardless of their network affiliation – and newspapers in various markets (usually no more than one owner per market) for the purpose of selling national (commercials) advertising to the major brands. National advertisers approach rep firms for the "local buys" to supplement network advertising. Also called *sales rep firm, unwired network* and *wireless network*.

R

repeat questioning – Technique (tactic) used by researchers to fish out untruths through inconsistencies. Many times, similar questions are asked throughout a survey. Inconsistencies reduce the *validity* of the survey.

repeat visitor – A unique visitor who has accessed a Web site more than once over a specific time period.

repertory grid method (RGM) – A technique for representing the attitudes and perceptions of individuals. It is also called Personal Construct Technique (use of matrix or paradigm). The technique can be useful in developing market research (and other) questionnaires. Also known as *Kelly Grids* – a tool for understanding how you think of people. Down the left hand side, write names of people and across the top their attributes. Using such techniques are important to public relations practitioners as they methodically and systematically design a PR plan.

reporter – A writer, investigator or presenter of news stories, employed to gather and report news for a print publication, wire service or broadcast station. A reporter's job is to paint reality as it is (Pulitzer Prize winning author James Stewart). Reporters should be accurate, fair and objective, and their stories should have meaning to the reader. They are "truth tellers who paint reality as it is," according to Pulitzer Prize winning author, James Smart ("Imus in the Morning" – Feb. 16, 2005).

repositioning – Arranging for a product or *brand* to occupy some other clear and distinctive position in the market and in the minds of target consumers than one it correctly occupies. The process of strategically changing the perceptions surrounding a product or service. Changing the placement of a company, its products or services in a market category or in relation to its competition. *Repositioning* may be necessary or desirable if sales expectations are not being met, or to allow for the introduction to the market of a new product or brand, or similar. See *market positioning*.

representative – See *sales representative*.

representativeness – The degree to which a sample of an audience in a marketing research study represents the characteristics of the population as a whole.

repristination – Returning a product to its *original* form. See *original*.

repro – A high-quality proof of an advertisement printed on glossy paper, which is suited for reproduction. In many cases, laser prints have

R

replaced *blue lines* as the final step before a printing job is shot and plated before printing. Also referred to as *ad slick*, *blue line*; *camera ready*; *laser print*; *matte*; *velox*.

repurpose a message – Taking a story that was used as a future in a newspaper, newsletter or on radio/TV, saving it in a file and then bringing it out and updating it for current use.

request for proposal (ROP) – Document from public or private entity containing specification required for a particular project or "job" and asking firms or individuals to quote or bid on the project.

request for qualifications (RFQ) – Answers the question, is your firm qualified to perform the duties needed in a *request for proposal* that it is bidding or quoting on?

resale price maintenance – A practice where the manufacturer fixes the price at which a buyer may resell the product. Many times, this is deemed illegal.

research – A scientific systematic investigation to gather information about *attitudes* (predisposition to act or inner feelings) that form *opinions* (expression of the attitude) and establish facts. It is a search for knowledge. *Research* is conducted to improve the effectancy of public relations and advertising. *Seminal research* is research never done before. *Research* is planned, carefully organized, sophisticated fact finding and listening to the opinions of others. (See *The Public Relations Practitioner's Playbook* – Kendall/Hunt – 2008).

research action – The survey or other research technique used to gather data to *research questions*.

research design – Sometimes referred to as *protocol*. The controlling plan for a marketing research study where the methods and procedures for collecting and analyzing the information to be collected are specified.

research objectives – The purpose of a marketing research study. Many times, "purpose" becomes the first step in the public relations process – even before *research* (*research, planning, implementation, evaluation* – known as PR-PIE when purpose is included). See *marketing research objectives*.

research questions – Carefully phrased inquiries designed to gather *research* data and other information.

researcher – The practitioner responsible for designing and carrying out the *research* project.

reseller – A *middleman* – one who buys merchandise to resell it at a profit.

reseller market – The market consisting of *wholesalers* and *retailers* who buy products for resale purposes.

218 Techniques to Succeed: Office romances and workplace efficiency

It is widely accepted that workplace romances cannot be avoided. So, to avoid the perception that an employee is getting preferential treatment because of an office romance, or to avoid accusations of sexual harassment, favoritism or discrimination, companies should have:

- Consensual Relationship Agreements. Some firms have them for employees who date as well as married couples in the same workplace.

- Other types of written agreements in which romantically involved workers acknowledge the following:
  - the relationship is voluntary and consensual
  - they agree to abide by the employer's anti-harassment policy
  - they will behave professionally and not allow the relationship to affect their work
- and to avoid behavior that offends others at work.

Companies should use them only when a relationship has already started to cause a problem or when the employer becomes aware of a relationship – especially one involving employees reporting to one another.

Companies wanting to discourage office romance are legally free to do so as long as company policy doesn't focus on one particular group. For example, don't punish only the women for engaging in office romance.

The workplace is a natural place to meet and even find your beloved. If you discover yours there, discuss how the relationship can affect your work. Communication – the key to a romantic relationship – will also be the key to a successful working relationship.

Andrea Kay - Author - *Greener Pastures: How To Find a Job in Another Place*
www.andreakay.com andrea@andreakay.com

R

residual public relations – *Silent publicity* or mentions an organization or company receives through the coverage of another organization. See *silent publicity*.

residential training courses (RTCs) – Used by many firms and organizations to consist of intensive coaching in courses and other classes. Many *RTCs* involve evening and weekend training sessions and include overnight stay and full accommodation.

residuals – A sum paid to a performer on a TV or radio commercial each time it is run, and is usually established by an AFTRA (American Federation of Television and Radio Artists) or a SAG (Screen Actors Guild) contract.

resolution – Refers to the clarity of an image as received by a television set or on a color photograph.

response (vs. reaction) – *Response* is an answer. *Reaction* is an action caused by another action.

response area – The last element of an ad. It includes the contact information (name, address, phone number, Web site, e-mail, *logo*, etc.)

response bias – The inclination of respondents in a marketing research survey to give the answer they believe the interviewer wants to hear. Well-trained survey takers can recognize *response bias* and note it on the responses.

response booster – Any device, token, *premium* or sweepstakes that will help raise the response rate.

response card – A postcard that urges the target audience to take action. See *direct response*.

response elasticity – A measure of the degree to which individuals or groups respond to a marketing program.

219 Techniques to Succeed: A good reputation sells *itself*

Remember, the Public Relations writer is "relating" the image, not "selling" it.

response list – Any list of individuals who have responded to a mailing/offer.

response panel – One panel of a brochure or other publication to be torn off and mailed back to the sender.

response rate – Percentage of responses received from a direct marketing campaign (typically the percentage of recipients who responded to a mailing).

response selling – An elementary form of selling, common in retailing, where the salesperson simply responds to the customer's demands. Little creativity or persuasion is used.

response time – The time taken by a firm or organization to answer a customer inquiry about the status of an order.

responsive writing – Correcting or clarifying a situation by filling in omitted details or adding information that better clarifies a subject, points out an error or promotes an issue.

responsiveness – The degree to which people control their emotions when relating to others. Used in public relations and selling as an indicator of social style.

retail advertising – A type of advertising used by local merchants who sell directly to consumers.

retail tracking – Researching why a product might not be selling (what went wrong) in a particular location or why it's being rejected by a target audience.

retainage – Money held back from contractors and/or vendors until all items on the *punchlist* ("to-do" items) are completed satisfactorily. See *punchlist*.

restraint of trade – Any action (usually illegal), which damages in some way another's opportunity to carry on a business.

restricted line – Sales items that are not legally sold in certain geographic areas, or only under special legal restrictions.

retail advertising – A type of advertising used by local merchants who sell directly to consumers. Also referred to as *local advertising*.

retail buyer – An individual employed by a retailer primarily to buy merchandise for resale through the store.

retail image – The perception that consumers have of a particular store and of the experience of shopping there.

retail mix – The mix of variables, including location, merchandise, communications, price, services, physical attributes and personnel, which form the overall strategic marketing components of retailing.

retail trading zone – Defined by the Audit Bureau of Circulations as the area beyond an urban area whose residents regularly trade with retail merchants within the urban area. Read more at *www.accessabc.com*.

retailer cooperative – A wholesaling operation established by a group of retailers to give themselves a buying advantage. In government and elsewhere, also known as buying groups.

retailers – Members of the distribution channel who sell directly to the consumer.

retailing – The activity of selling to buyers who are buying for their own consumption or (usually) for someone else in their household or family.

retainer – A flat fee that a client and public relations practitioner/ agency agree on as a monthly or yearly payment for services or a particular project. If it is primarily for a project, it would be a *project fee*.

retentive advertising – Advertising aimed at reminding a target market that a product is available rather than informing or persuading it. This method or technique is usually associated with products in the mature stage of their life cycle. Also referred to as *reminder advertising*; *advertising objectives*.

retool – Making adjustments to a speech or editorial copy to assure the message matches the audience.

retouching – To alter photographs, artwork or film to emphasize or introduce desired features and also to eliminate unwanted ones. Read more at *www.adobe.com/products/photoshop/main.html*.

retraction – Correction in the media information previously and erroneously reported.

return on assets managed – A measure of a firm's profitability – after-tax expressed as a percentage of assets used to make it.

return on capital employed (ROCE) – The value that an organization derives from investing in a project.

220

Techniques to Succeed: The art of rhetoric – learning how to use the 3 main rhetorical styles

Rhetoric (n) - The art of speaking or writing effectively.

According to Aristotle, rhetoric is "the ability, in each particular case, to see the available means of persuasion." He described three main forms of rhetoric: Ethos, Logos and Pathos.

To be a more effective writer, you must understand these three terms. Understanding them will help make your writing more persuasive.

ETHOS
Ethos is appeal based on the character of the speaker. An ethos-driven document relies on the reputation of the author.

LOGOS
Logos is appeal based on logic or reason. Documents distributed by companies or corporations are logos-driven. Scholarly documents are also often logos-driven.

PATHOS
Pathos is appeal based on emotion. Advertisements tend to be pathos-driven.

Rhetorical appeals can be achieved through:

• **Visual Information Structure** – Includes how the text looks on the screen. This is achieved through the appearance of such things as the titles and the headings.

• **Color** – Includes the color of the text, the background and the graphics. The contrast of the colors of each of these items is also important.

• **Graphic Images** – Includes the other information in the document aside from the text. This is achieved through such things as icons, buttons, and photos.

Read more at www.rpi.edu/dept/llc/webclass/web/project1/group4/

return on equity – A measure of a firm's profitability – profit achieved in a given period expressed as a percentage of the total amount invested in the firm by its owners.

221

Tips to Succeed:
25 words that hurt your resume

Words don't tell potential employers as much as deeds

So, you're experienced? Before you advertise this in your resume, be sure you can prove it.

Often, when job seekers try to sell themselves to potential employers, they load their resumes with vague claims that are transparent to hiring managers, according to Scott Bennett, author of *The Elements of Resume Style* (AMACOM).

By contrast, the most successful job seekers avoid these vague phrases on their resumes in favor of accomplishments.

Instead of making empty claims to demonstrate your work ethic, use brief, specific examples to demonstrate your skills.

In other words, show, don't tell.

Bennett offers these examples:

Instead of... "Experience working in fast-paced environment"
Try... "Registered 120+ third-shift emergency patients per night"

Instead of... "Excellent written communication skills"
Try... "Wrote jargon-free User Guide for 11,000 users"

Instead of... "Team player with cross-functional awareness"
Try... "Collaborated with clients, A/R and Sales to increase speed of receivables and prevent interruption of service to clients."

Instead of... "Demonstrated success in analyzing client needs"
Try... "Created and implemented comprehensive needs assessment mechanism to help forecast demand for services and staffing."

The worst offenders

It's good to be hard-working and ambitious, right? The hiring manager won't be convinced if you can't provide solid examples to back up your claims.

Bennett suggests being extra-careful before putting these nice-sounding but empty words in your resume.

R

• Aggressive	• Goal-oriented	• Professional
• Ambitious	• Hard-working	• Reliable
• Competent	• Independent	• Resourceful
• Creative	• Innovative	• Self-motivated
• Detail-oriented	• Knowledgeable	• Successful
• Determined	• Logical	• Team player
• Efficient	• Motivated	• Well-organized
• Experienced	• Meticulous	
• Flexible	• People person	

Laura Morsch - CareerBuilder.com - CNN.com

return on investment (ROI) – The costs of creating and running the advertisement versus the revenue it generates. A measure of a firm's profitability where profits are expressed as a percentage of investment: net profit divided by investment.

return visits – The average number of times a computer user returns to a Web site over a specific time period.

reusable container – A type of consumer sales promotion where potential customers are encouraged to buy a particular product because it is packaged in a container that can be used for some other useful purpose when empty.

reverse – To print text or art in white on a dark background.

R

reverse marketing channel – A marketing channel where goods (to be recycled or reprocessed) flow backward from consumer to intermediaries to producer. For example, bottles, cans and newsprint. It is also called a *backward marketing channel.*

reverse reciprocity – A selling arrangement where two organizations agree to sell their scarce products to one another. In some cases, the firm making the finished products gives selling preference to the firm providing supplies or raw materials used in the manufacture. See *reciprocity.*

reverse type – White type on a darker background.

RGB colors – A color model that stands for red, green and blue. Used by monitors, scanners, televisions and projectors.

ribbon – The facade that separates the seating in arenas, stadiums and other (concert) venues that electronically display (moving) advertisements.

rich media – A method of Web graphic communication that incorporates animation, sound, video and/or interactivity. It can be used either by itself or in combination with the following technologies – streaming media, sound, *Flash*® and with such programming languages as Java® and JavaScript®. It is deployed via standard Web and wireless applications including e-mail, Web design, banners and buttons. The technology supplements the traditional *GIF*, *JPEG* or *HTML* media.

right to know – Laws that make government or corporate data and records available to the public or to those individuals with a particular interest in the information.

rip 'n read – Derives from the days when wire-service stories came into the newsroom on a bulky, teletype machine that spat out the stories onto a large roll of paper. An anchor would rip the story off the roll and read it on the air – with little or no editing. The practice continues today except that copy isn't torn from a teletype, it is printed from a computer. It is the primary reason the newscasts of so many stations may sound the same – newscasts are using identical scripts – scripts written by wire news services.

rip-o-matic – A very rough rendition of a proposed commercial, composed of images and sounds borrowed (ripped-off) from other commercials or broadcast materials. If those images or sounds are used, fees, for the most part, must be paid.

risk – The chance a purchaser takes that the product will not function as expected or satisfy as intended. See *emotional risk*; *financial risk*; *performance risk*; *physical risk*; *social risk*.

risk avoidance – Measures including acquiring information, seeking reassurance from family and friends, obtaining advice from experts, etc., taken by consumers investigating a purchase to reduce the level of anxiety they experience when buying.

risk opportunity – In every crisis, there are risks and opportunities. Public relations counselors are trained to conduct research to turn risks into opportunities.

road block – A method of scheduling broadcast commercials to obtain maximum reach by simultaneously showing the identical advertisement on several different stations.

road map – Another term used for *public relations plan.*

robo calls – Political (and other telemarketing) automated phone calls – using computers and recorded voices – considered the most cost-effective way to reach constituents and get out the vote (*GOTV*). PoliticalCalling.com® is one of the companies providing customer service to campaigns and political consultants.

robot – A program that runs automatically without human intervention. Typically, a *robot* is programmed with some artificial intelligence so that it can react to different situations it may encounter. Also known as *bots.*

role playing – An exercise commonly used in sales training where one person acts the part of another – during media rehearsals or in sales where a "salesperson" and a "buyer" practice selling skills.

rollout – Day or time a product is launched or the day a publication "hits the street" for the first time. Many times, a *rollout* is preceded with the *drip, drip, drip method.* Also the launch of a new product on a region by region basis as opposed to a national introduction. Such a *rollout* is intended to minimize the risk, take pressure off of human resources and reduce the investment in production and marketing. See *national introduction; new product development.*

romance card – Written material that accompanies an advertising specialty – providing information about the product and its background.

Room, the (also called collective thinking) – The result of intellectual property, mind share, the thoughts of a committee or team. When all take equal credit, credit is giving to "the Room."

rope line (working the rope line) – which is what politicians other successful CEOs do as they attempt to breakdown barriers between themselves and their publics.

rotogravure – A magazine supplement that is printed by a *gravure* process and run on a rotary press. This process is useful for large runs of pictorial effects. The pictures, designs and words are engraved into the printing plate or printing cylinder. The printing is usually in color – as are many Sunday comic strips.

rotoscoping – The process of using live and animated characters within an advertisement – on television or the Internet.

rough – An unfinished layout of an advertisement, which shows only a general concept to be presented for analysis, criticism and approval.

222 Techniques to Succeed:

Make resume point quickly, but don't stop short – one page may not be enough

Some rumors just won't go away. Take the one that your resume is only supposed to be one page long. Since the late 1980s, I have given speeches and workshops to get workers to stop fretting about length and focus on content. I even wrote a book on it. But the rumor prevails.

So here, from my you-may-think-it's-true-but-it's-not file, is why you should erase this crippling belief from your mind.

Whenever someone brings up the one-page resume rumor – which is usually the first thing when I'm trying to help him or her develop a new and improved version – I ask, "Why do you think that?" Responses are always the same: "Employers only spend 10 seconds reading your resume."

Ten seconds? I don't know about you, but I can only read about 30 words in 10 seconds, let alone a one-page resume. What could an employer possibly glean from a 10-second read?

What these busy managers who are inundated with hordes of resumes are more likely to do, is glance, not read. They take a quick scan of the document to decide if it's worth actually reading at a calmer moment in their day.

To get them to that point with your resume, a short document is not the solution. Shoot for creating an enticing one.

In addition, if you've got experience, a one-page resume can't do you much justice. Let's say the employer is looking for someone with 10 years in public relations. If you're worth your salt, a one-pager does not leave room to summarize your knowledge about media and community relations and expertise in employee communications over 10 years.

Glance they do. That's why you need to highlight the most relevant information someone in your industry cares about with lively language in an easy-to-read format that helps the reader quickly see you're a contender. Even with the tendency to scan, if you can say boring things in an interesting way, zip up descriptions of yourself and share juicy facts that show you're a star, the manager might even forgo e-mail to read for three minutes.

One way to get and keep their attention is to offer a bird's-eye view of yourself in the first section of your resume where they will probably glance first. This is where you describe your experience, mention that you're self-motivated and can evaluate complex legal cases and express ideas succinctly and have a reputation for prosecuting difficult patent cases. You'll get into details of where you did all this in the experience section and later, show examples of how you made a difference.

If it captures your individuality, downplays potential liabilities and gives proof you have what it takes to do the job you want, then make your resume more than one page. So what if it takes two or three pages to separate you from the pack? If you don't get noticed, what's the point?

It's unfortunate that so many people are conditioned to create a short resume, believing the employer will give only a 10-second read. It would be much wiser to develop a document that easily captivates an employer upon first look so that he will give you the time of day.

Andrea Kay - Gannett News Service

rough cut – A preliminary edited version of a commercial – usually without voice-over or music. It's an early stage of editing.

rough layout – A layout drawn to size but without attention to the artistic, graphic and copy details.

rounds – Scheduled calls – made by news reporters – to area police (*pox*) stations, hospitals and other agencies as part of the news-gathering effort. *Rounds* are usually made several times a day – depending on the news organization. Checking the police (pox) blotters – or crime logs.

route sales force – A team consisting of salespeople who call on existing customers to take orders for the company's products. The *route sales force* does not sell in the traditional sense, but merely inspects a retailer's shelves and restocks them as required. TastyKake® and many bread companies use *route sales forces* for supermarkets and convenience stores.

router – In computer terms, a device that connects any number of *LANs*, wireless or otherwise. *Routers* communicate with each other to configure the best route between any two computers with possibly a server or host server.

routine problem solving – Buying situations, which require little or no effort thanks to the buyer having previous experience with the product or suppliers. See *extensive problem solving*.

routine rebuy – A purchase where the customer buys the same goods in the same quantity on the same terms from the same supplier. See *straight rebuy*.

routine response behavior – A buying situation where the buyer has had considerable previous experience. See *extensive problem solving; limited problem solving*.

routing – The planning of the best route to be followed by a sales representative in making a series of sales calls. Efficient *routing* raises both the number of calls the representative is able to make and the ratio of selling time to non-selling time.

rule of three – People connect elements in groups of three. For example, in publications, the *rule of three* would apply to the three elements – headline, graphic and text.

rules – Solid lines that separate editorial content.

rule of thumb – An easily learned and easily applied procedure for approximately calculating or recalling some value, or for making some determination. An example would be… as a "*rule of thumb*, insurance loss is usually twice as much as insurance coverage" (Al Neuharth – Gannett – Sept. 8, 2005).

rundown – A list of stories scheduled for inclusion in a newspaper, magazine or on a radio or television news program. *Rundown* in print usually includes the section or page. Radio and TV *rundowns* include length or story in minutes and seconds and where it will air on the show.

run of network (RON) – The scheduling of Internet advertising where an ad network positions ads across the Web sites it represents at its own discretion, according to availability.

run of paper or press (ROP) – An advertisement that can be placed anywhere in a publication at the discretion of the publisher, not the advertiser – unless the advertiser purchases a preferred position or space.

run of schedule (ROS) – Commercials purchased from radio or television station with no preferred (*daypart*) running times. Traffic (schedulers) may run commercials wherever there is available time – unless the advertiser purchases a preferred *daypart*.

run-of-site (ROS) – The scheduling of Internet advertising where advertisements run across an entire site.

run-out strategy – A strategic decision to allow a product in the decline stage of its life cycle to continue to be sold, especially if the product has a sizable dedicated market which insists on buying it – the marketer may raise the price to obtain a slight premium price from that particular market segment while paring all promotional costs. See *decline stage*; *product life cycle*.

runaround – The way type text is positioned around a picture.

running columns – A feature article that appears regularly in a newspaper, magazine or on a Web site – most times written by the same persons. Many have a specific theme or topic.

rushes – Rough, unedited versions, of a commercial to be used for editing purposes. Also referred to as *dailies*. **R**

R

s-type response – A response to an advertisement or an advertising campaign which is slow to take effect but gradually gathers momentum. See *c-type response*.

saddle stitch – A publication binding method using staples in the fold of the pages. Got its name because publications are placed over a saddle-type device so that staples are inserted in the center – much like a person straddling a saddle with his/her legs.

safe harbor – An agreement negotiated by the U.S. Department of Commerce and the European Commission that enables a U.S. company to receive data from Europe by voluntarily submitting to regulation by a U.S. government office.

safety needs – The desire of humans for safety, shelter, security and warmth. See *Maslow's Hierarchy of Needs*.

safety recall – The request by a manufacturer for the return of a particular batch or model of a product (for repair, replacement or credit) when the product has been found (or is suspected of being) to be defective or unsafe.

safety stock – A level of stock over and above expected requirements held in inventory as a precaution against unusually heavy demand or possible delays in shipping of additional supply.

salary plan – A sales force compensation method where people are paid a straight salary. Such an approach provides security and stability but may not provide the incentive associated with commission payments. See *straight salary*.

sale advertising – Advertising, common in retailing, which announces the sale of products at temporarily or permanently reduced prices. Also called *retail advertising*.

sale of goods acts – Various state legislation aimed at safeguarding consumers by ensuring that goods offered for sale are of reasonable quality and fit for their intended purpose.

sales administration-to-sales ratio – A marketing control measure used to determine whether the amount spent on sales administration in a given period is reasonable and acceptable. The total expenditure on sales administration is expressed as a percentage of total sales revenue for the same period.

sales agents – Manufacturers' agents and representatives, dealers, distributors, etc., available to supplement or replace a firm's own sales force. See *outside sales facilities*.

sales analysis – A control measure that breaks down sales figures by region, product, customer, market, etc. for a given period.

sales aptitude tests – Tests used to determine the suitability of applicants for positions in the sales force.

sales branch – A manufacturer's office established simply to facilitate sales. No manufacturing is done at this location.

sales calls – The visits salespeople make to a buyer's premises to sell their companies' products.

sales contests – Sales promotions aimed at members of a company's sales force. *Sales contests* are competitions designed to boost sales and lift performance by offering awards or prizes to top-achievers in a sales team over a given period.

223

Tips to Succeed:
PR counselors are
heard, but not seen

- We work behind the scenes
- We get our just rewards watching the people we work with get theirs
- We help our bosses succeed – we lead them to become strong leaders
- We advise
- We counsel
- We see the big picture
- Quite simply: It is our job to have relations with the public

Larry Ascough - National School Public Relations Association

sales effect of advertising – The effectiveness of an advertisement or advertising campaign in boosting sales of a product. It is generally hard to measure because sales may be influenced by factors other than advertising – such as the product's price, its other features, its availability and the actions of competitors. See *advertising effectiveness*.

sales effect research – Marketing research to assess the effect on advertisement or some other promotional activity is having, or has had, on sales of the product being advertised. See *advertising effectiveness*.

sales engineer – A salesperson hired primarily for engineering knowledge or strong technical skills.

sales force composite – A method of forecasting future demand for a product by adding together what each member of the sales force expects to be able to sell in his or her territory.

sales force mix – The mix of individual territory representatives, national account sales teams, telemarketers, etc. in a firm's total sales force.

sales forecast – An estimation of the likely volume of sales, measured in dollars and units, for a future planning period. Typically, sales forecasting is done on the basis of (previous) trends, sales force estimations, surveys of consumer buying intentions, managerial judgment or quantitative models.

sales itinerary – A written schedule of planned sales calls, specifying the date, location and objective of each call.

sales kit – A collection of sales materials, such as brochures, calendars, signs and posters, prepared to explain a particular *promotion* to retailers. It usually includes a full advertising schedule.

sales leads – Telephone inquiries, letters, responses to advertising or direct mail, etc. that direct a salesperson to a prospective customer.

sales literature – Printed materials (brochures, catalogues, price lists, etc.) used as selling aids. Many are contained in *sales kits*.

sales management – The process of planning, organizing, controlling and evaluating the activities of the sales force.

sales manual – A set of printed materials containing product descriptions and related information to guide sales representatives and their customers.

sales office – Premises of an organization used as a base for all or part of the sales team but not for carrying *inventory*.

sales orientation – The philosophy or orientation of an organization, which emphasizes aggressive selling to achieve its objectives and possibly the company or organization's goal. Firms characterized by this approach often rely on pressure selling and manipulative sales techniques to win business and reach a satisfactory bottom line. See *selling concept.*

sales party – A form of non-store retailing where a manufacturer's products are displayed, for group selling, at an in-home party. Examples would include Tupperware®, lingerie and various cosmetics companies.

sales personnel recruitment – Identifying appropriate sources of sales personnel and attracting applicants to the firm for employment.

sales planning – The assessment of the current situation in a sales region or nationally, the setting of objectives, the formulation of *strategies* and *tactics* and the establishment of control and evaluation procedures.

sales potential – An organization's expected sales of a product in a given market for a specified period. Also, the share of the total market that a firm can reasonably expect to attain in a given period. See *Market Potential.*

sales presentation – A salesperson's persuasive demonstration or display of a product to a prospective buyer to help make a sale.

sales promotion – A form of promotion that encourages customers to buy products by offering such incentives as *discounting, guarantees, contests, coupons, sweepstakes,* demonstrations, bonus commission, *sponsorship, cooperative advertising, samples,* free gifts, cents off incentives, etc. – one of the four major elements (with *advertising, personal selling* and *publicity*) of the *promotion mix.*

sales promotion-to-sales ratio – A marketing control measure used to determine whether the amount spent on sales promotion in a given period is reasonable and acceptable. The total expenditure on sales promotion in a given period is expressed as a percentage of total sales revenue for the same period.

sales quota – The expected level of sales for a territory in a given period. Also, a sales assignment, goal or target set for a salesperson in a given accounting period. Among the commonly used types of sales quotas are dollar volume quotas, unit volume quotas, gross margin quotas, net profit quotas and activity quotas.

sales rally – A meeting or conference held specifically to motivate members of the sales team to greater efforts with a particular product or product range.

sales report – A salesperson's detailed record of sales calls and results for a given period. Typically, sales reports include such information as the sales volume per product or product line, the number of existing and new accounts called upon and the expenses incurred in making the calls. See *call report*.

sales rep firm – A company that represents independent radio and television stations – regardless of their network affiliation – and newspapers in various markets (usually no more than one owner per market) for the purpose of selling national (commercials) advertising to the major brands. National advertisers approach rep firms for the "local buys" to supplement network advertising. Also called *rep firm, unwired network* and *wireless network*.

sales representative – A salesperson or an individual employed to sell goods on behalf of a producer or some other member of a marketing channel by contacting prospective customers and developing an interest in the company's products.

sales resistance – Anything the prospective buyer says or does to prevent or delay the salesperson from closing the sale. See *objections*.

224

Tips to Succeed:
Ease those public speaking jitters

Public speaking is many people's number one fear. These tips should help:

- Determine whom your audience is and what you want to say to them.

- Research your topic and find out what people want to know about it.

- Outline what you want to say.

- Practice your presentation – in the room where you will be giving the speech, if possible. Tape the rehearsal and play it back.

- Shortly before your presentation, make sure the equipment and props are ready.

- Take a short, brisk walk before your presentation. Breathe deeply and slowly. Drink water.

- Have confidence you will do well.

Mayo Clinic Healthquest

S

sales-response function – The effect of advertising on sales. A measure of the likely level of sales in a given period at different levels of expenditure on any of the major *marketing mix (synergy)* variables.

sales tactics – The planned day-to-day activities of the sales team when implementing the strategies it hopes will achieve its objectives and eventually a firm's goal.

sales tasks – The job activities carried out by salespeople. They could include direct selling tasks (making product presentations to prospective buyers, etc.), indirect selling tasks (mailing sales literature to new and prospective accounts, etc.) and non-selling tasks (attending sales meetings, writing call reports, etc.).

sales territory – The specific region or group of customers for which a salesperson is directly responsible.

sales territory performance modeling – A method of evaluating sales territory performance. A paradigm or model is used to depict the environmental factors that may have impacted on it and on the salesperson assigned to it. The model assists a sales supervisor to better understand the quality of the performance.

sales training – Formal or informal coaching in sales methods, product knowledge and account handling given to a sales representative by another more experienced salesperson, sales manager or specialist sales trainer.

sales volume – The total revenue produced or the total number of units of a product sold in a given period.

sales volume analysis – A detailed study of an organization's sales, in terms of units or revenue, for a specified period. Such an analysis (by sales region or territory, industry, customer type, etc.) is commonly used as an aid in determining the effectiveness of the selling effort.

sales wave experiment – A (tracking) technique used to test consumer reaction to new products prior to full-scale commercialization. New products are placed in consumer homes to determine the reaction to them. The rate at which the products are repurchased is tracked.

salting – Placing names in a mail, telephone or e-mail list solely for the purpose of tracking the use of the list to ensure that the list purchaser or renter does not break the sales or rental contract. Also call *seeding*. A name so placed is called a *decoy* (a real name) or a *dummy* (a fictitious name).

sample – In research, a subset of a universe (public) whose properties are studied to gain information about that universe.

samples – Products distributed free to prospective buyers to promote future purchases.

sampling – In public relations research, the use of a statistically representative subset as an indication of an entire population's attitudes and opinions. Also, a promotional activity, tact or technique where consumers are allowed to experience a good or service free of charge or at a greatly reduced cost.

sampling error – In research, a measure of the extent to which the chosen sample in a marketing research study can be expected to represent the total population on the characteristics being studied. For example, five percent margins of error means 384 people were surveyed and if the same survey were given 100 times to 100 different samples, the results would be the same 95 times. With a five percent margin of error, results that indicate 53 percent of those surveyed favor a person or product, 95 times out of 100, anywhere from 58 to 48 percent of the population favors the product – five percent above to five percent below. Politicians now use smaller margins of error to help achieve better results.

sampling frame – The source from which sampling units (respondents) are chosen in a public relations research study. Commonly used *sampling frames* are telephone books and electoral or tax rolls.

sampling plan – A scheme outlining the group (or groups) to be surveyed in a marketing research study, how many individuals within the group are to be chosen and on what basis that choice is to be made. The larger the sample number, the smaller the *margin of error*.

sampling principle – The idea that a small number of randomly chosen units (the sample) of a total *population* (the *universe*) will tend to have the same characteristics, and in the same proportion, as the *population* as a whole.

sampling unit – The individual members chosen from a total population as respondents in a public relations or marketing research study.

sandwich (doughnut) – A reporter's on location live intro and close with pre-recorded video or audio. See *wrap*.

sandwich spot – Two unrelated broadcast advertisers sharing 60 seconds of commercial time in which one advertiser uses the first and last

S

20 seconds and the other uses the middle (meat) 20 seconds. See *piggy-back advertising*.

sans-serif (type) – Two terms that apply to typeface and whether a particular typeface has "tails" (hands and feet) on it or not. *Serif* typefaces have tails on them – Times Roman is an example of a *serif* typeface. *Sans serif* typefaces have no tails; Arial and Avant Garde are examples of *sans serif* typefaces. See *serif*.

Sarbanes-Oxley Act of 2002 – Considered the most significant change to federal securities laws in the United States since the "New Deal." It came in the wake of a series of corporate financial scandals, including those affecting Enron, Arthur Andersen and WorldCom. Among the major provisions of the act are: criminal and civil penalties for securities violations, auditor independence/certification of internal audit work by external auditors and increased disclosure regarding executive compensation, insider trading and financial statements. Read more at *www.tech-listings.net/xlist/tech/bizsoft/compliance/sox?id=1*.

225 Tips to Succeed:
A publisher's view of journalism

Journalism is the first "rough draft" of history. Sometimes you wish it weren't so rough.

Philip L. Graham - Publisher - *The Washington Post* from 1946 to 1963.

satellite media tour (SMT) – Interviews offered to television and radio stations via satellite. TV satellite tours are usually made up of back-to-back interviews that run two to five minutes each.

satisficing – A planning philosophy implying a firm's intention to continue to carry on its present operations in much the same way as it has always done. The word is formed by combining satisfy and suffice. See *optimizing*.

saturation – Using a heavy schedule of commercial spots or print ads to get a message across to as many listeners, viewers or readers as possible.

scaled response – Questions on a survey that require respondents to rate a company, product, service, etc. on a scale provided (excellent, good, fair, poor, etc.). See *Likert scale*.

scanner systems – Electronic equipment which allows product *bar codes* to be read. Information recorded by the scanning devices is used in marketing decision making, including inventory control. See *bar code*.

scanners – An optical character recognition machine which consists of a scan head, a computer processor and an output device. Used for interpreting documents, invoices, *bar codes* and photos for use in *color separations*.

scanning – The act of using a scanner to digitally copy optical characters (text or photographs). Read more at *www.scantips.com/faq.html*. See *pre-press services*.

scene setting – The process of using realistic sounds to stimulate noise in backgrounds during radio production (such as car horns, sirens, recorded laughter, etc.).

scientific random sample – A sample where each member of the population has an equal chance of being chosen. Also referred to *chance survey* or *simple random sample*. See *random sample*.

scrambled assortment – An assortment strategy where a reseller decides to carry dissimilar or unrelated lines to generate additional sales. For example, a news agency might add indoor plants and housewares to its range of newspapers, stationery and books. Also known as *scrambled merchandising*. See *deep assortment*.

scrambled merchandising – The practice by wholesalers and retailers that carry an increasingly wider assortment of merchandise to generate increased sales. See *scrambled assortment*.

scrapbooking – Compiling a portfolio whose contents look more like a scrap book – broad assortment – rather than the best examples of completed work.

screen – A color printing method (boxes that are shaded) where ink is forced through a stencil placed over a screen that blocks out areas of an image and allows ink to adhere to the printing surface. Also, a printing process where a squeegee forces paint or ink through a screen which is transferred with stenciled designs onto the material – cloth or other fabric, paper, etc. Also referred to as serigraphy. Also, the surface onto which an image of a PowerPoint®, slide or television picture is shown.

screening – An early stage in new product development when ideas for new products are sifted or *screened* to identify those that the firm might profitably develop. Two broad approaches to (idea) *screening* are possible

– managerial judgment and customer evaluation. See *drop error*; *go error*; *new product development,*

screening interview – An early stage in the sales hiring process when supervisors meet with applicants to arouse further interest in the most promising and to identify those who are not suitable.

screening question – Questions designed to establish if the respondents have characteristics appropriate for the survey.

script – A prepared speech written on paper or the text of a play, broadcast or movie. Also, a type font (cursive) with individual letters that appear attached. Considered difficult to read in large blocks.

search engine – A program that helps Web users find information on the Internet – by using specified keywords. The search would return a list of documents that contain the keywords. *Search engine* examples would include Google®, Yahoo®, Ask® and Dogpile®.

search engine marketing (SEM) – Public relations, advertising and other communication efforts designed to aid the *search engine* industry.

seasonal discount – A reduced price to encourage the purchase of a particular product in the off-season – sometimes called out-of-season discount. See *discount.*

seasonal forecast adjustments – The adjustment of monthly sales forecasts based on projections drawn from of historical data taking into account short-term changes in volume caused by seasonal and other variations.

seasonal rating adjustment – An adjustment to rating numbers to reflect seasonal differences in television viewership and radio listenership. Factors that may be compensated for include weather, holidays and events that affect the news.

seasonal stock – Inventory added to meet the expected needs of an unusually heavy seasonal demand or for promotional campaigns. Also referred to as *promotional stock.*

seasonality – The variation in sales for goods and services throughout the year, depending on the season. For example, water ice is advertised more in the summer than winter.

second act – Slang for when a professional begins a new job after leaving the previous position either for positive or negative reasons.

S

226

Techniques to Succeed:
When output = outcome
synergy is achieved

SYNERGY'S COMPONENTS

- Advertising
- (Sales) Promotion*
- Public Relations*
- Direct Marketing
- Cause Marketing
- Sponsorship (Partnering) Marketing
- Positioning (Place)*
- Personal Selling*

- Price*
- Product itself*
- Packaging*
- Policy*
- Politics*
- Mind Share (Brainstorming)
- Brand Identity
- Interactive (Web)

Litwin's 9 Ps of Marketing
M. Larry Litwin, APR, Fellow PRSA - *The Public Relations Practitioner's Playbook*
(Kendall/Hunt – 2008)

S

Someone lands on his/her feet for a *second act* – or second career. Examples could include an athlete who become a sports announcer or a journalist who enters the public relations profession.

second act country – Political term for people who come to America to start a "new" life. They can change their name, their religion and their history.

second color – The *spot color* in a *two-color job* – *spot color* plus black.

second-day story – A "follow– up" story giving new developments on one that has already appeared in the newspaper.

second front page – The front page of a second section; also called the *split page*.

second life – Also called *virtual reality* – personalities (alter egos) created on the Internet – in cyberspace. Nearly 7,000,000 subscribe to such (3D online digital world) providers as www.secondlife.com. *Second Life* – employing a gaming interface that allows users to create a virtual character – presents an alternative universe where everyone can be what they want to be. In the form of avatars the Internet icons can meet, dance and explore in perfect (lifelike) physical form as any personality they choose. See *Web 2.0.*

secondary data – The collection of marketing research data using previously published sources. Also, information obtained from previously published materials such as books, the Internet, magazines, newspapers, government census publications and company reports and files. See *primary data*; *secondary research*.

secondary packaging – A box or other protective wrapping which protects the product's primary package until ready to be sold or used. See *primary packaging*; *shipping packaging*.

secondary research – The collection of marketing research data using previously published sources. Information or data available through another's research (U.S. Census Bureau; Gallup, a newspaper, etc.) See *primary research*.

section – Separate parts of a newspaper.

section lead – Top story in a *section*.

Sectional Center Facility (SCF) – A postal facility that serves as the processing and distribution center (P&DC) for post offices in a designated geographic area as defined by the first three digits of the ZIP Codes of those offices. Some *SCFs* serve more than one 3-digit ZIP Code range.

sectional story – A major news story with different aspects, featured under two or more headlines.

sector press – The media relevant to specific audiences, including special interest magazines and newsletters. Also called *trade press* or *vertical press*.

seeding – See *salting*.

segmentation – The division of a total market into groups, subgroups or sectors (*demographically* and *psychographically*) with relatively similar needs and wants. It's important that the proper message and channel be used to communicate to *market segments* at a time when the segments are available to receive the message. The purpose is to prioritize segments of the market to improve marketing profitability and to provide a means to choose the most appropriate communication media and messages for each target audience.

segmentation bases – The basic dimensions – *geographic*, *demographic*, *psychographic* and behavioristic – upon which a heterogeneous market can be divided into relatively homogeneous or similar groups.

S

segmentation strategies – Specific marketing approaches available to, or taken by, a firm or organization in relation to the market segment or segments it wishes to target. Four specific *segmentation strategies* are available – *concentrated segmentation strategy*, *market segment expansion strategy*, *product line expansion segmentation strategy* and *differentiated segmentation strategy*.

segue – The transition between two audio or video sources aired consecutively without interruption.

227

Tips to Succeed:
Job hunting – consider using an agency

- Target one or two agencies that are advertising positions you are qualified for and then call them - don't send your resume.

- Talk to the representative whose client has the openings you are interested in. Talk to the consultant about your experience and explain where your relevance lies.

- Don't send your resume out to each of their listings. Automated recruitment processes should be avoided because it doesn't help you build rapport and make you stand out from the other hundreds of candidates sending in resumes.

David Carter - www.job-hunting-tips.com

SELECT – Acronym for Situation analysis; Explicit statement of the problem; Laying out the research design and collecting data; Evaluating the data and making a decision; Creating a plan to implement the decision and Testing the correctness of the decision – a six-step approach to the process of public relations and marketing research.

selected friends – Term used to describe others who are like you.

selective advertising – Advertising intended to create demand for a specific brand rather than for the whole product category or class.

selective binding – The process which allows an advertisement to be inserted into only certain select issues of a magazine, or allows selected pages to be inserted in a catalog. National magazines use this technique to zone or regionalize their advertising.

selective binding programs for advertisers – The customizing of magazines and similar print media for specific groups of subscribers and advertisers. In *selective binding programs*, the same issue of a magazine can be tailored for different audiences by changing the "slant" of a story and targeting the advertising.

selective distortion – The interpretation of information in a way that is consistent with the person's existing opinion.

selective distribution – The policy of selecting dealers best able to serve a manufacturer.

selective demand – Demand for a specific brand within a particular product class.

selective demand advertising – Advertising that promotes a particular manufacturer's brand rather than a generic product. See *primary demand*.

selective distortion – The interpretation of information in a way that is consistent with the person's existing opinion. See *selective exposure*; *selective retention*.

selective distribution – Making a product available in more than one outlet, but not in as many as are willing to stock it. Nike®, Reebok®, New Era® and a number of electronics manufacturers use *selective distribution*. It allows manufacturers to maintain more control over the way their products are sold and discourages price competition among sellers of the products by distributing their products only to those wholesalers and retailers who follow the manufacturer's guidelines. Also referred to as *selective selling*. See *distribution intensity*.

selective exposure – The ability to process only certain information and facts contained in advertisements and other strategic messages and avoid other stimuli. Also called *selective perception*. See *selective distortion*; *selective retention*.

selective perception – The process of screening out information that does not interest us and retaining information that does. Also the process of remembering only a small portion of what a person is exposed to. See *selective exposure*.

selective retention – The process of screening out information that does not interest us and retaining only that information that does. Many times, the information we retain reinforces or confirms previously held attitudes. See *selective exposure*; *selective distortion*.

selective selling – See *selective distribution*.

self-cover – A cover printed on the same paper stock as the rest of the magazine or book.

self-liquidating premium – A premium offer paid by the consumer whose total cost including handling fees is paid for in the basic sales transaction.

self-liquidator – A form of consumer sales promotion where money and proof of purchase of a product (package tops, labels, etc) are traded in for an item of merchandise, usually sold below normal retail price. Also called a self-liquidating premium.

self-mailer – A brochure or other document, many times a direct mail or other advertising piece, that contains postal information (return address, bulk mail indicia or insignia or room for postage) and room for an address label so that it can mailed by itself, without having to place it in an envelope.

self-selected survey – Also known as *casual survey*. Respondents volunteer themselves. The Internet, newspapers, radio and television stations and magazines that encourage or allow listeners, viewers or readers to respond fall into this sampling technique.

sell-in – The process of educating the sales force and distributors to sell a new product as part of the preparation for its launch – development of *sales kits*, briefings on the target market and competition and outlining the organization's plans to create consumer demand may be involved. See *new product development*. See *selling-in*.

sell-off period – The duration of a particular sales promotion from the time of the sales promotion launch to the end of the special offer.

sell-through quantity – The quantity of merchandise required for a sales promotion.

sell-through rate – The percentage of ad or commercial inventory (space in print; time in broadcast) sold, as opposed to traded or bartered.

seller's market – A market where there is a shortage of particular goods or services for sale.

selling agent – An individual who represents a firm or company and sells to *wholesalers*, *distributors*, *retailers* or *end users*.

228

Tips to Succeed:
For entrepreneurs pondering a change

Some things you should know about starting and growing your business:

- Don't expect to become rich. If you want to make a lot of money in the next five years, go get a job. If you have the passion to see your ideas and actions succeed or fail, then become an entrepreneur.

- Know you will fail. It is not a matter of if you will fail, just when. Business is about the good times and the bad times.

Develop resiliency to ride the rollercoaster up and down. Celebrate the good times with your family and team. Transition through the bad times by learning what you can, then moving on for better days.

- Be humble. You meet the same people on the way up as you do on the way down in your business career. You are totally responsible for your success and failures.

Barry Moltz - Author - *You Need to Be a Little Crazy: The Truth About Starting and Growing Your Business*
www.barrymoltz.com

selling concept – The philosophy or orientation of an organization, which emphasizes aggressive selling to achieve its objectives and possibly the company or organization's goal. Firms characterized by this approach often rely on *pressure selling* and *manipulative* sales techniques to win business and reach a satisfactory bottom line.

selling formulas – Various formulae used by salespeople to guide their presentations to buyers. See *AIDA*; *formula selling*.

selling orientation – A company-centered rather than a client-centered approach to conduct of business. This orientation tends to ignore what the customer/user really wants and needs – and emphasizes *manipulating* (strategic) messages.

selling premises – The sales logic behind an advertising message.

selling process – The separate, but related, stages forming the activity of personal selling – including pre-approach (planning), approach, need identification, presentation, handling objections, closing the sale and post-sale follow-up.

selling proposition – A benefit statement about a feature that is both unique to the product and important to the user. Commonly referred to as the USP *(unique selling proposition)*.

selling-in – The process of educating the sales force and distributors to sell a new product as part of the preparation for its launch – development of *sales kits*, briefings on the target market and competition and outlining the organization's plans to create consumer demand may be involved. See *new product development*. Same as *sell-in*.

selling up – A practice in selling aimed at persuading the customer to buy a higher-priced item than the one originally inquired about. *Bait and switch* would be *selling up*, but *selling up* is not always illegal (bait and switch is).

semantic differential – A rating scale technique using pairs of words of opposite meaning.

semi-liquidator – A premium offer that is partially paid by the consumer as well as the manufacturer.

semicomp – A layout drawn to size that depicts the art and display type. *Body copy* is illustrated with lined rules (much like a finished rough copy).

seminal research – Original research never done before on that issue, topic or area.

seminar selling – Bringing together a number of prospective buyers at the same time for a sales presentation.

seminars – One day training sessions involving role play and group work exercises. See *training sessions*; *workshops*.

semiotics – Refers to theories regarding symbolism and how people glean meaning from words, sounds and pictures. Sometimes used in researching names for various products and services – a niche and profitable profession involving public relations, advertising and other aspects of *synergy*.

sender – The originator of the message process – the *encoder* or the source. The *encoder* or person, group or organization with a message to send. See *communication process*.

sensitive data – Information relating to racial or ethnic origin, political opinions, religious or other beliefs, trade union membership, health, sex life and criminal convictions.

sensory retailing – A recent trend in retailing where the retailer attempts to position the store and attract customers by making a visit to it an exciting visual, auditory, etc. experience. See *atmospherics*.

separation – The separating of a full-color image into the primary printing colors in *positive* or *negative* form. By overlaying the *separations* in the printing process, using the correct primary color for each, the result is a full color reproduction of the original. *Separation* must also be done in *spot color* work, too.

separator – A brief (usually two to 15 seconds) transition announcement – many times including high intensity graphics and sound – placed just before a television news story to gain the viewers' attention. Also called *bumper*. See *attentioner*.

sequential segmentation – The division of a heterogeneous market into relatively homogeneous (similar *demographic*) groups on one basis (for example, geographic, age, education, etc.), followed by further *segmentation* on some other basis (for example, end-user type).

serial comma – Comma before "and" – *Associated Press style* calls for "putting commas to separate the elements of a series," but no comma goes before the final conjunction, as in "red, white and blue" or "Rosie, Amy, Nicole and Rebecca."

series – A group of related stories generally run on successive days.

serif (type) – Short, decorative cross lines or tails at the ends of the main strokes in some typefaces (fonts), such as Times Roman lettering. A type font that has "tails" or hands and feet. This is a *serif* type. See *sans-serif (type)*.

served market – That part of the total market which a company decides to target. Also called *target market*.

server – A computer, which distributes files that are shared across a *LAN (local area network , WAN (wide area network)* or the Internet. A single server can run several different server software packages, providing many different servers to clients on the network. Also known as a *host*.

server centric measurement – A method of audience measurement retrieved from server logs, which are automatically tabulated.

server-initiated ad impression – One of the two methods used for ad counting. Ad content is delivered to the user via two methods – *server-*

S

initiated and *client-initiated*. *Server-initiated* ad counting uses the publisher's Web content server for making requests, formatting and redirecting content. For organizations using a *server-initiated* ad counting method, counting should occur following the response to the ad on the publisher's ad server or the Web content server, or later in the process. This is important because Web ad rates may be determined by *server-initiated ad impressions*. See *client-initiated ad impression*.

server pull – A process using an individual's browser which maintains an automated or customized connection or profile with a Web server. Much like many companies do, the *server* stores information consisting of *demographics* and specifications as listed by the individual or user.

server push – A process using an individual's browser which maintains an open connection with a *browser* after the initial request for a page. Through this open connection the *server* continues to provide updated pages and content even though the visitor has made no further direct requests for such information.

service – An intangible product – the work a firm does for a customer .

service bureaus – A company that will maintain lists for list owners. Services may include updating the list, merge/purge, data overlays and preparing the list for mailing or rentals. Also called *computer service bureaus*.

service call e-mail – An e-mail where the writer checks in to ask if there is anything he/she can do in the upcoming months.

service-firm-sponsored retail franchising – A system of service product delivery where an organization producing a service (termite control, plumbers, car rental, restaurants, income tax services, etc.) sets up a number of independently-owned franchised outlets or stores in locations convenient to its customers. See *franchising*.

service form competitors – Organizations offering products of different types, which can help an individual to fulfill a particular desire or need. For example, a person who wants to do a creative hobby course could enroll in a photography course conducted by the adult school or a painting course conducted by a town's parks and recreation department. These course providers are *service form competitors*.

service heterogeneity – One of the four characteristics which distinguish a service. *Variability* expresses the notion that a service may vary in standard or quality from one provider to the next or from one

S

occasion to the next. Also referred to as *heterogeneity*. See *services marketing*; *inseparability*; *intangibility*; *service perishability*; *service variability*.

service inseparability – One of the four characteristics which distinguish a service. *Inseparability* expresses the notion that a service can not be separated from the service provider. See *services marketing*; *service inseparability*; *service intangibility*; *service perishability*; *service variability*.

service intangibility – One of the four characteristics which distinguish a service. *Intangibility* expresses the notion that a service has no physical substance. It is something you just can't put your fingers on. For example, the difference between brands of flour or sugar. See *services marketing*; *service inseparability*; *service perishability*; *service variability*.

service management system – The equivalent of a product management system for service organizations.

service mark – A mark, sign, symbol, slogan, etc. that performs the same function for a service as a *trademark* does for a tangible product. Legal protection is through the U.S. Patent and Trademark Office. It is given to a *brand name*, *brand mark* and/or *logo*, term, design, symbol or any other feature that identifies the service, institution or idea. See *trademark*.

service mix – The range of services offered by a *services marketing* company.

service perishability – One of the four characteristics which distinguish a service. *Perishability* expresses the notion that a service cannot be made in advance and stored. See *services marketing*; *service inseparability*; *service intangibility*; *service variability*.

service sector – The part of industry or business that deals with the marketing and selling of intangible products rather than physical goods.

service variability – One of the four characteristics which distinguish a service. *Variability* expresses the notion that a service may vary in standard or quality from one provider to the next or from one occasion to the next. Also referred to as *heterogeneity*. See *services marketing*; *service inseparability*; *service intangibility*; *service perishability*.

services characteristics – The features of services that distinguish them from tangible products. See *service inseparability*; *service intangibility*; *service perishability*; *service variability*.

services marketing – The marketing of intangible products, such as cleaning services, haircutters, exterminators and travel companies.

229

Tips to Succeed: What amount of success is satisfying?

Question: How much is enough? Your answer may tell you that you need to make some changes in your life.

The authors wish to redefine our ideas about success and they argue that too many businesspeople try to group all their own ideas about success in just one professional basket, which places them on an endlessly revolving wheel where they chase more titles, deals and money. The result is an empty feeling because they can't grasp the unobtainable.

This leads us back to the question: "How much is enough?" The authors interviewed many people who passed through the Harvard Business School, and who, by most standards, would be called "successful," but they discovered that many of them weren't satisfied with their lives.

They felt as though something was missing. They sensed that there was far more to being successful than what their lives represented to them at the moment, but many could not say what that "something" was. The book says that kind of success is one-dimensional.

Success should be defined in four ways:
• Happiness. Being content with one's life.

• Achievement. Setting and reaching goals.

• Significance. Doing things that positively affect colleagues, family and friends.

• Legacy. In which a person's values and achievements are used to help others succeed in the future.

Success should be multidimensional - not built simply on work and money. If they were the answer, more people would be satisfied.

How do we define success? That depends on:
• Who we are.

• What we do for a living.

• How much we have of life's material possessions.

• How full or shallow we are in our personalities.

Laura Nash and Howard Stevenson -
Harvard University Business School - Authors - *Just Enough*
Newstrack Executive Information Service - www.News-Track.com - 800-334-5771

The ABCs of Strategic Communication

S

services selling – The selling of intangible products.

session – A measurement of Web site activity. A sequence of Internet activity made by one user at one site. Also a series of transactions performed by a computer user that can be tracked across successive Web sites. For example, in a single session, a user may start on a publisher's Web site, click on an advertisement and then go to an advertiser's Web site and make a purchase. Read more at *www.iab.net* for ad campaign measurement guidelines and at *www.netratings.com*. See *visit*.

session cookies – *Cookies* that are loaded into a computer's RAM (random access memory) and work only during that browser session. When the browser exits, these *cookies* are erased. They are "temporary cookies", and no *cookie* is written to a user's hard drive.

set – A constructed setting where the action in a commercial takes place.

set-top box – An electronic device that sits on top of one's TV set and allows it to connect to the Internet, game systems or cable systems.

set-up piece – A story reported on a radio or television news program that leads into another. The stories are usually related. For example, during an election, the *set-up piece* might be an overall story about the mayor's race to be followed by individual stories about the candidates.

sets in use (SIU) – The percent of television sets that are tuned into a particular broadcast during a specific amount of time. See *share*.

seven Ss – A framework or model, developed by the McKinsey Company, a leading consulting firm, for maximizing. The framework or model, which McKinsey considers an essential business strategy, refers to seven interrelated aspects of the organization – systems, structure, skills, style, staff, strategy and shared values. See *McKinsey 7- S framework*.

shade – A tint or *screen* used when you want to lighten the color used – 30 percent black is a light *shade* of gray.

share – The percentage of households or target audience members watching television or listening to the radio based only on the total number of TVs or radios turned on at that time. For example, if only 600,000 or the more than 1,000,000 homes that have TVs have their TV on and 200,000 homes are watching a particular program, the share would be 33 percent. See *rating point*.

share-of-audience – The percent of audiences tuned into a particular radio or television program at a given time. For example, the number of TV homes watching between the hours of 9 and 10 p.m.

share of market – The percentage of the total category sales owned by one *brand*.

share of Voice – The percentage of advertising messages in a medium by one *brand* among all messages for that product or service.

share-of-voice (SOV) – Percent of total category advertising contributed by each brand. How much money a firm or organization is

230 Tips to Succeed: Assertiveness skills help you de-stress

One way to de-stress at work is to improve your assertiveness skills. Here are some suggested strategies:

- Determine if you're passive or aggressive. Assertiveness is between passivity and aggressiveness. Gather information from others to figure out if you come across as passive and submissive or aggressive and intimidating. You want to fall in the assertive range.

- Learn how to say no. The ability to say no can relieve your stress at work. If saying no to work is difficult for you, begin slowly by working on not saying yes right away.

- Compromise for win-win solutions. Look for ways to create compromises that will work for everyone involved. If your boss wants you to have a project done in one week and that seems impossible to you, tell her the benefits of finishing within two weeks.

- State what you want. A major problem that leads to stress is not stating your goals. You then feel out of control of your work situation, but in reality you did not really try to be the leader of your own career.

- Ask for help. Look to others for assistance in decreasing your stress level.

Larina Kase - Doctor of Psychology, career coach and former counselor at the University of Pennsylvania - www.extremecommunicator.com

The ABCs of Strategic Communication

S

spending in the major advertising media compared to how much their competitors are spending. Read more at *www.givetogetmarketing.com/tips-sov.html*.

share order – In New Jersey and some other states, allows state authorities to turn over all materials in an investigation – transcripts of grand jury testimony, etc.

shared services – Joint or cooperative provision of municipal services between government entities.

shareholder value – The worth of a company from its shareholders' point of view. Maximizing *shareholder value* is a common objective for business management.

sheet-fed press – An offset printer that prints on paper which is fed one sheet at a time as opposed to a web press, which uses large rolls of paper (most newspapers use a *web press*).

shelf facings – The number of units of a product that are visible at the front of a retail store shelf. High-volume categories are usually allocated more shelf facings than low-volume categories. See *shelf management*; *slotting fees*.

shelf fee – A fee paid by a manufacturer to such major retailers as supermarket chains, big box drug stores, certain discounters, etc. for shelf space for a new product and/or to keep their products on store shelves. Typically, the more visible the spot and the more *shelf facings*, the higher the fee. Also referred to as the *stocking allowance, introductory allowance, shelf fee* or *street money*. See *slotting allowance*.

shelf life – The period of time that a product can remain on display in a retail store before the expiration of its "use by" date.

shelf-life – How long a document is held onto by the receiver. For example, an *evergreen* lasts forever.

shelf management – The process of determining the number and location of *shelf facings* in a retail store. See *shelf facings*.

shelf screamers (shelf talkers) – A printed advertising message that hangs over the edge of a retail store shelf, e.g. "On Special" or "Sale Item." With technology, *shelf talkers* are now literal – as shoppers approach a product, a device sets off an audio message.

shell – A folder that holds a *media kit*. It usually is printed with company or organization name, logo and other graphics, event, date and theme.

Sherpas – Experts in a particular area – communication, politics, world events, etc. Sous-Sherpas serve *Sherpas* as researchers and *niche* experts.

shield law – A law that protects journalists from disclosing their confidential sources. Thirty states have their own *shield laws*.

shipping packaging – Outer packaging (cartons, for example) in which products are packed for storage and transport. See *primary packaging; secondary packaging*.

shirt tail – A short, related story added at the end of a longer one.

Shockwave – For computer users, a browser plug-in developed by Macromedia® which allows multimedia objects to appear on the Web (animation, audio and video).

shoot – To take photographs.

shopbot – Computer software, available on the Web, that allows users to search for the best price. Read more at *www.wired.com/wired/archive/6.12/mustread.html?pg=9*.

shopping cart – On computers, software that allows the user to hold merchandise selected for purchase until shopping is complete and the user is ready to check out. Staples®, Victoria's Secret®, Jockey®, Amazon® and many other online retails use *shopping carts*.

shopping goods – Consumer goods that the customer typically compares for suitability, quality, price, features, etc. before selection and purchase. See *convenience goods; specialty goods*.

Short Message Service (SMS) – Mobile messaging. It enables users to send and receive text messages over their mobile phone.

short rate – A fee paid by an advertiser if it fails to buy the contracted volume of media space or time. The fee is charged because the advertiser received a reduced rate based on the contracted volume. For example, if an advertiser contracts with a newspaper for 200 column inches and receives a 200 column inch price but uses only 150 column inches, the advertiser would be obligated to pay a *short rate* fee.

short-run average cost – The *average cost* to produce each unit of an item or a set or group of products in the short term. Over a period of

231

Tips to Succeed: Speaking helps maximize growth

Participating as a speaker at business events can provide opportunities for you and your business.

You could gain more clients, greater name recognition and connections, which could offer you many long-term benefits.

However, it's important to carefully choose which events are worth taking the time to create and prepare a presentation.

Here are a few tips on when and where to share your expertise:

- Think outside your industry. Consider opportunities to present to people other than your own peers.

- Think business groups: Many organizations, such as chambers of commerce and Rotary clubs, have monthly programs that focus on education as well as networking. Take advantage of the chance to tell people about your work.

- Consider the time. When do you get your biggest influx of client calls? If your business is seasonal, consider doing presentations just prior to that time.

Speaking engagements work a lot like advertising. The more people hear and see you, the greater the chances of them buying whatever you're selling. Pick these opportunities carefully and you will be speaking your way to business success.

Valerie Schlitt - VSA - wwwvsanj@netcom.com

time (in the long term), the *average cost* may be reduced through experience of producing the product(s). See *average cost*.

short-term profit maximization – A pricing objective where a firm aims to make as much profit as possible as quickly as possible. In doing so, little attention is paid to maximum market penetration and long-term profit considerations.

shot sheet – A list of photo opportunities that can be provided to a newspaper photographer or one hired by the public relations practitioner coordinating an event.

shovel ready – A construction site that has been cleared and prepared for work to begin.

showing – A basic unit of measurement in purchasing television time, convention (display) space and such other forms of visual (advertising) communication as bus shelters and billboards. Also, a showing is the total number of *GRPs (gross rating points)* delivered in a market on a daily basis.

shrinkage – A term used in retailing to refer to the theft of merchandise by customers and employees. Many retailers and warehouse owners have attempted to reduce *shrinkage* by installing mirrors, video cameras, security guards and alarms that sound when tagged merchandise is carried out of the store.

sides – A print out of a script for a *video news release*, audition or other type of "shoot."

sidebar – A feature story appearing near a (hard) news article – giving the human interest or historical aspects of a story. Also a secondary news story that supports or amplifies a major story.

sig file – A signature block consistently used that includes a tag line about a company. Examples – "Good to the last drop"® (Maxwell House® Coffee); "I'm lovin' it"® (McDonald's®), "When it rains, it pours"® (Morton® Salt).

signature – In printing of books, booklets, newsletters, newspapers, etc., a single printing sheet which folds into 4, 8, 12, 16, and other multiples of 4 to be gathered and bound to form a part of the book, or pamphlet. Knowing *signature* make up is important because the first page of the signature is printed simultaneously with the last, the next with the next to last and so on. Thus, if a customer is paying for additional colors on page one, there would be no additional charge for color on the matching signature page. Also, an advertising locking power device (Kellogg's®) consisting of the name of a company or brand written in a distinctive type style and usually registered as a *trademark* or *service mark*. Also, a musical theme associated with a television program, radio show or a particular product or service; referred to as a theme song.

signature cards – Major characteristics associated with a product or service that sets it apart from others. Similar to *signature program*.

signature partner – Two or more corporations teaming up on such vehicles as credit cards – known as *signature cards* – Air Tran® Visa®, etc.

signature program – Major characteristics associated with a product or service that sets it apart from others. Similar to *signature card*.

signature song – A song that an artist is known for. An example would be Frank Sinatra's "My Way" or "New York New York," or the Beatles "I Want To Hold Your Hand." It would also be a television show's theme song, such as "Sex and the City" or "Dragnet." See *cover song*.

signature sound – A voice associated with a particular product, brand, radio or television station. For many years, the late Mason Adams was the voice of Smuckers® – "With a name like Smuckers, it has to be good."®

signature voice – The voice an individual uses – other than his/her normal voice – during special presentations. Sometimes called a staged or broadcaster's voice.

significance – Also referred to as *substantiality*. One of the four major requirements for useful market segmentation. *Substantiality* expresses the notion that the segment chosen as the target market must be large enough to be profitable. Other major requirements are *accessibility*; *actionability*; and *measurability*.

silent close – A closing technique where the salesperson presents or demonstrates the product to the prospective buyer and then deliberately stops talking – simply waiting for a favorable response from the buyer. See *close*.

silk screening – A color printing method where ink is forced through a stencil placed over a screen that blocks out areas of an image and onto the printing surface. Also, a printing process where a squeegee forces paint or ink through a screen which is transferred with stenciled designs onto the material – cloth, other fabric, paper, etc.

Simmons Market Research Bureau (SMRB) – A syndicated service that provides audience exposure and product usage data for print and broadcast media.

Simple Mail Transfer Protocol (SMPT) – In computers, the *protocol* used to transfer e-mail.

simple random (probability) sample – A sample where each member of the *population* has an equal chance of being chosen. Also referred to *chance survey* or *scientific random sample*.

simulated store test – A form of pre-testing of new product introductions prior to full-scale marketing. Tests are done to study consumer behavior towards the new products. Typically, consumers are selected from the target market and asked to shop in "test" supermarkets where the new products have been placed.

simultaneous submission – When (freelance) writers send a bylined article to more than one publication at the same time. Many publications discourage this practice.

Sinatra syndrome – The act of citing other's works rather than taking credit. Frank Sinatra would often cite composers and lyricists before singing a song during live performances. The better speakers sprinkle attributions through their "talks" and speeches. It avoids any hint of plagiarism. Also, referring to another human.

232

Tips to Succeed:
The basics of conducting a scientific survey

HOW-TO-DO-IT

1. Decide what *you* want to learn from the survey.
2. Ask why *you* want to learn this.
3. Ask *yourself* whether you could get this information without doing a survey.
4. Decide who your public or audience is going to be.
5. Determine the type of survey method you will use.
6. Establish confidence levels for your survey.
7. Develop a timeline from start to finish for your survey.
8. Decide how the information will be analyzed and disseminated to your publics or audience (especially those surveyed).

SINBAD – Single Income, No Boyfriend and Absolutely Desperate – A demographic grouping.

SINGAD – Single Income, No Girlfriend and Absolutely Desperate – A demographic grouping.

single brand name – A *brand name* not accompanied by any other family or corporate *brand name*. Sometimes called *individual brand name*. For example, Cold-EEZE®, Morton® Salt, and JC Penny®. See *corporate branding*; *family brand*; *product line brand name*.

single-line store – A retail store selling a wide assortment of goods in a basic line, such as women's clothing, hardware, cosmetics. *Single-line stores* are also referred to as boutiques.

single niching – A strategy followed by companies that operate in only one *market*

233

Techniques to Succeed:
Rather be somewhere else?
Your customers will too!

Commitment – true acceptance and dedication to a goal – makes a huge difference in the outcome of any course of action, whether in business, reaching personal objectives, or the quality of personal relationships.

Not all entrepreneurs love what they do. After all, they're their own boss, right? If they're not happy, can't they just change direction? It may not be that easy.

You may not be able to change your business – at least not immediately, but you can change your attitude.

What happens when you lose interest in your own business?
• First, the quality of your work suffers. Customers leave, but your overhead remains.

• You stop developing your skills, so you lose ground against your competitors.

• Most importantly, your lack of enthusiasm shows whenever you try to market your products or services. Even when new customers come to you they sense your indifference and leave.

Being passionate about your work is a competitive advantage. Customers and employees sense you're doing something you truly believe in, and they respond accordingly.

What can you do to reignite your enthusiasm for your business?
• Evaluate why you've lost interest.

• Decide whether you want to stay in this line of work.

If you decide to stay in business – and most of us will – here are other steps to take:
• Give yourself a goal.

• Develop a plan.

• Expose yourself to new ideas.

• Embrace your commitment.

Rhonda Abrams - www.rhondaworks.com/

S

niche. For example, Polident® markets, for the most part, to older people with dentures. See *market niche; multiple niching.*

single-piece rate – The "undiscounted" or "full" postage rate available for individual pieces of express mail, first-class mail, priority mail and package services.

single-product strategy – The decision by a producer to offer only one product with few, if any, options. For example, salt, snow shovels and cotton balls.

single-source data – Marketing research information, collected from the same source – by people-meters and scanning devices, for example – that makes it possible to link an individual's purchasing behavior to specific media exposure. Read more at *www.nielsenmedia.com.*

single-zone pricing – A pricing method, sometimes referred to as postage stamp pricing, where all customers pay the same freight costs regardless of their distance from the dispatch point. See *delivered pricing; uniform delivered price; zone pricing.*

singles market – A market segment, regarded as both a lifestyle and a demographic category that includes never-been-married singles, widowed and divorced people.

sink – A band of white space appearing at the top of the page.

sink-or-swim sales training – The practice of throwing new sales recruits straight into the field without *formal training* so that they have to learn quickly or risk losing their jobs. See *sales training.*

SITCOM – Single Income, Two Kids, Outrageous Mortgage – A demographic grouping.

site-centric measurement – Audience measurement derived from a Web site's own server logs.

situation analysis – The process of gathering and evaluating information on internal and external environments to assess a firm's current strengths, weaknesses, opportunities and threats, and to guide its goals and objectives. It sets the table for public relations planners by detailing necessary information gathered through scientific and nonscientific research – identifying target audiences and determining the strategic direction the organization should take. Some public relations practitioners define *situation analysis* as a one-paragraph statement of the situation and refinement of problem definition based on research; a second paragraph identifies potential difficulties and related problems to be considered. See *SWOT analysis*. (For examples, see *The Public Relations Practitioner's Playbook* – Kendall/Hunt – 2008).

situation (analysis), objective, strategy, tactics and targets (SOSTT) – When combined with a goal or global ambition becomes the "overall" public relations plan.

situational hero – An ordinary person who rises to the occasion in an emergency.

six degrees of separation – Also known as the "small world phenomenon." The concept that, if a person is one "step" away from each person he or she knows and two "steps" away from each person who is known by one of the people he or she knows, then everyone is no more than six "steps" away from each person on Earth.

six sigma – Takes such knowledge about individuals in the work environment and applies it to create a more productive and consistent workforce. Also called *human sigma*; *intellectual property*; team, .

sizing – Making a picture smaller or larger to fit a space.

skew – Weighting advertising activity towards a particular *market segment*.

sketch – A plan of where items will be placed on your page. A rough idea of the stories, graphics, etc. you hope to include in a publication.

Skills Level Analysis Process (SLAP) – In computers, an online tool to assess skills of marketing professionals and to measure them against business goals and objectives.

skim-the-cream pricing – A pricing approach where the producer sets a high introductory price to attract buyers with a strong desire for the product and the resources to buy it, and then gradually reduces the price to attract the next and subsequent layers of the market. See *market skimming pricing*.

skimming – Setting the original price high in the early stages of the product life cycle in an attempt to earn as much profit as possible before prices are driven down by increasing competition. See *market penetration pricing*; *market skimming pricing*.

skimming pricing strategy – Setting a relatively high initial price for a new product or service when there is a strong price-perceived quality relationship that targets early adopters that are not sensitive to price. The price may be lowered over time. See *prestige pricing*.

skins – In computers, customized and interchangeable sets of graphics which allow Internet users to continually change the look of their desktops or browsers, without changing their settings or functionality. *Skins* are a type of marketing tool.

skybox/skyline – A *banner* head that runs above the nameplate. Serves as a *teaser*. If they are boxed (with art), they are called *skyboxes* or boxcars. If they are only a line of type, they are called *skylines*.

skyscraper – In computers, advertisements on Web pages that are tall and thin – usually on the right side of a Web site.

slant – An angle of a story. A story is *slanted* when a certain aspect is played up for policy or other reasons.

sleeper effect – In advertising, recalling a *brand* long after seeing or hearing a commercial or advertisement. Many times, a word, picture or person (*transfer effect*) may have triggered the recall. Also called *top of mind*.

slice of life – A problem-solution message built around some common, everyday situation.

slate – A screen that identifies or introduces images to follow.

slicks – A high-quality proof of an advertisement printed on glossy paper, which is suited for reproduction. Also referred to as *camera-ready*, *laser print; matte, repro* or *velox*. They can be put in a pdf format and e-mailed.

sliding commission – A compensation method where salespeople are paid commissions at a changing rate depending on the quantity sold. See *progressive commission; regressive commission*.

sliding down the demand curve – A pricing method where the initial price is set at the highest possible level and then gradually reduced to attract successive waves of purchasers as demand diminishes.

slippage – In sales promotion, the percentage of purchasers who fail to redeem an offer made with the purchase. This could be viewed as either a positive or negative. If it drives additional sales, it is a positive – if not, it is a negative. Some manufacturers view the failure to redeem *rebates* a positive, but in the long term, that, too, could be a negative, because it may hinder future sales.

slogan – An advertising *locking power* device. Frequently repeated phrases that provide continuity to an advertising campaign. Also the verbal or written portion of an advertising message that summarizes the main idea in a few memorable words. If a *slogan* comes at the end of commercial, it is called a *tag* or *tag line*.

slot – Newsroom desk usually in the shape of a horseshoe – editor, assistants, broadcast producers and some others responsible for production of a newspaper or radio/television newscast sit in the *slot*.

slotting (allowance) fee – A fee paid by a manufacturer to such major retailers as supermarket chains, big box drug stores, certain discounters, etc. for shelf space for a new product and/or to keep their products on store shelves. Typically, the more visible the spot and the more *shelf facings*, the higher the fee. Also referred to as *introductory allowance, shelf fee* or *street money*.

slotting fee – Somewhat different from above. It is a fee charged to advertisers by media companies to get premium positioning on their site, category exclusivity or some other special treatment. It is similar to slotting allowances charged by retailers. See *slotting allowance*.

slow and steady – Used in the television news industry to describe the consistency in top-rated newscasts and other programs. Viewers develop an intimacy with the anchors and format because night after night the "show" is *slow and steady*.

slug – Short name or title given to a print or broadcast story used for identification purposes. It typically goes just above the start of the story on the upper left within parentheses – one to three words.

small order problem – The problem of coping with sales orders which are so small that the cost of filling them offsets the profit.

small to medium enterprise (SME) – Carries a number of definitions – according to one, it would be a firm or organization that employs fewer than 250 people with a turnover rate of about 15 percent.

smart board – Also known as interactive whiteboard – presenters write on them as they would a flip chart and the text and/or images appear on a large screen. It is known as DViT (Digital Vision Touch) technology.

234

Tips to Succeed:
Juggling at work? How to stay sane

Ever feel like you are juggling so many things that at any minute you will drop all of them and lose it? Constant multitasking at work can cause intense stress and pressure.

There are solutions:
• Stop juggling. You need to commit yourself to not multitask. Instead of juggling, think of yourself as bowling: one ball at a time. Once that ball is finished, you can move on to the next one. This helps you to feel that you can devote yourself 100 percent to the task at hand without constant distractions and the feeling that you aren't doing a good job.

• Juggle better. The key to multitasking is prioritizing. As a rule, the activities to multitask are the trivial, routine, or automatic duties that do not need all your attention and energy. You could check your e-mail while you are on hold on the phone. You can spell-check a document while listening to your voice mails.

The right solution depends on what works for you.

Larina Kase - Doctor of Psychology, career coach and former counselor at the University of Pennsylvania - www.extremecommunicator.com

smart ads – Digital billboards (advertisements) on the tops of cabs – technologically controlled – informing pedestrians that they are one block from a McDonald's®, other restaurant or retail store.

smart card – Identical in size and feel to credit cards, smart cards store information on an integrated microprocessor chip located within the body of the card. These chips hold a variety of information, from stored (monetary) value used for retail and vending machines, to secure information and applications for such higher-end operations as medical/healthcare records. *Smart cards* are used by many libraries and other such facilities by patrons using computers by the hour or printing hard copy from the rented computer. *Smart cards* are also the device used by public transit for rail tickets or for highway and bridge tolls.

smart growth – A set of standards for land-use and development planning that protects the environment and prevents suburban sprawl by using existing infrastructures and resources, recycled abandoned properties and preserving open space. Its purpose is to protect the future of established communities and improve the quality of life for residents. It accommodates population, housing and employment growth by adding a variety of housing types and price ranges, businesses that create new jobs, "walkable" town centers and neighborhoods and access to public transportation.

smart return – Device planted in the computer of cars that shuts down the engine if the cars owner falls behind in the payments.

smear campaign – A campaign intended to damage the opposition's reputation. They are usually premeditated and well thought out.

SMS message – See *short message service*.

snail mail – Regular U.S. Postal Service mail. Became a term with the advent of e-mail.

snap poll (survey) – A survey taken immediately after an action such as a corporate statement or event – containing only a few questions to determine the opinions of a specific audience or a representative sample of the audience.

sneaker crush – A secret crush or affection one has for another. It is said that Sen. Adlai Stevenson had a *sneaker crush* for *Washington Post* publisher Katherine Graham.

sniffer – Computer software that detects the capabilities of a user's browser (looking for such things as *Java*® capabilities, plug-ins, screen resolution and bandwidth).

soap box – Speaking one's views passionately or self-importantly. A temporary platform used while making an impromptu or nonofficial public speech.

social activity – Activity considered appropriate on social occasions.

social audit – A review and evaluation of the social benefits and social costs pertaining to a particular product. Products and services offer features which must be stressed in terms of benefits to the user – to help give reason to purchase.

social class – The level of society in which an individual belongs. Generally, society is viewed as being upper-class, upper-middle class, middle class or working class.

social marketing – Especially prevalent among non-profit organizations, government agencies, community-based organizations, private foundations, social/health/issue coalitions and any entity that wants to make social change. Also, the design, implementation and control of marketing activity intended to promote social causes or ideas within a target group in a society. A concept that requires balancing a firm or organization, consumer and public interests.

social media (Web 2.0) – A phrase coined by O'Reilly Media in 2004. It refers to a perceived or proposed second generation of Internet-based services – *social media*. Sometimes referred to as the "new media" targeted to the I-generation (Internet generation). But these *innovations* are hardly new. If Web 1.0 is about connecting computers, then *Web 2.0* is about connecting people – and the most popular and growing method is through social networking sites. See *Web 2.0*.

social responsibility in marketing – The recognition by public relations practitioners and marketers that the well-being of society and customer satisfaction is as important as profits in assessing marketing performance. Many more corporations are becoming socially conscious because of overall environmental and other health and well being concerns.

social risk – Concern or uncertainty in the buyer's mind that the purchase of the product under consideration will not be approved of by others. See *risk*.

socialization – The process where individuals are made aware of the behavior that others expect of them regarding such *psychographics* as the norms, values and culture of their society. Agents of *socialization* include the family, school, friendship groups, religious institutions and the mass media.

socio-cultural environment – That part of a firm or organization's external marketing environment where social or cultural changes (changes to the value system of a society) could affect the firm's marketing effort – the changing *socio-cultural environment* may pose threats or present opportunities.

socio-cultural, legal, economic, political and technological (SLEPT) – An economic term for a framework for viewing the macro and micro environments.

socioeconomic variables – Factors of a social and economic nature (occupation, income, etc.) which indicate a person's status within a community. See *demographics*.

S

soft bounce – An e-mail that has been sent back to the sender undelivered after it was already accepted by the recipient's mail.

soft copy – Copy seen on a computer screen.

soft news – Human interest stories that share a person's experience, tell a funny story or present a unique event or product. Most *soft news* stories do not need to be communicated immediately.

soft opening – Opening of a retail store or other business without fanfare. Usually the *hard opening* or grand opening follows – once many of the "kinks" are worked out. See *hard opening*.

soft sell approach – A low-pressure selling situation – a technique of using low pressure appeals in advertisements and commercials. An emotional strategic message that uses mood, ambiguity and sometimes suspense to create a response based on feelings and attitude. Also, a selling situation in which the buyer has no feeling of being coerced. See *hard sell approach*.

sole survivor – The final stage in the *family life cycle* – two sub-categories are used by marketers in examining consumer behavior – sole survivor, working and sole survivor, retired. Also called solitary survivor. See *family life cycle*.

Solicitor General's Office – Federal office that prepares and argues cases before SCOTUS (Supreme Court of the United States)

solid – An arrangement of type lines set vertically as closely as possible. Also referred to as solid set.

solitary survivor – See *sole survivor*.

solo mailing – A database innovation where a customized marketing piece is prepared to appeal to one individual's interests.

soporific – An event that lacks excitement – so boring it tends to cause a lack of interest. A turn off rather than a turn on.

sorting – The computerized process of reorganizing a list from one sequence to another. For example, a file can be sorted by last name, company name, ZIP Code, high donors, multi-buyers, recent buyers, etc. A number of computer programs are used for sorting – including Microsoft Access® and Excel®.

sound designer – person who puts sound effects under motion pictures.

235

Tips to Succeed: 10 steps to shame-fully successful self-promotion

1. Develop a strong belief system: Create better customer service, increase self-esteem and personal growth by promoting every aspect of your business.

2. Develop gutsy goals that make you stretch: Create a "crazy" file for those gutsy marketing ideas that could make your business stand out among your competition.

3. Seek out and act on opportunities: Sometimes the most important strategies appear to be so simple we tend to ignore them.

4. Stay active in your community by networking and volunteering: Work on your business in the community – not just in your business.

5. Take your expertise to another level: Have revolutionary thinking! Do more to service your clients with follow up, follow through and added conveniences. (What sets *you* apart from the others?)

6. Build a strongly connected group of strategic alliances: Look for opportunities to co-market and re-connect with similar business and/or your competition.

7. Break the mold then shamelessly promote your uniqueness: Share your marketing "commercial" and explain why people should do business with you.

8. Get out in front of your target audience on a regular basis and don't ever stop reminding them about your business: Ask and reward satisfied clients for referrals - in writing. Use them in your marketing materials.

9. Embrace technology and market yourself on the Internet: The opportunities to market your business worldwide are endless today. Don't miss this huge window of opportunity of a Web site for your agency or other business. Don't overlook a personal Web site

10. Apply for and achieve awards: Create an award-winning portfolio and seek out opportunities everywhere. This is a great way to promote your business to the media.

Shel Horowitz - www.frugalmarketing.com/libraries.shtml

The ABCs of Strategic Communication

S

sound effects (SFX) – Lifelike imitations of sound.

sound on tape (SOT) – The voice of a newsmaker related to a broadcast news story.

soundbite (soundbyte) – A newsmaker's voice on tape – as part of a news story (radio or television) – that usually runs seven to 15 seconds in length. Also the recorded words of someone who is part of a television or radio news story. Sometimes a very brief quote excerpted from a person's broadcast interview, used in the media to convey a certain idea or opinion. See *voice cut*.

236 Techniques to Succeed: The dreaded social kiss

Social kisses can be awkward – to both women *and* men. But they seem to be spreading everywhere – including business functions. In fact, they have become almost a universal greeting.

Peggy Post, author of the 16th edition of her great-grandmother-in-law's book, *Emily Post's Etiquette,* seems a bit concerned that social kissing has become "almost a universal greeting." At least when reserved strictly for those close to you, though, she approves of it as a method for greeting.

Emily Post's Etiquette suggests, "The social kiss is a charming way to greet family and friends…but not random people. Ms. Post's advice: "Do what you are comfortable with. There's no law that says you have to lay a social kiss when greeting anyone, and if you see one coming at you, just make sure to follow these basic rules. Try to kiss on the right cheek. Always aim to the right. That provides a sense of order, and helps you avoid smacking heads."

It is not *im*proper to gently take the hand of the other person just before the kiss. It is also wise to take the cue from the other person – which does not mean that just because he or she expects a social kiss, they are going to get one.

It is important in business, though, to master the technique, to avoid awkwardness.

source – The *sender* of a strategic message. Also called the *encoder*. Also, a person with information useful to the media. A supplier of information. A person, document, etc.

source attractiveness – In personal selling, the likeability or person-ableness of the salesperson. *Relationship marketing* can be key to *source attractiveness*.

source codes – An identifier used in direct mail and for other database purposes. Many firms and organizations use list servs (*list services*) which specialize in sorting – thus saving money. List servs assure that codes are unique to the particular segment and/or list being coded, so marketing and circulation efforts can be measured.

source credibility – Important to public relations – the use of someone who can be believed and trusted as the message carrier. Sometimes referred to as a *third-party endorser*. In personal selling, it is the *believability* of the salesperson.

source objection – An objection by a prospective buyer leveled against the firm represented by the salesperson.

space – Used in print and Web site advertising – location on a newspaper or magazine page, or the page of a Web site where an ad can be placed. There can be multiple *spaces* on a single page or an advertiser can purchase a full-page ad.

space holder – Any type of copy, text, graphic, etc., not to be included in a publication, but only to preserve the space until the intended product is completed and inserted.

spacing out – Daydreaming on the job.

spam – A term for unsolicited e-mail (sent in large volume without consent) that packs a computer's bulk mail or, as some refer to it, junk mail. Congress is grappling with legislation regulating *spam* and many *Internet Service Providers* (ISPs) are developing filters to limit unwanted e-mail while still allowing other (desired) bulk mail to get through. This is quite a challenge for *ISPs*.

spam filter – A computer program that attempts to prevent *spam* from entering an e-mail inbox.

speaking op – Opportunity arranged for a client or superior to speak at a conference, seminar, etc. to a target audience to heighten awareness through strategic messages or receive favorable media coverage.

spec sheet – A detailed description of requirements, dimensions, materials, etc., of a proposed publication, special event, etc. Once a "job" is assigned to a printer or other vendor, the *spec sheet* becomes a *contract*. (See Chapter 12 in *The Public Relations Practitioner's Playbook* – Kendall/Hunt – 2008)

special event – Activity arranged to stimulate interest in a person, product or organization by means of a focused "happening." Its purpose is to generate publicity, attract people or sell tickets – if that is a goal or objective of the event. *Special events* include such functions as conferences, seminars, workshops, corporate launches, fashion shows, exhibitions, road shows, theater productions, concerts and other activities where the goal is to attract an audience. A well-planned *special event* does not just happen. It requires careful planning and attention, which can include every detail from ordering invitations to promoting the actual event. Ideas for advertising *special events* may include a direct mailing to a list of targeted participants, placing newspaper ads and hanging banners near the special event site. Other ideas for promoting *special events* include using PR to get radio/television coverage, distributing promotional items to target groups, assembling volunteers to spread the word, providing free ticket offers and developing *special event* co-sponsorships and partnerships.

special event planning – Well thought out activities designed to create awareness, generate publicity, attract people or sell tickets – if that is a goal or objective of the event. A well-planned *special event* does not just happen. It requires careful planning and attention, which can include every detail from ordering invitations to promoting the actual event. Special event planning items to be aware of include developing and implementing logistics, strategic planning, public relations, sponsorship development, volunteer coordination, site management and marketing.

special event pricing – Reducing prices in retail stores at certain times of the year (e.g. immediately after Christmas) to attract customers.

special interest groups – Groups of consumers with concerns about particular products or product categories. For example, *special interest groups* have spoken out about the environment, too much and the wrong kind of television for children, computer sites that should be off limits to children, marketing of cigarettes, high-sugar breakfast cereals for children, fast foods with low nutritional value, etc.

S

special rate – A rate which is applied in any situation where freight is product specific rather than based on volume or weight. Also called a *commodity rate*.

specialty advertising – This is the older term used for promotional (products) advertising. Some firms and individuals still use it. It is an advertiser's message printed on such items such as cups, bags, note pads, key rings, pens, etc. usually given free to prospective customers – to promote a business or an event.

specialty distributor – A company or middle person (much like a merchandise *wholesaler*) who concentrates on one product line but carries a deep assortment within the line.

specialty goods – Consumer goods for which a customer has strong preference and is prepared to search for extensively to select and purchase the most suitable. See *convenience goods*; *shopping goods*.

specialty merchandise wholesaler – A *wholesaler* who specializes in one product line (or a few product lines) and carries the line or lines in considerable depth. For example, a sports *specialty wholesaler* may carry sports caps – nearly all teams and in a number of styles and sizes. Shoe *wholesalers* or *distributors* would do the same.

237

Tips to Succeed: Speaking in front of groups

1. If you have to use notes, don't use them in the first 60 seconds of your speech.
2. Number every page.
3. Never blow or tap on the microphone.
4. If you speak a little louder than usual, you will expend energy that will make you less nervous.
5. Don't use words in a speech that you wouldn't use in a normal conversation.
6. Be understandable.
7. Be memorable.
8. Move people to action.
9. Motivate them to tell other people about your message.
10. The more often you speak to large groups, the more comfortable you will feel.

Media Training Worldwide
www.topica-publisher.com

specialty retailing – Retail stores offering limited, specialized lines but carrying a deep assortment within the lines. For example, shoe stores, cosmetics shops, camera stores.

specialty store – Sometimes called *specialty retailing.* A retail store typically carrying only one, or part of one, product line but having considerable depth within the line. For example, stores selling only jogging shoes, cosmetics, or just men's shirts and ties.

specification (spec) sheet – A detailed description of requirements, dimensions, materials, etc., of a proposed publication, special event, etc. Once a "job" is assigned to a printer or other vendor, the *spec sheet* becomes a *contract.* (See Chapter 12 in *The Public Relations Practitioner's Playbook* – Kendall/Hunt – 2008).

speculative (spec) sample – A sample promotional product, with the prospective buyer's imprint on it, produced with the hope that the customer will purchase it.

spectaculars – Billboards with unusual lighting effects.

speed bump – A technique used in business to slow a group down so that it considers all aspects or reconsiders. The theory is, don't move too fast; it could cause problems.

spider – A program that automatically locates Web pages. *Spiders* are used to feed pages to *search engines.* It is called a *spider* because it crawls over the Web. Because most Web pages contain links to other pages, a *spider* can start almost anywhere. As soon as it sees a link to another page, it goes off and gets it. Large *search engines* (Google®; Yahoo®; Dogpile®) have many *spiders* working in parallel. See *robot.*

spif/spiff – In sales and marketing, it is a small, immediate bonus for a sale. While no one knows for certain, it is believed *spif* or *spiff* stands for "sales performance incentive fund (formula)."

spin – A slang term used when public relations practitioners attempt to manipulate the news or events in the media through skillful strategic messages and other public relations techniques. *Spin,* to some, is a derogatory term.

spitballing – Reporters or other members of the media throwing barbs at public figures – usually through commentaries or editorials, but many times during interviews.

splash page – In computers, a preliminary page that precedes the user-requested page of a Web site. It usually promotes a particular site feature or contains advertising. A *splash page* is timed to move on to the requested page after a short period of time or a click. Also known as an *interstitial*.

splicing – The process of joining together two pieces of recording tape.

split page – Usually the first page of the inside or second section (section B) of the newspaper carrying local, metro or area news; the second front page.

split run (test) – Two or more different versions of the same ad run in different copies of the same publication (newspapers which are zoned or magazines that might go to different target audiences or different regional or specific markets). Person "A" sees one version of the ad while person "B" sees another – to test the effectiveness of each version.

spoils system – Believed to have begun during Thomas Jefferson's presidency. It is the practice of giving appointive offices to loyal members of the party in power. The name supposedly derived from a speech by Senator William Learned Marcy in which he stated, "To the victor belong the spoils." When a political party comes to power, its leaders tend to place many of their faithful followers into important public offices. Simply put, it is the use of public offices as rewards for political party work.

sponsor – An advertiser who pays for all commercials in a television or radio program or who pays to operate a Web site. Also, an advertiser that has a special relationship with the Web site and supports a specific feature of a Web site, such as a writer's column or a collection of articles on a particular subject.

sponsor training – Pairing sales recruits with experienced salespeople who are responsible for their training in the field.

sponsored links – Ads on computer Web pages that take a user to a sponsor's site.

sponsorship – An arrangement where the advertiser produces both a television/radio program and the commercials inside the program. Also, a specialized form of sales promotion where a company will help fund an event or support a business venture in return for publicity – donating funds to an organization or event in exchange for supportive association in order to generate publicity (also known as *corporate sponsorship*; *partnering*). In computers, it is an association with a Web site in some way that

S

gives an advertiser some particular visibility and advantage above that of *run-of-site* advertising. When associated with specific content, *sponsorship* can provide a more targeted audience than a run-of-site ad buys.

238 Techniques to Succeed: For the self-employed or soon to be

While you're never going to eliminate the ups and downs of owning your own business, you can take steps to make the ride a little less bumpy and a lot less scary:

- **Discover your "bread and butter" business.** What pays your bills each month? Often the part of your business that covers your monthly overhead seems boring: The customer you've had forever, the product that keeps selling. Nurture these! Return the call from the long-time customer before you call the new prospect. Advertise the product that sells itself as well as the new one you're excited about. Remember what pays the bills.

- **Pay yourself a set "salary" every month.** Instead of spending wildly when times are good, give yourself a set monthly "draw" or salary every month, and put the rest of your income away. Draw from that savings account when times are tough.

- **Open a "tax account."** Sooner or later, tax time rolls around. Instead of waiting until the end of the year or the quarter and then having to frantically rustle up cash, put 20 to 40 percent of every dollar you earn directly into a tax account.

- **Take advantage of retirement plans.** One of the best tax advantages for the self-employed are tax-sheltered retirement plans.

- **Recognize there are cycles.** Generally, neither the good times nor the bad ones last forever, so try to keep perspective.

- **This is your life – live it!** While the first couple of years in business may be more intense than other years, you're always going to have too much to do and plenty of stress. It's tempting to tell yourself you'll get around to spending time with family, taking a vacation or exercising when work "lightens up." If you're really an entrepreneur, then this is the life you're going to lead.

Rhonda Abrams - www.rhondaonline.com

sponsorship marketing – An investment by a company in an organization or event in exchange for commercial benefits. *Sponsorship marketing* is used by companies to increase sales, target specific markets, increase customer and employee loyalty and enhance brand image. *Sponsorship marketing* is becoming a popular ingredient in the marketing mix to help firms and organizations achieve *synergy*.

spoofing – A "shady" practice used by some spammers who harvest an individual's e-mail address from someone else's address book or an online discussion group or who buy an electronic mailing list. The spoofer uses the individual's address to cover his/her tracks as he sends out his spam.

spoonerism – A play on words in which corresponding consonants or vowels are switched. It is named after the Reverend William Archibald Spooner, warden of New College (Oxford), who was notoriously prone to this tendency. Comedian Norm Crosby often uses spoonerisms – "fractured" English – in his performances.

sports promotion – The creation and implementation of event planning and marketing activities to attract audiences at sports venues. *Sports promotions* may offer integrated program *sponsorships*, including development of sponsor strategies, sponsor rights negotiations, event marketing, celebrity endorsements and appearances and strategic planning. Positive results and ultimate success are achieved through implementing a balanced mix of branding and fan entertainment. Well thought out, creative events provide maximum exposure.

spot/spot announcement – A commercial announcement aired on television or radio. *Public service announcements* are sometimes referred to as *spots* or *spot announcements*, but the term is usually reserved for paid commercials.

spot buy – In advertising, the buying of media time in a few selected markets only.

spot color – The printing technique of using color to emphasize an area of an otherwise black-and-white print piece. *Spot color* does not usually have the same close registration as processed color. In contrast, process color printing uses four inks (cyan, magenta, yellow, and black) to produce all other colors. Spot *color* printing is effective when the printed matter contains only one to three different colors, but it becomes prohibitively expensive for more colors. One widely used numbering scheme is known as the *Pantone® Matching System* (*PMS®*).

spot news – Current news, reported immediately. It is a news story based on facts, presentation, activity or interview. Also news obtained on the scene of an event, usually unexpectedly.

spot television (or radio) – Advertising purchased with individual television or radio stations, purchased on a market-to-market basis rather than through a *network* – which sends its programming to two or more stations (affiliates) simultaneously.

S

239 Tips to Succeed: Rules followed by the best writers

1. Prefer the plain word to the fancy.
2. Prefer the familiar word to the unfamiliar.
3. Prefer the Saxon word to the Roman.
4. Prefer nouns and verbs to adjectives and adverbs.
5. Prefer picture nouns and action verbs.
6. Never use a long word when a short one will do as well.
7. Master the simple declarative sentence.
8. Prefer the simple sentence to the complicated.
9. Vary your sentence length.
10. Put the words you want to emphasize at the beginning or end of your sentence.
11. Use the active voice.
12. Put statements in a positive form.
13. Use short paragraphs.
14. Cut needless words, sentences and paragraphs.
15. Use plain, conversational language. Write like you talk.
16. Avoid imitation. Write in your natural style.
17. Write clearly.
18. Avoid gobbledygook and jargon.
19. Write to be understood, not to impress.
20. Revise and rewrite. Improvement is always possible.

20 Rules for Good Writing from the Writers Digest School

spotter – A person who receives a fee for providing a salesperson with prospect leads to whom sales are made. Also known as a *bird dog*. A *spotter* is also the term used for the person who assists a sports play-by-play announcer identify participants.

spread – Advertising that runs across two contiguous pages of a publication. The display given to an important story; a double spread is one across facing pages. Also referred to as *double truck*.

spreadsheet – An accountant's worksheet. Such computerized electronic spreadsheets as Microsoft Excel® consist of a grid of rows and columns enabling specific marketing data to be organized in a standardized way. See *spreadsheet analysis*.

spreadsheet analysis – The analysis of data using computer software to anticipate marketing performance under a given set of circumstances.

spring break marketing – Public relations and other marketing campaigns designed to target college students. *Spring break marketing* attempts to reach students on the beaches and resorts they flock to on vacation. *Spring break marketing* is a major opportunity for reaching an extremely concentrated number of college students in a densely targeted venue. *Spring break marketing* tactics include giving out free samples, conducting product demonstrations, placing posters and stickers in high-traffic areas, staffing promotional tents, providing sample products inside the hotel rooms of college students, and patrolling beaches with such free promotional items as tee shirts, caps and towels.

squatter – A Web site that illegally occupies someone else's site.

squib – A short news item; a filler.

SRO (standing room only) technique – A closing technique in sales where the salesperson tries to get a quick commitment to a purchase by telling the buyer that the demand for the product is heavy and that only a limited quantity is left. See *standing room only*.

stabilizing price – A price set for a product with the intention of keeping prices steady within an industry to avoid a price war. This is legal so long as there is no evidence of *collusion*.

stagflation – A situation which exists in an economy when high unemployment, rising prices and wages occur together.

staggered schedule – A schedule of advertisements or commercials in a number of *periodicals* or on a number of television or radio stations which have different insertion (run) dates.

stakeholder – Anyone with an interest – financial or otherwise – in an organization. *Stakeholders* in a company may include shareholders, directors, management, suppliers, government, employees and the community. See *stockholder*.

stand-alone logo – A *logo* (symbol) – used by a brand or company – that does not contain words, but is easily recognized as belonging to the brand or company. Examples would include the Nike® swoosh, McDonald's® arches or the CBS® eye. See *logo*.

stand-alone photo – A picture that doesn't accompany a story, usually boxed to show it stands alone. Also called wild art.

Standard Advertising Unit System (SAUS) – A set of uniform advertising procedures developed by the American Newspaper Publishers Association.

Standard Generalized Markup Language (SGML) – In computers, the parent language for *HTML*.

standard industrial classification (SIC) – Defined by the U.S Department of Commerce to be a classification of businesses in a numeric hierarchy. Also used to indicate that a quoted passage, especially one containing an error or unconventional spelling, has been retained in its original form or written intentionally – in other words, the "spelling is correct" (SIC).

Standard Rate and Data Service (SRDS)® – A commercial firm that publishes reference books and other materials that include up-to-date information on rates, requirements, closing dates and other information needed for ad placement in the media.

standard test market – A form of test market where the company selects a small number of representative cities to try out the full marketing mix prior to a new product launch. See *test marketing*.

standardized marketing mix – A strategy employed by a multinational company attempting to use one *marketing mix* to sell its products world-wide. This approach minimizes cost but may result in a smaller (demographic) market than would be possible with a unique marketing program for each country. See *customized marketing mix*.

S

standing feature – A recurring piece found in newspapers, magazines, newsletters, etc.

standing head (department head) – *Headlines* (display type) that do not change and are usually kept in a library file on a computer so they are ready for instant use. Also a special label for any regularly appearing section, page or story in a newsletter or newspaper. Also called a *header*.

standing room only – A closing technique in which the salesperson tries to get a quick commitment to a purchase by telling the buyer that the demand for the product is heavy and that only a limited quantity is left. See *close*.

staples – A sub-category of *convenience goods* consisting of frequently purchased food products and such household goods as paper products. See *convenience goods*.

Starch readership report – A technique for post-testing advertising where interviewers ask selected readers of magazines to recall a particular advertisement's effectiveness. It was devised in 1923 by Daniel Starch, at that time a lecturer at the Harvard Business School. See *Starch scores*.

Starch readership service® – A research organization (Starch INRA Hooper®) that provides an advertisement's rank in issue and *Starch scores*.

Starch scores – A result of a method used by Daniel Starch and staff in their studies of advertising readership which include the percent of readers who viewed the tested ad and associated the ad with the advertiser. It also determines which ads are read most and the percent of readers who read half or more of the copy.

stars – Products in a firm or organization's portfolio characterized by high market share in a rapidly growing market. See *Boston Consulting Group (BCG) advantage matrix*.

stars and bars – Slang for Confederate flag.

starting date – The launch date for the entire public relations, advertising, marketing or business plan.

state-of-being segmentation – See *demographics*.

state-of-mind segmentation – See *psychographics*.

stated objection – The reason given by a prospective buyer for not accepting the product offered. The *stated objection* may conceal the true objection. See *objections*; *invalid objections*; *valid objections*.

571

Statements of Marketing Practice (SOMPS) – The Chartered Institute of Marketing's® (CIM's) grid of marketing competencies required to achieve business aims. CIM's new syllabus structure is mapped out against each marketing level as identified in the grid.

static ad placement/static rotation – Same as *embedded ads*. Also, ads that remain on a Web page for a specified period of time.

statistical bank – A range of statistical techniques used in analysis in a marketing information system to discover the degree of reliability of the data collected and the relationships within it. See *marketing information system*.

stationery package – A letterhead, business card and envelope.

Statistical Package for the Social Sciences (SPSS) – Released in its first version in the 1960s – is among the most widely used programs for statistical analysis in social science. It is also used by market researchers, health researchers, survey companies, the government, education researchers and others.

status quo strategy – A reactive marketing strategy characterized by a desire to avoid confrontation with competitors. A company seeks to keep things in the industry as they are – avoiding the expense of taking on a competitor.

stealth (parentage) marking – Nontraditional advertising such as *viral marketing* where people are paid to "talk up" a product using word of mouth and to create a *buzz*. Would also include *product placement* and *advertainment*. When a major manufacturer creates a second brand independent of the first and attempts to distance itself from that brand – for example, General Motors® and Saturn®. Also, paying someone to recommend (different from enforce) a product without revealing they are doing so. Using real people (referred to a *connectors*) to create a (manufactured) *buzz* for products or services – paid or otherwise, but most times paid (to recommend [word-of-mouth] a product or service).

stealth nominee – An individual, nominated by a president, governor or other in power, who is a virtual unknown – one whose track record is either unavailable or nonexistent – and one who has no paper trail.

stealth positioning – Sneaking a product into the market and gaining acceptance that might otherwise prove elusive. Two examples are Apple® and the introduction of the Mac Mini® in January 2005. Apple presented

Copy should always be prepared using the 30-3-30 principle. Is your copy aimed at the 30-second reader, three-minute reader or the 30-minute reader? To be effective, write for all three audiences.

it as something that could be left to the imagination as to how to use it: a server for a car, a dedicated Internet port for the kitchen, etc. Apple never said it was essentially a competitively priced machine that could compete in the low end PC market. SONY® introduced the EyeToy: Play – a video camera and game software – in July 2003 (in Europe). The camera sat on top of the TV, allowed people to put themselves "inside" the game via the PlayStation 2 console, engaged families in fun. The "stealth" positioning was the eventual introduction of the product as a video phone. The product's value has already been established. See *buzz marketing; stealth marketing; underground marketing.* Read more at *www.tremor.com.*

steeplechase ad – Ad that runs vertically up one side of a page or the other.

steering control system – Important to public relations and marketing. It is a system that detects unsatisfactory company or client performance during, rather than at the end of, a planning period so that quick corrective action can be taken. It is a reactive but effective marketing control system. See *reactive control system.*

step-and-repeat – A single image printed repeatedly in a pattern on a single sheet of paper. Sometimes referred to as giving the finished piece a better "bump."

stereotyping – Presenting a group of people in an unvarying pattern that lacks individuality and often reflects popular misconceptions.

stet – A Latin term (stetundum) meaning "let it stand," which instructs a printer or typesetter to ignore an alteration called for in a *proof.*

stickiness – A measure used in computers to gauge the effectiveness of a site in retaining individual users. *Stickiness* is usually measured by the duration of the visit.

sticker ad – See *dot whack, popper* or *sticky notes.*

The ABCs of Strategic Communication

S

stimulational marketing – Marketing activity intended to create demand for a product among those who are neither aware of it nor interested in it.

stimulus-response approach – An approach to selling which relies on the salesperson's ability to say the right thing (stimulus) to obtain a favorable reaction from the buyer (response). It is often referred to as the canned approach because a script is commonly used.

stock-keeping unit (SKU) – A product variant with its own distinctive attributes (price, packaging, etc.). See *product item*.

stock point – The level at which tangible inventory needs to be re-ordered.

stock-taking unit – A product variant with its own distinctive attributes (price, packaging, etc.). Also referred to as *stock-keeping unit*. See *product item*.

stock turnover rate – A measure of the operating efficiency of a business that indicates how rapidly a particular product sells out (sales of the average level of stock held in inventory) in an operating period. See *stockturn rate*.

stockholder – Anyone with a financial interest in a company. See *stakeholder*.

stocking allowance – A fee paid by a manufacturer to such major retailers as supermarket chains, *big box* drug stores, certain discounters, etc. for shelf space for a new product and/or to keep their products on store shelves. Typically, the more visible the spot and the more shelf facings, the higher the fee. Also referred to as the *slotting allowance*; *introductory allowance*; *shelf fee or street money*.

stockless purchasing – A practice where a vendor inventories and supplies products to a reseller on short notice. For example, such snacks as potato chips, corn chips and similar items would fall under this term.

stockturn rate – A measure of the operating efficiency of a business that indicates how rapidly a particular product sells out (sales of the average level of stock held in inventory) in an operating period. Also called *stock turnover rate*.

stop motion – A photographic technique used in video commercials and elsewhere where inanimate objects appear to move.

store atmosphere – The combination of store decor, physical characteristics and amenities provided by a retailer to develop a particular image and attract customers. See *atmospherics*.

store audit – A source of retail store information collected by marketing research firms (ACNielson®, for example) and supplied to manufacturers on a subscription basis; the information is compiled by subtracting end of period inventory for a product from inventory at the beginning of the period plus shipments. See *syndicated marketing research firms*.

store brand – See *mezzanine marketing*.

store decor – The combination of store decor, physical characteristics and amenities provided by a retailer to develop a particular image and attract customers. See *atmospherics*.

store image – The combination of store decor, physical characteristics and amenities provided by a retailer to develop a particular image and attract customers. See *atmospherics*.

story – The general term applied to any newspaper article written by a reporter; also called "piece."

story break – An interruption in a news story that is being transmitted by a wire service (Associated Press) via the Internet. Whenever there is an interruption, the work "more" is used to signify the story is not finished. When it is, usually three pound signs (###) or the number 30 will be used. See *take*.

241

Techniques to Succeed: Writers should use their heart *and* their soul

"Write your first draft from your heart. Write your second draft from the head…then polish it."

David Trottier - "The Screenwriting Center"

story has legs – Phrase that pertains to a news story that just won't go away. It stays on the front pages of newspapers and on television newscasts because of ongoing breaking developments, on-going controversy, story appeal, celebrity status, etc.

story list – An alternate word for story "budget." Also what reporters call their private list of stories they've written and where and when they've appeared in the paper.

storyboard – A series of frames sketched (rough illustrations) to illustrate how the story line will develop as commercials are created and produced. It is a tool (sometimes poster size) showing a series of miniature television screens depicting the sequence of scenes in a commercial with the words to accompany each picture written below it.

straight news – A plain account of news facts written in standard style and structure, without coloring or embellishments.

straight rebuy – A purchase where the customer buys the same goods in the same quantity on the same terms from the same supplier. See *modified rebuy; new task buying.*

straight salary – A compensation method where a public relations or advertising agency employee or a firm's salesperson receives salary but no commission on billings or sales. See *salary plan.*

strategery – First used in a *Saturday Night Live* sketch aired October 7, 2000, satirizing the performances of Al Gore and George W. Bush, two candidates for President of the United States, during the first presidential debate for election year 2000. A play on the words "strategy" and "strategic," it satirized Bush's reputation for mispronouncing words. The episode was later released as part of a video tape titled *Presidential Bash 2000.* After winning the 2000 presidential election, people inside the Bush White House reportedly began using the term as a joke, and it later grew to become a term of art among them meaning oversight of any activity by Bush's political strategists. Bush's strategists also came to be known within the White House as "The Department of *Strategery*" or the "*Strategery* Group."

Strategic Business Unit (SBU) – A separate operating division of a company with some degree of autonomy – commonly referred to as an *SBU*.

strategic control – The continuous and systematic checking that the company's strategies are appropriate to its public relations and marketing opportunities and resources. The ongoing assessment is based on the public relations or other marketing-type plan consisting of a goal, objectives, strategies and tactics – always taking into consideration changing market conditions.

strategic gap – The difference between a company's profit objectives for a given future period and its projected level of profit for the same period.

strategic group – Any group of firms or organizations that pursue the same clear strategies to achieve their public relations, marketing and other business-type objectives.

strategic market planning – The planning process that yields decisions in how a firm's business unit can best compete in the markets it elects to serve. The strategic plan is based on the total marketing process.

strategic marketing concept – A philosophy, focus, orientation or concept which emphasizes the proper identification of marketing opportunities as the basis for marketing planning and corporate growth. Unlike the marketing concept which emphasizes consumer needs and wants, the *strategic marketing concept* emphasizes both consumers and competitors. See *marketing concept*.

strategic marketing management – The planned process of defining a firm or an organization's business, mission and goals – identifying and framing organizational opportunities, crafting product-market strategies, budgeting marketing, financial and production resources and modifying or developing new products.

strategic marketing plan – A plan outlining marketing opportunities matched to the resources and abilities of the company.

strategic partner – A company, firm or organization that another company or organization aligns itself with to benefit both parties. This has become a common practice for nonprofits and profits to partner for major events. A number of *brands* owned by different corporations are now partnering by using the advertising technique *co-authoring*.

strategic planning – The public relations process of determining a firm or organization's goal (global ambition), objectives, strategies, tactics and other courses of action and the allocation of the needed resources (money and personnel) to achieve them.

strategic profit model – A tool used to assess a firm's profitability. It is the return on equity which is calculated by multiplying the net profit margin by the asset turnover to obtain the return on assets. That, in turn, is multiplied by the financial leverage. See *financial leverage*; *return on assets managed*; *return on equity*.

strategic window – The point of time when the right environmental conditions exist for a particular public relations or other marketing opportunity. Also referred to as a *window of competitive opportunity*.

strategy – The thought process that drives the plan – a general well thought out plan of action. What must be done, to whom (public) and how it will happen. It is a broad plan of action an organization uses to achieve one or more of its objectives. See *strategery; tactic*. (Chapter 7 – *The Public Relations Practitioner's Playbook* – Kendall/Hunt – 2008.)

stratified sample –A form of probability sample where respondents are chosen from a *random sample* of homogeneous (similar) sub-groups (according to a common characteristic) where the total *population* has been divided. Creating a *sample* by sorting respondents into groups that have a common characteristic – *demographics* and *psychographics* – distinguishing them from other groups. Characteristics could include age, income, use of a product, business size or type of business. See *cluster sample*.

stratified selection – An equally measured statistical sample which represents all the categories into which the population has been divided.

stratigilution – Arriving at a solution by taking a strategic approach.

streamer – A multi-column headline leading a page, but not necessarily across its full width. Synonymous with *banner*.

streaming – In computers, a technology that permits continuous audio and video delivered to a computer from a remote Web site. Also an Internet data transfer technique that allows the user to see and hear audio and video files. *MP3s* use *streaming*. The *host*, or source, compresses then streams small packets of information over the Internet to the user, who accesses the content as it is received.

streaming media player – A software program that decompresses audio and/or video files so the user can hear and/or see the video or audio file. Examples include Real Player®, Windows Media® and Quick Time Player®.

streaming video – The transmission of full-motion video over the Internet. Also, the transmission of video at the top or bottom of a television screen (during another program).

street furniture – Benches, tables, shelters, etc., that serve as advertising vehicles on city streets, in parks, zoos, etc.

street marketing – An innovative and aggressive tactic used by many firms and organizations as part of their street team promotions which involve activities that use a variety of *guerilla marketing* activities –hand-to-hand sampling distribution, massive postings of posters and stickers, product samples, CDs and other product giveaways. *Street marketing* is not limited to distributing promotional information on the streets, but also infiltrating clubs, labels, movie studios or any other location where influential peer members of the advertiser's target market may work. The *street marketing* group will also target high-traffic areas and places where their target audience may frequent. See *viral marketing*.

street money – A fee paid by a manufacturer to such major retailers as supermarket chains, *big box* drug stores, certain discounters, etc. for shelf space for a new product and/or to keep their products on store shelves. Typically, the more visible the spot and the more *shelf facings*, the higher the fee. Also referred to as the *slotting allowance; introductory allowance; shelf fee*.

street team promotions – An innovative and aggressive tactic implemented by an unconventional team of marketers. *Street team promotions* involve working the streets, reaching consumers where they live, work and play. A leader or "captain" typically heads the *street team* marketing operations. The leader usually is experienced in coordinating street team promotions and serves as liaison between the advertiser and the street team members. *Street team promotions* can be instrumental in getting the word out about new products and brands, concerts, events, upcoming movies, etc. Research shows street team marketing is highly effective because of its believability referred to as street credibility or "street cred" that advertisers can't get from mainstream media. *Street teams* are also able to infiltrate areas and groups that conventional advertising has a hard time reaching.

street team swag – *Street team swag* is the merchandise *street team* members receive in exchange for assisting bands, celebrities and companies market themselves on the streets (*street marketing*). *Street team swag* includes clothes, tickets to shows, backstage passes, gift certificates, sports

242

Tips to Succeed:
Marketing yourself online

1. **Don't lie** – Whether on a resume, application or personal Web site, make sure facts about you are accurate.

2. **Be professional** – For college or job applications, use a simple e-mail address with your name or initials that helps connect an e-mail to you.

3. **Censor yourself, and friends (if need be)** – If you know a college or potential employer might Google® you or search you out on MySpace®, make sure the content posted by yourself or others is appropriate.

Des Moines Register

equipment, etc. The *swag* is barter to street team members in lieu of money for distributing samples, etc. Since pay is often not provided to members of a *street team, swag* rewards are a way of saying thanks to the teams for all their hard work. See *SWAG*.

strengths, weaknesses, opportunities, threats – See *SWOT analysis*.

stringer – A correspondent for a newspaper or a news agency, usually part–time, who often covers a certain subject or geographic area. The person is usually paid according to the number or length of stories printed by the newspaper.

strip ad – One or two inch-wide ad across the bottom of a page. (Example would be front page of *USA Today*).

strip center – A shopping center where the stores are located along a suburban roadway and are open to the elements as opposed to be being in an enclosed mall.

stripping – A printers' term for positioning film *negatives* or *positives* of copy and illustrations for the purpose of creating a printing plate for that ad or page. At this stage, extraneous marks are removed from negatives using a process called opaquing.

structured research – Surveys that use a *questionnaire* as the basic tool.

stuffer– An advertising enclosure that is included in another media, such as in a newspaper, invoice mailings, merchandise packages, etc. Commonly referred to as *envelope stuffer*.

stump – Another term for *campaign*. For example, President Bush stumped through the heartland to gain support for his Social Security proposal.

stump speech – Campaign speech. "On the stump" means campaigning.

style flexing – A deliberate attempt on the part of a salesperson to adjust his or her communication style to suit the personality of the buyer. See *adaptive selling*.

stylebook – An organization's printed guide on the uses of grammar and style. *Stylebooks* are used by forms and organizations to maintain consistency. The *Associated Press Stylebook* has long been the standard of newspapers worldwide. Many newspapers and broadcast media use this style and supplement it with their own for their staff's use. See *AP style*.

styles – Many ways to manipulate a font – plain, bold, *italic*, capitals, underline, etc.

Sub-brand – See *brand within a brand.*

subcultures – Used in public relations research and audience targeting – broad groups of consumers within a society's culture that have similar values (*psychographics*) which distinguish them from the rest of society.

subheads – Sectional headline used to break up masses of type. An introductory line that offers supplementary information not included in the *headline* – sometimes used above paragraphs in longer newspaper and newsletter stories – to break up the monotony of a solid column of small type.

sublimation – Using heat and a color-type film material to transfer the color from the film to paper or some other material. During the printing process, the films are placed on the paper and heated up by the print head. This will cause the pigments to leave the film and enter into the paper where the color cools and re-solidifies. This is the *sublimation* part. There is little mess compared to ink. Sublimated images are extremely washable; scratch resistant and dishwasher safe because the image is protected within the surface. Printing with *sublimation* ink is not new; *sublimation* transfers have played an important role in the printing world for decades. What is new to the printing world, is the ability to digitally print sublimation inks rather that screen-printing them. Also called thermal dye. See *pre-press services.*

subliminal message – A strategic message transmitted below the threshold of normal perception so that the receiver is not consciously aware of having received it.

subliminal perception – An advertising or other strategic message transmitted below the threshold of consciousness. A visual or auditory message intended to be perceived psychologically, but not consciously.

subliminal persuasion – An advertising or other strategic message presented below the threshold of consciousness to persuade the receiver or encoder psychologically rather than consciously.

suboptimization – A situation carried out in some large companies when departmental or divisional leaders attempt to achieve the objectives of their particular sections at the expense of other sections.

subscription newsletter – A type of newsletter that includes specialized information not found anywhere else. Subscribers pay to receive current information in their specialty and quality information presented in easy-to-read articles. Does not include advertising – thus, subscription rates are usually higher than those of magazines and journals that accept advertising.

substantiality – One of the four major requirements for useful market segmentation. *Substantiality* expresses the notion that the segment chosen as the *target market* must be large enough to be profitable. Also referred to as *significance*. See *accessibility*; *actionability*; *measurability*.

substitute products – Products that buyers perceive as having some features and other characteristics in common (for example, salt, sugar, potatoes and cotton balls).

substitution – When a customer asks for one brand and another is served without the customer being told – Coke® is requested, but Pepsi® is served. This is illegal.

suggestion selling – A practice where the salesperson seeks to increase the value of the sale by suggesting related lines, special promotions or seasonal merchandise to complement the original purchase. Also called *suggestive selling*.

suggestive selling – See *suggestion selling*.

suitability studies – Research and other types of questioning and investigation to determine whether public relations and/or advertising agencies are compatible to work together.

summary annual report (SAR) – A shorter and less complicated annual report that is divided into brief summation sections.

summary deck – A sentence or two below a headline that introduces a story. Many times, *summary decks* are set in italics.

summative close – A closing technique where the salesperson summarizes the features and benefits of the product of prime interest to the buyer point by point. See *close*.

sunset – (As it affects legislation) A clause in a statute or bill proposal, regulation or similar piece of legislation that provides for an automatic repealing of the entirety or sections of the law once a specific date is reached. If the government wishes to extend the length of time for which the law in question will be in effect, it can push back the *sunset* provision date anytime before it is reached. (An example of a *sunset* provision is the U.S.

S

Patriot Act, which was intended to address relatively short-term security concerns following the events of September 11, 2001. When the act was initially drafted, it included a *sunset* provision for December 31, 2005).

Sunshine Law – Known in many states as the Open Public Meetings Act – state or federal law calling for "government in the sunshine" that requires most meetings of regulatory bodies to be held in public (rather than closed or executive session) and most of their decisions and records to be disclosed.

super-specialty store – A retail store selling only one line of a superior quality product or offering a superior quality service in a limited range of goods.

superimposition (super) – A technique in television production where an image, words or phrases are shown over another image – graphic overlay.

supersizing – Increasing the size portions of certain products to enhance their appeal – fast food is the most visible example. *Supersizing* began losing its appeal when medical research returned findings that the additional calories and "fat content" were unhealthy.

superstitials – Internet advertisements designed to work like television commercials. When you go from one Web site to another, a short animation (up to 30 seconds) appears in the window. Also, on television, the use of animation in a *crawl*. An example would be WPVI-TV (Philadelphia) which sends its "Action News" van streaming across the bottom of the screen to get viewers' attention for an upcoming video message.

SUPPIES – Senior Urban Professionals – A demographic grouping.

supplementary media – Non-mass media vehicles that are used to promote products. Examples would include distribution of promotional or specialty advertising items and point-of-purchase advertising.

supplements –Local or syndicated full-color advertising inserts that appear in newspapers.

supplier – Companies that sell goods or services to a public relations or an advertising agency for their use in creating and producing advertisements. Sometimes referred to *vendors* or *freelancers*, they would include design studios, color houses, printers and paper producers.

supplier relationship management (SRM) – Managing relationships with suppliers often through the use of IT (information technology) systems – a major component of *relationship marketing*.

243

Tips to Succeed:

Public relations practitioners

1. Analyze conditions
2. Assess policies
3. Inform
4. Develop programs
5. Make recommendations
6. Persuade
7. Get people to act

suppliers – Individuals or organizations from which businesses purchase the goods and services needed to operate and function.

supply (and demand) – While *demand* is the desire for a product or service at market price, *supply* is the quantity available at that price.

supply chain – The distribution channel of a product, from its sourcing, to its delivery to the end consumer (also known as the *value chain*). The *supply chain* is typically comprised of multiple companies starting with the creators, designers, manufacturers, (oversees) factories, shippers, retailers and consumers.

surfing – In computers, exploring the World Wide Web.

surprinting – Printing type over some other image.

survey – A method (or instrument) of obtaining primary data in a public relations or other marketing research study using interviews, either face-to-face, by telephone, mail, drop off-pick up or using the Internet. *Focus panels* are also a survey technique or method, but for the most part are nonscientific (qualitative rather than quantitative).

survey of buyer intentions – A forecasting technique where known purchasers of a product are asked to predict their requirements for a given future period.

survey research – Research using structured interview forms that ask large numbers of people exactly the same questions.

suspects – Slang term used for possible buyers or agency clients (sales prospects) who have not yet been qualified as buyers or who have committed to buy or sign on with the agency. Also referred to as *sales leads*. See *qualifying the prospect*.

sustainable competitive advantage – The competitive edge sought by a firm which will allow it to satisfy customer needs while maintaining an advantage over its rivals because of the uniqueness of its products or its lower production or marketing costs.

SWAG – Stuff We All Get – Promotional items given to media types (reporters, editors, etc.) to encourage them to cover events or stories.

swatch proof – A sample of the material for a promotional product, with the customer's artwork printed on it in the specified colors. Examples would include shirts, caps and bags.

244

Tips to Succeed: Survival of the fittest

- Assume a leadership role
- Gain experience – it's the best teacher
- Exude confidence – not cockiness
- Attitude – being positive is contagious
- Ask questions (the Aladdin factor) – get answers

sweeps – A time during the months of November, February, May and July, when both Nielson and Arbitron survey all local market broadcast media for the purpose of rating the stations and their programming. Several times each year, Nielsen Station Index (Nielsen Media Research's local market measurement service) collects demographic viewing data from sample homes in every one of the 210 television markets in the United States. Each home in the sample maintains a paper viewing diary for one week. Each household member writes down what programs they and their guests watch in their home during the course of that week. The term "sweeps" has been around since the beginning of TV measurement. These measurement periods are called "sweeps" because Nielsen Media Research® mails out diaries to certain households around the country, then collects and processes the diaries in a specific order. The diaries from the Northeast regions are processed first and then swept up around the country, from the South, to the Midwest and finally ending with the West. In some of the larger markets, there are as many as three additional months (October, January and March) during which diaries are used to provide viewer information. Read more at *www.nielsenmedia.com/sweeps.html.*

245

Tips to Succeed: 25 Unwritten Rules of Management

S

1. Learn to say, "I don't know." If used when appropriate, it will be often.

2. It is easier to get into something than it is to get out of it.

3. If you are not criticized, you may not be doing much.

4. Look for what is missing. Many know how to improve what's there, but few can see what isn't there.

5. Viewgraph rule: When something appears on a viewgraph (an overhead transparency), assume the world knows about it, and deal with it accordingly.

6. Work for a boss with whom you are comfortable telling it like it is. Remember that you can't pick your relatives, but you can pick your boss.

7. Constantly review developments to make sure that the actual benefits are what they are supposed to be. Avoid Newton's Law.

8. However menial and trivial your early assignments may appear, give them your best efforts.

9. Persistence or tenacity is the disposition to persevere in spite of difficulties, discouragement, or indifference. Don't be known as a good starter but a poor finisher.

10. In completing a project, don't wait for others; go after them, and make sure it gets done.

11. Confirm your instructions and the commitments of others in writing. Don't assume it will get done!

12. Don't be timid; speak up. Express yourself, and promote your ideas.

13. Practice shows that those who speak the most knowingly and confidently often end up with the assignment to get it done.

14. Strive for brevity and clarity in oral and written reports.

15. Be extremely careful of the accuracy of your statements.

16. Don't overlook the fact that you are working for a boss.
    * Keep him or her informed. Avoid surprises!
    * Whatever the boss wants takes top priority.

17. Promises, schedules and estimates are important instruments in a well-ordered business.
    * You must make promises. Don't lean on the often-used phrase, "I can't estimate it because it depends upon many uncertain factors."

18. Never direct a complaint to the top. A serious offense is to "cc" a person's boss.

19. When dealing with outsiders, remember that you represent the company. Be careful of your commitments.

20. Cultivate the habit of "boiling matters down" to the simplest terms. An elevator speech is the best way.

21. Don't get excited in engineering emergencies. Keep your feet on the ground.

22. Cultivate the habit of making quick, clean-cut decisions.

23. When making decisions, the pros are much easier to deal with than the cons. Your boss wants to see the cons also.

24. Don't ever lose your sense of humor.

25. Have fun at what you do. It will reflect in your work. No one likes a grump except another grump.

Here some "extra" rules from *Business 2.0*

1. You can't polish a sneaker. (notice when something hasn't got any real substance).

2. You remember 1/3 of what you read, 1/2 of what people tell you, but 100 percent of what you feel. (Leaders generate emotions that move people in the desired direction.)

3. Treat your company name as if it were your own (possibly the same as #19 above.)

4. When faced with decisions, try to look at them as if you were one level up in the organization. Your perspective will change quickly. (Your boss has to weigh more considerations than you do in making a decision.)

5. A person who is nice to you but rude to the waiter is not a nice person.

6. When facing issues or problems that are becoming drawn out, "short them to ground." (Solve problems instead of talking about solving problems).

Bill Swanson - CEO - Raytheon

sweepstakes – Sales promotion activities that require participants to submit their names to be included in a drawing or other type of chance selection. *Sweepstakes* are federally regulated. Also called a *lottery* because every participant should have the same chance of being chosen.

swing loan – A short-term loan is used until a person or company secures permanent financing or removes an existing obligation. This type of financing allows the user to meet current obligations by providing immediate cash flow. The loans are usually up to one year with relatively high interest rates and are backed by some form of collateral such as real estate or inventory. Also known as interim financing, gap financing or a *bridge loan*.

swing state – Also called a battleground state. It is a state where no candidate has overwhelming support – meaning any of the major candidates

246

Tips to Succeed:
Speaking in front of groups?

Speaking in front of a group is one of the best ways to enhance your career yet the biggest fears most people have. Here are three tips to help you overcome that fear:

1. Get excited about the topic.

2. You have earned the right to speak on this subject. It's a good bet that you wouldn't have been asked to talk about the subject if somebody didn't think you were capable.

3. Be eager to project the value to your listener. Decide what the one thing is you'd like to say about this subject and how it could change their view of a situation.

4. After hitting the key points on the subject, you should give your audience a chance to ask you questions. Answer the questions quickly and directly – again, showing the audience that you're the "expert" on the subject.

5. It's important that you learn to become comfortable when presenting in front of others. Practice your presentation with some of your colleagues or practice with a coach. Practice will enable you to feel more comfortable speaking in front of others.

Anita Zinsmeister - President -
Dale Carnegie Training of Central and Southern New Jersey

have a reasonable chance of winning the state's electoral votes. Could also be used on a local level – a swing district, county, etc.

SWOT (Strengths, Weaknesses, Opportunities and Threats) analysis – Often used as part of a public relations *situation analysis*. It is a formal framework of identifying and outlining organizational growth opportunities. *SWOT* is an acronym for an organization's internal strengths and weaknesses and external opportunities and threats. *SWOT* is an examination of the internal environment of a firm (mission, goal, objectives, strategies, resources, trends, tactics, etc.) to identify particular strengths and weaknesses, and its external environment (demographic, economic, technological, social and cultural, legal and political, and natural forces) to identify particular opportunities and threats.

symbiotic marketing – A marketing method where one manufacturer sells its finished product to another for resale under the second manufacturer's label where that manufacturer already has access to the market through a well-established distribution system. An example would be RCA Whirlpool® manufacturing Sears Kenmore® washers and driers. Many department store mezzanine brands are examples of *symbiotic marketing*.

symbiotic relationship – A *symbiotic relationship* is a relationship between two entities which is mutually beneficial for the participants of the relationship.

symbolism – Words and images that represent or trigger some type of response.

symmetrical digital subscriber line (SDSL) – A type of DSL (*digital subscriber line*) that uses only one of the two cable pairs for transmission. *SDSL* allows residential or small office users to share the same telephone for data transmission and voice or fax telephony.

synchromarketing – A marketing activity intended to bring supply and demand more in line with each other. For example, as demand increases, supply would be increased. It may or may not affect price up or down.

synchronize – Matching the audio to the video in a commercial.

syncratic decision – A purchase decision where both husband and wife (or other types of couples) have equal influence.

syndicate groups – Smaller groups of individuals or audiences formed from a large audience. It is a technique used in training sessions where role playing is an important aspect.

syndicated marketing research firms – Marketing research agencies that specialize in gathering consumer and product information and selling it to subscribers who use it as secondary marketing data for a variety of public relations and other marketing purposes.

syndicated program– Television or radio programs that are reruns or original programs purchased by local stations to run (usually) in non-prime time hours. Other than local news programs, most local stations find it cost prohibitive to produce their own programming.

syndicated supplements – Publications (separate sections) sold to newspapers throughout the country by independent publishers and included in Sunday or weekday editions as inserts. Examples include *PARADE*, *Family Weekly* and *USA WEEKEND* and contribute to what has become known as "print expansion."

syndication – Television or radio shows that are original programs or reruns purchased by local stations to air during open hours.

synergy – The principle in public relations and marketing that the whole is greater than the sum of the parts. Two or more "things" working together to achieve greater efficiency. Using as many of the *marketing mix* variables together in a way that achieves maximum effect. Ogilvy and Mather® refers to its *synergy* approach as 360 Degree Brand Stewardship® – a proprietary set of tools and techniques used to understand, develop and enhance the relationship between a consumer and a brand. See *cannibalization; marketing synergy.*

systematic sample – In research, a sample drawn strictly according to a pre-determined formula – for example, every eighth, or 14th, or 24th, etc. name is chosen. This is a random approach. Computer software is now available to select scientific (chance) and other random samples.

systems buying – Buying a complete (compatible) solution to a problem or need rather than a number of component parts – whether it is furniture that better fits together or computer hardware. For example, an organization may purchase an entire accounting system from one supplier rather than computers from one supplier, software from another, staff training from another, and so on. See *systems selling.*

systems selling – Selling a complete solution to a problem or need rather than one or more of the component parts. For example, a landscaping service might offer design and walkway construction and deck design and construction. See *systems buying*. **S**

24/7 – Around-the-clock operation. In news, *24/7* usually means an emphasis on breaking news – whether it be radio, television newspapers or, particularly, their Web sites. Print media are moving to *24/7* coverage to reflect how readers, users and advertisers use today's media.

30-sheet posters – Largest poster form (12 inches x 25 inches or 30 inches x 40 inches) – the two most widely available sizes.

30-3-30 – Copy should be prepared so it is targeted at the 30-second reader, three-minute reader and the 30 minute reader. The most effective publications and copy are written and designed for all three types of readers. For a full explanation, see Chapter 12 in *The Public Relations Practitioner's Playbook*/Kendall/Hunt – 2008.

360-degree branding® – Trademarked by Ogilvy North America. Similar to *synergy* in that all media contribute to the success of a campaign. Every point of contact builds the brand – the whole is greater than the summer of its parts. (See *The Public Relations Practitioner's Playbook* – Kendall/Hunt – 2008.)

360-degree performance review – Employee evaluation that involves review by those above you and those below – your supervisors, peers and subordinates – everyone on your team (including a self-evaluation). It reviews skills, strengths and those areas that need improvement. This type of multi-rater system has been found to provide consistent and accurate feedback and in combination with traditional performance reviews offers an all-around "360-degree" perspective of an individual's leadership skills.

T-1 – A high-speed (1.54 megabits/second) Internet connection.

T-3 – A very high-speed (45 megabits/second or higher) Internet connection.

T-commerce – Electronic commerce (buying and/or selling) on interactive television.

tab-on – Advertising technique using Post-It® type notes for page one advertising in newspaper. Also called *front page notes, note advertising, poppers, sticky notes* and *dot whacks.*

table – A grid, graphic or sidebar used for displaying data or organizing information in columns and rows. It is also used to control placement of text and graphics – possibly for comparison purposes.

table of contents – List of articles, features, departments, chapters, etc. in a publication. Acts as a *teaser* to entice readers inside the publication.

247 Tips to Succeed: Trade show prep

When all the costs are added up, showing off a company at a tradeshow can be expensive. So, how can you maximize your efforts? Here are several ideas:

• When you've signed the check for your booth, ask the show organizers for a PR/marketing sponsor opportunity kit. These usually feature special awards, and new product showcases that can add extra visibility and sponsorship packages.

• Since some tradeshows sell their pre-registered attendee list, or the previous year's list of attendees, a $75.00 to $150.00 investment is a small price to pay so you'll know who's attending to maximize your investment.

• Be creative. Make your space extraordinary to build traffic and potential sales.

• Tradeshow attendees often reserve blocks of rooms at hotels. Seeing that they receive your corporate premium at their hotel room is another super idea. It will cost between $1.50 and $3.00 per room to get your premium delivered, not including the cost of the premium itself.

Home Technology Products, December 2004/January 2005
Newstrack Executive Information Service - www.news-track.com - 800-334-5771

tabloid – A newspaper that is roughly half the size of a standard newspaper – five to six columns (12 inches) wide and 14 inches up and down. Term used to describe a smaller than standard size newspaper such as the *New York Post* and *Philadelphia Daily News*.

tabulation – Organization of research data in tabular form (display of several items or records in rows and columns) showing responses to all questions against banners.

Tachistoscope testing – A method used in advertising and packaging recall tests. Used to measure an individual's recognition and perception of various elements within an advertisement by using the different lighting and exposure techniques of a Tachistoscope – a device that projects a series of images onto a screen at rapid speed to test visual perception, memory and learning.

tacking – The legal practice of employees and private contractors combining two or more part-time government salaries into one public paycheck. That one paycheck has the effect of boosting an employee's final pension payment.

tactic(s) – The specific technique or course of action (activity or task) conducted to help achieve a *strategy*. It is part of a detailed public relations plan and involves the use of specific personnel (agent), time and cost.

tactical planning – Planning of the shorter-term activities or tools to be used to achieve strategies that will help achieve objectives and eventually the public relations plan's (organization's) goal.

tactile communication – A form of nonverbal communication or body language where touching, handshaking, kissing, etc. conveys a message from sender to receiver. See *facial coding*; *kinesic communication*; *nonverbal communication*; *proxemic communication*.

tag (line) – Clever phrase used at the end of an advertisement or commercial to summarize the ad's message. A sentence or phrase that provides a creative description of an organization's position (e.g., Red Cross – We save lives; Maxwell House Coffee® – Good to the last drop). In broadcasting, because it comes at the end of the commercial, it is also called a kicker or stinger.

tagging – The naming in a product advertisement of certain retailers who carry the product. The naming of dealers is done as a convenience to consumers and to encourage the retailers to carry higher stock levels.

T

Also referred to as *dealer listing*. Also a Web site where individuals can put their favorites Web sites – but they are there for public viewing. Delicious.com® relies on *tagging* where computer users can put their favorite Web sites a "click away."

tail wagon vehicle – Usually a car, used to have sex. Police and attorneys commonly use the term.

tailored training – A training program customized to help meet particular company/industry objectives.

take – A portion of *copy* in a running story sent down to the composing room in sections.

take away message (take away line) – The strategic message a speaker wants remembered by the audience once the event ends.

take-ones – Promotional literature found in racks, often at grocery stores, pharmacies, etc.

talent – People who appear in radio and television commercials.

talent reader – A news anchor reading a story over a *piece* of video or b-roll. Also called *tells*.

talking cutout – On a Web site – a person who greets you with dialogue. In print, it would be called a silhouette and on television, a *cutaway*.

talking points – A set of brief messages that explain your story or point of view. Talking points expand on your key messages.

talking head – Close up video of a newsmaker or newsperson speaking.

tally light – Red light on television studio camera to alert "talent" he/she is "on the air." Sometimes referred to as a *cue light*.

tamper-proofing – The sealing of packages of products in a way that makes deliberate, undetected interference with them, for malicious or nuisance purposes, virtually impossible. *Tamper-proofing* got a jump start in 1982 when Tylenol®, a Johnson and Johnson® product, was tampered with, leaving at least seven dead.

tandem retirement – When husband and wife retire at the same time.

tangible product – A bundle of need-satisfying tangible and intangible attributes offered to a buyer by a seller. The result of work or thought. Examples would include a magazine article of special interest, running

248

Tip to Succeed:
10 Tips from 'The Donald'

Entrepreneur Donald Trump says it takes more than luck to be a winner. He says, "To be winner – you have to think like a winner."

1. Stay focused

2. Think big
   • Sell only to those who pay their bills
   • Do the big jobs

3. Enjoy what you are doing – No, love what you are doing

4. Never quit
   • Go through the wall
   • Go over the wall
   • Go around the wall
   • Just get there

5. Be paranoid
   • At least a little paranoid
   • Watch out for people – It's either you or them

6. Don't lose your momentum
   • Know when you've lost it
   • Think of yourself as a one-person show
   • Don't believe anyone else is on your side

7. Always see yourself as victorious

8. Go against the tide – go with your gut

9. Hire the best people and trust (but watch) them

10. Work hard – Be lucky
    • "The harder I work the luckier I get!" - Golfer, Gary Player

Donald Trump

shoes with features that deliver a benefit to purchaser and diet drinks for an individual looking for a drink without sugar. See *core product*.

tangible product attributes – Elements of a product that have physical dimensions or are detected by the senses. See *intangible product attributes*.

tangible symbol – A *service mark* (registered with the U.S. Patent and Trademark Office) or design, usually of solid appearance, used by some service organizations to position intangible offerings. See *service mark*.

target audience – Selected group of people who share similar needs or *demographic* characteristics such as income, age, sex, occupation or education, and best represent the most likely potential recipients of an organization's message.

target audience rating points (TARPS) – The rating points delivered to a particular target audience for a specific time period.

target margin on sales – The desired profit on each sale. It is used to determine the selling price where the average total cost is known.

target market – A group of individuals whom, collectively, are the intended recipients of an advertiser's message. The market segment that is the strategic focus of a business or a marketing plan. Segment members usually possess common characteristics and a relatively high propensity to purchase a particular product or service. The target market is often defined in terms of *geodemographics*, *demographics* and *psychographics*.

target market identification – The process of using income, *demographic*, *psychographic* and other lifestyle characteristics of a market and census information for small areas to identify the most favorable locations to market products and services.

target marketing – The process of marketing to a specific market segment or multiple segments. *Differentiated marketing* occurs when an organization simultaneously pursues several different market segments, usually with a different strategy for each. *Concentrated marketing* occurs when a single market segment is pursued.

249

Techniques to Succeed: Pack without wrinkles

Whether you are going on a brief business trip or an extended vacation, you don't want to waste time at your destination ironing wrinkled clothing or spending money to have them pressed.

BEFORE YOU PACK:

• Hang each outfit and cover it with a plastic dry cleaning bag

• Fold each one over

• Place it in the suitcase on the hanger

When you unpack your suitcase, simply hang the clothes up and you are ready to go. If any of the clothes do wrinkle, hang them in the bathroom with a hot shower running for a few minutes.

www.cruisediva.com

target price – A price, established to achieve a set percentage return on investment or a certain level of profit on net sales. See *target return pricing.*

target public – A term used mostly by nonprofits when identifying the group whose needs and wants they serve. Not unlike a *target market* except that it refers more to individuals.

target return on investment – A pricing method that seeks a desired return on investment.

target return pricing – A pricing method where a formula is used to calculate the price to be set for a product to return a desired profit or rate of return on investment – assuming that a particular quantity of the product is sold.

targeted revenue – The desired income from sales of the goods and services produced.

targeting – The use of *market segmentation* to select and address a key group of potential purchasers.

tariff – A government tax or duty on imported goods.

task-objective method – A budgeting method that builds a budget by asking what it will cost to achieve the stated objectives.

tattoos – Tiny stickers placed on fruits and vegetables to assist with pricing at checkout. See *price look up.*

team selling – The use of two or more representatives from a selling company to present a product to a buying organization. The selling team may include sales and technical specialists and members of a promotion department.

tear sheets – A page cut from a newspaper or magazine – clipped by the ad vehicle, public relations practitioner or ad agency – and sent to the client and/or advertiser as proof that a story or advertisement insertion ran. Also used to check color reproduction of advertisements.

teardown – A house purchased with the intention of tearing it down to be replaced by something more modern and more expensive.

tease/teaser – An enticing lead to a story that tells just enough about the story to encourage the reader or listener to continue. In a public relations context, it is a promotion intended to arouse interest in the main PR campaign that follows. Also an eye-catching graphic element, usually on Page One or section front, that promotes an item inside. Also called a *promo*.

teaser – Copy printed on the outside of a direct mail envelope to encourage the recipient to open, read and act on the piece.

teaser campaign – A public relations or an advertising campaign aimed at arousing interest and curiosity for a product.

tech-fluential – A person who is a technical professional by trade with the ability to influence others to purchase electronic equipment, software, etc. This segment of the population helps carry a technical product company's message to novice consumers who know little about technology. (Source: *PRSA Tactics*, April 2005).

technical sales representative – A salesperson hired primarily for his or her technical or scientific expertise.

technology determinism – The belief that technology is the force that shapes society. It develops in a progressive manner – limited only by the resources available. Marshall McLuhan stated that we are living in a new age of technology that has never been experienced before. Read more at *www.oak.cats.ohiou.edu/~kh380597/TD.htm.*

technological environment – Part of a firm's external environment where changes in technology affect a firm's marketing effort. The changing technological environment may pose threats or present opportunities.

technophiles – People who know "everything" about the Internet.

telecommuting – The practice of working at home and communicating with fellow workers by computer and telephone. Firms that use *telecommuting* say it saves the employer from supplying support services such as heating and cleaning, and the employee getting to and from work – but it can also deprive the worker of social contact and support.

telemarketing – A form of *direct marketing* that uses the telephone to reach potential customers. Also, the use of the telephone as a medium to sell, promote or solicit goods and services.

telemarketing inbound – Any phone calls that come into a *telemarketing* call center.

telemarketing interactive voice response (IVR) – Recorded or digitized text messages that can be accessed electronically by using a telephone.

telemarketing outbound – Any phone calls made out of a *telemarketing* call center.

telemarketing predictive dialing – The automatic dialing by a computer of telephone numbers on a pre-selected list. The system can, with great accuracy, discern an answering machine from a human voice and will instantly connect a respondent to a telemarketing or telephone service (or sales) representative. If there is no answer or a busy signal, the computer will know to redial later.

T

251

Technique to Succeed:
The importance of *thank you notes*

As the inside cover of The *Public Relations Practitioner's Playbook* notes, "Public Relations is as simple as a thank you note."

You can never thank someone too much, or thank too many people in a day. Based on research, here are the seven most effective opportunities to send "thank you" notes to help develop new business:

1. **When someone offers suggestions.** It's a wonderful gift when you are given a suggestion on how you might do something better. Here's how to start this type of note: "Thank you for your suggestion. You make my job easier and so much more enjoyable when you provide input."

2. **When people try something you recommended.** When others buy into something new, solely based on your suggestion, they're going out of their "comfort zone." This calls for a note that could read, "Thank you for your trust in me."

3. **When customers do business with you, every time.** Write a short, personalized "thank you" on an interesting card, letterhead, or even a postcard that says, "I appreciate your business, thank you."

4. **When people compliment you.** When someone compliments you about something, it's an opportunity to jot off a little note of thanks. Compliments are given so rarely, so take the lead to say "thank you" when you get one.

5. **When someone recommends you.** This is the best form of advertising you can ever get. It's so easy to take the time and go back to our advocate, and say, "thank you for referring me to ___. I will keep you informed on what develops."

6. **When people are patient.** People help us when they give us time to learn how to best work with them. This often requires their patience. A note for this could say, "Thanks for your patience. I appreciate the opportunity to better work with you."

7. **When someone says "no" to you.** You've just presented your ideas to a co-worker or even a customer, and it was completely

telemarketing services – Firms that assist other firms, companies and organizations in the practice of marketing goods or services by telephone.

telephone interviews – One of the more popular techniques for conducting research and gathering data. It is a rapid and moderately inexpensive means of gathering marketing research data.

Telephone Preference Service (TPS) – A database of business and individual telephone subscribers who have elected not to receive unsolicited direct marketing calls. It is a service of the Direct Marketing Association for consumers who want to have their names removed from telemarketing lists. (Beginning in 2005, telephone subscribers could choose to opt out of *telemarketing* calls.) Read more at *www.dma.org.uk/content/home.asp*.

telephone survey – Research conducted by calling respondents by telephone and administering a survey instrument.

telephone service representative (TSR) – Anyone who sells, or services customers over the phone either inbound or outbound.

telephonically – Communicating by telephone.

teleshopping – A form of non-store or in-home retailing where the consumer can purchase goods and services shown on television. The purchaser telephones an order, or orders with the aid of a computer, and the products are delivered to the home. See *home shopping*; *non-store retailing*.

television generals – Retired generals serving as TV analysts during the Iraqi war and other "conflicts."

television market – An unduplicated geographical area to which a county is assigned for the purpose of measuring television use and viewership.

tells – A news anchor reading a story over a *piece* of video or b-roll. Also known as *talent reader*.

template – A document file containing layout, styles and repeating elements (such as *logos*, address, boilerplate, etc.) so that recurring documents can maintain a consistent look and feel. It could also be a model (blank form) publication that can be used as the basis for creating a new publication.

terminal dues – The payments between countries to compensate for imbalance in sending/receiving international mail.

terminal market – The market where commodity products are shipped from local and regional markets for processing and packing for eventual final shipment to *wholesalers* and *retailers*.

terms & conditions – The details of the contract accompanying an insertion order. Read more at *www.iab.net* for voluntary guidelines for standard *terms & conditions* of Internet advertising for media buys.

terra incognita – Exploration for "unknown territory" that has not been mapped or documented.

terrestrial radio – Traditional radio using public airwaves and frequencies (AM and FM bands). Became a term with the advent of Satellite radio (Sirius Satellite Radio® and XM Satellite Radio® check on actual name).

territorialization – The division of a sales region into *territories*.

territory – The specific region or group of customers for which a salesperson has direct responsibility. See *sales territory*.

territory management – Overseeing and coordinating a firm or organization's (sales) regions to achieve optimum results. It is widely accepted that organizations must have optimal coverage in all regions, including the proper distribution and management of sales representatives. Public relations and advertising agencies follow the same plan when they have multiple offices in different regions. It is the best way to properly service clients.

test – An order that is placed for a small quantity of names to determine how the list performs. If it performs well, a *continuation* order for more names is usually placed.

T

test market – A city, region or state used to evaluate market reaction to a new product and its public relations and overall marketing program before full commercialization begins. *Test markets* also can be simulated by bringing together selected individuals from the target market. See *new product development*.

test marketing – A limited introduction and marketing of a product or service to evaluate public reaction and projected success prior to establishing a full market strategy. Also, making samples of a new product available to see what certain consumers think of it. See *market testing*; *new products*.

testimonial – A positive statement (or written recommendation) made by a (satisfied) customer who has used the product or service. A *testimonial* may be a single customer quote or it may be integrated into other marketing material such as a case study about the customer's use of a company's product or service. Also, an advertising technique using celebrities or others to deliver a message about his/her positive personal experience with a product, brand or service. See *endorsement*.

text – Characters and words that form the main body of a publication. Also, the verbatim report of a speech or public statement.

text ads – Web site advertisements, such as those used by Google® that read vertically down the right side clearly identifying them as "sponsors." They are all text – similar to *classified advertising* – and not *display advertising*.

text inset – Moving text away from the edges of a box.

252

Tips to Succeed: That all important *thank you note*

Just a note to let you know the percentage of people who send you thank you notes.

Always 53%

Sometimes 34%

Never 13%

Source: Opinion Research Corp. for Lenox Inc.

textual ad impressions – The delivery of a text-based advertisement to a computer browser. To compensate for slow Internet connections, visitors may disable "auto load images" in their graphical browser.

theater testing – A method used in testing viewer responses of a large audience after being exposed to an advertisement. While the audiences chosen are selected randomly to achieve quantitative results, this audience does not qualify as a true "scientific" sample.

theme – What a story is about – its essential idea.

theme message(s) – A message(s) developed to help achieve objectives. Use one focus panel to develop message(s). Use another to test it (them).

theory-in-use model – A decision-making tool employing previous learning and experience. *Theory-in-use models* incorporate statements such as "if action X is taken, then result Y will occur."

thermal dye sublimation (sublimation) – Using heat and a color-type film material to transfer the color from the film to paper or some other material. During the printing process, the films are placed on the paper and heated up by the print head. This will cause the pigments to leave the film and enter into the paper where the color cools and re-solidifies. This is the *sublimation* part. There is little mess compared to ink. *Sublimated* images are extremely washable; scratch resistant and dishwasher safe because the image is protected within the surface. Printing with *sublimation* ink is not new; *sublimation* transfers have played an important role in the printing world for decades. What is new to the printing world, is the ability to digitally print sublimation inks rather that screen-printing them. See *pre-press services*.

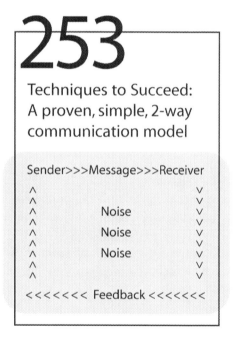

253

Techniques to Succeed: A proven, simple, 2-way communication model

Sender>>>Message>>>Receiver

Noise

Noise

Noise

<<<<<<< Feedback <<<<<<<

think piece – A background or opinion article.

T

254

Techniques to Succeed: Teamwork – a key to success

Delivering high performance is easier when everyone on the team takes responsibility for working together. Good team leaders know how to motivate others and keep everyone moving in the same direction. Here are some suggestions:

- **Empower when possible.** Give team members the opportunity to make decisions.

- **Delegate when appropriate.** Ensure that all team members have the same workload.

- **Teach when knowledge or skill is lacking.** When you see that training is needed in a particular area, take time to train.

- **Provide guidance when you are needed.** Always be available for questions.

- **Get out of the way when you are not needed.** If you see that your team is handling their workload efficiently, don't hover over them.

www.dalecarneigie.com

third-line forcing – An arrangement where a manufacturer sells a product to a reseller only on the condition that the reseller also buys another product from some other (chosen) manufacturer. For the most part, third-line forcing is illegal under the *Trade Practices Act.*

third-party ad server – Independent outsourced companies that specialize in managing, maintaining, serving, tracking and analyzing the results of online advertising campaigns. They deliver targeted advertising that can be tailored to consumers' declared or predicted characteristics or preferences.

third-party endorser – A person not associated with a firm, organization or another individual who offers an endorsement or testimonial (from personal experience or use) – honest opinion of the endorser. This third party validation – *known as third party endorsement* – carries considerable more weight in changing opinion than any form of communication. (It is true *face-to-face; word-of-mouth.*)

thought-leader survey – A technique sometimes used in the exploratory stage of marketing research where personal interviews are conducted with community leaders (*connectors* or *key communicators*) or experts who may be expected to shed some light on a problem to be investigated.

thousand yard stare – Deer in the headlights look.

threat matrix – A component of the *SWOT Analysis* – strengths, weaknesses, opportunities and threats.

three across – Term used when the three major network television anchors (ABC, CBS, NBC) are on the air at the same time.

three-color job – Printer's reference to a publication using black and two spot colors.

three-step flow – A communication method where a message begins with an organization's CEO or other chief spokesperson who sends it to *key communicators* who pass it on to the rest of the public. See *two-step flow*.

threshold firm – A company whose products serve segments too small to be of interest to firms with larger shares of the market. They are also called *market specialists, threshold firms* or *foothold firms*. See *market challenger; market follower; market leader; market nicher*.

threshold prices – The highest price most people are willing to pay for a product or service.

throughput – The amount of data transmitted through Internet connectors in response to a given request.

throwing out the trash – Government releasing bad news on Friday afternoons and evenings. Other organizations do it, too. It's commonly referred to as "*throwing out the trash*." Also called *Friday night dump*.

thrust marketing – Situations where sales managers change their titles to marketing managers, but continue to ignore the satisfaction of and relationships with customers and their needs and wants. Instead, these managers emphasize the selling of the products their firms can make most cheaply and easily.

thumb drive – A *flash, jump* or *thumb drive* – used to transport computer files – which connects to computers through a *USB port*.

thumbing (a message) – Use of thumbs (only) when typing a message on a *Personal Data Assistant (PDA)* or cell phone. (Thumb tribe members.)

thumbnail – Small preliminary sketches of various layout ideas – a rough, simple, often small sketch used to show the basic layout of an advertisement. Also a half-column picture. See *porkchop*.

thumbnail photo – Small version of a photo – a small (dimension) headshot.

tickler file – A public relations practitioner's (or other organized planners) ideas file kept in an organized fashion on a computer or in folders. Editors use them on "slow" news days for fillers and also as reminders.

tie-back – The part of the story that ties it back to something that has already been published. A tie-in is used to connect a story with some other, perhaps more important, story.

tie-in arrangements – An arrangement where a manufacturer sells a product to a reseller only on the condition that the reseller also buys another less popular product – not unlike the *tie-in advertising* technique where two (sometimes unrelated products) are tied together (a jar of peanut butter comes with a coupon for jelly). Also called a *tying contract. Tie-in arrangements* are not always legal. *Tie-in advertising* is an accepted and successful technique.

tie-in advertising – Two (usually related) brands/products advertised together. The intent is the incentive that the purchase of one will inspire the purchase of the other (e.g. a discount coupon for a jar of peanut butter inside the cap of a jar of jelly).

TIFF – A type of computer file used for graphic images or photos. *TIFF* (or TIF) stands for Tagged Image File Format. This type of file is one of the most widely used formats for sending high-quality images. Use the extension ".tif" for a *TIFF* file.

TIFs (Technology Involved Females) – A demographic on the rise. The TIF is a female from any background, any age, is smart, savvy and not afraid of technology. Intel® took the information to heart and has actively been marketing its technology to women as well as men. Now, according to a research project conducted by Cornell Law School, women are now making 50 percent of technology purchases – an industry once dominated by male consumers. The study shows that women are in the rising demographic because they're more likely to ask tech questions than men.

time analysis – A *time management* technique, used in public relations and many other professions, where the amount of time allocated to each job activity is recorded and later reviewed to plan for more productive use of the available time. See *time management.*

time codes – Generated from videotapes and used to reference specific places in the footage. Digital audio and video also generate *time codes.*

The ABCs of Strategic Communication

T

time compression – A technique used in broadcast production to delete time from radio and television commercials. It can be accomplished by editing space between words or technologically speeding up the message – which can now be accomplished without changing the quality of the recording.

time-efficient retailing – A recent trend in retailing where retailers attempt to position themselves by emphasizing the speed and convenience of their services – such non-store retailing as computer, credit card and telephone shopping.

time management – The perception of time as a valuable asset and the systematic structuring of the work day and week to conserve resources and maximize productivity.

time prices – The shopping time, travel time, waiting time, performance time and monitoring time that are part of the total price a consumer pays for a product. See *monitoring time; non-monetary price.*

time shifting (timeshifting) – Recording a television or radio program, *podcast*, etc. to a video or audio tape recorder, iPod® other storage

255 Tips to Succeed: Tips for tipping
Tip = To Improve Service

- Hotel maids: $2.00 per day

- Shuttle driver: $1-$2 for helping you with one bag; $5 for heavy luggage.

- Doorman: No tip for opening hotel door; $1-$2 for carrying bag or opening cab door

- Wine steward: 10%-20% depending on service

- Concierge: $10-$20 for assistance such as acquiring hard-to-get show tickets

- Limousine drivers, masseurs, caddies: 20% unless a tip is included in the bill

- Theatre ushers: They generally get tips in Europe

Eileen Smith (from *Emily Post's Etiquette*) - www.courierpostonline.com

medium to be viewed or listened to at a time more convenient to the consumer. Typically, this refers to TV programming but can also refer to radio shows via *podcasts*.

time utility – The value given to a product by virtue of the fact that it is available at the time it is required. See *utility*.

time warriors – Busy professionals who want their information in the quickest, most succinct strategic method available.

timing objection – An objection by a prospective buyer to the timing of the purchase of the goods offered by a salesperson – the buyer indicates that the goods are not required at this particular time. See *objections*.

TINKIE (Two Incomes, Nanny and Kids) – A demographic grouping.

TIP – According to Nancy Murphy, professor, Fuller Theological Seminary, Pasadena, Calif., "A Triumph In the Pursuit of knowledge." Used by fundamentalists who want to be the brightest and most educated. Murphy's theory, which pertains to public relations practitioner's objective to change behavior – "Those who pursue the truth will often end up having to change their mind."

tipping point society – The price that a product or service reaches before consumers "cut back."

tip-ins – Preprinted advertisements that are provided by the advertiser to be glued into the binding of a magazine.

title flow – The transfer of title or ownership of products as they pass from one member to the next in a channel of distribution. See *marketing channel*.

T-O technique – A closing technique commonly used in retailing where one salesperson "turns over" the customer to another if he or she fails to close the sale. See *close*.

token – A coin, peel-off stamp or a punch-out paper piece that can be inserted into a machine or order form. Referred to in public relations and advertising as an action device. The purpose is to involve the prospect in the offer.

top-down approach to planning – Planning where senior management determines *goal*, *objectives*, *strategies*, *tactics*, etc. with minimal input from subordinates. See *marketing planning process*.

top-down approach to promotion budgeting – Promotion budgeting where the amount to be spent on promotion is determined by senior management with minimal input from subordinates.

top-down approach to sales forecasting – Forecasting which takes the company's objectives rather than market conditions as its basis.

top of mind – In advertising, recalling a *brand* long after seeing or hearing a commercial or advertisement. Many times, a word, picture or person (*transfer effect*) may have triggered the recall. Also called *sleeper effect*.

top of story – The first paragraph or a paragraph near the beginning of a news story – the most important information. Usually it's in the lead. See *inverted pyramid*.

total ad impressions – The total of all advertisement impressions delivered, regardless of the source (print, radio, television, outdoor, etc.).

total audience plan – Advertising or broadcast commercial package consisting of a combination of ads and commercial spots in several sections of a newspaper or spread across each time classification so that ads and commercials reach more readers, listeners and viewers.

total costs – The sum of the fixed and variable costs incurred in the production of any given quantity level.

total market coverage – If a newspaper covers only a percentage of its market through paid circulation then a supplement has to be published/printed that would go free to the rest of the market.

total survey area (TSA) – Includes those counties penetrated significantly by signals from radio and television stations licensed to the metro survey area. The metro survey area definition plus the non-metro counties yields the *total survey area*. Read more at *www.krgspec.com/Library/TSA.cfm*.

total unique users – Different individuals who have either accessed a Web site (see *unique visitor*) or who have been served unique content and/or advertisements such as e-mail, newsletters and pop-under or pop-up ads. Unique users are identified by their registration or cookies. Reported unique users should filter out robots (automated users). Read more at *www.iab.net* for ad campaign measurement guidelines.

total visitors – In computers, the total number of browsers or individuals who have accessed a site within a specific time period. See *unique visitor*.

total visits – In computers, the total number of browsers accessing a Web site within a specific time period. Through specialized software, *total visits* should filter robotic activity and visits from repeat visitors.

town meeting – Where an entire geographic area is invited to participate in a gathering, often for a political or administrative purpose. It may be to obtain community suggestions or feedback on public policies from government officials, or to cast legally binding votes on budgets and policy.

track and trace – Theory behind technology used in tattooing produce which allows protection of the food supply at various stages of distribution because the *tattoo* helps trace product from birth to delivery.

256

Tips to Succeed: Preventing identity theft

- Buy a shredder and shred all mail and other material that contains personal information.
- Never give out personal information, such as Social Security number, to anyone unless you know and trust them.
- Lock your mailbox.
- Don't carry more than two credit cards.
- Never carry your Social Security card.
- Consider opting out of free credit card offers by calling 888-567-8688 or online at www.optoutprescreen.com.

Associated Press

tracking – The space between letters on a printed document.

tracking poll (survey) – A type of research study that follows the same group of subjects over an extended period of time.

tracking study – Research on the effectiveness of public relations and advertising campaigns. A tr*acking study* measures the effect that strategic messages, an advertisement or ad campaign has on organization, brand and/or company awareness, consumer recall, interest, attitude and purchase intentions. A tr*acking study* uses the same group or subjects over an extended period (regular intervals) of time.

trade advertising – Advertising designed to increase sales specifically for retailers and wholesalers – sometimes using the *push strategy* of public relations and advertising by directing advertising at *distribution* channels (*wholesalers, distributors, sales representatives, affiliates,* value-added resellers, *retailers,* etc.) rather than end-consumers.

trade barriers – Economic and financial measures, including tariffs, quotas, documentation requirements, etc. imposed by some countries to limit the import of foreign goods to protect local industries.

trade character – People, characters and animals used in advertising who are identified with the products – for example, Jolly Green Giant®, Tony the Tiger® and Michael Jordan.

trade deal – An arrangement where the retailer agrees to give the manufacturer's product a special promotional effort in return for product discounts, goods or cash. Also, advertisers who trade goods or services for advertising space or time. See *bartering.*

trade discount – An allowance or price reduction in payment for a channel member's participation in the distribution network. Also called a *functional discount.* See *discount.*

trade marketing – Marketing to the retail and distribution trades rather than to end-users. This can be included in a *push strategy.*

257 Techniques to Succeed: The 3-minute drill

The next time your boss asks you to solve a company problem, try the *3-minute drill* – keeping in mind that every 30 seconds = 75 words:

PREPARE AN EXECUTIVE SUMMARY:

1. Situation Description (the problem in 60 words)

2. Analysis (the issues in 60 words)

3. Goal (the destination in 60 words)

4. Options (at least three in 150 words)

5. Recommendations (from the options in 60 words)

6. Justification (unintended consequences – pluses and minuses in 60 words)

James E. Lukasewski, APR, Fellow PRSA - The Lukaszewsii Group - www.e911.com

trade name – The name under which a company operates.

Trade Practices Act – Legislation introduced to protect consumers from unfair dealings with sellers.

trade promotion – An *incentive* offered to resellers to encourage them to buy more of a particular product and to sell it more aggressively. See *trade sales promotion*.

trade publication – A magazine, newspaper, newsletter, journal, directory, etc. published by members of a specific industry. They are often used by salespeople as a source of leads. Also called a *vertical publication*.

trade sales promotion – An incentive offered to resellers to encourage them to buy more of a particular product and to sell it more aggressively. See *trade promotion*.

trade selling – Selling products to wholesalers and retailers for resale purposes.

trade show – An exhibition or fair where manufacturers display their products for the benefit of wholesalers and retailers attending the show.

trade stimulants – Sales promotions directed toward retailers and distributors designed to motivate them and increase sales.

trademark – Legal protection through the U.S. Patent and Trademark Office given to a brand name, brand mark and/or *logo*, term, design, symbol or any other feature that identifies the goods, service, institution or idea. See *service mark*.

traders – The earliest form of salespeople, existing in most ancient societies – typically, *traders* had ownership in the goods they sold.

trading areas – Major cities and centers of business or commerce – the garment districts of New York and Chicago; produce distribution centers in many cities.

The ABCs of Strategic Communication

T

trading down – Adding a lower-priced version of a product to the product range, generally to capture a new market segment not served effectively because the original version of the product was too expensive for it. In some instances, the practice of reducing the number of features or quality of an offering to realize a lower purchase price. For example, Toyota® added the Scion® and Chevrolet® the Cobalt®. See *trading up*.

trading stamps – A form of sales promotion used by retailers where customers receive stamps or coupons in proportion to the amount of their purchases – the stamps can be redeemed later for merchandise.

trading up – Adding a higher-priced, higher-quality version of a product to the range, generally to increase sales of the lower-priced model through consumer association of its image with the more prestigious model. In some instances, the practice of improving an offering by adding new features and higher quality materials or adding products or services to increase the purchase price. For example, Nissan® added the Infinity®. See *trading down*.

traditional delivery – Delivery of magazines to readers through newsstands or home delivery.

traffic – The department at a radio or television station that schedules commercials. In computers, the number of visits and/or visitors who come to a Web site. Known as the "bloodstream" of the agency, radio or television station because of its major operational responsibility.

traffic builder – The lowest-priced item in a product line. Also a promotional tactic using direct mail. Designed to draw consumers to the mailer's location. See *prestige builder*; *product line*.

trailers – Advertisements that precede the feature film in a movie theater.

training course – A course that focuses on the practical application of skills to improve productivity.

training qualification – A qualification for sales and marketing professionals that is assessed through work-based projects.

training sessions – Updating employees during the work day to keep them current. Also called in-service workshops.

transactional functions – One of the three kinds of functions (with *facilitating functions* and *logistical functions*) performed by intermediaries in a marketing channel. *Transactional functions* are the activities

T

associated with buying products and reselling them, and the risks incurred in keeping the products in stock.

transfer – In computers, the successful response to a (click) page request. Also, when a browser receives a complete page of content from a Web server.

transfer allegiance – Moving personal support from one person or brand to another. Research shows it is difficult to persuade consumers, loyal to a particular brand, to even try another brand.

Transfer Control Protocol/Internet Protocol (TCP/IP) – A software standard used by the Internet to understand all computer languages and most computers.

transfer effect – An advertising technique which makes use of celebrities or other well known people to endorse a product. The theory being that when a consumer sees the celebrity or hears his/her voice or name, the product being endorsed immediately comes to mind (*recall*). For example, Michael Jordan and Nike®; Wilfred Brimley and Quaker Oats®; Cindy Crawford and Pepsi®; Bill Cosby and Jell-O®. Also, the technique used by presidents during the State of the Union when they invite "ordinary" citizens to sit in the gallery and cite them for one good deed or another. See *gallery tribute*.

transfer price – The price charged by one division of a large company for the shipment of its goods from one profit center to another.

transformation advertising – *Image advertising* that changes the experience of buying and using a product. See *image advertising*.

transit advertising – Advertising that appears on public transportation or on waiting areas and bus stops.

transitional ad – An advertisement displayed between Web pages. In other words, the user sees an advertisement as he/she navigates between page "a" and page "b." Also known as an *interstitial*.

transitional pop up – An electronic advertisement that pops up in a separate window between content pages.

translation method – A method used by salespeople to respond to customer objections by turning the objection into a reason for acting immediately. When people object, turn them around by using what they

T

259 Techniques to Succeed:

Six career secrets you won't learn in school – to help you win at the business world's game:

Develop a marketable corporate person:
Think of yourself as a publicist with the task of promoting you. Learn to capitalize on your skills, succinctly assert your achievements and project a corporate persona – or your most mature, professional and competent face.

Establish profitable relationships:
Business networking is a valuable tool to gain information, increase your visibility in your field and make connections that will help you move forward in your career. Seek out new contacts and potential mentors whom you like and admire and whose interests you share. On the home front, don't expect your boss to figure out what you're all about. Determine her priorities, find out what she wants from you, and brainstorm ways to surpass her expectations.

Master transferable skills like goal setting, effective communication and time management:
You might not know exactly what you want to do with your life, but transferable skills will serve you well no matter what future path you decide to pursue. Make your time count now by working with your boss to set specific, reasonable and attainable goals for your present position that will help you advance to the next level.

Stay motivated despite trying circumstances:
There's no doubt that the business world can be frustrating, but remember that you can choose your response to your environment. If you make a conscious decision to begin each day with a positive outlook, negative conditions at work can't take that away from you. Aim to increase your self-awareness so you can better understand your emotional hot buttons.

Get people to cooperate:
Always keep in mind that other people don't care what you want – they want to know what's in it for them. By approaching negotiations with an attitude that allows both parties to win, you'll be more effective at eliciting cooperation and ultimately getting what you want.

say to prove that they are wrong. Use their own arguments like a boomerang, so they go around in a circle and come back to persuade them. See *boomerang method*.

transparency – A positive, color photographic image on clear film. Also clear plastic used with overhead projectors with information printed on the sheets or written on for presentations.

transparent ink – Ink used in a four-color printing process that allows for colors underneath the ink to show through. Sometimes referred to as varnish.

trap – To combine different layers of colors to create various colors in the four-color printing process.

trapping – Print slightly over the *knockout* area or white.

TravelDrive® – A brand of *flash, jump, key or thumb drive* – used to transport computer files – which connects to computers through a *USB port*. They are inexpensive digital storehouses.

traveler – An old term for a salesperson. A traveling salesperson – a salesperson who spends more time in regions outside his home territory than at "home."

traveling salesperson
– See *traveler*.

treatment – A written sketch outlining the plot, characters and action for a screenplay but not including certain elements of a finished screenplay, such as camera directions and dialogue. Also an adaptation of a novel or other literary work that serves as the basis for a screenplay. Used for producing such videos as documentaries.

trend analysis – A forecasting method where likely future sales are estimated by statistical analysis of previous sales patterns.

trial balloon – A project or idea tentatively announced in the news media in order to test public opinion.

trial close – A technique used in selling to assess a buyer's readiness to make a purchase decision. A trial close usually takes the form of questions that ask for decisions on minor selling points. If the salesperson gets favorable responses to these questions, he or she can more confidently attempt to close the sale. See *close*; *minor points close*.

trial objective – One of three possible aims or objectives of a consumer sales promotion – purchasers are offered incentives to try a new product. See *loading objective*; *loyalty objective*.

tribes – Electronic communities of kids with like interests around the globe.

trickle-across concept – The notion that the adoption of a particular fashion will spread horizontally within several socioeconomic classes at the same time. See *trickle-down concept*; *trickle-up concept*.

trickle-down concept – The notion that the adoption of a particular fashion will flow downward from one socioeconomic class of consumers to the next. See *trickle-across concept*; *trickle-up concept*.

trickle-up concept – The notion that the adoption of a particular fashion will flow upward from one socioeconomic class of consumers to the next. See *trickle-across concept*; *trickle-down concept*.

trim – To reduce the length of a story.

trim size – A size of a newspaper or magazine page or other printed "piece" after trimming.

Triple Bottom Line (public relations) Theory – The late Patrick Jackson coined the *Double Bottom Line Theory*. M. Larry Litwin, APR, Fellow PRSA, and author of this book and *The Public Relations Practitioner's Playbook*, has coined the *Triple Bottom Line Theory*. In summary, the *first* bottom line: developing (creating), enhancing or, at the very least, maintaining relationships. The *second* bottom line: revenue generated through those relationships. The *third* bottom line: profit – earned through relationships, revenue, and proper and effective management. Many times, when *synergy* is achieved, the proof is in the profit. See *Double Bottom Line Theory*.

truncate – Cutting off the end or shortening a term – many times to fit in a limited space (on the computer).

truth bending – Technique used in political advertising – where strategic message stretches the truth and, at times, borders on lying. The *Federal Trade Commission* has ruled that political advertising does not have to be "totally" truthful. Read more in *The Public Relations Practitioner's Playbook* (Kendall/Hunt – 2008).

truth squad – Term coined by political parties when they began sending workers to opposing conventions to clarify strategic message they believed contained "untruths" or false accusations by the opposition – quickly getting out the "truth." Major corporations also use this technique for clarification when they believe the competition has not been totally truthful.

truthiness – What you want "it" to be rather than what it is.

try-on-for-size method – A buyer-based approach to pricing where salespeople test resellers' reactions to the proposed price of a forthcoming product before a final decision on price is made.

tummler – An entertainer who is expected to entertain hotel guests all day, not just on the stage at night.

turnkey – Something purchased in a condition ready for immediate use, occupation or operation.

turnover – The rate of audience change for a specific radio or television program during a specific amount of time.

turnover method – A closing technique commonly used in retailing where one salesperson "turns over" the customer to another if he or she fails to close the sale. See *close; T-O technique*.

TV cool – A television program, network or otherwise, that appeals to a younger demographic – one with great spending power.

tweenagers (tweens) – The *demographic* group of 7 to 11 year olds.

twitter – A form of communication between friends (or strangers) near or far who send continual updates about moments in their lives (usually through text messaging). *Twitter* (personal social media Web sites) sites allow subscribers to have their messages – both sent and received – posted for everyone to view or they may be password protected.

two-color job – Printer's reference to a publication using black and one *spot color*.

two level channel – A marketing channel where there are two levels of intermediaries (for example, a wholesaler and a retailer) between the manufacturer and the end-user. See *marketing channels*.

261 Techniques to Succeed: Know the Product Life Cycle

A concept which draws an analogy between the span of a human life and that of a product, brand or retail store (outlet) suggesting that, typically, a product's life consists of a sequence of five stages:

• Introductory – Product/brand is born and introduced.

• Growth – Demand develops for the product and/or brand.

• Maturity – Product/brand gathers "steam" as it ages.

• Decline – Competition or other factors have a negative effect on demand and bite into market share.

• Withdrawal – Product/brand (or retail store) dies or goes out of business.

The concept is used as a tool to form marketing strategies appropriate to each of the stages. Also, the history of a product from its introduction to its eventual decline and withdrawal.

- Clarity: Say what you mean, mean what you say
- Correct: Avoid errors to avoid confusion
- Connection: Engage your reader
- Compelling: Motivate an action
- Conviction: Live the branding
- Consistency: Stay on message…always

Roger Shapiro - Mitchell Rose A Communications Consultancy - Lawrenceville, N.J.

two-step flow theory – Originally, it was a the term used by Katz and Lazarsfeld to describe their observation that media messages flow from the media to opinion leaders (*key communicators*) to the rest of the audience. The important point is that their research demonstrated that media effects are mediated by the pattern of our social contacts. They concluded that the media have limited effects. It is now accepted among many public relations practitioners that *two-step flow* skips the opinion leaders and goes directly to the rest of the audience. The method that uses *key communicators* is the *three-step flow* because the message emanates or encodes from a chief spokesperson for an organization, is sent to *key communicators* and then to the rest of the public. See *multi-step flow; three-step flow*.

two-way stretching – Introducing new products into a product line at both the higher and lower priced ends at the same time. See *downward stretching; product line stretching; upward stretching*.

tying contract – An agreement, usually illegal, that forces an intermediary (wholesaler, retailer, etc) to purchase other products in the line so they can obtain the product actually required.

type font (face) – Traditionally refers to the complete alphabet for a specific *typeface*. A specific set of characteristics that have the same look and design.

type specifications (specs) – Describe the type in terms of font, size, leading, column width, alignment and any other directions.

The ABCs of Strategic Communication

T

type styles – Ways to stylize a font: plain, bold, *italics*, underline, strike-through, outline, shadow, capitals, small capitals, superscript, subscript and superior.

typeface (font) – A designed alphabet with consistent characteristics and attributes – printing type or font (e.g., Helvetica, Times New Roman, Courier).

typo – An abbreviation for typographical error. Also, a keystroke error in the typeset copy.

typography – The designated setting of type for printing purposes. The style, arrangement and appearance of the copy in the final version of marketing material. *Typography* is a design element chosen for aesthetics, readability and, by setting a tone, reinforcement of the marketing message. **T**

T

ullage – The amount that a box (cereal), package (chips) or bottle (soft drink) falls short of being full.

umbrella pricing – A pricing technique common in *oligopolistic* (only a few sellers) market situations where the larger firms, by keeping prices high, create room for smaller companies to operate profitably below them. See *keep-out pricing*.

unaided recall test – The ability to recall information about an advertisement, product, service or brand without any prompting. A method of evaluating the effectiveness of a company's recent advertising. Without help from the researcher, selected respondents from the target market are asked to bring to mind advertisements they have seen or heard recently. See *recall test*.

unbalancing – The practice of bidding extremely high or low on some (government) contract items to win a job or make a larger profit (not illegal). A contractor who *unbalances* hopes to make up the difference by seeking approval for changes to the contract's *specifications* after the job begins through what is known as a *change order*. *Change orders* have become common on many large (government) jobs. *(Courier-Post –* Camden, N.J. Oct. 31, 2005).

unbundling – Eliminating one or more of the elements of a firm's product offerings. For example, a firm selling computers might discontinue its offer of free support with each computer sold, deciding instead to charge separately for it. See *bundle*.

under cover marketing – When someone stops you on the street to offer a free sample, ultimately, they are trying to sell you that product.

For example, if a "marketer" with a camera takes your picture, subliminally, they are really trying to sell you the camera.

underground marketing – Paying someone to recommend (different from enforce) a product without revealing they are doing so. Using real people (referred to a *connectors*) to create a *buzz* (manufactured buzz) for products or services – paid or otherwise, but most times paid (to recommend [*word-of-mouth*] a product or service).

underline – A subhead that leads from the headline into the body copy.

underwriting – Financial backing of a program or event – especially a program on National Public Radio or other non-profit radio or television station, or special event.

undifferentiated marketing – A view of the market that assumes all consumers are basically the same. A marketing philosophy where the seller views the market as a homogeneous whole, and, therefore, has only one marketing program (the same product, the same price, the same promotion and the same distribution system) for everyone. Also referred to as *unsegmented marketing* or *mass marketing*. See *differentiated marketing*; *product-differentiated marketing*; *target marketing*.

unduplicated audience – The number of unique readers, listeners or viewers of a publication, radio or television station. Or, those exposed to a specified domain, page or advertisement in a specified time period.

unfair advertising – Advertising that is likely to harm the consumer. The *Federal Trade Commission* has the power to regulate unfair advertising that falls within a very specific legal definition.

uniform delivered price – A pricing method, sometimes referred to as *postage stamp pricing*, where all customers pay the same freight costs regardless of their distance from the dispatch point. Also called *single-zone pricing*. See *zone pricing*.

Uniform Resource Locator (URL) – The *URL* is the address of a resource, or file, available on the Internet. It is the unique identifying address of any particular page on the Internet. Generally, when someone asks for your *URL*, they're asking for your Web site address.

Uniform Resource Locator (URL) tagging – The process of embedding unique identifiers into *URLs* (Web sites) which recognize new and return visitors to the site.

unfunded mandate – Governmental bodies making program demands of schools but without providing the funds.

union bug – A union logo or seal – usually very small – printed on a publication signifying that it has been printed by a union shop.

unique selling proposition (USP) – A benefit statement about a feature that is both unique to the product and important to the user. Commonly referred to as the *USP*.

unique user – Different individuals who have either accessed a Web site (see *unique visitor*) or who have been served unique content and/or advertisements such as e-mail, newsletters and pop-under or pop-up ads. *Unique users* are identified by their registration or cookies. Reported *unique users* should filter out robots (automated users). Read more at *www.iab.net* for ad campaign measurement guidelines.

unique visitor – A *unique user* who accesses a Web site within a specific time period. See *unique user*.

unit block – First block on a street (with an address below 100) usually with an address beginning with 1 and going no higher than 99 – for example, 5 Elm Street.

unit cost – The average cost per unit of production of a set or group of products. The total cost of production divided by the total number produced. Also called *average cost*. See *long-run average cost*; *short-run average cost*.

unit pricing – An aspect of labeling where, either by law or under voluntary industry codes, marketers are required to mark the price per unit of standard measure on certain product items, as well as the price of the item, so that shoppers in retail stores can compare packs of varying weight and volume. Regulated by the Food and Drug Administration.

unit volume quota – A common form of sales assignment, goal or target used to measure a salesperson's performance. The salesperson is

U

expected to sell a certain number of units of the product or product range in each budget period. Other commonly used types of quota are *dollar volume quota* and *gross margin quota*. See *sales quota*.

univers – A sans serif (Gothic) type font that resembles Helvetica.

Universal Mobile Telecommunications System (UMTS) – Broadband, packet-based transmission of text, digitized voice, video and multimedia at data rates up to, and possibly higher than, four megabytes per second. The *UMTS* offers a set of services to mobile/wireless computer and phone users no matter where they are located in the world.

universal product code (UPC) – The American system of computer-assisted product identification. *Bar codes* and *scanners* have now become the norm in retail stores, warehouses and for inventory control of products, company-owned furniture and other equipment.

universality – A feature of ideas marketing that distinguishes it from other forms of marketing. *Universality* means that ideas can be made (and, therefore marketed) by anyone. See *ideas marketing*.

universe – In marketing research, the total group that a researcher wishes to study and measure. Also, all people who are prospects for a specific product or service. See *population*.

universe count – The total count (i.e., number of names) on a list.

unmentionables – Groups of products that are considered too delicate or controversial to mention or to advertise. Examples once included sanitary napkins, condoms or incontinence pads.

unplanned cannibalization – The unexpected loss of sales from one product to another, more recently introduced, product in the same line. *Unplanned cannibalization* is more likely when there is little significant difference between the two products. See *cannibalization*; *planned cannibalization*; *synergy*.

unsegmented marketing – A view of the market that assumes all consumers are basically the same. A marketing philosophy where the seller views the market as a homogeneous whole and, therefore, has only one marketing program (the same product, the same price, the same promotion and the same distribution system) for everyone. Also referred to as *undifferentiated marketing* or *mass marketing*. See *differentiated marketing*; *product-differentiated marketing*; *target marketing*.

264

Techniques to Succeed:
More on business dining etiquette

In today's business world, a tremendous amount of business is conducted at a dinner table. Whether at home or in a restaurant, it is important to have a complete understanding of how to conduct yourself when entertaining or being entertained.

Anxiety while dining can be reduced by following guidelines on how to order your meal, what utensils to use and how to use them, and knowing proper table etiquette.

A. Knowing guidelines on what to order will help relieve dining anxiety.

1. When possible let the host take the lead.

2. Ask for suggestions/recommendations.

3. Do not order the most expensive or the least expensive item on the menu.

4. Avoid foods that are sloppy or hard to eat.

5. Avoid alcohol even if others are drinking.

B. Choosing the correct silverware is not as difficult as it may first appear. Knowledge of a formal table setting will allow you to focus on the conversation rather than what utensil to use.

1. Know the basic table setting.

2. Eating utensils are used from the outside in. Dessert forks/spoons are placed at the top of the plate.

3. Everything to your right you drink. Everything to your left you eat.

4. When you don't know what utensil to use, watch what your host does and follow suit.

5. When you have finished, leave your plate where it is in the place setting. Do not push your plate away from you. Lay your fork and knife diagonally across your plate and side-by-side. The knife and fork should be placed as if they are pointing to the numbers 10 and 4 on a clock face.

The ABCs of Strategic Communication

unsought goods – A category of goods and services which the buyer is unaware of, or would prefer not to think about buying. Examples could include cemetery plots, life insurance and encyclopedia sets. See *conven-ience goods*; *shopping goods*; *specialty goods*.

unwired network – In contrast to the wired networks like ABC, CBS, NBC and FOX, *unwired networks* are formed by companies that repre-sent radio and television stations – regardless of their network affiliation – and newspapers in various markets (usually no more than one owner per market) for the purpose of selling national (commercials) advertis-ing to the major brands. National advertisers approach rep firms for the "local buys" to supplement network advertising. Also called *wireless net-work* and *sales rep firm*. See *rep firm*.

up-front buy – The purchasing of broadcast or print early in the media buying season. See *upfronts*.

up-market consumers – Consumers who search for, and purchase, luxury or more expensive products. See *down-market consumers*; *prestige pricing*; *up-market consumers*.

up or down vote – When a governing body vote yes or no on a resolu-tion or an appointment of a person to a position, which needs approval.

up-or-down vote – Full body (Congress, town council, school board, etc.) voting on a nominee or issue after it is reported out of committee rather than a committee "killing" the proposal.

up-selling – Selling a higher priced item(s) to an existing customer or prospect who has already made a firm or mental commitment to buy another of the company's product(s) and/or service(s). For example, fast food workers are typically trained to *up-sell* fries or beverages to the next

265

Tips to Succeed: As a public relations counselor...

Build relationships

Keep a cool head

Be available (when the media comes calling)

Zack Hill - Senior Director of Communications - Philadelphia Flyers Hockey Club

largest size.

upfronts – Networks revealing and showing their fall shows and schedule in the spring to encourage advertisers to buy early.

uplink – A transmission path by which radio or other signals are sent from the ground to an aircraft or a communications satellite.

upload – To send data from a computer to a network or Web site. An example of uploading data is sending an e-mail.

upper case – Words in all capital letters.

upper third rule – A theory that sates that the top third of a page (or layout area) carries the most weight in attracting the reader.

upside elasticity – Used in reference to the sensitivity of consumers to an increase in the price of a particular product or service. *Upside elasticity* means there would be a significant drop in consumer demand as prices increase. See *upside inelasticity*; *downside elasticity*; *downside inelasticity*.

upstyle – Headline type where the first letter of each word is capitalized (except for prepositions and articles).

upward stretching – Introducing a new product into a product line at the higher-priced end of the market. Example would be Porsche® adding its SUV, Cayenne®, to its line of luxury cars. See *downward stretching*; *two-way stretching*.

usage rate – A measure of the quantity of a product consumed by a user in a given period. Users are categorized as heavy, moderate and light. See *behaviorist segmentation*.

The ABCs of Strategic Communication

URL – Uniform Resource Locator – The *Internet* address that tells a browser where to find an *Internet* resource. The URL for *this* book is *www.larrylitwin.com*.

USB (Universal Serial Bus) port – an external bus standard in computer language that supports data transfer. A single *USB port* can be used to connect peripheral devices, such as mice, modems, keyboards, *flash*, *jump*, *thumb* and *travel* drives. *USB* also supports *plug-and-play* installation and *hot plugging*. Starting in 1996, a few computer manufacturers started including *USB* support in their new machines. It wasn't until the release of the iMac in 1998 that *USB* became widespread. Eventually, because of its convenience or the portability of *flash* drives, the *USB port* will replace serial and parallel ports.

usenet – Internet bulletin-board application.

user – An individual with access to the Internet.

user – Individual in the buying center who will actually use the product being considered for purchase. See *buying center*.

user benefits – Understanding and appreciating that the basic reason an individual purchases a product or service is that he/she believes it will benefit him/her even if they are not totally certain of what that benefit may be (an intangible).

user-centric measurement – A technical term referring to a Internet audience measurement based on the behavior of a sample of Internet users.

user registration – Information gathered by Web site hosts from individuals which usually include such characteristics as the person's age, gender, zip code and often much more. A site's registration system is usually based on an ID code or password to allow the site to determine the number of unique visitors and to track a visitor's behavior within that site – and to prevent non-registrants from entering the site.

uses and gratifications approach to the media – How people use the media to gratify their needs. They emphasize the active use made of media by audience members to seek gratification of a variety of needs – monitoring what is going on in the world (surveillance), personal identity, personal relationships and diversion (entertainment and escapism).

utility – The inherent quality or ability of a product to satisfy a want. Also, the value a consumer receives from a product's design. See *economic utility; form utility; information utility; image utility; place utility; time utility; possession utility*. **U**

valid objection – A truthful *objection* raised by a prospective client to a good or service offered by a public relations practitioner or salesperson. Some valid *objections* are answerable, while others (I have no money), are not. See *objections; hidden objection; invalid objection; need objection.*

validity – In marketing research, obtaining the right and truthful information for the purposes of the study – the soundness and effectiveness of the survey instrument. Is the instrument measuring what it is supposed to measure? Is the sample being measured representative of the entire *universe* it is suppose to be reflecting.

valuation – Media coverage determined by calculating the length of articles (in inches) X number of *columns* (column inches) or the length of stories carried by television or radio stations. *Valuation* is qualitative rather than quantitative in that it doesn't determine behavioral change – it just helps to create it.

value – The ratio of perceived benefits compared to price for a product or service. It is widely accepted that if the value exceeds the cost, it is considered a bargain.

value added – Features added to a product or service to enhance the benefits so that a client or consumer can measure the true value – either real or perceived – or, a firm's increased worth as a result of positive public relations. Factors that generate the additional value are features, benefits, quality, reputation, *image* and exclusiveness. See *added value.*

value-added consumer orientation – Recognition by the company that the price consumers are prepared to pay for its product will depend on the benefits received and not just on the physical product itself.

value added reseller (VAR) —— Companies that combine (computer) components to build complete systems. For example, a VAR might take a computer chip, printer, hard drive, monitor and graphics software from different vendors, put them together, and package "it" as a specialized computer-aided design system. Sort of an electronic *mash up*.

266

Tips to Succeed: If the problem is *you*, climb out of that work rut

Perhaps it's not the place or the job – maybe *you* are the problem. Before you jump ship, it may be time to assess whether you're really putting everything you've got into the job you have.

• Maybe it's time to challenge yourself

• Come up with *new* ideas to create *new* excitement

• Treat the business as if it were your own.
  – Develop a plan
    • Where do you want to be in one or five years?
    • What duties would you like to have?
    • What skills do you need to accomplish those goals?
    • What are the obstacles in your way?

• How can you eliminate them?
  – Who are the key people you need to help you?
  – How much money do you want to be earning?

• At the same time, review your work over the last several years.
  – When did you start to feel bored or too complacent?
  – What factors were involved?
  – Did you feel as though some people were not helping or even trying to sabotage you? Treat the business as if it were your own.
  – Once you see where the traps are, you can work to avoid or overcome them so that they don't bog down your efforts to revitalize your job.

And finally, don't be afraid to ask for what you want. Ask the boss to work on a new project. Ask to train in other departments. Ask to attend a seminar, or to be taken off a dead-end task. Not all your requests may be granted, but continue to seek the changes you need to jump-start your career and fire up your enthusiasm.

Anita Bruzzese - Author - *Take This Job and Thrive*
(Impact Publications) - Gannett News Service

value added tax (VAT) – A tax based on the amount by which *value* has been added to a product at each stage of production. A general consumption tax assessed on the *value* added to goods and services. It is a general tax that applies, in principle, to all commercial activities involving the production and distribution of goods and the provision of services. It is a "consumption" tax because it is borne ultimately by the final consumer.

value-added wholesaling – Providing more wholesaler services and lowering the cost of these services to retailers to improve productivity and profitability.

value analysis – The rating by a buying organization of slightly different product offerings for the same task to determine which is the most appropriate.

value and life style system (VALS) – A (research) system developed at Stanford Research Institute and University of California, Berkeley, for classifying the American adult population into nine distinct groups on the basis of their values and lifestyles. It is the categorization of people according to their way of living, using such groupings as Belongers, Achievers, Emulators, I-am-me, Experiential, Socially Conscious, Survivors, Sustainers and Integrators.

value billing – Predetermined fees charged to clients by public relations counselors, attorneys and other professionals rather than a the traditional hourly fee. The advantages of *value billing* are debatable – some practitioners believe the set rate is the better approach while others support the traditional "time and materials." *Value billing* is predetermined by time, labor and skill required, experience, reputation and ability of the practitioner, and other factors that may come up during a *situation analysis*. See *value pricing*.

value chain – A list of activities in providing a product or service that ultimately creates *value* in the minds of the target audience.

value preposition – The set of qualities of a good or service that allows it to fulfill the customer's needs and desires – as opposed to simply benefiting the seller.

value pricing – A pricing approach where the selling price of a good or service is based on the company's assessment of the highest value of the product to the consumer – what the consumer is willing to pay for it. See *competition-oriented pricing; cost-plus pricing; target return pricing; value billing*.

The ABCs of Strategic Communication

V

value proposition – A clear statement detailing who the target market for a particular product is, what key benefits the product will deliver and the price that will be charged.

value retailing – Positioning a retail store as one where consumers receive greater overall value-to-cost benefits (if not necessarily lower prices) than in competitors' stores. It is widely accepted that if the *value* exceeds the cost, it is considered a bargain.

values – Enduring (internal) moral beliefs shared by members of a society and contributing to its culture that guide behavior.

values and lifestyle (VALS) research – A research method which psychologically groups consumers based on certain characteristics such as their *values*, lifestyles and *demographics*.

vampiring (vampire creativity) – An advertising problem where an advertisement is so creative or entertaining, or the production is so strong, that it overwhelms – sucks the blood out of – the product. An ad where a celebrity (from the media, arts, sporting world, etc.) is so dominant in the ad or ad campaign that the advertiser's message is lost, or the relationship (*transfer effect*) is not achieved.

van distributor – A specialty wholesaler making frequent and regular deliveries of fast-selling consumer goods, mainly milk, bread, etc., to retailers.

variability – One of the four characteristics which distinguish a service. *Variability* expresses the notion that a service may vary in standard or quality from one provider to the next or from one occasion to the next. Also referred to as *heterogeneity*. See *services marketing*; *inseparability*; *intangibility*; *perishability*.

variable costs – Costs that vary directly with the volume or quantity produced. *Variable costs* plus *fixed costs* equal total costs. See *fixed cost*; *total costs*.

variable imaging – Personalization done on a digital press.

variable pricing – A pricing method where the price charged for some consumer shopping goods and specialty goods, and for many industrial products, is open to negotiation between the buyer and seller. It is also known as *flexible pricing* and *multiple pricing*.

267

Techniques to Succeed:
Be skeptical of venture ads

The Better Business Bureau deals with 10,000 complaints every year from consumers who say they have lost money to business opportunity ads such as "be your own boss" and "earn money quickly." The bureau has these suggestions when looking at such advertised ventures:

- Look at the ad carefully and be skeptical of promises of lots of money in little time for little work.
- Get earnings claims in writing.
- Scrutinize franchise offers by studying the disclosure documents and looking for a statement from previous purchasers.
- Interview each previous purchaser or investor.
- Check on complaint records.
- Find out if the company involved is well known.
- Consult experts such as an attorney or accountant before you sign anything or give any money.
- Do not give in to high-pressure tactics.
- Follow the first critical step in the public relations process - research, research, research.

Remember – if something appears too good to be true, it probably is.

www.bbb.org

variety-seeking decisions – Purchase decisions made by consumers who are willing to try a diversity of brands for variety and to avoid boredom. Usually, *variety-seeking decisions* occur when the degree of involvement with a product is low. See *low-involvement products.*

variety store – A shop that sells many different items, usually at a low price.

vcast (vidcast) – A *vidcast* or video *podcast*. A video clip designed to be viewed in a portable device. A *vidcast* is the video counterpart of a *podcast* and uses the same *RSS* syndication method for delivering material to users.

The ABCs of Strategic Communication

vehicle (see MAC Triad) – A specific publication, radio station, television station, *billboard*, etc. within a *channel* (*medium* – print, broadcast, word-of-mouth) that carries an advertising message to a target audience. For example, one *medium* would be magazines, while one *vehicle* would be *TIME*® magazine.

velox – A high contrast black and white illustration printed on high quality paper used for its superior reproduction qualities. *Veloxes* are camera-ready. Can also be an *ad slick, slick, repro, laser print* or *matte*.

vending machine – A coin-operated device which can be used to dispense a variety of consumer products (food, drinks, etc.) and services (automatic teller machines at banks).

vendor – A seller or supplier.

vendor analysis – The rating by a buying organization of all possible suppliers of a product on a scale to select the best for that organization. Also referred to as *vendor rating*. See *value analysis*.

vendor loyalty – The allegiance a firm gives to a supplier. Straight rebuys usually reflect *vendor loyalty*, but they are sometimes due to resistance to change.

vendor rating – See *vendor analysis*.

vendor selection strategy – The decision-making that occurs when a firm selects a supplier to minimize the risk of choosing the wrong one. Strategies used include the rating of vendors on a scale, the practice of choosing vendors from an approved list, multiple sourcing and choosing the lowest- priced vendor to minimize the potential for financial loss.

The ABCs of Strategic Communication

V

268 Tips to Succeed: Leaving phone messages on voice mail

Always leave your name and phone number at least twice when leaving a voice-mail message – once at the beginning and once at the end. If you leave more than one phone number for call back, repeat all numbers. Speak slowly and clearly.

venture capitalist – A person who invests in a business venture, providing money (capital) for start-up or expansion – usually in return for a higher rate of return than might be available through more traditional investments. See *angel*.

venture team – Key people from various departments of an organization who are given responsibility for the development of a new product from concept to marketing.

venue – The scene or setting where something takes place.

verbatims – Spontaneous comments by people who are being surveyed.

vernacular – Language that reflects the speech patterns of a particular group of people.

vertical channel conflict – Discord among members at different levels of a marketing channel. For example, manufacturer-wholesaler or wholesaler-retailer discord. See *inter-type channel conflict*; *horizontal channel conflict*.

vertical cooperative advertising – Shared advertising by two or more members at different levels of a *channel* of distribution, each paying part of the total cost. A form of advertising where a national manufacturer reimburses the retailer for part or all of the retailer's advertising expenditures. See *cooperative advertising*; *horizontal cooperative advertising*.

vertical decisions – Management decisions which coordinate the flow of goods and services, title, information, payment and promotion along the *channels* of distribution.

vertical discount – A reduced rate offered to advertisers who purchase airtime on a radio or television medium for a limited amount of time, e.g., one week. See *horizontal discount*.

vertical diversification – See *vertical integration*.

vertical justification – The ability to automatically adjust the leading (interline spacing) to make columns and pages end at the same place on a page.

vertical integration – A strategy for growth in which a company adds new facilities to existing manufacturing or distribution facilities; vertical integration can be either forward or backward. Also called vertical diversification. See *backward integration*; *forward integration*; *horizontal integration*.

vertical market – A market for a product that is used in one or a few industries. See *horizontal market*.

vertical marketing system – An organized, structured and unified distribution channel system where producer and intermediaries or middlemen (wholesalers and retailers) work closely together to facilitate the smooth flow of goods and services from producer to end-user. See *contractual vertical marketing system; corporate vertical marketing system*.

vertical price fixing – Agreement between producers and retailers to maintain the producers' recommended retail price (generally considered to be illegal, although *manufacturers' suggested retail prices (MSRP)* are legal [used mostly in the new car industry]). Vertical price fixing is resale price maintenance. See *price fixing; horizontal price fixing*.

vertical publication – A business publication targeted toward workers who hold different positions in the same industry. For example, *Broadcast Engineering, National Petroleum News Magazine* and *Retail Baking Today*.

vertically integrated – Companies that control product production by controlling all steps in the production process, from the extraction of raw materials through the manufacture and sale of the final product. For example, car manufacturers who own or have an interest in the makers of tires, batteries and other parts.

viatical – A settlement contract that enables a life insurance policyholder to receive an immediate payment that is greater than he/she would get from its issuer by liquidating the policy, but less than the payout at the time of death. The buyer (usually another company/policyholder/investor) profits from the difference.

vidcast – A Weblog (*blog*) that includes video clips to be downloaded and viewed immediately or transferred to a portable player. Also called a "vog," "vid-blog" and "movie blog," the *vlog* can be exclusively videos with text used only for captions, or text entries may be included. A venue for people who like to remix audio, video and graphics in some artistic expression, as well as novice and experienced videographers and movie makers, the material is distributed in popular video formats such as Windows Media, QuickTime and *Flash*. See *blog*, v*cast* and *video blog*. (CMag encyclopedia).

video blog – A Weblog (blog) that includes video clips to be downloaded and viewed immediately or transferred to a portable player. Also

The ABCs of Strategic Communication

called a "vog," "vid-blog" and "movie blog," the vlog can be exclusively videos with text used only for captions, or text entries may be included. A venue for people who like to remix audio, video and graphics in some artistic expression, as well as novice and experienced videographers and movie makers, the material is distributed in popular video formats such as Windows Media, QuickTime and Flash. See *blog; vcast; vidcast* (PCMag encyclopedia).

video conferencing – Use of satellite, fiber optics or other type of transmission line to conduct business, news or other type of conference or, online meeting or distance learning. It allows for two-way communication.

video news release (VNR) – A broadcast version of a news release. A video program produced to promote or publicize a product, service or viewpoint. It is designed to resemble the same style as traditional television news reports (packages or wraps). Its purpose is to educate, inform and influence (if necessary). *VNRs* usually include a packaged news story between one minute and 90 seconds that is ready for on-air use and *B-roll* to allow producers to edit and create their own stories. News directors and producers who use *VNRs* say they fill in the gaps in news coverage. Effective *VNRs* are timely; newsworthy; have a local connection or can be localized; are excellent quality; contain powerful visuals; and include *B-roll*, real people, extra voice cuts and sound bites, names and titles, and a script. Television stations using *VNRs* should use disclaimers pointing out that the tape was supplied, but rarely do.

269

Tips to Succeed:
Using visual aids

1. Use visual aids sparingly
2. Use visual aids pictorially
3. Present one key point per visual
4. Make text and numbers legible
5. Use color carefully
6. Make visual big enough to see
7. Graph data
8. Make pictures and diagrams easy to see
9. Make visuals attractive
10. Avoid miscellaneous visuals

The ABCs of Strategic Communication

video on-demand – Commonly used by cable television providers. The ability to request video, audio or information to be sent to the screen immediately by clicking something on the screen referring to that choice.

video streaming – The transmission of full-motion video over the Internet. Also, the transmission of video at the top or bottom of a television screen (during another program).

video window – The cycle studios use to release motion pictures in sequence to the different media. Traditionally, a motion picture would first go to movie theaters, then to video retailers, pay per view TV and then regular television. Now it refers to the simultaneous release of motion pictures to movie theatres (theatre release) through digital distribution – DVD and TV Video on Demand. There were no windows prior to technology. Executive producers and other investors refer to the original distribution cycle as "delays." As movie audiences get smaller, in comes the *death spiral* – as it is known. There is a move that all steps in the release cycle be simultaneous – which would drive movie houses out of business – theaters need traffic not only to buy tickets but also to buy beverages, popcorn and other snacks. Experts say there will always be a core of movie buffs who like the theater just as there are people who still listen to vinyl records rather than or in addition to CDs.

videoblogging – A form of expression centering around posting videos to a Web site and encouraging an audience response. It is the next step from text *blogging* and *podcasting*.

videotex – A home shopping technology. An interactive system allowing subscribers to the system to access information about products on their normal TV screens by using of a small computer terminal and ordering items directly. See *home shopping*.

viewer – A person viewing content or advertisements on the Internet. There is currently no way to measure viewers. However, Nielsen Media Research and other firms can measure individual Web hits. Read more at www.netratings.com.

vignette – An illustration that has soft edges, often produced by using cutouts or masks. A photograph or *halftone* (photograph prepared for publication) where the edges, or parts of the edges, are shaded off to a very light gray.

viral marketing – An advertising and marketing technique or mechanism being used more and more for product and/or brand launches. In an attempt to establish the product among target audiences, advertisers and/or marketers use this technique that "spreads the message" like a virus by passing it on from consumer to consumer and market to market. It is the paying of someone to recommend (different from enforce) a product without revealing they are doing so. Using real people (referred to a *connectors)* to create a *buzz* (manufactured buzz) for products or services – paid or otherwise, but most times paid (to recommend [*word-of-mouth*] a product or service).

viral marketing (Web) – A marketing technique (usually the original message carrier does not identify him/herself as being paid) where *Web site* visitors or e-mail recipients are encouraged to pass along the compa-

270 Techniques to Succeed: Balance your life

Don't get out of balance in your life. Our lives are made up of seven vital areas.

✓ Health
✓ Family
✓ Financial
✓ Intellectual
✓ Social
✓ Professional and
✓ Spiritual

We will not necessarily spend time everyday in each area or equal amounts of time in each area. But, if in the long run, we spend a sufficient quantity and quality of time in each area, our lives will be in balance. If we neglect any one area, never mind two or three, we will eventually sabotage our success.

Much like a table, if one leg is longer than the others, it will make the entire table wobbly. If we don't take time for *health*, our *family* life and *social life* suffer. If our *financial* area is out of balance, we will not be able to focus adequately on our *professional*, etc. If we don't feel good about ourselves, our *intellect* and *spirit* suffer.

Is your life in balance?

Ed Ziegler - Director of Marketing - Rowan University - Glassboro, N.J.

The ABCs of Strategic Communication

ny's marketing message to friends, colleagues and/or family, thereby creating exponential growth in the message's reach. It is a strategy that encourages individuals to pass on a marketing message to others. *Viral marketing* creates the potential for rapid growth because it depends on one-on-one, person-to-person communication (highly effective because of credibility, trust and personal endorsement or testimonial). *Viral marketing* is effective for both building awareness and driving action. *Incentives* (free samples) are usually given to the early message carriers – which makes it *marketing* – to pass along the promotional strategic messages and offers, although the best viral marketing campaigns are the ones where people spread the word simply because the message is so compelling. When *viral marketing* is done via the e-mail, it is termed *"word-of-mouse (marketing)."*

virtual reality – "Second life" (personalities/alter egos) created on the Internet – in cyberspace – a computer simulated environment. More than 7,000,000 consumers subscribe to such (3D online digital world) providers as www.secondlife.com. Second Life presents an alternative universe where everyone (avatars) can be what they want to be. In the form of avatars – Internet icons or one's representation in a virtual world where people can meet, dance and explore in perfect physical form as any personality they choose. See *Web 2.0.*

virtual research – Gathers real-time information through online media and streaming video. It is low cost and quick.

vision (statement) – The long-term aims and aspirations of a company for itself. A guiding theme or message that communicates the nature of the business and its intentions for the future, based on how management believes the environment will unfold. A *vision* should be informed, shared, competitive and enabling. See *mission statement.*

visit – A measurement of Web site activity. Read more at *www.iab.net* for ad campaign measurement guidelines and at *www.netratings.com.*

visit duration – The length of time the visitor is exposed to a specific advertisement, Web page or Web site during a single session. Read more at *www.netratings.com.*

visitor – An individual or browser which accesses a Web site within a specific time period.

visual – A picture, clipart, graph, table or chart. A related photo (picture) or piece of *clipart* in a small ad.

visual connection – Created by the alignment of items on a page.

visual identity – The recognition of a brand simply by seeing a logo with or without the brand's name.

visual path – The direction where the reader's eye moves while scanning a layout.

visualization – The ability to see images in the mind, to imagine how an ad or a concept will look when it is completed.

Vlog (video blog) – A Weblog (*blog*) that includes video clips to be downloaded and viewed immediately or transferred to a portable player. Also called a "vog," "vid-blog" and "movie blog," the *vlog* can be exclusively videos with text used only for captions, or text entries may be included. A venue for people who like to remix audio, video and graphics in some artistic expression, as well as novice and experienced videographers and movie makers, the material is distributed in popular video formats such as Windows Media®, QuickTime® and Flash®. See *blog* and *vidcast* (PCMag encyclopedia).

voice cut – The recorded words of someone who is part of a radio news story (newsmaker). Also referred to as *actuality; soundbite.*

voice over – A reporter or other talent's recorded script used to narrate a broadcast news story or a commercial. The technique of using the voice of an unseen speaker during film, slides or other voice material.

voice over Internet Protocol (VoIP) – Telephone service using the Internet (and your computer). Telephone service using the Internet (and your computer).

voice over sound or VO/SOT (sound on tape) – A television news story with accompanying video read by the anchor that leads into the recorded words of a newsmaker. Much like a *voice over* and similar to a radio *actuality* except it is for TV.

voice response unit (VRU) – Hardware connected to the telephone through which *interactive voice response* messages are generated. Used by many firms and organizations for bill payment or to route callers to the correct department. It uses voice direction rather than touch tone keys.

voice-pitch analysis (VOPAN) – An advertising research technique of analyzing a subject's voice during their responses – to test feelings and attitudes about an ad.

voicer – A prerecorded radio news story voiced by a reporter.

voir dire – A preliminary examination of prospective jurors or witnesses under oath to determine their competence or suitability.

volume analysis – A technique or method of marketing control where sales volume in dollars or units or physical volume in units is measured over a given period, in an attempt to identify underachieving salespeople, sales territories, etc.

volume discount – A discount offered for purchases (product, newspaper space or broadcast time) in large quantity or agencies who offer discounts for the bulk purchase of retainer hours (payable in advance).

volume indicators – Umbrella term for methods used to measure advertisement or commercial effectiveness.

volume segmentation – The division of a market into segments on the basis of the varying volume of demand for the product by individuals, groups or types of customers. Like audience segmentation, these segments are ranked to denote heavy usage, medium usage or light usage.

voluntary chain – A group or chain of retailers working together on a non-contractual basis to achieve lower prices through *volume discounts* and purchasing power for both products, advertising, etc.

voluntary group – See *voluntary chain*.

voucher – A type of consumer sales promotion where *coupons* (or *vouchers*) sent by mail or included in newspaper advertisements, etc. can be exchanged for merchandise to encourage trial of a new product. In education, school vouchers, also known as scholarships, redirect the flow of education funding, channeling it directly to individual families rather than to school districts. This allows families to select the public or private schools of their choice and have all or part of the tuition paid.

wait order – An (insertion) order that includes holding an advertisement until a later date.

walking the line – When advertising agencies place individual storyboards on the floor and walk the client along as each board (representing a scene in a television commercial) is explained.

wants – The form, shaped by culture and individual personality, where basic human needs are given expression. For example, the need to satisfy hunger might be expressed as a want of fish by one person and as a want of chicken by another. See *needs*.

warehouse – A place in which goods or merchandise are stored. Also called a storehouse.

warranty – A guarantee by a manufacturer that a product will be repaired or replaced or the purchase price refunded if it is found to be defective within a specified period, if it does not perform the task for which it was intended or if it does not meet the purchaser's reasonable expectations. See *express warranty*; *implied warranty*; *promotional warranty*; *protective warranty*.

wash drawings – Tonal drawing, similar to watercolor, intended for *halftone* (photograph) reproduction.

Washington read – Simply reading the index or looking at the index of a book to see if your name or someone else's is in the book.

wastage – In advertising, that part of the audience or readership of a media vehicle which is "wasted" because it is not part of the target market. Also called *wasted coverage* because it is reaching unintended audiences.

waste circulation – Advertising in an area where the product or service is not available or has no sales potential. Also, people in an advertiser's audience who are not potential consumers.

wasted coverage – Advertising that reaches unintended or untargeted audiences – or people who are not potential customers or users.

watch-and-win sweepstakes – A sales promotion where consumers must watch a particular TV program to hear contest-winning numbers, etc. announced in commercials or promotional spots during the program.

watchdog journalism – The practice of reporters holding public officials and others in authority accountable – particularly if the individual might have an impact on the society. *Lapdog journalism* is the opposite – meaning those in authority control a reporter or entity.

watermark – Shaded art (usually 20 percent) that can be seen through the type.

271

Tips to Succeed: Lehrer writing approach

"I wake up every morning knowing I'm going to write. I know it's going to be typed and double spaced. The question is – '*What am I going to write?*' My head does the thinking – my fingers do the writing. Sometimes, though, I think better with my fingers than I do with my head."

James Lehrer
Journalist and Author - 2005

watershed moment – A turning point in history. See *jumping the shark*.

watershed state – In politics, *watershed states* attract big money, special interest pressure and heavy television advertising because they could influence a national campaign. Term can be used on a more local level – for example, watershed city or town during a statewide election.

wave scheduling – An advertising strategy that consists of scheduling space in the media in intermittent periods, e.g., two weeks on, two weeks off. See *flighting; hiatus.*

wave you off – Rather than speak, political figures and other newsmakers who would rather not speak would be asked by a reporter, "If this is incorrect, please *wave me off*. Otherwise, I'll go with it." It relieves the newsmaker of speaking to a reporter *off the record*. See *background; not for attribution; off the record*.

wearout – The point reached when an advertising campaign loses its effectiveness due to repeated overplay of ads – or a decrease in the effectiveness of an advertisement or promotional campaign due to boredom and familiarity. See *consumer wearout*.

weather forecast – Specifically, weather we should expect.

weather outlook – Generally, what can be expected (results) from the weather – residual effects. For example, rain may cause flooding; snow might disrupt morning commute.

wealth effect – An economic term meaning an increase in spending that accompanies an increase in wealth (earnings) – or perceived wealth.

weasel word – Low altitude word or phrase, like almost, nearly, sometimes, I feel, I think. Omitting *weasel words* strengthen public relations and other types of marketing *copy*.

Web 2.0 – A phrase coined by O'Reilly Media in 2004. It refers to a perceived or proposed second generation of Internet-based services – *social media*. Sometimes referred to as the "new media" targeted to the I-generation. These innovations are hardly new. If Web 1.0 is about connecting computers, then *Web 2.0* is about connecting people – and the most popular and growing method is through social networking sites.

Web browser – Software or service used for searching the Internet.

web bug – Software that can be introduced into an e-mail and transmit a Web log (*blog*) entry and associated *cookie* when the e-mail is opened. This enables tracking of the e-mail. *Cookie*-filtering software does not stop Web bugs from tracking the recipient's online activity.

web press – A printing press that is fed by a large roll of paper instead of individual sheets.

Web site – The domain – or virtual location – for an organization or individual's presence on the Internet. *AP style* is Web site.

webasode – Videos that can be downloaded from the Internet. See *webisode*.

webcasting – Real-time or pre-recorded delivery of a live event's audio, video or animation over the Internet.

The ABCs of Strategic Communication

webinar – An online (live) seminar.

webisode – A form of Web advertising. Similar to television programs with recurring episode in a developing story. *Webisodes* blend advertising and entertainment. See *advertainment*.

weblog (blog) – Internet-based opinion columns published by ordinary people. A web-based publication consisting primarily of periodic articles (normally in reverse chronological order see *www.larrysblog.com*). A Web log is an online diary or journal. Derived from *Weblog* and evolved into "we blog." A *blog* is citizen created content – unfiltered opinion. *Bloggers* use their expert knowledge based on categories. *Blogs* can act as a stimulus to traditional journalism. *Podcasts* and *vodcasts* are *blogs*.

weblog software – Tools for editing, organizing and publishing Web logs are variously referred to as *content management systems*, *publishing platforms*, *weblog software* and simply *blogware*.

weight – An adjustment made in a survey sample to correct for *demographic* or geographic imbalances. Also, the number of exposures of an advertisement.

weighted audience values – Numerical values assigned to various audience characteristics that help advertisers assign priorities when crafting media plans.

weighting – A method of rating the degree of importance of a factor or variable in a survey or other research instrument.

well to wheel – Oil taken from ground and refined into gasoline. Conception to birth or completion, meaning – idea to finished product.

whacker – A decision involving options that are so close, the decision could go either way.

"What if..." method – A closing technique where the salesperson attempts to isolate the last remaining objection or obstacle to the sale and closes it contingent upon being able to remove the obstacle. Also called the *contingent method*.

whiffle dust – A slang term referring to the ingredients, parts or accessories that manufacturers sometimes add to their products to enhance them, but for which no scientific basis can be found. Federal agencies regulate the use of *whiffle dust*. Also referred to as *mummy dust*.

The ABCs of Strategic Communication

whistleblower – Individuals who know of fraud being committed against the government or their employer. Also an employee, former employee or member of an organization – business or government agency – who reports misconduct to supervisors are law enforcement agencies who have the power and willingness to take corrective action. Generally the misconduct is a violation of law, rule, regulation and/or a direct threat to public interest – fraud, health, safety violations, corruption, etc.

272

Tips to Succeed:
Better writing through self editing

"The most valuable of all talents is that of never using two words when one will do."

Thomas Jefferson

"The secret of play-writing can be given in two maxims: stick to the point, and, whenever you can, cut."

W. Somerset Maugham

"I love words but I don't like strange ones. You don't understand them and they don't understand you. Old words is like old friends, you know 'em the minute you see 'em."

Will Rogers

"It behooves us to avoid archaisms. Never use a long word when a diminutive one will do."

William Safire

"Men of few words are the best men."

William Shakespeare

"A sentence should contain no unnecessary words, a paragraph no unnecessary sentences, for the same reason that a drawing should have no unnecessary lines and a machine no unnecessary parts."

William Strunk

"Use the smallest word that does the job."

E.B. White

"Think like a wise man but communicate in the language of the people."

William Butler Yeats

white balance – Zooming a television (video) camera in full frame on a pure white card to adjust color levels.

white goods – Large electrical devices (appliances) for domestic use, such as refrigerators, freezers and dishwashers. At one time, all were made of white enamel – hence the term.

white list – A list of e-mail addresses that are specifically allowed to be received by an e-mail inbox. A spam filter will pass messages from addresses on its white list even if the message has characteristics that would otherwise indicate it to be spam. See *black list*; *spam*; *spam filter*.

white paper – A document written in essay form that provides an in-depth discussion of an issue, technology, trend, product or process – a technical document that explains how a product or service functions and its purpose. *White papers* are predominantly informational rather than promotional. Information is usually based on scientific research – either primary or secondary, or significant experience.

273

Techniques to Succeed: Enroute to *synergy*

The right PR word!
By the right person!
At the most strategic moment!

white space – Blank area on a printed page between blocks of type, illustrations, headlines, etc. (Despite the name, it may be a solid color rather than white.) Also areas of any company where strategy and authority are vague, and where useful entrepreneurial activity can flourish.

wholesale merchant – An independent marketing middleman buying and taking title to goods and reselling them to retailers or industrial users. See *full-service wholesaler*; *merchant wholesaler*.

wholesaler – A marketing intermediary engaged in buying from manufacturers in bulk to resell to retailers or industrial buyers in smaller quantities.

wholesaler-sponsored voluntary chains – Groups of retailers formed by a wholesaler into a coordinated marketing system to save money by creating purchasing power (economies of scale) and to lessen conflict by building cooperation.

274

Tips to Succeed:
Make *your* Web site 'pop'

If you have a Web site and want it to "pop up" when someone searches for your name, product or service, you need to ensure that you set up your online presence properly. Search engines look for pages that have not only relevance, but the promise of rich content.

Here's how to get better results:

• Ask people to put a link to your site on their site. Besides direct traffic, the real benefit is that it raises your popularity . Ask for a text link with a good description.

• Put links to other relevant sites on your pages. This shows that you are enriching your site with outside resources and that you play well with others.

• Write good copy, and cover all of the high points on your opening page. Make the title of the home page relevant by including your business name, and perhaps product.

• Find a forum or mailing list where you can contribute occasionally. Anytime you contribute, don't pitch your product, but make sure you include a tagline with your site's full Web address and a short description.

• Put an FAQ (frequently asked questions) section on your site. It is likely rich with keywords that search engines will be looking for.

Terry Wilson - www.terryific.com

wholesaling – The activity of selling to buyers for resale or to further their own business operations.

Wi-Fi® – Wi-Fi® is a brand originally licensed by the Wi-Fi Alliance to describe the underlying technology of wireless local area networks (WLAN) based on the IEEE 802.11 specifications. It was developed to be used for mobile computing devices, such as laptops, in *LANs (local area networks)*, but is now used for more services, including Internet and VoIP (voice on Internet protocol) phone access, gaming, and basic connectivity of consumer electronics such as televisions and DVD players, or digital cameras. *Wi-Fi* and the *Wi-Fi logo* are registered trademarks of

The ABCs of Strategic Communication

the Wi-Fi Alliance - the trade organization that tests and certifies equipment compliance.

wide area network (WAN) – A group of computers connected together (a network) which are not located at the same physical location. It could include connecting *LANs* (*Local Area Networks*) together.

wide area telephone service (WATS) – A system of mass telephone calling at a discount rate. *WATS* lines usually prefix with 800, 866 or 877.

widget – Anything (icon, ad) embedded on a Web site – usually a short or "small" message.

widow – A single word or short phrase that sits alone at the end of a paragraph or at the top of a column or *white space* at the end of a paragraph when the last line does not fill the entire width of the column.

width of the product mix – The *width of the product mix* can be measured by the number of product lines that a business offers. For example, Frito-Lay® offers many types of chips. Pepsi® and Coke® not only offer line extensions, but also a number of different products – soft drinks, juices and bottled water.

wiki – A Web site that allows visitors to add, remove and edit content. According to Wikipedia®, an online encyclopedia and one of the best known *wikis*, *wiki* is a collaborative technology for organizing information on Web sites. The first wiki (WikiWikiWeb) was developed by Ward Cunningham in the mid-1990s. *Wikis* allow for linking among any number of pages. This ease of interaction and operation makes a *wiki* an effective tool for mass collaborative authoring.

wild art – A picture that doesn't accompany a story usually boxed to show it stands alone. Also called stand-alone photo.

wildcat – A business with a high level of opportunity and a high level of threat.

window – Box of information in a newspaper – used as a *copybreaking* devices and/or to highlight the information. *USA Today* made *windows* popular and helped revolutionize the newspaper industry.

window of competitive opportunity – The point of time when the right environmental conditions exist for a particular marketing opportunity. Also referred to as a window of opportunity. See *strategic window*.

wingman (wingwoman) – A *wingman* is a guy a man takes along with him on singles outings (like bars) who helps him out with the women. A *wingwoman* would be a woman who helps a man out with other women.

wink and nod – The exchange of information without saying a word – use of facial expressions. See *wave you off*.

wipe – A transition of scenes in a visual production where one image appears to *wipe* the previous one from the screen.

wire – News, now transmitted via the *Internet*, was once transmitted by Associated Press, Reuters and United Press International (UPI) using teletype (teleprinter) machines (resembling typewriters), which printed onto a large roll of paper. See *wire services*.

wire copy – Stories supplied to newspapers by news services.

wire services – Companies that supply news to various media on a subscription basis. Examples include Associated Press and Reuters. See *wire*.

wired network – In broadcasting, a network exists when two or more stations (affiliates) are able to broadcast the same program that originates from a single source. The programming may be transported by hard wire, fiber optics, satellite or wireless. Examples of networks include ABC, CBS, FOX, NBC and PBS. Affiliates are contractually bound to distribute radio or television programs for simultaneous transmission. Network also refers to two or more computer systems that are linked together.

Wireless Advertising Association WAA – Trade association promoting via wireless devices (known as wireless advertising). Members include hand held device manufacturers, software providers, carriers and operators, agencies, retailers and advertisers. Read more at *www.wssglobal.org*.

wireless application protocol (WAP) device – Any device (e.g., mobile phone, PDA [Personal Digital Assistant] or simulator) that allows access to wireless service.

wireless application protocol (WAP) – Mobile phones use wireless application protocol technology to access the Internet. The screen on a *WAP* phone can be used to deliver advertisements.

wireless applications service provider (WASP) – An organization that provides content and applications for wireless devices.

275

Techniques to Succeed:
Maximize your workers' potential

Employers can get their employees to reach their potential through energizing and motivational techniques. Here are some key techniques:

- **Communication.** When managers and employees communicate honestly and frequently, there are positive effects.

- **Support.** When managers are mentors and cheerleaders, employees feel support.

- **Energize.** Successful managers inspire visions from their employees. Let them dream, test and run with an idea.

- **Empower.** Great managers approach employees with trust and an assumed sense of capability.

www.firstcalleap.org

wireless bubble – Wireless (protocol network) network over such large areas as cities and/or towns and college or business campuses. Also known as *bubble*.

wireless marketing – Marketing to consumers via mobile phones. *Wireless marketing* works just like other channels of advertising – it sponsors or subsidizes content. *Wireless marketing* enables marketers to measure and track wireless response in real time and quickly respond based on the responses received, making wireless similar to e-mail, Web sites, call centers and other two-way channels that are direct to the customer.

wireless network – A company that represents independent radio and television stations – regardless of their network affiliation – and newspapers in various markets (usually no more than one owner per market) for the purpose of selling national (commercials) advertising to the major brands. National advertisers approach rep firms for the "local buys" to supplement network advertising. Also called *rep firm*, *sales rep firm* and *unwired network*.

with-pack premium – A type of consumer sales promotion where a free or low-cost gift is offered to purchases of a particular product. The gift can be either inside the package of the product or fixed to the outside of it. Polo® often offers sport bags or luggage with the purchase of after shave and cologne. See *premiums*; *in-pack premium*; *near-pack premium*; *on-pack premium*.

WOOPIES – Well-Off Older People – a demographic grouping.

word break – The division of a word at the end of a line – hyphenated between syllables.

word count – A word limitation placed on a written piece to govern its length.

word-of-mouse (marketing) – *Viral marketing* (paying people) to spread information about a product or service via e-mail. ABC's Charles Gibson calls it "word of Internet." Becomes *marketing* if the original sender is being paid to "spread the word" – especially in a secretly. See *viral marketing*; *word-of-mouth*.

word-of-mouth (WOM) – The spreading of information through human interaction alone.

word-of-mouth advertising or marketing (WOMM) – Advertising that occurs when people share information about products or promotions with friends. The spreading of information through human interaction alone. It is the most effective (credible and believable) form of public relations or advertising (although word of mouth is not normally paid for). It no one is paid it is *word-of-mouth*. If payment is involved it become *WOMM* or *word- of-mouth marketing*.

word painting – A technique used in radio (and to some extent, in print) that uses highly descriptive words to evoke images in reading material as an attempt to place the listener into the scene.

word spacing – The space between each word.

wordsmith – Someone known for his/her writing – especially a speech writer. An expert on words.

work for hire – Any creative product prepared by an employee as a normal part of employment. Its intellectual property rights belong to the employer.

workplace-selling program – A direct-selling strategy where manufacturers sell their products to consumers at their place of work. For example, Avon® employs workers to sell its cosmetics in their offices.

The ABCs of Strategic Communication

workshops – Interactive training sessions involving the combination of a lecture-type presentation or motivational speech, role play and group work exercises.

world brand – A brand that sells in many different countries. For example, Coca-Cola®, McDonald's®, Pepsi®. See *global brands*.

World Wide Web (www) – A system of Internet servers that uses *HTTP* to transfer specially-formatted documents. The documents are formatted in a language called *HTML* (*Hyper Text Mark-up Language*) that supports links to other documents, as well as graphics, audio and video files. One can jump from one document to another simply by clicking on *hyperlinks*. Not all *Internet* servers are part of the World Wide Web. Also know as just the "Web." Every web page is identified by a unique URL.

worldwide adaptation – A strategy used in global marketing where slightly different variations of a product are sold in each country – using promotion and distribution strategies which have also been modified to suit the particular needs of each country.

Wow – Offer the highest expectations and exceed them.

wrap – A radio or TV news report voiced by a reporter and containing the voice of a newsmaker. (Similar to a sandwich and a *doughnut*). Also an advertisement which fully covers a building, bus, car or truck. Many are appealing to the eye. See *building wrap*, *bus wrap*, *car wrap* and *truck wrap*.

writer's guidelines – A list of dos and don'ts, including word length, topic choice and format, that publications provide for writers who wish to submit articles.

wx – Weather.

eXtensible Markup Language (XML) – A richer, more dynamic successor to *HTML* utilizing *HTML*-type tags to structure information. *XML* is used for transferring data and creating applications on the Web. See *Hyper-Text Markup Language (HTML).*

x-Height – The height of the letter "x" in a font. The height of any letter without ascenders and descenders. X is used because it has no ascenders and descenders and sits directly on a baseline. **X**

276

Techniques to Succeed: Moderating a focus panel

ROLE OF THE MODERATOR
- Direct the discussion, ensuring that key topics are covered – yet remain flexible enough to allow for exploration of relevant issues that may come up spontaneously. Above all, the moderator must remain neutral.

MODERATING
- Establish a "safe" atmosphere, which encourages open, honest, thorough and valid participation. Participants should know that you are interested in their honest opinions – both positive and negative – and that there are no right or wrong answers.

- Be sure to cover the ground rules and get "head-nod" agreement on them. Groups may add their own rules to the list – if the moderator agrees.

- Encourage participation from all respondents – particularly those who are less likely to speak up.

- To gain early involvement by all members of the group, ask each participant to introduce him/herself.

- If everyone in the group seems to be saying the same thing, ask if anyone sees something differently.

- Do not reiterate participants' responses to clarify comments. If the moderator repeats back to the participant what has just been said, the moderator may not have understood the point exactly and may introduce an element of bias. Instead, ask the participant to clarify his/her own point.

- Remain neutral. Be careful not to nod your head in agreement or say "uh-huh" to those individuals whose opinions you agree with.

- Stick to time. You can move the discussion along by saying, "In the interest of time, we need to move to the next question."

- When you have several people who want to speak, you can "stack" speakers by saying, "First, we'll hear from Steve, then Jan and then Nancy."

- Move from a dominating speaker to another speaker by physically turning your body.

- Gesturing with your palm facing up encourages someone to speak.

- Don't be afraid of the "pregnant pause." It will encourage someone to speak.

Jennifer Wayan Reeve, APR - Director of Programs
Colorado Association of School Boards - Denver, CO 80203

YAPPIES (Young Affluent Parents) – a demographic grouping.

"Yes, ... But" method – Handling a buyer's objection by initially admitting the validity of the objection to maintain rapport, but then offering evidence to refute the objection. See *indirect denial method*; *objections*.

yield – A computer term meaning the percentage of clicks vs. impressions on an advertisement within a specific page. Also called *ad click rate*.

yield rate – In direct response marketing, the number of sales divided by the total *circulation* (number of pieces distributed) for a given campaign.

young marrieds – An early stage in the *family life cycle*. The *young marrieds* group is often targeted by marketers for being financially well-off and eager to spend – especially on *durables*. See *family life cycle*.

youth market – Young customers viewed as a marketing opportunity. Typically the term includes the *demographic* group 16 to 24 year olds. Other *demographic* ranges are 12 to 24 and 18 to 35.

YUPPIE (Young Urban Professionals) – Commonly used *demographic* term to describe a lifestyle-based market. See *psychographic segmentation*.

yuppie puppies – See *baby bouncers*.

277

Tips to Succeed: Starting or expanding *your* business?

Decide what you like to do. With your own business, you'll be spending a lot of time doing it.

• Know how much time you'll have to dedicate to your business. Running your own business doesn't always mean weekends off. So, be sure you have the time and energy to really make it successful.

• Identify technical skills or knowledge you have. You have to know what you're doing, and if you don't already know it, you must be completely willing to immerse yourself in learning.

• Determine what niche your business will fill. Just because you like something or are good at it, doesn't mean there is a market for it. Do some research to confirm or determine if there is a need for your product or service.

• Do your homework. Find out who your competition is, and how you will create demand for your product or service.

Andrew Glatz - Sun National Bank - www.sunnb.com

278

Tips to Succeed: Do for yourself

Tim's rules:

• Have fun

• Have it for yourself

• Share it

• Laughter might not be the best medicine, but it is preferred and the least expensive

• Tell yourself, each day, you are going to have fun – at work and at home – and no one is going to stop you

It's a ripple effect and you can be the "official" starter!

Tim Gard - www.timgard.com

zapping – The use of a television remote control to switch channels to avoid watching commercials.

zero-based budgeting – A method of budgeting where past sales and previous expenditure levels are ignored. The firm or organization forms its profit *goals*, determines the *tactics* (actions/costs) that will be required to achieve its *objectives* and *goal*, and estimates the expenditures that will be necessary to carry out the *tactics*. Assumes no present cost approved. Every item and cost must be justified as it enters the plan (total justification needed). Activities are evaluated yearly from a zero-base. It is probably a good idea to use zero-base every few years to eliminate unnecessary programs and expenses. This method can also be used from a public relations standpoint if the organization has no previous benchmark to refer to in previous years.

zero-based planning – The practice of analyzing the strengths and weaknesses of the various public relations, advertising and marketing communication tools and then matching them to the problem identified in the situation analysis.

zero level channel – Marketing directly to a target audience. *Channels* include direct mail, telephone, fax, e-mail and conference display booths.

zidane – Arguing with attitude (word was coined after Zinedine Zidanr, a French soccer player who head-butted an Italian opponent in the 2006 World Cup final).

zipping – Fast-forwarding through commercials when playing back a recorded program on a VCR.

zone pricing – A pricing method where customers within a defined zone or region are charged the same price while more distant customers pay a higher price than those closer to the company's dispatch point. Also called *multiple zone pricing*. See *geographical pricing*.

ZUPPIE (Zestful Upscale Person in their Prime) – a demographic group. **Z**

279 Tips to Succeed: Take time to smell the roses

"Life is what happens to you when you are busy making other plans."

Yoko Ono

280 Techniques to Succeed: Beefing up your credit report

Here are some suggestions for maintaining or improving your credit history:

• **Pay your bills on time.** Payment history is the single most important factor in determining your credit score, making up 35 percent of the total number. Missing even one payment can knock 50 to 100 points off a good score.

• **Pay down your debts and consider charging less.** Lenders like to see plenty of room between the amount of debt reported on your credit cards and your total credit limits. Charging less can also improve your score, even if you pay off your credit cards on a monthly basis.

• **Don't be afraid of credit counseling.** In 1998, the Fair Isaac Corp. changed its scoring formula to remove references to credit counseling in consumers' files after learning that receiving credit counseling was becoming less predictive of credit risk. Be sure to research, and only become involved with legitimate organizations.

• **Stay out of bankruptcy.** Bankruptcy can knock 200 points or more off your credit score. After filing, consumers are usually only able to secure credit through high-interest lenders, which can often lead consumers back down the path of bad credit.

Centers for Financial Education, a division of Consumer Credit Counseling Services of New Jersey - www.crediteducation.com

281

Techniques to Succeed: Event Planning – 10 key points

1. Decide event's purpose (goal and/or objectives).
2. Organize your volunteers.
3. Be ready for anything.
4. Create a timeline (Gantt chart – See Page 222).
5. Create an incentive to attract event participation.
6. Communicate (early on) with participants.
7. Make it a learning experience – determine what participants are going to "take away."
8. The event, if properly planned, will run itself. (Planning is everything).
9. Evaluate event and total plan at conclusion of event (exit survey).
10. Have fun!

282

Tips to Succeed: Do you have a brand? – Evaluate *your* 5 Ps

Your brand consists of a complex set of characteristics and dynamics that play out in thousands of scenarios each workday.

You can use your brand to positively influence your image to others and enhance your career using these five Ps:

Persona – The emotional connection and reaction you elicit from other people as a result of your personal style.

Product – The sum of your qualifications, experience, technical and/or functional expertise, ideas and results you've delivered over time.

Packaging – The presentation of your personal appearance, surroundings and tangible results of projects and assignments on the job.

Promotion – The way you inform your market about your value and impact.

Permission – The sense of legitimacy, confidence and core belief that you have important contributions to make.

Susan Hodgkinson - *The Leader's Edge*"

The ABCs of Strategic Communication

Z

Abbreviations and Acronyms –
Common to the Professions

AA = Average Audience

AAs = Author's Alterations

AAA = American Academy of Advertising

AAAA = American Association of Advertising Agencies

AASA = American Association of School Administrators

ABC = American Broadcasting Company

ABC = Audit Bureau of Circulations

ADI = Area of Dominant Influence

AIDA = Attention, Interest, Desire, Action

AIO = Attitudes, Interests, Opinions (Statements)

AMA = American Marketing Association

ANA = Association of National Advertisers

AP = Associated Press

APR = Accredited in Public Relations

ARF = Advertising Research Foundation

ASBA = American School Boards Association

AV = Audiovisuals

B2B = Business to Business advertising

BBB = Better Business Bureau

BBC = British Broadcasting Corporation

BCG = Boston Consulting Group

BDI = Brand Development Index

Blog = Web log

BPA – Border Patrol Agent

BUPPIE = Black Urban Professional

CARU = Children's Advertising Review Unit

CASS = Coding Accuracy Support System

CBBB = Council of Better Business Bureaus

CBD = Central Business District

CBS = Columbia Broadcasting System

CCO = Chief Communication Officer

CIO = Chief Information Officer

CIO = Chief Integrity Officer

CLV = Customer Lifetime Value

CMS = Content Management System

CMYK = Cyan-Magenta-Yellow-Black, and pronounced as separate letters C-M-Y-K

COBRA = Consolidated Omnibus Budget Reconciliation Act

COGS = Cost Of Goods Sold

CPA = Cost Per Action

CPA = Critical Path Analysis

CPC = Cost Per Click

CPC = Cost Per Customer

CPL = Cost Per Lead

CPM = Cost Per Thousand

CPO = Chief Privacy Officer

CPP = Cost Per Rating Point

CPS = Cost Per Sale

CPT = Cost Per Transaction

CPTM = Cost Per Targeted Thousand Impressions

CPV = Cost Per visit

CRM = Customer Relationship Management

CT = Click Through

CTR = Click-Through Ratio

DAGMAR = Defining Advertising Goals for Measured Advertising

DBA = Doping Business As

DEC = Daily Effective Circulation

DINKY = Double Income No Kids Yet

DIY Goods = Goods produced for the "Do-It-Yourself" market

DMA = Designated Market Area

DMA MPS = Designated Market Area Mail Preference Service

DMA TPS = Designated Market Area Telephone Preference Service

DMO = Destination Marketing Organization

DMP = Digital Music Player

DMU = Decision Making Unit

DOT = Department of Transportation

DPI = Disposable Personal Income

DPI = Dots Per Inch

DRA = Direct Response Advertising

DRTV = Direct Response Television

DSL = Digital Subscriber Line

DSS = Decision Support System

DTC = Direct to Consumer

DVR = Digital Video Recorder

EA = Environmental Assessment

EAS = Emergency Alert System

ECR = Efficient Consumer Response

EEC = European Economic Community

EFTP = Electronic File Transport Protocol

EFTPOS = Electronic Funds Transfer at Point of Sale

ENP = Expected Net Profit

EOQ = Economic Order Quantity

EPG = Electronic Programming Guide

EPK = Electronic Press Kit

EPOS = Electronic Point of Sale System

EPS = Encapsulated Post Script

ESP = Envelopes and Stubby Pencil

ET = Electronic Transcription

ETA = Estimated Time of Arrival

FAA = Federal Aviation Administration

FAB = Features, Advantages and Benefits (Analysis)

FABS = Features And Benefits Selling

FAQ = Frequently Asked Questions

FAST Marketing = Focused Advertising Sampling Technique

FCC = Federal Communication Commission

FDA = Food and Drug Administration

FEMA = Federal Emergency Management Agency

FERPA = Family Educational Rights and Privacy Act.

FFs = Freight Forwarders

FIDO = Forget it, drive on

FIS = Free In Store

FISA = Foreign Intelligence Surveillance Act.

FMCG = Fast Moving Consumer Goods

FOB = Free On Board

FOC = Front-Of-Counter

FOIA = Freedom of Information Act

FPS = Fax Preference Service

FSI = Free-Standing Insert

FTC = Federal Trade Commission

FTP = (Electronic) File Transport Protocol

FUD = Fear, Uncertainty and Doubt

GASP = Graphic Arts Service Provider

GIF = Graphics Interchange Format

GIS = Geographic Information System

GLAM = Greying, Leisured, Affluent, Middle-aged

GLB = Gramm-Leach-Bliley Act

GMT = Greenwich Mean Time

GNP = Gross National Product

GOTV = Get Out The Vote

GPF = Global Pet Finder (GPS device)

GPS = Global Positioning System

GRPS = Gross Rating Points

GSM = Global System for Mobile

GSR = Galvonic Skin Response

GUPPIE = Grossly Under-Performing Person

HDTV = High-Definition Television

HIPAA = Health Insurance Portability and Accountability Act
HTML = Hyper-Text Markup Language
HTTP = Hyper-Text Transfer Protocol

IAB = Interactive Advertising Bureau
IABC = International Association of Business Communicators
ID = Station identification during a commercial break in a television or radio program
IED = Improvised Explosive Device
IM = Instant Message
IMC = Integrated Marketing Communication
IMU = Interactive Marketing Unit
IP = Intellectual property
IP = Internet Protocol
IPA = International Priority Airmail
IPA = Internet Protocol Address
IPO = Initial Public Offering
IPR = Intellectual Property Rights
IPS = Institute of Professional Sales
IPTV = Internet Protocol TV
IRC = Internet Relay Chat
ISAL = International Surface Airlift
ISBN = International Standard Book Number
ISDN = Integrated Services Digital Network
ISP = Internet Service Provider
ISPR = Identify, Segment, Profile, Rank (audiences)
ITI = Information Technology Industry Council
ITS = In-service Training Sessions
iTV = Interactive Television
IVR = Interactive Voice Response
IVR = Telemarketing Interactive Voice Response

JIC = Joint Information Center
JIC = Joint Information Center

JIT = Just-In-Time Inventory System

JPEG = Joint Photographic Experts Group

KC = Key Communicator

KIPS = Key Influence People

KISS Principle = Acronym for "Keep It Simple and Straightforward"

KMPs = Key Message Points

KOLs = Knowledge Leaders (or Knowledge of those in Leadership roles)

KSA = Knowledges, Skills and Abilities

LAN = Local Area Network

LCC = Low Cost Carrier

LCD = Liquid Crystal Display

LLC = Limited Liability Company

MAC Plus (P & T) = Message, Audience, Channel, Purpose, Timing

MAN = Does the prospect have the Money to pay? Does the prospect have the Authority to buy? Does the prospect have a Need for the product?

MAPs = Message Action Points

Marcom = Marketing Communication

MBO = Management By Objectives

MBWA = management By walking Around

MIME = Multi-Purpose Internet Mail Extensions

MIP = Mobile Internet Provider

MIS = Marketing Information System

MLM = Multilevel Marketing

MOB = Mother of the bride

MOG = Mother of the groom

MOR = Middle of the Road

MOS = Man On the Street

MOU = Memo of Understanding

MPS = Mailing Preference Service

MRC = Media Rating Council

MRO Supplies = Maintenance, Repair and Operating Supplies

MSA = Metropolitan Statistical Area

MSM = Mainstream Media

MSRP = Manufacturer's suggested retail price

MVP = Most Valuable Player

NAB = National Association of Broadcasters

NAD = National Advertising Division of the Council of Better Business Bureaus

NAI = Network Advertising Initiative

NAM = National Account Marketing

NARB = National Advertising Review Board of the Council of Better Business Bureaus

NBC = National Broadcasting Company

NGO = Not a government organization

NILKIE = No Income, Lots of Kids

NPD = New Product Development

NQT = New Qualitative Technologies

NSPRA = National School Public Relations Association

NYLON – New York to London commuter – usually for business purposes.

OCC = Office of the Comptroller of the Currency

OINK = One Income, No Kids

OL = Opinion Leader

OOH = Out Of Home (advertising)

OOP = Out of Pocket (expenses)

OPA = Online Privacy Alliance

OPA = Online Publishers' Association

OPAL = Older People with Active Lifestyles

Op-Ed = Opposite Editorial Page

OPMA = Open Public Meetings Act

OPRA = Open Public Records Act

OTS = Opportunity to See

P2P = Peer to Peer Marketing

P3P = Platform for Privacy Preferences Project

PAD = Public Affairs Director

PAN = Pay, Authority, Need

PBR = Payment By Results

PCO = Public Communication Officer (Foreign term for PAD)

PCPs = Program Coordination Implanting (meeting)

PDA = Personal Digital Assistant

PDF (File) = Portable Document Format

PDM = Physical Distribution Management

PDM = Product-Differentiated Marketing

PDT = Potentially Dangerous Taxpayer

PDVR = Portable Digital Video Recorder

PEEST = Political, Economic, Environmental, Socio-cultural and Technological

PERT = Program Evaluation and Review Technique

PEST Analysis = Political, Economic, and Social Trends

PESTLE = Political, Economic, Socio-cultural, Technological, Legal and Environmental

PHR = Personal Health Record

PII = Personally Identifiable Information

PILOT = Payment in Lieu of Taxes

PIMS = Profit Impact of Marketing Strategies

PIN = Personal Identification Number

PIP = Personal Improvement Plan

PIT = Pursuit Intervention Technique

PLI = Privacy Leadership Initiative

PLU = Price Look Up

PMP = Personal Media Player

PMS = Pantone Matching System

PODS = Portable On Demand Storage

POP = Point Of Purchase

POSLSQ = Persons of Opposite Sex Living in Same Quarters – It is sometimes written as POSSLQ – Persons of Opposite Sex Sharing Living Quarters

POSSLQ = Persons of Opposite Sex Sharing Living Quarters - It is sometimes written as POSLSQ – Persons of Opposite Sex Living in Same Quarters

POTUS = President of the United States

POX = Police

PPM = Portable People Meter

PR = Public Relations

PR-Pie = Purpose, Research, Information, Communication, Evaluation

PROGS = Progressive Proofs

PRSA = Public Relations Society of America

PRSSA = Public Relations Student Society of America

PS = Postscript

PSA = Prostate-specific Antigen (protein) Test

PSA = Public Service Announcement

PSL = Personal Seat License

PSP = PlayStation Portable®

Pub = Short for publication

PUT = Persons Using Television

PVR = Personal Video Recorder

PVT = Persons Viewing Television

Q&A = Question and Answer

Qangos = Quasi-autonomous Non-government Agencies

QC = Quality Circles

Q-TIP = Quit Taking It Personally

R&B = Rhythm and Blues

R&D = Research and Development

RACE = Research, Action, Communication, Evaluation

RAPPIES = Retired Affluent Professionals

RDC = Regional Distribution Center

RFI = Request for Information

RFQ = Request for Qualifications

RFP = Request for Proposal

RGM = Repertory Grid Method

ROAM = Return on Assets Managed

ROC = Return on Capital

ROCE = Return on Capital Employed

ROI = Return on Investment

RON = Run of Network

ROP = Run of Paper

ROS = Run of Schedule

ROS = Run of Site

RPM = Resale Price Maintenance

RPM = Revolutions per minute

RSS = Really Simple Syndication

RTC = Residential Training Courses

SAR = Summary Annual Report

SAUS = Standard Advertising Unit System

SBU = Strategic Business Unit

SCOTUS = Supreme Court of the United States

SDSL = Symmetrical Digital Subscriber Line

SEM = Search engine marketing

SEO = Search Engine Optimizing

SFX = Sound Effects

SGML = Standard Generalized Markup Language

SIC = Spelling (content) Is Correct

SIC = Standard Industrial Classification

SINBAD = Single Income, No Boyfriend and Absolutely Desperate

SIQ = Sick In Quarters (U.S. Military)

SITCOM = Single Income, Two Kids Outrageous Mortgage

SITCOM = Situation comedy

SIU = Sets In Use

SKU = Stock-Keeping Unit

SLAP = Skills Level Analysis Process

SLEPT = Socio-cultural, Legal, Economic, Political and Technological

SME = Small to Medium Enterprise

SMPT = Simple Mail Transfer Protocol

SMS = Short Message Service

SMT = Satellite Media Tour

SOMPS = Statements of Marketing Practice

SOSTT = Situation, Objective, Strategy, Tactics and Targets

SOT = Sound On Tape

SOV = Share-of-Voice

SPSS = Statistical Package for the Social Sciences

SRO = Standing Room Only

SRDS® = Standard Rate and Data Service

SRM = Supplier Relationship Management

SUPPIES = Senior Urban Professionals

SWAG = Stuff We All Get

SWOP = Specifications for Web Offset Publications

SWOT = Strengths, Weaknesses, Opportunities, Threats

TARPS = Target Audience Rating Points

TCP/IP = Transfer Control Protocol/Internet Protocol

tiff = Tagged Image File Format

TIFs = Technology Involved Females

TINKIE = Two Incomes, Nanny and Kids

TIP = Triumph In the Pursuit (of knowledge)

TO = Turn Over (technique)

TPC = Trade Practices Commission

TPS = Telephone Preference Service

TSA = Total Survey Area

TSR = Telephone Service Representative

UAB = Universal Accreditation Board

UMTS = Universal Mobile Telecommunications System

UPC = Universal Product Code

URL = Uniform Resource Locator

USB = Universal Serial Bus

USP USP = Unique Selling Proposition

VALS = Values and Lifestyle System

VAT = Value Added Tax

VNR = Video News Release

VMS = Vertical Marketing System

V/O = Voice Over

VoIP = Voice over Internet Protocol

VOPAN = Voice-pitch Analysis

VPN = Virtual Private Network

VRU = Voice Response Unit

WAA = Wireless Advertising Association

WAN = Wide Area Network

WAP = Wireless Application Protocol

WAPs = Web Access Phones

WASP = Wireless Applications Service Provider

WATS = Wide Area Telephone Service

Wi-Fi® = Brand for wireless technology

WOM = Word of Mouth Advertising or Marketing

WOOPIES = Well-off Older People

WX = Weather

XML = eXtensible Markup Language

YAPPIE = Young Affluent Parent

YUPPIE = Young Urban Professional

ZBA – Zoning Board of Appeals

ZUPPIE = Zestful Upscale Person in their Prime

INDEX

More Third-Party Endorsements

For information and *ABCs'* updates and additions:
www.larrylitwin.com

All Tips and Techniques are on the *Companion CD* available at www.larrylitwin.com